Imogen Holst

A LIFE IN MUSIC

ALDEBURGH STUDIES IN MUSIC

General Editor: Christopher Grogan

Volume 7

ISSN 0969-3548

Other volumes in this series:

Our contributions to this book we dedicate to

Rosamund Strode

with love and affection on her 80th birthday

CHRISTOPHER GROGAN

COLIN MATTHEWS

CHRISTOPHER TINKER

Contents

Part I ~ 1907–31
Rosamund Strode

Part II ~ 1931–52
Christopher Grogan & Rosamund Strode

List of illustrations

Foreword

Imogen Holst – Imo to everyone – was inimitable. Although I had done a little work for her in 1970, I met her for the first time in 1971, at a private showing of the television film of Britten's *Owen Wingrave*. Most of the audience was a little uncomfortable with what was perceived as a not wholly satisfactory experience ('O what a terrible medium' was Britten's private comment) but Imo listened only to the music, and danced with excitement. Watching this seemingly austere, thoughtful person positively explode with enthusiasm was something I would become very familiar with.

I saw her subsequently in Aldeburgh, when I was working for Britten, and in the autumn of 1971 she invited me to Church Walk to ask if I would work on the Thematic Catalogue of her father's music, which she was preparing for publication in Holst's centenary year of 1974. This was the beginning of a collaboration which was to last more than twelve years. We prepared new editions of Holst's music – including *The Planets* in 1979 – and four volumes of a critical facsimile edition between 1974 and 1983; we initiated recordings – notably the first (and still only) recording of *At the Boar's Head*; and, anticipating the end of Holst's copyright after 1984,[1] conceived the Holst Foundation as a charitable trust whose main aim would be the support of living composers.

Her devotion to Britten – so evident from her Aldeburgh diary – meant that for the first four years of our working together she was always concerned that I should be available at any time that Britten needed me. She was very scrupulous to avoid too much contact with Britten herself, not only for the reason – with her ability to compartmentalize her life – that she had resolved that this was a time she would devote almost exclusively to her father, but also because, just as in the 1950s, she felt that his work was too important for her to intrude on. I only recall one occasion when I was alone with the two of them, at a meal in the Festival Club, where the atmosphere changed dramatically as they walked in. (I have a fond memory of a lunch with Imo in the Club, where she watched with fascination two elderly Aldeburgh residents carefully negotiating the single step in the middle of the restaurant: 'I love coming here,' she whispered, 'it makes me feel so *young*!')

---

[1] The change in copyright legislation in 1996 meant that Holst's music unexpectedly came back into copyright, which finally expired at the end of 2004.

The double and triple underlinings in her diary, together with the exclamation marks, give just a little indication of what her speaking voice was like. But she had two voices (and personalities to match): one for public occasions and broadcasts, almost excessively careful and precise – this went with the figure who would walk along Aldeburgh High Street with her eyes fixed on the far distance, anxious to avoid anyone who might distract her from more important things. But in private she could be both voluble and uninhibited, intense yet relaxed, with a capacity for hoots of laughter when something pleased or amused her, which was very often. The switch from one to the other could be dramatic: when you phoned her, the frail voice saying 'Aldeburgh 2865' sounded like someone at death's door; the moment she knew who it was there would be the drop of an octave or more and the most welcoming of greetings. I don't believe any recording of her father's voice survives, but I imagine that their manner was very similar.

And, like her father, she had many unexpected interests. After her death I found that she had saved for me a book about particle physics which she had been recently reading (all her library was marked with how it should be disposed), and which she had annotated throughout. She would not read things unless they could be useful to her – there wasn't enough time for that – but she retained a wonderfully open mind. Though her opinions were always strong ones, she was never inflexible, and took a particular delight in being persuaded to change her mind. This was the case even where music was concerned, and she was always open to the new: I remember seeing her copy of the Proms Prospectus for 1972, where she had marked the concerts she was most interested in, with one marked as a 'must' – the performance of John Cage's HPSCHD at the Roundhouse.

Imo's musical tastes were very decided, and very much her own. She was notably a pioneer in the revival of 15th and 16th century church music, and the programmes that she regularly devised for the Aldeburgh Festival broke much new ground. By the time I knew her this largely belonged to the past, both because she was taking more of a back seat as artistic director and because she was content that others were continuing the work she had begun. But she had other things to concentrate on: her father's approaching centenary made her conscious that she could do more on his behalf (in spite of having written two books, *Gustav Holst* in 1938 and *The Music of Gustav Holst* in 1951). This didn't imply a blinkered view of his music. Quite the opposite: her often disparaging remarks in *The Music of Gustav Holst* caused controversy, and went largely unretracted. She could never reconcile herself to the pervasive influence of Wagner on her father's early music. With some difficulty I persuaded her to agree to a recording of the large-scale Walt Whitman setting, *The Mystic Trumpeter*, of 1904 (to my mind an early near-masterpiece) and she did grudgingly allow a few other early works to emerge from obscurity. (Even Holst had labelled some of these as 'Early Horrors'.)

Her perception of the occasional weaknesses in Holst's music was, in many cases, accurate, although she tended to overreact because of her love for the late works, which she felt to have been been unfairly neglected. But nothing would have persuaded her to allow the disastrous *Phantastes Suite* of 1911 to see the light of day (apart from its slow movement, of which she was fond). And she made it quite clear that she did not want Holst's royalties (so much more substantial than they had been in his lifetime) to be used to record *The Perfect Fool*. She felt that this opera was dramatically inept, and its revival would do her father's reputation no good.

Her trenchant criticisms were not restricted to her father, and she had scant regard for many English composers whose reputations have since flourished in the age of recording. As for her own music, she could be just as critical of that, and my queries about it were usually gently brushed aside. I was delighted when in the mid-1970s she began composing again (although a glance at the Catalogue will show that at no time, apart from the years either side of 1974, did she stop). I suggested to Faber Music that they publish her 1982 String Quintet in honour of her 75th birthday, and this brought her great pleasure. ('I feel like a *real* composer', she said.) There was quite a flowering of music in her last years, and after her death I partially completed a Recorder Concerto that she was writing for the 1984 Cricklade Festival.

At Britten's funeral, in 1976, I rounded a corner of Aldeburgh Church to find Imo bursting with excitement because the bell ringers had just executed a particularly felicitous change. It was not possible to be too mournful at her own funeral, because she would not have wanted it: and would have rejoiced both at the words (from Holst's *Hymn of Jesus*) that Rosamund chose for her headstone – 'The heavenly spheres make music for us / All things join in the dance'– and at its proximity to Britten's grave. She was more 'alive' than almost any person I have known, and she remains so. More than 20 years after her death I still approach Imo's Church Walk house and expect to find her inside, making the strong coffee that she always served the moment I stepped in the door.

Acknowledgements

This book is the result of the coming together of three individual projects, each intended to pay tribute to Imogen Holst in the year of her centenary. Rosamund Strode, perhaps IH's closest colleague and, since her death, the guardian of the Holst archives at IH's house in Aldeburgh, had already dedicated a number of years to annotating documentary sources and conducting interviews with a view to writing a full-length biography of her friend and mentor. In the late 1980s she worked in close conjunction with Christopher Tinker, who produced in 1990 a catalogue of works that was subsequently revised for publication. Meanwhile, students of the life and music of Benjamin Britten were gleaning considerable insights into the mind of that composer from the uniquely insightful diary kept by IH during the first eighteen months of her time as his music assistant. The appearance of excerpts in studies of Britten's life prompted many calls for the diary to be edited and published in its complete form. A meeting at the Britten–Pears Library in 2005 brought these three strands together, and work on this single volume began.

It soon became clear that the first, and greatest, debt of acknowledgement must be to Imogen Holst herself. She was a writer of huge gifts, and produced over the years a series of autobiographical essays and interviews in addition to the Aldeburgh diary. These bring to life many of the events and stages of her long and varied career more vividly and truthfully than any account drawn from secondary sources could ever hope to realize. In consequence, what follows is to a great extent a 'documentary biography' that allows, as far as possible, its subject to speak for herself in recounting her musical achievements, triumphs and disappointments. While thus bequeathing a wealth of writing that has made the task of those attempting to trace her footsteps infinitely easier, perhaps even more enduringly she left behind her such a fund of goodwill that everyone who has been approached to assist with details or anecdotes for this volume has done so with ready enthusiasm and warm memories; their stories have done much to add colour to this portrait of IH.

As befits a volume written to celebrate its subject's centenary, the portrait is an affectionate one, born of admiration for IH as a musician and an individual. It is also, as the title suggests, primarily the story of a life lived through, and for, the music to which IH dedicated her entire being with surpassing generosity and utter selflessness. In contrast, of her private thoughts and emotions she spoke very little and, after the end of her schooldays, wrote even less. Friendly and welcoming to all, she always kept a part of herself at a distance, and this survey makes little attempt to break through the defences that she so deliberately built up to prevent anyone getting too close.

Of my fellow contributors, I must first thank Rosamund Strode, IH's friend, colleague and her successor as Britten's music assistant, not only for narrating a colourful and detailed account of IH's early years, but also for the wealth of knowledge and insight regarding the whole of IH's life, career and musical output, which she has freely shared. She has devoted love and care to preserving the memory of IH and perpetuating her legacy, and as we commemorate IH's centenary we rejoice in equal measure in the celebration of Rosamund's own eightieth birthday. And if this book belongs to Rosamund almost as much as to its subject, it is also hugely indebted to Helen Lilley, IH's devoted secretary from 1963 until her death and an essential part of G. & I. Holst ever since. Helen has played a major part in organizing the Holst Archives at Church Walk, and in making these available to researchers over the years; I am very grateful for her help, both in locating numerous items from the archive, and especially for contributing her memories of IH's last moments, of which she was the only witness.

To Colin Matthews, another close colleague of IH during her last years, I am especially grateful for providing ready access to his correspondence with IH, for sharing memories and filling in numerous gaps in the narrative, and also for providing an introductory essay that brings vividly and affectionately alive his own years of friendship and work with IH.

Christopher Tinker's painstaking work on IH's musical output goes back more than fifteen years, and he has given generously of his time and skill to help bring the catalogue of works to publication, as well as adding an informative and insightful essay about IH's musical style. The biographical chapters are also much enriched by his pioneering research, which included interviews with a number of friends and associates of IH.

Anyone attempting to write the life of a subject as unique and multi-faceted as Imogen Holst must be prepared to encounter a massive and diverse range of documentary sources, which require distillation and synthesis if they are to aid the creation of a picture at once recognizable to friends and colleagues and illuminating to those who never had the opportunity to meet her. Fortunately IH knew from experience how important it would be to maintain some notes and primary papers on her own career, activities and journeys, and it was good luck that the most important elements in her life, up to 1941, were enshrined in a series of large scrap-books, probably left at her mother's house in Essex when she herself was without a permanent base. Maintaining the scrap-books was a habit introduced to her by Lady Reid, mother of Vicky, her great friend at St Paul's Girls' School in about 1926, just before IH went to the RCM. There are nine volumes in all, recording the events of her life in some detail up to the spring of 1941. The books hold a mass of information, all carefully positioned and pasted onto the substantial card pages, and if not self-explicit (by dated concert programmes, etc.) have some kind of contemporary identification or comment written by IH in ink. Late in her life, after she gave up active work in 1977, she added further notes in pencil when there was not quite enough detail for others to unravel. On her foreign travels she collected many view cards, and she had learned from the Reids that it was possible, in those days, to split the backs of commercial postcards from the fronts, pasting in both sides (views and correspondence) thus losing nothing. Subsequent important materials from 1941 were kept and annotated as before but not pasted into books. These all comprise much the same sort of detail as those used in the scrap-books themselves, with the addition of pieces sent in by the Press Cuttings agency to which she subscribed for many years up to her death in 1984.

Towards the end of summer of 1984 Rosamund Strode began to assemble an occasional series of interviews with IH's friends, on the basis that such a remarkable person should not be allowed to recede into obscurity unrecorded. One friend recommended another, and over the next ten years she was able to talk to well over fifty people who had known IH, some from her childhood onwards. This body of information, much of it on taped interviews, has proved to be invaluable and a great deal is owed to all those who were happy and willing to talk about IH and their memories of her. For assistance with a myriad details in the narrative, Rosamund and I extend our particular thanks to the late Helen Asquith, the late Bernard Barrell, Ronald Blythe, Barbara Burrell, Kathleen Butt, Peter Cox, Nicola Grunberg, the late Victoria Ingrams, the late Arthur Marshall, Sue Phipps, Julian and Valerie Potter, Janet and Ian Tait, Marion Thorpe, Helen Wiggington of the Royal Opera House Archive and Benjamin Zander. Becky Cape of the Lilly Library, Indiana University, provided copies of letters between Britten and Heywood Hill, and Vicki Perry, Assistant Archivist at Hatfield House, tracked down correspondence relating to Britten's visit there with William Plomer.

The diary of Imogen Holst is © the Estate of Imogen Holst, and is used by permission of G. & I Holst Ltd. The letters of Benjamin Britten are © the Trustees of the Britten–Pears Foundation, and are used by permission. The extended interview between IH and Jack Dobbs that forms the basis of Chapter 7 previously appeared in *Imogen Holst at Dartington*; I am grateful to Jack Dobbs and to the Dartington Hall Trust for allowing us to reproduce it here. The unpublished diaries of Stephen Potter are © the Estate of Stephen Potter, and I am especially grateful to the author's son Julian for permission to quote from these, as well as for allowing me to include the very fine illustration of Britten and IH by his mother, the artist Mary Potter. I would also like to thank Thomas Gibson Fine Art for permission to include Edward Seago's atmospheric portrait of IH as a frontispiece, and to Milein Cosman for allowing us to include her etching of IH on the jacket cover. Tim Fargher's evocative drawing of IH on Aldeburgh beach first appeared in the Festival programme book in 1980, and I am grateful for the artist's permission to reproduce it here. The music examples in Chapter 14 are © the following and used by permission: Boosey & Hawkes (ex. 6); Faber Music (exx. 4 and 18); G. & I. Holst Ltd. (exx. 5, 7, 8, 11, 13, 14, 16); Novello/Music Sales (ex. 3); Oxford University Press (exx. 1 and 2) and the William Morris Society (ex. 9). For permission to use photographs, I would like to thank Sharon Boswell at the *East Anglian Daily Times*, The Britten–Pears Library, Francesca Franchi of the Royal Opera House Archive, The Holst Foundation, Nigel Luckhurst, Roger Mayne, Edward Morgan, Brian Seed and Yvonne Widger of the Dartington Hall Trust.

For help in my attempts to decipher erased passages in the Aldeburgh Diary, I am indebted to Dr Julia Craig-McFeely, Project Officer for the DIAMM project, who invited me to her home in Oxford, painstakingly made a photographic record of the necessary pages, and introduced me to the potential of the Adobe Photoshop software as a tool for recovering 'lost' text. Vicky Oxby word-processed the text of the Aldeburgh Diary and IH's other writings, and Richard Northedge contributed his great skill and expertise to the compilation of the index; I am very grateful to them both. The team at the Britten–Pears Library – Jude Brimmer, Nick Clark, Jon Manton, Lloyd Moore, Joseph Phibbs, Andrew Plant, Eleanor Pridgeon, Cerys Shepherd, Judith Tydeman, Lucy Walker and Barbara Wallington – have all had a hand in what follows, and I am especially in debt to Anne Surfling and Pam Wheeler, for their tireless and insightful work in reading and annotating the entire text in draft, which has greatly enhanced both the clarity and sense of the narrative. I must also thank Peter Clifford and Caroline Palmer at Boydell & Brewer for their belief in the project and their patience and dedication in seeing it off the ground, and to Anna Morton and David Roberts for guiding it through the press.

The following list gives the principal sources of information used during the compilation of the catalogue of works, and we would like to thank the archivists and librarians of these institutions past and present. The BBC Written Archive, The British Library and National Sound Archive, The British Music Information Centre, The Britten–Pears Library, The Elmhirst Centre, Dartington Hall,

The Library and Resources Centre at Dartington College of Arts, The Holst Foundation, The Holst Library at Snape, The National Federation of Women's Institutes, The National Union of Townswomen's Guilds, The Old Girls' Associations of Roedean and Eothen Schools, The Royal College of Music Parry Room, The Rural Music Schools Association, St Paul's Girls' School, Hammersmith, and The Vaughan Williams Room at Cecil Sharp House. Excerpts from Christopher Tinker's essay on IH's musical style have previously appeared in *Tempo* and are reproduced here by permission.

Finally, I must express my warmest thanks to my wife Katherine, and my children, Lucy, Hannah and Ben, for allowing me so often over the past months to disappear and 'spend time with Imogen'. Without their patience and love, this book would never have been completed.

CHRISTOPHER GROGAN
Kettleburgh, February 2007

A note about names

Such was the intertwining of the lives of Gustav and Imogen Holst that it is inevitable that they should appear throughout this narrative very frequently not only in the same paragraph, but also the same sentence. It has therefore not proved possible to use the common device 'Holst' to refer to either. The names 'Imogen' and 'Gustav' would also have been inappropriate, as they imply a level of familiarity to which, regarding Holst senior at least, none of the contributors can lay claim. They would in any case convey an inaccurate impression, given that Imogen Holst was 'Imo' to all who knew her, while her father's familiar appellations ranged from 'Gussie' to simply 'G'. Taking a lead from this last abbreviation, and to avoid confusion between the two composer-Holsts, the abbreviations 'IH' and 'GH' are therefore used throughout.

Notes on contributors

Christopher Grogan was born in London in 1962, and studied music at Royal Holloway, University of London, where he completed his doctoral dissertation on Elgar's oratorio *The Apostles*. He has been Librarian of the Britten–Pears Library since 2003. He has published articles on Elgar and Grainger in *Music & Letters* and other journals, contributed two chapters to the symposium *Edward Elgar: Music and Literature* and edited Elgar's *Wand of Youth* suites for the Elgar Complete Edition. He has also reviewed extensively for *Music & Letters*, *Musical Times* and *Brio*. He is currently managing a major project to develop a Benjamin Britten Thematic Catalogue as a web resource, timed for the composer's centenary in 2013.

Colin Matthews was born in London in 1946. He studied music at the Universities of Nottingham and Sussex, where he also taught, and subsequently worked with Benjamin Britten and Imogen Holst. He collaborated with Deryck Cooke on the performing version of Mahler's Tenth Symphony. Since the early 1970s his music has been played widely both in the UK and worldwide, with recordings on Unicorn, Collins Classics, NMC and Deutsche Grammophon. He is active as administrator of the Holst Foundation, Chairman of the Britten Estate, and trustee of the Britten–Pears Foundation. He has close links with the Aldeburgh Festival and the Britten–Pears School, particularly as co-director with Oliver Knussen of the Contemporary Composition and Performance Course.

Rosamund Strode (ARCM, Hon MA (UEA), Fellow of Dartington Hall) was educated at St Mary's, Calne, the Royal College of Music and the Arts Department at Dartington Hall, where she studied under Imogen Holst, from whom she took over the role of music assistant to Benjamin Britten in 1964. She went on to be Keeper of Manuscripts and Archivist at the newly formed Britten–Pears Library, retiring in 1992, and she continues to chair the Holst Foundation. She has written numerous articles on Britten, and recently contributed the essay on Imogen Holst to the *Oxford Dictionary of National Biography*.

Christopher Tinker was educated at Uppingham School, the Royal College of Music and the universities of Durham and Lancaster. His PhD thesis was on Imogen Holst; his subsequent writings include articles on her in *The New Grove Dictionary of Women Composers*, *The New Grove Dictionary of Music and Musicians* and *Tempo*. He has had teaching posts at Sedbergh and Whitgift schools, and is currently Director of Music at St Joseph's College, Ipswich.

List of abbreviations

Names and organizations

B&H	Boosey and Hawkes
BCP	Book of Common Prayer
BPL	Britten–Pears Library
CEMA	Council for the Encouragement of Music and the Arts
EFD(S)S	English Folk Dance (and Song) Society
EOG	English Opera Group
GH	Gustav Holst
HF	Holst Foundation
IFMC	International Folk Music Council
IH	Imogen Holst
NUTG	National Union of Townswomen's Guilds
OUP	Oxford University Press
RAM	Royal Academy of Music
RCM	Royal College of Music
RMS(A)	Rural Music Schools (Association)
RVW	Ralph Vaughan Williams
SPGS	Saint Paul's Girls' School

Instruments and voices

A	alto		perc	percussion
B	bass		ob	oboe
bsn	bassoon		picc	piccolo
cel	celeste		rec(s)	recorder(s)
cl	clarinet		S	soprano
corA	cor anglais		str	strings
C-T	counter-tenor		T	tenor
d	descant (recorder)		ten	tenor (recorder)
d.bass	double bass		timp	timpani
dbsn	double bassoon		tpt	trumpet
fl	flute		tr	treble (recorder)
hp	harp		tri	triangle
hn	horn		vcl	violoncello
instr	instruments		vln	violin
pft	pianoforte		vla	viola

Part I ~ 1907–31

ROSAMUND STRODE

1 'She do favour 'er Pa': Infancy and early schooldays, 1907–20

Attempting to give a true picture of Imogen Holst is a daunting task. I was lucky enough to have known her first as a teacher at Dartington Hall (where, from 1948 to 1950, I was a post-Royal College of Music trainee) and then worked closely with her, both as a member of her Purcell Singers for ten years, and also on matters connected with Benjamin Britten and the ever-growing Aldeburgh Festival. She was always clear and precise in explaining just what had to be done, whether in rehearsals or, say, in her requests for a London-based search to report on the availability of some more obscure piece of music to be included in a Festival programme, but in her normally completely open personality she had hidden depths which were somehow difficult to explain, so contradictory did they seem.

When 'off duty' and relaxed she had a great fund of memories, and she evidently enjoyed revisiting many of her experiences, built up between World Wars I and II, when she had travelled widely on the Continent. Rail travel then was cheap, and while at the RCM she had earned various prizes (most of these expressed in cash awards of what now seem tiny amounts) which she used exclusively for foreign excursions and broadening her horizons generally. She had an unusually retentive memory, and could always bring out some long-remembered experience in conversation, or perhaps satisfy her own enquiring mind by asking an expert, met by chance at some social event, the solution to a long-held puzzle in a manner that could not possibly offend.

But occasionally she could surprise by claiming total ignorance about a subject she patently knew all about; when challenged, her disclaimer would be 'I have cut that right out of my life.' Often these rather dramatic words would be accompanied by a grand stage gesture of rejection with her right arm – which effectively closed down that particular line of conversation and made one think of a locked door of which she had thrown away the key. It is important to remember that Gustav Holst's younger brother, Emil (who settled in the USA) was a successful actor under the stage name of Ernest Cossart; his daughter Valerie was also on the stage. IH herself evidently shared that particular gene, and had a good deal of acting experience and stage work as a dancer when at the RCM. She was perfectly aware of the impression she could make on people and audiences, backed by her genuine charm and likeableness. So what was that 'cutting out' actually covering up? Although she appeared to be inde-structible and ever the same, in fact she had needed, quite early on, to come to terms with the limitations of her own physical strength, managing her life in such a way that her students and audiences had no idea of the rebuffs she had met and overcome.

Imogen Clare was born on 12 April 1907 at 31 Grena Road, Richmond, Surrey, to Gustav and Isobel von Holst. Her proud father announced the arrival to all his friends thus:

N.B. A daughter

GH's earnings as a teacher of music were not great. He had some regular school jobs (for instance, at James Allen's Girls' School, Dulwich, and St Paul's Girls' School, Brook Green) and gave evening classes at Morley College, Westminster, but none of these brought in much in the way of a salary. Besides, he knew all along that he wanted to make his way as a composer, and for that (as he often said) he needed solitude and silence. A new baby in the house provided neither; soon after IH's birth he wrote to the singer Maja Kjöhler, who lived nearby, that 'Imogen is practising coloratura – the sort that foghorns usually perform – and my brain feels pulpy whenever she lets fly.'[1]

When his daughter first appeared, her father, still deep in his Indian phase, suggested that she should be named 'Sita' (The Daughter of the Earth) after the subject of his recently completed opera. But when her mother pointed out that the baby not only had bright blue eyes but had obviously inher-ited her own blonde hair, he had to concede that perhaps his idea was not such a good one after all. A family saying, alluded to in letters from time to time, also stems from this period; the Holsts' charwoman, when looking at the baby, was heard to say 'She's a pretty li'l thing, pore li'l thing, though she do favour 'er Pa.' (It was true that IH's oval face resembled her father's, but her undeniably rather prominent nose seems to have come from her mother.)

[1] Short, *Gustav Holst*, p. 69.

There are tantalizingly few accounts or photographs of IH's early child-hood in the Richmond and Barnes area of London, just on the south side of the Thames. The Holsts soon had to move from 31 Grena Road to no. 23 close by, but were not there for long; probably the fact that this second house was in the middle of the row rather than semi-detached at one end meant that GH would have had more intrusive noise to cope with. Fortunately an aunt of his, who kept a small school nearby, made no. 10 The Terrace, Barnes, available to the little family. Here GH used the bare top-floor room as his music room and study, while the family lived on the lower floors. IH later recalled:

> I first got to know my father as someone who played tunes on the piano for me to dance to. This was in an old house on the river at Barnes. He had his composing room at the top of the house, and that was a room that one didn't go into. But downstairs I got to know him as a person. He invented the right sort of game to play: – my favourite was the one where we stood on one leg with our bedroom slippers on, and tried to kick the other slipper to the far end of the room.
>
> By the time I was four he was teaching me to sing folk-songs – a difficult business when one had a lisp and couldn't pronounce the letter 'R'; I can still remember struggling with 'Ath I wath going to Shtwarbuwy Fair'.
>
> Then there were the walks on Sheen Common and in Kew Gardens. He was a very patient companion, and would stop when I wanted to smell every flower we came to. But there were times when he thought of what he was composing, and would forget that my legs were much shorter than his, and would go on striding ahead. I knew that composers were people who mustn't be interrupted, so I learnt to keep pace with him by bending my knees at every step.[2]

Among the tunes he played were the *Lyric Pieces* of Grieg, which IH remembered dancing to even before she could walk.[3] GH encouraged his infant daughter's musicality in other ways also, taking her along to one of his classes at James Allen's Girls' School, and, at home, sitting her on his lap at the piano, where she would play pentatonic tunes on the black keys while he improvised accompaniments.

---

[2] IH, notes for a BBC Woman's Hour Talk, February 1965; HF.
[3] Interview with John Amis, BBC, 23 July 1982.

IH's early enthusiasm for dancing was rewarded by her parents sending her to dance classes before going to school, and she never forgot her first public appearance at, she thought, about four years old. This was as a small toadstool in a large wide-brimmed hat, dancing barefoot in Kensington Gardens (or was it Hyde Park?) and knowing that, whatever she found underfoot – broken glass, etc. – she must on no account cry or stop. (Luckily this danger was safely averted.) In 1967 she received a letter from an old acquaintance, who had actually also been involved in that event and had a clear recollection of IH then. 'We once, as children, went to the same dancing class, and also danced in a Ballet of Ruby Ginner's. You, and another very small person were toadstools I remember.'

In the summer of 1912, at the age of just five, she went to the Froebel Demonstration School in Colet Gardens (quite close to St Paul's Girls' School, where her father taught), which had been built in 1895 to accommodate both the students the Froebel Institute was training to be teachers and the young children, up to the age of twelve or thirteen, who were their pupils. The Froebel approach, derived from pioneering work begun in Germany towards the end of the nineteenth century, was then considered a very modern way of teaching young children. Arthur Marshall, a near contemporary of IH's at the school, wrote of his time there:

> My two years there were an enchanted time. I remember no punishments, no rows, no squabbles. We seldom sat at benches or desks. Our schoolmistresses never frowned at us. All were sunny and in this happy and harmonious paradise we sang, we painted, we made cardboard models, we stuck chestnut buds in jam jars, we acted *Hiawatha*, we became Knights with shields and swords, we kept animals. We skipped on fine days and bowled hoops (and where have hoops gone to?). There were puppets and a water-tank and a revolving summer-house and a sand-pit for the youngest of all. There was a library (somewhere along the way I had learnt to read) and we were encouraged into it. One absorbed a great deal and almost without realising it. The building itself lacked beauty (it is still there) but we hurried to it in the morning with joy and left it at tea-time with regret.[4]

Also surviving from IH's Froebel years is her first school report, from the Summer term, 1912:

[4] Marshall, *Life's Rich Pageant*, p. 34.

THE INCORPORATED
FROEBEL EDUCATIONAL INSTITUTE
KINDERGARTEN
REPORT

Summer   Term, 1912

Name   Imogen von Holst.

Age   5 years 3 months.

Imogen has made a good beginning in the Kindergarten & is now entering more fully into its life. She speaks well for her age; in 'News' her descriptions are good & easy to follow.

She has a good sense of rhythm & in singing, her voice though small is tuneful & she easily learns a new melody. In all handwork she is careful & accurate & shows that her idea of form is developing. She shows an interest in plant & animal life but with the latter she is rather timid. At free play she usually plays some quiet game alone though now & again she catches the interests of other children & has an energetic romp with them. Her movements are slow & controlled.

Imogen is an affectionate little girl with very tidy & careful habits.

Doris C. Ironside   Class Mistress

Imogen will pass into the Transition Class & should go steadily forward.
A dear little girl & full of promise.

A. Yelland   Head Mistress

In the same form as IH at this time were the brother and sister Robert and Margaret Donington, both of whom were to become experts in their own fields of Baroque music and Elizabethan dance respectively; many years later IH was to consult Margaret to assist her and Benjamin Britten in devising the dances for *Gloriana*.

In an *Old Froebelian News Letter* from 1951, under the paragraph heading 'I remember ...', a Miss Walton Smith gave her memory of IH at the school. It concerns a Spring Pageant, given as part of their Spring Festival in 1915 to a script by Margaret Stone, a student of the time: 'In that pageant Glen Byam Shaw was a graceful Hyacinthus, his brother David played the young Pan to perfection, Imogen Holst just became a daffodil.'

In the same year, 1915, IH contracted typhoid: was that daffodil already sickening for it, one wonders? Luckily by then the Holsts had the tenancy of a small ancient cottage in the country, near Thaxted, Essex. Monk Street Cottage proved to be the perfect place for her to recover. She later wrote of these Thaxted years:

> Holst's first glimpse of Thaxted was in the winter of 1913, when he was on a five-days' walking holiday in north-west Essex. He stayed a night in the 'Enterprise' in Town Street, and he liked the place so much that he made up his mind to return there. In the following year a friend told him of a cottage belonging to the writer S. L. Bensusan, which was to let. Although it poured with rain on the day when he and my mother went to see it, they immediately knew that Thaxted was the right place to live, and Monk Street Cottage became our home for a short time.
>
> Unfortunately it was burnt down more than forty years ago, and the recent road-widening has destroyed all trace of the garden. The cottage dated from 1614; it had a thatched roof, and open fire-places, and a wonderful view across meadows and willow trees to the church spire in the distance. In the fields beyond our garden we could watch the farmer sowing the seed broadcast. Farm-horses moved at a leisurely pace between the high hedges of what is now the A130, and there was a carrier's cart on Wednesday afternoons. Here, in this quietness, my father, who had been rejected by the recruiting authorities as unfit for war service, was able to work at *The Planets*.
>
> The neighbours were at first suspicious, because our name was then 'von Holst'. They told the police dramatic stories of the stranger who walked alone for mile after mile. The police, however, merely noted in their report: 'Many rumours are current about this man, but nothing can be traced against him.'[5]

IH was able to spend her long convalescence there all through that summer, happily looked after by two young women, Jessie and May Beames, daughters of friends of the family from Ashford, Middlesex (then in the country, but now under Heathrow Airport), a regime which left her with a real understanding of what a country childhood could be like. Her parents would come at weekends, taking the train from Liverpool Street Station, and then the little branch line to Thaxted itself. They kept Monk Street Cottage until 1917, and then rented another house, The Steps, in the centre of Thaxted itself, which they were to retain until 1925.

[5] IH, 'Gustav Holst and Thaxted'.

On returning to Barnes IH remained at the Froebel School until Easter 1917, when she became a boarder at Eothen, a smallish private school near Caterham, Surrey, run by the Misses Pye. The school was already known to Holst, since Jane Joseph, his most promising ex-pupil from St Paul's, taught there, as did Miss Eleanor Shuttleworth, a well-regarded teacher of the piano who also had pupils at SPGS. IH was her pupil at both schools. From Eothen on 13 July 1917 IH wrote her father a graphic letter which provides a glimpse of her daily life at the school:

> Thank you so much for your letter. The red-books and black-books I got, are not books, but they are honors, at least the red ones are, and the black ones are disgraces. I have got 5 red, and 2 black. One of the girls has got 9 red and one black, and another has got 19 black and one red. I do not like Rewards and Fairies as much as Puck of Pook's hill, either. I have got a piece to play to you when you come. We did not hear much of the raid, but what worried me was that mother could not come. But she is coming on Sunday to make up for it. Jane, the now Miss Joseph, said that she was coming to Thaxted, and Jessie wrote and told me that she was coming to stay with us for a fortnight if she could.[6] We are going to have exams next week, and we are all getting madly exited. I worked it out, and I got 50400 seconds to the hols, 8400 mins 240 hours and 10 days, so there is not long to wait, but I reccond it out from Monday. There is going to be a party this afternoon, the birthday of one of the day girls, and all the boaders are going to it.
>
> My room-mate says that they have one every year, and we allways have a ripping time, she says we hunt for sweats, and we have a bag each. And we are going to have compertishions, and ripping prizes, and strawberries and cream for tea. But I must go and get ready now ...
>
>> With love and Kisses
>> from
>>> Imogen

GH, rejected for military service on account of his poor eyesight, had been noted by Percy Scholes as an ideal candidate for inclusion in the YMCA (Education) music programme of which he was in charge. In 1918 he put GH forward as suitable for service in Holland, but his appointment there was not accepted on account of his Teutonic-seeming name, although GH's forbears

---

[6] 'Jane, the now Miss Joseph' refers to the fact that IH would have had to use the formal mode of address for Jane Joseph, whom she had called 'Jane' all her life. 'Jessie' is Jessie Beames.

were in fact more Swedish than German. Scholes, with another post already in
mind, advised GH that the British army, too, might look askance at his name,
so GH took the trouble to change it by deed poll, legally removing the enno-
bling 'von', which had anyway become an increasing embarrassment to him by
then. During the course of this procedure it was discovered that all along there
had never been any right to the offending prefix, which had just been assumed
by an ancestor eager, ironically enough, to improve his family's image.

That matter dealt with, GH, now forty-four, was appointed YMCA Musical
Organiser for the troops in the Eastern Mediterranean. Before taking up the
appointment he was able, through the generosity of Henry Balfour Gardiner, to
be present at the first private performance of *The Planets* in Queen's Hall on 29
September 1918; IH was also there and later vividly recalled 'sitting in the dark-
ened auditorium, looking down on the performers from her seat in the circle'.[7]

By the time his appointment had actually been put into effect in the autumn
of 1918 the war was almost over, and the Armistice was signed before GH had
even reached Salonica, his destination. Extracts from some of his letters to Isobel over the next few months give graphic descriptions of the frustrating situations he had to deal with, and they are in themselves a touching record both
of the relationships which bound this family together, and of GH's firm conviction of what he wanted to do, rather than what other people felt he should be
doing. None of Isobel's letters to him seems to have survived. He gives advice
on the way he feels IH's curriculum should develop – if Miss Pye agrees – and
in those letters one can see the experienced teacher at work.

IH herself had begun violin lessons with André Mangeot, and had already
started to write her own music, with the guidance and help of Jane Joseph,
starting with a Sonata in D minor for strings and piano, composed at Thaxted
that summer and proudly designated her 'Op. 1'. GH encouraged this development from the start, first asking Mabel Rodwell Jones, a member of staff at
James Allen's Girls School, where he taught, to make copies of the sonata, and
then presenting his daughter with a copy of Edith Rickert's *Ancient English
Christmas Carols, 1400–1700*, inscribed 'To Imogen to help her do her Opus
II and in honour of Opus I from Father, Thaxted, August 1918'. IH duly wrote
tunes for three of the carols, adding a fourth to a text by J. A. Symonds, entitled
'A Christmas Lullaby'. This was included in the programme for the distribution
of Prizes and Certificates at James Allen's Girls' School on 19 December 1918.
The succession of compositions that followed then formed part of the packages
that IH and her mother sent regularly to GH while he was away.

---

[7] Short, *Gustav Holst*, p. 162.

On 5 December 1918 GH wrote from Salonica:

> Dear Isobel
> In my letter yesterday I never thought of Xmas. And today is the last day for mails.
> So a very happy and peaceful one to both my fair Eyes with many blessings on them and may they enable me to continue to look on the world through them with all the joy they have brought me in the past which is rather a selfish way of putting it but there are times when one does feel for oneself as it occurred to me the other night when our troop train ran into a Greek one and none of us were injured so we got breakfast then and there while the man responsible for the event was placed under arrest and I'll tell you all about it some day but just now I think it is time to add a full stop because I've lost my way in this sentence almost as completely as I did in the rain on Monday night when I fell down between GHQ and home three times and have not got my coat clean yet but it doesn't matter because I've borrowed one and anyhow my new boots are splendid and the sun is shining and peace is coming and also a happy New Year to all and so all I says is why worry because we are all coming home some day and until then Best Love and now for a
>
> •
>
>   B L
>   G [8]

He wrote again on 29 December, anxious about the sort of work he should take up when he returned to England, and also for his wife's health. Isobel had been ill through the Christmas period and was worried about how to increase the family's income; GH wrote to her on the last day of the year:

> I'm so sorry to hear of all yr trouble – poor old dear you have been in the soup this time. And the eye trouble is really very serious because the ill effects last so long. Keep me well posted up with news about you and get Imogen and Vally [9] to do the same.

---

[8] In most of the letters home to Isobel, and later to IH, GH uses a simple private code, particularly when signing off. Always in capitals, there are 'B L' (Best Love), 'G' (Gustav), occasionally 'V' (Very), and 'O D' (Old Dear), and guessable riddles such as 'SYS' (See you soon) and even 'almost SYN' (Now) as he gets nearer home.

[9] Vally Lasker, a good friend of the Holsts and a colleague of GH's at SPGS.

Don't worry about getting any work – just concentrate on getting
Well and don't imagine you are really so just because you feel all right
for a day or two.

The news about Imogen is splendid. Bless Her she is a joy for ever
as well as a thing of beauty. Of course we don't want her forced into a
prodigy but under people like Miss Pye and Miss Shuttleworth I should
be quite willing for her to specialise in music even at her present age.
So if you care to discuss it do so. I feel that like everything else it is a
question of people entirely. She is under the right people and if they
think she could be excused certain school work it would be certain to be
successful. Mind you settle about the violin. And could she have private
theory lessons from Jane? I mean something that would stimulate and
guide her creative powers. Jane would do this better than anyone else I
know.

Don't you think Imogen ought to try and write a little better. It is all a
question of habit and habits grow on people – in a few years she would
find it very hard to improve ...

How splendid of Nora to score Imogen's carol!

Nora Day, one of GH's colleagues at SPGS, had orchestrated IH's recently completed arrangement of 'Resonet in Laudibus'. In her next letter Isobel sent her
husband some more of IH's recent outpourings in prose, verse and music; he
responded on 15 January 1919 that 'considering Imogen's age, I think her report
very good indeed. Also her poem isn't at all bad but not as good as her music'.
Then on 9 February he wrote a more considered letter on the subject of his
daughter's education:

Don't be always apologising for not writing or not sending interesting
news. Your letters are not as numerous as Jane's – nobody else's could
be – but you and Imogen are both bricks at writing when you have so
little time and you yourself write such long letters which in itself is a joy.
When I see your fist I settle down to a good long read and you never
disappoint me. And I don't want 'interesting' news – I want just what
you always send me. Ordinary details of home life become quite thrilling out here! ...

I've had a very kind and wise letter from Jane about Imogen. I hope
you quite understand that I only suggested Imogen specialising if Miss
Pye and Miss Shuttleworth really recommend it. I expect it is all right.
Little points can be so easily confused when one is 2000 miles away!
Still I thought I would mention it. Personally I am delighted that she is

learning the violin instead of geometry but I do hope that you and Miss Pye are equally delighted because I should be very sorry if I had unconsciously persuaded you against your judgement.

I wonder if Imogen will be as big a duffer at languages as her father! Anyhow she must have a good struggle. Each time I go abroad I realise that English and French will take you over Europe if you know them well enough but you must know both.

I've just re-read your letter and I see that it's all right and that you and Miss Pye are doing what you feel to be right. I won't tear this up but you can ignore all this part.

GH's next letter, from Athens on 2 March, continues the theme, as well as addressing the equally important issue of what to buy IH for her birthday in April:

I enclose Imogen's letter. I have had three from her – all splendid. The last one ends
> PS I simply love the violin.
> PSS Monsieur Mangot is topping.
> PPSS Theory with Jane is ripping.
> Cheerioh !

(I wonder which is the greater compliment, topping or ripping.) Jane has told me about the theory lessons which seem a great success. I thought they would be ...

I've had no flue and no fleas and only a few bugs just to let me know what to expect in the spring. Do send Imogen's viola piece. I wish I could have had it in Salonica as Vowles (see program) plays the viola. Could you advise me as to Imogen's birthday present? My only idea is to walk round the bazaars seeking for inspiration. Something that can be turned into something else for charades – and something pink. Where shall it be sent? Her writing is very good now. I hope you don't disapprove of my checking her old scrawling. It's my first offence. I hope Jane will never give her homework. I have suggested to Jane that Imogen should be played to. She doesn't hear much music as I never play. Otherwise I've left it to them both to do as they please ...

P.S.
I have thought it better to send Imogen's birthday present now as I have a certain amount of free time and I know some of the shops.

I am sending her

1) A nice tin to hold everything. This is to be passed on to you as you need tins more than she does.

2) My 'goat'. I thought that perhaps you would like Imogen to wear him – of course with due alterations – next winter. If not she can pass him on to you. He is a noble looking beast and so is your husband when he wears him! He may smell a bit when he is let loose but don't be alarmed – he is pure goat. (This last sentence refers to the goatskin, not to your husband.)

3) A 'Corsage turque' that you must work into a dress for her.

4) Some picture postcards. Among them some duplicates to be sent to Miss M. Clark James Allen's Girls' School for her small people.

5) Some pictures of Athens done up in a cardboard roll. I hope she will pass on any she does not want to you. The same applies to the postcards. Those of the Parthenon ruins are a bit 'grown up' and you will appreciate them more.

I am labelling the parcel "to be opened on April 12th." Shall you be with her then?

IH's 'viola piece' was her Duet for viola and piano, written at Eothen and designated 'Op. 3' by the young composer. In her reply Isobel sent GH some more of IH's poetry, this time in the form of a valentine to her mother; GH responded on 12 March, from Athens:

Thanks so much for Imogen's letters. The valentine just came at the right moment: I had just realised with horror that I was a fond weak parent who could see no wrong in his daughter. And now I know to my relief that she writes valentines in geography lessons!

The Valentine read:

> She is as pretty as the peacock
> And as happy as the day
> And as loving as the birds
> That love one another
> You'll guess right away,
> By the meaning of these words
> She is my darling <u>Mother</u>
> Valentine!

(I couldn't do this better as Im doing it in Geography.)
(Risky Business)

By 3 April GH had still not received the promised viola piece, and was growing impatient:

> Yr news of Imogen – barring the earache – is splendid. In fact the news of her has been the nicest of the many nice things I've had out here. Mangeot must be very good. I also get delightful accounts from Jane who is doing just what I wanted – enlarging her horizon in music without filling her head with 'facts'.
>
> But where's Opus III ? I was promised it long ago …
>
> If the news of Imogen is the nicest thing I get the news of you is the worst. And the absence of news makes me fidgety. I wish you could have a little of the sunshine here – it is glorious and there is a gentle breeze from the sea that just makes it right.

Two months later GH was on his way home. Before his return he had organized and conducted a large competitive music festival of army personnel, most of them awaiting their own repatriation. It was a great success, but took an immense amount of effort. He wrote from Constantinople on 16 June: 'The festival is over and I am still alive – or nearly so … and I sail for home tomorrow !!!' On 20 June, aboard ship, he wrote to say that he was 'in terrific form and full of thoughts of you and Imogen MS paper and other pleasant things … If you don't arrange that I see my daughter within 24 hours of my arrival there will be trouble!!!' His final letter before arriving home from Italy was written on the Holsts' wedding anniversary, 22 June, when his arrival back in England was imminent:

> I got up long before sunrise this morning and have been thinking of you and this day all the time. Many many happy returns of the day my dearest and many many thanks for all you have done for me and for all you have been to me.
>
> It seems quite ridiculous to think that we have been married eighteen years. Also it is quite nice. And it is also nice that it is so ridiculous!
>
> My train starts in a few hours and although I have few hopes of arriving on Saturday it is not impossible. And it ought to be Sunday or Monday at the latest.

He did indeed arrive back in London on Saturday 28 June, saw his Aunt Nina and half-brother Max the following morning, went down to Caterham to see his daughter that afternoon, and finally got back to Thaxted and Isobel on Monday 30 June 1919.

   Little is recorded of the final eighteen months of IH's school life at Eothen, with one notable exception. The school magazine for 1920 lists, in its Calendar of Events, the following entry for 9 July: 'Dance of Nymphs and Shepherds, composed and arranged by I. Holst'. At this time IH hoped to be a dancer, so her talents were combined in this school performance; as well as composing the music (no doubt with a little help from Jane Joseph) and arranging the dancing, she took the part of first nymph; contemporary photographs show her to have been very much centre stage in the production. GH attended the performance and commented: 'I wish I could have written anything as good at that age'.

2 'Corn-coloured pigtails and very blue eyes': St Paul's Girls' School, 1921–6

Imogen left Eothen at Christmas 1920, hoping to attend the Ginner-Mawer School (of Dance and Drama) immediately thereafter. Ruby Ginner was a well-known teacher of the freer 'modern' dance (loosely known as 'Greek Dance'), as opposed to strict ballet: it was she who had organized that children's event in Hyde Park in 1911, when IH had represented a very small toadstool. But now, in January 1921, IH was rejected almost at once on health grounds, and her parents were advised that she should spend as much time as possible out of doors over the summer, before going to St Paul's Girls' School in the autumn term. That period must have been the time when Miss Tosh, familiar to IH from the nearby Froebel School, acted as her governess, just to keep her going with school work. While IH was away at Eothen, Miss Tosh had trained and qualified as a teacher of Dalcroze Eurhythmics, which would have recommended her all the more to the Holsts. There is no written proof either of this or of any piano lessons at this time, but as IH was to continue with Miss Shuttleworth for piano when at St Paul's, she would surely have carried on through the summer. As to Miss Tosh: in the 1960s IH, staying overnight with an ex-pupil friend, listened to her describing her near neighbours, including two Misses Tosh. IH suddenly exclaimed 'Not *my* Miss Tosh! She was once my governess!' – a point which could only be resolved by her calling on the house and seeing for herself; alas, neither of these ladies turned out to be 'her' one.

At Whitsun 1921 GH put on a well-documented outdoor production of Purcell's *Masque in Dioclesian*, the first time that the work had been performed since Purcell's day. It was given in the spacious grounds of Bute House, a large eighteenth-century building next to St Paul's which served as the boarding house for the school, and the singers included adult voices from GH's Morley College choir. The production was a great success and was repeated a week later in Hyde Park; memories of IH dancing, with her long fair hair loose round her shoulders, seem to have added to the magical effect felt by the audience.

In September IH went to St Paul's, and was placed in the Lower V form; her form mistress was Miss Muriel Potter, the elder sister of the writer Stephen Potter. (At SPGS the form mistresses remained with the same group of girls all the way up the school, from the time that they entered until they reached their final year. This certainly must have given those teachers a better insight into their pupils' progress than the more commonly found 'year-teacher' system might have done.) The High Mistress was Miss Frances Ralph Gray, who had held the post since the school was founded in 1903. IH would have met several people from her Froebel school days, including one of the teachers (Miss Wigg, whose reports betray prior knowledge of her) and Jane Schofield. She was just six weeks younger than IH, and her father was the Holsts' general practitioner. But her two particular friends were to be Victoria Reid (Vicky) and Helen Asquith.

IH's first day at the school was recalled after her death by a friend with whom she had kept in touch, Dr Joan Wray, née Dancy.

> Imogen arrived ... when she and I were about 12 years old.[1] A girl with corn-coloured pigtails and very blue eyes gazed at me as I said 'I <u>love</u> your father, Mr Holst' and she retorted 'I call him Gussie' – to put me at ease! – and she added '<u>and</u> I call my mother Iso.[2]

For many years the girls at SPGS had referred to Gustav as 'Gussie' among themselves, but here IH seems quickly to have staked her claim to her father, just to make the position quite clear. This was the time when the tight bands of convention were giving way; after all, we are now in the 'twenties.

The Holsts had no London home at this time, and for her first term IH apparently stayed with the family of Jane Joseph, at least during the week. In the Spring term of 1922 she became a boarder at Bute House, where the House Mistress was Janet Cunningham, remaining there in term time until early July, when the family's new London home became available. For the Easter holidays she stayed with the Asquiths at their country home at Mells, near Frome, which was a delight: IH enjoyed tree-climbing and being in the country. One of the Holst family routines seems to have involved going away in school holidays if possible – or at least sending IH away for part of the time – leaving the coast clear for GH to have the solitude he needed so badly for composition. His sound-proof music room at SPGS, to which he always had access, and a refuge in Vally Lasker's nearby flat at 104 Talgarth Road, suited him well.

In mid-July the Holsts moved into 32 Gunterstone Road, Barons Court, which was to be their London home until IH left school in 1925. She and her mother had ideas for brightening up the house, as she wrote to Helen Asquith: 'Iso and

---

[1] IH was in fact fourteen years old.

[2] From a letter to Rosamund Strode, reprinted in *Aldeburgh Festival Programme Book*, 1984, p. 14.

I have got the most inconcievable ideas for decorating the house. She is going to paint the Music room green and gold, and the kitchen vermillion, while I am pondering deeply over my room.'[3] Many years later, a friend commented that Isobel was 'born out of her time', and that twenty years later she could have had a good career in interior decorating and furnishing. She certainly seems to have had strong leanings in this direction, and obviously enjoyed strong colours, a trait she passed on to IH (whose own tastes, however, were to mellow significantly as she got older).

The rest of IH's summer was recorded in lengthy letters to Helen Asquith, the beginnings of a remarkable sequence of correspondence which, for the next two years, provides an important window into her life and thoughts. She began with a letter dated 'Thursday-end-of-term' and outlining an impending visit to hospital:

> My operation is on Monday ... It seems an awful waste of time somehow, to have to take a lump out of the beginning of the hols. And the worst of it is when we <u>do</u> get to Thaxted I shan't be allowed to climb trees or paddle, or even go walks and play tennis at first.

IH's need for an operation remains unexplained. On 8 August she wrote again, from Thaxted:

> Many thanks for your letter which I received <u>ages ago</u> but have been unable to answer till now. Gussie brought it to me ten minutes before I went up for my op. and it comforted me greatly when I was feeling in a perturbed frame of mind.
>
> We have at last escaped from London ... it is glorious to be in the country again. I had forgotten what Life is, in London; the last glimpse I had of it was in Mells at Easter.

Her next letters, on 20 August and 2 September, give the first inkling of her interest in two occupations that were to dominate her future life – country dancing and teaching:

> I have discovered three things. First, the Bach Prelude and Fugue in F minor (Book II). Secondly, the astounding fact that there is country dancing three times a week in the Vicarage garden, on the most beautiful lawn I have ever seen. Twenty or thirty of the villagers turn up at about 7.30 or 8 in the evening, and we dance in a graceful though mildly immoral manner until it is too dark to see, and the bats and ghosts come

---

[3] July 1925. Copies of all the Helen Asquith letters are at HF.

out and mingle with the scent of a tremulous twilight … It is rather fun, although the music for the affair is supplied by a gramophone that has seen better days.

I am very busy trying to instruct my elders and betters and youngers and also betters in the Art of Music. I find it a tedious job … It must be ghastly to teach. Thank goodness all my present pupils are She-males though. Last year I was teaching the present organist, and he was always bribing me with large boxes of chocolates. You will wonder why I try and teach anyone? Well, you see, its all Gussies fault. He sees that people are anxious to learn, so he has pity on them, gives them one lesson, and then finding that he has no time to spare, hands them on to me. Its rather fun at present, but it must be absolutely awful to have to go on all day and every day …

Here one can surely see GH's teaching methods at work: he would have known just what she was capable of doing, but tried out the unpromising village class himself first, just to make sure. All his SPGS pupils were to find out, unexpectedly, how much they actually could do – while he mildly assumed that almost anything was possible. Considering the way her own career was to develop, the remarks of his fifteen-year-old daughter about the awfulness of teaching are amusing in retrospect.

Since 1921 IH, no longer learning the violin, had been having lessons on the French horn with Adolph Borsdorf, a founder member of the London Symphony Orchestra who had also taught Aubrey Brain. But Borsdorf's death in April 1923 put a sudden end to her study of this instrument. In the same month, when she turned sixteen, she became a member of the English Folk Dance Society, and in July her musicianship was recognized when she won the Alice Lupton (Junior Piano) Prize at SPGS. That summer the family went to stay at Paycockes, in Coggeshall, Essex, an ancient merchant's house rescued from ruin and owned by a relation of Conrad Noel, the vicar of Thaxted. In August IH travelled further afield to attend the EFDS Summer School held at Aldeburgh – her first visit to the town that would later become the centre of her life – and unforgettably heard Cecil Sharp play the piano. Then towards the end of the month she continued her travels up to Ellon, Aberdeenshire, by overnight train, for a three-week stay with Victoria Reid, whose father, Sir James Reid, had died at the end of June. IH wrote in anticipation from Paycockes: 'My dearest Vixie, I am counting the minutes to Wednesday night, I have never been in a sleeping carriage before, it will be great fun as I shall read all night and sing at the top of my voice.' From Scotland she wrote to Helen on 5 September, after having 'just returned breathless and exhausted from a Café Chantant (Chong-tong!), where Vixie has played several violin solos, accompanied by me (on a piano which may have seen better days but has certainly forgotten all about them!)'.

By the beginning of 1924 IH's enthusiasm for folk music and dance had deep-ened: over the New Year she spent a week in London, before writing to Helen on 5 January: 'We have had the most glorious week, folk-dancing absolutely every minute of the day, and we have returned to Thaxted to recover.' At the end of February GH fell ill and, suffering from overwork, was obliged to can-cel his teaching commitments and other engagements for the rest of the year, which he spent instead for the most part on his own in Thaxted (with a capable man to look after him) working on, among other things, the Choral Symphony. His SPGS colleagues, Vally Lasker and Nora Day, had to take over much of his work in the school, including the orchestral rehearsals. In March IH wrote to Helen:

> Vally and Nora have been to see me. Poor dears, they will have an awful time of it now that Gussie isn't coming back. I do hope the form will be kind to them, especially Nora …
>
> My dear, THE most thrilling prospect. We may be going to Bruges in the hols, just Iso and I!! Isn't it too exciting for words. What on earth shall I do about speaking French ? Or is Belgan a totally different lan-guidge? I do hope it is, 'cos then one won't be supposed to know it.

Although in later life she was quite comfortable in German, IH never did really come to terms with French. It seems that GH's prophecy that his daughter would prove to be 'as big a duffer at languages as her father' had come home to roost after all.

For the next few months the ups and downs in the lives of the Holst family are vividly brought to life in the correspondence with Helen. In March IH reported that

> the most glorious thing has happened. Gussie has been awarded the Howland Memorial Prize, a gold medal, from Yale University in Con-necticut. It is supposed to be a very great honour, as it is given to a person in any country, for any endeavour in the region of art, literature or music. The only two people it has been given to so far are a French painter called Jean something who was blinded in the war, and Rupert Brooke!!! … Gussie will have to go over and receive it and conduct a few things and make speeches etc. some time, but he won't be well enough

this year. If he goes the summer after next I <u>may</u> go with him !!! Won't it be thrilling.

But GH's absence in Thaxted was a cause of regret for his daughter, who, with her seventeenth birthday looming, was now thinking about the options for the rest of her school education; she wrote on 25 March to tell Helen that

> Gussie ... has developed a sudden passion for Thaxted scenery, before he treated it with a mild indifference. That is all very well, but it leaves him in complete possession of the place, and as he has to be absolutely alone, his family is/are banished. Hence the visit to Bruges ... Pottie is coming to tea today to discuss how many subjects I can conceivably leave out, henceforth ... I suppose one has to go on with Latin and French to the end of one's days, but History – Do you think its necessary for the good of one's soul? Because I don't.

'Pottie' was the pupils' affectionate name for Miss Potter. IH thought that a course of strict harmony and counterpoint would compensate for not doing mathematics, but despaired of having to learn about Reform Bills and Temperance Acts. The next day she cast her sights even further into the future:

> Pottie has a wild notion that I should shove music into a second place, take up English, and go to <u>Oxford</u> after the VII !! Did you ever hear anything like it? Of course neither Gussie or Miss Gray will listen to that, but the awful thing is that <u>that</u> is what I would really like to do! ... Meanwhile, the only things that are decided are that I shall <u>not</u> do Matric at all, and give up History next term. 'Ooray! – English and Music. And <u>that</u> is my idea of Heaven upon Earth ...

On 29 March, she wrote again:

> It was great fun going to orchestra on Thursday. But <u>oh</u>, the Bach is going so badly. The performance is next Thursday, and only a miracle can make it anything but a failure ... Did I tell you how I got on with my first course of treatment from Mr Michael Thomas, the man who is curing my arm? I went to him on Thursday afternoon, and it was most thrilling. I lay and basked under a powerful electric lamp for twenty minutes: – it was like a summer holiday at the sea. He then pinched me and pummelled me all over, and in the intervals kept up a highly instructive conversation ... He is a wonderful person, with the brightest eyes I have ever seen: – even more twinkly than Rutland Boughton's. I like him awfully.

This is the first mention of any kind of the trouble in IH's left arm, which was to plague her for the rest of her life. At this time it must have seemed a nuisance if nothing else; she was already practising the piano for hours every day, and hoped to become a concert pianist if she could. It was an irony of fate that GH should have suffered from severe neuritis in his right (writing) arm – putting an early end to his own dreams of becoming a concert pianist – and his daughter from what turned out to be phlebitis in her left arm, quite unrelated to his condition.

A worse worry for the Holst family was caused by a financial blow in the spring; IH reported to Helen on 6 April that

> I don't know what we are going to do in the hols: – the Bruges expedition is off, worse luck. You see Gussie's gramophone people have gone bankrupt, which means that we have lost over £100 in royalties on the "Planets" during the last year. This is rather a blow, of course, as we had rather been counting on it.
>
> Gussie won't let us come anywhere <u>near</u> him at Thaxted, so I expect we shall spend the hols. in London. We might go down to Oxford for a few days, to stay with some friends there. That would be great fun, as I have never seen the place.

But Mrs Asquith came to the rescue, and invited IH to stay at Mells in the holidays. IH wrote an enthusiastic letter of gratitude: 'How perfectly HEAVENLY … <u>Do</u> thank your mother <u>ever</u> so much. I'm so wildly excited, I can't think, far less write … shall bring tennis racket. What about bathing dress???' Whatever the problem had been, by the summer GH was recording again for Columbia and looking forward 'to my gramophone royalties to keep me from bankruptcy'.[4]

Something of IH's life at this time can be gleaned from the journal of Jane Schofield. Jane and IH had known each other as small children from their Froebel School days, and she too had gone on to SPGS, where they were in the same form. In January 1924 Jane began to write a daily journal. She shared IH's passion for folk dancing, and indeed her brother, Kenworthy Schofield (six years older than Jane), was an expert morris dancer. She also played the violin. Jane herself was enormously enthusiastic, slightly accident-prone, and not such a fool as she often appeared to be. IH flits across her pages from time to time, especially when it comes to the various Folk Dance Vacation Schools which

[4] Letter to W. G. Whittaker, 7 September 1924, quoted in Short, *Gustav Holst*, p. 224.

they both enjoyed.⁵ On 23 June Jane recorded: 'A dreadful day. Just before the exam Imo met me with the dreadful news of Mr Sharp's sudden death.' Cecil Sharp had died quite unexpectedly, after a very brief illness.

Meanwhile in Thaxted GH was recovering, and at the half-term break in June it was possible for Vicky Reid to come to stay at The Steps. There was a good deal of dancing on the vicarage lawn, and other midsummer Thaxted events. Back in London IH's life is picked up in Jane's diary, with another life-long enthusiasm – for the music of Johann Sebastian Bach – now coming to the fore. On 11 July Jane recorded that 'After school the Musical Society betook itself at Imo's invitation to Gunterstone Rd for a 'Soul array thyself'⁶ – most of the time, as is usual on such occasions, was spent eating tea.' A week later the 'Musical Society went to tea with Imo to practise "Soul, array thyself" under the direction of Joan Gibbon ... Imo administered some weird home-made ices – we all ate them to be polite, but they tasted most strange, and smelt like citric acid. Imo discovered afterwards that the whole contents of the flavouring tin had been upset into them by mistake. We hope to live through it, or failing that all depart together.' The performance took place on 23 July, and was not without incident: 'Leila Andrews, who was sharing a stand with me, turned over at the wrong time and knocked the music off the stand – I therefore had to continue without music – but as I knew it by heart by this time it didn't make much difference. There was an election afterwards, and Imo was elected Secretary for the coming year and Viccy Treasurer.' After the SPGS Speech Day six days later Jane recorded wryly that 'Imo got her usual music prize.'

The following month both IH and Jane attended the Cambridge EFDS Summer School, held from Saturday 2 to Saturday 23 August. Jane wrote that 'Imo arrived with hair up! – in two screws round either ear'. 'Putting your hair up' was, of course, a sign of maturity, and obligatory for long hair in the top form at St Paul's – although a fashionable short haircut was also, it seems, acceptable. So IH adopted this hairstyle in the summer holidays, practising for her last year at SPGS in the VIII form. The onset of maturity brought other problems, however, as she wrote to Helen on 26 August from Thaxted:

> It is great fun exploring Essex like this [on a bicycle] but oh and alas, let me whisper it close to your ear, lest anyone shall chance to hear me, and hoot me mercilessly for ever after: – I AM SO LONELY – Awful

⁵ The diary itself is deposited in the RVW Memorial Library at Cecil Sharp House, where there is also a transcript.
⁶ Bach's Cantata no. 180, *Schmücke dich, O lieber Seele*. IH's enthusiasm for the work was to extend forward nearly thirty years, when she performed it with the Aldeburgh Music Club in 1953.

confession, but quite true, I'm afraid! You see, it was all brought about by an unfortunate occurrence which happened at Cambridge. A Greek God (I think it was Apollo, but I'm not sure) was reincarnated, he dropped from the skies, he danced beautifully; – he captured – not my heart, for I decline to carry such a thing about with me; – but my senses! ... I have tried all the usual cures, without much success: I have had my hair up all the hols, so there's not much novelty in that. I have tried smoking, but it's awfully disappointing. And so, as a last resort, I have been devouring novels, "Far from the madding crowd," etc, and "Shirley", which is excellent. But oh! I yearn for intelligent conversation ... I haven't read a note of music for a month, except on Sundays and at choir practices: – Mrs O'Neill would ejaculate "Mon Dieu!" with much feeling if she knew this, but she is safely packed away in the South of France, busy practising Gussie's new piano piece.

By this time IH had transferred her piano studies from Miss Shuttleworth, who had taught her ever since she went to Eothen, to the principal piano teacher at St Paul's, Adine O'Neill. A well-known concert pianist, Mrs O'Neill (née Ruckert) was French by birth and, after she left the Paris Conservatoire as a gold medallist, had become one of the last pupils of Clara Schumann. She met her future husband, the composer Norman O'Neill, while they were both studying in Frankfurt. Appointed the first music teacher at SPGS, it was Mrs O'Neill who, in 1906, had recommended GH to Miss Gray as a possible singing master at the newly founded school.

Sunday 21 September 1924 was GH's fiftieth birthday. The previous day IH had written to tell Helen that 'we are having a Country Dance Party at the Hall tonight: – a kind of last wild fling to finish up the hols. It ought to be rather fun, the dancers here have improved tremendously, and they have learnt heaps of new dances.' Depression set in after the birthday celebrations, however, and she wrote again on Monday: 'Alas and alack! Why do holidays ever come to an end ... I am spending these last hours folk-dancing at every conceivable moment. ... Shall we get up a F.D. Society on the leads,[7] to perform in the 5 minute intervals, except after History?'

In the autumn IH began a year of serious study in the VIII form, aiming for admission to the Royal College of Music. She did little conventional academic work apart from English with Mrs Watkins, whom she found an inspiring teacher. She was now having composition lessons with Herbert Howells and

---

[7] A reference to the lead-covered flat roofs at SPGS, favourite haunts for basking in the sun.

remained very busy with the Musical Society. At half-term in November Vicky came to stay in Thaxted for a few days. GH's condition had evidently continued to improve, though the two girls seemed to be out of the house most of the time, as IH reported to Helen on 6 November: 'We are having a glorious time: – we danced till ten last night and this morning we cycled for miles and miles and miles, and the weather has been glorious. Since then we have played Bach until we are both too weak to know how to stand.' In December the Musical Society put on a concert. IH, who had been reprimanded for slouching, pointedly included Morley's three-part canzonet 'Though my carriage be but careless' in the programme. Alas, her irony passed unnoticed.

The following February IH had her first encounter with Joan Cross, an ex-pupil of SPGS and a musician with whom she was to come into closer professional contact later in life. The Musical Society went to an opera in London, and IH gave an account it in the SPGS journal, the *Paulina*:

> It is not often that we have the pleasure of seeing an old Paulina take a leading part in an opera. Such a pleasure, however, was granted to the few members of the Musical Society who made an expedition to 'The Marriage of Figaro' at the Old Vic, on February 14th.
>
> Joan Cross's acting and singing afforded us great delight, and she is to be congratulated on her well-earned success as 'Cherubino'.[8]

Joan Cross had been at SPGS about ten years earlier than IH, during the War. She had played the violin at school, though she did not noticeably participate in singing, according to one informant a little senior to her. But she went on to work closely with Benjamin Britten in the 1940s and 1950s, creating the roles of Ellen Orford (*Peter Grimes*), Lady Billows (*Albert Herring*), Queen Elizabeth I (*Gloriana* – at which point, late in 1952, she came back into IH's life) and Mrs Grose (*The Turn of the Screw*), and founding the Opera School in London once she had retired from the stage. Like IH, she was to end her days in Aldeburgh.

By Easter 1925 the Holsts had moved from The Steps in Thaxted, to Brook End, Easton Park, Dunmow, Essex – not very far away. This ancient half-timbered house had a small separate barn-like building (with a proper fireplace); with the timely aid of a substantial gift from Balfour Gardiner, this was converted into a music room for GH. On Maundy Thursday that year IH wrote to Helen to tell her about the new house:

> This place reminds me at every turn of Mells, because it is the only place I have ever seen comparable with Mells. The park is huge, massive,

8 *Paulina*, no. 61 (March 1925).

austere and not too aristocratic. By which I mean that there are deer, but not too many; − that the trees are ancient, but not too old to be clumb up; − the lakes are deep, "day-vilish" deep, but not too weedy to be swum in, in the event of a heat-wave. All this is, of course, as it should be, and I hope that one day when you have nothing in particular to do, you will come down and form your own opinions … You can't think how alarming it is to get a report all in Miss Gray's handwriting![9] … Frightfully "wash", as one might say, all except Herbert's remark: − "I. has worked well enough to establish a real friendship with counter-point." Don't you think that's very original?

Have you read this week's "Punch"? Don't you think "You shure slob-bered a bibfull" is a supreme remark? I think I shall try it on next term, when I meet people talking on the stairs. Must stop: − post going.

The next edition of the *Paulina* recorded the fulfilment of IH's desire the previ-ous autumn to found a Folk Dance Society

open to all members of the League. Miss Gray has very kindly consented to be our President, and we are also most fortunate in having, for our Vice-President, Miss Stoddart,[10] who is on the staff of the English Folk Dance Society. Meetings are held at school every week, and though at present our activities are confined to country dancing, we hope that in time we may be able to practise morris and sword dancing, with Miss Stoddart's help and guidance.

The Society now boasts twenty members, but we are naturally anx-ious for more enthusiasts to join, so would those who are interested in the scheme communicate with the Secretary, at the school, for further particulars. Beginners are most welcome, for we have not yet acquired much in the way of technique, our chief aim being to enjoy ourselves as much as possible.[11]

The final weeks of IH's school career were filled with music and dance. On 10 July 1925 Jane Schofield recorded that

---

[9] At SPGS form mistresses, using the words of the teachers concerned, copied out into the pupils' reports all the comments on that term's progress, so that a girl's report was almost entirely in the same handwriting throughout. Miss Gray was the 'form mistress' for the VIII form, but she would still, as High Mistress, have endorsed the report as usual.

[10] Amy Stoddart, recently appointed Geography mistress, was herself a skilled dancer; she carried on teaching at SPGS until well into the 1950s.

[11] *Paulina*, no. 62 (July 1925).

Imo read a paper to the 'Musical' on 'The Dance' which was very well written. There were various illustrations some of which were by us doing country dances ... Also Amy [Stoddart] did 'Princess Royal' to Imo's accompaniment on pipe and tabor, but she did caper music when she should have played side step & then by the time Amy had adjusted herself very skilfully she changed back to side step. Poor Amy she looked very heated.

Ten days later there was a performance of *The Rehearsal*, a short comic play (purporting to be the first-ever rehearsal of *Macbeth*) by Vicky's uncle, Maurice Baring. GH attended and, his daughter remembered, 'laughed all the way through'. 28 July was Speech Day, in which, according to Jane, 'Imo was the heroine of the hour – as it's her last term we performed one of her works for choir & orchestra. She also played piano with great vim.' The IH work performed was *An Essex Rhapsody*, and her 'vim' at the piano that day was targeted at Chopin's *Etude* in E major and the first performance of GH's *Toccata*, 'dedicated to Mrs O'Neill and her Pupils.' Finishing her school career as she had begun it, IH was awarded the Senior Alice Lupton Piano Prize, and left SPGS a few days later, at the end of July. On 31 July she wrote a vivid account of her final days to Helen Asquith:

> What a relief it is to have left school, after all. We had a hectic time on Wed. after everyone had gone home. I dreaded saying goodbye to Miss Gray, as everyone always comes out in floods of tears after that ordeal. However, I found her terrifickly cheerful, – one might almost say flippant, and the only thing she did was to offer me a post on the music staff in three years' time. This caused me great joy at the time, but on thinking it over I have decided that I would rather accept a post as chief handmaid to Phlegyas in the cerchio quinto of Dante's hell, any old day of the week ...

After a swim and a picnic lunch in their old form room, the leavers then started to enjoy themselves in a variety of ways. Miss Patrick (History) took a group photo of them all, wearing unlikely outfits (based on elements of the school uniform), after which the much-loved School porter, Ruthven, took them on a guided tour of all the forbidden corners of the building – a 'terrifying proceeding', as she recalled to Helen:

> I nearly fell through the roof of the hall, and was only just rescued by Ainsworth's long, lean arm. Crawling through the dirty little passages under the baths was quite the most agonising experience I have ever had.

We all felt so dirty after this that we decided to go to the baths again. I learnt to dive, but with very little success, I'm afraid … During the picnic tea, the company began to feel slightly depressed, so Diana and I sang all the songs we could remember from 'By the Way', and I produced Jack Hulbert's photo from within the folds of my rough note book, and they cheered up miraculously.[12]

Then we went home and changed, and <u>then</u> the fun began. They <u>all</u> came to supper with me: – I can't <u>think</u> how we managed to fit them all in, and we talked scandal and smoked and eventually departed for the Beggar's Opera. It was a fitting end for such a day, term, year, epoch …

She gave Helen her address for the next three weeks, when she would be at the EFDS Summer Vacation School in Cambridge. Then:

THE MOST TREMENDOUS thing has happened; – so tremendous that it will take at least five minutes for it to sink in. So pull up your socks and listen: – An American person came to School on Speech Day, lost his head completely, with the result that he is going to do my Rhapsody <u>in</u> <u>America</u> next spring!

Did you ever hear of such a thing? Public performance, copyright, performing fees and everything. I'm so wildly excited about it: – I walk with my head among the stars and my feet among the poppies in the cornfields.

It's just as well I am going to settle down and do a little hard work at Cambridge. Picture me lolling in a punt on the backs, with a frivolous novel and a bag of chelsea buns, or lying full length and smoking in some field near Granchester.

With school behind her, IH was formidably well placed for her chosen career in music. She was having composition lessons from Herbert Howells, and studying the piano with Adine O'Neill. She knew her way around the organ, but no longer played the violin; for two years she had had lessons from Adolph Borsdorf on the French horn. She could train and conduct a choir or small orchestra, so that by this time she knew from experience something about the difficulties inherent in learning almost any musical instrument, and also how

[12] *By the Way*, 'one of the brightest specimens of *revue intime* that London has ever seen', had been running at the Apollo Theatre since January 1925; it starred and was directed by the entertainer Jack Hulbert and his wife Cicely Courtneidge (*The Theatre World and Illustrated Stage Review*, November 1925, p. 14).

to write for them. Most auspiciously, she had been promised a performance in the USA of one of her works.

Nothing more was heard from America, however, and IH got down to the 'hard work' of accompanying country dance class sessions every morning in Cambridge. But at least she was paid and could write enthusiastically to Helen on 6 August that

> Cambridge is the best place in the world: – second only to London, Thaxted, Mells, and half-a-dozen or so of the other best places in the world.
>
> I enjoy earning my living most tremendously: – it gives me a creepy feeling down my spine every time I think of that 4gs [guineas] a week, even though it means getting up at an incredible hour in the morning.

Before IH went to Cambridge an old school friend had visited her at Brook End. They went for a drive around Essex, and then called in to see another old Paulina, staying in a cottage out in the country with a friend of hers. The experience was a strange and revealing one for IH, showing her a new world of which she had little knowledge, as she wrote to Helen:

> We all sat on the floor and smoked and drank strong black coffee, and those two read things out of the Oxford Book[13] and ever and anon they said the most amazing things, which I endeavoured to remember, but with very little success. Perhaps it was the coffee that had got to my head, or the cigarettes. I don't know …
>
> I have never seen anyone smoke so many cigarettes as those three. They kept the chain going for over two hours. After my seventh I began to feel as if I had had a glass of old port on a hot afternoon, so I thought it wise to desist. The others, however, went on well into the 'teens.

They continued, reading poetry, and IH 'realized what a lot one misses by not going to Oxford or Cambridge. I envy you'. (Helen was to go to Oxford in due course, to read Classics.)

> However, there is precious little time to regret things or grow sentimental, as all day is taken up with folk dancing and singing.
>
> I should be impossibly happy if only I had not gone and fallen violently in love with one of the folk dancers. This sad state of affairs renders my working hours fraught with agony and my sleeping hours nil. It is quite

---

[13] *The Oxford Book of English Verse, 1250–1900*, ed. Arthur Quiller-Couch (Oxford: Clarendon Press); the most recent edition had come out in 1924.

the worst dose I have ever had, and at intervals throughout the day and night I am filled with dismay and long to rush from this city. It is rather amusing: – his mother[14] and Gussie were in love when she was seventeen and he was nineteen, and <u>my</u> mother was running about in a pinafore with two plats down her back. On the strength of this old alliance his mother (who is a dear, by the way) has asked me to lunch on Sunday. I don't know how I shall get through it; – I'm sure I shall lose my head. Do pray for me, will you? 1 o'clock next Sunday.

And, incidentally, don't forget to write and tell me everything. I'm afraid I shan't get down to Mells, – I can't possibly learn to drive in my present frame of mind; – it would be too risky!

She never did learn to drive, though she tried once or twice. Gear levers and handbrakes would not, anyway, have helped that troublesome left arm.

On her return to Brook End from Cambridge, on 26 August, IH wrote to Helen:

O, but I have had a wild time; a madly exhilarating time, an intoxicating time at Cambridge. Perhaps it is just as well that I have returned once more to this rusticity. During the last three weeks I have earnt £13.11s.9d by the sweat of my brow, and in the intervals I have succeeded in getting my affairs hopelessly entangled. When you next see me, I shall be sadly changed. I have grown <u>thin</u>, – almost willowy, one might say. It is owing to the constant lack of sleep and total loss of appetite. Some day, in the far distant future, I may emerge from this misty sea of melancholia, in which I am splashing about rather ineffectively; – and I shall look once more upon the world in general, and my friends in particular; – (you, who will be greyhaired and a grand-mother by then.) As it is, I sigh wearily, and set some of the shorter poems of De la Mare's to the most acrid and nauseating series of discords.

She signed herself off as 'your tiresome, and rapidly decaying Imo'; there now ensued a gap of two years in this remarkable sequence of letters, as the two friends went their separate ways. IH had applied her 'acrid and nauseating' discords to three of de la Mare's poems, set for treble voice accompanied by two violins and cello.

At this time the Holsts had no London home (they had left 32 Gunterstone Road earlier in the year), so in the Autumn term of 1925 IH once more stayed at

---

[14] Mabel Forty, GH's 'adored Beloved Sweetheart' to whom he had dedicated his *Introduction and Bolero* for piano duet in 1893.

Bute House as a boarder, studying hard with Herbert Howells and continuing her piano lessons with Adine O'Neill. She carried on with EFDS classes and some out-of-school activities, and would no doubt have returned to Brook End at weekends when she could. Isobel remained in Essex all the time, enjoying the spaciousness of the house and its garden, and welcoming her family when they came. Now, at this crossroads in her life, between school and the RCM, IH received a letter from her father, the contents of which she valued so much that when she much later gave the letter away (to someone in need of similar advice) she first copied it out to keep:

> Dear Imogen,
> Half term is a good time to overhaul one's affairs and if you indulge in doing so it ought to be a pleasurable occupation. As far as I can see you have drawn up a stiff program and stuck to it which means that you have got grit and perseverance, two things very difficult to acquire if you haven't got them in you to begin with. But from what Iso told me I fear there is a little danger of rigidly following out the letter and thus sacrificing the spirit. The latter consists of Parry's definition of education – 'making the best of oneself for oneself and for one's fellows.'
> Now if one is naturally flabby the only thing to do is to try and follow a fixed program rigidly. But in your case this is not as essential as keeping oneself in the tip top of physical fitness. You can't make the best of yourself in any other way whatsoever any more than you can get the best of music out of a YMCA piano during a Salonica winter. The analogy is very close because in both cases the mechanism gets clogged and doesn't respond to one's will.
> And just as there are keen young ignoramuses who despise looking after their physical fitness, so there are sentimental novelists (or there used to be) who talk twaddle about the hands of a master drawing sweet music from a piano with half its notes broken. The point being that both could do better with proper mechanism. I'm very glad you have stuck to your program but I suggest that you constantly overhaul it with a view of getting more and more music with less and less effort. And for the next six weeks sacrifice everything to general health and stop practising <u>before</u> you get tired. Then in 1926 see how long you can go on without getting tired. Later on see how much result you can get in a short time.
> For the rest I feel happy and proud in and of my daughter. I think life is not going to be too easy for you which is a matter of great importance

as I am always sorry for people who have not been knocked about while young and have never learnt that happiness is something springing from within and not something applied from without like a mustard plaster.

If you like your present life and if you can keep tremendously fit I don't see why you shouldn't have a whole year of it.

But in Sep 1926 you've got to go to College and I'm going to play the stern PA over it because there is much that you can only learn from your fellow students.

Ask Herbert [Howells] if you are to try for a scholarship.

Composition is a wicked gamble – one cannot foresee results. But you are going the right way to work by writing lots. Most young people nowadays don't write enough and in particular they don't write enough Early Horrors —— Mind you do!

> B. L.
>
> Gussie[15]

There is not a great deal of information about IH's working pattern for the first half of 1926. She may have tried unsuccessfully for the RCM scholarship which she was to gain the following year. Certainly her musical education continued; she went to a performance of *Parsifal* over two nights at the RCM ('my first Wagner opera') early in July, and she would have carried on with the EFDS classes to which she was already committed. On a wet day in the summer there was a fund-raising fête in aid of the restoration fund for Great Easton Church tower at which IH led some country dancing, and played in a concert – that, at least, was indoors, one hopes. Another of IH's pre-RCM activities was to provide the music for a pageant held near Thaxted in July. The goal of this fund-raising effort was to build what became Cecil Sharp House, headquarters for the EFDS, on the north side of Regent's Park. The preliminary announcement for the event reads as follows:

> A message from the Marquis D'Oisy: "A festival will be held under the auspices of the Essex Branch of the English Folk Dance Society at Pledgdon Green on Saturday, July 10th, at 3.30 p.m., wet or fine. In the event of very bad weather we hope to adjourn to a neighbouring barn. An old fourteenth century Monk (Mr. A. A. Thomson) has written a chronicle of St. Thomas of Canterbury – the borders of his MS he has beautifully

---

[15] The copy in IH's hand is on a page of foolscap-size paper using royal blue ink, and may date from *c.* 1950 or a little later. Her heading runs 'Copy of a letter from G, written in October or November 1925'; HF. 'Early Horrors' had been GH's description of his own earliest attempts at serious composition.

illuminated with miniatures of the principal scenes of the story, using that wealth of pure colour so dear to the mediaeval illuminator. It is these miniatures that have come to life in our play. Folk Dances led by Miss Morris will be shown in mediaeval dress. The Letchworth Morris team, in traditional costume will dance to the pipe and tabor played by Mr. K. Schofield. Miss Imogen Holst is arranging and conducting the old music which accompanies the play. After tea we will return to the twentieth century and have a folk-dance party from 6.30 to 10 pm., to which all dancers are invited."[16]

The Marquis D'Oisy was a somewhat ambivalent, flamboyant character, known for painting plain furniture with Italianate decoration (the 'beautifully decorated MS' mentioned above could well have been one of his pieces of work) and with a flair for staging events and pageants such as this one. He was to disappear off the Essex scene rather suddenly and apparently without explanation a few years later. Joan Morris and Kenworthy Schofield, Jane's brother, were to be married just two weeks after this event; all the Holsts went to the wedding in Bishop's Stortford church, and GH played the organ.

Meanwhile Adine O'Neill was enquiring at the RCM as to whether the pianist Kathleen Long would be able to take IH on as a pupil; she replied positively on 25 July 1926 from her home at Bury St Edmunds:

> I am so very sorry that I had left town on Wednesday and your letter has only just followed me here. Mr Holst spoke to me some time ago about this and I shall be delighted to take Imogen at the College next term. I have given up taking 'second studies' in general but I think she will probably prove interesting. I remember quite well hearing her play at St. Paul's. I suppose there is no hope of her taking piano as an additional 'first study' is there? as I am sure you will agree that it is very difficult to make much headway with one 20 minute lesson a week …
>
> I shall be most interested to do anything I can to help Imogen and I hope she will prove a good worker.

O'Neill forwarded the good news to IH with some advice about how she should spend the summer:

> I enclose Miss Long's letter you need not return it – just pick up those pieces in September and work at the Ile Joyeuse so as to be in good trim when you play to Miss Long …

---

[16] *English Folk Dance News*, no. 11 (April 1926), p. 343.

I hope you will enjoy your Holidays and take rest in Music in August (apart from Folk dancing)!

In August the EFDS Summer Vacation School again took place in Cambridge, and as usual IH was there. At the same time there was another event going on in the city, a Summer Course in Music Teaching, and IH made a particular note of having heard one lecture, given on 4 August by Dr George Dyson, marking it in her records as 'The first time I saw Dyson'. He would be one of her professors at the RCM a few weeks later. And at the beginning of September 1926 she went to stay in Dublin as the guest of Janet Cunningham, House Mistress of Bute House, where she had been lodging since leaving school (an arrangement that was to continue for a few months longer). She was taken to a first night at the Abbey Theatre, saw an exhibition of paintings by Jack Yeats (brother of the poet) and no doubt thoroughly enjoyed her first visit 'abroad'. Certainly, there were to be many more to follow.

3 'To be best when all are good': The Royal College of Music, 1926–30

It is undeniable that, as GH's daughter, IH did gain a certain amount of attention from the musical profession and press, especially as recognition of her father's achievements, and his reputation abroad, grew over the years. But she never at any time traded on their relationship, and, being of independent mind and quite capable of holding her own, it was soon discovered that, as a musician, she had no need to depend on her parentage. On the other hand it could be useful to be the bearer of this unusual name, and when she travelled abroad GH would write notes of introduction for her to some of his Continental colleagues and friends whom he felt she should meet. He knew she would never abuse such privileges.

When she entered the RCM in the autumn term of 1926 IH embarked at once on a very busy schedule. For the first year her first study was to be piano, with Kathleen Long, and her second composition, with George Dyson. As an 'extra' second study she undertook conducting with W. H. Reed. The importance of first and second studies at the RCM was entirely to do with the weekly individual time allowance given to professors for each student. 'First studies' had a basic 40 minutes, but 'second studies' rated only half that. No wonder that Kathleen Long complained about the miserable 20-minute allocation before IH entered the college. IH's other classes and professors were:

Score Reading	Aylmer Buesst
Paper Work	George Dyson
Aural Training	Stanley Stubbs
Music Class	Percy Buck
Choral Class	Hugh Allen (the Director)
Ballet Class	Penelope Spencer
Folk Dancing Class	Mrs Kennedy

William H. Reed, who took the conducting class, was a very well-known violinist and teacher, and had been leader of the London Symphony Orchestra for many years. A great friend of Elgar, under whose baton he had frequently performed, his pupils would have learned much about how conducting should be done, as well as how it should not. Students began in his 'junior' class – conducting the Third Orchestra – for two years, then, if continuing with conducting, moved up to confront the two more senior orchestras. IH had, of course, already picked up a good deal from her father at SPGS, where the girls had to conduct choral and instrumental groups as a matter of course – a valuable grounding for later life. Years after, when teaching her own students at Dartington, IH was particularly fierce with the women, insisting that on no account should conductors ever bend 'gracefully' at the knees as if curtseying or dancing to the music: legs should always be kept as straight as possible in a natural standing position, and movement across the podium, if really necessary, just simple, single paces as if walking. When conducting, her own hand gestures were always clear and positive, easily followed by musicians of all calibres, and were no doubt influenced by her years of dancing. At the RCM she much enjoyed Penelope Spencer's ballet class, and was to receive good notices for several of her appearances on stage in the class presentations.

Informal Concerts, given by the Third Orchestra, were held at 4.45 p.m. at regular intervals, and were known as 'jazz concerts' by the participants. Two or three big works (or a variety of smaller ones) were programmed each time, and these were directed by a selection of members from the class, who shared out between them the responsibility for the performance of works in several movements. IH's first opportunity was in December 1926 (at the 103rd Informal Concert), when she conducted the first movement of Mozart's 'Prague' Symphony. Iris Lemare, a few years older than IH and herself to become well known as a conductor, took part in the same concert, with Vaughan Williams's *Norfolk Rhapsody* no. 1. At the end of IH's first term all the comments on her report were good, very encouraging for all concerned.

Although she was now at College, IH's enthusiasm for, and involvement with, the EFDS and folk-dancing continued to grow. She fitted in as much as she could, in addition to the 'official' classes held at the RCM by Mrs Kennedy (whose husband, Douglas Kennedy, was the EFDS Director). As an EFDS representative from Essex, IH took part in an All-England Festival held in London in December. At the beginning of 1927 she danced in RCM performances given by the ballet class to music by Bach and Rutland Boughton, and folk dances, and there was a Royal Performance in February 1927. She also went to several concerts in London; here a student pass was a great help. GH's choral ballet *The Morning of the Year*, written for the EFDS, received its first concert performance in the Royal Albert Hall on 17 March; it was the first work to have been commissioned by the music department of the BBC, but would have to wait several months for its first fully staged performance at the RCM. Cheltenham, the town of GH's birth, put on a big concert of his works on 22 March; IH was there, photographed sitting demurely near the end of the front row in a large group of people. GH, pictured next to the Mayor in the centre of the same row, has the usual vaguely unhappy look which he wore on such occasions. IH's end-of-term report at Easter was again very good.

In April, just before her twentieth birthday, IH obtained her first passport – a highly significant event. She describes herself as a 'Student of Music', 5 feet 4 inches in height, with blue eyes and flaxen hair. Her photograph shows a serious young woman, wearing her fair hair in the plaited 'earphones' style fashionable at the time, with a crowning ribbon encircling her head. This document was to work hard on her behalf until its expiry ten years later, and she put it to good use almost immediately. The previous summer a group of Basque musicians and dancers had come to London, and now, just after Easter 1927, there was to be a return visit by a group of fifty EFDS enthusiasts as 'camp followers', there to support the small official party and skilled morris dancers, and to perform English country dances from time to time. They left England on 24 April, crossed the Channel, travelled across France by train (there was just time to walk a little in Paris between stations) and reached Bayonne the next day. The Basques are an ancient people, living at the north-west foot of the Pyrenees in the furthest corner of Spain. Once a part of the kingdom of Navarre, their culture derives from distant ancestors, and the language is quite distinct from others. But some of their traditional dances share elements with English morris and folk-dances, so this visit to the French side of the Pyrenees (where similar dances might be found) was not as far fetched as it might seem. After an exciting and active few days, the EFDS party returned to London on 1 May. IH would have been thrilled by this introduction to an unfamiliar, ancient tradition of music and dance, still living on its home ground; this was an aspect of folk music which she increasingly found enthralling.

GH's *The Morning of the Year* had its first full (staged) performance in the Parry Theatre at the RCM on 1 June. The programme also included some short pieces in which IH danced, one of which she choreographed herself to Scarlatti's *Tempo di ballo.* But composition was also occupying much of her time, and during the spring she completed two orchestral suite movements under the eye of George Dyson to add to the Mass in A minor that she had completed before Christmas for her 'paperwork' class. This work was to be one of the lengthiest products of her entire composing career, and it pleased her teachers, with

Herbert Howells commenting, 'Good, I like it.'[1] The style is quasi-Elizabethan, and indebted also to Vaughan Williams's Mass in G minor, but it demonstrates a new technique and confidence in applying her material to larger structures. In May she entered an RCM competition for an Open Scholarship for Composition, and heard the next month that she had won; the scholarship awarded her £60 per annum for three years. (The *Herts and Essex Weekly* reported this success of a local student, giving the recipient's name as 'Mr Ogen C. Holst of Dunmow'!) At the beginning of July IH joined an outing arranged by her father to visit Robert Bridges, the Poet Laureate. The *Paulina* gave a detailed description of the event:

> Early in the term, Mr Holst invited several mistresses and girls, with Nellie Meyrat as soloist, to sing and play his settings of some poems by Robert Bridges to the poet at his home near Oxford. So, with Miss Strudwick's permission,[2] a merry party travelled down to Boar's Hill on Saturday, July 2nd. Dr. and Mrs Bridges welcomed us very kindly. Between 12 and 3 o'clock we had two short rehearsals in a large music-room, while in the interval the sound of talking and laughter came from little groups enjoying their picnic lunch in different corners of the beautiful garden. In addition, the discovery of a swing provided much amusement for the younger members of the party.
>
> A few visitors arrived soon after 3 o'clock, including, to our joy, Miss Gray, who came from the Headmistresses' conference at Oxford. We had hoped that Miss Strudwick would be able to come, but she was unable to spare the time. After the performance Dr. Bridges said that he hoped we would come again.[3]

IH was there as one of the singers and noted, 'This was the first time I met Masefield' (with whom GH would shortly collaborate on *The Coming of Christ*). Three days later, back in London, IH played one of her own works, the Theme and Variations for piano solo, at an RCM Informal Concert on 5 July; two weeks later, on 19 July, she conducted Howells's *Puck's Minuet*. Her conducting ability was by now attracting serious attention; on 6 July 1927 the *Daily Telegraph* critic observed in her

---

[1] Termly report, Christmas 1926.
[2] Miss Gray, after twenty-three years as High Mistress of SPGS, had retired at Easter.
[3] *Paulina*, no. 68 (July 1927), p. 6.

a conductor of something more than promise. No woman has yet managed to establish a secure tenure of the conductor's platform, so that Imogen Holst may prove the first of her sex to do this. The fact that she is a score-reader of exceptional brilliance is a hopeful augury. The time may not be so far distant when the British Women's Symphony Orchestra places its baton again in female hands.

In July and August, during the summer vacation, IH was again involved with the EFDS Summer School, as before playing for classes in the mornings and joining in the dancing when free; this year it was held at Buxton for four weeks, from 30 July. Jane Schofield, now a Cambridge undergraduate, recorded some details of the events, though from time to time pages are tantalizingly missing from her diary. On 4 August she wrote:

> I went off to the band practice … Imo insisted [that Jane should play her violin] and went on insisting as she was running the band, so I did … In the evening was the country dance party – out of doors this time – it was glorious – there was a lovely blood red setting sun, and Imo stood with her back to it conducting the orchestra in an orange coloured dress – and the sun made an orange halo round her head so that she looked like Osiris arrisern.

In this excerpt Jane Schofield has conjured a wonderful scene, with a most observant description of IH wearing her favourite colour. (There was very often some blue as well, but perhaps not this time.)

After Buxton IH went to stay again with the Reids at Ellon, from where she and Vicky Reid wrote a last letter to Helen Asquith, now studying Classics at Somerville, Oxford. It is a jointly composed document, turn and turn about, and mixing sound information with pure gibberish. IH begins:

> My dear Helaina,
>
> *Imo and I are writing alternate sentences.*
>
> No, do you? *Chiefly North.* What do you mean by telling Diana that Vicky and I have changed? *How do you mean?* Don't you think this is an affected letter? *Imo has got a scol, and I am going to Leipzig in 3 weeks.*
>
> That's all the news we've got to tell you.
>
> *Are you haven a good time?*
>
> Does Bill say "Have bit choc?" before breakfast every morning? *and does Per still come down her doze?*

Gussie has been a walking tour in Dorset: – he went to see Thomas Hardy, and he's dedicated his new work to him: – it's all about Egdon Heath and the first chapter of "The Return of the Native."

What a long sentence. Goodbye. *This requires an answer*

Definatel – – –*Sst sst Pshaw* Definitely.

Love from Imo and *Vicky*

P.S. Nunc, nunc, *o Daedale bixuit*

After the holidays IH's timetable at the RCM was as full as before. But, as the holder of a scholarship for composition, this (and not piano) became her official first study, and piano 'equal second' with conducting. On 22 November in an Informal Concert she played the solo part in Beethoven's Piano Concerto no. 1 (with three conductors, one for each movement) and also conducted her father's *A Fugal Concerto* with her school friend Sylvia Spencer (sister of Penelope) as the oboe soloist. On the afternoon of 26 November she played the orchestral piano part in a performance of GH's *Hymn of Jesus*, conducted by the composer, in the Royal Albert Hall. The same evening, also in the RAH, there was a Folk Dance Festival involving massed country dancing by 500 performers, and Basque Folk Dances given by traditional teams from France and Spain on their first visit to England. The event was held in aid of the Cecil Sharp Memorial building fund, the aim of which was to provide the EFDS with worthy headquarters; hitherto the Society had had no home of its own suitable for its routine activities, and had been using a variety of halls across London for its classes and meetings.

An entry in IH's passport recording her disembarkation at Dunkirk on 16 December 1927 marked a week that she spent in Flanders, apparently travelling alone, and visiting Brussels and Bruges – replacing that trip which, back in 1924, had to be abandoned when GH's recording company had let them down. While she was away her father left for Germany for one of his periodic breaks, this time for a whole month, and IH returned home on 23 December, to spend Christmas at Brook End with her mother. She recorded that they were snowed in for three days over the holiday. At the end of that term Kathleen Long had again bemoaned the fact (this time in her official terminal report) that, now that the piano was IH's second study, there had not been nearly enough time to get through all the work of which she was capable. That her next report was to show piano as an 'equal first study' with composition reveals that someone was finally paying attention. The Director's report at the end of this Christmas term reads: 'A worker who brings good wits and good will to bear on all she does.' Those attributes stayed with her all her life.

1928 was ushered in by another EFDS event: an All-England New Year's Eve Festival held in the Imperial Institute, a neighbour of the RCM. And on 19 January a private performance of *The Jew in the Bush* was given in the Parry Theatre at the RCM Union's AGM. The story was taken from Grimm's fairy tales and set to music by Gordon Jacob; IH enacted the part of the Youth, who outwits the evil witch. GH returned to London from Germany towards the end of January, and on 1 February he accompanied his daughter to a Bach Choir concert in the Queen's Hall, conducted by Vaughan Williams, and concluding with RVW's own *A Sea Symphony*. The programme also included a performance of Gerald Finzi's Violin Concerto played by Sybil Eaton, a musician IH would later get to know well. She went to several other concerts with Vicky through the month, culminating on 23 February in the first London performance of *Egdon Heath* at the Queen's Hall given by the Royal Philharmonic Society's Orchestra, conducted by Václav Talich. The death of Thomas Hardy less than a month before would have added to the work's impact that evening. IH noted that her mother also came to this important concert, and that at the reception afterwards she herself met Talich.

By the end of February IH at last had a London address of her own, a bed-sitting room at 42 Craven Road, not far from Paddington Station on the north side of Kensington Gardens. At the beginning of March she danced in two public performances of *The Jew in the Bush* (having some good critiques), bringing a brief note from her father just saying, 'Last night was delightful. It is a great experience and a rare one to be best when all are good. Many congratulations.' Later in the month she went to Winchester to act as an official accompanist for the Women's Institute Class entries in their competition Festival (earning 3 guineas for one morning's work), and on 26 March she made her last appearance conducting at an RCM Informal Concert, directing the overture to Mozart's *Così fan tutte*. Her own compositional activities were now focused on the production of chamber music, and in the course of the next few months she completed a violin sonata, an oboe quintet and a suite for wind quartet.

Early in April IH received a letter from the 'Squire' of the Cambridge Morris Men inviting her to join them in a two-week cultural tour to Germany at the end of June; as well as dancing (morris for men only, and English country dancing for both men and women) the programme was to include some singing. Meanwhile IH and her father attended the EFDS Easter Vacation School, held in Chester. On 12 April, her twenty-first birthday, GH wrote a promissory note to her: 'I O U a piano piece. Gussie. NB No folk tunes allowed.' (IH had specifically asked him for 'some piano music without any folk tunes'; GH eventually fulfilled his promise with the *Nocturne*, written in 1930.) Two days later she left with Iris Lemare for a two-week holiday in Italy; they visited Milan, San Gimignano, Siena, Perugia and Assisi (staying for five nights in both Siena and Assisi) before departing for home via Strasbourg and Dunkirk. She then returned to the RCM for the summer term, but travelled with her mother to Canterbury for the Whitsun weekend, staying in the Close, in order to attend the first performance on 28 May of John Masefield's new work *The Coming of Christ*, written for the Cathedral, with music by GH, who conducted. The following day she and Vicky played her own Violin Sonata in G at an RCM Informal concert. On 1 June she danced to 'Clair de Lune' (fortuitously and memorably lit by real moonlight) in a late-night RCM cabaret at the Imperial College Union, an event which she noted as 'my first appearance in a Cabaret'.

Plans for the tour of Germany were now well advanced; the group was to travel under the name of The Travelling Morrice. The aim of the visit was to repair and reinforce Anglo-German relationships through music and dance; the organizer on the German side, Georg Götsch, an experienced musician and conductor, was immensely dedicated to the project. The group from England comprised the Cambridge Morris Men, with a few women and three non-dancing musicians. They set off on 24 June via Harwich to the Hook of Holland, journeying to Rotterdam; thence they travelled to Spandau, Berlin, Halle, Weimar, Göttingen, Hannover-Münden, Marburg an Lahn, Bonn, Cologne, Arnhem and Oosterbeck, staying long enough in each place to establish some rapport with their audiences as they performed in the locality (often several times) of each large town. IH directed the English musicians (her choir of dancers, two staff violinists and a recorder player) in performances of pieces by Byrd and Purcell, and of English madrigals. By the time they returned home on 7 July the group had given twenty-one separate performances to welcoming and appreciative audiences. The RCM term was not yet finished, and in addition to the usual schedule there was time for IH to enjoy a few summer season extras such as the Ballets Russes, and to repeat her 'Claire de Lune' dance at a special evening on 21 July at the Garden Club, arranged by Mrs Louise Dyer.[4]

Following the end of the college year, from 4 to 18 August the EFDS summer Vacation School was again held at Buxton, with IH playing for the morning classes as before. When that ended she travelled up to Scotland to join the

---

[4] Louise B. M. Dyer, née Smith (1884–1962), a generous Australian patron of the arts, who founded The Lyrebird Press (later L'Oiseau Lyre). Her aims were to make available early music that had never been printed in a good modern edition, and to support contemporary composers, including at this time GH.

Reids, this time going first to the west coast, to Gairloch in Ross-shire and staying with relations of Lady Reid at Flowerdale, then returning to Ellon, where
she prepared the fair copy of her *Phantasy* String Quartet, intended as an entry
for the Cobbett Prize. The prize – for the composition of a short piece of chamber music – had been established by W. W. Cobbett, a philanthropist and lover
of the genre; he stipulated that the word *Phantasy* should be used in the title,
but did not specify any particular instrumentation. There were to be first and
second prizes both for composers and ensembles, and strictly 'no coaching'
was allowed in rehearsal; this condition was designed to test both the composer's clarity in writing, and the ensemble's ability to search out and interpret
a new work. For the competition IH produced her most technically assured
score so far. Although rhapsodic in style, with harmonies reminiscent of Ravel
and with multiple sections linked by fanciful passages for the solo instruments,
the thematic structure is close-knit, with all the material being developed from
two motifs that occur at the beginning. With the *Phantasy* completed, IH came
back from Scotland in time for the autumn term at the RCM and the second
London performance of *Egdon Heath* at a Queen's Hall Promenade concert on
20 September, conducted by GH.

For the new term Vaughan Williams replaced George Dyson as IH's composition teacher. Gordon Jacob was put in charge of her 'paper work', but in
fact he switched with RVW almost at once. It would seem that RVW felt a
little uncomfortable at having IH as a pupil – he thought he was too close to
the family – but the 'paper work' position enabled him to keep a close eye on
her progress. On 12 October came the announcement that she had won the
Cobbett Prize, with Grace Williams's *Phantasy* Quintet for Piano and Strings
placed second. The prize-winners were awarded 15 and 10 guineas respectively.
Hard on the heels of this success, IH learned that she had also been awarded
the Morley Scholarship 'for the best all-round student'. Founded in 1883, this
provided tuition fees and a sum of £52 10s. yearly 'for maintenance during College terms'; it was tenable for one year, or longer, at the discretion of the Council. In IH's case it was to be renewed the following year.

Despite this success, GH was worried about the effect his daughter's piano-
playing was having on her arm. She was due to take her ARCM in solo performance in the spring, and, mindful of the work that this would entail, GH
took it upon himself to write to her teacher, Kathleen Long, on 16 October:

> Mrs Holst and I have discussed Imogen and the piano and we feel that
> she really ought not to practise any more. Thanks to you, neuritis has
> never been more than lurking, but this autumn she has had one or two

nasty little attacks. I know from bitter experience that when it once gets hold of you there is an end to all piano playing, so hope you will not mind if we keep her timetable as it is. I suppose the Ravel is not too difficult for her?

Forgive me for asking this: you are by far the better judge and we are more than grateful for all you have done.

Although it seems likely that the matter was settled satisfactorily at the time, this was not to be the end of the problem; indeed, the writing was already on the wall for IH's dreams of a future as a concert pianist.

Over the course of the next few months IH's musical experiences and activities outside her RCM timetable were to be exceptionally wide-ranging. In mid-October she was asked by the EFDS if she would take a weekly class at Royal Holloway College, a teacher training establishment for women at Englefield Green in Surrey. There would be seven lessons before Christmas, and she would earn £1 10s, plus expenses, each evening. On 24 October she attended an evening of 'Music by Humans, Puppets and Instruments' at the RCM, when Georg Götsch brought a party of singers over from Germany, with Harro Siegel's puppets. The performance included Mozart's little opera *Bastien und Bastienne* (acted by the puppets) with a variety of madrigals, motets, canons and instrumental pieces by Purcell, Schein, di Lasso, Cherubini and others. The puppets also performed a morris dance (with commentary by their manager) – and in addition magically sang canons and played recorders. IH's concert schedule in London at this time included a programme conducted by Furtwängler in the Royal Albert Hall on 4 November, and three days later a violin recital by Adolf Busch and Rudolf Serkin at the Aeolian Hall. The following week she was the official accompanist for the Class Singing section (all under fourteen years old) of the Sixth Children's Festival, part of the Kensington Musical Competition Festival, with Bernhard (Boris) Ord as adjudicator, returning at the end of the month to fulfil the same role for the Adult Choirs in the Festival. On 28 and 29 November she danced in the ballet for the RCM performances of *Aïda*. Despite all this activity, composition was not neglected, and on 3 December she heard the first performance of her own Suite for wind quartet played at the County Secondary School, Clapham, by an ensemble including Sylvia Spencer. It must have been very gratifying that both her teachers and GH liked and approved of the work; in her Christmas report Gordon Jacob described it as 'charming' and noted that IH was 'getting a good grasp of scoring and shows good aptitude for it'.

Just before Christmas 1928 IH set off on her travels again, spending the 15 guineas of the Cobbett Prize on a holiday in the Swiss Alps, travelling in the company of Iris Lemare and Sylvia Spencer. They began the journey also with IH's father, who was to be away in Italy for a couple of months, seeing him into his train once the Channel had been crossed, before catching their own train for Bern, and Adelboden. Iris Lemare was about four years older than her travelling companions, and used to skiing, and took her role of 'elder sister' very seriously. Her friends, inexperienced and speaking hardly any useful German or French, enjoyed themselves (and the seasonal festivities) very much, rather trying her patience and almost getting into scrapes, but coming to no harm. One of these scrapes, recalled by Lemare, sheds some rare light on IH's romantic pursuits at this stage of her life:

> In the evening we went to a New Year's Eve Ball at one of the big hotels. Midnight came, the little squealing pink pig was released to bring luck to the first person to touch it. When the scrum had subsided, I searched for my two friends. I found that they had both by then acquired faithful admirers and were dancing only with them and all seemed to be well. It must have been 1 a.m. when Sylvia sought me out. 'Iris, you can speak a little German; what kind of drink is a Zimmer? Is it very strong, as my man has just gone to reception and ordered "zwei", that's a double, isn't it?' It was clearly time to be gone. I collected the protesting Imogen and we beat a hasty retreat. We were not unobserved, though and … had to make our escape through the high square window of the cloakroom, dropping onto the snow.'[5]

Though the plan had originally been to spend two whole weeks with her friends, while she was at Adelboden IH received a pressing invitation from Miles Tomalin (the recorder player for the 'Travelling Morrice', also in Switzerland, on a family holiday) asking her to join them at Splügen, on the Italian border, for her second week. This was an irresistible chance, so she travelled across the country and had an enjoyable time there, before returning home on her own.

Back in London IH heard Schnabel play Beethoven's 'Diabelli' Variations at the Queen's Hall on 8 February 1929, and her own *Phantasy* String Quartet, played for the first time on 27 February 1929 at an RCM College Chamber Concert by three string quartets, who were competing for the second half of the Cobbett Prize; Grace Williams's *Phantasy* Quintet for Piano and Strings was similarly performed. The winning ensemble, led by Reginald Morley, broadcast IH's work on 20 March. That spring IH also heard Handel's *L'Allegro* for the first time, a work she was later to edit and perform several times, and at the

---

5 A 'zimmer' is not a drink, of course, but a room. Iris Lemare, 'Sylvia Mortimer Spencer' (memorial article); HF.

end of term she danced in Vaughan Williams's *Sir John in Love* at the RCM. She attended the EFDS Easter Vacation School for a week at Keswick, with GH directing the singing, and in mid-April took her ARCM diploma for solo piano-forte, playing Bach's Prelude and Fugue in F minor (Book I, no. 12), Beethoven's Sonata in E, op. 109, and Holst's *Toccata*, of which she had given the first performance at SPGS back in the summer of 1925. She passed the diploma with 250 marks out of a possible 300, and Kathleen Long wrote her a congratulatory letter:

> Heartiest congratulations! I am delighted that you passed & I don't think that it was altogether to do with softening of the brain on the part of the examiners & I think you thoroughly <u>deserved</u> to pass. Yes! I agree that exams are enormous fun but I am afraid that our opinion isn't unanimous! I was amused & gratified at receiving a 'testimonial' for 'soup-lesse' from you – & I only wish you weren't such a many-sided young woman …

True to form, IH immediately went on holiday by herself to relax, this time to the Scilly Isles. She was there for about ten days, enjoying the people and the early spring. Having no camera, she produced a number of little watercolour sketches of the dramatic scenery to hand. As a girl, sketching was something she did for several years, but of course a chatty crowd is not helpful. There is a snapshot of her at Ellon at work, wearing spectacles, and evidently engrossed. If picture postcards were available of the more spectacular views, she would sometimes place them next to her own efforts in her big scrapbooks: they compare very well, but she appears not to have continued with this agreeable skill as she grew older.

On her return to London IH applied herself once again to composition, and to hearing distinguished foreign artists visiting London in the summer season. In June she was on a short-list of three for the Mendelssohn Travelling Scholarship, but was not awarded it, the prize going instead to David Moule-Evans. On 13 June she heard Eugene Goossens conduct Brahms's Symphony no. 4, Respighi's *Roman Festival* (in its European première) and the first public performance of Stravinsky's Piano Concerto, with the composer himself playing the solo part, an event that failed to enthuse the London critics at the time. A fortnight later, on 25 June, Diaghilev's Ballets Russes performed *Les Sylphides* and *Petroushka* at the Royal Opera House, preceded by the first performance of Eugene Goossens's opera *Judith*. Later that week she attended the laying of the foundation stone of Cecil Sharp House on 29 June, before returning to Thaxted to take part in some morris dancing. In Essex the Holst family were on the move again, leaving Brook End and taking up residence at The Cottage, Great Easton, Dunmow, where they were to stay for a year before moving to Hill Cottage in the same village.

During the summer term IH received an exciting letter from Douglas Kennedy inviting her to join the EFDS group which was to tour in Canada and the USA for six weeks in the autumn, from 26 October to 13 December. She accepted the invitation enthusiastically. Meanwhile, on 5 July her overture *Persephone*, her last and most flamboyant flirtation with Ravelian impressionism, was included in a Patron's Fund rehearsal performance played at the RCM by the New Symphony orchestra conducted by Malcolm Sargent. These events were instituted to allow young composers hear how their works could come to life with the best possible interpreters, an invaluable help, and with critics present. IH had several good critiques, but they could not, of course, refrain from mentioning her relationship to GH, one way or another. The beginning of July saw an open-air production of her father's choral ballet *The Golden Goose* at Warwick Castle. The three performances also included the *St Paul's Suite* as a tribute to the memory of GH's favourite pupil, Jane Joseph, who had died on 9 March 1929 while GH was still away in Italy. Then before the end of term IH learnt that she had been awarded the Sullivan Prize of £10 for 'best proofs of ability and progress in Composition at the Annual Examination'. On 15 July IH and the two Reid girls, Vicky and her elder sister Margaret (who was also a good violinist), put on a small recital for two violins and piano at the Reids' London house, for invited friends.

Once the term had finished IH's summer 'routines' followed much as before. The EFDS Summer School was held at Norwich at the beginning of August, followed immediately by another tour to Germany by the Travelling Morrice, led by Rolf Gardiner. This time the tour was based well to the east of Berlin, and the group were due to stay in the newly built Musikheim at Frankfurt an der Oder. But the accommodation was not yet quite ready for occupation, so the first week took place at Bärwalde in der Neumark, a village about 60 miles further to the north, on the right bank of the river Oder, not far from Küstrin, now Kostrzyn.[6] The touring programme was not nearly so strenuous as it had been the previous year; IH took charge of the purely musical aspects, this time working with the singers at Purcell's *Dido and Aeneas* (for Harro Siegel's puppets to enact), three of Bach's unaccompanied motets and some English madrigals, all repertories with which she was to become indelibly associated through the course of her career. Then for the second week the company moved down

[6] Since 1945 the Oder has formed the eastern border separating northern Germany from Poland; in 1929 the river was then well inside Germany itself.

to Frankfurt into the brand new Musikheim, finding it well appointed, though
with a somewhat irksome daily regime to be followed. On the whole it would
seem that the visit lacked the joy that was so evident the year before, and an
impression of slight malaise creeps into IH's accounts of it written soon after
the fortnight was over.

Back from Germany, IH enjoyed a holiday in Scotland with the Reids, visiting both Ellon and Gairloch before returning to London. At a Promenade
concert of English music on 4 October she heard Paul Hindemith give the
first performance of William Walton's Viola Concerto. A few days later GH
invited her to accompany him to Paris, where *Egdon Heath* was to receive its
first French performance, played by l'Orchestre Symphonique de Paris, conducted by Pierre Monteux. The Dyers (now based in Paris) entertained them,
and between rehearsals there was time for IH to be shown a little of Paris and
its surroundings. At the performance on 20 October (given in the afternoon)
the work itself went well, but the audience failed to understand the music, and
loudly hissed its disapproval. Father and daughter returned that evening, the
ever kind Dyers on hand to see that they caught the train. On 21 October IH
learned that her Morley Scholarship had been renewed, and the next day she
went to hear Schnabel playing Beethoven's fourth concerto and Brahms's first
at the Queen's Hall, conducted by Malcolm Sargent.

Three days later, on the morning of 24 October, the EFDS party, bound for
the ss *Montrose* at Southampton, assembled at Waterloo station, seen off by a
number of EFDS friends and relations, including GH. It took a week to reach
Canada. The *Montrose* then cruised up the Saint Lawrence River (the party
spending an hour and a half on shore in Quebec on the way) as far as Montreal,
reaching there in time to catch an overnight train to Boston, arriving on the
morning of Sunday 3 November. From that moment the group was kept very
busy, dancing its repertoire of morris and country dances, with the singing of
Clive Carey adding welcome relief to the dancers between the groups of dances.
IH managed to keep a descriptive diary of the various places she visited; sometimes staying in private homes, or in hotels, or spending nights on the trains.
The evenings included the usual post-performance receptions, with over-eager,
good-natured hosts delighted to talk to the dancers after the show, but not
always realizing how their guests were longing to sit, or, quite often, how much
they would appreciate a square meal after all the strenuous exercise. But there
were other times when old friends turned up, and there were agreeable gatherings in interesting surroundings, and – even at this time of year – stunning
views to be seen. Ten days in the USA included performances in Boston, at
Harvard and Yale universities, and in Greenwich Village and the Carnegie Hall,

New York. A tourist day at Niagara Falls was followed by more performances in Rochester and Cleveland. 'Show not good … Evening even worse … Not a brilliant finale to our ten days in the States', IH commented in her journal, followed by 'Nightmare trying to catch the train to Toronto.' But they did, and she concluded: 'And so – Farewell to America.'

On 13 November the party reached Toronto, the city which had originally suggested the participation of the EFDS in an English Music Festival week and was funding their trans-Atlantic travel. The English Singers, an excellent six-voice consort, were also in residence and shared some of the concerts; otherwise there was much the same mixture of personalities and shows, with two performances a day. Three days later the party set off on a 45-hour journey by train to Regina, with 45 minutes at Winnipeg. Looking out of the window on the first day of the trip, IH enthused: 'Marvellous, looking out at emptiness, etc.' all day. But by the next morning the novelty had begun to pall, and she complained: 'Deadly! Miles and miles of flat, barren prairie, and snow.' They finally reached Regina on 19 November; they stayed for one night, with a performance the next day. Then they embarked again, this time for Yorkton, returning via Regina (where the temperature was 5 degrees below zero), before getting the train to Vancouver, where a very friendly family, stemming from Gloucester-shire, hosted IH for the next four days. The steamer from Vancouver to Victoria accommodated the party for the night of 25 November; on their arrival a very full day took in some sightseeing and two shows – including 'the best Canadian performance we'd given' – before the midnight steamer took them back to Vancouver, with the foghorn going all night (no sleep), and IH realizing 'the terrible truth: we are now homeward bound.' At Vancouver on 27 November there was a 9.00 a.m. train to catch, and some of their hostesses (from the first few days) came to wave them off. They were now bound for Calgary, where they spent two days before returning to the east by train. At this point, IH later wrote 'This is as far as I got with this diary.'

The party returned home on the RMS *Duchess of Atholl*, leaving Saint John, New Brunswick, on 6 December, and arriving at Liverpool on Saturday 14th. Back in London that day IH was met at the station by her father, who whisked her off to the Chelsea Palace Theatre to see *A Joyous Pageant of the Nativity* by Charles A. Claye, a stalwart of the English religious drama movement then in vogue. IH had Sunday off, and then travelled to West Hoathly in Sussex for a Christmas-tide holiday week of dancing and good fellowship in the company of some of her EFDS friends who had not been on the tour. The week was described as a 'camp', though the activities took place mainly in a large ancient barn, evidently used as a village hall; as the accommodation there was rather primitive, local residents put up the girls. William Ganiford, who had been on the North American tour, joined the camp a day later. He was an excellent classical violinist, and since he also danced very well, had the knack of playing for dancing with understanding and authority. He and Priscilla Worthington, an RCM student and cellist, formed a trio with IH, and during the week they played several times for all – including themselves, no doubt – to enjoy. IH and Priscilla's brother Barton Worthington, the 'Squire' in charge of the party, also devised a ballet for all to perform telling the tale of the Fatted Calf; IH, at the piano, provided the suitably inventive music. This was quite a success, and a repeat performance took place at the end of the week, when an audience of local well-wishers was entertained. The week was officially over on Monday, Christmas Eve, after which IH went home to Essex. She would have had much to tell the family.

During her last two terms at the RCM IH, now living at 15 Queensberry Place, South Kensington, seems to have packed even more into her timetable, especially in regard both to developing her skills as a conductor and in broadening her musical experience through judicious concert-going. The roll-call of famous musicians whom she heard play and conduct in these months provides eloquent testimony to the quality of concert life in London between the wars, and gave IH a series of unforgettable concert experiences which were to stand her in good stead for the rest of her life.

On 31 January she went to the Queen's Hall to hear the BBC Symphony Orchestra under Ernest Ansermet play Vaughan Williams's *Flos campi*, with Bernard Shore as the viola soloist. At the end of February there was a performance of Bach's Mass in B minor in the Royal Albert Hall given by the Royal Choral Society conducted by Malcolm Sargent, quite possibly the first time she had ever encountered this great work. On 3 March there was more contemporary English music, including Walton's *Façade*, recited by Edith Sitwell and Constant Lambert. 13 March found her at the Queen's Hall again for a Royal Philharmonic concert with John Barbirolli conducting, in which Pablo Casals played the Schumann Cello Concerto; the following day she returned to hear the BBC Symphony Orchestra, under Sir Henry Wood, give the first performance of Bax's Third Symphony, which she attended 'with G. and Helen Waddell'.[7] She also found time to attend a rehearsal of a Sargent concert and a string

[7] Helen Waddell was an expert in medieval Latin, and author/translator of *The Wandering Scholars,* published in 1927, and *Mediaeval Latin Lyrics* (1929). At this time GH was working on his short chamber opera *The Tale of the Wandering Scholar,* and about to set some of her *Mediaeval Latin Lyrics,* a choral group for male voices, and another (canons) for three-part female voices.

in a programme of new works by members; critics from the *Daily Telegraph* and *The Observer* both singled out IH's piece as the most interesting. Finally, the string version of *The Unfortunate Traveller* had its first performance at the RCM by the Third Orchestra on 15 July, conducted by Alan Bartlett and Hector McCurrach, two movements each, under the tutelage of the watchful W. H. Reed.

For IH's final RCM report in July 1930 Gordon Jacob wrote of his composition student that she 'continues to do good work. Her new ballet promises to be exceedingly effective.' Vaughan Williams, perhaps still uncomfortable in his position as both family friend and teacher, confined himself to a few 'ditto' marks in support of Jacob's comments, but Kathleen Long was more expansive, writing: 'I lose Imogen with many regrets. She has been a most enjoyable & musical pupil & in spite of other "irons in the fire" has developed into a charming player within a necessarily limited range & I shall watch her progress with interest.' The 'new ballet' mentioned by Jacob had come out of IH's acquaintance with the newly established Camargo Society. Entitled *Meddling in Magic*, it was based on the story of the Sorcerer's Apprentice. Immediately after the end of the college year, IH went to stay for a few days in a small, unmodernized, country cottage at Henkins Hill, near Finchingfield in Essex, lent by a friend, in order to finish the score before embarking on the travelling scholarship.

4 'Wandering about Europe', 1930–31

August began auspiciously with a luncheon at the Savoy, put on by the *Daily Mail* in honour of the aviator Amy Johnson; IH was invited as one of the 'Distinguished Representatives of British Youth and Achievement in all Activities of Life'. Following this, the routines of her summer life continued, centred on the EFDS Summer School, which was held at Malvern. On 23 August she went to the wedding of her good friends Barton Worthington and Stella Johnson, before finalizing her plans to be away in Europe until Christmas, spending her travelling scholarship money on a trip to learn more about Continental music and musicians. On her return the following May she delivered a lecture to the Society of Women Musicians, entitled 'Some Impressions of Music on the Continent', the earliest in a series of vivid and insightful autobiographical essays that she was to write through the course of her long career. She began the lecture by musing on her reasons for wishing to explore music in Europe:

> At the end of last summer, when I was given the opportunity of wandering about Europe, some of my friends said to me: – "How wonderful: now at <u>last</u> you will hear real orchestral playing" – or– "now at <u>last</u> you will hear opera as it should be given." But a few of my friends, and they were very, very few, said: – "you are certain to have an amazingly good time, but if it's music you're after, I'm not sure that London isn't the best place." It is a vexed question. There are two schools of thought – one holds that English music must necessarily be bad, just because it happens to be English, while German music must unquestionably be good just because it is German. The followers of the opposite school of thought go through life with a perpetual grievance that British music has not got a wider reputation, and they refuse point-blank to go and listen to any of the world-famous foreign orchestras who pay a yearly visit to the Albert Hall, merely because these distinguished visitors never trouble to publish their programmes until three-quarters of an hour before their concerts begin. Having been brought up in this latter school, I began to have secret leanings towards the Anti-Britons, and went abroad with high hopes of the excellence of all things continental.

For her initial expedition IH set off on 30 August with the British party for
the ISCM (International Society of Contemporary Music) Eighth Congress
and Festival, to be held at Liège in the first week of September; the event was
also to include the First Congress of the International Society of Musicology.
IH, an Associate Member of the ISCM, found herself in the company of several
musicians she already knew, listening to new music and performing groups
of all sorts. To her delight Mrs Dyer was also there, as well as the critic Edwin
Evans, and several other friends and acquaintances. One concert, given by
the Schola Cantorum of Brussels under Eugène Van der Velde, would have
struck her in particular; the programme, with works by Josquin, Ockeghem,
Gesualdo, Lassus and Tomkins, was just the kind of music she was to include
in her own concerts with the Purcell Singers many years later. But the performance impressed her less. She noted: 'But oh, they sang so badly. They simply
had no idea of getting a common chord in tune. Evans remarked that he didn't
see why people made such a fuss about the novelty of quarter-tones when we
were forced to listen to them every day of our lives.' The highlights of the Festival, as well as its most amusing curiosities, were to be found in the new music
that she heard:

> The outstanding event of the week was the performance of Alban Berg's
> opera: – 'Wozzeck'. This devastating work took place in the middle of a
> heat-wave, and was punctuated by a series of thunderstorms. Even the
> hardened critics in the audience seemed to lose a little of their calm and
> aloof dignity. It is difficult to speak of 'Wozzeck' after only one hear-
> ing, as the drama is so packed with horrors, and the characters are so
> exceedingly neurotic that it is almost impossible to listen to the music
> dispassionately. But the composer has certainly accomplished what he
> set out to do: – he has succeeded in riveting the attention on the chief
> character from beginning to end.
>
> After 'Wozzeck', perhaps the most outstanding event was the per-
> formance of William Walton's viola concerto, with Lionel Tertis playing
> the solo. This was the first piece of real music that we had heard at the
> Festival, and there can be no doubt that it was a triumph for British
> music. Most of the other works were purely percussive: – earnest young
> composers from all the corners of Europe had vied with each other in
> the novelty and variety of the percussion they employed. One of them
> introduced a large sheet of wrought iron: – it was fixed in a vertical and
> somewhat perilous position, and was worked to and fro by a foot lever.
> Unfortunately the player was rather too short for his instrument, and

his anxious face kept bobbing up and down over the edge of the sheet of iron, while he endeavoured to keep an eye on the conductor. It was the noisiest festival on record: – towards the end our nerves got somewhat frayed at the edges, and the mere sound of a bicycle bell was enough to make us leap and turn pale.

The tour party arrived back in England on 9 September. For IH, 'having crowded six receptions, five lectures, four operas and eleven concerts into the space of one week, the need of some sort of rest-cure was imperative', and the very next day she set off on her own travels on the ss *Britannia*, beginning in Sweden, the Holst family's ancestral home. Her route was from Göteborg in the west, with time just to take a look round, then back on ship for the two-day journey via the Göta canal and waterways across country to Stockholm on the eastern coast. There she met old family friends, the singer Maja Kjöhler and her husband, Sven Sternfeld (who had been near neighbours of the Holsts in Grena Road when IH was born), who were now back in Sweden for a holiday. IH had also been given a letter of introduction, via Bishop Bell, to the Archbishop of Uppsala, who kindly invited her to lunch one day; while there she saw the Archbishop's palace and the cathedral. Maja and IH went to a performance of *En Midsommarnattsdröm* (in Swedish) with Mendelssohn's incidental music, and on 20 September IH heard a pupils' concert at the Stockholm Conservatoire, the same evening going to a 'really good performance' of Tchaikovsky's *Eugene Onegin* at the King's Theatre. The musical life of the city impressed her, as she commented in her lecture: 'The opera in Stockholm is good, and they have an excellent orchestra. Perhaps it is because Sweden is so far away that we don't hear much about music in Stockholm, though the fame of their very beautiful concert-hall has managed to reach us.'

On the next leg of her journey she crossed over to the island of Gotland, where she had time to look at the main town, Visby, and significant ruins nearby telling of a once important past. From there she went to Denmark, where she explored Copenhagen, Lyngby, Frederiksborg and Helsingør before moving on to Germany and Old Hamburg by train on 30 September. The next day she attended a concert given by the Philharmonic Society of Hamburg, conducted by Eugen Papst, with the Overture to *Tristan und Isolde* and Bruckner's Fifth Symphony, a notable event, if not always for the right reasons:

> After a surfeit of architecture and sculpture in both Sweden and Denmark I was ready to listen to any amount of music by the time I reached Hamburg. So I went to a symphony concert: – my first symphony concert in Germany. The programme began with the prelude to Tristan. At

the opening I found to my horror that *all* the 'cellists were looking at
their notes instead of at the conductor. They played with great feeling,
but with entirely their own choice of tempo: – and the result can better
be imagined than described. Next came Bruckner's 5th Symphony. In
the Scherzo one of the first violins lost his place, and had to stop playing for about thirty bars before he could catch up with the others. And
then the fourth horn lost his breath, and faded out of existence, turning
a perfectly innocent chord of 5–3 into a 6–4, with disastrous results.
But the climax was reached in the finale, when the timpani player, in
the middle of a fortissimo roll, actually lost one of his sticks, and had
to dive into the middle of the wood-wind to retrieve it. And I began to
wonder why I wasn't at the Queens Hall, listening to the Promenade
concert.

From Hamburg she went on to Cologne, where she 'had the good luck to
hear' the opening performance of the winter's opera season, *Die Fledermaus*
(in Max Reinhardt's new production and 'a sheer joy from beginning to end')
and *The Bartered Bride*. Her visit to Germany was clouded, however, by her
growing awareness of an incipient change in the political climate; in her scrapbook for this leg of her journey, she inserted a cutting from an English newspaper which now reads ominously:

Steel Helmets – a military organisation to keep alive the old military
spirit – numbering 120,000 – were reviewed at Coblenz to-day, and
passed before the tribune in which stood the ex-Crown Prince of Germany. The leader of the Steel Helmets, Herr Seldte, proclaimed the
identity of aims of the Steel Helmets and the National-Socialists (Herr
Hitler's party). "For the Steel Helmets," he said, "there is only fight, and
once more fight, until finally the disgraceful treaties are revised, until
the German people can have the army they desire, until Germany has
again the space to live in that she demands."

The report reinforces the impression of how lucky IH was to embark on, and
be able to complete, her Continental schedule when she did – at a time when
Germany appeared to be recovering from its defeat in 1918, the performing arts
were taking new directions, and the 'Steel Helmets' and their like did not yet
hold the whole nation to ransom. In another two years or so those who were
able to read the early signs were already making their way out of their home-
land, while the less fortunate remained behind to face the terrible events ahead,
of which they were still unaware.

IH's next stop was Frankfurt am Main, where she spent a few days, including going to a recital by Kathleen Long in the small hall of the Saalbau on 7 October. She was also able to visit, in its original home, the great musicological library assembled by the industrialist Paul Hirsch. Jewish by birth, Hirsch had, as a life-time hobby, made a huge collection of important and rare editions of music and books on music. When in the mid-1930s it became apparent that he should leave Germany, with the encouragement of his friend Professor E. J. Dent of Cambridge, he managed in 1936 to bring his family to England, and all the precious 20,000 volumes as well. His wife had seen to the careful parcelling up of the whole collection in harmless-looking brown paper lots, and they were shipped by rail to England without awkward questions or comment, the entire consignment in due course arriving safely in Cambridge (where the Hirsch family was to live) and lodged in the University Library for the next ten years. In 1946 it was purchased by the British Library, where it has a place of honour. But IH was always proud to have seen the collection on her student travels, when she was first discovering the scholar's thrill of seeking out original materials to study.

Every town IH visited seems to have kept its ancient, medieval houses, and here again she was lucky to find so much of the old Germany still extant. Her next target was Nuremberg, afterwards taking in Ansbach, Rothenburg and Regensburg on the way to Munich, where she arrived on 13 October. There she went to a symphony concert conducted by Hans Knappertsbusch, which included Tchaikovsky's Violin Concerto played by Nathan Milstein. On 14 October she heard a violin recital given by her old friend Adila Fachiri with Friedrich Wührer, and four days later saw an opera by Clemens von Franckenstein, *Des Kaisers Dichter*, again conducted by Knappertsbusch. In the course of the visit she learnt about some of the extra-musical, and not always positive, forces that were driving German opera at this time:

> Talking about music in Europe means talking about opera in Europe, because on the continent, although concerts may be few and far between, there will always be an opera every night of the week. This is largely due to State support, for which so many people have been clamouring in England. It was not till I got to Munich that I learned some of the disadvantages of State support. Programmes are chosen, not from artistic, but from political motives. A certain tenor, although obviously the right man, may not be allowed a big part in a Wagner opera, because he happens to be a Jew. Or a popular modern opera may not be produced because the composer happens to be Czechoslovakian, and the

anti-Czech feeling is strong at the moment. But even worse than this is the bribery and corruption that goes on in the press. There is a composer in Germany who has written a vast number of bad operas: – <u>very</u> bad operas. And they are always being produced, one after another. In my innocence I wondered why, till I learnt from a very high authority that the composer is closely related to the head of one of the leading newspapers, and unless one of his works is put on at <u>least</u> once a month, the press would make life unbearable for the producers. So that State support can hardly be called an unmixed blessing.

Leaving Germany behind her, but promising to return, IH next travelled on into Austria, visiting the Tyrol, Innsbrück and Salzburg, where she made a Mozart pilgrimage before aiming for Vienna, where she took a room in a pension for a month. On 23 October she saw a performance of *Der Rosenkavalier* with Elisabeth Schumann in the cast, and was invited by the singer to tea the next day. *Die Zauberflöte* followed two days later, and Weinberger's popular *Schwanda der Dudelsackpfeifer*[1] on Sunday 26 October. Of the Viennese and their music, IH later recalled:

In Vienna one can go to the opera for the price of a cup of coffee. Sometimes the opera is very good: – sometimes it is surprisingly bad. There are certain standard works which they turn on at regular intervals without bothering much about them, using faded scenery and worn-out costumes and stereotyped gestures. But when they take trouble over a work, and spend time and money and thought on a production, the result is glorious. 'Fidelio' is the best Vienna has to offer, and this is largely thanks to the Philharmonic Orchestra. Clemens Krauss is now the conductor-in-chief of the orchestra: – he is not spectacular as a conductor, but he gets what he wants. The concert programmes of the Vienna Philharmonic are disappointing. There is a certain sameness about the lists of their forthcoming events: – Bruckner, Mahler: – Mahler, Bruckner; – Beethoven No. 5, Mozart in G minor; – Mahler, Bruckner, Bruckner, Mahler – And so on. Occasionally they have the courage to play a more modern work. Once, while I was there, they were daring enough to play a little early Schönberg; but it was very, very early – Op. 4 in fact.[2] One of the few modern works that has met with whole-hearted approval in Vienna is Weinberger's opera, "Schwanda". The overture was played at

[1] 'Schwanda the Bagpiper'.
[2] *Verklärte Nacht* (1899).

one of the Royal Philharmonic Society's concerts in London last season. The story has great possibilities ... It is a refreshing opera, and is full of tunes.

The audiences at the Vienna opera house are enthusiastic, but not what we should consider well-behaved. Not only do they applaud during the Scenes, but they will actually clap in between the verses of a song, leaving the orchestra suspended on a chord of the dominant seventh. On the nights when a famous celebrity is singing they will queue up for the cheap seats for hours before the performance begins; – but not in the orderly queues that we are accustomed to see at Covent Garden, with rows of little camp-stools and mid-day editions of the evening papers. In Vienna the enthusiasts are tightly packed in a narrow passage, standing seven or eight deep, and when it gets near the time for the box office to open they push and push with all their might, and go on frantically pushing, being determined to get into the house or to perish in the attempt.

Apart from the opera and the Philharmonic concerts there is very little regular music going on in Vienna. The other symphony orchestras – and there are several of them – are all incredibly bad. I was once rash enough to go to a popular symphony concert where a man got up and endeavoured to play the Beethoven violin concerto. It was a performance that would never have been tolerated at any concert in London. It reminded me of the sort of noise that goes on behind the closed doors of the Royal College of Music when well-meaning young students are in the early stages of practising for their associateship. Yet Vienna seemed to enjoy it. They had been to Fidelio at the opera house the night before, and yet here they were, listening to those excruciating sounds with rapt attention; – and the player had glowing press notices the next morning. The Viennese are enthusiastic, but they can hardly be called discriminating.

In addition to attending musical events, IH visited art galleries and soaked up the atmosphere of the city, but still kept closely in touch with home, receiving letters and news cuttings from London, where her *Phantasy* Quartet, played on 21 October in the Armitage Hall in Great Portland Street, had once again been very well reviewed by the press. The *Daily Telegraph* in particular praised the work for being 'completely free from the tricks and eccentricities too often practised by the non-musical composers of today', and listeners generally enjoyed the relatively unchallenging musical language of the Quartet at a time when they were struggling to comprehend the contemporary advances in European composition that IH herself had come to Europe to encounter at first hand. Her father, who was there, managed to get the signatures not only of the four players onto the back of a picture postcard, but also of W. W. Cobbett himself, and the Sternfelds, now back again in England. GH wrote on 27 October:

> Excuse dictated letter; I have been scoring ... Last Tuesday was unforgettable. There was a splendid rehearsal of 'Job' in the morning at Norwich and R. was quite happy about things at the end. The Kutcher Quartet played quite perfectly the whole evening, and your Quartette ... was a revelation to us all. In spite of the extreme provocation on the last performance, I cannot forgive myself for not realising how good it is. We all disgraced ourselves when it was over. Maya and Mabel[3] did a war dance, Sven gave an imitation of my daughter's reactions to Stockholm on first landing, and as for your poor Pa, he suddenly realised that he had started autograph-hunting! I trust you received the result. The critiques are excellent.
>
> I am asking Iso to send the notices on to you. What I like specially is that they treat you with dignity and take the trouble to criticise as they would any other artist and they do not pat you on the head, and above all they have discovered that you do not favour your Pa!

Still in Vienna, IH met Grace Williams, who was spending her scholarship award studying there with Egon Wellesz, and went to more operas: at the end of October there was *Die Meistersinger*, conducted by Clemens Kraus, followed by *Parsifal*, then *Fidelio*, and *Schwanda* again on 6 November. Then she went to Budapest for a few days, accompanied by Leslie Russell, her fellow winner of the Octavia travelling scholarship. Here on 10 November she went to an orchestral concert of works by Bach, Schubert, Bartók and Haydn, and 'met Dohnanyi after the concert'. Other aspects of the music to be heard in the city she found disappointing, however:

> Budapest is a miraculous city, and is fortunate in possessing three very great musicians: – Dohnani, Bartok and Kodaly. But its State orchestra doesn't bear comparison with the Vienna Philharmonic – technically they are nothing like as good. The thing I liked best in Budapest was the ballet. The Hungarians have a genius for colour and design, and theirs was the first really good dancing I had seen since leaving England. They

[3] Mabel Rodwell Jones, a good friend of the Holsts.

did a very modern ballet containing several entirely new ideas in choreography, and it was interesting to notice that the guest-producer was the director of the ballet at the Stockholm Opera House. The famous Tzigane, or gypsy musicians of Budapest are deadly dull. They play in most of the restaurants every evening, because they consider it is the thing to do, but there is an audible sigh of relief when their places are taken by the ordinary jazz band.

Returning to Vienna she heard *Die Entführung* on 18 November, and on her last day there, 23 November, a Philharmonic subscription concert of works by Weber, Schoenberg, Dukas, and Beethoven's Fourth Symphony. This was followed in the evening by a complete change, a performance of Shakespeare's *Measure for Measure* (*Mas für Mas*) in German.

Her month at the pension over, IH moved on to Prague, where she first heard a Philharmonic concert at the German Theatre with Georg Széll conducting and Rudolf Serkin playing the piano. She went with her friends the Löwenbachs to a concert in the same theatre to honour Vitislav Novák's sixtieth birthday with a performance of his *Serenade* for small orchestra, followed by Max Reger's Piano Concerto in F minor, once again with Serkin, and Mozart's 'Jupiter' Symphony. She also had an enjoyable, if somewhat offbeat, introduction to modern Czech opera:

> I found people very enthusiastic about modern music, but it was nearly always the modern music of their own Czechoslavakian composers. It was in Prague that I heard 'Mechanist Hopkins', a modern opera by Max Brand, a German composer. It was a highly-coloured affair, full of detectives and thefts and murders and cabaret shows and factory workers going on strike. But unfortunately both the dialogue and the programme notes were in Czech, so I never managed to make out who was the murderer, or which wife was married to which husband, or why the workers downed tools. There was some very effective scenery – especially a large purple machine with wheels that went round; and there were some very effective noises going on in the orchestra. At the end of the last scene, when the strikers had gone back to work, they let off a real factory hooter, which successfully drowned the entire chorus and orchestra. The long-suffering members of the audience stuffed their fingers into their ears, while the building shook to its foundations.

After these excitements IH returned north, where she found herself once more 'puzzling over the legend that Germany is the most musical nation in

Europe'. In her London lecture she called on her experiences of her previous visit with The Travelling Morrice to explain her difficulty:

Two years ago I was invited to a summer festival at the opening of a new School of Music in an industrial town in Germany. It was a beautiful building: – very modern, very practical, and admirably suited for its purpose. It had cost £25,000 to build. Half this sum had been granted by the German government – the rest had been raised by local subscriptions in the town itself. The students led a strict life, which I confess I found somewhat trying to live up to. They got up at six o'clock every morning, and having sung a five-part Alleluya, they donned bathing dresses and practised physical exercises on the front lawn, ending up with a cold shower under the garden hose. Their diet consisted very largely of lettuce leaves and tepid weak tea. Smoking was strictly forbidden. They talked at length, and with obvious sincerity, about such things as 'Rhythm of Group Emotions'. They went to bed at nine o'clock every evening, and all lights were turned out by nine-thirty. Most of the day was spent in unaccompanied choral work, and this they did superbly. Whether it was Bach motets, or Palestrina, or German madrigals, they sang with a beautiful tone, and great ease, and perfect timing.

They were thinking of producing Purcell's 'Dido and Aeneas' as a compliment to their English guests, and I was asked to coach the soloists. I was amazed to find that they were incapable of learning their parts. When they were in the choir they could learn a difficult Bach fugue without turning a hair, but once they were by themselves they couldn't master the simplest melody: – they could neither read the notes nor learn them by ear. Instrumental music was practically non-existent in the school. The man who was at the head of that department once achieved the really remarkable feat of conducting a minuet with four beats in every bar: – and he seemed quite pleased with the result. Any sort of technique was definitely discouraged. To be found practising scales in one's bedroom was almost as serious a crime as to be caught smoking a cigarette. Also there was no piano in the building, for the piano was considered to be a soul-destroying instrument. And this was an institute that had the moral and financial support of the Ministry of Education. Students at the Royal College and the Royal Academy may not all rise at six and go for the higher life, but quite a number of them manage to learn something about music.

People in Germany have a very poor opinion of music in England. There is a popular belief that we in England have never heard a real orchestra, except on those rare occasions when Herr Furtwängler pays a visit to our shores with the Berlin Philharmonic Orchestra. And they have never heard of most of our composers. They used to ask me politely who I'd been studying with, and when I told them with Vaughan Williams, they looked blank, and asked: 'Oh, is he a composer?' And I got quite used to the question: – What *sort* of music does your father write? Mostly <u>songs</u>, I suppose?' There are three British composers, however, with whom they have become acquainted, and these three represent for them the sum total of our music. They are: Mr Cyril Scott, Dame Ethel Smyth and Mr Constant Lambert. They have heard of Delius, of course, but they refuse to believe that he is English. Yet these are the people who have read all the plays of Bernard Shaw, and most of the novels of Hardy and Galsworthy, and who wait impatiently for the arrival of each new book from the pen of Mr Aldous Huxley.

However much they may underestimate our musical capacities, there is one thing that they simply <u>cannot</u> believe, and that is that we don't have regular grand opera going on every night in London and the important provincial cities. When the fact dawns on them that we haven't got a permanent State Opera in <u>London</u>, they shrug their shoulders and tactfully change the subject. For in Germany every large town has its opera house, and the competition is terrific. 'Oh yes', they say, 'of course the opera <u>is</u> good at Munich or Berlin and Vienna, but wait till Sunday evening when you hear <u>our</u> Götterdämmerung!' In Berlin there are three State opera houses, or rather, there <u>were</u> three, a few months ago. For now, owing to the bad times, the magnificent Kroll opera house, directed by Otto Klemperer, has had to be closed.

In Germany IH travelled first to Dresden and then on to Leipzig, paying homage to J. S. Bach and the Thomaskirche. Thence she started on the journey home. Berlin was the last city she visited in Germany, going on 2 December to a concert played by the Busch Quartet at the Singakadamie. She heard *Prince Igor* with ballet at the Staatsoper on 4 December, followed by a remarkable sequence of *Salome, Boris Godounov* and *Die Meistersinger* on the following three nights. On 8 December there was the Berlin Philharmonic under Bruno Walter, with Rachmaninov playing the first performance of his own Piano Concerto no. 4, placed between Mendelssohn's *Midsummer Night's Dream* Overture and the *Symphonie fantastique* of Berlioz. For the Busch Quartet and the

Berlin Philharmonic she had high praise, but she was less impressed by another incident that demonstrated for her once again a German disregard for English music and its history:

> There is nothing I can say about the Berlin Philharmonic Orchestra, for it is familiar to Londoners. There are some things in Berlin, however, which we can't get in London, and one of these is the Busch String Quartet. It is worth travelling a great many miles to hear this quartet play Beethoven. Even Berlin, though, has its occasional lapses, and one of the worst shocks I ever had was when I went to a play called 'Elisabeth von England'.[4] The play had caused a stir throughout the whole of Germany because during part of the time a double stage is used, and the action takes place simultaneously in Spain and England. It was a wonderful production. The acting of Elizabeth was unforgettable. The costumes and the scenery and the gestures exactly fitted into the picture of Elizabethan England. There was no incidental music, but in one of the scenes which took place in a small anteroom, Francis Bacon was supposed to be listening through an open door to music that was going on in the next room. I had expected that they would have a lute or a virginal, as they had paid such scrupulous attention to details of period. Imagine my dismay when a violin and piano struck up 'Herr Ober, zwei Kaffé!' – a 1930 foxtrot.

On Wednesday 10 December her orgy of musical experiences in Berlin finally came to an end at the Staatsoper, with the première of *Fremde Erde* by Karol Rathaus under the direction of Erich Kleiber. This was the day when the string orchestra version of her own suite *The Unfortunate Traveller* was being performed in the more modest surroundings of a public concert in Bromley, conducted by the indefatigable W. H. Reed. Two rare days without music now ensued, as IH travelled across Germany to Amsterdam. Here she heard the Roth Quartet play in the Concertgebouw on Saturday 13 December, and the following day she accompanied a friend to a Sunday afternoon concert to hear Mahler's Seventh Symphony, conducted by Willem Mengelberg, whom she met afterwards. She finally arrived back in London on 20 December. Very nearly four months away from England, her self-imposed musical education had been thorough and intensive; no one could have accused her of spending her time abroad idly. She went to Essex for Christmas itself, and must have revelled in the familiarity of it.

---

4 By Ferdinand Bruckner (1930).

Early in the new year, 1931, IH went to stay with the Reids at Ellon. While there she received a telegram which said 'Grant of fifty granted congratulations', which signalled the renewal of her Morley scholarship 'at the discretion of the College'; the RCM authorities evidently approved of her foreign exploits thus far. Back in London she briefly resumed her concert-going while planning her next trip abroad; the Camargo Society's second ballet season at the Apollo Theatre on 25 and 26 January programmed five ballets, including *Capriol Suite*, a tribute to the memory of Peter Warlock, choreographed by Frederick Ashton (one of the dancers in the company), and *Rout* by Arthur Bliss, dating from 1922 (choreographed by Ninette de Valois), the whole conducted by Constant Lambert. She also attended a Royal Choral Society concert conducted by Malcolm Sargent on 31 January, consisting of Parry's *Blest Pair of Sirens*, her father's *The Hymn of Jesus* and Vaughan Williams's *A Sea Symphony*.

But Europe beckoned once again, and on 1 February IH began her final scholarship tour, this time to Italy and Sicily, a journey that would last almost two months; she was joined by Leslie Russell, finishing-off his own Octavia scholarship. They started off in Milan, where Chaliapin was singing *Boris Godounov* at La Scala, before taking in Verona on the way to Venice, where the Italian Tourist Office (CIT) helped with working out a schedule and transport for the four days it would take to reach Sicily, starting on 10 February. The route took them briefly to Bologna, Orvieto (on its spectacular, surprising, rocky site), Rome and Naples. In Sicily they visited the spectacular ruined temples at Segesta, Selinunte and Girgenti on the way to Syracuse. On then to Taormina, on the east coast, where IH was photographed with Mount Etna in the background. IH and Russell now went their separate ways, he to return home, and she to revisit Rome, where she stayed for a few days. News from London included advance notice by the Camargo Society that they would perform her ballet *Meddling in Magic* in April and possibly also later in the year. (In the end nothing was to become of this proposal.) She visited the Vatican and the Sistine Chapel, and on 8 March went to an orchestral concert, conducted by Antonino Votto, including music by Weber, Schumann, Albéniz, Roussel, Respighi and Dukas.

Of her musical experiences in Italy, IH wrote on her return:

After a wealth of music in Berlin and Amsterdam, it was perhaps a mistake to expect very much from Italy. I was lucky enough to be in Milan when Chaliapine sang in the first performance of 'Boris' at the Scala. It was a great occasion, but it was not without its drawbacks. For Chaliapine was unsafe in his Italian words, so they put the prompter in the middle of the footlights and he recited the words a beat and a half in front of the music throughout most of the important scenes. And then I found it difficult to cope with the extraordinary hours that the Italians keep. For in Milan they don't approve of going to the opera at half-past six in the evening. They like to have their meal at a reasonable hour, and they like to linger over it, so that it was nine o'clock at night before 'Boris' began, and five-and-twenty to one the following morning before the last curtain had fallen.

In Rome I was not impressed with the symphony orchestra, though they certainly [played] Respighi very well. I went to a chamber concert where a modern Italian string quartet was played, and I found that most of the audience talked the whole time: – quite loudly, and quite happily, and taking it very much as a matter of course. I thought the symphony orchestra in Florence better than the one in Rome: – they were admirable when they played Spanish or Italian music, but when they attempted Bach or Beethoven the results were disastrous. The audiences in Florence are highly enthusiastic. They will hurry over their mid-day meal on Sundays, and queue up in the streets (often in the rain) and having paid their fivepence, they will run up seven flights of stone steps and stand on the edge of a high balcony, peering down through the iron bars. Here they will stay quite cheerfully for two and a half hours before the concert begins.

It is politics rather than any artistic merit that moves them to applause. On one occasion when I was there the orchestra played a short, harmless, inoffensive little piece, the sort of little piece that one couldn't imagine would rouse any violent feelings of admiration or disgust in the mind of the listener. But it happened to be by a Russian composer, and it was scarcely over before the whole of the gallery and the two upper circles leapt to their feet and hurled abuse at the orchestra, booing and hissing and throwing orange peel about, so that it was quite ten minutes before peace was restored and the programme could be continued.

One has only to listen to the choir of St Peter's at Rome to realise that music is something quite different in Italy. It is impossible to compare the singing at St Peter's with that of our own Westminster Cathedral. We should consider that the one is singing, while the other is not. But then perhaps the Italians would say the same thing. There can be no doubt, though, that whatever one thinks of the sort of noise they make, the Italians are a nation of singers. In the markets they sell their vegetables in impassioned cadenzas, and they encourage their hard-worked donkeys to climb up-hill by crooning chromatic scale-passages to them, while down in Sicily one can often hear folk-songs in the evenings, when the doors of the cottages are open. But music is a different language in that part of the world.

While still in Rome IH received a letter from the Marchesa Lanza, who had helped in finding her a pension in Florence, her next port of call. She was expected there on 10 March, and the Marchesa hoped to see her for tea on the following day. IH stayed in the pension for several days, and attended an orchestral concert conducted by Vittorio Gui of works by Bach, Beethoven, Borodin, Albéniz, Wagner and Liszt. Travelling north on her way home, she took in Pisa and Arezzo; one of her picture postcards is carefully labelled 'Guido d'Arezzo was born in the house next to the tower'.[5] Her ticket to St Pancras Station, booked in Florence on 15 March, took her via Modane, Dunkirk and Tilbury; on the way she was met briefly in Paris by Louise Dyer. As she later recalled: 'I passed through Paris on my way back to England, but of music in Paris I fear I can say nothing, for by this time my pocket only contained a third-class ticket to St Pancras and the sum of three shillings and sevenpence halfpenny. So I came home, having had an amazingly good time, but having come to the conclusion that if it is music one is wanting, there is no place like London.'

IH arrived back in good time to attend an RCM first orchestra concert on 27 March. She then resumed the pattern of work that had become familiar to her over recent years. Central to this was her involvement with the EFDS. An Easter School took place from 4 to 11 April at Belstead House School, Aldeburgh, with GH in charge of the folk singing and IH accompanying the dance sessions. On her return to London she had ample time to work up her 'official' account of her months spent abroad, and to prepare the lecture on the subject that she was to deliver to the Society of Women Musicians at their Annual Composers' Conference on Saturday 30 May. The talk was warmly received, with one newspaper report commenting that it engaged its audience by saying 'wise things in a witty way', a trait that was to become a distinguishing characteristic of IH's writings and public lectures as the years progressed.

---

[5] Guido was an eleventh-century music theorist who first developed a system of precise pitch notation through lines and spaces, and who propagated a method of sight-singing that relied upon the syllables *ut, re, mi, fa, sol, la.*

Part II ~ 1931–52

CHRISTOPHER GROGAN
&
ROSAMUND STRODE

5 'Life is not going to be too easy for you': London and elsewhere, 1931–8

Once back from her European wanderings in May 1931 IH, now twenty-four, with her years as a student behind her and her financial resources at a low ebb, began to look at her options for employment. She knew that she wanted to continue working at the piano (if that ever-present weakness in her left arm would allow it), but also that she was quite capable of teaching music in its widest sense to both children and adults, making use of everything she had already learned. She now had confidence in her abilities as a composer, accompanist and conductor, both from her RCM work and, less formally, from her experience with the EFDS promoting the folk music and dance that she so much enjoyed. It was not long before an opportunity arose for her to put some of these skills into practice, as she heard in June of an offer, made through the RCM, of a vacant position for a pianist at Citizen House, Bath.

Citizen House was a theatrical enterprise providing 'Facilities in Dramatic Production and Training', covering all aspects of practical production work in the theatre, including acting, scenery, lighting and costumes, with performances staged at The Little Theatre in Bath and the Everyman Theatre, Hampstead, in August and September each year. The institution's letter of introduction to the RCM, dated 10 June 1931, offered the prospective pianist opportunities for playing, arranging and providing the musical accompaniment to mimes, dances and ballads. There would also be the chance to contribute solo piano work. Full board would be covered and a small salary paid 'according to age, qualifications and work undertaken'. More ominously the letter continued:

> As the pianist's work is mainly in the evening ... it would only occupy a part of the time, and we should ask her to assist during the remainder of the day with some department of our work, either the secretarial matters dealing with plays and tours [or] stage costume loan department. All these matters, in so far as they are part of the general working of the house, are of great interest, and we feel sure that any candidate would be assured of a very interesting life'.

Choosing to ignore these last sentences, IH applied for the post and received a positive response from the director, Miss Marion Radford, who expressed a particular interest in her enthusiasm for ballet and folk dancing. A meeting in London was arranged, and by the last week in June IH, now described as 'Musical Director', found herself in Bath at the large eighteenth-century mansion that was Citizen House.

Once settled, IH naturally gave of her best, seeking out, arranging and playing suitable music to fit the dramas, but over time the whole enterprise – idealistic and worthy in its aims though it was – proved to be exasperating and impossible for her to live with. Luckily her working schedule allowed her to attend some of her regular gatherings, including the ISCM meeting from 21 to 28 July, which took place in Oxford with two final concerts at the Queen's Hall in London. Back in Bath, she worked on a Citizen House programme entitled 'Pavilion Tour', suitable for presentation in village and church halls in the region. Some of this was broadcast in 'Children's Hour' by the Western Region of the BBC on 4 August, while a second broadcast three days later featured IH playing seven pieces from Howells's *Lambert's Clavichord*. During the summer she was also able to escape to the Reids at Ellon and attend a chamber music summer school in Bangor, where she teamed up with two old friends – Margaret Reid and Peggie Thomson – to form a piano trio.

By September Citizen House had moved its centre of operations to Hampstead, enabling IH to attend some London concerts; she then went with the Company on tour to the South West. In the middle of October she took more leave to fulfil an engagement in Yorkshire, where the Huddersfield Glee and Madrigal Society were mounting a big concert in honour of her father, who conducted some of the programme; IH played a group of his piano pieces and the concert was broadcast by the BBC Northern Region. Tired by now of the onerous duties imposed on her by Citizen House, she took the opportunity of being away to resign from her post, and left in mid-November.

For a while she mixed freelance conducting and accompanying with seeing family and friends. Since returning to England she had put considerable effort into supporting her father's projects and had gradually assumed the role of his musical confidante, which had been vacant since the death of his friend and pupil Jane Joseph in 1929. For GH, Jane Joseph had 'come nearest to his ideal of clear thinking and clear feeling', and he continued to miss both her company, and on a more practical level, her 'passion for accuracy' and 'instinctive capacity … for taking pains'.[1] Later in life IH came to regret that, in her own view at least, she had not filled the empty space sufficiently, preferring to pursue her

[1] IH, *Gustav Holst*, p. 136.

own career, but for the last few years of GH's life she was at least able to take her place beside him and witness some of his triumphs and frustrations. In June, for example, she accompanied him to a private preview of the film *The Bells*, for which he had written the music, and observed the 'white-faced look of dismay' that came over him as they listened in the viewing room to a sound-track recorded so badly that it bore little resemblance to what he had written.[2]

Early in 1932 IH joined the staff of the EFDSS,[3] an appointment that stemmed from the huge amount of work she had done for the Society since joining at the age of sixteen. The work suited her, and the skills that she brought to it as a pian-ist and accompanist, conductor, public speaker and organizer, together with her immense enthusiasm, did much to raise the profile of the Society and its work over the next seven years. That summer she and Vicky Reid took a cottage in Borth, a small village on the Welsh coast north of Aberystwyth. Here they took chamber music lessons from the cellist Arthur Williams, by all accounts a remarkable teacher. Before this she had taken a few days out to accompany her father, while he was recuperating from illness, on a tour of the Cotswolds, for which they were joined by GH's brother Emil (the actor Ernest Cossart), on one of his very rare trips to England from the USA. IH later recalled:

> They planned a glorious week, beginning at Oxford and ending at Cirencester, and I was able to get off work to join them. Walking was out of the question, as Holst was not strong enough. But at Oxford, dur-ing the very first day, Douglas Clarke suddenly appeared from Montreal with a large high-powered car, offering to drive us wherever we wanted to go … It was a good holiday. One of the last, and one of the best.[4]

IH travelled next to St Andrews, where she deputized for Douglas Kennedy at the Scottish Summer School of Music and Dancing; from there she went to stay with the Reids in Ellon. Returning to London in October she performed once again in support of her father when she played some of his piano compo-sitions at a concert following his appearance as guest of honour at the Annual General Meeting of the Music Teachers' Association in London. That summer GH had finally completed the two piano pieces that he had promised her for her twenty-first birthday, by adding a 'Jig' to an as yet unnamed piece which

---

[2] IH, *A Thematic Catalogue of Gustav Holst's Music*, p. 190.

[3] The English Folk Dance Society (EFDS) became the English Folk Dance And Song Society (EFDSS) in December 1931, when it merged with the English Folk Song Society. The journal of the Society kept its title of *EFDS News*, however, until June 1936, when it was renamed *English Dance and Song*. IH wrote a regu-lar column, 'Music Notes' for the journal from September 1936 to June 1939.

[4] IH, *Gustav Holst*, pp. 160–1.

he had written, and she had performed, in 1930 (later to be published with the title *Nocturne*). At this time she still had ambitions to make her way as a pianist, but these were shortly to be dashed by the recurrence of the phlebitis in her left arm that had troubled her for so long. To begin with, it seemed as if treatment might remedy the problem; GH wrote to his cousin Mary Lediard that although 'Imogen's left arm has collapsed and she has had to abandon all piano playing for the present … as far as we know it is not my complaint and we are hopeful that she can be completely cured.[5] In December GH discussed IH's condition with Dr Donald Roy, a consultant physician, in the light of a surgeon's report. He wrote to IH on 20 December, prompting her to make a decision the consequences of which would remain with her for the rest of her life:

> The surgeon holds out no hope for you as a pianist unless you have an operation. The operation <u>ought</u> to make your arm quite fit for work in time. But he cannot <u>guarantee</u> that it will because the trouble is a rare one and nobody knows much about it …
>
> And we both think that you should decide what you would like to do. I mean by this, that it is a purely personal matter. You must think only of yourself.

In the absence of any guarantee of success, IH declined the opportunity and the hoped-for cure was never to be. For GH, whose own aspirations to develop a career as a concert pianist had been dashed in 1893 by worsening neuritis, it must have been a bitter blow to realize that a similar fate had befallen his daughter. Nevertheless, IH continued to act as an accompanist at EFDSS events for several years, developing strong ideas about the role, which she later shared in one of her 'Music Notes' written in 1938 for the Society's news-sheet:

> On the one hand we get players so reticent that they almost sink through the piano stool … On the other hand we are faced with dictators who drag their singers along the route, ruthlessly enforcing their own time limits and rejoicing in the knowledge that protest is impossible.
>
> But real accompanying is a very different matter. It is closely related to the art of accompanying a friend on a walk. The pace that is set will be just right for both; silences will be mutual, and the exchange of ideas will be unforced … and we, who are first and foremost a body of amateurs, are fortunate in having known such accompanists within the EFDSS.

If the misfortune of having to abandon one career seemed to echo the

---

[5] Undated letter, 1932; private scrapbooks.

experience of her father, so did IH's response, which was to follow him into the world of teaching, and to combine this, for the next decade, with working with amateur musicians, a task for which she proved to have a remarkable gift. A few years after GH's death she wrote that he had found 'among amateurs ... a way of making music that had given him more delight than any other'. She saw this as an aspect of his musical legacy which, in the uncertain times when she was writing, 'might endure'.[6] At this fledgling point in her career, with her idealism riding high, his was an example that she was keen to follow.

Neither was it coincidental that 1932 should prove to be the year in which IH quite suddenly revealed her talents as an arranger, completing five instrumental titles, of which four were published, and working on numerous vocal arrangements. Clearly one of her main motives was to earn herself a living, having embarked on a freelance career. But she was no doubt equally inspired by a sense of responsibility towards the young, the amateur and, indeed, the preservation and spread of the folksong heritage itself in the generation after the death of Cecil Sharp. Through her work for the EFDSS she had developed an almost missionary zeal to help ensure that folksong permeated every level of practical music-making, and although the benign figures of Vaughan Williams and, at first, her father, were standing in the wings and encouraging her at every turn, her main influence was undoubtedly that of Sharp himself. She had never forgotten hearing him accompany folksongs at the piano in Aldeburgh, and, although her own arrangements and accompaniments were to differ markedly from his, she remained a staunch defender of his pioneering work and methods, which had by the 1930s come in for much criticism. Her admiration, and much of her own enduring belief in the value of folk music, was to be encapsulated in an article nearly thirty years later, written to celebrate Sharp's centenary:

> My father used to say that when the time came for the history of twentieth-century English music to be written, Cecil Sharp's name would stand out above all others. That was thirty-five years ago, when English composers were still overwhelmed with gratitude for the miracle of the revival of English folk song, which had saved them from a surfeit of nineteenth-century translations and had taught them to listen to the musical possibilities of their own language.
>
> To-day we take our folk songs for granted. Cecil Sharp would, I think, have been one of the first to agree that this is as it should be – for he was wise enough to know that work such as his could never be completed

[6] IH, *Gustav Holst*, p. 169.

until it had become unnecessary. Those of us who have been brought up on the revival of folk song and dance can never be grateful enough for what he has done for us. Perhaps one of our chief reasons for gratitude in this centenary year is the fact that he was so often right when other people thought he was wrong.

When he decided to publish his largest selection of folk songs in a series entitled *Novello's School Songs*, there were cries of dismay. People thought that it would be the death of folk songs to have them sung in compulsory classes in LCC schools. But the songs survived. Like the Bible and Shakespeare, they could stand the test of being a 'set subject' and could bear any amount of repetition. In the year 1908, when the first book of *School Songs* appeared, there were few genuine English tunes available for singing classes. (My father used to go to the British Museum to find sixteenth and seventeenth-century songs for his pupils to learn.) But from 1908 onwards the supply has been inexhaustible, and harassed teachers of junior schools, conductors of village choirs and adjudicators of competition festivals have all been able to find exactly the right song to satisfy their needs.

The accompaniments to the songs have also been a cause of dismay. Critics have complained about having the tunes dressed up in mild-sounding harmonies with a conventionally pianistic texture. But fifty years ago Cecil Sharp's harmonies were revolutionary; he managed to escape from chromaticism far sooner than most of his contemporaries. He chose to publish his songs with accompaniments because he was a practical musician and he wanted the tunes to reach thousands of homes as well as thousands of school children. And he knew that not many parents or teachers would have been able to make up their own accompaniments. The pianistic texture was inevitable in 1908, when the piano was used much more than it is now. A 1959 collection of folk songs for schools would probably be arranged for unaccompanied voices in parts, or for voices in unison with *ad lib* recorder parts. But in 1908 very few people sang unaccompanied part-songs; E. H. Fellowes had not yet brought out his edition of the English Madrigal composers. And not even the Dolmetsch family had dreamed of the possibility of the recorder ever becoming a mass-produced instrument for schools.

Cecil Sharp's dance accompaniments have been criticized even more than the songs. It is true that the piano is not the easiest instrument to dance to, but it was the only possible instrument when the dance books were first published. The energetic Morris men of to-day would not be able to dance through the streets to the pipe and tabor if their teachers had not learnt their steps and figures to the thump of a well-worn Broadwood in an ill-ventilated Polytechnic or church hall. The piano accompaniments to the Playford dances are still beautifully satisfying to dance to. Their lasting delight is a reminder that musicians as well as dancers owe a debt of gratitude to Cecil Sharp for his apparent inconsistency in including these sophisticated country dances among his collections of genuine traditional folk dances. The Playford dances are our surest practical guide to the phrasing of English seventeenth-century instrumental music, particularly the music of Purcell … It is a happy coincidence that Cecil Sharp's centenary should occur in the same year as Purcell's tercentenary, since they both owe each other so much.

Of all causes for gratitude, none can compare with the debt that the English composers of fifty years ago owed to Cecil Sharp. Composers in other countries had been helped in their struggles to escape from too much Wagner-worship by the strong national traditions of their own folk music. Without Cecil Sharp's help, English composers might still have been engulfed in the silence that descended on them after Purcell's death. This was the debt that my father had in his mind all his life. And it seems more than likely that his prophecy will come true. Although Cecil Sharp's actual name may not stand out above all others, his work will stand out, for it will have been immortalized in the best of the English music that has been written and is still to be written during this century.[7]

From the beginning of her own career IH's approach to arrangement was directed above all at enhancing the freshness of the original tunes, and her light harmonies were always calculated to maintain a close association with the modal spirit of the original melodies. In a lecture to the EFDSS in Carlisle in 1935, she spoke of the 'appalling mistake of trying to fit folk tunes into Wagner harmonies', and simplicity was always her watchword, a trait which, indeed, would sometimes lead her into austerity. Like Sharp she was a pioneer, especially in her choice of material; many of the tunes and dances that she chose to arrange were obscure, and her settings thus often represented the first time that the music had been widely disseminated. Arranging brought together her passions for educating, inspiring amateurs, and propagating folk music which she knew could be appreciated by people of all backgrounds, and for much of the next decade she turned her back on 'original' composition and directed her

[7] IH, 'Cecil Sharp and the music and music-making of the twentieth century'.

creative energies to producing what she was to describe as 'useful' music, written for educational purposes and amateur groups, and working in the fields of folk music and dance. The unique strengths of her contribution to the field were captured in a review in *The Times* of her carol setting 'Cherry, Holly and Ivy' of 1943: 'Imogen Holst's setting does exactly what is needed to give the folk song a wider currency; she preserves its simplicity, supports it with appropriate harmony, and gives vent to the tune's own efflorescence.'[8]

Foremost among her earliest arrangements were her settings for pipes. Begun in 1932, these first came about through the requirements of her folk music bands, which were made up of 'humbler instruments … such as the tinwhistle and its more relaxed first cousin, the celluloid whistle; the home-made bamboo pipe which is still in its infancy; the concertina, which can sound as noble as a clarinet at times, and even the mouth organ.'[9] IH used the opportunity of the summer school at St Andrews in 1933 for her first public pronouncements on the subject, giving a lecture on 'the making of pipes from bamboo' and providing

> instruction in how to play them. In the first of her course of lectures Miss
> Holst explained that these pipes were the result of an experiment by
> Miss Margaret James, a Gloucestershire teacher. She had been attracted
> by the Sicilian pipes which are made of bamboo, and in trying to make
> one herself realised the educational value of her task.[10]

Developing Margaret James's idea, IH was imaginative enough to foresee the educational value of pipes, an initiative that helped to pave the way for the introduction of the more sophisticated Dolmetsch recorder to schools at the end of the decade, an instrument for which IH was herself to contribute a significant body of educational music. The initiative encapsulated an attitude to the teaching of young children that never changed; in 1955, in response to a question from the audience during a lecture to the Chelmsford Townswomen's Guild, she suggested that small children should be encouraged to learn only very simple instruments, with more difficult challenges like the violin and piano following later and only if the child showed real enthusiasm and aptitude.

IH's earliest published collection, the *First Book of Tunes for the Pipes*, combined her interests in education and folk music, bringing together tunes from Playford's *Dancing Master*, some English country songs, and the music of

[8] *The Times*, 26 November 1943.
[9] IH, 'New ways of making music'.
[10] Report on the Summer School, St Andrews, 1933; private scrapbooks.

Thomas Morley and her father, to build a repertory designed to extend the
musical experience of the novices at whom the pieces were aimed. The second
book exposed her intended public to an even wider range of music, including
arrangements of pieces by Purcell, Lawes and Weelkes, as well as folksong and
one of her own compositions. The *Five Short Airs on a Ground* of 1934 were
written mindful of Margaret James's wish that children should be involved in
making their own instruments, and incorporate to that end a ground which
can 'be played by beginners … on unfinished pipes with only two holes'. Two
years later came the *Canons for Treble Pipes*, the earliest published examples of
one of IH's (and indeed her father's) most favoured musical devices, and where
the emphasis is very much on the encouragement of ensemble playing.

Alongside her arrangements for pipes (and knowing by now that she would
never make a career as a pianist herself), IH began to contribute to the educational piano repertory, which gave her another opportunity to demonstrate
the appeal of folk music. Her first such work, the *Eighteenth Century Dances
for Piano* of 1932, was clearly aimed at the folk dancer: the music is illustrated
with diagrams of how the dances should be performed in the spirit of the originals. Mindful of the need to attract younger performers, IH wrote in her preface that 'new dances have been invented in the style of the older forms of the
country dance, which fit the music equally well and are much more interesting
to dance'. Some original compositions, also with an educational slant, were
produced in the same period, including the *Five Short Pieces* of 1934, which
give particular attention to strengthening fingers and independence of hands,
and the beautiful and highly pictorial *Six Pictures from Finland* (1934), written
after a visit there with the EFDSS in September 1933. In writing this music IH
was keenly aware of the need for some commercial benefit, and she would have
been pleased and encouraged to receive reviews such as the following, for the
Two Scottish Airs for cello and piano (1932), which one commentator praised
as 'unhackneyed and well-contrasted, the first being a plaintive lyric and the
second an energetic dance. The arrangements are neatly made, and are com-
mendable for their restraint.'[11]

Through the course of 1932 IH quickly made her mark in the EFDSS, and
on 6 December 1932 her *Morris Suite*, a continuous arrangement for orchestra
of four dance tunes collected by Sharp, was performed by the BBC Theatre
Orchestra at Cecil Sharp House in a concert to celebrate the coming of age
of the society. The following summer she performed her *Eighteenth Century
Dances* at the society's Summer Festival in Reading, playing the virginals. She

[11] *Musical Times*, March 1936.

also helped to organize the first Folk Music course to be run by the EFDSS. This took place at Cecil Sharp House between 21 and 23 July 1933, and attracted more than a hundred enthusiastic participants. The quality of the speakers was high, with Reginald Jacques, Harold Craxton, Maud Karpeles and Douglas Kennedy all contributing, and IH herself delivering talks on 'Learning Folk Songs by Rote' and 'Folk Dance Bands'. The illustrations for the latter, as the *EFDS News* recalled, 'were given on unorthodox instruments by unrehearsed performers who brought out the points of the argument with an emphasis which surprised them as much, or more, than all the rest'. She spoke of the importance of these bands with an eloquence derived from experience, for as a member of staff at the EFDSS one of her duties had been to turn her conducting skills to working with them. Notwithstanding the inclusion of basic instruments such as mouth organ and tin whistle, such live music was encouraged in preference to wireless and recordings, and IH's knowledge of the idioms of folk dance marked her out as an ideal person to lead ensembles in this repertory.

The beginning of 1933 presented IH with a further opportunity to employ the conducting experience she had gained at the RCM. One of the last compositions she had written there, her suite *The Unfortunate Traveller*, had been scored originally for full brass band, but it was first performed in a version for string orchestra so that IH could hear the piece before she left the college. When GH was planning a concert in Carlisle to be given by the local St Stephen's Band in February 1933, he remembered his daughter's work, included it in the programme, and invited her to conduct it; she thereby became, by her own account, the first woman to conduct a brass band at a public concert.

With her father's career and example before her, it was perhaps inevitable that IH should now choose to settle for a while into the role of music teacher at girls' schools. In March 1933 she began to teach at Eothen School in Caterham, Surrey, where she had once been a pupil, and where her old headmistress Miss Pye was still in charge. Here, together with a few composition and piano pupils, she was principally in charge of class singing, a role that gave her a huge sense of fulfilment; in 1937 she wrote to the headmaster of another school that 'the eight to ten year old classes have been the greatest joy of the week'.[12] At Eothen she was able to encourage the children to play the music of Bartók, a favourite since her RCM days, Debussy and Delius. She could also rely on the active support of Vaughan Williams, who, based nearby in Dorking, became a regular visitor to the school and attended the concerts she gave, which included a rearrangement of Bach's *Christmas Oratorio* for girls' voices and a single bass,

[12] Letter to Mr Curry, 15 November 1937.

a part provided by the school's gardener. One of her pupils, Daphne Hereward, recalled that during these visits 'Vaughan Williams was not allowed to have Miss Pye's chair because he was very fat and the chair might have collapsed.'

Another pupil summed up IH's contribution to music at the school, where her distinctive approach, if still viewed askance by some, at least had the approval of the head mistress. 'She blew away the crabbie spiders of music teaching at Eothen … she never walked, she danced … [and was] frowned upon for allowing girls self expression and treating them as equals, except by the far seeing Miss Pye'. Her conducting was remembered as 'infectious' and her singing classes as 'sheer joy', and there can be no doubt that she was highly successful in enthusing her pupils and firing their musical imaginations. Following in her father's footsteps, she was distinctly unconventional in her methods and, as another pupil recalled, 'did not do much in the way of academic exercises … her method was to encourage one to write music and then to try it out … the main thing about Imo was her tremendous enthusiasm and her conviction that music was for everyone and composition a natural form of expression'.[13] The school also stimulated IH's own creativity, and with the need to provide suitable material for girls' choirs to sing, she began increasingly to write folksong and other arrangements for SSA (two soprano parts with alto), a grouping that seems particularly to have appealed to her. True to her spare, light harmonic style and her contrapuntal leanings, she would have enjoyed the enforced economy of the medium, which also – and no doubt to her great relief – proved to be popular with the range of publishers to whom she had now begun to send her work on a regular basis. In gratitude for this creative spur, she dedicated the fourth of her *Four Somerset Folk Songs* 'to the singers at Eothen'.

To supplement her income from her post at Eothen IH also accepted a music teaching post at Roedean School in Sussex, where she took on about twenty piano pupils and some aural training classes. Aware of her commitments in Surrey, the school did its utmost to accommodate their new member of staff, who would need to stay overnight for part of the week. In her letter of confirmation, written on 26 July 1933, E. M. Tanner informed IH that her fee would be 'about £50 per term'. She continued:

> I think you will find that it will be necessary for you to give us Monday, Tuesday and the morning of Thursday. As I explained to you, we shall be very glad to put you up for Monday and Tuesday, and also, if it fitted in with your work at Caterham (as I think it will) for Wednesday night …

---

[13] Recollections of Katherine Moore (née Hunt), Marion Coxon (née Grieg) and Helen Bucknall, all in correspondence with Christopher Tinker.

I am delighted that you are coming to us; I hope that you will enjoy the work and be happy here.

Her old piano teacher Kathleen Long wrote to congratulate her on the appointment, but warned that 'the music is not thrilling at that school from all accounts, so there'll be a chance for you to put some opinion into it'.[14] This challenge proved to be insurmountable, however, as unlike at Eothen, the staff at Roedean actively discouraged her attempts to introduce her students to new European music. Despite this frustration IH stayed in the post for two years, leaving at the end of the summer term in 1935.

The year 1933 had seen a significant decline in GH's health, with both his diet and mobility becoming increasingly restricted; he spent Christmas of that year in New Lodge Clinic in Windsor, being treated for a duodenal ulcer, and did not emerge until the end of February. Nevertheless, at the beginning of March 1934 he made the effort to be present at a concert at the Assembly Rooms, Oxford, which featured a performance of his daughter's arrangement for two sopranos and piano of the Oxfordshire folk-song 'Pretty Caroline'; in the event this was to be the last concert that he ever attended. Later in the month IH's skill as an arranger was further recognized when she was invited to venture for the first time into a recording studio, conducting three records of her folk dance settings for the Gramophone Company. In the same month, her school friend Jane Schofield married Henry Fosbrooke, and IH contributed a wedding hymn to the service, held on 17 March in Stoke D'Abernon, Surrey. She then went to the EFDSS School at Windermere, directed by Douglas Kennedy, where she took charge of the singing. But the spring was clouded by her father's deteriorating state of health. He eventually submitted to a major operation in Ealing on 23 May for the removal of the ulcer, but although the procedure itself was successful, the shock to the composer's system was too great, and he died of heart failure two days later.

GH was cremated at Golders Green on 28 May 1934. On 19 June the staff and pupils of SPGS held a memorial service at St John's, Smith Square, at which Bishop George Bell paid tribute to his life and work. Then on 24 June his ashes were interred in Chichester Cathedral. Singers representing several of GH's choirs joined together under the baton of Vaughan Williams in a selection of pieces by Weelkes, Vaughan Williams and GH himself.

Once the formalities were completed, IH resumed her established pattern of work. Very soon afterwards, however, she made a decision that was dramatically to affect the course of the rest of her life: to dedicate herself to the cause

[14] Letter of November 1933; private scrapbooks.

of preserving her father's legacy and promoting his music. GH had bequeathed a small estate to be divided between his wife and daughter. But IH, reasoning that she could earn her own living whereas Isobel, already showing signs of arthritis, could not, elected to accept only a small percentage for herself, diverting the rest to her mother and later on, as resources allowed, to the promulgation of her father's scores. Having set out on this course, it was inevitable that her career as a composer would be eclipsed, and she henceforth became increasingly self-effacing and diffident about her own work. The shadow of her father's reputation, and her desire to emulate his example in other fields, had already contributed, together with her preoccupation with arranging folksong and dance, to her largely turning away from original composition in the years following her departure from the RCM. Although she later regained the self-confidence to write major works, she always remained guarded about her talents and achievement. Towards the end of her life her father's biographer Michael Short attempted to break down this guard and was sharply rebuffed:

> When asked why she had not followed up her promising début as a composer (was it because of having a famous father, or the difficulties of being a woman composer, or the necessity of earning a living by teaching?) she parried the question with the brusque retort 'Wasn't good enough!'[15]

But her student works, so well received at the RCM and in the press, belie this assertion; indeed, the original compositions that she produced through the 1930s in addition to her educational work continue to display individuality and a personal style, constrained only by the absence of opportunities that she afforded herself to develop and refine it.

Through the course of 1934 IH began to spend time at Westhall Hill, on the edge of Burford in Oxfordshire, the home of Captain and Mrs W. R. W. Kettlewell, influential members of the EFDSS and themselves enthusiastic musicians and dancers. Their house had become the focus for much musical activity, and a grieving and vulnerable IH found herself drawn into these hospitable surroundings, where she formed new friendships and began to conduct and train a small group of local singers and direct them at occasional weekend gatherings. That December she arranged for the Westhall Hill Singers a carol, 'Nowell and Nowell', originally collected by Cecil Sharp; a second performance was given at Christmas in a carol service at Chichester Cathedral, where the ashes of her father had already been interred.

---

[15] Short, *Gustav Holst*, p. v.

Once the rush of obituaries and commemorative articles in the national and musical press had receded, IH watched as GH's music fell into neglect, despite the best efforts of champions such as Vaughan Williams, Adrian Boult and Havergal Brian. It was left to her to pick up the gauntlet as his main champion. One of her first tasks was to fulfil her father's outstanding obligation to provide music for a Hollywood pageant entitled *The Song of Solomon*, which GH had only partially completed. She submitted the score promptly on 30 August, but disappointingly the project was subsequently abandoned and the score never returned. Then in January 1935 she included one of GH's scores in a concert of ballet music at the Rudolf Steiner Hall, organized as a fund-raising event for the EFDSS by Amy Stoddart. The programme comprised *Petticoat Lane*, choreographed to her father's *St Paul's Suite*, Thomas Dunhill's *The Fairy Ring* and her own new ballet score *Love in a Mist*, 'strung together' from the music of Scarlatti. Two months later, on 24 March, she took part in a memorial concert to GH at Cecil Sharp House, conducting her own orchestral arrangement of the 'Intermezzo' from his First Suite in E flat for brass band.

In the spring of 1935 IH gave the inaugural lecture to the Eothen Music Club for Amateurs. A report of her lecture, entitled 'Modern Music', encapsulated her views on music in England during this time of economic depression, informed by her recent European experiences, and emphasized once again her belief in the importance of the contribution of amateurs to the musical health of the nation:

> She lay great stress on the necessity for vitality in any work of art and showed that many modern composers had this vitality, but that it is often difficult for us to recognise it owing to the unfamiliar idiom which they use … She mentioned Sibelius, Vaughan Williams and William Walton as great modern composers. Miss Holst said that we were in an experimental state in England, comparable with that of the Elizabethans; then there was a state of unrest similar to the unrest of the present day, when people turned to music as relief from their troubles. Finally she showed that amateurs were to a large extent responsible for the music of the nation, and it was no use for a man of genius to compose a work unless there were people willing to study and perform it.

Underlying her reference to the 'man of genius' was no doubt the image of her father, whose music in the year after his death notably lacked either willing students or performers. IH's own music, on the other hand, was increasingly attracting both performance and publication. That year saw the appearance in print of both original works and arrangements, issued by Cramer, Augener and Novello. In October, feeling more financially secure than at any time since leaving college, she was able to move to a new flat at 54 Ormonde Terrace, Primrose Hill, and on 15 November her Concerto for Violin and String Orchestra, founded on traditional Irish tunes, received its first performance; Elsie Avril was the soloist, with IH conducting the London Symphony Orchestra at an RCM Patron's Fund 'rehearsal'.

Throughout 1936 IH's star in the folk music firmament continued to rise steadily. In January the National Festival of English Folk Dance and Song took place at the Royal Albert Hall, a major event for which she arranged the music. That spring she drew up the syllabus and acted as the chief judge for a Folk Music competition at Cecil Sharp House on 14 March, and in the last week of April she adjudicated at the Leith Hill Music Festival with Vaughan Williams. On 15 July the Society of Women Musicians, keen supporters of IH and her music, celebrated its twenty-fifth anniversary with a concert that included several new part-songs for female voices by IH, including 'My Bairn sleep softly now' and 'Now will I weave white violets', conducted by her friend Iris Lemare. Once again, both these songs found a ready publisher in Cramer, and thus helped to bring in welcome supplementary income to her earnings from teaching. She had also begun to produce arrangements for recorder groups, an educational initiative that she, together with the Dolmetsch family, did much to promote, and which was receiving strong support from the music publisher Schott. The returns from these pieces and the publication of her successful SSA arrangements and piano teaching music were by now quite generous, the royalty on her publications in the Oxford Piano Series of 1934, for example, being 12.5 per cent. Her income received a further boost when she was commissioned, together with Gordon Jacob, to provide arrangements for band of a series of country dances to be recorded by Columbia to celebrate the coronation of King George VI on 12 May 1937.

Not all of IH's compositional activity, however, was geared so directly towards bolstering her income. In 1937 she embarked on a substantial score of incidental music for *Nicodemus*, a mystery play by the Presbyterian minister Andrew Young. The work, which involved writing a full orchestral score with organ, would have seemed laborious in the context of its likely return; she was only to receive 2.5 per cent on each copy sold at 3s. 6d. She must therefore have been driven by other motives, which may have stemmed from her acquaintance with Young through their shared connection with Chichester Cathedral, where Young had been a canon, and from the inspiration of her father, who had undertaken a similar project in composing the score for Masefield's *The*

Coming of Christ. In any case the work, first performed on Palm Sunday (21 March) 1937 at St Andrew's Presbyterian Church in Cheam, where Andrew Young was the minister, achieved considerable success and received many performances across the country. The score is a notable achievement, combining vitality and tenderness, and providing further demonstration that IH's gifts as a composer of original music, although largely dormant during this period, might under different circumstances easily be revived.

For the time being, however, folk music remained her chief preoccupation, although this was rivalled increasingly by her passion for rediscovering and editing lost and neglected music from the Renaissance and the Baroque. Her interest in early music repertories extended back to her time at the RCM. Many years later, at a time when her reputation as a pioneer of early music scholarship and performance was secure, she was to record the sense of exaltation that she found in exploring this music for the first time and coming to grips with the issues of notation and performance practice that it raised:[16]

> Half a century ago, when I was a student at the Royal College of Music, a visitor walking along one of the corridors past those over-resonant music-rooms would almost certainly have heard the sound of Bach or Handel being practised with energetic determination. My fellow pianists and I used to work hard at the accompaniments of the violin sonatas, endeavouring to obey all the instructions on the printed page, and seldom questioning anything that the editors had asked us to do.
>
> Then someone suggested that we should go into the college library and look at the Bach Gesellschaft edition. What we found there was exciting but unsettling. Some of our accompaniments had no right-hand part for the keyboard player, which meant that the expressive bits we had practised so carefully must have been composed at the end of the nineteenth century. For page after page there were no indications of loud or soft, although in the copies we were using the editors had given us definite instructions to begin, say, mp or mf and to mount up, through a long hairpin crescendo, to ff at the climax. In the Gesellschaft, the words ritt and rall never appeared. There were, it is true, a few slurs, but nothing like the number of bowings and 'expression marks' that we had been faced with. Thrilled by this discovery, we began to make pencil corrections in the copies we were using, crossing out all unwanted slurs and dynamics. The result was a mess, and it was difficult to read the notes. So we tried scratching out the editor's contributions with a

---

[16] 'Learning to edit baroque music', *ESTA News & Views*, vol. 1 no. 2 (1976).

penknife, but the result was a worse mess (and it wore holes in the pages). We then decided to make our own manuscript copies for our own use. And, in that instant, we became embryonic editors.

Our ignorance was abysmal, but our zeal was tremendous. (I can remember taking two hours over two bars of a Bach Trio Sonata, trying to guess which of the left-hand quavers should be legato and which should be semi-staccato.) One of the things that helped most in those painful struggles was the chance of hearing a lively and sensitive performance of baroque music. Adolf Busch's series of Bach programmes at the Wigmore Hall in the early 1930's taught us a great deal. This was the first time most of us had heard the Brandenburg concertos played as chamber music. (At Promenade concerts in the Queen's Hall, Brandenburg No. 3 used to be performed by the same number of string players who had been engaged that evening for the Fourth Symphony of Brahms or for the Tchaikovsky Piano Concerto in B flat minor.) The Busch ensemble played with an effortless sense of well-being: the counterpoint was clear, and the dance movements sounded like real dances. The continuo, beautifully realised by Rudolf Serkin, was of course played on the piano, because that was the normal keyboard instrument in those days. It was only among members of the Dolmetech family and their pupils and followers that the harpsichord was considered essential in Bach.

As time went on, we gradually learnt a little more about what was needed. Exploring pre-Bach music was a help. In Purcell's manuscripts we had to grapple with many problems of notation, such as the time-signature of 6/4 for six quavers in a bar; or the key-signature of one flat for a piece in G minor; or the frequent and bewildering absence of necessary accidentals. While trying to solve these practical problems by trial and error we began to see that it is as well to forget all about 19th-century text-book rudiments when studying baroque scores.

Problems of pre-Bach style were much more difficult to solve than those of notation. Monteverdi's music let in a great light. The recording of some of his madrigals under the direction of Nadia Boulanger, came as a revelation. For many of us, this was the first Monteverdi we had heard. Here again, the continuo was played, as a matter of course, on the piano; though by this time some of us were beginning to wonder why it couldn't have been the harpsichord.

By the early 1930s IH had already taken time to explore collections of manuscripts in Italy during her travelling on the Octavia scholarship, and in

1936, when on tour with the EFDSS in the USA, she took the opportunity of visiting the Huntington Library in California, a visit that led to her first published arrangements, of music by Pelham Humphrey, for her favoured recorder groups. Further editions of Humphrey followed in the form of three songs which appeared in 1938, published by Louise Dyer's Lyrebird Press. At their first performance on 20 March that year the *Musical Times* critic noted that 'Miss Holst's enthusiasm for this hitherto neglected composer [has] become infectious'.

For all her own success, the perpetuation of her father's legacy in the years immediately following his death remained of prime concern to IH. Since 1935 she had joined with Vaughan Williams and others in spearheading a campaign to build a lasting memorial to GH in the form of a new soundproof music room at Morley College. The necessary sum of £1,100 was raised through the course of the next eighteen months, and by the spring of 1937 the new facility, to a design by Edward Maufe, was ready to be opened. Queen Mary visited the College to perform the ceremony on 6 March, and IH conducted the choir in some of GH's part-songs. By this time she was already forming in her mind plans for another enduring memorial to her father. Over six weeks that summer she brought the writing experience that she had developed over the previous decade (largely from contributing articles to EFDSS publications) to bear on the much more demanding task of authoring her father's biography. Entitled simply *Gustav Holst* and published by Oxford University Press in 1938, it was immediately recognized as a model of its type, and marked the first step towards the rehabilitation of the late composer's reputation.

The book was received rapturously by friends and press alike. Donald Tovey admired its 'Holstian directness and economy', Vaughan Williams pronounced it 'splendid' and Clifford Bax praised the author for producing an account of GH's life 'which brings him to life again'.[17] Edmund Rubbra's considered review in the *Monthly Musical Record* of November 1938 praised IH in particular for avoiding the pitfalls encountered by offspring when writing about their parents:

> It is usually perilous for a daughter to take it upon herself to be her father's biographer. Either the years between them make real understanding difficult to achieve or vision is clouded by sentiment. Imogen Holst has, however, inherited from her father not a little of his sense of proportion, so that her biography is at once intimate and objective. She has wisely refrained from discussing Holst's works except in a very

[17] Undated letters, 1938; private scrapbooks; HF.

general way, not from an inability to do so (on the contrary, occasional asides show how acute her judgement is) but from a desire to write nothing that shall divert attention from her picture of Holst the man.

After a decade in which GH's presence and influence had been a constant source of support and strength to her emerging career, the achievement of such a measure of objectivity in this book was particularly significant. For IH herself the writing seems to have proved a necessary cathartic experience. She was now ready to emerge from his shadow and stand on her own feet to embark, with renewed self-confidence as an independent woman and artist, upon the next stage of her life and career.

6 'A present from the Government': Travelling with CEMA, 1939–42

There can be little doubt that IH herself regarded the period in 1938 following the publication of her biography of her father as a crossroads in her life. In an extended interview given to Ronald Blythe nearly twenty years later, she spoke of her need at that point to take stock of her life and achievements and to ponder the way ahead:

> She [had] travelled a good deal, on the Continent – France, Germany and Austria –and as an accompanist to the English Folk Dance Society when it toured Canada, the United States and Finland. In 1938 she made a great decision, which was to 'cut loose' from all amateur associations in music. There was nothing out of character in such a decision, nothing which involved pride or the *volte-face* of a personality which had been for many years the inspiration of so many amateur choirs and musical events. It was just that the time had come for a deeply personal assessment of her hopes and her aims. What was she? What did she want to be? There were many artists of all kinds who wondered similarly in 1938. She had been gaining an increasing reputation as an adjudicator of the best amateur musical field, but eventually this very success would be the thing which might hinder her greater career … Her father's eminence had brought her rapidly into contact with the most remarkable names in literature and music. Now she felt she must prove herself to herself – always the most searching of tasks.[1]

In the event, it would take IH more than a decade to disentangle herself – and then only partially – from making music with amateurs. At Easter 1939 she resigned from her post at Eothen and decided to travel to Switzerland to study quietly and to think things out; she was also keen to improve her German. She first had some commitments to fulfil, however, including a big adjudication engagement at the beginning of May, at the climax of

---

[1] Blythe, 'Imogen Holst – perfectionist'.

which she heard 'her favourite song' sung thirty-nine times. The EFDSS Folk
Music Festival kept her in England until 20 May; three days later she finally
left for Switzerland. From June to August she travelled through the country, hoping to stay into the early autumn, but she had to hurry back at the
end of August as the war clouds broke, reaching home with two days to
spare.

IH later described her September war work as 'picking and packing apples
in Essex', but this overlooked her much more important activities for the
Bloomsbury House Refugee Committee, which, headed by Vaughan Williams,
worked to secure the release from internment of musicians who had escaped
from Austria and Germany. Then, in December, she was drawn into a much
larger and more far-reaching initiative to promote music-making during
wartime, begun by the Pilgrim Trust. Founded in 1930 by the American philanthropist Edward Harkness in admiration for what Great Britain had done
in the 1914–18 war, the Trust was endowed with an initial gift of 2 million
pounds, which Harkness wished to be used to support some of the country's more urgent needs and to promote her future well-being. When war
broke out the Trust's secretary, Dr Thomas Jones, was one of the first to realize that a likely effect of prolonged conflict could be the abandonment, and
even extinction, of a host of English cultural values and traditions. To prevent
this happening, he conceived a scheme to send out practitioners of the arts,
theatre and music into rural communities where they could work to ensure
the public's continuing interest and participation. He took the idea first to the
Chairman of the Trust, Lord Macmillan, and then to Lord De La Warr at the
Board of Education, who between them devised a plan whereby the Pilgrim
Trust would fund the initiative with £25,000. Sir Walford Davies, Master of
the King's Musick, agreed to organize the music branch of the scheme, and in
January 1940 he appointed IH to be one of six 'Music Travellers', charged with
inspiring and organizing musical activities among civilians in rural areas. In
the wartime situation it was inevitably women that took the lead, and among
IH's colleagues, working under the leadership of Sybil Eaton, would be Ursula
Nettleship, the flautist Eve Kisch and the singer Anne Wood.

Once the scheme was under way, its themes were soon taken up by central
government. A memorandum written to the Board of Education on 18
December 1939 had already argued that

> This country is supposed to be fighting for civilization and democracy
> and if these things mean anything they mean a way of life where people
> have liberty and opportunity to pursue the things of peace. It should be

part of our national war policy to show that the Government is actively interested in these things.[2]

The Government responded in January 1940 by establishing the Council for the Encouragement of Music and the Arts (CEMA) with two key objectives: 'The preservation in wartime of the highest standards in the arts and the widespread provision of opportunities for hearing good music and the enjoyment of the arts generally.'

In agreeing to take on the role of a Pilgrim Trust (and later CEMA) Traveller, IH – who was assigned to the west of England, from Oxfordshire to the Scilly isles – was accepting a huge challenge. Not only did the project fly in the face of her recent decision to leave behind her work with amateurs; it also presented severe logistical difficulties to a London-based non-driver. But Walford Davies had been astute in his choice, recognizing in IH both the missionary qualities that the scheme would require, and the ability to enthuse and encourage sometimes reluctant amateur music-makers. Such zeal would be crucial to the morale-boosting which, from the Government's point of view at least, was central to the success of the project. Her work with amateurs had also demonstrated a commitment to the democratization of music that set her views well in line with the national agenda.

Several years later IH wrote an extended autobiographical account of her time as a Traveller, bringing vividly to life the ups and downs of the itinerant existence that she then led, setting the idealism with which the project started against the sometimes grim realities that she faced, yet also highlighting the enthusiasm and the astonishing results that this method of music-making could achieve:[3]

It was in December 1939 that the Pilgrim Trust decided to help people in the country districts of England to make music for themselves during the war. So Walford Davies was consulted about the best way to set about it, and he sent out six music travellers, whom he judged to be 'missionary-minded', under the inspired guidance of Sybil Eaton. He had had a vision that music would spring up in all the villages through which the travellers passed on their journeys. No plans were made: no policy was outlined. We were told to go where we liked and to do what we liked when we got there.

So we set out on our travels. By great good fortune I was allowed

[2] Quoted in Sinclair, *Arts and Cultures*, pp. 26–7.
[3] *Making Music*, no. 2 (October 1946), pp. 10–11.

to explore Somerset, where I soon learned that all the legends about
West Country hospitality are founded on fact. I was ill-equipped for my
first county committee meeting, being ignorant of the meaning of such
words as 'agenda' or 'minutes', never having heard of the initials L.E.A.
or R.C.C.,[4] and feeling utterly mystified when asked to define my 'terms
of reference'. However, I soon discovered that 'organizing' was not as
formidable as it sounded and that it mostly consisted of making a lot
of new friends. And these friends were all musicians. There was the village grocer who conducted a madrigal choir in the small sitting-room
behind the shop. There was the village postman who had taught himself
to play the violin and the viola and the cello and the bass, and had then
founded and conducted a flourishing string orchestra which met every
Sunday afternoon by invitation of the proprietor of the ironmonger's
shop. The members of the orchestra miraculously fitted themselves into
his back parlour (which had to be emptied of all its furniture for the
occasion), and played with an astonishing warmth of tone and intensity
of phrasing.

There was the organist whose chief joy in life was to collect half a
dozen friends on a Saturday afternoon and sing unaccompanied motets
by Palestrina and Byrd and Gibbons until well after midnight, being for-
tified by a strong cup of tea every two hours or so. There were middle-
aged market-gardeners who came straight in from work in the evenings
to play 16th century German recorder music.

One of the most exciting experiences was hearing Somerset folk-songs
sung in their own traditional way in the villages where they had always
belonged and where Cecil Sharp had first heard them in the eighteen-
nineties. In a tiny village school, over a thousand feet above sea-level, I
heard the authentic tempo and phrasing of 'Up wuz I on my furrrthr's
furrrm', sung by the eleven children in the school, whose ages ranged
from the skinny little girl of five to the big robust boy of fourteen who
was already working on his furrrthr's furrrm. Their 'uncertified' school-
mistress was a genius who kept them happy all the time – singing was
their favourite occupation.

As a Pilgrim Trust Traveller there were many different ways in which
one was asked to help people to make music; perhaps it would be a
Women's Institute meeting in a remote village, with fourteen very old
women in hats sitting round the edge of a dark, empty, hideous tin hut

---

[4] Respectively, 'Local Education Authority' and 'Rural Community Council'.

with the rain beating on the roof. There would be no piano – not even a harmonium. Their faces would be set in a glum or ironical frown of disapproval at the suggestion that they should sing. But when they were safely embarked on their first round, 'Hark, the bells', their eyes would become wide with astonishment as they heard themselves drawing the magic harmonies out of the empty air around them.

Next day there would be a request to coach the local brass band, as the conductor had suddenly been called up. Or it would be a request to take a congregational hymn practice during evensong at the parish church. This was always something of an adventure, since many members of the congregation were filled with dismay at the thought of a woman's voice being raised in church. They were also terrified at hearing their own naked voices bereft of the familiar covering of the all-embracing 16-foot and Swell to Great. But as soon as they had begun to thaw it was an inspiring sound to hear the Tallis eight-part canon soaring up through the pillars, with the soldiers' voices filling the back of the church.

Perhaps the request would be to take a sing-song at an evacuee hostel for mothers and babies from the east end of London, exiled miles from anywhere on a bleak, desolate stretch of the moor. Here there was no question of 'thawing'. The rhythm of their singing was intoxicating; they conducted with their hips and punctuated each chorus with the soles of their shoes, while their black-eyed, woolly-haired babies gurgled and beat their fists in the air.

The war had made very little apparent difference to Somerset in 1940. Most of the men were working on farms, and in several village choirs there were *too many tenors*. But one never knew what would happen next, and with evacuees coming and going all the time the easiest way of making music for combined groups of people was to hold 'drop-in-and-sing' festivals all over the county. Our festivals invariably clashed with some world calamity: the first one coincided with the German invasion of Holland and Belgium and all the altos had to walk out in the middle of the rehearsal to make a house-to-house collection of blankets for the refugees who were expected to arrive by boat at any minute. But it made an unforgettable performance of 'Turn back, O man'. Another festival took place during the retreat from Dunkirk, and our leading viola's only son was among the thousands who were waiting on the other side of the channel, but not for one instant did she allow her attention to wander from the orchestral accompaniments.

C.E.M.A. had come into being by then, and the Pilgrim Trust Travellers were now C.E.M.A. Travellers. It was good to be related to the Rural Music Schools Council. And it was good to be able to visit the Women's Institute group meetings (poor dears, they were struggling to disentangle the intricacies of the Sugar Scheme) and to be able to say to them: 'This half hour of singing is a present from the Government, because they believe that making music is a thing that matters, even in war-time'.

Fortunately we were still allowed to go where we liked and do what we liked when we got there. Work had to be limited owing to the difficulties of transport, but this, in a way, was an advantage. Musicians from London are seldom acclimatized to the speed of country life. If one takes three hours over a journey of twenty-two and a half miles one learns a good deal about one's fellow travellers in the crowded, slow-moving bus. In the summer of 1940 one was lucky to find a bus going in the right direction. 'There *used* to be one that went there every Wednesday', they'd say, 'but that was before the war'.

Travelling by bicycle, or even on foot, had a lot to recommend it. It meant that there was time to stop and talk to the old man who had been singing in the same church choir for 81 years and who remembered the musicians sitting in the gallery when he was a boy and playing the hymns on the clarinet and the serpent. And having talked to the old man, there was time to go into the church and listen to the organist practising Bach: he was a tailor by profession and he had played the organ every Sunday for forty years, but now he was filled with a desire to get his 'letters' after his name. And the great difficulty was the paper-work, because he couldn't understand the ill-written, ill-printed little pamphlet they had given him on Fugal Analysis. So we analysed his Bach fugue for three quarters of an hour and his face shone with excitement.

There was time in those idyllic days to sit over a cup of tea and talk to the individual enthusiasts about their own hopes and dreams and difficulties. So many of these solitary musicians were self-taught, and they were ploughing their way through the wrong text-books and longing for advice on what to sing or play or conduct. There was time to talk to them all and go back later on and see how they were getting on.

But by the end of 1940 C.E.M.A.'s work was spreading very rapidly and each Traveller was responsible for the music of five or six counties at once. It was inevitable that the work should become more organized. We could no longer wander from place to place with a fortnight's luggage strapped to our shoulders, without any fixed plan and without any clear notion of where we meant to sleep that night. From then onwards we were chained, however intermittently, to a telephone.

Today [1946] the work of the Arts Council has expanded far beyond the wildest dreams of those who set out as Travellers in January 1940. But over a large part of England there are individual enthusiasts who are making music for themselves and struggling on without the help of an R.M.S., waiting, whether they know it or not, for a Sybil Eaton to drop in for a cup of tea and a talk and a little music.

One day, perhaps, it may happen again.

Despite the upbeat tone and optimistic ending to her retrospective account, IH soon became more and more worn down by the workload and travelling associated with the post. Moreover, once CEMA had been established, and funding for the project transferred from the Pilgrim Trust to the Board of Education, she also found herself immersed in the unwelcome bureaucracy that came with the new structure, which required her to submit documentation, attend tedious committee meetings and accept directions from Whitehall. Some idea of her weekly burden of travelling, meetings and rehearsals can be gleaned from a surviving report that she wrote of her work in Somerset at the end of 1940 (see Figure 1). From this it is clear that she was working under the stress of other pressures too, notably her recurrently painful arm and the thought that far away in London, her father's legacy was under threat from German bombing. Eventually she was able to find a more permanent solution to the latter problem at least, as she recalled many years later:

I had to find somewhere safe to house my father's manuscripts which I'd inherited after his death. And I asked at the Bodleian and they very kindly allowed them to be – I don't know where they were, but obviously below ground, somewhere quite safe. And when the war was over and I went to take them away I decided to give them *The Planets* as a gesture of thanks for that help.[5]

Over two and a half years IH had become physically overburdened, disillusioned and finally ill with exhaustion, and by July 1942 she had reached the point where she felt bound to resign. It would, however, be wrong to conclude from this final disappointment that her time as a Traveller had been wasted, either for herself or for the communities she visited, who benefited immeasurably from her presence and activities. Her unconventional teaching methods,

---

[5] Interview with Christopher Headington, 1979.

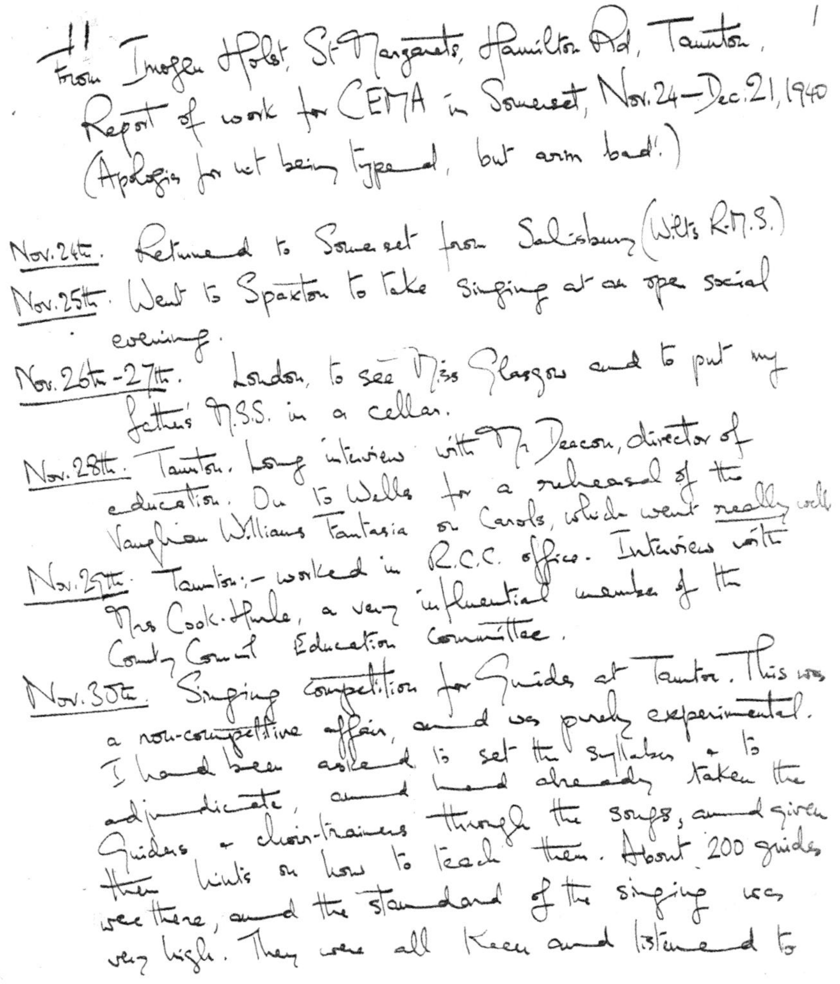

H.
from Imogen Holst, St Margaret's, Hamilton Rd, Taunton.
Report of work for CEMA in Somerset, Nov.24–Dec.21, 1940
(Apologies for not being typed, but arm bad!)

Nov.24th. Returned to Somerset from Salisbury (Wilts R.M.S.)
Nov.25th. Went to Spaxton to take singing at an ope social evening.
Nov.26th–27th. London, to see Miss Glasgow and to put my father's MSS. in a cellar.
Nov.28th. Taunton. Long interview with Mr Deacon, director of education. On to Wells for a rehearsal of the Vaughan Williams Fantasia on Carols, which went really well
Nov.29th. Taunton:– worked in R.C.C. offices. Interview with Mrs Cook-Hurle, a very influential member of the County Council Education Committee.
Nov.30th. Singing competition for Guides at Taunton. This was a non-competitive affair, and was purely experimental. I had been asked to set the syllabus & to adjudicate, and I had already taken the Guides & choir-trainers through the songs, and given them hints on how to teach them. About 200 guides were there, and the standard of the singing was very high. They were all keen and listened to

Figure 1 IH's report on her CEMA work in Somerset, 24–30 November 1940

viewed askance by some of her colleagues at Eothen and Roedean, came into their own during these years, when she confirmed for herself the importance of being able to teach without books and brighten people's lives by teaching them rounds rather than counterpoint. But if her music-making relied heavily on the oral transmission of the tunes, rounds and canons she had acquired for herself over many years, she also began to realize the need for these resources to be available to local communities in a printed form. She later wrote of her work in the villages:

There were never any song books and seldom any pianos, so I soon found that the best way of getting people to enjoy themselves was to teach them easy accumulative folk songs such as 'The first time I went to Donnybrook Fair' or 'My name is Jack Jintle' … where the tunes went with a swing and the words were simple enough to pick up by ear. We also sang short rounds such as 'Hark, the Bells!' or 'Lady come down and see, the cat sits in the plum tree'. At the end of each visit, people used to ask me, 'Where can we buy copies of those songs and rounds?' and I had to say 'You can't. The English folk songs are from journals which are available only to members of a Society – the Appalachian songs are from volumes published at 35s. each (melody only) and the rounds are out of print and would need to be searched for in the British Museum'. Their disappointed faces have haunted me ever since …[6]

It was this experience that was later to lead her to the preparation and publication of her enduring volume of songs for female voices, *Singing for Pleasure*, in 1957, devised for the Women's Institute.

Leadership qualities were as vital as musical ones for the travelling musicians, and IH seemed naturally gifted in directing the various mixed assemblies which she encountered, developing an innate understanding of people's needs. She was proud of some of the results that she achieved, recalling later the 'unforgettable experience' of hearing a Tallis canon sung by 200 people. And her pride was reciprocated by those with whom she worked; following an afternoon of madrigal singing in Taunton, arranged with the Somerset Rural Community Council on 13 October 1941, the *RCM Magazine* reported the participants' 'eager co-operation in some of the best things in music'.[7]

It is perhaps not surprising that during this period of her life IH's own flow of compositions and arrangements should slow to a trickle, or that the music she did produce should be closely related to her work as a Music Traveller. In particular she arranged traditional carols for female voices, providing 'short simple settings' for 'village choirs and Women's Institutes'. Ever the practical musician, she designed these settings to ensure not only that 'each part is easy enough to be learnt by rote' but also that 'choirs can learn the carols by heart for singing out of doors in the dark'.[8] She also found time and leisure to write two suites for her favoured ensemble, recorder trio. The first, the *Offley Suite*, took its name from Offley Place, near Hitchin in Hertfordshire, where the CEMA Music

---

[6] IH, 'Singing for pleasure'.
[7] *RCM Magazine*, vol. 38, no. 1 (1941), p. 21.
[8] From IH's note to her *Six Traditional Carols*.

Travellers held their conferences, while the second, the *Deddington Suite*, was written for Marjorie Wise, headmistress of a large school in Dagenham which had been evacuated to Deddington in north Oxfordshire.

Marjorie Wise knew IH well, having taken part in her orchestra at Cecil Sharp House. More significantly for IH and her future development, she had in 1938 introduced her to Leonard and Dorothy Elmhirst, the founders of Dartington Hall, near Totnes in Devon. At Dartington the Elmhirsts were trying to create an ideal community, influenced by Leonard's work in rural India and in sympathy with the Arts and Crafts movement of William Morris. IH, like her father, was much in sympathy with Morris's socialist ideals, and when Marjorie Wise had first brought her to Dartington in 1938, initially to draw on her expertise in leading community singing, IH immediately grasped the potential for using the Elmhirsts' unique setting to create an arts centre where 'music and the other arts could be a living experience for the locality'.[9] Now, four years after that visit, IH arrived in Devon once again, on what would prove to be the last leg of her journey as a Music Traveller. The Elmhirsts invited her to make Dartington her home while she worked in Devon and Cornwall. To have the offer of a permanent base, after the constant travelling of the past three years, and to be in such a sympathetic environment, was both a relief and a great pleasure; she accepted wholeheartedly. Neither she nor her hosts, however, could have predicted that her sojourn would be the prelude to an association with Dartington which would dominate the next eight years.

[9] Cox and Dobbs, *Imogen Holst at Dartington*, p. 31.

7 'A wonderful opportunity': Dartington, 1942–50

At Dartington IH's life as a Music Traveller was swiftly transformed, as she was able to bring her amateur and novice musicians into an environment much more conducive to music-making than the assortment of village and church halls with which she had become familiar during her previous travels. Her achievements were quickly recognized by Christopher Martin, the Administrator of the Arts Centre at Dartington Hall, and when, shortly afterwards, an exhausted IH returned to Devon for an extended period of recuperation having been 'encouraged to give up' her CEMA responsibilities, he asked her to become involved in an Arts Enquiry report into musical life in England that Dartington was sponsoring. Many years later she gave an interview to Jack Dobbs regarding this period of her life,[1] and described her introduction thus:

> While I was here, Chris Martin asked me if I would work on the Arts Enquiry. That was marvellous, because I had been around in this side of England and I was able to do a bit. I remembered that Leonard Elmhirst had been so pleased about some rude remarks I had made about church singing. I had said that people in church services quite often sang so badly that it was only the Almighty that would have put up with it. To my horror I found that he had written to the Archbishop telling him about this.
>
> Anyway, that was the way I began working in Dartington and one day, as I was crossing the courtyard, I got a message that Chris would like to see me in his office ... He said, 'Imo, how can we start at Dartington the sort of thing that your father did in the old days in Morley College?' Well, Morley College nowadays has a very high standard of music education ... but when my father started in 1905, before I was born, it was really amateur. He achieved a great deal because he cared passionately about lovely music being done by anyone who wanted to do it, whether they were good at music or not, as long as they were keen and turned up regularly every week for rehearsals. So they did Purcell's 'King Arthur'

[1] Cox and Dobbs, *Imogen Holst at Dartington*, pp. 10–27.

and Purcell's 'Fairy Queen' and Bach Cantatas with people who could
hardly play at all. That was the tradition in which I was brought up. The
other thing that I would like to mention he did at Morley College in
those days (because it does link up with Dartington) – he started a composition class every week for grown-up beginners, some of whom didn't
know their notes. They could hear a tune in their minds but had never
thought how to write it down. They were that elementary, and were of
all ages – some retired, some still working as tram drivers, office workers or school teachers. That impressed me a lot. So, when my father
died in 1934, I thought, if ever I had the chance to carry on that tradition I would do so because no one else was doing that. Teachers were
beginning to think about composition in schools; now it is a matter of
course. But when Chris Martin said 'How can we start at Dartington?' I
thought, what a wonderful opportunity! It linked up with the work for
C.E.M.A. I had been doing with amateurs, because we had been working
in the early days before it was taken over by the Government, through
the Rural Music Schools with my friend Mary Ibberson whom I already
knew and admired so much.

 I suggested … that this would be a golden opportunity to train young
music students to be future Rural Music School teachers, but we didn't
want to limit it to that. I had learnt from my father before I learned it
from anyone else, that you don't want to have either just Rural Music
School teachers or just brilliant young singers or violinists. In such a
community as Dartington there was a wonderful chance to mix them all
up together and let them learn from each other.

Martin not only took up IH's suggestion, but invited her, with the Elmhirsts'
approval, to stay at Dartington and run the music course within the Arts
Department. The programme that they devised together was advertised thus:

 Four scholarships for training in leadership in rural music under Imogen
 Holst are offered at the Arts Department, Dartington Hall, to candidates
 aged 16–18 who show inclination and ability for leadership in amateur
 music-making … work will include regular lessons … in accompanying,
 sight-reading, transposing, elementary conducting, harmony at the keyboard, simple orchestration, and the arranging and transcribing of easy
 music for groups of amateur singers or players.

The proposal was for a one-year course for young women with a vocation
to lead the singing and the local orchestras in village communities, but the

realities of recruitment in wartime Britain resulted in a more mixed outcome, as IH recalled:

> Of course, it was war time and to get students they had to be sixteen years old and no older, because of conscription. So we started in September 1943 ... with four sixteen year olds, one boy and three girls. Two of the girls had come from the local school in Totnes. Oh! we had a part time older student who did some teaching of music in Foxhole, so then we were five. We were very ambitious – we did Benjamin Britten's *Ceremony of Carols* before it was published. Right from the beginning we had open evenings of music every night of the week during our term for anyone who was living at Dartington or round about who would like to come ...
>
> We had land girls, very keen they were, and they used to come in apologising for not having had time to remove the mud off their clothes. We had evacuee school teachers, because Leonard and Dorothy gave up nearly the whole of their house, as you know, to young school children. The children couldn't come because they had to go to bed by that time, but their teachers came, and of course were thrilled because they had come from London and were used to having things happening in the evenings. Later on, when America came into the war, we had wounded American airmen who were convalescing here. That was another of Dorothy's wonderful ideas, and I will never forget when they came to our composition class.
>
> We had an orchestra open to anyone ... At one time we were sixty strong but hardly any of us could play. I remember – I don't think she would mind if I mention her name, as she is such an old friend – Marjorie Fogden, who played second violin. I used to have her, as she hadn't done much music, just under me, as it were, when I was conducting. She played with another second violin who, again, was rather elementary. Every now and then one or the other of them would get out in their bowing arm, so I would see Marjorie doing an up bow and her partner doing a down bow. I would be horrified that they were going to hit each other ... However bad we were, we went on. I had to write out the parts myself. Then, as we got more students it became part of their training as future Rural Music School teachers to learn how to arrange and write the parts out. That was where Winsome was so marvellous ... I quite immorally stole her away from her work there and said I must have her in the Arts Department ...

Winsome Bartlett, who was to become one of IH's closest friends, was work-ing as the Welfare Officer at Dartington when IH arrived. Using methods pio-neered by Rudolf Laban, she ran movement classes for sawmill workers during the war, designed to ease the muscular tensions caused by repetitive manual labour. But IH soon seized upon her altogether different talents for music handwriting, and soon discovered another of Bartlett's talents – her immense skill in playing the pipe and tabor for folk dances. She found another close ally and friend in Florence Burton, who acted as her secretary but was also a teacher of ballet to scores of small girls in the district.

For all the enthusiasm and momentum with which IH drove the develop-ment of music teaching at Dartington, one of the most beneficial effects of her early years there was the opportunity that the atmosphere of peace and solitude gave her to embark once again on her stalled career as a serious com-poser. Comfortably distant from London, she found her confidence returning, and she began to revitalize and develop her style, building upon her forma-tive achievements as a student in the 1920s and the wealth of experience as teacher, conductor and arranger that she had accumulated through the subse-quent decade. The austerity of wartime England created an ideal backdrop for her increasingly tight-knit, linear and frugal style, and her music became once again an attraction for performers. In July 1942, led by Marjorie Wise, some of the many friends IH had made in the field of amateur music wrote to her to say: 'We all feel that it is high time that you had a LONDON CONCERT, both as a COMPOSER and as a CONDUCTOR, but it must be professional not amateur. We are prepared to do the work of getting the necessary funds and audience.'[2] More than 300 people subscribed, and the concert given at the Wigmore Hall on 14 June 1943, consisting exclusively of her music, included first perform-ances of three substantial works composed in a remarkable burst of creative activity during the first half of that year: the *Serenade, Suite for String Orches-tra* and *Three Psalms*.

The event was widely and positively reviewed by both the London press and national music magazines, and did much to restore IH's faith in herself as a composer. Over the next few years she not only wrote some of her most important works but was able to hear many of them performed. Inspired by the musicians who came to work at Dartington, her compositional choices were to a great extent defined by her wish to write for them. In the autumn of 1943 she composed the solo violin *Theme and Variations* for Joyce de Groote, and the next year an oboe concerto for a pupil, David Tucker, who

---

[2] Private scrapbooks.

gave the first performance in Wembley in February 1945. The First String Trio was written for the Dartington Hall String Trio, and premièred by them at a National Gallery concert on 17 July 1944, while the *Four Songs*, with words from the sixteenth-century anthology *Tottel's Miscellany*, were composed for the voice of Mary Williams, who had been one of her first students at Dartington.

This period of creative endeavour, the richest of her compositional career, saw IH balance her obligations to her students with a more private develop-ment of her technique. For the latter, she subjected herself to the rigours of chamber music, writing two string quartets (the second unfinished); but she also continued to produce 'useful' music on many levels, ranging from simple violin canons and the *Offley Suite* for elementary string class, through numer-ous folksong arrangements, to a series of extended stage works written for the larger forces available to her. These include the puppet opera *Young Beichan*, performed in an 'open rehearsal' in the summer of 1946, incidental music for the *Prometheus* of Aeschylus, written for an American University Sum-mer School in August 1950, and the one-act Shakespeare opera *Benedick and Beatrice*. Finally, she wrote pieces for friends, among which was a notable curi-osity, a part-song for Winsome Bartlett's birthday in August 1947. The dedica-tee, then an adult beginner, was having trouble understanding the rudiments of music, and so IH wrote for her a song (to words by Robert Southwell) 'with NO time signature/ NO bar-lines/ NO key-signature/ NO sharps/ NO flats/ NO naturals.'

As the peace and isolation of Dartington, together with the stimulus of new creative partnerships, helped to free IH's compositional spirit, so after the tur-bulence of the 1930s, her newly settled lifestyle had a consolidating effect on her personal life. When she arrived in Devon she was thirty-five and single. She was distinctive in appearance and demeanour, and had proved herself adapta-ble and adventurous, being exceptionally well travelled. She disliked small-talk, and was reclusive in the public arena, in spite of her gift for lecturing and for encouraging amateurs in their musical pursuits. To those who knew her, she was a delightful friend to all, while never allowing anyone to get really close to her. When interviewed she would speak freely about her professional and public work, but never about the private side of her composing and writing, or indeed her personal life. Since her student days, there had been little in the way of romance in her life. Indeed, marriage may never have suited her unusu-ally independent nature. She confided in a pre-war diary that she had already decided on a celibate life, but she was undoubtedly lonely at times, and cer-tainly remained capable of deep affection. These characteristics of the mature

IH were to change little during the remaining years of her life. Above all, at Dartington she had found a job that suited her perfectly and where, at least from a professional point of view, she could be deeply fulfilled and genuinely happy. As she later recalled ruefully, at a time when she was heavily involved in administration and fund-raising:

> Life then did not consist of one committee meeting after another as it had done in C.E.M.A. jobs, and also this problem of discussing where the money was to come from. That was all right, and my only worries were musical ones. When it is one's job and one is allowed to choose the music one wants to do, those worries are not worries – they are part of living. The exhaustion at the end of the day is not desperate exhaustion but is really the exhilaration at the end of a lovely day of lovely music.

One of her signal achievements at Dartington was founding an orchestra of which she became justifiably proud, despite its inauspicious beginnings:

> We had at one time something like seventeen descant recorders, all out of tune, very shrill; hardly any of the players could read notes, but of course the orchestra helped them to do so. You must have the picture of a row of percussion, some of them quite small children, some of them Estate workers who simply couldn't read a note of music but were given a tambourine, and every time I smiled at them they played the tambourine. Then we had Leonard Elmhirst playing the cello ...
>
> We had one of our original students, the boy, playing trumpet. He had always wanted to play the trumpet, so he played the trumpet and that was rather loud. We had a sprinkling of strings, and later on we got some good strings because they were connected with the Rural Music School ... Later on, after a few years, we had Muriel Anthony who ... was Director of the Kent Rural Music School before she retired. She played violin and viola here. We had April Cantelo as one of our singers and she played the viola very well in the Orchestra. I can remember when we were still in this studio and rather elementary, the extraordinary sounds going on behind her head and, without stopping, she turned round to see what it was, while still going on playing.
>
> Now I want to link up this orchestra, which then got so big, with the fact that Winsome, among all the other things she was doing, taught us instrument repairs. When anything went wrong, all the string players went up to Winsome's workshop. She not only did the repairs, but held classes in how to do instrumental repairs. Also, we had Mr Harris of

Harris Osborne come in and teach the elements of piano tuning and repair.

IH's emphasis on such practical skills was entirely characteristic of her methods and demonstrated her great understanding of rural musical life, an environment in which the ability to repair and maintain a village hall or school piano was as valuable as it was rare.

Other skills taught by IH were also drawn very much from her own experiences. Students sat no compulsory examinations, but instead learnt by 'doing', in disciplines that included unaccompanied singing, arranging and conducting. Unsurprisingly it was not long before IH's methods fell under the scrutiny of the Board of Education:

> Of course, we sang. We sight-sang unaccompanied every morning – Palestrina, di Lasso, Vittoria – from 9am to 9.30am but nobody dreamed of calling that compulsory, because it was such a joy.
>
> Now, this business of arranging everything took a lot of time but it all leads up to teaching students how to arrange music. One of the things we had in this studio was a rural orchestra amongst the students but with no outsiders. Each week one student would be in charge as a conductor, having arranged and written out the music. We would sit around with an instrument in our hands that we didn't know how to play – the noise was horrendous. I remember how our distinguished cello teacher, Sylvia Bor, had decided she would like to play the cornet and the sounds she made! Well, it would happen, but the Tuesday composition class which was going to render something with a cornet part for Sylvia was on the day we had our first inspector, our first HMI ...
>
> ... one of the inspectors who came to listen to a composition class sat next to me on the sofa while it was going on and said 'What textbook of improvisation do you use here?' Can you imagine? A different inspector – a rather higher up one – came on the day that Sylvia Bor was going to play her cornet, and of course everyone got hysterics – just everybody. But it didn't matter because we got accepted, which astonished a lot of our students.
>
> You see, some of them couldn't believe that the way I taught them was going to get them through exams. They didn't mean to be rude, but the look of absolute astonishment on their faces when they came back at the beginning of a new term and said, 'But Imo, I've passed my exams, I've got ARCM'. Absolute astonishment, but it did help them, and it helped in an extraordinary way. For instance, this business of the

rural orchestra when you play an instrument that you don't know. You learn how long it takes to get your instrument ready when you've had it down, and the conductor has been saying, 'when you get there, you must do that better and that better – now let's go from letter C'. You have to find letter C and then you have to pick up the instrument and pick up your bow and find the first note and look at the beat. It takes an awfully long time. Well, unless you have experienced that, you go out into schools with a lot of elementary school children around you and you say, 'letter C' and wonder why they are not ready. Those things really did help enormously.

Now we also had one of our evenings open to the Estate – Friday evening was singing evening. There had always been a tradition of singing on the Estate and I was asked to carry that on. We did Bach Cantatas and we did Handel's *L'Allegro*, a shortened version, in the Great Hall. That was lovely. We had quite a large choir and I remember particularly one of our best basses was Mr Tucker, the police constable from Totnes … I don't think I ever heard such beautiful amateur singing, with perfect Bach phrases. I can just hear it in my mind.

In addition to Bach and Handel, IH led her students in performances of a wide range of music. This included pieces by her father, and no less a score than Verdi's *Requiem*, boldly undertaken with only a piano for accompaniment and with Rosamund Strode singing the soprano solos, as IH recalled, 'most beautifully'.

But of all her performances it was Bach's B minor Mass that was most fondly remembered by those who took part in its preparation and performance, and which, indeed, is still regarded as the pinnacle of her achievements as a conductor at Dartington. Preparations began in the summer of 1947, and various sections were performed informally in the succeeding months, but it was not until July 1950 that the work was heard in its entirety, marking the 200th anniversary of Bach's death. That such a performance was possible is testimony to IH's particular brand of leadership, characterized by a striving for high standards and a determination to overcome the potential inadequacies of performers. She could be lavish with her praise to those with little skill who made up for their deficiencies through commitment and effort, but she could also be 'severely critical … with more advanced students and devastatingly dismissive to anyone who was either complacent or pretentious'.[3] As she was later to recall, the performance owed much to the unique teaching environment at Dartington, which allowed for detailed preparation over an extended period:

[3] Cox, *The Arts at Dartington*, pp. 36–7.

We took three years to rehearse the B Minor Mass, and people were astonished at that and thought it would get stale but we had the chance that could only have happened in Dartington. For instance, we had our violin technique class, bowing and fingering the difficult bits in the B Minor. We also had the young solo singers among the students having singing lessons on their solos. We had, of course, the choir divided up into the main chorus and then the semi-chorus of our own students doing the difficult bits in between. We had harmony at the keyboard working out all the figured bass. We also had what I hate teaching as a subject and never have, the subject of musical analysis. My father never taught musical analysis, so I never did it as a subject, but we went right through the B Minor Mass living every note and finding the most extraordinary links with keys. For instance, whenever Bach went into E flat it would be the Incarnation, and the message coming down from Heaven and that would link up with some quite different chorus or solo when the E flat phrase came in again …

IH's constant encouragement of young musicianship at Dartington, together with her championing of musicians who had escaped from Germany and Austria during the war, came together in one particularly lasting achievement, the founding of the Amadeus String Quartet. Soon after the end of the war, IH had attended a concert given by Hans Oppenheim, the Director of Dartington Hall Music Group, in Cambridge

and he had Norbert Brainin playing in a small orchestra for the Bach Cantata they were doing in a church concert. Norbert was staying in the Blue Boar Hotel in Trinity Street and I had to go in with a message. As I walked along the corridor of the hotel I heard the most beautiful violin practice I have ever heard in my life. It was just two notes, to and fro, very slowly, very beautifully played, and I just stood there with my ear to the keyhole. Well, later on I heard the Church performance and was introduced to Norbert, and I thought this is a real violinist.

Now, soon after that, when we got our students and Sylvia Bor, she said, 'I think you should ask Norbert to stay a few days here at Dartington.' He was having a very hard time when he was out of work and was having difficulty really in finding the next meal. She said, 'He is very fond of food, ask him here.' So we asked him and straight away he began playing with our sixteen year old students. They weren't all sixteen year olds, but some of them were very young. Norbert just stood there on that spot of the Music Studio leading them and helping them, and I sat on the floor, as it might be there, watching him and seeing how he helped them with everything. And his relaxation before coming in and that extraordinary power of continuity of the rhythm going through – I learned so much which has helped me ever afterwards when I have tried to conduct. And also I was so moved to find it happening with these young elementary students because it is so rare to get a very great player with such gifts. We talked for a bit and I asked him what he was going to do now that the war was over. Was he going back to Vienna? He said, 'No, I think the centre of music in the future will be in England'.

I think it was on the visit after that (because he came back several times) he said, 'Imo, I would like to start a string quartet'. He had already got his great friend, Peter Schidlof, who, as I expect you know, had so generously given up the chance of a career as a solo violinist in order to play viola in the quartet. He had got his great friend, Siegmund Nissel, and he had just found this new young cellist, Martin Lovett, who hadn't been a refugee but who had the same kind of playing. I said, 'Yes, Norbert, that is a marvellous idea, come and give a concert here in Dartington'. And he said, 'Yes, we will begin rehearsing'. And we talked about programmes and we then got this series of concerts in memory of Christopher Martin. We had a summer festival of concerts in the Great Hall and Peter Cox [the new Administrator, who had come in after the unexpected death of Christopher Martin] and Dorothy welcomed the idea. Now, where else would you get people saying, 'Yes, let them give a concert in six or eight weeks time', when the quartet hadn't even begun to be put together? But that was the sort of thing that happened, they took my word for it that this would be something terrific. So they came and gave their first concert in the Great Hall. And after that they would come on visits and play with us informally. It's been a wonderful link.

Despite the personal fulfilment and the great sense of artistic achievement that IH experienced at Dartington, the demands of bureaucracy and considerations of finance inevitably began to impinge more and more closely on her life as the years went by. The Music Department had grown significantly under her leadership, and she began to perceive the need for its methods and syllabus to match up to national standards, especially if it was to attract the local authority and government funding it would need to expand further. In 1947 she wrote a revealing letter to her employers which displays if not insecurity, then certainly an acknowledgement that her own unique approach to teaching should be subject to external oversight and objective scrutiny:

The need that I'm most aware of is the need for criticism. I would ask you not to let me go on for another year without getting some detailed criticism from first-rate working musicians. My methods are unorthodox. I never use textbooks, and never divide musical history up into periods, and I teach harmony and counterpoint as living sounds rather than written notes ... Then there is the choice of music. Having a free hand I naturally teach them the music I love best, i.e. a lot of sixteenth and seventeenth century stuff, a fair amount of Bach, a bit of medieval church music, folk songs and dances and as much Britten as can be done by amateurs. This is all very well but there is inevitably a danger that the influence may get too one-sided, Apart from individual piano pupils they get very little nineteenth century stuff.[4]

This appeal also masked a deeper and more personal concern that her own musicianship was no longer being tested, and that her potential to learn and improve was being stifled in what was too comfortable an atmosphere. The yearnings that she had experienced in 1938 to break away from her associations with amateurs, but which she had suppressed in order to support the war effort as a Music Traveller, now returned even more strongly. As early as 1945 she had confided in Leonard Elmhirst her wish to 'break free from teaching before I am too old and ... from the particular sort of amateur music-making that has been my main thing in life ever since I can remember. There is so much other music still to explore ...' Although she retained her belief that amateurs provided the backbone of musical life in England, she had also become convinced that her father's achievement had been compromised, and his life possibly shortened, by the exhaustion brought on by his dedication both to teaching and amateur music making; moreover she had begun to feel isolated without the surrounding presence of musicians of her own calibre, as she later explained:

> ... when one is always teaching amateurs and future professionals who are still immature, one needs constantly to be criticized on one's own music by someone who one knows is a better musician than oneself. Now, in South Devon, we had so many blessings but we hadn't many musicians better than me at that time. We had visitors, wonderful visitors who would come into our lives – Benjamin Britten and Peter Pears giving recitals, the Amadeus and other great musicians who would come here. They would come for a day or two and then they would go away again. And I thought, I must not get into the habit of this. I remember walking

---

[4] Document at the Elmhirst Centre, Dartington.

round this exquisite garden in early Spring and thinking 'now, you could live here for the rest of your life'. It seemed a kind of heaven on earth, and then thinking 'no, because you are a musician, and you have to go on learning and you have got to go on having really strict criticism'.

Undoubtedly, the 'better musician' she had most in mind was Benjamin Britten, whom she had come to recognize as the only composer of the twentieth century whose achievements matched those of the Renaissance and Baroque masters whose music she most admired.

IH had first come into contact with Britten and Peter Pears through their shared involvement with CEMA during the war, when the composer and his partner, as conscientious objectors, travelled the country giving concerts. Their commitments took them to Dartington in October 1943, where they gave a recital that included Michael Tippett's *Boyhood's End* and Britten's own *Seven Sonnets of Michelangelo*. Following the concert, on 12 October, IH wrote to Britten:

> Your music seems to me the only reliable thing that is happening today in a world where everything else goes wrong all the time. It is a real security and one can hang on to it as one hangs on to Bach and Mozart and Schubert. It oughtn't to make any difference that you are English, but I can't help being glad about that too, because I was brought up to believe that there would one day be a renaissance of English music: – my father thought it would happen after the reprinting of the Tudor composers and the revival of folk-song and then year after year he got more and more disillusioned as one 'young' English composer after another turned out nothing but mild and pleasant little tone-poems. And now it's all right.

Almost from the first time she heard his music, IH decided that Britten was the man who could bring to fruition the work begun by her father. As for Britten, at this stage of his career, he retained a mistrust of anyone whom he felt was part of the Royal College of Music establishment or the Vaughan Williams circle, and he was thus somewhat taken aback to find his music so well received by 'a musician of your standing, & from a section of musical life which I have hitherto imagined so unsympathetic to me'.[5] Over the next few years IH organized regular visits and recitals from Britten and Pears, and began to take on 'various odd jobs' for the composer.[6] A profound mutual respect was soon established,

5 Letter of 21 October 1943; BPL.
6 IH, 'Working for Benjamin Britten', p. 202.

founded partly on a shared love of neglected English Renaissance and Baroque repertoire, but more keenly on IH's well-informed and finely articulated understanding of Britten's new music. After attending one of the earliest performances of *Peter Grimes*, she wrote to him:

> There are no words to say thankyou ... We knew it was going to be a wonderful experience, but we were not prepared for anything as wonderful as that. It is the wholeness of the thing that is so overwhelming. This perfect balance between the moments of intensity and the moments of lyrical beauty is such a very rare thing: – Shakespeare could do it, but very few other people have got anywhere near it.
>
> You have given it to us at the very moment when it was most needed ... as the full flowering of the renaissance in music ...[7]

The following year she wrote in similar terms about *The Rape of Lucretia*, prompting Britten to respond in glowing terms, thanking IH for her 'appreciation and understanding of my work [which] ... gives me great pleasure, & great encouragement' especially 'from someone whose personality & mind I admire as much as yours.'[8] Such was IH's enthusiasm for Britten's work that for a brief time in 1945 it even appeared that the new opera company planned by Britten and others, to become the English Opera Group, might open at Dartington in 1946, before John Christie at Glyndebourne put forward an offer that seemed to guarantee the venture much greater financial security and the possibility of a permanent venue.

Despite her increasing restlessness, IH agreed with Leonard Elmhirst and Peter Cox that she would stay at Dartington until the music course was more firmly established. She did so, however, on the condition that she could undertake other projects, including some work with Britten and, even closer to her heart, completing work on a study of her father's music, to complement her earlier biography.

During the months that followed IH came into contact with a new student whose life and career was soon to become closely intertwined with her own. Rosamund Strode was then at the RCM, studying viola and singing, and uncertain what she should do after graduating. Many years later, she recalled her first meetings with IH and the development of their relationship in an essay that sheds much light on IH's character and her working methods during these later Dartington years:

[7] 12 June 1945; BPL.
[8] 22 August 1946; BPL.

In my first few encounters with Imogen, strung out over several months in 1948, she demonstrated many of those characteristic approaches to people, music, and life in general which were, as I later realised, absolutely fundamental to her. Why should such first impressions still be so easy to recall, even after almost forty years? Partly, no doubt, simply because they <u>were</u> so Imo-like, but mainly because of the challenge and impact that this unique person made upon one's own rather woolly approach to a career in music.

Halfway through my last year at the RCM, where I'd been studying singing and viola (neither with much distinction), I had realised that some decision needed to be made, and had had a useful talk with the composer Christopher le Fleming, still the director of music at my old school, whose wisdom and advice seldom failed. 'Why not go in for County Music Organising – I think you could do that – and you must get on the only course where you can learn about that, it's at Dartington Hall, and Imogen Holst runs it. She knows everything you need to know about that job.' Well! What an idea! I'd already heard a little about the music at Dartington (culled from Joanna Harris, a family friend who enthused almost too much about Dartington, and about Imogen herself) and immediately responded by saying 'What, <u>that</u> place??' But Christopher countered with 'No, I really mean it – it would be just right for you.'

So the interview was arranged, and after a College orchestral concert I travelled in a sleeper (but sleepless, kept in a mental turmoil of general apprehension and the Brahms D minor piano concerto in equal proportions) on the overnight train to Totnes. Arriving in the early morning of 6 February I was met by Shirley Eyre, familiar from school, who drove me up to the Hall in time for breakfast. The 'interview' turned out to be a full day's participation in the normal Arts Department routine, with a talk to Imogen after lunch. There seemed to be no doubt about my acceptance at Dartington; she assumed that I should come in September, and most of the time was spent in talking about how to apply for a financial grant from my home county, and what could be done, while I was still in London, to fill in some of the gaps in my own training. She gave me, on the spot, a handwritten note of introduction to Gertrude Collins, then (in those pre-Suzuki days!) working miracles in violin class teaching, and before leaving for home the following morning I had already been booked to return six weeks later, all expenses paid, as a chorus soprano in the memorable performance of the Bach St John Passion which Imogen conducted on 20 March. Dartington had already taken charge of my career.

During the summer term there was another glimpse of Imogen, who conducted a day's music making in London at Cecil Sharp House for the Rural Music Schools Association. I don't remember what the programme was, but between the rehearsal and the final run-through (not a formal concert) Imogen disappeared into the little garden – 'Don't talk to me, I'm busy' – in order to conjure up a horn part for an unexpected player; first things first, as always.

The new Dartington year began on Thursday 23 September, and Friday was a day of introduction – and of the first shocks. There were, I think, about twenty-three music students that year, and from being a decidedly non-starry student at the RCM I suddenly found myself among the most experienced in the Dartington group, many of whom, though certainly talented, had never had the chance of any formal musical training at all. Imogen gave us two simple test papers that first day, to help in sorting everyone out; one was on the rudiments of music, and the other in harmony – a subject in which I'd made disgracefully little progress at the RCM and which continued to baffle me. The second shock came on Monday, when we learned the results of the test papers. I came third (or was it second?) in the harmony test, and top in rudiments ... how could this have happened? And what on earth *was* this place, from which I'd been expecting so much, if such results could be achieved by someone of only average attainment? There was time to chew that one over before the following day's private session with Imogen, at which she was to provide the biggest shocks of all. (Later, the rudiments success was explained, assuming, that is, that the rest of my replies had been generally accurate. In trying to define the difference between 3/4 and 6/8, that favourite tricky question, I'd unwittingly added the one phrase guaranteed to gain Imogen's fullest approval: 'You can dance to 6/8 time'. It wasn't long before we all discovered the importance to her of the dance, and just how her own music making was founded upon this one thing.)

Those last, numbing, shocks, were to do with my own timetable and the various jobs on it, designed to turn me into a useful practical musician. We both sat in Imo's room on the first floor of the Barton wing, overlooking the courtyard, while she went remorselessly through the list in her hand, day by day, allowing no protestations or cries of alarm, until she had got to the end. It went something like this: 'On Monday at 10 you will take a very elementary harmony class in the Blue Room

[Harmony – help!] and start a children's violin class at the Adult Education Centre after tea. (When not doing anything for which you are particularly responsible you can, by the way, attend any of the other classes
that you can fit in.) On Tuesday afternoons there will be a W.I. choir at
Berry Pomeroy; you can use the Arts Department car [this was then a
solid, pre-war Morris Minor belonging to Mrs Holst and on loan for
the time being] and the office will tell you about petrol coupons. [Petrol
was still rationed in 1948.] Wednesday is orchestra night; I want you to
supervise, now, the addition of extra rehearsal numbers to all the instrumental parts of the Haydn symphony we'll be playing – use all the students, it'll be good for them [Hooray! Something I *can* do] – and then
I shall want you to make new parts for one horn, one trumpet and two
recorders, which we have in the orchestra, out of those woodwind and
brass which Haydn used but which we haven't got, and please cue into
Pam's cello part the timpani notes not covered elsewhere. [Help!!] From
half term there'll be an extra orchestra practice every week; the School
is doing Bach's Christmas Oratorio [Part I only, was it? Probably.] and
we are providing the orchestra – you will be conducting the preliminary
rehearsals for this before Emil Spira takes it over at the end. [HELP!!! I
can't ... can I?] On Thursdays you'll be going to a village west of Crediton:
Bow, forty miles from here, to carry on with the work Gerald McDonald
began last year. You'll have a W.I. choir in the afternoon, a mixed orchestral class [it was indeed <u>very</u> mixed!] after tea, and a choral society in
the evening. Someone there will put you up for the night, and you'll
come back the next morning; use the car for that, of course. Fridays are
Singers' night, and we shall be starting to learn Benjamin Britten's latest
choral work, *St Nicolas,* which he will conduct here next spring. And
as you may know, I am writing a book about my father's music which
has to be finished over the next few months, so I shall have to rely more
than usual on those of you who have already had a good musical training.' (Imogen several times said to me, much later, that she'd regretted
having to give this particular generation of Dartington students less of
her time than others, on account of the book.) 'But anyway, this will
give you the best possible practical experience, and that's really why you
came. The Music Library has plenty of material for your choirs, and you
will probably have to make special parts and arrangements for the Bow
orchestra. I'm here to answer any questions and give any advice you
need, but please give me a little warning – after lunch is usually a good
time.'

That, roughly, was my introduction to Imogen as a teacher; from the immediate open acceptance and helpful advice of the first meeting in February, past the exhilaration of her dedicated and extraordinary St John Passion and the relaxed enjoyment of the day of music at Cecil Sharp House in June right up to the shattering, coldly realistic assessments of those first days as a student in September, as she confronted me with tasks for which I felt quite unqualified. But of course she was right. She knew exactly how, and when, to push her victims in at the deep end, and she knew, also, that although they would flounder and splash about at first, it wouldn't be long before her confidence in them took over, and they would be swimming easily while she beamed approval from the bank. And Imogen would have been thrilled and delighted ... to have seen for herself how well the lessons she taught in those nine Dartington years had been assimilated, and how they are still being handed on by her students.[9]

While remaining committed to Dartington, IH increasingly moved beyond its confines after 1947, expanding her range of interests and musical contacts. By this time she was much sought after as a lecturer at one-day courses of the EFDSS and at various new Summer Schools which were then in their infancy. Of these the most important was at Bryanston, where in 1948 she was on the staff, together with such luminaries as Nadia Boulanger, Paul Hindemith, Alan Bush, William Glock and Jack Westrup. Spending time in this company would no doubt have stimulated her, but it must also increased her sense of isolation from other professional musicians and thus her restlessness. Most significantly of all, IH was able to attend, briefly, the inaugural Aldeburgh Festival in 1948, and return the following year. She was immediately intoxicated by the atmosphere and surroundings, as she was later to recall in an essay, 'Recollections of Times Past', for the Aldeburgh Festival programme book in 1976:

> My Aldeburgh 'Times Past' go back to a visit on the first afternoon of the first festival for the unforgettable first performance of *St Nicolas*. I had to go straight back to work that evening, but during the next two festivals my employers let me off for a whole week. There was a dream-like quality about those weeks; the house in Crabbe Street had been decorated with yellow tree-lupins, and it seemed entirely appropriate that the festival choir, rehearsing a Purcell anthem in the church, should have reached the verse about 'the time of the singing of birds is come'

[9] Rosamund Strode, 'Meeting Imogen'. Unpublished typescript, March 1986. HF.

when two birds flew into the porch and began chirruping in time with
the music ... In those dreamlike days there was time, between concerts,
to sit on the beach, and time to look at the exhibition of Henry Moore
drawings in the Church Hall.

That was the last festival in which I ever had time for anything ...

Beyond the Aldeburgh Festival, IH's conviction of Britten's genius was reinforced by her attendance at the first performance of his *Spring Symphony* in
Amsterdam in July 1949, following which she wrote to him:

I felt that by far the most exciting thing about it was its form. H O W
R I G H T I T I S! ... And what a relief it is, to be given the right thing, after
all those years of listening to people trying to build up a symphony as if
it were Brahms with wrong notes ...

The biggest miracle of all is the way you have brought complete happiness into music again ...[10]

In 1950 the Elmhirsts celebrated their twenty-fifth wedding anniversary.
Their daughter Ruth had commissioned some part-songs from Britten to mark
the occasion, and these arrived just in time for IH to copy out and distribute
parts on Leonard Elmhirst's birthday, 23 July. IH later recalled how she and the
singers went quietly

on to the bit of lawn behind the private house and sang them for the first
time. We couldn't manage all of them but we sang three of those *Flower
Songs* with Leonard at his study window there and the windows open.
And to be able to do that sort of thing – great music, commissioned for
great people such as Leonard and Dorothy – and to have their own students singing it on their own lawn. That was a lovely feeling.

This episode demonstrates that IH's affection for the Elmhirsts was profound, and her loyalty to the cause at Dartington unwavering. Nevertheless, by
the middle of 1950, and with the Aldeburgh experience enhanced by repeated
acquaintance, she decided that for the sake of her own development and fulfilment she needed to get away from Devon for good, and so gave a year's notice.
At about the same time, she accepted a commission from Britten to write a
piece for female voices for the following year's Aldeburgh Festival. Selecting
texts from the poems of John Keats, she devised a song cycle for SSA and harp,
which she entitled *Welcome Joy and Welcome Sorrow*. She sent the completed
score to Britten, who wrote to her on 31 October to acknowledge the arrival

[10] 18 July 1949; BPL.

of the 'six little treasures. Peter happened to be here for a day or so when they arrived, & we played them over with the greatest pleasure. I think they sound quite beautiful ...' To her unbounded joy, he went on to invite her to come to Aldeburgh the following June and conduct the first performance. She had also undertaken to prepare with Britten a new performing edition of Purcell's *Dido and Aeneas* for the English Opera Group, and she worked on this through the autumn, completing her contribution at the end of November. Writing to Leonard Elmhirst nine years later she recalled the magic of this time:

> I've been thinking of you all so often: we've been doing Dido and Aeneas
> for the B.B.C. Transcription service ... and I kept on remembering that
> that was the first full score I'd ever copied out for Ben – in the evenings
> at Dartington in the studio above the School with the wonderful view
> of your garden.[11]

To her great delight, Britten himself prepared a version for an expanded orchestra of GH's *The Wandering Scholar* for the EOG in 1951.

With her notice submitted to Dartington, and no firm plans of what she might do afterwards, IH had once again reached a crossroads in her life. Just as she had punctuated the passing of her college days by taking time out to wander across Europe, and marked the end of her teaching at Eothen by visiting Switzerland, so she again felt the need for travel to give her a fresh perspective. This time, however, she sought a wider horizon, and asked Leonard Elmhirst if she might spend a term at the end of the year on a visit to Santiniketan, the international university in Western Bengal founded by the poet Rabindranath Tagore.

[11] 6 October 1959; HF.

8 'She is quite brilliant':
India to Aldeburgh, 1950–52

IH's decision to go to India for two months in the winter of 1950 to 1951 sprang directly from the restlessness she had first confided to Leonard Elmhirst five years earlier. But in addition to her simple wish to explore new territories, both geographical and musical, she had begun to develop a scholarly interest in the links between Indian music, for which her enthusiasm could be traced back to her father's influence, and the early Western music repertories that she was so actively engaged in reviving. She also had an ethnomusicological purpose which was, as she explained to her prospective hosts:

> to try and get hold of records of traditional songs such as the boatsmen's tunes Tagore used to listen to. It matters enormously that these folk songs should be preserved in their traditional style of performance, because every new radio set that is manufactured threatens to destroy the tradition. This also has a particular interest for me personally, as I have been working at folk music for the last twenty-five years.[1]

Tagore's University had had Ghandi as its President, and one of the first things the Mahatma recommended for the institution was that everything possible should be done to bridge the cultures of the East and West. Prior to his marriage, Leonard Elmhirst had helped with the setting up of the university in the 1920s, and Tagore's work had in turn helped to inspire the foundation of Dartington Hall. Elmhirst was thus in sympathy both with IH's request and her motives. He granted her leave and she was thus able to join a line of European musicians and teachers invited to come and share their knowledge of western traditions with the students in India. She left England in early December and returned two months later, when she contributed an extended, and typically vivid, account of her time in India to the Dartington *News of the Day*:

> It was a wonderful experience to have the two months of December and January in Northern India. I was staying most of the time in West

---

[1] IH's letter to Santiniketan was reproduced in the Dartington *News of the Day*, 6 December 1950.

Bengal at Santiniketan University, founded by the poet Tagore, where
Mr. Elmhirst worked more than twenty-five years ago. One of the greatest joys was the sunshine; I never quite got used to having to move into
the shade by eight o'clock in the morning! And the colours were another
joy; the flame-coloured flowering shrubs and trees (Borgainvillea, Poin-
settia, and Bignonia) and the enormous rainbow-coloured butterflies.
But the best joy of all was making so many new friends. Faces used to
light up whenever I mentioned that it was Mr. Elmhirst who had sent
me to India. And the members of the music staff were lovely people to
work with. I was allowed to go every day to the elementary music classes,
which began at 6.15 a.m. (!) Later on I was given individual coaching by
several of the music teachers; they became so interested in European
music that they asked me to help them to get to know more about it.
After a fortnight of these exchange lessons the head of the music in the
Teachers Training Department said to me: 'Now I realise that there is
only *one* music'. I found that the Indian style of singing took a bit of
getting used to – their habit of what we should call 'scooping' sounds
distressing to Western ears until one has learnt to accept it as inevitable.
While I was staying at Benares, where I was a guest of the University, I
had the good fortune to sit at the feet of a very great singing teacher,
Pandit Onkaamda Thakur. He looked exactly like J. S. Bach: he wore
his hair in long silver-white ringlets which bobbed up and down on his
shoulders, he taught with lively gestures and a passionate attention to
detail, and he had a sense of humour that could be enjoyed even when
one didn't know a word of Hindi. Owing to his magnificent singing I was
able to understand far more about Indian music than I had dared hope
would be possible in such a short time. Many of the things I learnt from
him belong equally well to our sort of music, and the students at Dartington are already beginning to apply several details of his teaching to
their own studies. My few days in Benares were among the most exciting I have ever known: there were such beautiful palaces overlooking
the Ganges, and such beautiful boats on the river, and so many beautiful
people walking about who looked as if they had come straight out of
the Old Testament. And it was exciting having to squeeze oneself out of
the way of the camels in some of the narrowest streets of the city. Other
cities that I saw were more depressing than exciting: I was appalled by
the overcrowding and poverty in Calcutta, where there were two million refugees from East Bengal. Whole families were sleeping on the
pavements in the busiest parts of the city, less than a yard away from

the traffic, and were having to wash themselves in the gutters, letting their one set of clothes dry on them. The memory of the poverty is more vivid than the memory of the sunshine and the colours. But with it is a memory of the extreme grace of all the people I saw, from the aboriginal villagers dancing in the moonlight to the distinguished scientists discussing technical problems in their lecture hall. And, inseparable from that grace, is the memory of a friendliness that has to be experienced to be believed.

On IH's arrival in West Bengal, her hosts were initially dismayed that she could stay for two only months, as they thought that she would be unable to assimilate enough of Indian music culture in that time. But with characteristic energy and boundless enthusiasm, she threw herself into both learning and teaching. On being invited, first of all, to introduce the students to some Christmas music, she demonstrated the tendency of her own thought at this time by choosing to teach them the plainsong 'Alleluia' used by Britten in *A Ceremony of Carols*. On 16 December she wrote to Britten to tell him this news hinting at where, were she not in India, she would most rather be:

> I wish I could send you some of the sunshine as a Christmas present! But on second thoughts, the Aldeburgh sea is even better than the warmth and the jasmine and the banana trees and the fireflies!

At first IH noticed a great deal of common ground – especially in the use of pentatonicism – between the folksongs that she knew, and those sung to her by Prabhakar Chinchore, the head of the teacher training department at the University. But when she was introduced to classical Indian ragas, both the music itself and its performance conventions drew her into an entirely new world. The use of drones and microtonal scales she found at first disconcerting, but she was enthused by other aspects of the music, especially the skill of drum players who could 'conjure up an incredible range of harmonics on the surface of their two small drums, varying each phrase with subtle changes of dynamics and tone-colour that could reach from the thunder of the storm to the rustle of the wind in the trees'.[2] In exchange for learning much that was new about the importance of rhythm, IH taught her students about Western harmony, which her hosts, on listening to records of Beethoven before her arrival had found 'undisciplined and disturbing'. Characteristically she threw Beethoven aside and instead demonstrated the joys of harmony through the practice of

---

[2] This and subsequent quotations relating to IH's visit to India are taken from her essay 'Indian music'.

singing a round, much to the surprise and pleasure of the Director, who found the sound that she conjured from her pupils 'so beautiful, I had to go and listen to it from a distance, under the trees'. Not all her instruction was quite so successful, however; in particular, the 'stumbling-block' of equal temperament ensured that her 'rash attempts to teach them to sing tenth-century organum in parallel fourths were doomed to end in disaster'.

Dance, on the other hand, was an area of musicianship and performance where IH could be sure to find common ground with her hosts. She was delighted to discover that the link between music and dancing was taken for granted at Santiniketan, and when asked to lecture the students on the history of European dance she called on her years of experience and her innate skills as a performer, once more adopting a pragmatic, rather than theoretical, approach to the lesson that she knew would hold their attention:

> On a small patch of carpet no larger than a sheet I demonstrated the Rumanian sword dance representing the death of the old year and the birth of the new; I described the Basque Hobby-Horse neatly stepping upon a glass of wine without spilling a drop; and I showed them the courteous gestures of the Abbot's Bromley Horn Dance, where the men bow to each other with the tips of their reindeer horns just touching. My audience, sitting tightly packed on the floor, gazed at me in polite but blank incomprehension. Then, with the sweat running off me in rivulets, I showed them what I could remember of the movements of that great dancer Argentina,[3] and described her smooth black hair, her flame-coloured silk shawl drawn tightly across one shoulder, and the curve of her wrist as her fingers felt their way through the pattering whisper of the castanets. A sudden gleam came into their eyes and a murmur of approval rippled around the room. This was something belonging to their own world, and one more barrier between East and West had been successfully removed.

Returning to England via Calcutta, IH was disappointed to discover in the city the existence of other attempts to bridge the gap that did not possess the same level of integrity, based on mutual respect between different traditions, which she had encountered at Santiniketan. She heard a Westernized Indian

---

[3] Antonia Mercé y Luque (1890–1936), known by her stage name as *La Argentina*, was a flamenco dancer, who originated and helped to establish the neoclassical style of Spanish dance as a theatrical art. Starting out in ballet, she moved on to performing native Spanish and gipsy dances, developing a distinctive and much-imitated style.

orchestra, whose borrowed European harmonies sounded to her 'patched on to the surface of the music', and was saddened to be told by artists and writers that there was no future for the traditional music about which she had learnt so much. But these disappointments did not mar the overwhelming effects of her visit, which had given her a fresh perspective on her understanding of her own musical traditions. On her return to Dartington she immediately marked the experience by making arrangements for recorders of *Ten Indian Folk Tunes from the Hill Villages of the Punjab* collected, and sung to her, by Prabhakar Chinchore. In her preface to the published score, she wrote:

> The recorder is the right instrument for bridging the gap between eastern and western folk music, for Indian villagers play home-made bamboo flutes ... which are fairly similar in tone to our treble and descant recorders. And there is a welcome flexibility of intonation in the recorder which suits the Indian scales far better than the equal temperament of the keyboard.

On her return to England IH was greeted by the appearance in print of her study of GH's music, which was published in February by Oxford University Press under the title *The Music of Gustav Holst*. Like her earlier biography, the book was well received; *The Listener* found it 'candid, equally balanced and objective, informed throughout with sound professional judgement',[4] while the *Daily Telegraph* considered its criticisms 'knowledgeable [and] to the point'.[5] The same reviewer also considered, however, that occasionally IH had pushed her criticism of GH's music 'too far'. In fact, writing more than fifteen years after his death, IH was able to apply a significant degree of critical detachment to her evaluation of her father's music and found herself forced to conclude that his achievement in solving the problems he had inherited as an English composer born in the last quarter of the nineteenth century was, from posterity's standpoint, probably more important 'than the fact that he wrote very few works that are entirely satisfactory'. These problems had involved unlearning the inherited techniques of Romanticism and developing a new language which transcended the 'snares of pleasant English neo-modalism'. In his daughter's view, GH had successfully fought his way from extravagance to economy and undertaken a lifelong search for 'the musical idiom of the English language', for which he had to 'dig for his own materials'. Ultimately, however, his approach to composition had been hampered by over-intellectualism, and his achievement

4 *The Listener*, 15 March 1951.
5 *Daily Telegraph*, 3 February 1951.

compromised by an insistence on 'spending most of his time and energy on teaching' and working tirelessly with, and in the cause of, amateurs. She regretted, finally, that while he had 'dreamed of the possibility of a renaissance of music in England', he had 'died before he could be certain that it was going to happen'.[6] These conclusions are significant in their analysis of the state of English music in 1951. In particular they demonstrate that IH had come to view her father almost as if he were something of a John the Baptist figure, making the mistakes that needed to be made and clearing the path for a greater composer to follow. For her the saviour had arrived in the person of Benjamin Britten, and it was to him that she dedicated the new book.

Since 1943 Britten had been well aware of the exalted position in English musical history to which IH had assigned him, contenting himself with expressing the more cautious view that 'whether we are the voices crying in the wilderness or the thing itself, it isn't for us to know'. But he was deeply affected by the dedication and wrote to the author:

> You cannot imagine, my dear Imogen, what deep pleasure that has given me. The dedication, your touching letter, & the joy of having it all the time around & reading & re-reading it. It is so good. So wise & just, & so deeply sympathetic. I feel he himself ... would have loved it & agreed with it. What is most remarkable, & perhaps most valuable, about it, is that it sends me straight back to the music itself. How unlike most critical surveys! It is because of the love (which our dear Morgan Forster so truly says is the only critical approach) which shines through every page.[7]

The ever-tightening bond of affection and respect between IH and Britten was given a further twist the same month, when Peter Pears, while in Dartington on a teaching assignment, attended a class in which she studied a Bach chorale with her students. He enthused to Britten: 'She is quite brilliant – revealing, exciting ...'.[8] At the end of his stay he wrote again: 'I am quite sure that somehow we have to got to use Imo in the biggest way – as editor, as trainer, as teacher, etc. – she is most impressive.'[9] No firm plans were made, however, and for the next few months IH plunged herself into the musical and administrative life of Dartington, taking a full part in the discussions that led to the appointment of her successor, John Clements, who was to start

[6] IH, *The Music of Gustav Holst*, pp.145–9.
[7] 12 February 1951; BPL.
[8] 21 February 1951; BPL.
[9] 1 March 1951; BPL.

in September 1951. She also returned to composing, and through the spring and early summer wrote her one-act Shakespeare opera *Benedick and Beatrice*. The first performance was given on 21 July 1951 to an invited audience in the Barn Theatre at Dartington Hall, as the second half of a double bill which also included a work by one of her favourite and most accomplished pupils, James Butt. This was IH's last weekend as Director of Music at Dartington, and the performance marked her farewell. IH acted as both producer and conductor, and the performance involved all her staff and students: the singers included Noelle Barker (Beatrice), Kathleen Kelly (Hero) and Roger Newsom (Claudio), and, in three spoken scenes, members of the amateur drama group as Dogberry, Verges and other supporting characters. But IH was dissatisfied with the work, and despite its success was adamant that it should never be performed again.

Peter Cox summed up IH's achievement at Dartington in a personal recollection written forty years later. He recalled that

> within two or three years of her arrival we were confident that the principles around which we were building were right for Dartington. Excellent opportunities were being provided for local people to enjoy music, both as participants and listeners. The new course was meeting a national need … The staff and students on the course provided a central core which leavened every aspect of music-making and contact was being forged with some of the most creative musicians in the country, including Britten and Tippett.

Equally significant was the mark that IH had made upon the atmosphere and ethos of Dartington, characterized by Pamela O'Malley as 'a harmony [between] all the staff and students. There seemed to be a peacefulness and excitement in the air which grew from mutual appreciation of people and things around which I will never forget'.[10] Of IH's achievements as an educator, both at Dartington and elsewhere, Rosamund Strode later wrote: 'She was one of the world's great teachers and was able to communicate to all who met her her knowledge and love of music and exactly what she required from her players and singers.'[11] And, as Christopher Tinker has pointed out,[12] IH herself was to provide the perfect summation of her philosophy and methods when she chose to set, in one of her last works, *Homage to William Morris*, the following text:

---

10 Cox, *The Arts at Dartington*, p. 37.
11 *Aldeburgh Festival Programme Book*, 1984.
12 Tinker, 'The Musical Output of Imogen Holst', p. 77.

I do not want art for a few, any more than I want freedom for a few, or
education for a few. I want all to be educated according to their capacity,
not according to the amount of money their parents happen to have'.[13]

IH had no firm plans for her employment once she had left Dartington. She
proposed first to travel to Europe again, this time not to hear music but to
study it: as she told Leonard Elmhirst on 2 July 1951, she wished to

> spend several weeks studying in the music library at Venice, reading the
> earliest editions of the late sixteenth century Italian composers whose
> work showed an influence of eastern scales. And I hope to have several
> weeks in Solesmes, learning about fifth to ninth century Gregorian chant,
> with possibly several weeks in the library at Paris, transcribing mediae-
> val polyphonic music of the twelfth and early thirteenth centuries.

The trip was a fruitful one, and the music that she collected in Italy that
summer, and subsequently edited for performance, was to feature in concert
programmes that she devised and conducted regularly over the next thirty
years.

On her return to England IH bided her time by taking on freelance editorial
and copying work for Britten and others, writing to her friend and pupil James
Butt (who had also studied with Britten): 'O Jim it is HEAVENLY not being a
director of music any more! It's so lovely to be allowed to start right in doing
music first thing every morning and then be allowed to go on and on and on.'
On 30 September she told Butt that 'I've got the first two-thirds of the vocal
score of Billy Budd. And Erwin is going to allow me to correct the full score
before it's published, which will be very exciting'.[14] After the first performance
of *Billy Budd* at Covent Garden, she wrote to Britten 11 December 1951 from
Paris that it was 'quite impossible to say anything coherent to you about it,
because it's so very much the greatest thing you've yet written'.

Then in April 1952 IH came to Crag House, Britten's seafront home in Aldeburgh, to work on an orchestration of his *Rejoice in the Lamb* 'for that year's
festival, as he hadn't time to do it himself'.[15] Britten 'enjoyed every minute'[16] of
her visit, and she returned at his request to help out at the Festival itself. 'I'm
still in a state of wild intoxication after the excitement of working with Ben', she
wrote to Butt soon afterwards: 'you're about the only person who can realize

[13] From 'The Lesser Arts', a lecture Morris gave in Birmingham in 1878.

[14] 30 September 1951; BPL. Erwin Stein was music editor at Britten's publishers
Boosey & Hawkes.

[15] IH, 'Working for Benjamin Britten', p. 202.

[16] Britten to IH, 16 May 1952; BPL.

just <u>how</u> exciting it is to be allowed to do things for him'.[17] Britten seems to have enjoyed the experience in equal measure. He wrote to express his gratitude to IH for her

> contribution to the Festival – both <u>behind</u> the scenes & very much <u>on</u> them. It has been an indescribable comfort to us to have you with us, working so closely. It has been wonderful to know there was someone we could trust, not only to do the things, but to do them with a skill & efficiency which amounts to genius … I have heard paeans of praise from organisers, singers, players & audience.

Looking to the future, he continued:

> Now the next thing is – next year! … always supposing you would like to come in & help us, & in future on a really professional basis, will you count yourself as definitely engaged – in the preparations & running of Aldeburgh Festival nos. 6, 7, 8, 9 …? Please say yes! … Peter & I get back at the end of August, & then we must settle down to plans. Could you come & stay some days with us – to post mortem, & in the light of experience (some bitter) map out next year?[18]

Once back in Aldeburgh, on 26 August, Britten wrote again, asking her to visit on 4 September for a more extended stay to discuss plans for the 1953 Festival. During this time he was able to persuade her to move to Aldeburgh for the whole year. Four days before she was to arrive, he wrote to the young opera producer Basil Coleman, expressing his relief that IH would soon be 'taking up residence to help straighten things out'.[19] In accepting Britten's invitation she had achieved a dream that she could hardly have dared hope for. Even so, when she arrived in Aldeburgh on 29 September, she could not have guessed that she would stay in the town for the rest of her life.

[17] 3 July 1952; BPL.
[18] 7 July 1952; BPL.
[19] 25 September 1952; BPL.

1 *above left* Gustav Holst, 1923

2 *above right* Isobel Holst, passport photograph, 1918

3 *left* IH in her pram, late summer 1907

4 *below* IH in a mushroom field with Jessie and May Beames, Thaxted, 1915

5 *top* Centre-stage with her Nymphs and Shepherds at Eothen, 1920

6 *bottom left* In the porch at Thaxted Church, 1919

7 *bottom right* With Isobel at Brook End, *circa* 1925

8 *top left* IH in 1926

9 *top right* Playing an early piano, Primrose Hill, *circa* 1936

10 *bottom* IH's study at Primrose Hill, *circa* 1936

The Heretics

ABOUT eighty keen folk dancers from all parts of the land were at Cecil Sharpe House for the week-

MISS HOLST MADE A CONFESSION.

end. They practised the Coronation dances.

They were addressed during their stay by Miss Imogen Holst, daughter of Holst, the composer. In her talk she confessed, though she suggested that it was heretical at folk dance headquarters, to liking waltzes by Straus.

I gather that most of the eighty assented to the same heresy.

11 *top* Playing the recorder, on her greetings card, Christmas 1933

12 *bottom left* Cartoon from the *EFDS News*, 1937

13 *bottom right* 'Imo', a cartoon by her friend Diana Batchelor

14 *top* With Mary Ibberson and an unidentified man, while working for CEMA

15 *bottom left* Conducting at Dartington, 1942

16 *bottom right* Relaxing at Dartington

17 Learning Indian dance at Santiniketan, Western Bengal, January 1951

18 The opening page of IH's vocal score of Britten's *Gloriana* (1953)

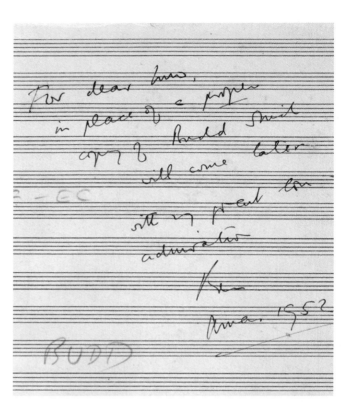

19 *right* Britten's Christmas present to IH, 1952, the composition sketch of *Billy Budd*, inscribed 'in place of a <u>proper</u> copy of Budd which will come later'

20 *below left* With Basil Douglas, August 1955

21 *below right* With her bicycle on Crag Path, Aldeburgh, *circa* 1954

22 *top left* In the Crush Bar at Covent Garden, discussing *Gloriana* with George Harewood, Erwin Stein and Joan Cross, 1953

23 *left* Playing recorders at Crag House with Julian Potter, Britten and Mary Potter, *circa* 1954

24 *below* Outside a café in Venice, after the first performance of *The Turn of the Screw*, September 1954 (clockwise from left) Marion Harewood, Peter Diamand, IH, Lord Harewood, Anthony Gishford, Sophie Stein, Mrs Diamand, Benjamin Britten

25 *top left* With Britten, Pears and Clytie, Aldeburgh, mid-1950s

26 *top right* With Britten at Crag House, mid-1950s

27 *bottom left* At Aldeburgh, 1955

28 *bottom right* Conducting 'Music on the Meare', Thorpeness, June 1955

Part *III* ~ 1952–4

CHRISTOPHER GROGAN

9 'The excitement of working with Ben': an introduction to the Aldeburgh Diary

Once in Aldeburgh, IH was to stay in the town for the rest of her life, becoming inextricably linked both with Britten's music and legacy, and with the wider Aldeburgh Festival. For the first eighteen months she kept a diary on an almost daily basis, writing in the evenings while her memories of her day with the composer were still fresh, and pouring out her thoughts and feelings in a spontaneous rush of vivid prose. The resulting document is a uniquely intimate testimony, not only for the insights it gives into Britten's life and thoughts, but equally significantly, for the light it sheds on IH herself, whose personality is revealed in all its dazzling and troubled complexity. Utterly dedicated to music ('I'd much rather be dealing with crotchets and quavers' than people, she tells Britten), she remains hugely loyal to her friends; forever anxious about money and leading a frugal existence, she repeatedly declines to accept payment for work done or lessons given; forthright and determined, she is infinitely sympathetic; jovial and outgoing to almost everyone she meets, she maintains a distance; and when by herself, she is often contemplative, experiencing times of frustration, sadness and loneliness.

That the diary reveals so much about IH would have surprised its author, who was at great pains throughout to pass over the details of her own life in the service of what she saw as a greater mission – chronicling the words and deeds of the living composer she admired above any other and for whom she felt wonderfully privileged to work. Whenever Britten goes away – on tour, on business, or on holiday – the diary stops until he returns. His ailments are treated extensively and in sympathetic detail, but IH's own physical difficulties are never mentioned, startlingly so in the case of the phlebitis in her left arm which must have replicated, in symptoms if not in diagnosis, the bursitis that dogged Britten throughout these years, and which became a preoccupation and the cause of depression in the autumn and winter of 1953. Her own life as a composer came to a standstill for the first few years of her life with Britten, yet this too is passed over without comment. When Britten mentions it – asking her if she has ever composed for piano, for instance – she sidesteps the question; and when he praises her Baroque continuo realizations as better than his, she is embarrassed and anxious to get back to the 'comparative relief' of talking about *Gloriana*. Similarly, she describes in glowing terms every performance given or directed by Britten during the course of the 1953 Aldeburgh Festival, but makes no mention of her own major contribution – conducting Handel's *L'Allegro* on the final Saturday – beyond praising Britten for being very helpful at the rehearsal.

Through the course of the narrative IH comes to view Britten as near perfect, and (rightly or wrongly) as a perfectionist in all areas of life. As a result, she is extremely self-critical, 'giving herself the sack' when she spots mistakes in her preparation of orchestral parts from which he is to conduct, and castigating herself for over-beating the eggs when preparing his breakfast. Her complete self-effacement is tempered only when she feels that the music itself is at stake; as she was later to recall: '... the most difficult thing [in working for him] was judging whether I could risk criticising details that I felt passionately were wrong ... to risk it without interrupting the flow of his ideas; and because of this marvellous thing that music matters most, I had the courage to do it.'[1]

And yet – composition aside – these eighteen months covered hugely important ground in IH's own creative life. They saw the foundation of the Purcell Singers, the growth of the Aldeburgh Festival and Music Club, and her editorial work on music ranging from the championship of neglected English Baroque composers such as Henry Carey and Pelham Humphrey, through to the performing texts of Purcell, Schütz and Bach that would provide the foundations for her published editions of the 1960s and 1970s. Most of all she advanced tirelessly the reputation of her father's music with Britten and anyone else who would listen, arranging for recordings and performances, and herself conducting broadcast performances of *Sāvitri*, performing the same work with the Opera School in a double bill with *The Wandering Scholar*, and introducing *A Fugal Concerto* to the Aldeburgh Festival. But all this work and formidable achievement has to be teased out from between the lines of the diary, so determined is she not to distract the reader away from what she perceives as its main theme and focus.

To understand the diary, however, it is essential to bear in mind IH's relationship not only with Britten but with the memory and legacy of her much-loved father. For her complete devotion to the two men and their music was linked by a complex chain of love, loneliness and guilt. There can be little doubt that IH continued to miss her father terribly, and that she came to see Britten, in some ways at least, as a surrogate. Her joy in observing him in everyday

---

[1] Interview with Donald Mitchell, January 1980; BPL.

life is often punctuated with the remark that she has witnessed him say or do something 'just like G', whether it be his readiness to work with amateurs (even to cajole them into playing Schubert's String Quintet in C), in his admiration for Schubert's 'Great' C Major symphony (GH's 'favourite') or his self-avowed indebtedness to GH for a particular harmonic progression. Britten was both well aware of the perceived link, and encouraging of it, taking time to discuss GH's scores with her, and, in his own moments of stress and need, asking if her father 'always enjoy[ed] working' or ever got 'terribly depressed'. In a reflective moment in the wake of the widespread critical rejection of *Gloriana*, he even goes so far as to see his career as following the same 'pattern' as that of GH, perceiving *Peter Grimes* and *The Planets* as their respective high water-marks, with the public being generally 'disappointed with what came afterwards'. That IH's love for her father should have been so compounded by guilt is more surprising, given GH's own very independent spirit and his wish that his talented daughter should make her own way in the world; yet IH, twenty years after his death, felt she had neglected him at the end of his life, 'being ambitious about jobs instead of ruling bar-lines for him', and so now found penance and drew solace from performing such creatively menial tasks for Britten. Even her willingness to take on a sequence of composition pupils from Britten harks back to similar selfless gestures that she had made for her overburdened father. And it is her guilt over GH's early death that prompts her to take her courage in her hands to tell her overworked and suffering employer, who is about to embark on a concert tour even though he can hardly move his arm, not to 'just get through on endurance, like G. tried to do'.

At some point soon into the narrative of the diary, IH's unconditional belief in Britten's achievement and status, and her absolute devotion to his work, tips over into infatuation and then love. After spending an entire evening with him less than a fortnight after coming to Aldeburgh, she confides to the diary that 'it will last a life-time, such an evening as that'. She soon becomes tongue-tied when discussing anything more intimate than music, is unable to hear his compliments about her work, and goes off for her 1952 Christmas holiday on the train 'in such a state of bliss that the other people in the carriage looked a bit doubtful', after he has written her a warm and affectionate letter of thanks. As late as February 1954 she confesses that 'when he talks to me confidentially about personal things I still suffer from paralysis even after all these months'. And though she is frequently light-hearted and gently self-mocking in her accounts of individual events – grateful for a dark night or the excuse of having run to his house to conceal her blushing, for example – there remains a pervasive unhappiness underlying this strand of the narrative. Praising Britten (six years her junior) for his physical youthfulness and athleticism, she feels herself bound by the constraints of middle age, a state of mind that gives a sad twist to her narration of conversations between them such as the planning of her proposed American tour: Britten, trying to write her a letter of introduction for the visit alights on the description of her as 'stimulating' to which she responds that 'there [are] few things worse than a stimulating middle-aged spinster'.

All this begs the question, of course, of to what extent IH was suppressing her awareness, at this stage in their friendship, of Britten's homosexuality and the permanence of his relationship with Peter Pears. IH deals in summary fashion with her predecessor as Britten's female confidante, Elizabeth Sweeting, not only replacing her in the composer's affections, but ousting her over time from her role in the organization of the Festival; thirty years later she still felt strongly enough to erase every mention of Sweeting from her edited version of the diary, much as she had done Eric Crozier from the first edition of her biography of Britten. But with Pears it is very different. IH was conscious from the start of how much Britten looked forward to the 'delicious relaxation of the light-hearted enjoyment of having Peter on Sunday', yet during the singer's frequent absences in London, the provinces or abroad, IH and Britten talk openly, if always in the abstract, about marriage and children. While Britten tells IH that he thinks it 'unlikely that he'd ever marry and have children of his own' the fact of his sexuality does not impinge upon the discussion, which centres instead on whether he ought to adopt; even more remarkably he tells IH on one occasion that if Peter were ever to find 'the right girl to marry he supposed he'd have "to lump it"'. But when Pears and Britten are together, IH both knows and keeps her place, most touchingly when she leaves the two together in tears after the departure of the young Paul Rogerson to a Jesuit seminary. And Britten is quite open with IH about his feelings for Rogerson at least, describing in detail how the two 'fell in love with each other, if that is how you can describe it' at a London performance of Britten's *Serenade* in 1950, sung by Pears. Whatever her feelings for Britten, or her understanding of his sexuality, what is certainly true is that IH, who had worked hard to suppress her own sexual identity since her teenage years, endeavoured to put in place a number of coping mechanisms, chief among them hard work. Over time there emerged a maternal quality in her affection for Britten, the beginnings of which can be observed in the diary as she takes inordinate pleasure in packing his suitcase or doing his washing-up: Britten, who missed his mother as IH did her father, is portrayed as being quite comfortable with this arrangement.

On a practical level IH and Britten appear to have had very similar attitudes to getting things done. IH admired the composer's lightning-like mind, his ability to range swiftly from one initiative to another, to contribute clear-headedly to a detailed meeting discussing plans for the Festival, for example, immediately after finishing a scene for a new opera. Britten for his part found in IH at this time a more natural ally than the instinctively cautious Pears in developing his ambitious plans for a new theatre and a music school in Aldeburgh, plans that were to be fulfilled much later, very largely through the energy and dedication of all three. And they came together also in sharing GH's dedication to amateur and community music-making, primarily through the Aldeburgh Music Club, to which they both devoted great quantities of time and energy. Britten would practise vigorously between rehearsals and even get nervous before performances of a group whose standards were not high.

In many other ways IH and her employer prove to be well matched. IH was a wonderfully good listener, and from her first day in Aldeburgh, when Britten opens up to her on the subject of death and posterity, it is clear that their relationship will be unique and very special. Perhaps for the very reason that he could talk to her so openly, however, the impression the diary gives of his being frequently depressed is one that other contemporary observers might find hard to recognize. His announcement near to the start of the narrative that 'life is good' was undoubtedly true for him much of the time, and most of those in regular contact with him found him more often to be cheerful, witty, positive and good company than IH's account would allow. Stephen Potter, whose diaries do much to complement and sometimes counter-balance IH's versions of events, certainly found him so.

For all its inevitable subjectivity, however, IH's portrait of Britten in the diary gives an insight into the mind and work of a great composer that can have been rarely matched either in its range or the depth of its detail. Britten's views on other composers, for example, are strongly represented. With some, such as his friends and contemporaries Tippett and Berkeley, he is considered in his criticisms, but others, such as Sibelius, are treated more harshly. A few are beyond criticism, especially Purcell, but Schoenberg is dismissed as 'not what you would call a "magic" composer'. Britten shared with IH a devotion for the music of Bach that leads to several insightful conversations, matched only by the discussions regularly initiated by IH about the music of her father – including at one point the revelation that Britten considers *The Planets* to be a better work than she does.

Of Britten's own music and creative processes IH writes a great deal; she found it 'the most exciting thing to hear his music growing, not just week by week, but day by day'[2] and used the diary to record a host of uniquely valuable observations and insights. Much of this material, especially in relation to *Gloriana*, has been treated elsewhere in the Britten literature,[3] and is not the primary focus of this study, but there are many enlightening asides that are worthy of mention. After a successful performance of *Saint Nicolas*, for example, Britten announces that he is planning to write a life of Christ, news by which IH is 'so excited that I nearly knocked him off the wall' on which they are both sitting. Elsewhere he agrees with her assessment that depression is 'part of the business' of being a composer; he resigns himself (without the benefit of hindsight) to *Billy Budd* never being popular; he wishes that he could write a 'real' tune, after hearing *Norma*, and he writes whole scenes of *Gloriana* which he then finds 'monotonous'. And in a moment of depression about the opera, he finds both solace and creative stimulus in digging out and showing to IH some of the songs and piano pieces from his childhood, the enduring value of which he saw as the 'chance [they] gave of seeing how a child's mind worked'. The self-imposed discipline of Britten's working days has been much commented on, but there in fact emerges from the diary a striking contrast in his approach to the commissioned opera *Gloriana*, and the work that followed it, the song-cycle *Winter Words*. Composition of the opera was tightly controlled; IH later recalled that 'it was astonishing to see how strictly he could keep to his time schedule',[4] even when faced with setbacks such as his librettist William Plomer going into hospital for an operation, or his house being flooded. *Winter Words*, on the other hand, begun as a relaxed 'under the desk' diversion during a period of enforced holiday, developed in a more spontaneous and improvisatory fashion, only becoming a 'cycle' as it neared completion. Britten sought out a new poem each day, struggled unsuccessfully to find a less 'depressing' one to open the sequence, and was apparently spurred into setting 'Proud Songsters' by a desire to outdo the version by Gerald Finzi. Yet from this process emerged songs that IH and the composer could agree were among 'the best thing[s] he'd written', and in which the composer was particularly pleased 'to be able to be so relaxed'. Referring to the last song, he remarks 'I couldn't have written that a year ago.'

Composition apart, into these eighteen months are crammed some of the most significant and determining experiences of Britten's life – his rejection of the Covent Garden directorship, the Aldeburgh floods, the critical mauling suffered by *Gloriana*, the prospect of having to give up the piano because of his

[2] Interview with Donald Mitchell, January 1980.
[3] See especially Reed, 'The creative evolution of *Gloriana*'.
[4] IH, *Britten*, 3rd edn, p. 53.

bursitis, and the suicide of Pears's accompanist Noel Mewton-Wood. He was also astoundingly busy at this time, as a performer, administrator and community figure. Yet one of the most important insights offered by IH's intimate portrait is the importance of leisure and relaxation to Britten's creative life. In addition to relaxed music-making, the composer somehow finds time for reading, listening to records, walking, sketching, bird-watching, church-crawling, and a wide range of games and sporting activities (often in defiance of the pain in his arm). Yet, as Stephen Potter observed (and contemporary photographs and documentation also testify), Britten, 'like the majority of men who create a lot of work and can turn themselves into a factory [remained] punctual and tidy and ordered [and had] the correspondence side of his life well under control.'[5]

If Britten's life was well ordered, this in no sense implies that he was unemotional, and although IH describes him as the 'calmest & most patient person in the world' the diary portrays the composer across a wide range of emotional states: from elation to black despair in the last months of 1953; from behaving like a sixteen-year-old prankster singing carols loudly outside the house of an objectionable local resident, through to the quiet seriousness of late-night discussions about life and death; from deep anxiety when Pears goes missing on the way to Cornwall, to profound contentment when his partner is at home with him; from anger about issues surrounding *Gloriana* and the Aldeburgh Festival, through to intense sympathy on many other occasions. And just once, a moment of 'absolute fury', when IH suggests inappropriately that he should take over the podium for the first performance of *Gloriana* and is met by Britten's 'hard, set face … no love in his eyes and a feeling of utter removal to an immense distance'.

Yet for all its darker moments, one of the main characteristics of the diary is its humour, often intentional and delivered with a twinkle, but at other times the product of IH's over-enthusiasm and unstinting devotion. Britten's almost Messianic appearance to a waiting public, when IH observes 'the crowds waving to him on either side of the road which was just right' following a concert in Lowestoft perhaps belongs in the latter category, but her constant if gentle mockery of her own age, mental condition and foibles displays a keen eye for the ridiculousness of life. William Plomer adds some amusing anecdotes, as does Britten himself, but perhaps the central focus of the narrative's comedy is Britten's relationship with his housekeeper Miss Hudson, who is observed making him eat his food, arguing with him about his trousers, catching IH

---

[5] Stephen Potter, 'Aldeburgh Festival 1952 Diary', unpublished typescript, p. 8.

innocently kissing him, and, to everyone's horror, serving up tinned peas at the height of the fresh runner bean season. Food and drink are common themes of the story, with IH, as a frequent guest at Britten's table, relishing Miss Hudson's cooking and enthusiastically contributing her own rations of meat and butter as required. Rationing apart, other occasional glimpses into life in the 1950s are afforded by the narrative; for example, Britten's fast and free attitude to driving, despite a catalogue of near-misses. Of such stuff was much of Britten's and IH's daily life made, and its presentation in the diary is consistently delightful in its mix of warmth, vitality and humanity.

Editorial note

Imogen Holst's Aldeburgh Diary comprises two spiral-bound exercise books, written throughout in pencil. Once the narrative had been abandoned, it lay unread for the next twenty-two years, until IH brought it out to assist her recollections in writing obituaries of the composer and giving interviews in 1977. Four years later, she returned to it again, and began to edit it. Although, as she told the Trustees of the Britten Estate, the diary 'was not intended to be seen by anyone else'[6] when she wrote it, she had come to realize how important it was in shedding light on Britten's world, its unique perspective being 'the result of my having noted each day exactly what Ben had said to me in his own words … just a couple of hours after he had said it'. Her intended readership at this point was unclear; she believed that it might be shown to 'research students under supervision' – many of whom, she must have realized, would never have known Britten – but at the same time felt that 'it is <u>not</u> suitable reading for strangers'.

IH's editing of the diary comprised a number of visible stages. Firstly, she went through the text, separating it out into three types, which she distinguished as follows:

(1) Text that she thought appropriate for transcription into the edited diary she underlined in green pencil, and surrounded in square brackets to create paragraphs; very occasionally she corrected a word in the text, added a word for continuity, or added a brief explanatory note.

(2) Text that was to be suppressed was left outside the square brackets and not underlined in green pencil.

(3) Text that she regarded as particularly personal, or 'anything that would have been libellous or embarrassing' she erased entirely from the page with india rubber, replacing the text with sequences of dashes.

[6] Letter of 2 August 1982; BPL.

She then gave the diary to a friend, Lloyda Swatland, to transcribe. Once this was done she annotated the typescript copy with further comments, corrections and occasional footnotes; these were then added by Swatland to the typescript which she finally gifted to the trustees of the Britten Estate, with the title:

> Diary of Imogen Holst. Sept 29 1952 to March 21st 1954 (Edited in 1981 with cuts, deleted details, and explanatory footnotes where needed.)

The trustees accepted the gift. Isador Caplan wrote to a colleague after a meeting with Rosamund Strode:

> We doubt if there is anything at all defamatory or particularly embarrassing … but it is her privilege to provide us with an edited typescript … If she does not destroy the original before her death, we shall then be in a position to consider the substance of this. It could be that the only other person whose feelings would need to be considered if he survived is Peter Pears …[7]

For the next few years this edited transcription was made available to a few chosen scholars by the Britten–Pears Library.

Then, in October 1991, more than seven years after IH's death, Rosamund Strode wrote to Isador Caplan reminding him about the omitted material, and of their shared view that 'Imo was probably being extremely cautious over the defamatory/embarrassing aspects of the passages which she decided not to have typed when she edited the text in 1981.' This led to a decision by the Holst Foundation to have the rest of the diary typed out as 'supplementary material', to be made available 'to selected persons only' for the purposes of research, on the grounds, as a memorandum by Strode in November 1991 says, that 'the remaining unused text contains much that illuminates the characters of both Benjamin Britten and Imogen Holst and is of great value to those undertaking serious biographical studies of them'. In this context, the diaries in their complete form (but with the texts split up) were then made available to scholars and researchers 'at the discretion of the Holst Foundation' and began to be quoted in published works, most extensively by Humphrey Carpenter in his ground-breaking biography of Britten published in 1992.[8]

The current text presents the first opportunity to view the Aldeburgh diary in a text that is as complete as possible. No distinction has been made between

---

[7] Letter to Peter Carter, 9 August 1982; BPL.

[8] Carpenter, *Benjamin Britten: a Biography*.

the text that IH allowed to be seen, and the supplementary material which she originally suppressed but was transcribed in 1991. Where it has been possible to recover definitively (either from the text or the context) words and passages erased by IH, these are indicated by placing a grey background behind the text. IH's determined use of her india rubber has, however, in many cases defeated all attempts to recover her thoughts, and some gaps remain. IH's revised paragraph structure in the original transcript is not maintained as it no longer makes sense in the context of the complete text; instead the paragraph structure of the original is followed (which in any case gives a better visual representation of the original, reflecting the way that the words poured spontaneously from her in the late evenings when she was writing).

IH's editorial annotations are of two kinds. When editing the text itself for Lloyda Swatland to type up, she added a few clarifications and comments in green pencil. Once the diary was transcribed, she then added a few footnotes. These have been retained where they add meaning to the text, but because her transcription was so radically cut, her first reference to a particular surname, for example, is often no longer the first occurrence, so in these cases her note has been omitted. IH's occasional misspellings have been left in the text without comment, as has her inconsistent use of round and square brackets, and the different format, and sporadic underlining, of dates. These have no significance, but provide further evidence of the spontaneity of the writing.

IH's views about what should and should not be excluded from the original transcript altered in the course of her own editorial process. To begin with, almost everything of a personal nature is omitted, as the first two entries demonstrate. 29 September is transcribed completely; 30 September is complete apart from the first sentence, 'He called in during the afternoon'; but 6 October is omitted completely. Her editing of the 8 October entry omits the opening, and begins with 'He said very helpful things …', with the name 'Jim' in the next line being substituted for 'a student's'. Throughout the text IH is consistent in omitting many domestic references (especially to drinking, a regular if never excessive event) and discussions of the politics of the Aldeburgh Festival. Complete erasure was reserved for passages where she felt her feelings for Britten came out too strongly, for the names of people in Aldeburgh of whom she was critical and, more or less systematically, for references to Elizabeth Sweeting.

An example is provided by the entry for 11 December 1952. The entire first paragraph, much of it innocuous, is omitted, while of the second section, only the sections shown below in bold type survived IH's editorial rigour, with both the alcohol reference and the personal comment about Malcolm Sargent excised:

> **When I went round in the evening he didn't look too good**, *and he was angry with Malcolm for his wrong tempi in the Berlioz. We listened to the first half, and in the interval he drank rum & I drank Drambuie and* **he talked about voices and conductors and how wretched it is that composers took the trouble to write just what they wanted and then they so seldom got it.** *When the second half began some of the choral singing was so bad that he switched off.*

As the diary progresses, however, fewer and fewer passages are omitted, so that by 5 February 1954 the complete discussion between Holst and Britten about unhappy marriages and the importance of children is included, together with Britten's unashamed plying of IH with glasses of St Emilion. It is this inconsistency of approach which justifies the recovery of the erased text which, where it has been restored, has proved to be very similar in content to passages left in elsewhere by IH herself.

10 Aldeburgh Diary
   September 1952 – March 1954

September 1952

On her arrival in Aldeburgh on 29 September 1952 IH moved into a small bed-sitting room in a house in Brown Acres, which had once been the Vicarage, behind the parish church and a short walk up the hill from Britten's house on the seafront. Her pupil Benjamin Zander later recalled that the room contained no more than a 'bed, chair, table and the Bach *Gesellschaft*'.[1] She at once threw herself enthusiastically into the musical activities of the town and the 'infinity of things great and small which every year must be done to keep the Festival running'.[2] She was welcomed first as a member of the recently formed Aldeburgh Music Club, a group of locals of all abilities who met regularly at Crag House to make music. Pieces were rehearsed and then performed on Club Nights, which were strictly for members only. When IH joined, rehearsals were already under way for a performance of Purcell's *Timon of Athens*, planned for 26 October.[3]

Britten himself was heavily immersed in the composition sketch of the opening scenes of a new opera. *Gloriana*, to a libretto by the South African poet and novelist William Plomer, had been promised to Covent Garden as part of the celebrations for the new Queen's coronation year, and the vocal score was due to be delivered in February.[4] IH quickly picked up the pattern of Britten's disciplined working routine, by which 'he planned a timetable for getting each act finished. Each morning he wrote from about 8.30 to 12.30; then he took the manuscript to the piano and played through what he had written. He usually went back to work at 4, and kept at it until 7.30 or 8.'[5] Almost immediately she found her own life beginning to revolve around the rhythms of Britten's day.

---

[1] Interview with Christopher Grogan, 19 October 2006.
[2] IH quoting Britten; quoted in Burrows, *The Aldeburgh Story*.
[3] For the early history of the Aldeburgh Music Club and a list of its performances, see Walker and Potter, *Aldeburgh Music Club*.
[4] The composition history of *Gloriana*, and IH's part in it, is fully explored in Reed, 'The creative evolution of *Gloriana*'.
[5] IH, 'Working for Benjamin Britten', p. 202.

Sept 29th '52. (first day as an inhabitant of Aldeburgh) Ben asked me in after a choir practice of Timon of Athens. We were talking about old age and he said that nothing could be done about it, and that he had a very strong feeling that people died at the right moment, and that the greatness of a person included the time when he was born and the time he endured, but that this was difficult to understand.

Sept. 30th. He called in during the afternoon: Scene I nearly finished, and he expected to finish it after tea. It was pouring with rain and he said he'd got very wet indoors because he hadn't noticed that the rain was coming in on him while he worked! He looked at G's 3-key canons and said "Yes, it really works; it's not just an intellectual excersize." He also said, of polytonality "I suppose I've been influenced a good deal by it."

The abbreviation 'G', here and throughout the diary, represents IH's father, the composer Gustav Holst. Ever since his death in 1934 much of IH's time and energy had been spent in promoting his music and legacy, and she was quick to try to encourage Britten's interest in his scores. In 1948, after hearing *The Planets*, he had told her that 'I do now want to get to know *Egdon Heath*', upon which hint she sent him the score.[6] Three years later she dedicated her study of GH's music to him. Now, on her arrival in Aldeburgh, she presented him with a copy of her earlier biography, inscribed 'For Ben with love from Imogen September 1952';[7] over the next years she went on to give him a variety of other materials, including manuscripts and notebooks.

October 1952

Once settled in her new surroundings, IH wasted no time in getting to grips with the planning of the Aldeburgh Festival. She was later to recall: 'As soon as I began living in Aldeburgh … I realised what an immense amount of hard work had to go on, eleven months of the year, planning and preparing for those weeks in June.'[8] Overseeing the Festival's organization and management was a Council, chaired by Fidelity, Countess of Cranbrook, and including also in its membership the Mayor, Mr. E. E. Grundy, the Vicar, Rupert Godfrey, the manager of Barclays Bank, H. W. 'Tommy' Cullum (as honorary treasurer), the manager of the Wentworth Hotel, Lyn Pritt and Britten's sister Beth Welford, together with a dozen other people from the town and an Arts Council Assessor.

[6] 27 October 1948; BPL.
[7] *The Music of Gustav Holst* (1951) preceded by *Gustav Holst* (1938). The '3-key canons' form part of Holst's *Eight Canons for Equal Voices*, written in 1932.
[8] Interview with Donald Mitchell, January 1980; BPL.

From the Council was drawn an Executive Committee, which met regularly to plan the detailed arrangements, and there was also a paid Festival Manager, Elizabeth Sweeting. In the week before her arrival in Aldeburgh IH had been the subject of discussions at the Executive Committee, which minuted its 'great pleasure that Miss Imogen Holst had very kindly agreed to work in close collaboration with the Committee in the planning and general arrangements for the Festival 1953.'[9]

> *Oct 1. Business meetings to discuss committees. Scene I finished & he's begun Scene II.*

> [*Oct 2–6th London*]

On 2 October Britten travelled to London for a series of appointments that provide ample evidence of the wide range of his preoccupations at this time. He first had a difficult meeting with his publishers Boosey & Hawkes, not primarily about his own music, but in support of a younger composer, Arthur Oldham, who had worked as his amanuensis in the 1940s. Boosey's were threatening to withdraw the retainer they were paying Oldham, unless he could commit to writing an orchestral piece, rather than completing his EOG opera *Christopher Sly*. Britten saw the firm's approach as indicative of their attitude towards young composers, and expressed his apprehension that he would end up as 'the last of the young composers'[10] in the Boosey catalogue. Britten also discussed another opera project, *The Turn of the Screw*, to be based on the novella by Henry James, which had originally been considered for the EOG in 1951, before being shelved to make way for *Gloriana*. He now intended to complete the work by the autumn of 1953 for the Venice Biennale Festival, the organizers of which had written in July to 'express great interest'[11] in mounting the first performance. Boosey's were concerned that they would be unable to process the work in time, coming so soon after the first performance of *Gloriana* in June, so Britten was seeking an interim arrangement whereby the EOG could control the work. In any case he was not prepared to 'gear [his] composing to suit the comfort and convenience of [his] publishers.'[12] Over the next two days, the composer went on to meet with Basil Douglas, the General Manager of

[9] The minute book covering meetings of both the Council and the Executive Committee is at the BPL.
[10] As paraphrased by Anthony Gishford in a letter to Britten, 5 October 1952; BPL.
[11] Memorandum by the General Manager of the English Opera Group of the meeting on 15 July 1952; BPL.
[12] Anthony Gishford to Britten, 5 October 1952; BPL.

the EOG, William Plomer, Isador Caplan, his solicitor, and his physician Dr Michael McCready, with whom he discussed the pain and discomfort he had recently begun to experience in his right arm.

IH's weekly routine was also beginning to take shape. Working in Aldeburgh from Monday to Friday, she spent most weekends in London, where she stayed with a variety of people, including her old schoolfriend Vicky Ingrams, and held rehearsals on Saturday afternoons 'in a London mews office'[13] for a newly formed, partly professional, group of young singers that Pears had encouraged her to start, to be available to perform at the Festival and elsewhere. Pears himself had originally been approached to form such a group himself by his niece Sue Pears and her college friend Gillian Collymore, but because of his other commitments had passed on the idea to IH, who embraced it enthusiastically.

With this group she began to rehearse repertoire that she had come to love at Dartington, especially the music of Monteverdi, Purcell and Schütz, the Bach cantatas and motets, and more contemporary Dartington favourites such as Britten's own *Five Flower Songs*, written for the twenty-fifth wedding anniversary of Leonard and Dorothy Elmhirst in 1950 and first performed at Dartington with IH conducting. She would then travel back to Aldeburgh on Sunday, usually calling in on Britten during the evening to plan the working week. On this first weekend she was also busy devising a concert to be given by the EOG at the Victoria and Albert Museum on 16 November and then repeated for broadcast by the BBC four days later. Entitled 'Songs from the Gardens of Ranelagh, Marylebone and Vauxhall (1745–1830)', the concert would feature music from the pleasure gardens of eighteenth-century London, sung by Pears and other members of the Group accompanied by George Malcolm.

> Oct 6th. Ben rang in the evening to ask about Vauxhall programme & B.B.C. Said he'd been in a tantrum for five days and needed me to quieten him. Asked me to go to lunch next day.

Arriving for lunch, IH found Britten in familiar company. In addition to his housekeeper Miss Hudson, he had Jim Butt staying for a few days to discuss his new opera *The Laughter of the Gods*. Butt had known Britten since he was a schoolboy in 1944, when Britten had suggested that he 'should start more advanced serious study of composition as soon as possible', inviting him to 'come and stay ... so that I can begin to teach you about counterpoint, if you

[13] Strode, 'Working for Britten (II)', p. 52.

would do some copying for me in exchange'.[14] This arrangement continued for
a time, until Butt went into the RAF. When he came out Britten wrote to IH at
Dartington, asking her to take him on as a pupil. IH agreed, and later wrote to
thank Britten 'for having sent Jim Butt to us. It's a great joy to have him: – he's
just the right mixture of simple and complicated, and he thinks for himself'.[15]
Also in the house was Mary Potter, a distinguished artist and wife of the writer
and broadcaster Stephen Potter, who was embarking on a portrait of the composer. The Potters lived a mile away at The Red House on the outskirts of the
town with their sons Andrew and Julian, and were members of the Music Club;
they also had a tennis court, an attraction which drew Britten and Pears (who
until then had used the public courts) to the house frequently.

Britten's 'tantrum' had been brought on largely by problems surrounding the
proposed gala night first performance of *Gloriana*. Kenneth Clark, one of the
first directors of the EOG, on the Committee of Covent Garden, and recently
appointed Chairman of the Arts Council, was hinting that *Gloriana* might be
scrapped for the gala performance in favour of a more populist work and possibly a ballet; the Royal Ballet had expressed its unhappiness at being excluded
from the planning of the celebrations. Britten entered into a feud with Clark
which was to last for several months, with Mary Potter 'the unwilling ambas-
sador between the two'.[16] In fact Clark was displaying a great deal of presci-
ence in his belief that, as he told Stephen Potter, 'the Queen's night next year
is a gala night, with royals in white ties who won't understand music'. On a
more optimistic note, the EOG were planning two broadcasts of GH's *Sāvitri*
in November, and Britten and Pears were considering whether to stage the
work at the Aldeburgh Festival in 1953 in a triple bill that would also feature a
ballet, devised by the young choreographer John Cranko, and Stravinsky's *The
Soldier's Tale*.

> *Oct 7th. Went to lunch. He said he'd just finished reading my biography, that
> it was much too short and that perhaps one day I'd write another when people
> had died off and I could say more. He also said that he liked G's humour. Then
> Jim came in and over lunch Ben told us some of the depressing things that had
> happened in London, including K. Clark saying to Covent Garden that Gloriana
> shouldn't be done at the Gala performance! Also that he'd been to his lawyer
> to try & make a will and that the lawyer had said that the most likely thing
> to happen would be for Ben & Peter both to be killed in the same air disaster.*

[14] 3 April 1944; BPL.
[15] 6 December 1949; BPL.
[16] Diary of Stephen Potter, 17 November 1952.

*Cheerful! Then he said that they were thinking of doing Savitri at the Aldeburgh
Festival. After lunch he had a sitting – Mary Potter painting him. So I took Jim
for a walk. Ben came in to tea, and afterwards told me in the kitchen that he was
bewildered by Jim's manner & that they'd had a real fight the evening before. I
tried to persuade him to send him home & not let him take too much of his time
& energy from Gloriana. Then he said he'd go through Jim's opera with him & I
said I'd go home & work, and while seeing me out Ben said would I make a habit
of calling in on him & I said no because I'd lived with a composer, but agreed to go
to supper with him on Wed & he said he <u>might</u> play Gloriana. Got home & after
about half an hour's work Ben rang up to say what did one do when Jim had a
blackout, so I went down and he was just putting him to bed. I went up and had
a long talk with Jim when he was in bed and he seemed calm but a bit muddled:
– I think he partly realised what was wrong. But when I told him he mustn't be
rude to Ben he didn't know he had been. The same mixture of reasonableness
amounting to wisdom at times, but all mixed up with vagueness. I couldn't do
anything for him except tell him he was all right & not to worry. When I went
down the stairs Ben was putting on his shoes to walk uphill with me – he said
wouldn't I stay but I said no and then when he got to the door he looked so
depressed that I said yes. So we had a drink and I told him all the symptoms I
could gather from Jim's incoherent account and he was dismayed that I'd told
him he'd been rude to him but I <u>hope</u> he saw the point. Then he said he'd ring up
Barbara[17] to try & get advice about the right Dr. to send Jim to, and he suddenly
got quite cheerful when he thought that even if it cost £100 he'd be able to do it
so we drank to wealth and he said "Good old Peter Grimes" and we laughed a lot
and he said he hoped I wouldn't think that life at Aldeburgh was <u>always</u> like this
so I assured him it was nothing after life at Dartington. Miss Hudson had cooked
a superb meal and we both felt better and then he told me that he was thinking of
adopting two children from the Hessen's displaced persons camp in Germany:[18]
– he wanted a girl and a boy but it would probably have to be two boys because of
regulations about a predominantly male household. He said he'd been thinking
about it for ages because he realised that it was unlikely that he'd ever marry and
have children of his own, and he'd got such an immense instinct of love for them
that it spilled over and was wasted. Also that he felt that otherwise he might*

---

[17] Barbara Britten, the composer's sister, who was a nurse and qualified social
worker.

[18] UN camps in the Hessen region of Germany had originally been stopping-off
places for the displaced persons of World War II, but by 1951 some were also
sheltering Eastern Europeans fleeing across the Iron Curtain, including many
children.

*get more and more selfish. That he'd try & find the right school for them & then
would arrange all his concert tours in the term time so as to be free for them in
the holidays. He said he'd probably spoil them, but I said no, he wouldn't. Then
we came and sat by the fire and he rang up Barbara and got advice & decided
to ring his own doctor and I said I'd take Jim to London & see his parents. He
wanted to send us by car but I said no v. firmly & in the end we compromised on a
car to Ipswich going & taxi from Sax. coming back. It was the most I've ever had
of him in one day – even more than when I stayed in April, because more crowded
with things. His calmness and clear-headedness when things need doing are on
the same sort of level as his technique in music.*

*Oct. 8th. Went down directly after breakfast and found Jim up and much better
and well enough to travel alone. Ben had fixed up an appointment with his own
doctor for him. I took Jim off into the garden and we sat in deck-chairs in the sun –
it was the most* marvellous *day, and to my dismay Ben came and joined us instead
of going straight to work on Gloriana. He said very helpful things about Jim's
new opera,[19] and advised him to try and get more definite contrast in his next
libretto between recits and arias etc, because one of the reasons why too much
recit was a bore was that the singers couldn't ever sing loudly which meant that
the orchestra could never play out, so it became monotonous. It had struck ten
and I* longed *to tell him to go and work but* just *managed to resist the temptation
and then he himself said he must go. So I went through the last two scenes with
Jim and criticised some practical details, and then we went for a walk and bought
Ben some toothpaste, and it was the most wonderful day and the sea looked better
than I've ever seen it before and the air was even more invigorating than usual. I'd
said I'd go to Saxmundham with Jim, so I stayed to early lunch, and we all enjoyed
the* superb *first fresh herrings of the season, brought by Brian[20] and then we went
to Sax and the colours were wonderful. I felt a bit anxious about letting Jim travel
alone, but he seemed perfectly calm. Ben wanted me to go to supper as arranged
in spite of all the upheavals of the day, so I went at eight, prepared to wait for him
to stop working (Miss Hudson's evening out so cold supper) and he'd just stopped
having had a terrific session at great pressure, and said he'd got to unwind. So*

[19] 'Jim's' subsequently altered by IH to 'a student's'. Britten thought highly enough
of *The Laughter of the Gods* to suggest that it might be done at Aldeburgh in a
concert performance, and as late as 10 October 1958 asked Butt: 'What happened about "The Laughter of the Gods"? Was it ever performed?', and suggested that the EOG might take it on. In fact the work had been performed
at the Cowdray Hall, Aberdeen, in April 1955, and displayed, according to a
review in the *Western Morning News* 'a power that was most exhilarating'.

[20] Brian Cotton, one of the local fisherman. Saxmundham is the nearest train
station with a direct line to London.

he had a drink but I didn't because I wanted to remain intelligent, and then he said he'd like to play it to me and it was <u>quite</u> *the most exciting thing that's ever happened; – the piano got almost red-hot when he did the trumpets: –* <u>marvellous</u> *entry for Q.E. and wonderful tune for her. Then the second scene as far as he'd got; conversation with Cecil, rising phrases with quiet top note at end of them, two-against three, and the last bit which he'd only just done that morning and afternoon was the best of all and he knew it because he said "*<u>that's</u> *all right isn't it!" So we held onto each other and then drank to it, and when I said he'd got the right Elizabethan flavour with contemporary materials he said I was to swear to tell him directly it began to turn to a pastiche. Then he went to put the soup on, and I remembered it* <u>just</u> *in time before it boiled over, and when we began the meal he looked* <u>really</u> *happy and said that life was good. And we ate excellent cold ham with superb orange and celery salad, and red wine to celebrate, and Peter rang up in the middle and Ben told him all the news, good and bad, and then when he'd rung off Ben began talking about Joan's voice and how he had it in his mind all the time he was writing. He said he'd rather play his things to Peter and me than anyone else (!!) because we knew at once what he was aiming at. I insisted on washing up so he dried and we talked about Mount Wilson observatory, and how solid the moon looked, and then he said it was* <u>very</u> *important to have one's own home (this was not really so disconnected, it all joined up beautifully.) Then we went and sat by the fire and he went on drinking wine but I couldn't because I was too excited, and he* <u>nearly</u> *finished me off by saying he was so grateful to me for letting him play it to me and I shouted "Come off it" but he said "no, I mean it, it's not false modesty or anything stupid, it's a fact, because I'd been so depressed about it – it's so near the bone, and this is the first time I've felt happy: – you're so encouraging." This was* [words erased] *unbearable to listen to, but it was all right because we are now so completely at ease with each other that not only does it not* [words erased] *say to him, but also it is getting easier not to disintegrate* [words erased] *when he says lovely things to me. Then we talked about technique of Elizabethan dancing, what to do in the Masque scene, and he played the Dowland Lachrimae* <u>superbly</u> *on the old piano which was frantically out of tune but it didn't matter a bit. And he produced volumes of Elizabethan keyboard stuff, but* <u>so</u> *badly edited – I must try and do something about the Fitzwilliam Virginal Book.*[21] *Then he was anxious that I shouldn't be too late in bed, so he walked up the hill with me and said that he* <u>thinks</u> *the doctor has cured his arm (!!!) because*

---

[21]   Britten's annotated score of five pieces from Dowland's *Lachrimae*, edited by Walter Budelko (Kassel: Bärenreiter, 1931) is preserved at the BPL. The edition of the *Fitzwilliam Virginal Book* was that of William Barclay Squire and J. A. Fuller-Maitland (London: Breitkopf & Härtel, 1899).

Queen Elizabeth. IH had identified 'Sellenger's Round', used by William Byrd as the basis of a set of keyboard variations and familiar to her from the *Fitzwilliam Virginal Book*, as an appropriate tune, and undertook to transcribe it for strings.

Plans for the gala performance of *Gloriana* continued to vex Britten. David Webster, the Administrator of Covent Garden, came to stay for the weekend on 14 October to discuss the opera and the possibility that the gala performance might also include a ballet. IH, meanwhile, seized on the opportunity provided by Britten's difficulties with writing the Masque scene to do some research herself into Elizabethan masques and dances; this was to prove invaluable to the progress of Britten's thoughts.[27]

> *Oct. 15th. Ben rang up early, at 9.15, to say Elizabeth was going to lunch & would I go too, to discuss the next move in the festival plans. But when I got there she wasn't there, as she'd had to go to Cambridge, so I took notes of everything he said, even during the meal. He is doubtful about Savitri – would those singers have enough authority on the <u>stage</u>? "If we do it, it must be <u>really</u> good." He said Peter had a frightful economy campaign on: – wanted to turn the Tchaikowski chamber concert into a piano recital. We agreed that we don't like piano recitals. Then it was 2 o'clock and time for his sitting with Mary Potter, but as we'd only just begun he said would I go on while he sat. So we had over an hour, with her painting him at his writing table, looking out to sea, and me sitting on the floor where I couldn't see him so that he shouldn't move, and we did lots of details, and I said all I wanted to about Evensong & the Vicar, and made him promise to fix a meeting with the Vicar this Friday and he loathed the thought of it and said why not Monday. We covered quite a lot of ground – the new variations are to be on an instrumental theme by Byrd (I'm to fetch this from Essex) and he's going to let me go to the Third Programme and try and sell them several concerts in the week. He approved of my suggestions about appealing for more money from Arts Council & getting local education authority people to finance dress rehearsal audiences. The only thing he sounded doubtful about was when he said he didn't want Herring with anyone else but Peter and I said that was one of the things we'd have to face – he agreed but didn't like having to agree. It was awful having to do all one's arguing without looking at him and as a result I got flippant. But we managed.*

Of Tchaikovsky's works, only the Piano Sonata was eventually to feature in

[27] IH's extensive notes are preserved at the BPL. Her main sources of reference were E. K. Chambers *The Elizabethan Stage*, I. Nichols *Progresses of Elizabeth* (1823) and W. Kelly *Royal Progresses and Visits to Leicester* (1884).

the 1953 Festival, played by Noel Mewton-Wood. But the Evensong was fixed upon, and Pears was in the end able to sing the title role in *Albert Herring*. Over the next few months IH successfully negotiated with the BBC to broadcast an Amadeus Quartet chamber concert on 23 June, the first half of the programme on 25 June on the Home Service, and the Festival Evensong. In addition, the BBC would broadcast a concert from London on 16 June, before the Festival, which would include some of the works to be performed there, particularly the new *Variations on an Elizabethan Theme*. They would also commit to making a feature programme to catch the atmosphere of the Festival, to be narrated by Alec Robertson.

> *Oct. 17th Early train to London. Ben appeared at Saxmundham, having taken David Webster in to the train. He said there were "alarming repercussions" of my date with Elizabeth the day before!*

IH had been to see Elizabeth Sweeting to discuss IH's view, already shared with Britten, that the Festival organizers needed to plan further ahead and in particular look at the possibility of earlier bookings for concerts. At the time, Sweeting didn't comment, but instead told Tommy Cullum, and 'next time Ben went into the bank to cash a cheque, to his dismay Mr Cullum was furious to him ... about my interfering with the way ... the Festival was run and everything ... he was so angry that his heart beat so violently that he was frightened'.[28]

It would be three days before Britten had the opportunity to tell IH the whole story; in the meantime he had a busy weekend ahead. On Saturday 18 October George Lascelles, the Earl of Harewood, and his wife Marion came to stay at Crag House for a few days. A friend of Britten since 1949, Harewood was President of the Aldeburgh Festival and had played a major role both in arranging for Britten to be asked to write the Coronation opera and in choosing the subject. He had also been asked to devise and introduce an evening of opera excerpts for the end of the Festival.

The next day they all went to a concert given by the EOG at the Odeon Cinema in Britten's home town of Lowestoft, where the programme featured Joan Cross, Anna Pollak, Pears and Trevor Anthony, with Britten at the piano, in a wide-ranging selection of arias and duets including excerpts from Verdi's *La forza del destino, Il trovatore, Simon Boccanegra, Un ballo in maschera* and *La traviata*. IH went in the company of Norah Nichols, a member and future secretary of the Music Club, and widow of the poet Robert Nichols.

---

[28] Interview with Donald Mitchell, 22 June 1977; BPL.

Sunday Oct 19th. Went to the Lowestoft concert with Mrs. Nicholls. Hideous place; – tried to guess which house Ben had been born in, but impossible to imagine. The usual cinema, with awful glaring lighting. Very good concert, especially the Verdi, which was superb. Ben said to go to tea with one of his councillor friends afterwards, so we followed his car and saw the crowds waving to him on either side of the road which was just right. At the tea party Peter said Ben might be playing act I of Gloriana at about 9.30 that evening, so I went in, in hopes, and got the information I wanted about the Aldeburgh operatic concert from George Harewood. Ben looking desperately tired and in no fit state for anything except bed, but to my dismay he agreed to play Act I, chiefly because George hadn't heard it yet. The end of Scene II is WONDERFUL.

Meanwhile Dr McCready, who was continuing to see Jim Butt, had become convinced that his patient's problems were more than physical: as he was to write later, he believed that Butt's 'glandular imbalance lay originally in some emotional factor',[29] and enquired of Britten if he knew, or could find out, what this was. Britten used the opportunity of a visit by IH to discuss a proposed Haydn concert in the Festival to open up the subject.

Oct. 20th. Ben rang & said would I go in at 8.30 that evening as he wanted to discuss the Haydn programmes. He came in late in a marvellous new coat with a fur collar, which miraculously doesn't look like Hollywood! He was in the depths of depression owing to wearyness: – had had a vile headache all thro' the concert and had been so depressed by Gloriana when he played it. After we'd been through the Haydn he told me of the row he'd had with Mr Cullum as a result of my suggestion about earlier booking for the festival, and said that he'd been so angry that his heart had beat so violently that he could hardly speak or move. He also talked about Jim: – the doctor says it was deficiency of pituitary gland brought on by worry. The gland can be treated, but what about the worry. He asked me about Jim's personal life, so I told him all I knew, which was the first time we'd ever discussed emotion apart from music. I came away early because he looked so weary. He said he'd play me Act I properly some time, but that just at the moment he was in the depths of depression about it: – I said that was part of the business, and he agreed.

Oct 21–22 London

On her return to Aldeburgh IH found a new guest at Crag House. Thérèse Mayer was the wife of Tony Mayer, the Cultural Attaché of the French Embassy

[29] Letter to Britten, 20 November 1952; BPL.

in London. Britten and Pears, together with the Harewoods, had stayed with the Mayers at their house in Aix-en-Provence in July, and taken part in the Festival there.

IH was now beginning to stamp her individual mark on the musical content of the Festival, over which her knowledge of medieval, Renaissance and Baroque repertoires was to have a profound influence for the next thirty years. Having identified 'Sellenger's Round' and devised the music for Evensong, she was now trying to interest Britten in a little-known piece by Thomas Arne, 'Now all the air shall ring' from *The Fairy Prince*, a duet for two sopranos with chorus and orchestra which she thought would be apt for the Coronation Choral Concert that was to open the Festival on 20 June.

> *Oct 23. Ben had asked me to go to lunch there. His french friend Thérèse who is recovering from concussion was there: – very nice and obviously truly grateful for all the help she is getting from Ben. He looked at the unknown Arne and said "yes", and suggested Sop & Tenor instead of 2 sops. Mary Potter came for a sitting and let me see it – she'd just washed out the eyes so it was difficult to judge, but it's going to be good. Went back to tea, before the Council Meeting. This, on the whole, wasn't too bad. Ben did it very well, and only once got dangerously near being upset by them. He brought home lots of points very clearly. The subject of earlier booking was raised by one of the non-executive members, & then discussed in full: – Mr Pritt very helpful. When it was all over, and I left for a Timon rehearsal, Ben gave me a large wink of relief.*

The artist was in fact less confident about the quality of her portrait of Britten than the admiring IH; a month later Stephen Potter noted his wife's self-critical observation that 'for deep reasons she cannot get him – though she always gets a side of him. "If only you will leave out my face", says Ben.'[30]

William Plomer was due to arrive early the next evening, and Britten had offered to collect him from the station in Saxmundham. But he found time to relax with IH, taking her out to the shingle spit at Slaughden, south of Aldeburgh, which divides the sea from the River Alde. On the river side, near a Martello Tower, was the picturesque wreck of the fishing boat 'Ionia'. IH decided to take the opportunity to cajole Britten into partnering the Amadeus Quartet, Pears and the contralto Anne Wood (who was also an Artistic Director of the EOG) in a concert of Hugo Wolf's music at the Festival.

> *Oct 24th. Ben walked in just before 4 and said come for a walk: he'd only got till 4.30, so we drove to Slaughden & walked along the ridge beyond the boat.*

---

[30] Diary of Stephen Potter, 30 November 1952.

He talked about the flight of birds, how they all kept perfectly together, never touched each other, and all without a conductor! "And we talk about orchestral technique & ensemble but we haven't <u>begun</u> to get near it!" Then he told me about his Uncle Willy[31] *who'd been a teetotaler until he was over 40 and the Dr ordered him to take a drop every now and then and he'd ended up by being 30 years in an alcoholic's home: – Ben at the age of 7 was sent as a hostage to try and cure him, and <u>almost</u> succeeded – he kept off it for a week, but then had to be taken away – there were bumps in the night, & someone wrapped Ben up in blankets and he was taken home. Then he talked about rehearsals – I'd been trying to persuade him to play for the Hugo Wolf in spite of having too much to do – and he said what he <u>could</u> do was to do a <u>very</u> little rehearsing and then just mesmerize them into doing it properly. "That's probably what I'm meant for," – "I'm no good at rehearsing, I just get bored and irritated. I can rehearse with Peter till the cows come home: and I can rehearse with Joan. But not other people".*

He thought he'd done the Council Meeting badly: – Beth had told him he was too casual. He asked me if I'd noticed how nice he was being to Elizabeth.

It was a <u>heavenly</u> walk; – very high tide; – waves on the river, and the air caressing. Then he played beginning of Act II Scene II ABSOLUTELY SUPERB. *Plomer was thrilled with it.*

Oct 25th London

From the beginning of the *Gloriana* project Britten and Plomer had been keen to imbue the setting with Elizabethan authenticity. Together they had visited the National Portrait Gallery in July, whence Britten returned with a handful of postcards of paintings of his main characters, and he was now planning a trip to the 5th Marquess of Salisbury at Hatfield House to see a letter written by the first Queen Elizabeth. A month earlier he had told Plomer that 'George & Marion (H.) have recently met & been charmed by Lord Salisbury & they (& he) are keen for us to pay a visit'.[32]

Meanwhile *Timon of Athens* was to be given at the Club Night at Crag House the next evening, with Pears playing the piano and Britten the viola.

26th. Spent quite a lot of the day going through Aldeburgh festival things with Peter, while Ben was at Hatfield looking at Queen Elizabeth's letter. Music Club

---

[31] Henry William Hockey, the brother of Britten's mother Edith, and an organist in Ipswich. Britten occasionally stayed with the Hockeys from the age of 8 and later described Uncle Willy as 'a rather reprobate old uncle, but … intensely musical'. Carpenter, *Benjamin Britten*, p. 11.

[32] 14 September 1952; BPL.

Timon in the evening – went right through – not too bad on the whole, though
bits were scared. It was lovely following the score in the Overture & listening
to Ben's viola playing. Peter did the piano part beautifully. Then when it was
over Ben suggested doing it all over again and wanted me to conduct because it
was difficult to follow from the piano. I didn't want to do the overture because
I'd never worked at it and didn't know the first thing about speeds or even cuts,
but he made such a fuss, like a small boy, scraping his bow on his open strings,
so I had to, and most, but not all of it went better the second time. Everyone
radiantly happy. It is wonderful *for the amateurs in Aldeburgh to have those two*
to play & sing with. Hadn't had anything like it since G in Thaxted thirty years
ago. Ben was thrilled with Q. Eliz's letter, but I came away directly, because he
was weary and hadn't had supper yet.

At Hatfield Britten, Plomer and George Harewood were shown round the house,
and invited to a lunch party. Of the other guests, Lord Hood found the visitors
'from the musical world quite charming', as did Mary, the Dowager Duchess
of Devonshire, who was pleased moreover that Lord Harewood was not 'once
allowed to mention music & so was very agreeable'. Plomer found the day
'unforgettable … we were talking all the way back to Aldeburgh, & later, about
the splendid things we had seen & the conversations we had had …' Britten's
own letter of thanks foreshadows the notorious reception given to *Gloriana* on
its first night the following June: 'It is hard to exaggerate how inspiring these
beautiful contemporary objects are. I hope you won't be too shocked when you
finally see the opera (as I hope you will)!'[33]

The next day Britten went to London, where on 28 October he went to the
EOG Ball at the Royal Festival Hall in the company of the Harewoods and
Potters, dressed as Pedrillo from Mozart's opera *Die Entführung aus dem*
Serail.

(Ben in London.)

Soon after moving to Aldeburgh IH had been advised by Britten that 'I couldn't
just do things for the Festival, I should have to earn some money, and he asked
me to be his … amanuensis … to help him get his scores written and prepared'.[34]
Until this point her involvement in *Gloriana* had taken the form of general
encouragement and imparting expert advice about sixteenth-century music

---

[33] Letters to Lady Salisbury from Lord Hood (28 October), Mary, Dowager
   Duchess of Devonshire (30 October), Plomer (28 October) and Britten (30
   October). All at the Archives of Hatfield House.
[34] Interview with Donald Mitchell, January 1980; BPL.

and dance. But her contribution now began to intensify as Britten started work on the dance sequences in Act II. She first lent him her copy of a translation of Thoinot Arbeau's dance treatise *Orchesography*,[35] while Britten for his part started to involve her in more general discussions about the score.

> *Oct. 30th. Ben rang up & said would I go round in the middle of the morning because he was stuck with the problem of the dances in Gloriana. When I got there he began talking about the orchestra on the stage for the ball-room scene: what instruments would they have had; – he'd decided to have violas for viols, so as to get away from the "sloppy brilliance" of the violins! He also talked about wood-wind and suggested 2 flutes in unison, high up, with the slight out-of-tuneness adding to the ⟋ loudness.[36] He talked about trumpets, and I mentioned the E♭ sop. cornet of the brass band which he didn't know, & I told him how I hoped it would one day be used in Bach. Then he talked about trumpets in Gloriana – he was enviously reading the lists of the numbers they'd had in 1600. I asked him how many he'd got on the stage and he said only three because he didn't think in all conscience he could ask for more, and I said of course he could, what else were the tax-payers paying for, and he said "well perhaps I could", and I said yes, for the Gala night, & then be able to have fewer when necessary, and he said "yes, I think I'll have twelve"!! (This is so far my only tangible contribution to Gloriana). Then he played me the end of the second scene in Act II which is most beautiful. After that it was awful to have to ask him about Aldeburgh festival, but I had to tell him all that Peter had said in the car coming home from London. He asked me to go round in the evening to dinner with Therese and Elizabeth. When I got there he was deep in Arbeau and feeling quite mystified about speeds and lengths of dances, so I said I'd go to Oxford the next day to have lessons on the Pavane, Galliard, Coranto and La Volta. Then after dinner we played Happy Families and were frivolous.*

Britten's enthusiasm for childhood family games was characteristic, and one of a number of domestic recreational pursuits that he enjoyed; IH and Mary Potter were among the circle of close friends with whom he shared this pleasure. The next day, as promised, IH travelled to Oxford to take lessons in the dances of the period from Margaret Donington, a contemporary from her school days at Froebel and a specialist in Renaissance dance and the recorder.

[35] Thoinot Arbeau, *Orchesography: a treatise in the form of a dialogue: whereby all manner of persons may easily acquire and practice the honourable exercise of dancing*, trans. Cyril W. Beaumont (London: C. W. Beaumont, 1925).

[36] In the original text this hairpin is filled in; in her list of notes for Lloyda Swatland, IH states that 'The ⟋ should not be solid!'

On 31 October the artist John Piper and his wife Myfanwy came to stay at Crag House. John Piper was discussing with Britten and Plomer the décor and costumes for *Gloriana*, which he was to design. Myfanwy for her part had been approached by Britten to write the libretto for *The Turn of the Screw*, still promised to Venice for the following autumn. But with both *Gloriana* and the Aldeburgh Festival lying between him and any real prospect of beginning work on the new opera, this commitment was becoming ever more burdensome.

(London & Oxford)

November 1952

By the beginning of November Britten was ready to pass on to IH the task of preparing the vocal score of *Gloriana*, so that the singers could begin to rehearse as planned in February. William Plomer was about to go into hospital for an operation, which further threatened progress on the opera, while other projects continued to jostle their way into Britten's preoccupations. Foremost among these was the EOG. As artistic directors, Britten and Pears were party to talks with the Arts Council about the future of the Group and its financial sustainability. They were also involved in a new initiative to set up festivals on the Aldeburgh model in Lowestoft, Henley and Devon, the last of these in collaboration with Britten's erstwhile librettist Ronald Duncan.

> *Nov. 3. I went round directly after breakfast & found the Pipers and Peter still over breakfast (Ben was dictating letters.) So I made Peter do the La Volta straight away! They talked about Ballets in general and Covent Garden in particular, and when the Pipers had had to go I showed Ben the dance steps, and he loved the cross-rhythm in the Galliard, as I knew he would. Spent over two hours going through everything thoroughly, and it was worth all the effort of all the journeys in the world.*

> *Nov. 4th. Ben walked in about 4 o'clock and said he was stuck in the dance tunes and would I go down and hear them. Half-way down the hill he told me there'd been another Elizabeth crisis – saved this time by Beth who'd had 2 solid hours with her. It had happened while Ben was in the middle of Gloriana, and he'd had to go on writing while quivering. When we got in he played over the two tunes – the Pavane very lovely; there was one new attack on a forte chord which cut across the middle of a double [bar?][37] & wouldn't do, so he's going to get a gradual crescendo up to it. Galliard, which he'd only just written that moment, was excellent, with Dowland-like scale passages, but thoroughly Ben. There*

---

[37] '[bar?]' added editorially by IH.

was a cross-rhythm which made the ordinary coming to rest on the sixth beat
very difficult in the middle: – at first I thought it wouldn't do, but decided the
choreographer could wangle things round it. Then he asked about the tumbler,
and in the same breath talked about the morris, so I leapt at it, and he showed
me a paragraph in Arbeau which mentioned a small boy dancing a morris jig in
aristocratic circles! So I showed him some steps and told him why they painted
their faces black.[38] *Then he made tea, & we talked a bit about the meeting next*
Sunday. And about the Arts Council. He talked about the difficulty of getting the
Devon festival started without someone there, and I said what about Peter[39] *&*
then before I knew where I was I was telling him about Peter being afraid of my
tactlessness. He was very reassuring and said it was the only qualification that
mattered. Just as I was coming away he appalled me by saying he'd got to go to
a piano recital in the Jubilee Hall and I said <u>must</u> *he & he said yes it was one of*
the things that had to be done if one wanted other people to come to one's things.
I think he's wrong, but couldn't argue then. Must <u>try</u> *& persuade him that he*
already does more than enough for people in Aldeburgh.

That night in the Jubilee Hall, a week before Armistice Sunday, Joseph Cooper
gave a piano recital of Bach, Liszt and Debussy, in aid of Earl Haig's Fund.

Peter Cox was the Administrator at Dartington Hall, and IH thus had extensive first-hand knowledge of his working methods. In fact Cox was unconvinced
by the EOG's plans to use Barnstaple as the centre for the Devon festival; he
considered the town 'unattractive', with 'too many second-rate people', and
with a type of holiday-maker who would not be interested in an arts festival.[40]

Britten summarized IH's advice regarding the morris dancers in a letter
to Plomer: 'Do you mind if instead of a "Tumbler" (which reference books
& Imogen Holst suggest was slightly lower class) we have a small boy (with
blackened face) doing a Morris dance? Arbeau (in Orchesography) has a good
description of one (in "fashionable circles") & the music is excellent and a
complete contrast to what's gone before.'[41]

Nov. 7th. Ben asked me to go round at 8.30 in the evening to hear the dances and
say whether they would do. I just managed to finish Act I Scene I in time and
took it round. He hadn't finished supper so I went & sat with him and we drank

[38] Morris dancers painted their faces black to conceal themselves both from evil
  spirits, and from local clergy and gentry, as many dances would have been
  performed when the dancers should have been working in the fields.
[39] I.e. Peter Cox.
[40] Minutes of an EOG meeting held at Fawley Bottom Farmhouse, 4 May 1952;
  BPL.
[41] 7 November 1952.

red wine and he was a bit distrait and said he was feeling horribly depressed
so I said I oughtn't to be sitting at the same table because I was feeling so much
the opposite that it would have an unsettling effect and he said "that's all right,
it'll unsettle the depression". Then we took the wine into the sitting-room and
went through some of my queries in the score and I told him he couldn't fit those
particular words "If Gloriana etc" for Peter in the ensemble because the rhythm
of ♪ | ♪ ♪ was so bad, also "hath made us brothers" on a rising phrase
   more than a
sounded wrong and he agreed & suggested it should be ironical! He said he'd
take them to William Plomer when he was recovering from his operation. Then
he played me the 1st half of the Lavolta and the little bit of recit leading up to it.
I tried to tell him how grateful I was for the weeks of working on Gloriana. He
walked up the hill with me in his beautiful new coat and I sent him home when
we got to the churchyard and he said "You've saved my life this evening".

[*Nov 8th–9th in London. Back in the afternoon.*]

As part of the economy drive for the Festival, Britten and Pears had offered
at the Executive Committee meeting on 12 October to host a tea party on 9
November to launch the 'Friends of the Aldeburgh Festival', to which they
would invite 'Aldeburgh people known to be interested in the Festival'.

IH, meanwhile, was throwing her energies into the EOG performances
of *Sāvitri*, to be broadcast from the BBC's Maida Vale studios on 14 and 16
November. The BBC had initially expressed 'strong objections' to her as a
conductor, but these had, for now at least, been resolved.[42]

Nov 9th Meeting of Friends of Aldeburgh Festival – Ben v. nervous saying "my
hands are already beginning to sweat!" But he did it beautifully, and people were
most impressed. After the whole crowd of 50 had gone we drank a marvellous
concoction that Peter mixed – Barbara was there, looking happy, and Peter Cox
came in and drank three on end!

The following evening the Annual General Meeting of the Aldeburgh Festival
was to take place.

Nov 10th. Ben said would I go in at tea-time & discuss points for Annual General
Meeting. He said he'd come to my Savitri rehearsal – bless him. Meeting very
good, in spite of appalling weather. Had to leave half-way through to catch the
9.55 at Ipswich.

---

[42] Memorandum by the General Manager of an EOG meeting, 15 July 1952;
BPL.

The meeting that evening was well attended and expressed strong local support for the Festival. One major item of concern, however, was the EOG's plans, reported in the *Leiston Observer* of 26 September, to establish a second Festival at Lowestoft. Britten and Pears countered local disquiet that the Lowestoft event would be in competition with Aldeburgh by saying that it would most likely take place at the end of September.

The meeting also discussed a proposal that a Veteran Car Rally be held on the last Sunday of the Festival. Pears observed enthusiastically that 'the strip of road between Aldeburgh and Thorpeness would make a fascinating track'.[43] Following a newspaper report of the meeting, however, this idea met with strong opposition; Douglas Goodrich-Meech wrote to the *Leiston Observer* that while he had few problems with the scheme itself, 'Sunday belongs to God'. Despite some uncharacteristically energetic support from the vicar, Rupert Godfrey, in the following week's paper, the proposal had eventually to be dropped from the Festival plans.

[*Nov 11th–17th. in London. Ben came to Savitri rehearsal at the B.B.C. on the 14th and made some very helpful suggestions and criticisms.*]

Britten had gone to London primarily to see Verdi's *Un ballo in maschera* and Bellini's *Norma* on 12 and 13 November at Covent Garden. He was in search of a conductor to whom he could entrust the first performance of *Gloriana*, and Anthony Gishford, a director of Boosey & Hawkes and one of Britten's most sympathetic advisors, who had seen *Un ballo* a few weeks before, thought that the young John Pritchard had 'much promise and might become very good'.[44] Britten was in fact more impressed by Pritchard's conducting of *Norma*, which featured Maria Callas's début role at Covent Garden, in a landmark production that also included Mirto Picchi, Ebe Stignani and Joan Sutherland.

Meanwhile Britten had written to David Webster about delays with *Gloriana* caused by 'the choice of choreographer. I have had to omit the first scene of the second act (the mask scene) because before writing it I must be able to discuss in detail the shapes and styles of the dances. If the idea of having a ballet in the programme on the gala night still holds, it will seem that Freddy Ashton will be all absorbed in it. In which case I should be only too happy if I could work with John Cranko ... He will also have by then worked with Basil Coleman at Sadlers Wells and they will know each other well. I know he is sympathetic to my music, and so would make a very strong plea for having him join

---

[43] *Leiston Observer*, 14 November 1952.
[44] Letter to Britten, 26 October 1952; BPL.

in what I am certain is going to be a very happy "working party".'[45] The young South African choreographer John Cranko had been introduced to Britten by John Piper and had already worked with the EOG and Basil Coleman on the production of Arthur Oldham's performing version of *Love in a Village* at the 1952 Aldeburgh Festival.

On his return to Aldeburgh Britten hosted a visit from a young friend, Paul Rogerson, a sixteen-year-old Roman Catholic who was committed to joining the Jesuits as a novice (although Britten did not yet know this). On a previous visit in April Rogerson had got to know Fr William Jolly, the local Catholic priest, who was a member of the Aldeburgh Music Club and also owned a yacht on which they went sailing.

> *Nov. 17th. Got back to Aldeburgh in the afternoon and coming back from the post met Ben in the garden – he said come to tea so I went to collect Act I Scene II. Miss Hudson very illuminating about him in the kitchen while he was making the tea: – he'd been saying that Paul looked sea-sick while out in a boat yesterday, so Miss Hudson said "Well Mr Britten has looked sick all Saturday and Sunday, and it's worry, that's what it is." So Ben admitted that he'd felt ill because William Plomer was having his operation, & said "But I'm feeling better today, so Mr Plomer must be feeling better too." A very breathless shy person arrived at the back door with a receipt for the subscription Ben had given to the chapel, and when she'd gone Ben said "That chapel! They've written to the papers complaining about our holding an Old Car Rally on a Sunday." Then Miss Hudson had a long harangue about a pair of woolen pants which Ben swore weren't his & she said they must be: – all in wonderful Suffolk dialect that got more and more like Essex every minute. Then we went upstairs to have tea in Ben's work-room because there was a fire there. He talked about Savitri – he hadn't heard last night's performance, & got back just in time for Friday's which he thought good but not as good as he'd hoped at the rehearsal. He talked about the bits of Wagner in it, and said how beautiful and haunting the simplicity of "I am with thee" is. Then he talked about Paul, who'd spent the weekend with him to cheer him up, and how he'd been very loving and it had been good to have him because he was so good and so beautiful. Then he said he'd play me as far as he'd got with the third scene in Act II – and said "I don't think I can bear it if you don't approve today, because it's been so awful writing it". But of course it was just right: – the morris[46] superb and the continuity between the dances and the agonisingly*

embarrassing bit with Q. Elizabeth & the borrowed dress. He said he hoped he'd
got Cranko for the dances. Also that he thought he'd found the right conductor,
because he was really impressed with the way Pritchard had done Norma. "So I'll
be able to sit in the stalls and listen!" I said "But you'll conduct the first night?",
and he said no, very firmly.

The Aldeburgh Music Club was now preparing for a repeat performance of *Timon of Athens* on 23 November, to be performed with an overture by Gossec and the Minuet and Trio from a G minor string quartet by
Haydn.[47]

Nov. 19th Ben rang to say would I go to supper before the string rehearsal for
Timon. Found him very distracted having only just got rid of a lame duck who'd
wasted all day – Also he'd had no news from William and was worried. We talked
about Gloriana – he's decided to have a Coranto at the end of the scene. I was so
delighted that I leapt up from the meal to kiss him and just at that moment Miss
Hudson came in to say why hadn't he found the shepherd's pie in the oven: it was
a very comic meal! He talked about Norma and said "If ONLY I could write a real
tune: – one day I will." I thought of several answers but none were adequate. It
was lovely to be warm. The players came much too early: – I only got half-way
through the washing-up (it was Miss Hudson's night out.) Timon rehearsal good,
& then they did their Haydn 4tet which was lovely to listen to. We were meant to
go through bits of Act I Scene II to see what I'd got wrong, but it was nearly 11 &
he looked so tired so I went home.

Nov. 20th. Went to listen to the broadcast of the Vauxhall programme with Ben
which was agony because it wasn't good enough & I felt desperate. But he enjoyed
hearing Peter sing. Afterwards we ate and there was red wine and he told me
how angry he'd been because of another message from K.C. about having a ballet
on the gala night at Covent Garden. Then he corrected my Scene II as far as it had
gone and he asked me to dance a Coranto and I could hardly move having eaten
& drunk so much: – (he wrote down the rhythm for the drum, & told me about
the ironical march he's writing for the Queen's second entry in the scene.) Among
other things, he talked about the sick state the world was in and how many evils
seem to be coming back again.

Despite her own misgivings, the Vauxhall concert, and in particular IH's choice
of music, was very well received in the press, with the *Western Morning News*

---

[47] Possibly Haydn's op. 74 no. 3, for which both Britten's miniature score
(acquired in 1929) and Pears's set of parts survive at the BPL.

calling it a 'refreshing experience', and the *Times* critic praising the 'delightful programme' beautifully sung by the members of the EOG.⁴⁸

Britten wrote to David Webster on the same day: 'Can nothing be done to stop K. Clark's silly mouth? I have, five minutes ago received yet <u>another</u> second-hand message from my Lord of Upper Terrace about the Ballet v. Gloriana situation (it was thro' the 'usual channels' of course). I am now informed that there is going to be a short ballet on June 8th – <u>before</u> poor old Glory Anna. Just like that. Anyhow you know that only over my dead body, dead opera too, will there be a ballet before Gloriana that night. Let them prance on their points as much as anyone wants <u>after</u> – but <u>not</u> before … Excuse scribble please – but I'm still shaking with temper!⁴⁹

Two days later, Britten celebrated his thirty-ninth birthday.

Nov. 22nd Got back from London at 10 pm & went into Crag House for the last bit of Ben's birthday party. It had already been going on for some time – champagne & lots of other drinks including Drambuie which was just right after a cold bus journey. Peter in good form looking younger & very beautiful. Tony Gishford was there, also the Potters. Everyone quite absurd: – Stephen whistling God Save the King & humming the bass – Ben doing flutter-tongue whistled trills on late 19th century walzes.

Nov. 23rd. Ben had asked me to go round with the score of Gloriana after breakfast, & to stay to hear him play it through to Tony. But when I got there they weren't up, so I left the MS & went for a walk. When I got back Ben had begun rewriting the new recitative in Act II Scene III – he told me how he'd decided that Essex <u>must</u> have something to say after the announcement that he was to go to Ireland – he couldn't just remain in a stupified silence. He'd been so full of what he wanted to write that he did the music before the words, and when the words came from William they fitted <u>very nearly</u> perfectly, with one or two tiny adjustments! While he was making the adjustments Tony & Peter went on having breakfast and I got Miss Hudson to let me dust the sitting-room. Then Ben came down and played the whole of Act II Scene III: – he couldn't resist beginning the wrong end although Tony hadn't heard any of it, because he'd got his mind full of what he'd just been writing. The new bit is superb – wonderful ironic march, and parody of an official announcement; terrifyingly agitato bits for Essex – then a wonderful recitative with comments from the chorus – leading up to the final coranto with the full orchestra drowning it at the curtain. Then he

⁴⁸ *Western Morning News*, 18 November 1952; *The Times*, 22 November 1952.
⁴⁹ 20 November 1952; BPL. Clark's address was Upper Terrace House, Hampstead.

played the second scene in the second act which gets more and more beautiful at
every hearing. He said he'd give anything not *to have to write the Mask for Scene*
I – and he thought Scenes II and III would make a complete act in themselves. But
obviously this is because he's still weary with the effort of having written the
dances in Scene III, and dreads having to do it all over again. Peter very insistent
that Scene II isn't right for the beginning of the act. Then Ben began at the
beginning of Act I and then just as he was finishing it the new dining-room table
arrived so we all looked at it – it is beautiful.[50] *Then Ben played Act II Scene*
II and I listened hard *for all the bits I'm working at at the moment. Peter very*
much moved by the second lute song, and obviously longing to begin work on his
part, and Ben terribly happy that he should be so thrilled by it. They discussed
casting and points about production. Ben asked me to stay to the meal off their
new table. Tony produced a bottle of Bols – it went straight to my head so that I
couldn't find the right word to say. However it wore off during the meal & I was
able to ask Ben if there'd be time for Peter to test his lute strings on the pause on
the low E♭ just before the 1st lute song & he said the first 2 chords were meant to
sound like a trial trip, but I insisted that he'd never have played a chord without
first testing[51] the open strings, so Ben said there'd be plenty of time during the
bar & a half before the pause. After the meal Ben talked business with Tony and I
asked Peter about Aldeburgh carols. Ben wants to come to Thaxted for Midnight
Mass on Christmas Eve!!! That would be lovely. *Committee meeting of Friends*
of Aldeburgh Festival at the Potter's house. Stephen did it very well. But it went
on awfully late & there was only ¼ hr between it and the Music Club. The Gossec
went well and looked *so lovely: – they lit the Salzburg candle & put it on the old*
piano & the players looked just right. Timon went better in most ways though
not in all. Haydn 4tet was more frightened than at rehearsal but the trio was
heavenly. Afterwards Rhoda told me that Ben wants to work at the Schubert C
Quintet!!!!! With the 2 Miss Rowes!!! No-one else in the world *would be as rightly*
crazy as this: – I didn't think anyone but G would have done that. Got so excited
that I lost all control & had a sleepless night in consequence.

The opportunity to play the Schubert quintet, with its two cellos, would
have appealed to Britten, with both Shirley Bayles and Dot Row among the
Music Club strings. And the composer's easy familiarity with the locals of
Aldeburgh extended well beyond these amateur musical circles. Another

---

[50] An elm refectory table, designed and made by Ralph Saltiel of Long Stratton,
    Norfolk, specifically for Britten and Pears, who paid £60 for it. The table is
    now at the BPL.
[51] IH typescript note: 'i.e. silently with gestures'.

frequent visitor was Billy, or Bill, Burrell, a local fisherman and friend since 1947, when the composer had first moved to the seafront. Burrell ran a bathing station immediately on the beach outside Crag House, and frequently took Britten and his friends out on his boat. Britten for his part was a ready listener to Burrell, who had problems of his own, and occasionally took him and his future wife Barbara for drives in his car, to get them away from the sea.

> *Nov. 26th. Ben asked me to take Act I round after breakfast as George Harewood & David Webster were coming down for the day & the night. When I got there he was finishing his coffee, with Bill sitting with him – very peaceful. Then Miss Hudson came in and was firm with him about everything, including paying his bills, and Bill teased him about his legs being too thin for the fancy dress he wore at the opera ball and Ben said, "The trouble with you is that you have no respect for your elders and betters" and that led Bill off on the old joke about Sir Benjamin, and altogether it was <u>exactly</u> the right sort of breakfast for him when he'd got a Covent Garden crisis on in the middle of "pushing" ahead with Act III Scene I. It is lovely to know that he has such peaceful domestic moments as this, as well as the occasional delicious relaxation of the light-hearted enjoyment of having Peter on Sunday. Then he gave me Act II Scene II for a few hours until the others wanted to hear it, and just as he was handing it to me he looked agonisingly doubtful because he wasn't sure about the end of the scene, so I reminded him that my copy wasn't final and was only meant for second thoughts. Terrific muddle of papers on his big table in his work-room: – yet he manages to know where things are most of the time, and if one asks for a score or a book he can <u>nearly</u> always put his hand on it straight away. I wish he'd get his work-room hermisealed like the rest of the house: – the east wind was getting in at all the cracks and he said "this is the sort of day when I have to sit on the stove all the time."*

David Webster's visit in the company of George Harewood was motivated by more than a desire to keep up with the progress of *Gloriana*. He came to offer Britten the post of musical director at Covent Garden, in succession to Karl Rankl. The composer had to consider the offer seriously, balancing the advantages, in terms of recognition and the opportunities the post might afford for performing his own work, against his loyalties to Harewood and the EOG, his perceived inexperience as a conductor and the demands of his composing schedule.

*Nov. 27th. Went round at breakfast time to collect Act II Scene II & found Ben &
Bill deep in earnest discussion. Ben asked me to go for a long walk with him that
afternoon as he wanted my views on the thing that was worrying him. It was
pouring with rain, but by 3 o'clock it had stopped, and he said we'd walk by the
marshes. As soon as he got out of the thick of High St he began to tell me about
the Covent Garden crisis – David Webster wanted him to decide then & there
whether he'd accept the post of musical director or not. Ben had told him that he
wanted not to have to think of it while his mind was on Gloriana, but Webster
insisted on having an answer. He had also said the most frightful things about
Ben's "duty" to music in England, etc! Ben had said that the only thing that would
make him do it would be if Covent Garden would take on all of them, ie the Group,
with George as manager. Webster said he wouldn't do that because people would
say it was turning into a clique. Ben furious, and said that everything that ever
got done in music was done by a clique – that that was the word that was used
when people disapproved, and that when they approved they called it a "group"
or something else. What <u>amazed</u> Ben was that Webster had objected even before
Ben had asked for the group as a whole: – he'd only asked for George when the
word "clique" was thrown at him. So he immediately felt that he wanted to say
No straight away. And he asked me what I thought. I said it would be wrong
for him to do anything that got in the way of composing, and although he did
lots of things that <u>appeared</u> to interfere, they didn't <u>really</u>: – whereas being an
administrator would be fatal. He agreed. He said it would mean 6 months of the
year, working in an office from Monday to Friday, which was of course impossible.
At this moment he caught sight of his favourite barn owl flying over the water
just beyond the ruined boat, so he stopped thinking about Covent Garden while
he looked at it. Then he went on to say that he couldn't be a "public figure", and
that he hated parties. And that he couldn't manage dealing with people, except
when he loved them or was interested in them – ("I'm not like you", so I quickly
said that I only managed to deal with them because it was a job that had to be
done, & I'd much rather be dealing with crotchets and quavers.) It was very wet
under foot, and every step sank right into the mud, but we got beautifully warm
walking against the cold wet wind. Then he said that when he was through with
Gloriana he wanted to do more concerts with Peter. And that anyhow it was
absurd to have a director who wasn't a conductor. So I said he was a conductor,
& he said he <u>wasn't</u>, & I tried to make him see that he only felt like that because
he'd not been at it long enough: – that there must have once been a time when
he couldn't play the piano, but it was too long ago for him to remember. I said
that if he could conduct a Mozart season for three years running it would make
a difference to music, & he said "I'll only do that in the Jubilee Hall." Then we*

met Bill's father[52] *out with a gun, and somehow, when we'd left him, we began*
talking about Ireland and Yeats & A.E. And the long line of willows with the sky
behind it, and how the very slight changes of level in the Suffolk horizon made
it so much *more beautiful than the flat skyline in Holland. Then we got back to*
Covent Garden again and he said that the trouble was that it was much too large
for anything except Norma and possibly Wagner. He said it was impossible to
time things like the end of a recit. & the beginning of an aria with such a vast
stage as that. He said he'd much rather be writing for Sadlers Wells than for
Covent Garden. By that time we'd got back to the house. He asked me to do bar-
lines, & voice parts in the full score of Gloriana. (Hurrah!) Over tea in front of a
blazing fire he suddenly said "Did your father get terribly depressed?" And then
before I knew where I was I told him how I'd neglected G during the last 2 years
of his life, being ambitious about jobs instead of ruling bar-lines for him, and how
it was one more reason why it was lovely to be doing barlines in Gloriana. Ben
said he'd been quite sure that he'd been responsible for his mother's death & it
had taken ages to realise that he hadn't been.[53] *Then he began talking about his*
compositions that he wrote when he was a child, & tried to find the full score of
his first symphony. He was still looking for it in his room when the clock struck
five, so I went up to say not to look anymore as it was time for Gloriana; – but
he was still depressed about Covent Garden & in the mood for playing me his
early piano pieces (including the tunes he used in the Simple Symphony.) And
then he went on to songs: – A marvellous *one called "Beware!"*[54] *Stacks & stacks*
of manuscripts written while he was at prep. school: – immense *full scores with*
beautifully clear writing and everything written in in detail. I asked him how
he ever had time for his school work & piano practice and he said "I don't know;
– and there were all the elevens[55] *as well: – I wish I'd got as much energy now."*
Some of the very *early things were pricelessly funny: – directions such as*
"semper ad lib." He told me that when he was fifteen he'd gone to London for a
lesson with Frank Bridge & while he was there he heard The Planets & he was
so excited that he came straight back and put in a discord in the symphony he
was writing! He said the only value in the stuff he kept from those early years
was the chance it gave of seeing how a child's mind worked. Then I left him to

[52] Hector Burrell, who liked to go out shooting on the marshes.
[53] Britten's mother had gone to London in January 1937 to nurse Britten's sister Beth through a bout of influenza. Beth recovered, but Mrs Britten contracted bronchial pneumonia and died on 31 January.
[54] 'Beware', to a German text translated by Longfellow dates from 1923, when Britten was nine or ten. Britten revised the song very slightly in 1968 with a view to publishing it; it was eventually published by Faber Music in 1985.
[55] IH typescript note: 'i.e. games'.

Gloriana and went away until the business meeting in the evening where he seemed weary.

Unsurprisingly, Britten chose to decline Webster's offer.

That weekend the visitors at Crag House were Erwin and Sophie Stein, parents of Marion Harewood. The Austrian-born Erwin Stein was a conductor, writer, publisher and at this time music editor at Boosey & Hawkes, and had become one of Britten's closest colleagues and most valued music advisers. Having now been asked by Britten to work with him on the full score of *Gloriana*, IH was also keen to see Stein, as she wanted to discuss the details and terms of her copying of the opera for Boosey & Hawkes. Her financial situation at this time was precarious. Since leaving the security of Dartington, she had lived from day to day, telling Jim Butt: 'In another four or five weeks it will have reached the stage of "where's the next meal coming from?" Of course there are lots of friends who will always give one a meal, but now that fares have gone up it's difficult to get from one free meal to the next. I'm looking for another job, but have vowed that it shan't be whole-time teaching, OR the BBC!!'[56] She had taken the work at Aldeburgh instead of this full-time job and Britten – who seems to have been oblivious to the state of her finances – was paying her piecemeal, while she lived in spartan conditions in her single room at Brown Acres.

Nov. 28th. Went round at 6.30 to talk to Ben & Erwin about copying Gloriana for Boosey & Hawkes. Covent Garden want to have the vocal score by the middle of Feb. Ben said he hoped he'd have finished writing by Jan 5. & could begin scoring then. I had to go before Erwin had talked about payment, as I was taking rounds and madrigals for the Friends of the Aldeburgh Festival. Ben came & sang with us (!) also Sophie & Erwin, and the Potters. Luckily the studio had warmed up, and everyone enjoyed the singing which was rough & ragged but occasionally quite good. They all looked happy. Ben was <u>immensely</u> impressed, and said so many lovely things to me on the way to the car that I was thankful it was a <u>very</u> dark night. The most practical of the things he said was that my beat was very clear to follow. I went back to Crag House to continue the conversation with Erwin: – the Potters were there, and luckily managed to get all the business with Erwin settled before we began drinks. Home late.

That night Stephen Potter penned a vivid picture of the evening, and of IH in particular, in his diary: '... the Aldeburgh beauty chorus is arranged for Imogen Holst to conduct them in madrigals. Imogen looks like an intellectual of the

[56] 19 April 1952; BPL.

20's cartooned by Osbert Lancaster, with a ... bun the size of a hen's egg. But she conducts very well ... Back at Ben's after ... instead of the ... suppressed feeling, a huge vulgar hearty laugh breaks from her from time to time'.[57]

December 1952

IH spent the last weekend of November in London, rehearsing Bach motets with her new group of singers. The previous week she had also spent some time at Uppingham School in Rutland, visiting Benjamin Zander, who was a pupil there. Zander had briefly studied composition with Britten before the composer passed him on to IH in September 1951, as one of his 'babies', as he had done with James Butt and would do again. IH had initially declined to take Zander on, as to do so would mean her travelling from Aldeburgh to Gerrard's Cross on a regular basis to do so. Soon afterwards, however, Zander and his father were taken by Britten on a rowing trip on the sea outside Crag House, and Britten offered to 'have a word' with IH, after which she accepted him as a pupil, characteristically refusing any payment.[58] This generosity, which was repeated many times, went back to her schooldays and was, as IH had remarked to Helen Asquith at the time 'all Gussie's fault ... he sees that people are anxious to learn ... and then finding that he has no time to spare, hands them on to me'.

> *Monday Dec 1st. Went into Crag House as soon as my train got in, to collect Act II Scene II: – Ben seemed depressed, but talked again about how much he enjoyed Friday's singing. I came away quickly because it was Gloriana time: – he asked me to dinner next evening. Told me of the* Elizabeth [illegible word]: – *damn the woman.*

> *Tuesday Dec. 2nd. Tried hard not to get to the house too early, and for once succeeded. Lovely fire: – during sherry he asked about my Saturday so I told him about Jesu meine Freude and he talked about "Trotz" saying it was so like a recitative. He also spoke of the $\frac{6}{8}$ section of Komm Jesu Komm, with its sequences.[59] He asked about Uppingham, so I told him all I could, about the down, about chants to organ and Stanford in B♭[60] (which he'd been brought up on but I'd never heard before) and small boys in black clothes, and he said it wasn't*

[57]   Diary of Stephen Potter, 28 November 1952.

[58]   Benjamin Zander, interview with Christopher Grogan, 19 October 2006.

[59]   *Jesu, meine Freude* is Bach's motet BWV 227; the fifth movement begins 'Trotz dem alten Drachen, Trotz dem Todes Rachen'. *Komm, Jesu, Komm* is Bach's motet BWV 229.

[60]   Sir Charles Villiers Stanford's Morning, Communion and Evening Services in B♭, for four voices and organ (1879).

*so bad when they had fantastic black clothes as at Eton because these were
comfortable to wear and looked charming, but the trouble was when they tried
to "civilise" the clothes because it made the children look like little old men on the
Stock Exchange.*

*Then at dinner he said he'd been depressed <u>all</u> the time. I said hadn't he been out,
because it had been a <u>glorious</u> day with wonderful colours and dry cold air, and
he said yes, he'd been a long walk on the marshes and the light was beautiful
and he'd seen about 20 curlews which had produced a slight incline of an up,
though not a real lift out of the depression. He talked about several rare sea-
birds – divers, but being ignorant I couldn't follow him. There was Niersteiner to
drink – 1949 – <u>excellent</u>, which made me so exceedingly happy that I talked too
much: – however, I made him laugh at the thought of Cyril Wynn[61] inspecting my
students at Dartington. Then he told me the story about how he'd been staying
at Harewood House at the time when the Stone of Scone disappeared from
the Abbey,[62] and one morning at breakfast when he'd been sitting next to the
Princess Royal she suddenly said "I think it's been stolen by communists who have
taken it away in a small boat." Ben rocked with laughter, thinking it a joke, and
said "What a <u>wonderful</u> idea, mam; wouldn't it be funny if they had!" "<u>Funny!</u>"
exclaimed the Princess. There was a ghastly silence, followed by: – "I am <u>most</u>
displeased!"*

*It was a superb meal: – Miss Hudson at her very best: – one of the things I like
best about eating there is that one is allowed to take one's wine into the sitting-
room and spend 2 hours over it instead of hurrying over it before it's cleared away.*

*Ben said he'd spent a whole evening playing viola & piano sonatas with Erwin,
including the Brahms! (clarinet).[63] I said <u>must</u> he, and he said there wasn't
anything else to play except some <u>very</u> bad pieces by Schumann. Then he told
me he'd been reading Sibelius symphonies as a bedside book every night from 11*

[61] Cyril Winn, music educationalist, writer, and at this time HM Staff Inspector
for Music at the Board of Education. Winn had visited IH at Dartington in
response to her application for more funding to pay for teacher training for
her students. He expressed some misgivings about IH's unconventional teaching methods, especially the 'absence of text books for teaching harmony and
counterpoint', but nevertheless gave Ministry approval to the scheme. Cox,
The Arts at Dartington, p. 34.

[62] On Christmas Day 1950, when Britten was staying with George and Marion
Harewood, and Harewood's mother, HRH Princess Mary, four Scottish nation-
alist students stole the Stone of Scone from beneath the Coronation Chair at
Westminster Abbey. It resurfaced some four months later following a huge
public outcry, having been deposited by the thieves in Arbroath Abbey.

[63] Brahms's sonatas for clarinet (or viola) and piano, op. 120.

onwards, and I got into a <u>fury</u> with him and he said he couldn't help having a conscience, and every now and then he had to get out the things he disliked and take another look at them to be quite sure he hadn't been mistaken. "Anyway I've done Brahms now and needn't get him out again for another three years or so." He'd been through the Arch-Duke[64] that afternoon. Sibelius, he decided, probably wrote when he was drunk. He realised why people liked him: – because he went on and on and it was sufficiently like the nineteenth century not to be upsetting, but with a suggestion of something "new", and a certain amount of "atmosphere". He said he'd read one of the symphonies twice running without realising his mistake: – he thought there was something vaguely familiar! This "chastisement" as he called it had gone on for a whole week. I said no wonder he was depressed and rowed him about it as firmly as I could. Luckily I'd brought the score of G's Choral Symphony with me, so I offered to lend it him as an alternative, and he cheered up and said he'd enjoy reading it. He opened it at random and said "I like the <u>look</u> of the thing, on the page." And then he said "<u>How</u> well he wrote for chorus: – I wish I could write like that." Peter rang up – he was anxious about Macheath,[65] saying it wasn't his part – Ben said "I don't know what he means; – it's good enough for me." Peter suggests doing the Vauxhall programme as a serenade at the Aldeburgh festival on the Sunday night. Ben said we shouldn't be able to get George Malcolm & he'd have to play himself – "two concerts in one day. I shouldn't be able to play the Mozart rondo as well as George did!" Then Beth rang up. I asked how she was, and Ben said "Depressed". So I said "[words erased] the family but she's got more excuse than you have because she's got a loser for a husband but you haven't written a loser of an opera." And he said "Well an opera isn't with one as much as a husband: – at any rate it's easier to start a new one."

He said he'd played the whole of Gloriana to Erwin on Sunday, straight through as far as it had gone, and he'd felt desperately bored by it and was convinced that it was "monotonous". There was no point in arguing about this, so I opened the score & I asked him to correct my Act II Scene II. He approved of my suggestion for seconds resolving onto unisons instead of the unplayable trills. Then he talked about piano playing, and told me how once he'd been playing Mozart with Clifford[66] (presumably the

[64] Beethoven's Piano Trio in B♭, op. 97, 'the Archduke'.
[65] Pears was singing Captain Macheath in Britten's realization of *The Beggar's Opera* in a broadcast by the BBC with the EOG on 5 and 8 December.
[66] IH typescript note: 'Curzon'. Clifford Curzon had first met Britten in 1942 (introducing his fellow pacifist to the Peace Pledge Union), and the two had performed in a two-piano partnership for a number of years.

D major)[67] and when it was over Clifford had been thrilled and had insisted on taking his chair & sitting by Ben's piano and asking him how he'd done certain phrases, and when he asked him how he'd fingered something Ben not only didn't know but was physically incapable of playing the passage in order to find out!

Then he said should he play me Act III Scene I as far as it went, and he obviously <u>hated</u> the idea of bringing himself to having to play it, so I said nothing at all, and he hesitated and decided first yes & then no, and then he said he'd play it but he'd probably stop. So he opened the score & sat down at the piano and was in more of a state than I've ever known him before in the way of being nervously wrought up (other than quarrelling with people – after all it was only me and he's used to me by now.) He stopped after the first dozen bars and shook himself and said "I'll begin again: – it was too fast." This time he played right through as far as he's worked it out, and he managed to calm down after the voices had begun. The music is <u>much</u> the best in the whole opera – truly great – immensely dramatic, with the personal conflicts in the characters extraordinarily vividly brought out, yet the whole thing, of course, depending on its <u>musical</u> needs the whole time, and the economy of material more staggering than ever. The C minor funeral march arpeggio chords in the bass of the quotation from the second lute song the most moving thing in the whole work. It was quite impossible to tell him of the overwhelming effect of the music, because there were no words for it – but I had to try and break through his depression somehow because after all what else am I here for so I held onto him and he bless him knows what one is feeling. After a bit he said "I'm pleased with the <u>silences</u>: – <u>they're</u> the right length anyway!"

Then we went back to the fire and he said he thought one reason for his depression was weariness, because apart from one or two business meetings in London he'd not stopped work for 3 months. Then we drank more wine and got <u>very</u> frivolous, and he told me about the Danish for Hamlet being "omelette" and "Ghost" being "Spook". And then he told me how once in Denmark he'd been desperate to know how to get rid of the vast laurel wreath he'd been given before going on to Oslo, so he'd staged a ritualistic ceremony and had cast it into the sea off the danish coast in homage to Shakespeare, with press photographers and all! He said he'd often left his laurel wreaths apologetically outside his hotel bedroom, only to have them returned by some bright-eyed page-boy! Then he told me he'd just had a letter from the Antwerp opera-house asking which was the more important character, Florence Pike or "Syd the Butcher", & we decided it sounded just like Happy Families, so we laughed a lot, and then we wondered

---

[67] IH typescript note: 'Sonata for 2 pianos' [K448].

what the Flemish translation of "Me father shot the brute in '63"[68] would be,
so we laughed a lot more. Then somehow we began talking about St Paul, and
being drunk with excitement even more than with Niersteiner I told him about
Sarastro[69] & he saw the point. Then I tried to go home, but he began telling me
about a discussion he'd had with Erwin about form, and how Erwin found it very
difficult to follow Purcell's forms: – Ben had played him "My beloved spake," and
he'd loved the music but had been bewildered by so many short and apparently
unconnected sections. I asked if Erwin had ever found it difficult to accept the
form of the Spring Symphony, and Ben said "No; – it's a good point. After all,
that scene I've just played is nothing but short sections one after another." Then I
said that I thought people who'd been brought up on the 19th century, especially
Germans & Austrians, & who couldn't get hold of Purcell's form could probably
come to him as a result of knowing Ben's music, & he liked the idea. He said he
found it impossible to imagine what it would be like <u>not</u> to follow Purcell. Then
he said "Aren't we lucky?" So that was too good an opportunity to be missed, so
I seized his hand and held it hard and said "Yes aren't we lucky, thank you" and
he looked embarrassed but pleased at the same time. Then it struck eleven, so I
went home. It was the most exciting evening he's ever given me: – I didn't think
anything could ever be more exciting than the first time he played me Act I, but
this was.

Amidst the stresses of *Gloriana* Britten still found time to relax, taking
out his viola for informal chamber music sessions with members of the
Aldeburgh Music Club, listening to gramophone records and reading. Two
young scholars, Donald Mitchell and Hans Keller, had recently published a
symposium about him, to a mixed critical reception. The volume included
articles by many of Britten's closest associates, including Pears, George
Harewood, Arthur Oldham, Erwin Stein, Lennox Berkeley, IH herself (a
'racily'[70] written piece on 'Britten and the Young'), George Malcolm (on
the Purcell realizations and *Dido and Aeneas*), and Paul Hamburger, whose
study of the chamber music included a number of diagrams of Britten's
formal and key structures. And in his own essay on 'The Musical Character',
Keller had written: 'What is this new personality? It does not show Bartók's

---

[68] Florence Pike, a housekeeper, and Sid, the butcher's assistant, in *Albert Herring*.
In Act II Lady Billows appoints Albert Herring to be May King with the words:
'Albert! Albert! Stand up to receive / This purse of otterskin – my father shot /
The brute in 'Fifty-six on Christmas Eve – / With five-and-twenty sovereigns
inside!'

[69] The wise priest of Isis and Osiris in Mozart's *Die Zauberflöte*.

[70] According to Eric Blom in *The Times*, 21 December 1952.

straightforward sadism. It does not show Stravinsky's equally uncomplicated sado-masochism ...'[71]

The book was a welcome diversion from Britten's increasing concerns over his commitments not only to *Gloriana* and the Aldeburgh Festival, but to *The Turn of the Screw*. He particularly felt his obligations to the EOG, who had been less than enthusiastic about him diverting his energies away from their need for new chamber operas in order to fulfil Covent Garden's request for the coronation opera.

IH, meanwhile, had begun to rehearse the Aldeburgh Festival Choir in Ipswich, in preparation for their concerts the following June. She had taken on this responsibility the previous year, holding auditions for new members in the Suffolk Rural Music School in Soane Street, somewhat against her instincts as she was, like her father, reluctant to restrict entry to anyone who wanted to participate. She later recalled that, following the rehearsals in the cold hall she would 'get off the bus near Britten's home ... "well, Imo, what was it like tonight?" he would ask: she would pour out to him her troubles and excitements, for he was always passionately interested in her progress with the choir'.[72]

Thursday 4th. Dec. Ben rang up to ask me to take Act II Scene III down in the evening, so I went in at about 9.30 and he was playing a Mozart trio (string trio) with Rhoda and the young American girl. It was late when they left, getting on for 11, but he was wide awake & produced Drambuie and wanted to know about the Ipswich choral rehearsal, so I told him how it had gone. Then he showed me the copy of the book about him & laughed a lot at the v. elaborate analysis of his early oboe quartet,[73] and read out a terrible sentence about "sado-masochism": – he said they must have noticed in my chapter that his favourite instrument was the whip! On the whole he was pleased with the book: – said he liked George Malcolm's chapters v. much. But the analysis diagrams in Paul Hamburger's made him think of one of Bill's nets. He said he'd no idea he was as clever as that: – "I've come to the conclusion I must have a very clever subconscious".

Then he talked about the summer and said he wished he hadn't got to write The Turn of the Screw in time for the September performance in Venice. I said couldn't Venice wait, and he said "Venice could wait, but I doubt if the English Opera Group could." He said he longed to do concerts in April with Peter and Kathleen Ferrier. He also said that he was wanting to stop and think a bit about

[71] Mitchell and Keller, *Benjamin Britten*. The Keller quotation is on p. 350.
[72] Wren, *Voices by the Sea*, p. 29.
[73] The *Phantasy*, op. 2, for oboe, violin, viola and cello.

composing, ("now that I know how clever I am".) I <u>had</u> to go, because of early
train next morning: – he walked up the hill with me and said that he'd had such
a pain in his head the night before that he was quite certain it must be a tumour
in the brain & had stayed in bed all the morning (Miss Hudson had said "it's
only <u>nerves</u>, isn't it," when I went in that evening.) So I told him it was one of
the things that happened when one was middle-aged, & he must remember he
was 39 now. So we laughed up the <u>very</u> silent hill – people go to bed <u>very</u> early in
Aldeburgh.

Britten and Pears already had a tour planned with Kathleen Ferrier for mid-
April, set up by Basil Douglas the previous March.

   William Plomer, now recuperating after his operation, was expected at Crag
House that weekend. IH had been spurring on the librettist's recovery, writing
to him in late November and receiving a reply thanking her for saying 'such
encouraging things – a great help towards getting well'.[74] Meanwhile, IH had
promised an article to *The Times* on her father's early music and sketches,
interest in which had been awakened by the discovery of his 1903 wind quintet. Entitled 'Holst's Unpublished Music: Discarded and Revised Compositions',
the piece appeared in the newspaper on 9 December.

Sunday 7th Dec. Went round to collect Act I & found them sitting over breakfast,
William Plomer looking wonderfully well after his operation, & Peter looking
weary after singing in the London fog. They gave me Greek honey to eat, on
the wrong end of a desert spoon. And then we went into the music-room & Ben
planned the day and I rang up Elizabeth for him, and then he played us Act III
Scene I which Peter hadn't heard. The <u>most</u> <u>beautiful</u> new bit after Essex's last
exit, where the ladies-in-waiting soothe her as they finish dressing her: – it's as
ravishingly tender as anything he's ever written, and <u>absolutely</u> right. Then I
went home to write 800 words for The Times, & went back at 4.30 for the first
committee meeting about the Music Club: – when it was over there was five
minutes before the next began: – Ben & William were discussing Penelope &
the Queen's dialogue in Act III: – William said that Penelope would flatter her
– "but Elizabeth was intelligent" said Ben; – "Yes, but even an intelligent woman
can't resist flattery" William began, but corrected himself by saying "oh, but she
was old, so she would have known better." Then they discussed words: – William
changed "Begone" to "Out", saying that it was what one would shout at a dog,
"or rather a bitch." Then the next committee meeting began. Went round to the
Friends of Aldeburgh Festival meeting in the Wentworth in the evening, and

[74] 29 November 1952; HF.

several very depressing things were said: – oh dear I hope it's not going to turn
out like a Festival committee! After it was over Ben took my arm & walked back
to Crag House & I congratulated him on not having lost his temper: – he was
obviously depressed, so I tried to soothe him by reminding him that they were all
right underneath, & he said "Yes, but if only they hadn't got the English habit of
having to hate what they love." Then he asked me if I really thought Act III was
going to be all right, so I told him how lovely the dressing-table song was and he
said "yes, I was pleased with that". By then we'd reached Crag House, so we drank
& Stephen Potter & William exchanged stories about early films, and William
made us cry with laughter.

IH later recalled that Britten's temper had been particularly stretched at the
meeting by 'Elizabeth Sweeting and Mr Cullum giggling … that sort of thing
upset him an enormous amount'.[75]

Basil Douglas, the General Manager of the EOG, was now working on the
Group's agreed plans for 1953. He rang Britten to tell him that he had to go
to Venice to begin the arrangements for *The Turn of the Screw*. Britten would
soon be forced into making a decision as to whether he could still complete the
work for the late summer.

Tuesday Dec 9th. Ben rang up in the middle of the morning and said would I
go to lunch because he'd got the titles of the sections for me. He was looking
weary, having just finished Act III Scene I. And worried, because there's so
much work to be done on the libretto of the last scene of all, & William's had
to go back to London to see his doctor. But the worst worry of all came out
over coffee, when he told me that Basil has been ordered to Venice to discuss
terms of the contract for the new opera for Sept. 53. Ben had been putting
off thinking about it, and now it's rushed at him. Obviously he won't be able
to write it in time; – he went through the arguments just for the sake of arguing
with himself. The worst of it is a Scandinavian and German tour depends on
Venice, and they won't take anything except a new work by Ben (for "snob value",
says Ben.) It's madness ever to have thought he could do it during the spring
& summer of rehearsals and performances of Gloriana. As things are going at
present, he thinks he'll be ready to start scoring by mid-January. He asked my
advice for ballads in Act III scene II and I didn't know a tune of the rhythm
he wanted, and I didn't know what acc. if any they'd have had in Elizabethan
England so was no use. He wants a fiddle to embroider round the straight tune
of the song. His first idea for the tune had a falling major 6th, sub-mediant to

[75] Interview with Donald Mitchell, 22 June 1977; BPL.

tonic, which he thinks too "hill-billy". He doesn't know the Appalachian ballads.[76]

He corrected my final queries in Act I and was very illuminating about dynamics: – said that with a voice it's so often more a matter of quality than volume. Then just as I was coming away he suddenly said he wanted to do a Mozart concert instead of a Haydn at the Aldeburgh festival, so we're going to start all over again! He said he'd like to do the Kleine Nachtmusik and I leapt at the idea but he said "Yes, but what would those few strings sound like?" So I said it would be all right if he didn't agitate them as he did in the Adagio last festival, so that they tried to do more than they could.[77] *I had to say it, but wished I hadn't when he was feeling so weary: – but my tactlessness is what I'm employed for, so must risk everything when music is at stake. I wish he weren't getting worn down by the constant pressure of writing against time.*

It was to be the end of January before Britten finally decided that *The Turn of the Screw* would have to be put back until 1954.

The following night Pears was in London, taking part in a broadcast performance of Berlioz's *The Childhood of Christ* at the Royal Festival Hall, with the BBC Symphony Orchestra conducted by Sir Malcolm Sargent.

Thursday Dec 11th. Ben rang in the middle of lunch and said he was going to London next day to see John Pritchard & wanted to play the whole of Gloriana as far as he's got, & would I let him have the sketches & neat copies: – he said to come & listen to Peter broadcasting in Berlioz's Childhood of Christ at 8.20. He said he'd been in bed with a cold for a day & a half, but had got on with the scene. I asked about the ballad, & he thought it was all right, even the falling 6th, which is good news.

When I went round in the evening he didn't look too good, and he was angry with Malcolm for his wrong tempi in the Berlioz. We listened to the first half, and in the interval he drank rum & I drank Drambuie and he talked about voices and conductors and how wretched it is that composers took the trouble to write just what they wanted and then they so seldom got it. When the second half began some of the choral singing was so bad that he switched off. He looked at some

[76] IH's own knowledge of the Appalachian folksongs collected by Cecil Sharp went back many years. In 1937 she had written the piano accompaniments for his *Twelve Songs for Children from the Appalachian Mountains* (London: Oxford University Press, 1937).

[77] Britten had performed Mozart's *Adagio and Fugue* for strings, K546, with the EOG Chamber Orchestra at the 1952 Festival.

*of my Scene III act II and then talked a bit about what he was working at and
said he hoped it was all right and did I think his music was getting better and he
wasn't fishing for compliments "at least I don't think I am" so I said very firmly
that I didn't go in for giving compliments and he looked so comically crestfallen
that I saw that laughing at him wasn't enough so I held his hand and put my
book down [words erased] and then I told him how thrilled I was with the detail
of light in "and how my lady shines": – the spacing and context of that chord of
the added 6th make it shine, as in the "Etruscan palace" chords in Lucretia, and
the delirious[78] light behind the eyes. It was helpful to have practical details. Then
he said he was always aware of what went on on the stage, as if he himself were
involved in it. Then we got to talking about Bach, & I said we'd raise lots of money
in the Friends of Aldeburgh Festival so that he could do more cantatas with
solo voices. And that got to talking of the future, and he said couldn't I possibly
arrange my work to stay here next year, and where did I really want to live. So
I told him Thaxted was the only place but that I was too emotionally involved
to live there just yet. And he said could I teach in London & live here the rest of
the week & I said I could probably manage another year as freelance: – but that
I'd have to learn to put my feet on the ground because I'd never been so happy
for 3 months on end before. Then he switched on again for the end, which Peter
sang very beautifully. Then I thought it was time to go, because he'd got a day in
London. And he looked so depressed [word erased] but it was all right and he
said "You've helped with Gloriana in more ways than you know."*

*Friday Dec. 12th. Went in at 10.15 pm after carol rehearsal, to collect Gloriana
and found Ben distressed because Peter was ill with a feverish cold.*

On Saturday Anne Wood arrived at Crag House to talk about EOG plans and
to look at some Hugo Wolf songs with Britten and Pears. Meanwhile, following the success of *Timon of Athens,* the members of the Aldeburgh Music Club
were starting to rehearse for their next Club Night on 15 February, which was
to include a selection of Brahms's *Liebeslieder* waltzes.

*Sunday Dec 14th. Peter better. Went round in the middle of the morning and
heard Peter, Anne & Ben rehearse Hugo Wolf for the Aldeburgh Festival. Then
Ben played Act I Scene II & Act III Scene I for Anne to hear – the second duet
is incomparably the best thing he's written. I went back at 5.30, when he was
playing it all to Basil. The effect of hearing it, more or less straight through, from
Act I Scene I to Act III Scene I, was quite overwhelming – Peter tremendously
moved, and when they clasped hands after Act III it was obvious that every*

[78] IH typescript note: 'or ?delirium'. The written text remains ambiguous.

*shadow of doubt about it had now disappeared for ever. We were all limp with
exhaustion, and then the <u>bell</u> rang, & the first of the Aldeburgh Music Club
turned up to rehearse the Brahms Liebeslieder. I let them in as slowly as possible
while Peter removed the drinks and Ben put on his tie. Then we rehearsed,
right through <u>twice</u>(!) Ben & Peter playing the piano duet, & the club members
standing round & singing in various stages of nervous apprehension. When it
was over (nearly 10 pm) they <u>would</u> stand round in groups & talk, so I whispered
to several of them that Ben & Peter hadn't eaten yet and had been working for 3
hrs non-stop before the rehearsal began. So then they went, and we had supper
– an excellent supper, but Ben was too tired to eat, which was wretched.*

*Monday Dec 13th,[79] went up to London with Peter; luckily Ben sent us to Sax in
a taxi instead of driving us, because the snow on the roads was slippery. During
the journey Peter suggested doing Lucretia in Thaxted church!!!*

*Got back by 8 pm & went down to Crag House at about 9 pm[80] to collect
Gloriana. Ben feeling ill and off his food. He was thrilled with the suggestion of
Lucretia in Thaxted.*

*Talking about helping people who were desperate, he said "one can't pick up <u>every</u>
pebble on the beach, because one's hands aren't large enough to hold them."*

*Tuesday Dec 16th. Spent the morning going through Savitri with Basil Coleman.
He is <u>just</u> right: – v. intelligent & sensitive. When I went to fetch him, he & Ben
were having a depressing conversation about the English Opera Group and
how difficult it was to keep it going. We went back to the house at about 12.30,
by Ben's invitation, but to my horror, when we walked in from the Crag Path
entrance, he was working in the music-room at Act III Scene II. He seemed
quite cheerful at the thought of stopping, and when I said shouldn't Basil & I
go upstairs & talk in his room, he said "don't be so school-mistressy about my
stopping work" – so I said I'd go to any lengths of awfulness when it was Gloriana.
Then we discussed the casting of Savitri. At one I came away, & he said would I go
in that evening to go through details in the final copy of Act I sc. I before it went
to Boosey & Hawkes, & when I said yes he did his usual polite thing of saying "are
you <u>sure</u> it's not a bore for you my dear," so I was determined to get even with
him for his remark about being schoolmistressy, so I said: – "Well, it's a choice
between you and your music: – just at present your music comes first, but you are
not <u>very</u> far behind!" He said "Pig!" and looked completely nonplussed: then he*

[79] Actually 15 December.
[80] 'pm' added later by IH in green pencil.

said: – "I don't know the answer to that one." (This was the first time I've silenced him!)

Went back in the evening and found him more depressed than I've ever known him – really exhausted with the effort of doing Act III Sc. II. He looked so weary that I wanted him to go straight to bed but he said he'd rather correct my neat copy. It was hopeless to try and cheer him up. When I asked if I could take Act III Scene I away with me he said "Yes, before I tear it up," – he apologised for being so "uncivilised".

Wed 17th Went in to collect libretto. His room has now been hermisealed and is lovely.

On top of her other commitments IH had taken on the task of rehearsing and leading the Aldeburgh Music Club and the newly formed Friends of the Aldeburgh Festival in their first venture to raise revenue, carol singing around the town. There was local opposition, however, to the proposal that the singers should be allowed to make a collection.

Thursday, Dec 18th. Ben rang up in the morning to ask about the carol rehearsal: – I told him not to come. He said he'd been having an awful time with Act III, Scene II; – had gone on working till 9 pm the night before, but that he didn't like what he'd written and that he couldn't hear what he'd written. So I said hadn't he been going at it too much non-stop, and he said perhaps, and I said I thought he'd probably need to recover after writing the very best scene he'd ever written, and this seemed to cheer him a little. He said I could hang on to Act III Scene I until Friday afternoon.

Friday Dec 19th. Went to tea; – Ben still depressed: said he'd had one of the worst weeks he'd ever known, owing to Act III Scene II. We talked about the book about him: – he said it made him feel like a small and harmless rabbit being cut up by a lot of grubby school-boys when he'd much rather be frisking about in the fields. I quoted one or two of Keller's inaccurate generalisations, and he said that it was distressing when people made arrogant statements – that he'd almost rather have the English "perhaps" or "possibly": – that Michael Tippett was given to wild mis-statements. Also Auden. And when he'd been seeing a lot of Auden, and Auden had been holding forth to a lot of "swooning" admirers, Ben would wait till they'd gone and then say "But Wiston,[81] did you really mean that?" and Auden would say "did I say that?" Ben added that it was all right in poetry, but it wouldn't do in prose. He said what a relief it was after wading through Keller on

[81] I.e. Wystan.

him, or Rothschild on Bach,[82] *to go back to William – he'd not been able to sleep a couple of nights ago (this was the evening he'd worked till 9 o'clock) and he'd read a whole volume of William's poems at 3 in the morning, and had enjoyed it. He also talked of Denton Welch's "Journals" – said it was much his best book.*[83] *Then we did a bit of corrections in Act III scene I and I tried to tell him a little about how thrilled I was with it, but it was quite impossible. He made some <u>very</u> helpful suggestions about the piano reduction, such as tremolo for the crescendo in the sustained brass entries. He said it was the octave E♮*[84] *which had given him the idea of the Coda: – he hadn't had a notion of what to do, & then when he heard the E♮ he knew the first bit had got to come back again. Then Mary Potter came in to take him to Badminton.*

After the carol practise I was desperate about the crisis in the Friends of Aldeburgh over taking a collection so I <u>had</u> to get Ben's advice though I loathed interrupting them with Peter & William both there: – door was locked & Miss Hudson gone to bed, so I had to knock on the window of the sitting-room & it happened that they'd been talking about ghosts! Ben & Peter both <u>very</u> sympathetic: – Peter got me a drink of wine & Ben agreed that the snobs <u>mustn't</u> think they've won, "or it will be the end of the festival." He said could we go & look at the portrait of Essex in Washbrook next day.

Britten's continuing research took him next day, together with Plomer, Pears and IH, to a house in the small village of Washbrook, just to the south of Ipswich, and then on for some Christmas shopping.

<u>Sat. 20th Dec.</u> Went down at 1.45 and drove to Ipswich with them: – pouring with rain, & prospects of carol singing very low. They all liked the picture, & thought it <u>might</u> be Essex. We shopped in Ipswich – crowds milling about in the streets and hardly an inch to park the Rolls. (Ben said "I wished I'd got a small Austin!") He asked me to get him some rosin, & when I'd been very particular about it being the <u>best</u> rosin, for violas, it turned out that he wanted it for badminton! We went to a second-hand bookshop in Silent St with some good things in it, but not as exciting as Bath or Bristol or Exeter or Penzance. Peter & William thrilled, and

[82] Fritz Rothschild, *The Lost Tradition in Music: Rhythm and Tempo in J. S. Bach's Time* (London: A. & C. Black, 1953) was about to be published. Britten and Pears had acquired a pre-publication copy.

[83] *The Journals of Denton Welch*, ed. Jocelyn Brooke (London: Hamish Hamilton, 1952).

[84] Both this and the next are clearly a ♮ in the original text, but appear as ♭ in the edited typescript. E♮s correspond with the score, and have been reinstated here.

would have stayed for hours, but Ben was cold, & we came back. It <u>poured</u> all the way home. They asked me to dinner, before the carols. <u>Marvellous</u> meal, but I daren't drink wine before working. William absolutely <u>priceless</u>, reading bits of the Leiston Observer out aloud during the meal. There was an account of a house that was going to be an Anglican retreat: – its motto was to be "Come ye apart".[85] "Hum, sounds a bit disintegrating" said William, and I laughed so much I had to leave the table. I went early to be there before the carol singers arrived, and it had <u>stopped</u> raining and the stars were shining! We sang up & down the High St & from the top of the town steps, and we were doing the round "For us a child"[86] while walking in the direction of the hospital – I was just fading them out when Ben rushed up & said "why are you stopping – that's Mrs Close's house!" (Mrs Close being one of the worst of the snobs who'd objected to the carol singing.) So I collected them under the light just opposite her huge house[87] & we sang Masters in this Hall & the marcato "Cast adown the proud" was <u>so</u> terrific that I've never heard anything like it:[88] – Ben behaved just as if he were 16 and I adored him for it; – I've never seen him being outrageous before. Then we sang in the hospital and ended up at Mrs Hales where she gave us drinks (soup!).[89] I had to explain that the singers didn't want a collection, & I had to say something about how we were glad the Festival needed our help because it was our only chance of saying thankyou. When we came out, and Peter had sung "I wonder as I wander"[90] in the starlight, Ben took my arm – and squeezed my hand very hard [words erased] it didn't matter because he was obviously happy and we walked together to the church porch and the best thing of all was that he began talking about Act

[85] Plomer had found the report in the section 'In Town and Country', which detailed an announcement by the Bishop of St Edmundsbury that a committee had obtained permission to run the nearby Leiston Abbey as a conference and retreat centre. A member of the committee prefaced a description of the 'aims and aspirations of the promoters of the project' with the title 'Come Ye Yourselves Apart'. *Leiston Observer*, 19 December 1952.

[86] An anonymous five-part round, later included by IH in her collection *Singing for Pleasure* (1957).

[87] Grey Walls, on Park Lane, near the hospital.

[88] GH's arrangement for equal voices of a French folk carol. Part of the text reads: 'Noel, Noel, Noel, / Noel we sing loud, / God today hath poor folk raised / And cast adown the proud.'

[89] Mrs Elsie Hale lived at Longcroft, on Priors Hill Road.

[90] Britten had made a setting of this in 1941, having seen it in a Schirmer collection entitled *Songs of the Hill Folk,* and believing it to be a folksong and in the public domain. Although a favourite in their concert programmes, however, Britten and Pears were not allowed to broadcast the song or have it published because of copyright difficulties with the original composer, John Jacob Niles.

III Scene III. Then we sang Break Forth[91] *under the church porch & went home
weary but happy.*

*Sunday Dec 21st. Went to Crag House at 2.30 to give Peter a recorder lesson but
it was such a wonderful afternoon that I suggested he ought to go out. So they
said "let's all go for a walk", but I'd got my best clothes on, having had Sunday
dinner with Capt. & Miss Basham,*[92] *so Ben brought me up in the Rolls & I tried
to change as quickly as Joan will have to in Act II Scene III.*[93] *Then we walked
over the marshy bit to the north of the town; Ben took his binoculars to look at
birds, but there were never the right ones at the right moment: – the light was
beautiful. When we got back I gave Peter a lesson & he solemnly played his 3
tunes to Ben & William, Ben being* very *rude. I made them promise not to come
to carol singing again that night, & left them in the middle of their tea-party
with Pamela & her children.*[94] *But when we'd* just *finished singing Break Forth
outside the almshouses at Thorpeness they both turned up, and came with us
to Aldringham almshouses and Mrs Agate's party*[95] *(v. painful with guests in
evening dress which made us feel like the "yokels" in a Hardy novel, shuffling our
feet because we were conscious of our boots.) The best bit was ending up with
Bach in front of the Moot Hall.*

*Monday Dec. 22nd. Ben asked me to go in at 9 pm to meet John Cranko & talk
to him about the dances in Act II Scene III. When I got there they were still
eating so I dried myself in front of the fire. Ben came in and gave me the libretto
of the end of Act III Scene III to read, to keep me going. When they emerged,
clutching glasses of champagne, they were all looking hot & happy – Peter with
a particularly wild glint in his eye and his hair standing up on end. John Cranko
with boy friend*[96] *in flame coloured sweater: – William more ribald than ever,
making outrageous puns. Peter gave me what was left of the champagne, which*

[91] An English version of the chorale 'Brich an, O schönes Morgenlicht', from
Bach's *Weihnachts-Oratorium.*
[92] Captain Kenneth Basham was a the founder of the Aldeburgh Players and a
member of the Aldeburgh Festival Council. Lilian Basham was much involved
with dramatic and musical life in Aldeburgh, including the Pierrot Players,
and was on the committee of the Aldeburgh Music Club.
[93] In *Gloriana*, Queen Elizabeth, in a show of spite, changes quickly from her
own dress into that of Lady Essex, in the space of a brief morris dance.
[94] Pamela Hope-Johnstone (later Cadogan), and her children Charles and Philip.
They lived at Framlingham, a market town about 15 miles west of Aldeburgh.
[95] Mrs W. B. Agate, a member of the Council of the Aldeburgh Festival and
Secretary of the Aldeburgh Women's Institute. Aldringham and Thorpeness
are villages to the north of Aldeburgh.
[96] Frank Tait, an Australian psychiatrist.

*helped a lot. Then they calmed down a bit, & eventually Ben played right through
to the end of Act III Scene I.*

IH was planning to travel to Essex for Christmas to visit her mother Isobel
('Iso'), now living at Westbury House in Great Dunmow, and to see friends in
Thaxted. The Crag House Christmas guests now began to arrive, including Iris
Holland Rogers, a friend of Pears and a linguist, who had made translations
of Britten's French folksong arrangements, and Charles Erdmann, William
Plomer's partner.

*<u>Tuesday</u> Dec. 23rd. Ben had asked me to go in at about 4 oclock, to collect
Gloriana, but when I got there he and William were deep in Act II scene I so I
waited till Peter came in and then we had tea. Ben said they'd done a lot on the
Masque scene and he was now feeling better about it. He said he'd correct my
first copies over Christmas and leave them for me to collect when I got back from
Dunmow. Peter fetched Iris, the first of their Christmas guests, and then I went
to finish packing – Ben gave me a large untidy parcel for a Christmas present,
with a letter "explaining it", and said he'd pick me up at the end of my drive at
a quarter to seven as he'd got to go to Sax. to meet the 7.10. When I got home &
opened the parcel I found that it was the original M.S. of Billy Budd, so I <u>nearly</u>
died, and when I'd read the letter I still more nearly died. It was a good thing
I'd done nearly all the packing or I'd never have caught the train. I sat over the
remains of the fire and drank the hot milk Mrs Farrington had given me, and
then when I was saying goodbye to them at the front door they pointed out the
lights of the Rolls, earlier than 6.45, so I ran the length of the drive and what
with emotion and middle age I was quite incoherent by the time I tried to thank
him – however, <u>as</u> <u>always</u>, he sees what one means when one means the real thing.
He said he'd come early because Basil Douglas had rung up about Venice and it
would have meant telephoning for a solid two hours, and Peter, who'd answered it,
thought that he'd already gone to the station, so that had momentarily saved the
situation. He said he didn't think that they'd get to Thaxted for midnight mass
because they were both very tired, "especially Peter", and it was quite a strain
having five people in the house over Christmas and things had already begun
badly because Charles had been too shy to come downstairs and William was
looking drawn & worried. We got to the station <u>much</u> too early for his train or my
train, so he parked the car outside and we sat in it right in the glare of a street
lamp which was very difficult. He said he hoped I wouldn't get exhausted working
for him so I said I'd never felt so strong because I'd never been so happy, and he
again said that he hoped I'd stay on. It was lovely and calm. Then he thought he
heard my train so we got out but it was only the Aldeburgh flyer and he said he*

envied me coming back so soon. He was kinder than even he has ever been before.
Then his train was signalled so he crossed over to the other platform and I went
to Chelmsford in such a state of bliss that the other people in the carriage looked
a bit doubtful.

Britten's letter to IH read: 'It is quite impossible to thank you for what you have
done for me & meant to me these last months – nor for what you've done for or
meant to so many of our dear friends in Aldeburgh. Everywhere one goes one
hears praise & affection for you, it is heartily echoed in my own heart. Over &
over again you have saved my sanity in so many different ways, by your energy,
intelligence, infinite skill & affection. My great worry is that it may be sapping
your own strength – but I have far too much respect for your own wisdom &
judgement not to trust you in that respect, as in all the others. And so I won't
bother you with misplaced avuncular advice! I haven't got a real Xmas present
for you, but I send you the enclosed with my love (I haven't got a proper copy of
Billy Budd which you want).' IH reciprocated by presenting Britten and Pears
with the autograph fair copy of GH's setting of the folksong 'Here's adieu' from
1905–6.

Charles Erdmann eventually came downstairs and enjoyed his visit: Plomer
wrote to Britten after they had left that 'Charles has continued to go over many
details of his stay at Aldeburgh in happy retrospect, with deep appreciation of
all your kindness'.[97]

January 1953

After Christmas Britten travelled to Leeds and stayed with George and
Marion Harewood through the New Year, in the company of Harewood's
mother, HRH Princess Mary, the Princess Royal. For the last few days they
were joined by William Plomer. At Harewood Britten finally completed Act III
of *Gloriana* and corrected IH's work on the vocal score, writing on 3 January
to compliment her on her work, which he found 'most beautifully written;
I was quite overcome with admiration for your writing; what neatness &
character!'

In his absence, on 9 January IH attended the meeting between the commit-
tees of the Aldeburgh Festival and the Jubilee Hall to discuss Britten's plans for
enlarging the Hall. The plans were rejected on the basis of cost and inconven-
ience, and because it was felt, the minutes recorded, that 'the character of the
Festival might be harmed by a more pretentious building'.

Pears, meanwhile, was in London, hunting for a town residence for the

---

[97] 29 December 1952; BPL.

couple, to replace a series of temporary arrangements they had shared with the Steins over a number of years, most recently sub-letting two rooms at 22 Melbury Road, Kensington. Their search had started the previous spring, when Britten had told Elizabeth Mayer that his sister Barbara was 'helping Peter & me find a flat somewhere because reluctantly we have all, mutually, decided that Melbury Road is not satisfactory anymore'.[98] Britten now wrote to him: 'I hope all goes well with the Flat arrangements. It'll be lovely to have something of our own'.[99] Pears also reported that he had been asked to sing in a projected production of *Billy Budd* at the Städtische Oper in Berlin. Britten responded enthusiastically: 'I was thrilled that you were asked to do 'Vere' in Berlin. Please do it, if you can. It means so much to all of us if you will'. Pears, however, mindful of his commitments to the EOG schedule for 1953 and 1954, declined.

[Ben at Harewood till Jan. 12th.]

Tuesday Jan 13th. Ben asked me to lunch. He was looking well. As soon as he'd poured out a drink I told him about the result of the committee meeting with the Jubilee Hall people expecting him to be furious, but he was grateful instead. I then told him I'd thought of doing an American lecture tour to raise funds for the festival and he was really thrilled & thought it an excellent idea. We went into the dining room & he suggested wine but I said no – that his first day back went to the head sufficiently and he said "well I must say I find you go to the head rather". Then during the meal he described life in Harewood, how all the rooms were terribly over-heated: – how he got up early & had breakfast in his own room and worked till lunch without seeing anyone. How meals were sometimes painful, because of the Royal Temper: – it felt rather like being in No Man's Land trying to dodge the blows when sitting between George & his mother. They'd got a lovely old Steinway in perfect condition, & he said "my music sounded quite good on it – awfully disappointing to get back to the one in the next room." Then he talked about Act III and said it was good in its form as a whole – each scene leading very well from one to the other with the right balance & contrast.

Then he talked about Christmas and asked about Thaxted, and also asked about [name erased] and I told him I thought [name erased] was pretending to himself that all was well. "Should we shake him?" asked Ben, & I said I thought Gloriana would shake him. THEN he said he wanted to write another full-scale

98 14 March 1952; BPL.
99 9 January 1953; BPL.

opera with William, on a contemporary subject.[100] *This was so exciting that I got up and danced round the room.*

Over coffee I told him about the Mozart Trio with the Misses Row. And he told me how depressed he was that Peter had turned down the invitation to sing Vere in Berlin. Then I asked his advice about Jim Butt & he was very reassuring and said it was weakness of character not of mentality. He said that the young seemed to think it was their right to get what they wanted. Also that they grew up much earlier than we did, so I said I'd found the man I wanted to marry by the time I was 15 and he said that was remarkable. He said there was no need to be frightened about Jim I must just tell him everything.

Then he played me Act III Scene III and it was so moving that he had to then practise scales out of it afterwards till we'd both calmed down. Then he played a little bit of Scene II which is absolutely *right – can't think why he made such a fuss about being depressed by it. Then he said come for a walk, so we went along the back lane*[101] *which I hadn't done since the Spring when he took me there in April and the nightingales were singing in broad-daylight in the bushes. He said it was good to be home, that it was lovely to take a long time opening one's letters, and looking at the pictures again. He described the Ravel opera he'd been hearing on gramophone records,*[102] *& said it was much the best thing of his that he knew. Then he went on to talk about the American tour again, & how I'd be able to go to the places where his operas had been produced.*

Then we walked along the field behind Brown Acres[103] *to look at a possible site for a festival theatre & he said I must live there. He talked about Peter's wisdom. (I'd told him that Peter had said that he mustn't be too angry about the Jubilee Hall and that we mustn't any of us get sour grapes over it.) "But", said Ben, "I'm wiser about Peter than he is about himself. If it weren't for me, he'd never have been a singer, and although* he *might have been happier, lots of other people wouldn't have been." Then we talked about press notices – this arose because I'd said it was odd that Peter got so depressed by bad criticisms, and Ben said George Harewood had shown him some press notices of about 40 or 50 years ago about Chaliapin, etc., making out that they were none of them any good at all.*

---

[100] *Tyco the Vegan*, to be based on a pioneering science-fiction scenario, had originally been promised to the EOG for Christmas 1952.

[101] IH typescript note: 'At the edge of the marshes by the allotments'.

[102] *L'Enfant et les sortileges*, of which Britten had acquired the pioneering recording conducted by Ernest Bour on Columbia, recorded in 1948.

[103] IH typescript note: 'Behind the church. Since built over with small houses'.

Then we went into the jeweller's shop as he wanted to buy a present for Marion
and then went back to tea and I told him the thing I loved him best for was
wanting to do the Schubert 5tet with the Misses Row. Then we looked at the score
of "Schmücke dich" and he agreed that the Violoncello piccolo obbligato would do
perfectly on the viola, & he was thrilled at the idea of Peter playing bass recorder
in the opening chorus. Then I asked him the pitch of the Tabor notes to put in the
dance scene, and as I was going he said how he was aware of Peter throughout
the last scene, even though he never appeared on the stage.

IH was planning to perform Bach's Cantata no. 180, *Schmücke dich*, with the
Aldeburgh Music Club in April, and needed Britten to play the viola. Britten,
meanwhile, seems to have anticipated the rejection of his scheme for expanding
the Jubilee Hall, and was already moving forward in his mind with much grander
designs, involving the development of a Festival Theatre in Aldeburgh.

> *Friday 16th, went in at 2.30 for a discussion of details about the festival.*
> *Elizabeth was away. Ben made facetious jokes about her having gone off to*
> *Boulogne for the weekend with Mr C. Ben was looking weary and depressed:*
> *– we agreed about programmes and singers and he knocked out the Trumpet*
> *Sonata.[104] He went for a walk to try & clear his head while Peter & I went to*
> *rehearse recorder quartets.*

On Saturday IH went to Thaxted, while Britten's own diary records that 'Basils
C & D' arrived at Crag House to discuss progress on *Gloriana* and also the plans
for EOG activities, which were now increasingly bound up with the developing
Aldeburgh Festival programme. *Sāvitri* remained an important part of the plan,
but in IH's absence it was decided that Norman Del Mar would take over the
conductor's baton. Away from Aldeburgh, the Internationale Maifestspiele in
Wiesbaden had committed to putting on the EOG production of *Albert Herring*
on 9 and 10 May, to be conducted by Britten with Pears in the title role, and
it was becoming clear that it would make sense both financially, and from a
rehearsal point of view, to repeat the production at Aldeburgh the following
month. The Amadeus Quartet had also been booked, to join Britten, Pears
and Anne Wood in the Hugo Wolf recital; IH was deputed to contact Norbert
Brainin, the leader of the Quartet, and Sigmund Nissel, the second violinist, to
confirm the date for this concert.

---

[104] Probably Henry Purcell's. Britten may have been considering this for inclu-
    sion somewhere in the Festival as a replacement for a trumpet sonata which,
    according to a letter from Leonard Isaacs to Robert Simpson in the BBC
    Archives of 6 January 1952, he was 'about to commission from John Addison',
    but which never materialized.

Sunday Jan. 18th. Ben & Basil Douglas met me at Sax. & took me back to dinner.
It had been a wonderful day (Thaxted had looked heavenly in the sunshine, and
fortunately they'd all managed to get walks in, during the intervals of their
discussions. When I got to Crag House & we began drinks they were all deep in
searching for bloody ballads for Ben to set for Peter & Kathleen Ferrier. We had
an excellent meal, and then sat round discussing opera for the Aldeburgh festival.
Wiesbaden wants Herring after all. It was decided that Norman shall conduct
Savitri after all: – this is a disappointment, but I'll be more use during festival
week if I'm not a performer. At 11.30 pm Ben suggested that we should break off
until the following morning, and he insisted on taking me home in the Rolls, right
to the door in spite of the tree-felling down our drive.

Monday Jan 19th. Went round at 9.30 & found them still at breakfast – that is,
the two Basils – Ben & Peter had been up & about for some time. I lent Ben my
Appalachian ballads. Then we had further discussions, and about 11 o'clock he
played the whole of Act III straight through. We were all limp with emotion, &
he produced coffee. He took Basil Coleman off for a 20 minute walk, leaving Basil
D & Peter & me to deal with Elizabeth & the next bout of discussion. Meanwhile
Covent Garden had rung up Peter to ask if he could sing in Zauberflöte that
night! We searched for his copy of the vocal score, but it couldn't be found. Then
Elizabeth appeared and we tried to get down to a business meeting but it was
desperately difficult with Act III still going on in our minds. When Ben & Basil
came back we had drinks, & in spite of my rule about never drinking during work
I was so desperate that I had 2 sherries & then had to have a cigarette to sober me.
As Peter had to leave at 1.15 I broke up the meeting at 10 to 1.

Pears had first sung Tamino at Sadlers Wells in 1943, and had been very well
received in the role at Covent Garden under Erich Kleiber in 1951; he was thus
well placed to stand in for the indisposed John Lanigan that night alongside
Geraint Evans, Ilse Hollweg and Joan Sutherland, under the baton of John
Pritchard.

   In addition to his other visitors, Britten had Leslie Periton staying at Crag
House. Periton worked for Chenhalls, the firm of accountants who dealt with
the composer's income tax returns. IH was also to benefit from Periton's advice
about her personal finances; spare pages in her appointments diary are filled
with the notes she took from their meeting.

Tuesday Jan 20th Went round at breakfast to tell them the Amadeus were
leaving for America next day – asked if I could ring up Siegmund about the Hugo
Wolf. To my horror Siegi said they couldn't do Aldeburgh after all! I was slinking

out of the house without letting them know when Ben caught me at the front
door & said "Was that all right?" & then saw by my face that things were wrong,
so said "They can't come?" Then he looked very worried so I smoothed the frown
out of his brow with the tips of my fingers & then when I'd got rid of it he made
a face on purpose, so I said it was <u>our</u> headache not his, & went off. Back that
afternoon at 5.30 for the committee meeting. Not as bad as some, but this was
possibly because very few were there. Most of them had to go early, and only
Fidelity & Elizabeth were left by the time Norbert rang me up. I got him to say
"Yes".

Fidelity & Elizabeth[105] began putting on their coats to go, & I went in to the hall
to fetch mine and Ben followed me & said "pretend to go & then have a meal with
us & go to the films with us." (Leslie Periton was staying there to do accounts.)
I said I'd rather go on with Gloriana than see any film, but he enticed me into
saying "yes" ("it's an awful bore <u>not</u> falling for temptation" he said). So I ran up
the hill & changed into my Cresta frock & ran back and was there just before
7.30 & was looking at the pictures over the fireplace when he came in looking <u>so</u>
beautiful that my heart turned over so that it was thumping when he embraced
me but I explained that I'd run down the hill too fast. Then Peter came in in his
old blue sweater & Ben made him go and change which I thought <u>very</u> odd of him.
Then we had a second sherry & I said I was going to take things in hand for the
Aldeburgh festival & not hang back, & that it was absurd that my phone call that
evening had been my <u>first</u> contact with the Amadeus about the festival, and he
agreed. Then he said that the decision about the ballet at Covent Garden would
have been made by then, & he was waiting for George to ring up. Then we went
in & had a marvellous meal with <u>wonderful</u> red wine & Leslie Periton talked
about wine which was very soothing and then the telephone rang & it was David
Webster & I couldn't bear the suspense of waiting in the pauses between Ben
saying "Yes?" and "<u>What?</u>" because it was agony knowing that it meant so much
to him, so I left the room. When I got back he'd just put down the receiver & was
going on carving as if nothing had happened. When we asked what the verdict
was he said "<u>Most</u> extraordinary," and told us that the decision had been reversed,
and there was to be <u>no</u> ballet before or after the opera. Immense relief all round,
& we then got down to the meal.

The film was frightful beyond belief – as Peter said, films <u>are</u> obscene. So we had
another drink.

They had seen the 8.30 showing of Jean Renoir's *The River*, starring Esmond

---

[105] Subsequently altered by IH to 'The committee members ...' in green pencil.

Knight and Nora Swinburne, a coming-of-age story of two English girls living in India and loving the same young officer wounded in World War II.

That evening, Pears reported to the committee that the EOG still intended to present a triple bill at the Festival, comprising a ballet, *Sāvitri* and *The Soldier's Tale*. In the revised schedule, the proposed Haydn series had been replaced with a Mozart concert, and the Veteran Car Rally was finally dropped from the plans. Discussions were meanwhile continuing as to how to set the Festival on a more secure financial basis, and Leslie Periton had been called in to advise while he was staying with Britten, who remained, as he wrote to Plomer, 'up to my eyes in the yearly tax figures'.[106]

> *Thursday 22nd. Ben rang in the middle of the morning & said would I go to lunch to discuss the finances of the festival[107] American tour with Leslie. I asked if I could have more Gloriana and he said "Ye-e-es" and then said "I'm being torn in small pieces." He didn't say why, but when I got there I discovered it was income tax. Peter had looked haggard with effort the evening before, but Ben was not only haggard but peevish. With a <u>great</u> effort he just managed to be civil, & we discussed making the Aldeburgh Festival a "charity" so that we could covenant for it. Leslie very helpful. I went away early & left them to it. But when I called in at 5 to collect Peter for a rehearsal, Ben looked himself again, – years younger & quite flourishing, as it was all over.*

[*Ben went to London Friday 23rd to Sat night 24th*]

In London Britten saw first David Webster and then William Plomer, in an attempt finally to resolve the issue of the dances in *Gloriana*. Now that the Royal Opera Board had dropped the idea of a separate ballet, Ninette de Valois had written to Britten to plead with him to expand the dances in Act II, and to replace John Cranko with Sir Frederick Ashton. Back in Aldeburgh later that week, Britten complained to Webster: 'I saw William Plomer on Saturday morning, and discussed the ballet situation in Act 2 Scene I with him. We will go as far as we can towards meeting the ballet's demands, but as the opera is planned (and the rest of it completely written) we cannot enlarge this scene out of proportion and wreck the work, nor can we do something out of the period and style. The work is a serious one and has never been planned as a hotch-potch ... About the Freddie v. Johnnie battle: I do not see why, if Johnnie were originally good enough to do the work in the opera (and I have

---

[106] 21 January 1953; BPL.
[107] 'festival' added later by IH in green pencil.

Dame Ninette's blessing on his collaboration in it in writing) he should now be inadequate.'[108]

While in London Britten took the opportunity to go to a performance at Covent Garden on Friday 23 January of Tchaikovsky's *Pique Dame*, with Parry Jones, Ronald Lewis and Otakar Kraus, conducted by Vilem Tausky. He also met the sculptor Georg Ehrlich, to discuss showing the artist's work in a sculpture exhibition being planned for the Festival, together with works by Gaudier-Brzeska, Jacob Epstein, Reg Butler, Lynn Chadwick and Elisabeth Frink.

Sunday 25th. Ben rang & asked me to go in for a drink before he went on to Woodbridge to have lunch with Beth. Said that the ballet situation was pretty bad, I asked if they wanted to introduce some Delibes into Act II Scene I and he said "Well, very nearly."

Monday. Jan 26th. I learnt from Basil Douglas, who rang up from London about Wiesbaden, that Ben was ill. So I went round to ask Miss Hudson how he was and she said he was in bed; – it was flu. She said would I go up & see him, but I said no, he'd only got to ask for me if he wanted me, & would she ring if there was anything I could do. She rang up later & said he would like to see me, & would I go round that evening. I'd got Julia[109] followed by Music Club rehearsal but said I'd be at Crag House by 8.30. Found him looking very mouldy but not in the least peevish. Lovely pictures in his bedroom, which I'd never been into properly before. He said he'd had an awful night. His worst dreams were hearing commonplace sequences going on and on. Bill had been in to see him and was very gentle. When I said I preferred not having company when I was ill, he said "it depends on the company." I told him the story of Lady Warwick calling on G. and he enjoyed that.[110] I left after about three-quarters of an hour as I hoped he'd go to sleep. He was terribly kind and seemed really grateful for company.

Tuesday Jan 27th. Looked in on Miss Hudson at breakfast time & he'd had a better night. I called in at tea & he was up but not looking v. grand. Mary Potter was there, & they talked about Whistler.

Wed. 28th. Went in at tea-time and he'd not had such a good night. I wished he'd have stayed in bed instead of getting up.

[108] 27 January 1953; BPL.
[109] Julia Keys, Secretary of the Aldeburgh Music Club.
[110] Lady Frances Warwick, the patron of the Revd Conrad Noel, the socialist vicar at Thaxted when GH was living there.

That night Pears, together with Dennis Brain and Noel Mewton-Wood, broadcast a recital on the Third Programme comprising Schubert's *Auf dem Strom*, Beethoven's *An die ferne Geliebte*, Hindemith's horn sonata and Tippett's *The Heart's Assurance*.

Soon after settling in Aldeburgh, IH had begun giving piano lessons to supplement her lack of regular income. One of her first pupils was H. W. Cullum's son Jeremy, who lived with his parents in Aldeburgh and had recently begun to work for Britten as secretary and driver.

> *Thursday 29th. Went in at tea-time and he was much better. He'd been out, but felt 150, with wobbly legs. He talked about Michael's "The Heart's Assurance." I tried to persuade him not to go to London next day, but he was adamant. It was such a warm afternoon that he said he'd walk a bit of the way with me (I was going to give Jeremy a piano lesson). So we walked down Crag Path very slowly, & I wished more than ever that he needn't go to London.*

Britten travelled to London the next day and went straight to Covent Garden to deal with the ballet situation. From there he went on to the Pipers' house at Fawley Bottom, near Henley, where he met up with Basil Coleman and William Plomer. While he was away, disaster struck Aldeburgh on the night of Saturday 31 January, as the town, together with much of the east coast of England, was hit by 'a storm surge of hideous ferocity'[111] and experienced severe flooding.

> [*Friday 30th. I went to London by the early train. Got back Sat. night. That same night there was the hurricane & the river burst its banks. On Sunday, Feb 1st, I went down the hill at midday & there was a raging river down Crabbe St. I asked a young man called Keith[112] to carry me across as he'd got fisherman's waders on, & I found Miss Hudson had had an awful night. I moved all the music from the lower shelves on to the first floor, stripped Ben's writing desk & collected all his manuscripts I could find & put them in the attic, between rooms in a passage without glass, & buried them in pillows. Keith came to fetch me: – I rang Ben at the Pipers in Henley and tried to reassure him. Then Keith took me back & I got home about 3.30.*]

---

[111] Summers, *The East Coast Floods*, dust-jacket.

[112] IH typescript note: 'Cable'. Keith Cable was a member of an Aldeburgh seagoing family, many of whom served on the lifeboat. In the 1970s he became secretary to the Aldeburgh Festival, and then House Manager.

February 1953

> *Monday Feb 2nd. Went round to Crag House – water had gone down, & nothing*
> *but mud in the streets. Ben arrived just after 12, looking ill and worried. I got*
> *him to give me Act III Scene III, & was glad to know he was going to sleep at the*
> *Potters.*

On the way back from Henley to Aldeburgh, Britten stayed overnight with Basil Coleman in Coleman's 'very uncomfortable flat which I shared with three other people in Fitzroy Street … He was very distressed – and very cold'.[113]

> *Wed. Feb. 4th. Met Ben at the corner of High St & he asked me to go in.*
> *Everything still in a state, and Miss Hudson looking weary. Ben had spent most*
> *of Tuesday trying to clean out the cellar. He said that after dark (the electricity*
> *was off) he went up to the Potters and Mary gave him an extra stiff drink and he*
> *managed to write Concord's song "all concords – that's the sort of joke one* can
> *make, I think." He was pleased with the scene on the whole; "sometimes God is*
> *kind." He said we'd got to have a meeting about the Festival that evening as Peter*
> *was coming down specially. Where could we eat? So I invited them up to my room*
> *& bought a bottle of the right sort of sherry, & a good Berncastle,*[114] *& stoked up*
> *a fire and lent them rugs & we got quite drunk & I wrapped the eiderdown round*
> *Ben's shoulders & Iso's fur coat round Elizabeth's. The discussion was depressing,*
> *because it hinged round economy. Ben lost his temper with Peter several times,*
> *which is I suppose what happens when nerves are on edge. I produced my half*
> *bottle of Drambuie & that helped. And he liked the story of the 2ndhand book-*
> *catalogue's description of "Girl of the Golden West. A little shaken. Spine weak.*
> *Otherwise nice." They left about ¼ to 11, Ben looking* very *weary.*

Pears had brought with him to Aldeburgh a sculpture by Georg Ehrlich entitled *Die Bruder*, for which he had paid £95 on 2 February. The piece was to feature in the sculpture exhibition during the Festival, and was photographed for the programme, before becoming a fixture on Britten's writing desk for many years.

> *Thursday Feb. 5th. There'd been a gale warning for midnight, but no more floods.*
> *Went round with Scene III just after 2, & found he was planning to spend most*
> *of the afternoon down the cellar again. Implored him to leave it to other people*
> *& get on with Gloriana, but no good. He looked better, however. And he said he'd*
> *play me the bit he'd done of the Masque scene before I went to my W.I. choir. It*

---

[113] Interview with Rosamund Strode, 4 May 1993.
[114] Altered to 'Berncastel' for the edited typescript.

was lovely – the bells at the beginning one of the most wonderful sounds I've ever heard, and the Concord song most melting. He said I could call back at 6 for Act III scene II. When I got there he was just going to take Miss Hudson up the hill to her brother in laws, so I went up to the study which was warm and practised Bach. He'd got his Ehrlich group of children on his writing desk. He made several suggestions for Scene III & said he'd go through it properly that evening. I asked if I could take Scene II & he was agonised because he's still got doubts about it. He said it would need time to get it right, and there wasn't time. He said a year ago he'd have tossed it off without any difficulty, so I said that was part of the business because since Budd it was sure to take longer, & he agreed. He said "You would tell me, wouldn't you, if it won't do: – you know how much I rely on your judgment." I tried to set his mind at rest, and told him something of how thrilled I was with the characters in Gloriana, & how it was beginning to emerge in Budd, but that was prose characters, like a novel, and Gloriana is opera. He talked about Budd and said that although it would never be a popular success he was very glad he'd written it, and to a few of his intimate friends it would always mean a great deal. He was very kind, and again said what a help it was having me. There were no words to answer this, so luckily he suggested having a drink, and while we drank it he said how difficult it was to settle down to work with all the devastation round us, and how he was longing to get back to normal and sleep at home again. Then he drove me up the hill on his way to the Potters. It was a very lovely hour, and as always in moments of emotion with him, it is the calmness that was uppermost, just as though that particular slice of life was already half-turned into material for music.

In addition to her other local musical activities, IH had also taken on the task of preparing a local Women's Institute Choir for their participation in a regional competition.

Friday Feb 6th. I went down just after 2 to go through Act III scene III before posting it and he criticised several things and was very patient with my mistakes. Said that he'd have to give up writing trill for timp when roll was meant – still OK for side drum, but nowadays when an actual trill was possible on timps it was confusing to go on using the old sign. He was going to spend that night at Crag House.

[Sat 7th in London.]

During her weekends in London, IH had been rehearsing her London singers for a performance of Schütz's *St Matthew Passion* to be given with Pears at St Margaret's Westminster in the spring. Meanwhile, in Aldeburgh, Paul Rogerson had been invited for the weekend before the floods had occurred, and although everything on the ground floor of Crag House was 'filthy & soaking' Britten asked him to come anyway '& cheer us up'.[115]

Another element of normality that Britten tried to maintain during these difficult days was keeping up with Pears's travels through his radio broadcasts: on 8 February the singer was scheduled to perform in a concert of Bach's cantatas nos. 180 and 189, with Szymon Goldberg, John Francis, Joy Boughton, Terence Weil and George Malcolm, broadcast from the Raphael Cartoon Gallery at the Victoria and Albert Museum.

> *Sunday Feb. 8th. Went down to Crag House at 9.30 am to see how they were getting on & to take Miss Hudson my present of real farm-house butter. Found Paul there, which was* excellent *because I'd just been wishing he could be there to help. I wasn't going to stay because I wanted to get on with Act III scene II, but Ben said would I help them get the Festival chairs & screens out of the flooded store. So I went back & changed into trousers & Wellingtons & we spent the whole morning in mud – luckily the sun shone. Miss Hudson produced* marvellous *hot coffee for 11ses & later we had Guinness. Ben was furious that the passers-by stopped and stared. He worked* very *hard & would insist on carrying things that were too heavy for him, but he looked much better. He wanted me to go for a drive with them that afternoon but I insisted on getting on with Gloriana. So he said would I come in for supper & listen to Peter's Bach broadcast. It was snowing when I got there at 7 & he'd skidded on the road taking Paul to the station & then some idiot had left his car* just *outside Ben's garage so we had to push it[116] through the snow. We then went in to the* warm *kitchen & drank rum while watching the soup and the rum went straight to my head but all the same I had sherry with the soup. As always he wanted to know all about everything, including how the Schütz had gone. He* almost *made me choke my rum by describing* [name erased]*'s[117] record of the Mozart Duo Concertante as sounding like an "elderly bullock"! I was completely light-headed by half-way through the soup & told him how I enjoyed the quaver rest at the end of each line in the boys song in Act III sc II, & how, having taught 13yr olds, I could appreciate its realism, and he said "it's because I'm still 13." He also said that tune was the only bit of the scene he liked. Then he began telling me about Paul – "Do you know, Paul & I fell in love with each other, if that is how you can describe it, a whole*

---

[115] 3 February 1953; BPL.
[116] Later changed by IH to 'his car', in green pencil.
[117] Probably a reference to the recording of Mozart's *Sinfonia concertante*, K364, by Albert Sammons, Lionel Tertis and the London Philharmonic Orchestra under Hamilton Harty, on Columbia Records.

year before we met." It was at a concert when Peter was singing the Serenade,
& they just looked at each other. Then a year later Paul went to the 1st night of
Budd & they met & Paul said "Do you remember going to that concert?" Then I
accepted a 2nd glass of sherry & we went into what used to be the sitting-room
to listen to the broadcast, & the damp struck a chill to the heart. Ben minded
terribly. Peter sang beautifully. We drank more rum in the interval, to keep the
damp out & he again talked about Tippett. And because I was drunk I said things
about texture & form which normally I'd have said to other people but not to him,
but luckily he agreed. I also said how lovely it was to know Peter, & he said "Yes,
one can't appreciate him enough." He enjoyed the Bach, but was looking weary. I
came away directly it was over.

The next day Britten was playing host to a visit by Leslie Boosey and his wife.
Boosey, who was sixty-five and had more than forty years' experience at Boosey
& Hawkes, had a dual interest in the progress of *Gloriana*, as he was both the
Chairman of the firm and a major benefactor of the Royal Opera House.

Tuesday Feb 10th. Ben walked into my room at mid-day while I was working
at Gloriana – said it was the stupidest fire-place he'd ever seen: – said he'd
been frantically tired all the day before, and said he'd reached rock bottom of
depression that morning owing to the dance for girls and fishermen.[118] *He asked*
me to go round in the evening when Leslie Boosey & his wife would be there. He
looked at my copying, although there was hardly any phrasing in it so that it
looked ghastly, and he made several suggestions. I went round at 8.15 but they
were still at dinner. Read 15th cent poetry in his study & then Miss Hudson came
in to make up the fire. I asked her to let me help wash up – in the middle Ben
came in having packed them off upstairs – he was absolutely desperate & quite
frivolous – he gave Miss Hudson & me a glass each of MARVELLOUS *claret just*
the right temperature & then I went up with him. Desultory conversation and
then Boosey asked Ben to play him bits of Gloriana. They didn't know the story
so Ben began telling them & then Peter rang up so I had to go on with the story
– very heavy going. Then at last Ben came back & played them bits of each act
– Boosey yawned openly and jingled the coins in his pocket during the 2nd Lute
Song, and when it was over he said "Very effective. You've managed to get away
from your usual style, haven't you? But I suppose when we hear the orchestration
it will sound more like the usual Britten." (!) I nearly hit him. Ben behaved
beautifully throughout: no-one can say that he's impatient – even G. couldn't
have been more longsuffering! It was too late to begin talking about America, so

[118] The fourth and fifth dances of the Masque in Act II scene 1.

> *Boosey said he'd come round <u>directly</u> after breakfast but had got to leave by 9.*
> *So I asked Ben if I might come to breakfast. There was a gale warning so I helped*
> *him sandbag his doorsteps before I went home.*

Britten wrote to Anthony Gishford that day to say that 'the last traces of mud
and slime are fast vanishing, thank God. We shall not be able to use the downstairs room for some weeks to come, but upstairs we are nice and cosy'.[119]

> *Wed. Feb. 11 Went round about 8.20 am, Ben not yet down – Miss Hudson*
> *allowed me to help which was a <u>real</u> joy. Then Ben came in and said the miracle*
> *had happened –Walton had actually sent his Variation for the Festival!!*

> *Wonderful coffee. He said dinner the night before had been absolute hell because*
> *Mrs. B had done the heavy wife "You know, Leslie knows <u>much</u> more about*
> *singing than some of the others, but they <u>never</u> consult him: – after all, he <u>did</u>*
> *choose all the singers for the Ballad Concerts" (!!) And then Leslie saying "Well,*
> *I don't know about music" – (pause in the hopes of denial) "and I don't know*
> *about wine, but I know a good wine when I taste it and I know a good voice when*
> *I hear it."*

> *Somehow the conversation got on to Harriet Cohen, & Ben described how when*
> *he was in his early twenties he had a work performed at the Carnegie Hall & she*
> *came into the artists' room afterwards, in front of everyone, & said "Let me be*
> *your mistress."! He said she was just like a snake, and it would be terrifying for*
> *any inexperienced young man to be left alone with her. Then Boosey came in and*
> *we went up to the study & he was friendly but not very hopeful about America*
> *& then he said he wanted to talk to Ben so I said goodbye & was going but Ben*
> *asked me to wait. 10 minutes later he came in, exuberant with the bravado of*
> *despair, and said "<u>Well</u>, I've had my talking to, and that's over. I've been told I'm*
> *<u>very</u> expensive to the firm." I almost wept with rage, but he took it calmly (he is*
> *<u>essentially</u> a CALM person!) and said "Oh well, it's worth it if they're going to*
> *keep Erwin on, & I think they are." Then Jeremy came & I went up to his room*
> *to copy out the 2 bars of side drum transcription he'd scribbled out for me, & he*
> *came up and <u>asked</u> <u>my</u> <u>advice</u> about a tune he'd given the chorus sops (!) and*
> *then played me the canon between Concord & Time. He's very nearly finished.*
> *I thanked Miss Hudson for letting me come to breakfast and she said "Oh, I like*
> *someone to have it with him – takes his mind off when he's depressed."*

The pianist Harriet Cohen recalled in her own memoirs how she had been
invited to a party given by Ralph Hawkes in New York for Britten and Pears,

[119] 10 February 1953; BPL.

and how she had 'had a marvellous time. There were great whisperings going on in their midst but the reason for this was deliberately not revealed to me until several weeks later'.[120]

> *Thurs Feb. 12th. Long discussion with Ben, Peter and Elizabeth*[121] *about festival programmes – lasted nearly all day, from 10.45 AM to 7.45 pm!*

> *Friday. Feb. 13th, Went in during the morning to give Ben the finished neat copy of Act III scene II and he asked me if I'd like to go to the Covent Garden rehearsal next morning. The wind was still raging, but it had died down by the time I caught the 3.30 train. He talked about planning the full score.*

With the composition draft now complete, Britten was taking *Gloriana* to London the next day for its first play-through at Covent Garden. The same afternoon, Lennox Berkeley's new opera *Nelson* was to be given a 'concert reading' at the Wigmore Hall. Pears was to sing the title role in a performance with piano alone, directed by the composer. Britten arranged to have lunch with Plomer before going to the reading together.

> *Sat. Feb 14th. (in London.) Went to Covent Garden at 11 for the playthrough of Gloriana in one of the chorus rooms – mercifully it was warm, as it was snowing. Ben arrived only 5 mins. late having left Aldeburgh at 7.30 that morning (Jim Balls*[122] *driving, thank God.) He asked me to turn over for him: – about 25–30 people there – Covent Garden directors, music staff and some of the caste. Frightfully noisy wornout piano. Ben played brilliantly right through without a break, to the beginning of Act III, better than I've ever heard him before. I had to leave at 10 to 1 for my Schütz choir at 1, so missed the last 2 scenes & the listeners' reactions. Then there was Lennox Berkeley's Nelson at the Wigmore at 3 – Peter sang superbly in it. When it was over, & we were in the artists room, Ben said "Bist du fertig?"*[123] *which made me feel quite homesick, so I put on all my warm clothes and waited by the Rolls at the back entrance. William Plomer in terrific form – it was lovely to see him again. It was a very exhausting drive back, & bitterly cold. We drank rum at intervals which helped. But it was good to get back to a calm Aldeburgh at 8.45. In spite of his extreme exhaustion Ben's mind had been full of the score on the journey and he asked about fencing, and what percussion there should be with it, – also what to do about viols in the stage orchestra – were violas the right answer – and so on. Miss Hudson had cooked*

---

[120] Cohen, *A Bundle of Time*, p. 281.
[121] Name erased and replaced in green pencil by IH with 'and the committee'.
[122] A local man, the son of a well-established Aldeburgh family.
[123] 'Are you ready?'

a miraculous meal and we drank v. good red wine (I'd had nothing to eat since
breakfast so was grateful.)

Now that the work had been heard at Covent Garden, Britten was ready to
begin the full score of *Gloriana*. IH later recalled the hectic routine into which
they fell: 'We … had to work for at least ten hours a day in order to get through
it in a month. I prepared the 34-stave pages for him, spacing the bar-lines, writing the clefs and signatures, copying out the vocal lines, and eventually filling
in any instruments that were to be doubled. We sat side by side at separate
tables …'[124]

Meanwhile, the Aldeburgh Music Club had met to discuss whether to
cancel their 15 February Club Night because of the floods, but had decided
to go ahead, relocating to the Potters' house. The programme comprised the
Andante from Bach's Brandenburg Concerto no. 4 (with Britten playing viola);
a cello sonata by DeFesch, three songs by Henry VIII arranged for recorder
quartet (including IH and 'Peter Pears playing Bass Recorder for the first time')
and the Brahms *Liebeslieder* waltzes, conducted by Pears.

Sunday. Feb 15th. Ben had said "don't exaggerate the 9.30 start" so I turned up
at 10 and they were still at breakfast. Then we got down to work on the score
and I realised that I shall never be able to keep up with him. He writes it quicker
than one could ever believe would be possible. He's leaving doublings for me to fill
in, and he thinks he can get through by the time they go away in mid-March. He
was feeling v. depressed as a result of being so weary, but he cheered up a bit after
he'd had a walk with Peter. They asked me to stay to supper before the music club
meeting, so I took the bottle of champagne Peter produced after the floods in the
hopes that it would cheer Ben, but he was still very low. The music club went well
on the whole, and Peter's bass recorder was a great success.

Monday. Feb 16th. The hardest day's work I've ever done. Began scoring at 9 &
worked feverishly to keep pace with him – then at about 11.30 got absolute panic
because I'd numbered his pages wrong, but by a miracle the music was OK so
all was well but it was the worst moment I've ever had with him & I expected
the sack. As I couldn't keep pace with him I went back at 2 and worked till the
Festival discussion at 4.30, and again from 6.30–7.30. Ben had written 28 pages
of full score in one day. I suppose I shall learn to be quicker as it goes on, but I
hope to heaven I don't keep him waiting. He was v. kind and never got peevish.

Rapid though Britten's scoring undoubtedly was, one reason that IH was unable

---

[124] IH, 'Working for Benjamin Britten', p. 202.

to 'keep up' with him was her self-imposed practice of unaccountably drawing a separate bar-line for every instrumental stave, rather than across the system or the page. IH later recalled that her only opportunities to catch up occurred when 'he happened to notice a rare bird flying out to sea: he would then break off work for a few minutes to look at it through his binoculars'.[125]

> *Tuesday Feb 17th. Got to Crag House at 8.45 & began working feverishly to catch up, but was saved by the fact that Ben had to think for nearly an hour about the contrapuntal entries in "Green leaves", because the tune had such a large compass that it ran over the edge of practically every instrument. Owing to this I got enough done to supply him, & began to breathe again. Peter wanted to practise recorders in the afternoon, so I stopped for ½ hr & then went to see how far Ben had got and to my horror I hadn't left him nearly enough room for the semiquavers in the fishwives wrangle – this was awful, but he was still calm & kind. And then I'd squashed him up too much for Raleigh's song. V. tired by 7.45 and didn't get much vocal score done that evening.*

The next day Pears was leaving for a recital tour of Scotland with Noel Mewton-Wood. Over the next ten days he would perform recitals in Dundee, Milngavie and Edinburgh, before singing Bach and Mozart in a concert in Glasgow with the Scottish National Orchestra under Karl Rankl.

Attempts to buy a flat in Harley Street were causing renewed difficulties for the couple, but Britten was distracted nearer home by an impending visit by Eric Crozier, co-founder of the Aldeburgh Festival and EOG, producer of the first *Peter Grimes* and librettist of *The Little Sweep*, *Saint Nicolas* and, with E. M. Forster, *Billy Budd*. Once one of Britten's closest colleagues and friends, the composer's relationship with him had now cooled considerably.

> *Wed. Feb. 18th. Ben had an interrupted morning with builders coming to look at the flood damage and Peter going off to Scotland, and news that their London flat may not materialise after all. He looked very tired and dreaded his evening with Eric. He couldn't remember which trombone position change was the awkward one, & had to work it out. This was the first time I'd ever known him not know something about music. In spite of being rushed and weary he kept up a priceless intermittent conversation throughout the hours of work, saying how glad he was that he'd refused that Dr. of music the day before. He said he needed a stiff drink before Eric came, so I had one too because I was desperate – and when I thanked him for the day he leaned his hot-from-the-bath cheek against mine and said "thank you a million times; you are very wonderful help to me."*

[125] IH, *Britten*, 3rd edn, p. 55.

Thursday Feb 19th. He was still feeling depressed about Eric when I went down to begin the morning's work. And there were <u>so</u> many notes at the end of Act I Scene I! But I plucked up all my courage to say that I thought the 3½ bars in the "behold the sower" bit in the Masque scene were weak: – he said "I don't think you're right, but I'll look into it." Then I had a telegram from Curwen's[126] and he was very kind & let me ring up & fix a meeting next day. It was a lovely afternoon, and he said "let's go for a walk", so we drove out to Snape and walked along by the marshes and the colours were lovely, he was particularly thrilled with the purply-brown of last year's heather which he thought was a mournful colour. He said that stretch of the marsh always reminded him of the end of Peter Grimes because while he was writing the last scene Beth & her children asked him to spend the day with them on a picnic & he said he couldn't but would try & join them by lunch time, and he finished it that morning & was with them by 1. He was priceless in his description of Lennox walking up & down that path in his dark London clothes all the years they lived at Snape.[127]

When we got back he said that there'd be no need for me to have got all the doublings in the score before he went abroad, and I said I could have it all ready for him to correct as soon as he got back & he said "Oh but there'd be no need to correct it" and I said I didn't trust myself an inch and he said "but <u>I</u> do!"

[Friday 20th, Sunday 22nd, in London & Dorset.]

The London property situation remained unresolved. Britten wrote to Pears:[128] 'I had expected you to ring about the flat … Do let me know, because if it (the Harley St) has fallen through, then I've got a plan of flat-hunting which I can set in motion, (friend of Imo's – as you might imagine).' He added: 'We've got a Friends meeting to-morrow night. Hope it'll go alright. They'll need pushing abit I think, but Stephen is quite keen & energetic.'

Sunday Feb 22nd. Got back from Dorset in the evening, went into Crag House to collect the Masque scene – Ben & William working at the libretto. Ben said stay to supper, but I said I was too dirty. However, he said "Why not have a bath", so I did, & recovered immediately from old age and exhaustion. Had a quick supper with <u>wonderful</u> soup and white wine & garlicky salad & then we had to rush to

126 J. Curwen & Sons, the music publishers, who had agreed to issue IH's edition and arrangement for female voices and orchestra of Handel's *L'Allegro, il Penseroso, ed il Moderato*.

127 Lennox Berkeley had lived with Britten at the Old Mill, Snape, in the late 1930s.

128 The letter is dated 22 February 1953, but may be 21 February, as Britten refers to the Friends' meeting as occurring 'to-morrow night'.

*the Friends of the Festival meeting and to my dismay Ben insisted on staying
to part of the gramophone recital out of politeness. But I went back to William
who said it was no good fretting, Ben would always be like that and one wouldn't
want to change anything about him. But I still felt it was a mistake and that he
oughtn't to squander his energy on things that don't matter. He came in, half an
hour later, quite desperate, and soon after I went home.*

Stephen Potter recalled that Britten slipped out of the gramophone recital half-
way through, with IH following, 'wide-eyed and secret with the anticipation of
more work for the Master'.[129]

*Monday Feb 23rd. Got to Crag House before he was back from Saxmundham,
seeing William off. He came in and worked very hard but moaned and said he
was <u>bored</u>: – "the trouble about me is that I'm catastrophically lazy" !!! I had to
work v. hard to keep pace with him. Then in the afternoon he motored to Ipswich
to fetch George Harewood: when they got back he played us the Masque scene as
George hadn't heard it, and the bells sounded lovelier than ever, and he'd altered
the 3½ bars, going to C instead of G – <u>much</u> better. I took it home to copy it.*

Britten's 'boredom' was exacerbated by the fact that he was missing not only
Pears's company but also their recitals together, reluctantly suspended for the
duration of *Gloriana*. He wrote to Pears on 23 February: 'however good Noel
is, I am certain that you & I together have something very special, & it won't be
long before <u>that</u> happens again!' Also featuring in the composer's plans was a
holiday in Greece with Pears and the Harewoods to celebrate the completion of
the full score of *Gloriana*, but further delays now threatened as Jeremy Cullum,
his secretary, contracted shingles.

*Tuesday Feb 24th. One of the best days I've <u>ever</u> had. As I was ahead with
planning and barlines I was able to fill in some doublings, and do a bit of
correcting – absolutely <u>thrilling</u>. Poor Ben very weary as he & George had talked
far into the night. He asked me to stay to lunch and during the meal he talked
about the disadvantages of a public-school upbringing because of always having
a feeling about loyalty, which got in the way so often – for instance Peter being
"loyal" to the English Opera Group and not singing Vere in Berlin. He then said
that it was probably only this conventional loyalty that had made him stay on
to the gramophone recital on Sunday night, & I leapt into the air and said YES
and that I didn't agree with William and that it was one of the things that Ben
had got to learn, so that he needn't always be exhausted. It was a wonderful*

[129] Diary of Stephen Potter, 22 February 1953.

*day – spring at its best, so Ben suggested driving out & having a walk, & he had
to write some letters first (Jeremy being ill was another setback) but we started
about three and went off in the direction of Dunwich. When we got just beyond
Leiston he took a small turning to the right & we went through Eastbridge and
then suddenly the country got miraculously beautiful – a double row of willows
leaning over and a small boy holding a large dog. He stopped the car just over a
bridge & we decided to walk by a dyke towards the sea. He'd never been to that
particular bit before, & he wanted to find the ruins of a very ancient chapel.*[130]
*The colours on the dykes & the flooded meadows were quite extraordinary and
then I realised that it was a bit of my dream of four nights ago when I'd been
reading Morgan's short story about heaven,*[131] *and Ben said "Well, if I thought
heaven was like this I wouldn't mind dying." It got better & better, a beautiful
brick bridge over the dyke,*[132] *and the warm apricot-coloured water, and a
windmill and lots of birds – curlews and (or) wimbrels – he wished he'd got his
binoculars with him. And then he saw the chapel – so we* had *to go further in
spite of Gloriana, and when we got there he was so distressed that they'd built
a gun implacement right inside the ruin – he said if they tried to hack away the
concrete the whole thing would probably collapse. There was a wonderful view
of the sea beyond the sand dunes, and of the bird sanctuary at Minsmere. On
the way back the birds began flying homewards, and the sun turned all the dried
grasses to scarlet. It was well after 5 when we got in. He'd promised to go out to
a cocktail party, so I did the first few pages of the next scene & went home to the
Masque scene.*

On the same day Britten received news which, as he wrote to Pears, 'makes
the Greek tour a little doubtful'. The couple were sponsors of the League for
Democracy in Greece, which had been established with the aim of rebuild-
ing friendship between the two countries and promoting the cause of democracy. In the post-war climate, the activities of the League were not supported
by the Government, although they were championed by a number of Labour
MPs. Britten told Pears that George Harewood had been 'summoned' to the
Foreign Office to be questioned about 'the thing we're sponsors of (League

[130] On the coast east of Theberton, the chapel had connections with the nearby
Leiston Abbey.

[131] Altered by IH in green pencil from 'short stories' to 'short story about heaven'.
A reference to E. M. Forster, *The Celestial Omnibus and Other Stories* (London:
Sidgwick & Jackson, 1911).

[132] IH typescript note: 'I commissioned Mary Potter to paint a water-colour of it
and gave it to Ben as a thank-you for having worked at Gloriana'. The painting
is still held by the BPL.

for Democracy in Greece) – as the Foreign Office take a dim view of it, & the Greeks (in spite of the fact they've given us visas) are angry'.[133]

With most of the concert programmes for the Festival now decided, IH was continuing to travel to Ipswich on most Wednesday evenings to rehearse the Festival Choir, first calling in on the home of Barbara Gibbons, the accompanist, to go through the piano parts. IH's dedication to improving the choir was complete, but the challenge was a huge one, as one member recalled of the 1952 rehearsals:

> Often the weather was wintry or wet, or both, and the hall was icy cold. She did not make a fuss, because no-one did in those days, things being so difficult even seven years after the war. But [she remembered] seeing the singers' noses gradually turning blue, their voices getting quieter and quieter, their teeth chattering, their breath condensing in visible clouds to blot out their faces. She herself was quite warm, leaping about on the platform in her enthusiasm. At one singer's request, she led the whole choir in physical jerks to warm them up, though she afterwards realised that this had possibly been a risky thing to do. For, as she said, 'It's no good my pretending that they weren't on the old side, quite a lot of them, because they *were*, and they might have broken a leg or had a heart attack'. Her 'elderly, bald and white-headed friends', as she described the tenors and basses, were often matched in age by the sopranos and altos, many of whom had begun to develop hard edges on their voices ...
>
> There was one alto – 'a dear soul, but no longer with us' – who was christened by her fellows 'The Boomer'. She had been professionally trained, but she bellowed: the unfortunate altos on each side were either drowned, or felt that perhaps they should be making that kind of noise too. Much of Imogen Holst's time and energies, those Wednesday evenings, were spent trying to prevent 'The Boomer' from causing too much damage to the choir sound'.[134]

Wed. Feb 25th. Among the things that he wasn't sure about in orchestration
– could trombone gliss a 4th fairly low down? – could the bass clarinet flutter-
tongue? – what were the shakes that the bassoon couldn't manage? And what
was the downward compass of the celesta? I remembered this from the Planets &
he found he'd got one passage a 3rd too low & had to have the 1st 8 notes 8va. His
work was continuously interrupted by builders and electricians and so on – I felt

---

[133] 24 February 1953; BPL.
[134] Wren, *Voices by the Sea*, p. 25.

desperately sorry but at the same time was grateful for a chance of catching up with him. However desperate he got he always remained <u>very</u> kind.

Thursday Feb 26th. He wanted to know all about the Ipswich rehearsal the night before. He was distressed that Peter had got something wrong with his eye. Also he was disappointed not to be able to get to Greece for a holiday – they were refusing him a permit because he'd signed a petition about the prisoners who'd not had a fair trial. He took Mary the Eastbridge walk during the afternoon, & I had my W.I. choir for the last time. Came back to find Pam & Charles for tea. Ben late back, & played Pelmanism[135] on the floor with Charles. When they'd gone he asked about the W.I. & when I said they'd sung so well that I'd got swelled head he said "well it's about time you got swelled head."

While sedate domestic pastimes, such as Happy Families with IH and Pelmanism with the young Charles Hope-Johnstone, helped Britten deal with the stress of *Gloriana,* he also found relaxation in more strenuous forms of exercise, including tennis at The Red House, squash at Framlingham College and badminton in the Jubilee Hall; of this last sport Stephen Potter recalled that the composer was 'totally impossible to get a point off by being made of india-rubber and having played for Suffolk'.[136] The Aldeburgh Music Club, which was moving into new and more adventurous musical territory under IH's influence, also continued to provide a welcome diversion; it was now about to embark on rehearsals for Bach's Cantata *Schmücke dich*, 'Rise, O Soul', for a Club Night on 12 April.

Meanwhile the problems surrounding Britten's Greek holiday plans proved insurmountable, and Pears, Britten and the Harewoods decided to visit Ireland instead.

Friday Feb. 27th. Went down early & worked all day at getting Act II scene III ready for him. He cheered up in the evening after having had an energetic game of squash, & said how he enjoyed the relaxation, not only of games, but of being with ordinary normal public-school people. Then in the evening we had our first rehearsal for the Music Club's Schmücke dich – the Potters piano was down ¼ tone & the recorders got sharp with anxiety & by the time Ben came in to play viola we'd got about 7 different pitches & his face was a study. He was a great help, especially when the strings had the tune in unison. When it was over he got hold of me by the neck (which was exceedingly sweaty with the effort of making

[135] A memory game in which a pack of playing cards is spread out face down; players turn over cards two at a time, attempting to discover pairs.
[136] Diary of Stephen Potter, 21 November 1952.

them come in at the right moment even if not on the right note) and said "You are an angel." There was no answer to that one, so I went home where it was so cold that I thought I should die.

(Sat in London)

The cold in IH's room was a stark reminder of how frugally she was living. Britten, who since visiting the room had become more aware of her situation, was now discussing with Boosey's how IH should be paid for her work on the vocal and full scores of *Gloriana*. Later that week Ernst Roth suggested to Britten that 'a lump sum would be best. Does something like £50 seem adequate to you? She must not forget that if she gets £50, she will probably not need to pay any tax, while if you would pay her a sort of weekly salary, she would have to return it to the tax'. Against Roth's suggestion, Britten wrote '£100'.[137]

On the last day of February Britten's sister Barbara came to stay at Crag House.

March 1953

Sunday March 1. *Went round before he & his sister Barbara had had their breakfast, & did the last 12 pages of Act II Scene III for him. Then worked at home on Masque scene from 11 to 4.30. When I went back Beth & the children were still there. It was after 5 when Ben settled down to work – he'd meant to go to the Fishermen's service in the church but couldn't face it, as he was feeling cold and weary and said he couldn't see. He asked me to stay to supper with them. While planning the pages of Act II Scene I I got hopelessly muddled because of the running conversation between Ben & Barbara – Ben saying how when he was a small boy Frank Bridge used to keep him for a lesson from 12 to 4 without a break! He made lots of mistakes because he was so weary, & got fed up. But an excellent claret helped: – we fought over the last glass – I thought I'd won because I poured mine into his glass when he was in the kitchen, but as soon as I turned aside he poured it back into mine. I said "do you* always *have to win?" and he said "Well, I get very cross if I don't." We worked till 10, with Barbara knitting socks, and then I stopped and luckily he stopped too, as he was beyond concentrating any more.*

Monday March 2nd. *Went round at 8.45 hoping to get Masque scene finished for him to take to London, but couldn't manage it. He reckoned to get the dance scene finished by 4, but he finished it at 12.20!! Absolutely incredible. As usual, he turned round from putting in the last note and said "Now in the* next *scene"*

[137] 2 March 1953; BPL.

– but I told him to take Barbara for a walk, <u>which</u> <u>he</u> <u>did</u>! Went back at 2 and he
planned the orchestration of Act III Scene I so that I could go ahead with bar lines.
He and Barbara drove off to London at about 3. He'd had a moment's down about
the end of the dance scene, because Peter had thought it a mistake having the
Coranto: – but he said the orchestra during the slow curtain would be absolutely
terrifying, and was necessary to the drama. (He also said, during the course of
the morning, that he was afraid the double-bassoon's[138] *semiquavers during the*
recit. might sound like the hot water system gurgling!)

Wed March 4th. They had had an awful journey back from London in the fog the
night before – Peter was still in bed when I got there, & Ben very weary. Later
Peter blew in and they discussed festival plans. During the conversations Ben
said of Schönberg that he was "not what you'd call a <u>magic</u> composer." There were
two committee meetings that evening but I had to leave ½ way through the first
to get to the Ipswich rehearsal.

In IH's absence, at the meeting of the Executive Committee on 4 March, Pears
announced that *Sāvitri* and *The Soldier's Tale* had finally been dropped for
financial reasons, to be replaced by *Albert Herring*, which Britten would be
rehearsing in any case for the Wiesbaden Festival in May. *Sāvitri* would now
have to wait until 1956 for its first performance at Aldeburgh. The evening
of ballet, devised by John Cranko, would be kept as a separate programme.
Britten and Pears reported that they had also had a successful meeting with
the Decca Record Company, which wanted to issue recordings of some of the
concerts in the Festival.

Meanwhile David Webster was planning to tour Rhodesia with the Royal
Opera House production of *Gloriana* in August 1953, as part of the Cecil Rhodes
centenary celebrations; in addition to Covent Garden, the Hallé Orchestra and
Sadler's Wells Theatre Ballet had also been invited. He was hoping that Britten
would conduct and Pears sing Essex. But Britten, Pears and IH were plotting
a more local project for August – bringing students to work and perform at
Aldeburgh as the first step towards founding a school of music in the town.

Pears's property negotiations in London were finally moving towards a resolution. He wrote to his friend Oliver Holt that he and Britten had finally made
an offer for a house in Chester Gate after '6 months dithering'.[139]

Thursday March 5th. We discussed possibilities of a week in August with

---

[138] Appears as 'double bass's' in the edited typescript, but it is definitely 'bassoon's'
in the original.
[139] Headington, *Peter Pears*, p. 172.

students – Ben was quite mad, saying "Let's have the Amadeus" – Peter saying that he wouldn't dream of going to Rhodesia if there was a chance of students in Aldeburgh. Peter had gone by the time I got back in the afternoon. Ben, in spite of working at terrific speed, was in a very communicative state & told me his doubts and hopes about their new London house. He said he'd leave me the not-quite-repetition bits in Act III Scene I to fill in. He also said that he kept on having to refer to my vocal score whenever he couldn't read his own pencil sketches! I went back in the evening to work while he was out. He was obviously v. weary; & said, among other things: "did your father always enjoy working?"

Friday March 6th. Went down early, feeling ill – Ben very sympathetic and also very helpful, dispelling panic as usual. He asked me to stay to lunch, and during the meal he talked about the inevitability of old people getting querulous, & I refused to accept it as inevitable, if they'd been great, & he said that querulousness didn't interfere with greatness. He suggested we should go for a short walk before beginning work again – it was lovely out – he asked me if I could feel any sense of wholeness about Gloriana – he couldn't himself, because he was still too close to it. He was sure that the drama was convincing and hung together all right, so I said I couldn't separate the drama from the music in my mind: – this cheered him.

During the afternoon he asked me if I thought Gloriana was better than the Spring Symphony, & when I said yes and why, he said "you are very encouraging." Peter came back from London, and after I'd taken the Bach cantata rehearsal I went back to join the last few minutes of their recorder session & found Ben conducting the four of them in Peter's bedroom. It was very helpful having a beat in the first chorus of the Bach, which otherwise would have been chaotic. Ben kept giggling whenever Peter tried to get his top D.

IH, Britten and Pears were all rehearsing for the Club Night on 12 April, in which the Bach cantata was to feature Pears as pianist and Britten playing viola *obbligato*, conducted by IH; the programme was to be supplemented by a recorder quartet (including IH and Pears) repeating the Henry VIII song arrangements from the February concert, and a Handel sonata in G minor for violin, viola and piano, with Rhoda Backhouse, Britten (viola) and Pears (piano).

Moving seamlessly between his amateur and professional duties, Pears returned to London on Sunday to sing in the first performance of a new work he had himself commissioned, Lennox Berkeley's *Four Ronsard Sonnets*, with Hugues Cuénod and George Malcolm, broadcast from the Raphael Gallery at the Victoria and Albert Museum.

Monday March 9th. Got to Crag House just after 8.30 & found that Ben had already got to Page 25 of the street scene. How on <u>earth</u> he managed it I can't imagine, because when he came in he told me he'd been out quite a lot during the weekend. He spoke of the broadcast concert & thought the Lennox Berkeley songs were good, especially the last, though the 3rd suffered from vagueness.

The sun came out in the middle of the morning and the sea turned bright blue & he wanted to go out and hated having to go on working. He talked a lot about Schubert – the night before he'd listened to the L.P. record of the C major symphony conducted by Kripps,[140] *& he'd been "bowled over" all over again & had read the score afterwards in bed. He said it was extraordinary the way so much of his orchestral writing was at least 50 years ahead of its time – and how Schubert heard so little of his own orchestral stuff – yet he gave the instruments things to do that they'd never been asked to do before – for instance, the sensuousness of the strings. He asked if G. had liked the C major, & when I told him that it was his favourite symphony of all, he said "I can understand that."*

When he'd finished off the street scene & was beginning on the last scene he said "I MUST have trombones alone, don't you think? It's no good being safe and doubling everything. He was, as always, endlessly kind and patient, and it was lovely to be able to bask in the joy of working for him, without anything to worry about.

On the same day Britten wrote to David Webster, finally declining the trip to Rhodesia; he was eventually replaced by Reginald Goodall. Meanwhile, planning for the trip to Ireland was nearly complete. Britten's keen anticipation came out in a letter to Plomer, with an oblique reference to their recent Greek tragedy: 'Ireland next Monday week! Why 'Ireland' is a long & sad story, which can wait till we meet …'[141]

Tuesday March 10th. Ben arrived late at work having sprained a muscle in his back & not slept a wink and unable to bend. <u>Wretched</u> trying to work. He decided to go up to London at midday with Peter to see his doctor. He complained that every time he wrote a note in the score it was a wrong note. So I said that if he were the sort of composer who <u>only</u> depended on a first-rate brain he'd be writing <u>all</u> the notes correctly & we shouldn't be any better off. This cheered him quite a lot, & he said "You <u>do</u> say the right things!" Then after a bit he said "All the same, I think there's room for a bit more intellect." I said I thought Gloriana's balance

140 Josef Krips's recording of Schubert's Symphony no. 9 with the Concertgebouw Orchestra had been issued by Decca in May 1952.
141 8 March 1953; BPL.

couldn't be bettered, and he said "Well, I only hope the unseen powers are as charitable as you: – whoever the unseen powers are; – St Cecilia perhaps."

He got back from London at 8.30 that evening, having had the muscle put back where it belonged. It still hurt a bit, but he was able to get around and looked <u>years</u> younger. We had a lovely meal, with white wine. (Pouily? spelling?)[142]

Wed. March 11th. He was much better – still hurt a bit but able to move. As I'd finished preparing Act III sc.III I went back to Act I & filled in and tidied up –

[Thursday 12th – Friday 13th in London for Schütz]

On Thursday IH went to London for the final rehearsal and performance of Schütz's *St Matthew Passion* at St Margaret's Westminster. The performance was at 10 o'clock in the morning on Friday 13 March, allowing Pears and IH to travel back to Suffolk together for the evening. Their return coincided with the achievement of a milestone for Britten and *Gloriana*.

Friday 13th. Ben met Peter & me at Saxmundham and was <u>very</u> sympathetic about the crises in the Schütz. He'd finished Gloriana at 3 o'clock this afternoon!!! I went in for 3 minutes after my Bach rehearsal just to see the score & to drink Cognac: – they were both very tired so I came away almost immediately.

Sat. March 14th. Went round at 9 to go on with filling in gaps in the score. Ben came back from taking Peter to Sax and said we must write a letter to America about my lecture tour – he was <u>very</u> fussy[143] *about how to describe me – should he say "famous" and I said no v. firmly: – he refused to say "experienced" lecturer & suggested "stimulating" but I said there were few things worse than a stimulating middle-aged spinster and he said "you will embarrass me so much". In the end he put "a brilliant & charming lecturer" (!?!) He found it very difficult to settle down to any other work: he rang up William who said "What does it feel like to have finished Gloriana – is it like having parted from your wife?" He asked me to stay to lunch and there was excellent red wine which made me reckless so that when he began saying, about composition, "do you think we can go on now without worrying?" I couldn't resist coming out with my thing about how he'd given us what English music needed, which was the equivalent of romanticism, & how it was all very well for Vienna to have to evolve 12-note systems, but English music had stopped at Purcell & we'd got to live through it. He agreed and said that that was what Erwin felt. It was <u>terribly</u> exciting, but the worst of it was*

---

[142] Altered by IH to 'Pouilly' for the transcript.

[143] IH typescript note: '[?funny]'. IH was apparently not able to read her own writing when she came to edit the passage.

I was too intoxicated to keep calm. Afterwards he went to have his hair cut & I bought him some shoe-laces & then we went to Framlingham & he showed me the church & the castle & we had a lovely drive back through villages and it was very peaceful. Went to dinner at the Potters, and when we got there he apologised for being in such a state & I said he was the calmest person I knew & he said he was afraid he <u>always</u> showed exactly what his state of mind was. V. good food & drink and he cheered up over a game of ping-pong.

Sunday March 15th. Went round in the morning, he was very business-like & trying to write letters before going off for a holiday. In the middle of it all he insisted on writing a cheque for me for £100 and began thanking me all over again but I couldn't bear it so I told him to stop or I'd weep over Gloriana. In spite of having so much to do in so little time he said "let's go for a walk" and we walked by the sea in the brilliant sunshine and he said he wished he wasn't going away because there was no place like Aldeburgh, but of course one <u>had</u> to go away in order to relax. He then began talking about money and what to do with it in his will: – how he'd got a large income but no capital whatsoever, and he and Peter both hated the idea of investments and so they bought pictures. And they were both leaving everything to each other but their lawyers pointed out that they'd quite likely meet an air crash at the same moment. Then he talked once more about his adopted children. But it was time to go back. I waved him off just before 1.30.

[He was away in Ireland until March 29th]

On his last full day in Ireland, 28 March, Britten sketched out a setting of Thomas Hardy's poem 'Wagtail and Baby', marking the start of a project to which he would return later in the summer. When they returned from County Cork Britten and Pears walked into an encounter with Margery Spring-Rice, a member of the Aldeburgh Festival Council with somewhat entrenched views about modern art. IH, meanwhile, finally came to the end of her first massive undertaking as Britten's amanuensis.

Sunday March 29th. I finished the full score of Gloriana at mid-day, having worked practically non-stop. Went in to Crag House at 9 pm after the Friends of Festival meeting & found they'd only <u>just</u> arrived after a desperate journey – car had broken down – refused to go at less than 70, and they'd had to abandon it & take a taxi from Oxford!! They were both dead tired. There were various telephonings to be done & then Margery Spring-Rice came in and stayed for <u>ages</u> and when they were both nearly dropping with fatigue she began – while they were all standing to see her off – a long discussion about the Reg Butler sculpture *prize, & said how it was "too easy" and Ben in spite of his weariness argued most lucidly about how you might just as well say that "Dove sono" was too easy, and it was no good being scornful about twisted wire because it was no "simpler" than pencil on paper. At last she went and they were able to get to bed.*

Reg Butler, whose work was to feature in the sculpture exhibition at the Festival, had recently won an international competition for a Monument to the Unknown Political Prisoner held at the Tate Gallery. Butler's winning sculpture, described by Herbert Read as 'an emblem purged of pity and terror, a luminous and enduring act of meditation on the liberating significance of sacrifice' had provoked a public debate of unprecedented vigour, that had reached even Aldeburgh.

March 31st. He said he hoped it wouldn't be the last opera I helped him with, & gave me a copy of the 2nd Canticle,[144] and talked about The Turn of the Screw being a subject for Blake.

April 1953

[During the week Ben had to go to London on business.]

Good Friday. He'd asked me to go to the Messiah in Norwich with them, because Peter was singing in it. Went round in the morning & found Ben rehanging the pictures and Peter pruning the rose-bushes. Ben terribly depressed about John Cranko & the Gloriana dances. But thrilled with Piper's designs. Lovely journey to Norwich. Ghastly Messiah – we got the giggles badly at one moment when the cellos & basses lunged onto a low B♭ & missed it. Then afterwards, when walking back to the close, there was a thrush singing superbly.

IH was visiting her mother for Easter, and as Britten was going to London, he offered to drive her to Essex. He then went on to spend the weekend at Glyndebourne, before heading off to Lancing College, where he attended the Easter service and visited David and Steuart Bedford, the sons of Lesley Bedford, who as Lesley Duff had been a member of the EOG from its outset until 1949, creating the roles of Lucia in *The Rape of Lucretia* and Emmie in *Albert Herring.* Britten wrote to her a fortnight before the visit: 'I was glad for news of the boys, whom incidentally I expect to see (the younger 2 at least) at Lancing over Easter, if my plan to go to Glyndebourne & on there materialises! It'll be lovely to see them happy in their surroundings'.[145]

---

[144] Britten's Canticle II: 'Abraham and Isaac', op. 51.
[145] 15 March 1953; BPL.

Sat. April 4th; – Ben asked me to go to an early lunch before leaving for London. We talked again about ballet dancing & I tried to defend it as an art. He said that if it were a serious art it would have a notation by now. It was sunny & showery by turns & we had the hood open for a bit of the way but had to close it. When we got into Essex he began talking about why did Iso live in Dunmow [lines erased] I told him about A. [words erased] As he was late for his London appointment he didn't come in but said he would when he picked me up on the Monday.

'A' was Arthur Caton, a Thaxted associate of the Holsts, and one of IH's most valued friends and advisers. A shepherd's son and by trade a weaver, Caton did much to care for IH's mother and had previously had a romantic interest in IH herself.

Monday April 6th. He arrived about 6 & came in for a glass of sherry and then when we'd started he said how young Iso looked and how nice she'd made the house. He'd had an awful journey & had nearly had a smash near Ongar – heart beating furiously. He talked about his Easter at Lancing, and how he'd enjoyed it & what a good school it was, & how if he didn't get so involved with other things he'd like to be a school teacher & I tried to tell him how exhausting it was but he didn't sound convinced. Round about Ipswich he made a very shrewd comment [words erased]. He was terribly tired with driving and it was awful not being able to do anything for him. Then just near Snape he became more confidential than ever before & talked about Peter & how if he found the right girl to marry he supposed he'd have "to lump it" and that nothing would ever interfere with their relationship.

The next day E. M. (Morgan) Forster, Eric Crozier's co-librettist on *Billy Budd* and a regular visitor at Crag House since 1949, arrived. Joan Cross was also in Aldeburgh to go through the part of Queen Elizabeth with the composer and the accompanist Viola Tunnard. IH, meanwhile, had expanded her piano teaching to include Sally (Sarah) and Roguey (Elizabeth) Welford, the daughters of Britten's sister Beth; when Roguey was told that IH was going to be teaching her, she apparently asked 'Is that the lady who runs through the sea getting her skirts wet?'[146]

Wed. April 8th. After a whole morning of Festival details in Elizabeth's office I went round to Crag House & heard Joan rehearsing Act III scene III from the other side of the door. Ben was thrilled with her, and said "Well, whatever it's like as music, I've certainly managed to write something that suits Joan."

[146] Wake-Walker, *Time and Concord*, p. 57.

Britten wrote to Plomer the same day that, during his rehearsal with Joan Cross, 'most of the time I was too excited to play the piano properly.'[147] IH meanwhile was planning a visit to Dorset for her birthday weekend, to visit friends she had made when she had participated in the Bryanston Summer School of Music the previous year. When she returned, she planned to be involved with Britten and Pears in the writing of the programme book for the Aldeburgh Festival.

> <u>Thursday</u> *April 9th. Went in during the afternoon to give a piano lesson to Sally & Roguey – Ben just going to take Morgan to Framlingham. He told me that Peter had managed to collect Acts II & III & would be bringing them down that night.*

> *(in Dorset Friday 10th to evening of Sunday 12th.)*

With the orchestration of *Gloriana* complete, Britten at last felt able to fulfil his desire to resume recitals with Pears. IH's birthday on 12 April found them both immersed in rehearsals for a recital tour later that week, which would take them to destinations including Bristol on 15 April and Manchester four days later. The tour had originally been planned to include Kathleen Ferrier, but the contralto, now in her final illness, was not well enough to take part, although her initials remain pencilled in next to Pears's in Britten's diary for the tour, and the dates are included in her own diary. Just before the tour she wrote to Britten saying that she felt 'heaps better'[148] and still hoped to take part in a planned recording of Canticle II, but this was never to take place.

Before they set off, Britten and Pears first fulfilled their more immediate commitment to IH and the Aldeburgh Music Club, taking part in the Club Night performance of Bach's Cantata no. 180, *Schmücke dich.*

> <u>Sunday 12th</u> *(Journey from Dorset) Got to Crag House late for the Music Club concert[149] and was desperate with weariness & couldn't cope with having to arrange the singers in their places. Ben very sympathetic & patient – we rehearsed the Bach & then did it straight through – some of it was good: – it was lovely having Peter as continuo and Ben as viola. After coffee & business they went away & we tidied the room & Ben said what will you drink so I said yes because it was my birthday & it had been such a bloody awful day until the Bach. So Ben produced brandy & Peter produced cake & we sat by the fire & Ben said the rehearsals had been difficult for the tour, & he'd lost his temper with Morgan the day before, & had been awful. It was late, so I went home.*

---

[147] 8 April 1953; BPL.
[148] 10 April 1953; BPL.
[149] '(Journey from Dorset)' and 'Music Club' added by IH in green pencil.

Monday April 13th. Business meeting all the morning at Crag House, trying to fix final details about programmes for festival. Then back again at 5 oclock to go through programme book. Ben harassed and so weary that he could hardly speak, but still making <u>excellent</u> suggestions whenever the rest of us were defeated. He had a violent quarrel with Peter about their Thursday evening programme – he wanted to do "An die ferne Geliebte" and Peter didn't want to – at one moment he called Peter "Petehoven" by mistake. We didn't get through till 8.30 – they both looked utterly exhausted & had got to leave the house by 8 next morning.

[They were away on tour all the week]

On his return Britten received the news that Boosey & Hawkes wanted the vocal score of *Gloriana* as soon as possible; they were planning to engrave a limited edition in advance of the first performance, so that a copy could be presented to the new Queen. At very short notice, IH was soon to find herself correcting the proofs.

Sunday April 19th. Ben rang in the morning, admitting that they were "only just surviving", and asked me to go down to Crag House at 12.30 with Elizabeth and stay to lunch in order to go through the programme book. When I got there I found they'd both got colds, Peter's worse than Ben's, and Ben was obviously upset about something because all the beauty had gone out of his face. He was v. philosophic about Rubbra having said he couldn't do a [Festival]¹⁵⁰ Variation at the <u>very</u> last minute, and suggested Arthur [Oldham] and Humphrey Searle. Got through our stuff at about 3.30, and just as I was going he broke it to me that Boosey's wanted the vocal score of Gloriana <u>immediately</u>, in order to bring it out by the 1st night. I said was he depressed about this, because he'd said that he wanted to hear it first before committing himself to print, – but he said "No, I don't think so; – but anyway I'm depressed to begin with!" They asked me to go in at about 9 pm but when I got there they'd only just started their meal so I waited and went through the Morley Canzonets.¹⁵¹

When they came in they both looked desperately tired, & Peter's cold much worse. So I came away almost immediately: – Ben insisted on seeing me to the door, & then came out into the street with me in order to have a heart to heart about the crisis over the house: – it was <u>bitterly</u> cold with a howling north-east wind

¹⁵⁰ '[Festival]' and '[Oldham]' added by IH in green pencil.
¹⁵¹ Britten and Pears owned both books of the canzonets in the *English Madrigal School* series, edited by Edmund H. Fellowes (London: Stainer & Bell, 1913), and a more recent edition of the first book by Donald Boalch (Oxford: George Ronald, 1950).

> *and he'd been sitting right on top of the fire so I was quite sure his cold would be*
> *worse, but he seemed to want to get it off his chest: – I held his hand and seemed*
> *I'm afraid very flippant about the permit for the bathroom – but told him that*
> *anyway the affair would have had to blow up anyway, and once it <u>had</u> blown*
> *up it would be over. Then I quickly sent him in out of the cold. The stars were*
> *marvellous.*

Rubbra's variation was to be replaced with contributions from Arthur Oldham and Humphrey Searle. The following day, Britten and Pears returned
to their tour, now covering the Midlands and the North East, where they
gave a concert in Leeds on 20 April and another in Newcastle two days
later.

> *(Ben in London and on tour all the week.)*

> *Friday April 24th. Looked in on them after my music club rehearsal and they both*
> *looked <u>much</u> better than the week before, tho' Peter still had a cold. Ben had lost*
> *his hunted look. We drank liquers and then I left them.*

> *Sunday April 26th. Went round at breakfast time to go on with correcting Acts II*
> *& III. Ben said would I stay to lunch to go through final details for the festival. He*
> *said the house crisis was at <u>last</u> over and poor Peter was telling him it wouldn't*
> *do. Ben had been searching his conscience over & over again, but he didn't think*
> *it was just that he was jealous "though I am very jealous." Thank goodness it's*
> *decided, anyway. In the afternoon he helped me over several technical problems*
> *when I'd got stuck in notation, and then he tried to persuade me to go for a picnic*
> *with him & Beth & the children but I wanted to finish Gloriana so that he could*
> *take it to London the next day. After the Friends of the Festival meeting in the*
> *evening he helped me sort out the Gittern rhythms in the street scene, which*
> *were all over the shop, and he put one bar with a ♩♪♪ ♩♪♪ in ⁶⁄₈ saying*
> *"<u>that'll</u> give all the musicologists something to talk about." When I left at half-past*
> *ten they were having a wonderfully domestic conversation with Miss Hudson on*
> *the staircase – both looking weary, but more at peace.*

Britten spent the next few days in London, discussing Festival arrangements
with the percussionist James Blades, who was to play in Bartók's Sonata for
Two Pianos and Percussion in a concert on 24 June, and John Cranko, with
whom he also discussed the dances in *Gloriana*. He then met with the directors of the EOG, to finalize details of the Group's coming trip to Wiesbaden
for *Albert Herring*, and conducted rehearsals with Pears and the rest of the
cast. These were not straightforward, with difficulties being caused by the

non-appearance first of Nancy Evans, who was singing Nancy, and then Roderick Jones, cast as Sid.

On Tuesday 28 March Pears took part in a concert of 'Music to honour the memory of Edmund Horace Fellowes, Priest and Musician' in the Livery Hall of the Worshipful Company of Goldsmiths. Back in Suffolk, IH continued to prepare the Festival Choir for their significant contributions to the Choral Coronation Concert that was to open the Festival.

(Ben & Peter came back Wed. evg. April 29th.)

Thursday April 30th. Ben rang up in the morning and characteristically his first question was about the Ipswich rehearsal the night before. He asked me to go round at 11 and talk about titles to sections in Act II Scene II. When I got there he told me about Cranko and I asked him about proofs. When we went through titles he wanted to call the scene Ballad-Rondo, but thought Rondo suggested instrumental music too much. I said not if it was Ballad-Rondo and so he put it. Then he began searching for the right titles to the sections and he said "don't say anything" so I said "mm?" feeling exactly like Papageno,[152] & then when I could hardly bear it I asked how long I'd got to go on not saying anything and finally he released me and I pointed out that he was confusing the form by putting verse-labels that described the episodes, and he gave in, saying "You win," and left it as it is.

He said what a frightful discipline it was for him & for Peter to have to be rehearsing Albert Herring at this moment. He'd only just begun to enjoy it. Nancy had refused to come to rehearsals,[153] and Syd had gone on strike rehearsing day after day without his girl. I raged and fumed and said it was outrageous that just because people were his friends they treated him like that & if he was a foreign dictator of a conductor-composer they'd turn up at every rehearsal, and he said: "Oh well."

Then he asked me if I'd "like" to come to the rehearsal on Sat afternoon at Orme Square, when Peter & Joan are going right through their parts.

---

[152] In Mozart's *Die Zauberflöte*, Papageno, as a punishment for lying about saving Tamino from a poisonous snake, has his mouth padlocked by the Three Ladies. Before his eventual pardon by the Queen of the Night, he sings a duet with Tamino in which he can only utter the sounds 'Hm, hm, hm'.

[153] Nancy Evans's diary records only one rehearsal for *Albert Herring* during the week, on 29 April. On the other days she was taking Helga, her daughter, to the dentist and to school, and had a meeting with the theatrical impresario Harold Fielding. BPL.

> We were meant to have lunch with 2 men from Deccas but they never turned
> up, so we had an excellent meal at the Wentworth with Peter and Elizabeth
> discussing the very final details for the programme book. Ben was talking about
> the Fellows Memorial concert, and he said the Byrd Masses shouldn't be sung
> with solo voices, because they needed to feel and sound more impersonal, & more
> universal, which is just what G. used to say.

The 'Kyrie', 'Gloria' and 'Agnus Dei' from Byrd's Mass for Four Voices had
been sung at the Fellowes Memorial Concert by four soloists, on the grounds,
according to the programme that 'they may well have been intended for private
devotion rather than for choral singing.'

That weekend, IH, Britten and Pears went to the Harewood's London house
in Orme Square, Bayswater, for a play-through of *Gloriana*.

May 1953

> *Sat May 2nd.* In London. Miss Hudson had told me that Ben had felt ill on
> Thursday night and oughtn't to have gone to London on Friday morning, but I
> was relieved to see he was all right again. They went right through the opera in
> Orme Square, Joan singing superbly.

> [*Ben away in London and Wiesbaden, May 4th – 16th.*]

While Britten was away IH took a rehearsal of the Music Club. Stephen Potter
remarked on her 'sad enthusiasm and slight dislocated eagerness … the shadow
over her, which halts her, her bizarre, even ludicrous appearance … We do a
Weelkes madrigal – "Hark all ye lovely ladies (?)", with a rather difficult rhythm
… "Think of the rhythm, not the bar lines" says Immo …'[154]

In Wiesbaden Britten conducted the EOG in two well-received performances of *Albert Herring* during the Internationale Maifestspiele on 9 and 10
May, with Pears in the title role. On their return Pears stayed in London to
supervise the move into the new London house at Chester Gate, and Britten
went to Aldeburgh, where he had Paul Rogerson to stay.

The following weekend the Aldeburgh Music Club was coming to Crag
House for a Club Night to celebrate its first year of existence. The members
were to share a cake decorated 'with a bar of music from Mr. Britten's 'Young
Person's Guide to the Orchestra'', and sing madrigals and carols, while IH
would accompany the Row sisters in a Mozart trio. Meanwhile IH had received
an invitation from the International Music Council to attend their conference

[154] Diary of Stephen Potter, 8 May 1953. The title of the madrigal is in fact 'All at
once well met faire ladies'.

in Brussels at the end of June and 'contribute a paper on "The importance of listening".'[155]

May 16th. As Miss Hudson was wanted in London to help move into Chester Gate, I offered to cook for Ben over the weekend, with Mrs. Goddard's help.[156] He arrived in the middle of the afternoon, with Paul. As I'd only got enough food for him I felt a bit anxious, but he said he wanted to take Paul over to Beth's on Sunday midday – so I prepared the Sunday dinner for Sat evening. Paul was a great help, and Ben most encouraging, and every bit as patient as he was over the full score of Gloriana! The potatoes wouldn't brown, and the gravy was non-existent and the cauliflower sauce was too thick – also I put too much Maraschino in the fruit salad. But otherwise it wasn't so bad and we had a bottle of the most superb 1947 Nuits St. George, so on the whole it wasn't as bad as I'd expected.

Sunday May 17th. Ben walked into the kitchen while I was getting the breakfast, looking very weary and terribly thin in his dressing-gown: – can't think how he manages to work so frantically hard when he doesn't weigh nearly enough. Breakfast was all right, and the coffee was excellent, but of course it was much too hot for Ben, and when I told him I usually warmed the cups he was flabbergasted. He asked me to go over to Beth's with them, and we had a wonderful journey and a v. good picnic lunch in the garden. Afterwards we walked through the fields and the children & I picked cowslips (which they don't call paigles in Suffolk) and I discovered that Ben is quite bad at climbing trees![157] He was very happy lying in the sun and doing nothing. The drive back in the late afternoon was absolutely beautiful – a magic over everything, and nightingales singing all the way. The evening meal was easy as it was only warmed up, but he began work on the extra dance for Gloriana, and that made us late and the soup was so hot that he nearly died of it. The Music Club began to arrive halfway through, so we left the rest of the meal till after the music. The Mozart Trio was a bit hectic but might have been worse – I was so agitated that I played lots of wrong notes and Ben insisted on turning over for me which I thought was going to make it much more agitating, but surprisingly it didn't – he is a calming person at all times, (except when he himself is agitated.) Some of the madrigals went well. Ben took the chair for Peter and did it very well, though he said afterwards that he hated having to speak in public. When they'd gone, about

155 Letter from Jack Bornoff to IH, 11 May 1953; HF.
156 Mrs Katie Goddard, a local lady who helped Miss Hudson with the cleaning at Crag House.
157 IH herself was very good at climbing trees, and had been since her school days.

> *10.15, we ate the rest of the meal, and had a drink, which made life easier. They*
> *wanted to help wash up, but I drove them to bed and then spent over an hour*
> *trying to clear up the kitchen. Went home at mid-night.*

The next day Britten was to return to Orme Square, where the Harewoods were hosting a dinner party at which the Queen and the Duke of Edinburgh would be present, and where Pears and Joan Cross were to introduce excerpts from *Gloriana* to the new monarch and her consort.

> *May 18th. Took Ben a cup of tea at ten past 7 – he said he'd been awake for a long*
> *time. The sun was making a pathway on the sea from the horizon to his bedroom*
> *window. He looked very beautiful and was so grateful* [words erased]. *Breakfast*
> *was all right, though the scrambled eggs suffered from too much beating. Directly*
> *after breakfast he asked me to look at the wrong chord in the score, in Act II Sc.*
> *III – he couldn't remember what it was supposed to be. I turned up the page in*
> *my 1st M.S. copy, and it was F♮ B♭ B♮ E♮ He didn't think this was right at first,*
> *but then he said it was – and I said wasn't it C♭ and F♭ instead of B♮ E♮ & he*
> *said "Yes." He wrote it in the score & I copied it for him to take to London. Then*
> *he asked me to pick some flowers to take to Peter in London. By 9.30 they were*
> *ready to go. It was a beautiful day, and he said "it's so lovely I can hardly bear it."*
> *On the doorstep he looked so disconsolate that I wished him good luck and he said*
> *"You'll think of me tonight?" so I said that I wasn't supposed to know anything*
> *about it but that Sophy[158] had let it out by mistake, and he said "Oh! I was only*
> *going to ask you to pray for me."*

> [*Ben played Gloriana to the Queen that evening, and was in London till the end*
> *of the week.*]

Joan Cross was later to recall of the royal party: 'I don't think they enjoyed the evening any more than we did'.[159]

June 1953

The beginning of June found IH in London, immersed in checking and correcting proofs of the vocal score of *Gloriana* with Erwin Stein, while Britten attended rehearsals. He was becoming increasingly exasperated by the apparent lack of organization at Covent Garden, and on 1 June he wrote an angry letter in response to a last-minute request from David Webster that he should write a fanfare for the Gala performance, despite having asked Webster weeks

---

[158] Sophie Stein.
[159] Headington, *Peter Pears*, p. 166.

before to find someone else. He concluded: 'And don't, David, go round saying I've let you down, because it isn't true'.[160] He was equally dissatisfied with the conductor John Pritchard who according to Joan Cross, simply 'didn't know the score well enough'.[161] Pritchard had been fulfilling conducting engagements in Vienna, and rehearsals had begun without him. These frustrations were to boil over as IH saw a side of the composer under pressure that she had never witnessed before.

Date?[162]

In London for rehearsals of Gloriana; – trying to correct proofs against time. At the second orch. rehearsal Ben said he was going to conduct the 1st ½hr and as we were alone in the passage I said "Oh, now it will be <u>right</u>!" and he blew up in an absolute fury, the first time he's ever lost his temper with me: – absolutely terrifying – hard, set face and no love in his eyes and a feeling of utter removal to an immense distance. I was so shattered that I could hardly listen. Lots of mistakes in the parts; alas, some of them were mistakes in the score which I should have corrected while he was in Ireland. In the pub, over a meal, while correcting the newest batch of proofs, I realised that he'd been angry because I'd said what was in his own mind, which he didn't want to think. He said "Everyone will have to help me to think that Pritchard is going to be all right." He also said "I wish I didn't get so angry", so I said that he was the calmest & most patient person in the world.

It was a very difficult week – we had to send the last set of proofs to the engravers without Ben seeing them, so as to get through in time.

[Back to Aldeburgh, with Ben in London.]

Went to dress rehearsal on June 6th – <u>wonderful</u>

8 June was to be the climax of IH's work for Britten so far: the day of the Gala first performance of *Gloriana* at Covent Garden. Yet the morning found Britten, characteristically, already looking beyond the evening's events to the forthcoming Aldeburgh Festival.

June 8th Ben rang up in the morning, while I was at Chelsea, & asked if I'd go to lunch next day to discuss festival things. He said that all things considered he

[160] 1 June 1953; BPL.
[161] Carpenter, *Benjamin Britten*, p. 318.
[162] IH transcript note: 'End of May and beginning of June'. 'Date?' has been added in green pencil.

didn't think the dress rehearsal was too bad. He said the vocal score was looking
beautiful – the Queen's copy had just arrived for him to sign – and he said he
hadn't yet found any mistakes, so I said he'd find those later when he'd got a freer
mind, and then he thanked me for my help and said "it belongs to you as much as
to anyone", so I told him that I'd cry down the telephone if he went on so he asked
me to go round behind after the performance, and rang off. Saw him for half an
instant after it was over, but no time to talk.

In fact, although the engraved score looked impressive, IH regarded it only as
a proof, and was dismayed that it had been engraved and issued. Rosamund
Strode recalled her saying that it was 'looked on as a complete waste of everybody's time, musically … it was not reckoned by Imo and Ben, and anybody
else, really, as being a very good buy … They hadn't had time [to correct it].
And … putting engraved things right takes a very long time'.[163] Once the
first performances were over, Britten and IH would have to dedicate considerable time and effort to preparing a second edition for publication in
November.

The reception of *Gloriana* that night proved to be one of the most cruelly disappointing moments of Britten's career. The work was received half-heartedly
by an unsympathetic audience of society figures who 'were unused to opera,
let alone modern opera'.[164] Tony Mayer, who with his wife Thérèse had successfully pleaded with Britten for tickets, found himself bewildered by the lack
of understanding and intolerance shown by the first-night audience, and by
the press that followed.[165] But the following morning, Britten had yet to see
the reviews, and his own frustrations found their vent, implicitly at least, in
criticism of the conducting of John Pritchard.

June 9th. Went to Chester Gate at 1; – lovely house. Ben & Peter both looking v.
tired, and Ben feeling like death. They were desperate because they couldn't get
another rehearsal before Thursday. Ben said "I suppose I was a fool not to conduct
it myself." I said that other people had got to learn to do his things, & it wouldn't
have been the answer: he agreed. Then we had a meal and it was so lovely
being with them both that I said how calm it was and that they were the only
really calm people I knew and they looked surprised but pleased. An agonising
telephone call with Basil Douglas, and several tiresome details to arrange about
rehearsals. I couldn't get away till nearly 3, though I longed for them both to be
able to sleep for a bit. It was one of the loveliest times I've ever had with them.

[163] Interview with Basil Coleman, 4 May 1993.
[164] Malloy, 'Britten's major set-back?', p. 52–3.
[165] Malloy, 'Britten's major set-back?', p. 50.

Once the opening week of performances of *Gloriana* was out of the way, Pears was committed to travelling to Cornwall to take part in the St Ives Festival of Music and the Arts (the musical directors of which were Tippett and Priaulx Rainier). He was scheduled to give a song recital with Noel Mewton-Wood on 14 June at 3 p.m., including Beethoven's *An die ferne Geliebte* and Tippett's *The Heart's Assurance*.

Although now frantically involved in writing out parts for the orchestral concerts, IH remained fully committed to preparing the Festival choir; Britten undertook to accompany her to Ipswich for a rehearsal of Mozart's 'Coronation' Mass, which would comprise the second half of the opening choral concert.

> Ben got back to Aldeburgh late on Friday evening June 12th, having had a desperate day – Peter involved in a car collision but no-one hurt, & then he himself delayed 2½ to 3 hrs by train. Saw him only for a few minutes on Sat 13th, & he then went back to London for the evening performance. He'd asked me to go round next evening, Sunday 14th, to go through orch. parts etc. for festival. I went down at 10 & Miss Hudson told me he was terribly agitated because they'd rung up from St. Ives to say Peter hadn't yet turned up, & Ben of course was having visions of taxi smashes & disasters. I went up to Peter's room to try & find the telephone number of the St. Ives office to tell them to ring through directly he arrived: Ben was pacing up & down in his dressing-gown looking distraught. He said should he ring the police, but I told him that if anything <u>had</u> gone wrong they'd have let him know immediately. He tried to settle down to learn the scores of the Variations while I did Bassoon parts for the Haydn Horn Concerto & the Mozart Mass, but it was an hour before St. Ives rang up, & he nearly passed out with worry. When he'd heard that Peter had arrived, having missed his train, he had a huge brandy & said "let's go for a walk" so we went along by the sea & he began to recover. I tried to persuade him not to go to the Ipswich rehearsal that evening as he was so desperately tired, but he said he wanted to. The drive there was very beautiful – in talking about his agitation of the morning he said "if anything happened to Peter or Erwin or you I don't know what I'd do". On the whole the Ipswich rehearsal might have been worse – he was pleased that they knew their notes, and inspired them to sing better than they'd ever done it before – his suggestions were always <u>perfect</u> – in the Gloria he said "put an exclamation mark after the word 'Gloria'". We had supper when we got back, and he said "Isn't the body marvellous in the way it recovers! A few hours ago I couldn't have faced that rehearsal for a thousand pounds.

IH's own preparation of the choir had been painstaking; one member recalled that she was 'particularly keen on improving the clarity of consonants and the correct sound of vowels, principles which Gustav Holst had drummed into her when she was very young ... The correction of the thin, flat East Anglian vowel-sounds took a lot of her time. "Choirs living on the east coast" she explained, "only half-open their mouths, to prevent the cold north-east wind from blowing in and giving them toothache".'[166]

The Festival was now looming large, and Britten had much to do, not least learning the scores of five other composers for the *Variations on an Elizabethan Theme.* Together with Holst's *A Fugal Concerto* – to be conducted by IH – Priaulx Rainier's *Cycle for Declamation* for unaccompanied tenor and Bartók's Sonata for Two Pianos and Percussion, the new variations were to have their first performance in a broadcast concert by the BBC in London on 16 June, prior to all four works being given at the Festival.

> _Monday June 14th_[167] _Motored up to London – Jeremy driving & Ben learning the scores of the Variations in the back of the car._

> _Tuesday 16th at the BBC all day, rehearsing. The performances very agitating – I muddled a cello lead in the slow movement of the concerto & it almost came to pieces. We motored back after it was over, having a wonderful picnic supper by moonlight in a lane, with champagne. Ben insisted on driving nearly all the way, but at Ipswich he was so stiff with tiredness he couldn't manage any more & Jeremy took over._

The next day rehearsals began in earnest for the Aldeburgh Festival concerts. For the next week the lives of IH, Britten and Pears were to be a whirlwind of rehearsal and performance. At the top of the list was Mozart's 'Coronation' Mass, which was to complete the concert on the opening afternoon, and the Haydn and Mozart orchestral programme that Britten was to conduct on 21 June, and in which he was to lead the orchestra from the piano in Mozart's Concerto in B flat major, K456, playing Mozart's own cadenzas. But his conducting had begun to be affected by a return of the troubling pain in his arms.

> _Wed 17th June. Rehearsals began – Mozart Haydn strings in the afternoon, & an agonising Mozart Mass rehearsal in church in the evening with parts still incorrect – I gave myself the sack quite definitely that night._

> _Thursday [18th]._[168] _The evening rehearsal was far better than I'd dared to hope. Ben asked me to go down to supper with him after it was over. Both arms were_

---

[166] Wren, *Voices by the Sea*, p. 25.
[167] Actually 15 June.
[168] '[18th]' added in green pencil.

troubling him and he couldn't pour out his beer. I had to do everything for him,
even squashing up his strawberries. Arthur Oldham rang in the middle of the
meal, saying he'd re-written his Variation. Ben was <u>endlessly</u> patient with him.
I tried to go home so that he could go to bed, but he was too tired to relax. He
even sat on a hard chair until I insisted that he should get into a comfortable one.
Peter was driving down after Gloriana, so he said he couldn't go to bed till he
arrived (at about 2AM.) I wanted to copy out his Mozart cadenzas for him but he
said it would help him to learn them if he did it himself. He was terribly worried
by the pain in his arms & said "I'll have to learn a different way of conducting if
I'm to get through this weekend." He also said "I suppose it's because I'm too tense
nearly all the time". So I said it was an occupational disease & he couldn't expect
anything else after doing Gloriana in 6 months. When it was 11 I said I'd have to
go home and he was so kind that I could hardly bear it, and thanked me for the
"cherishing".

<u>Friday 19th.</u> A very bad day for him. Arms worse, & Dennis Brain never turned
up for the afternoon rehearsal.

Dennis Brain was scheduled to perform on the first Sunday, in Haydn's Horn
Concerto in D.

The Aldeburgh Festival opened the next day. In the afternoon IH's Festival
Choir was singing the Mozart Mass in the opening Coronation Choral Concert, together with Arne's *Ode in Honour of Great Britain* and 'Now all the
air shall ring', and Purcell's anthem 'O Lord, grant the Queen a long life'. The
concert also featured IH conducting her father's *A Fugal Concerto* and Britten taking the podium for the *Variations on an Elizabethan Theme* for string
orchestra. The concert was followed in the evening by a performance of *Albert
Herring*.

<u>Sat. 20th.</u> Was too agitated to take anything in until it was all over, but the
performance went well. Albert Herring <u>brilliant</u> in the evening.

Britten had no time to rest his arms after this triumph. The following day he
was playing the piano and conducting the Aldeburgh Festival Orchestra and
Dennis Brain in concertos and symphonies by Haydn and Mozart. Later that
evening, in the gardens of Eaton House, the home of Lyn Pritt, a morris troupe
from Thaxted performed a range of dances, including the 'Abbots Bromley
Horn Dance'.

<u>Sunday 21st.</u> Heard the last bit of the Mozart G Minor rehearsal – absolutely
<u>wonderful</u>. Ben terribly agitated, & having kept the orchestra till 1.20 he then

began practising the piano feverishly & much too fast although the concert began
at 2.30. Luckily Peter was there to drag him away. Concert went well, tho' not as
inspiring as the rehearsal, but that was inevitable. He was very lovely afterwards.
After the Thaxted morris dancing (which went well) he came round to thank them
– he was thrilled *with the Abbots Bromley.*

Norman Del Mar took the reins on 22 June, Pears's birthday, for a concert
concluding with Lennox Berkeley's *Stabat Mater*, giving Britten a day away
from performing. The following morning he was back on stage with Pears,
Anne Wood and the Amadeus Quartet for the Hugo Wolf concert. That evening
he joined the Amadeus again to perform Mozart's Piano Quartet in E flat, K493,
in a programme that also included his own String Quartet no. 2.

> *Tues 23rd. The Hugo Wolf was beautiful – he played superbly. And more than*
> *superbly at the Amadeus concert in the evening. He asked me to go round after it*
> *was over & feed the 4tet.*

On Wednesday Britten had the day off, although his music could still be heard:
the film *Night Mail*, an early collaboration with W. H. Auden, was given at
the cinema, and Joy Boughton performed the *Six Metamorphoses after Ovid*
for solo oboe on the Meare at Thorpeness. The following evening, Pears and
Britten gave a wide-ranging recital including a Mozart cantata, Purcell's Divine
Hymn 'O Lord, rebuke me not', Alban Berg's Four Pieces for Clarinet and Piano,
songs by Schubert, Priaulx Rainier's *Cycle for Declamation* for solo tenor and
Beethoven's *An die ferne Geliebte*.

> *Thursday 25th. Ben & Peter's recital in the church – the Berg v. exciting and the*
> *Shepherd on the Rock quite intoxicating. Also the Purcell anthem – the silences*
> *before the Alleluya were wonderful.*

IH, Britten and Pears now had nearly two days to prepare for their next big
concert, Handel's *L'Allegro, il Penseroso, ed il Moderato* to be given in the
Parish Church on Saturday afternoon. IH was to conduct, Britten to play the
harpsichord continuo and Pears to sing one of the tenor parts. Prior to the
Handel, Britten was to conduct a second performance of the *Variations on an
Elizabethan Theme*. Then on Sunday, Pears and Britten were both involved in
the final concert of the Festival, an opera programme devised and introduced
by George Harewood, comprising music from operas by Gluck, Rossini and
Britten himself, including some excerpts from *Gloriana* sung by Pears and
Joan Cross.

Friday 26th. Went round in the morning to ask Ben where he wanted the harpsichord moved. He was obviously feeling <u>much</u> better now that the worst was over, but Peter not too good & still troubled by his thumb. The rehearsal that evening was v. agitating but got through it better than I'd expected – Ben said he was bewildered by the harpsichord, but the sounds he made on it were ravishing & it was <u>terribly</u> exciting hearing him playing my continuo parts.

Sat 27th. He was the <u>greatest</u> help during the day, suggesting how things could be better, & giving me confidence.

Characteristically, IH did not mention the success of the performance of Handel's work under her baton that evening.

Sunday 28th. The opera concert went <u>very</u> well in spite of the hastily revised programme owing to Geraint's illness. Ben's playing of the end of Gloriana was by far the loveliest thing that had happened during the festival.

Trevor Anthony stood in for Geraint Evans and 'with the assistance of Monica Sinclair, a re-shaped programme was introduced by the Earl of Harewood'.[169] Monica Sinclair had just created the role of Lady Essex in *Gloriana*, and the new programme included extensive excerpts, about which the *Leiston Observer* commented, echoing IH's sentiments: 'Mr Britten's pianoforte accompaniments were a joy in themselves, and it all culminated in a series of scenes of unforgettable power and beauty, a worthy climax to a fine festival.'

With the turmoil of the Festival finally over, IH's domestic life entered a period of uncertainty as she moved out of the bed-sitting room at Brown Acres, and stayed temporarily with Music Club friends. Her first port of call was Herons, the riverside home of Betty Pritchard, a recorder player and chairman of the Club. Having been called in by Britten for one year, first to help with the 1953 Festival, and then with *Gloriana*, IH's initial period of tenure in Aldeburgh was coming to an end. But Britten had been urging her to stay on, and she was now gathering the courage to ask him formally if she could do so. In the meantime she had to fulfil her obligation to give a paper at the 'Conférence Internationale sur le Rôle et la Place de Musique dans l'Education des Jeunes et des Adults' at the Palais des Beaux-Arts in Brussels on 6 July.

Monday 29th. I had to go to London to fix up about Brussels. Back in evening, to stay at Herons. Message would I ring Ben – he said could they come round after they'd finished clearing up the sculpture. So I went to the Church Hall & helped, & then they came & eat strawberries – both looking terribly tired.

[169] *Leiston Observer*, 3 July 1953.

July 1953

During the early gestation of *Gloriana*, Pears had repeatedly expressed unease with the project, arising partly from the effect it would have in diverting Britten away from the EOG and their recital partnership, and partly from his own discomfort with his allotted role of Essex, which he always believed that 'somebody else should have done … rather than me'.[170] On 2 July the BBC broadcast *Gloriana* again from Covent Garden, and these tensions rose to the surface once more. George Harewood recalled Britten confiding to him that following the first performance of the opera he 'had received a broadside' from Pears to the effect that the reception had confirmed 'his worst fears … Should they not stick in future to the public that wanted them, the loyal Aldeburgh friends, and not get mixed up with something that was none of their concern?'[171]

> *July 3rd, Friday.* I got back from London – Ben rang in the early evening & I said how thrilled I'd been with Gloriana and he said he'd been terribly depressed about it _all_, (including Peter and Basil Coleman and began having a _long_ thing about how he felt he ought(n't) to have dragged Peter away from the Matthew Passions and things that he loved doing, since he was obviously unhappy in opera; – and how he wanted to have a long talk about it because I was about the only person he _could_ talk to about it. But he'd got Elizabeth for dinner. So I said I'd run in for a few minutes at 9 after my music club rehearsal: – but it was 9.30 or more before I got there and the atmosphere was so gloomy that I felt perfectly _frightful_ to be cheerful. I asked him the technical things I had to know about – Gloriana revisions and postponing America until March – and then I went away, saying I'd got to pack for Brussels. Ben saw me out, and in the cool night air I plucked up courage and asked if I need have the sack & if I could stay another year and he said "if you _will_". It was tantalising having to go, because he obviously needed to let off steam, and there was no chance of it.

As IH was later to recall, Britten's sentiments regarding Pears derived from disappointment with the singer's performance that night. This 'depressed him enormously because … a bad performance for a composer matters more than anything else … Ben, I remember, said to me, 'You're about the only person I could've talked to about it'.[172] Stephen Potter recalled Pears's own despondency at this time, 'because he's made a lot of mistakes in Gloriana'.[173]

[170] Headington, *Peter Pears*, p. 166.
[171] Harewood, *The Tongs and the Bones*, p. 138.
[172] Interview with Donald Mitchell, 22 June 1977.
[173] Diary of Stephen Potter, 4 July 1952.

(Ben & Peter away, London & Devon festival.)

The Taw and Torridge Festival, the first successful outcome of the EOG's plans to establish festivals away from Aldeburgh, ran from 11 to 19 July. George Harewood was one of the Festival's patrons and Ronald Duncan was Chairman of the Council. The opening concert on 11 July, at St Mary's Church Bideford, featured anthems by Handel and Purcell, Arne's *Ode in Honour of Great Britain* and Britten's own *Saint Nicolas*. Pears sang the tenor solos and Norman Del Mar conducted local choirs and the EOG Orchestra. Britten then performed as pianist in a recital of opera arias featuring Joan Cross and Nancy Evans and including excerpts from *Gloriana*, and Del Mar conducted both *The Beggar's Opera* and *The Little Sweep*. Pears and Britten rounded off the Festival with a 'Soirée Musicale' at Moreton House, Bideford on 19 July.

> <u>Tuesday July 21st</u>. *Ben & Peter walked in at 10 at night while I was copying out Schütz – both looked weary but they said the Devon festival had been a success. Ben said Peter had sung very beautifully at his recital. And he'd been happy with the Pickled Boys*[174] *& had taken them to Let's Make An Opera. They were in a frivolous mood for gossip: – Ben described ——'s girl*[175] *as "one of those with* <u>studied rudeness.</u>" *They asked for all the Aldeburgh news and I told them what I could.*

With no improvement in his arm, Britten's doctors were now insisting that he take at least a month off to recover. The composer acquiesced and decided to spend August on holiday at home, using the remainder of July to complete outstanding projects.

> <u>Wed. July 22nd</u>. *Went to lunch at Crag House – both of them feeling very low with weariness, not having slept. Ben very depressed because he'd just heard that Paul was going to be a Jesuit – 15 years away from everyone. They cheered up a bit after Miss Hudson's food – we talked of the possibilities of the Aldeburgh Opera House and I warned Ben that if we got American help it would mean a stunt comparing him with Wagner, and he said "I want it so much that I think I could stand* <u>anything</u>." *After we'd had coffee Ben went upstairs and Peter & I began talking about Monteverdi but he was so weary I told him to go to bed, & went off home. Then at about 5 oclock when I was walking on the beach I met them both and Ben said he'd been meaning to do Gloriana. However, he'd had a* <u>bit</u> *of sleep. I said how glad I was that he was going to have a holiday in August*

---

[174] The 'three small boys' who sing an 'Alleluia' refrain in Britten's *Saint Nicolas*, having been murdered and 'salted down' but then revived by the saint.

[175] Not a text deletion; IH has written a long dash here in the original.

and hoped he was glad too and he said "Well I expect I <u>shall</u> be". We began
discussing plans for the 1954 Festival – I suggested Bishop Bell for a festival
service and they thought it a good idea. Peter went in and while Ben & I were
standing on the wall opposite the garden gate he began telling me what he
meant to write next, and how the Devon festival had proved that St Nicolas is
the answer to a great need, and he'd been discussing with Ronald Duncan the
possibilities of other Saints, and then afterwards he'd decided that he'd do a life
of Christ. I was so excited that I nearly knocked him off the wall. He said that
he & Peter would do the libretto themselves, using the Apocryphal acts.[176] And
that it would be for the 1955 festival; – that he'd have to do it fairly soon because
there'd be a lot for the chorus to learn, and that I must promise to stay for it.
Then Peter called out that Tony Gishford had arrived, so I went home.

Knowing the local community as she did, IH was being somewhat mischievous in making this suggestion for the Festival Service speaker, although Britten himself would undoubtedly have welcomed it. George Bell was Bishop of
Chichester, and a good friend of GH, whose funeral service he had conducted.
A committed pacifist, he had been a supporter of Dietrich Bonhoeffer, had con-
demned the persecution of Jews in Europe and criticized Churchill and Harris
for the policy of area bombing. His views had made him unpopular in many
areas of the Anglican Church and ruined his chances of becoming Archbishop
of Canterbury; they would certainly not have gone down well among some
sections of the Aldeburgh community. Nevertheless, in the end IH was able to
invite Bell to conduct a Festival service in 1956.

On 25 July IH departed Brown Acres for good. She also started a second
exercise book for her diary, even though there were a dozen pages left in the
first one, suggesting that it might have been mislaid during the move. She was
now working on corrections to the vocal score of *Gloriana*, which Boosey &
Hawkes wanted to publish by the end of the year.

The next day Britten and Pears went to Norfolk with Jennifer Vyvyan to give
an 'Operatic Recital', including the Second Lute Song from *Gloriana*, as part of
the King's Lynn Festival. Britten was also having further consultations about
his arm.

Monday July 27th. Went to Crag House after breakfast but a message came
through that they couldn't get back till tea-time. They arrived just before 5, both
looking very weary and a bit depressed about the concert in Kings Lynn which

---

[176] Britten owned *The Apocryphal New Testament: being the Apocryphal Gospels,
   Acts, Epistles, and Apocalypses / with other narratives and fragments*, trans.
   Montague Rhodes James (Oxford: Oxford University Press, 1926).

hadn't gone too well. No chance of doing Gloriana mistakes, so I left almost
immediately.

The local *Lynn News and Advertiser* took a different view of the concert, describing the Lute Song in its review the next day as 'an impressive finale to a brilliant concert'.

Britten and IH now met to turn their minds to the necessary corrections and revisions to the vocal score of *Gloriana*, including the addition of metronome marks.

> *Tuesday July 28th. When I arrived at breakfast they were in the throes of a 20*
> *minute telephone call with Basil Douglas about programmes for the V. & A. and*
> *the Festival Hall. Then Ben suggested that we should work at Gloriana in the*
> *garden. The sunshine was lovely. He was very patient about the mistakes I'd let*
> *through, and made a good many suggestions for improving things in the 2nd*
> *edition. I suggested altering "for its bread" and he agreed.*[177] *But when I told*
> *him my doubts about Penelope quoting from Q.E.'s dilemma in Act III Sc III he*
> *said I'd missed the overall drama of the music in that section but I said that he'd*
> *created such characters that one couldn't forget their personalities & that Q.E.'s*
> *cry from the heart was a v. different sort of heart from P. Rich's. The food arrived*
> *so we had to stop arguing. Lovely picnic in the garden. But Ben was depressed*
> *& began talking about the problems of the Festival committee. Peter said that it*
> *was no good worrying about it before Sept. I said "but he'll have to think about*
> *something during his month off" and Peter said "no, his orders are not to." which*
> *is grim: – I was hoping he'd only got to stop actual work & not use his arm. They*
> *are trying to diet him by cutting off fats which sounds disastrous when he's so*
> *thin.*
>
> *We then got to work putting in metronome marks in Gloriana – it was a great*
> *help having my silent metronome instead of a ticker. He produced his watch with*
> *second hands, and then he played through ½ a minute of music with me saying*
> *"Now" and "stop" and it always fitted in exactly to the beginning of a bar, and the*
> *speeds were always related to each other as in Bach. It was very exciting. And it*
> *was so lovely hearing it with the right phrasing again. Especially the trombones*
> *at the soliloquy at the end of Act I, which sounded so different from the Covent*
> *Garden performances that I wept. He was very business-like & kept me to it,*
> *but after the end of the scene, having found that the Prayer really was the same*

---

[177] In Act III scene 2 of the opera, a group of old men, on hearing that Essex is drumming up support for rebellion, comment 'Poor ravening knaves! / A boy runs mad when for its bread his belly craves'.

*speed as the bit before, he was silent for a long time and came back from an
immense distance.*

*"Flood music" he said, when it came to the Recorder's rheumatic bit in the Masque
scene. When he played the Concord dance he said "Are we <u>ever</u> going to hear
it right, do you suppose?" And in the final dance of homage he wanted to put
━━━▶ on the word "tokens" to help them to phrase but I said that he'd done all
that a composer could by setting those words in that way & by putting "Smooth
and gracious" at the top, & that it was the chorus-master's job to teach them to
sing it properly. He agreed, & left it.*

*Half-way through Act II scene II he stopped and said "I can't think why people
dislike this music so much". I said that it was because they hadn't heard it yet.
[words erased] In reply to the thing about not having heard it yet he said "but
there have been some very remarkable individual performances in it", but I said
that it was all-of-a-piece and until they'd heard it like that they couldn't know
it. He didn't answer that one, and we went on to time the next bit, but then
Myfanwy turned up so we had to stop. He asked me to go back next day and
finish the remaining 4 scenes.*

With his mind free of the Festival, Britten's thoughts were now already looking beyond his holiday to the 1954 Festival and *The Turn of the Screw*. First,
however, the corrections to the vocal score of *Gloriana* had to be completed,
and he went with Pears to Chester Gate, from where he arranged meetings
at Boosey & Hawkes. Pears, meanwhile, resumed his concert schedule; on 30
July he was to sing in a Promenade Concert from the Royal Albert Hall, with
the BBC Symphony Orchestra conducted by Sir Malcolm Sargent and John
Hollingsworth in a programme including Mozart's aria *Per pièta, non ricercate*,
K420, and Britten's *Serenade* (with Dennis Brain) and the *Four Sea Interludes*
from *Peter Grimes*.[178]

*Wed. July 29th. Jeremy rang up to say Ben was too busy to finish the metronome
marks that day & would I be at Boosey & Hawkes at 2.15 on Thursday.*

*<u>Thursday July 30th</u>. London. Got to Boosey & Hawkes & found Erwin waiting.
Ben came in a few minutes late, looking weary, depressed, agitated & cross.
He began going through the Gloriana corrections <u>almost</u> peevishly, sitting tense
and rigid, and saying what had to be said in a cold voice. I was determined not to
get upset by it, and after a while, just through the sheer necessity of having
a practical job to do, he began to relax, till by the time he got to* 𝄢 ♩ ♩ ♩♭

for its

---

[178] This performance is available on CD as BBCL 4192–2.

he was laughing at both of us, and telling Erwin it would <u>have</u> to be altered
"because I have to live in Aldeburgh with Imo".[179] *He found several small*
corrections in Act III sc. III but nothing devastatingly wrong, so I began to feel
better. He tried the 3rd scene of Act II but then he had to stop to go home & give
Peter tea before his concert. He'd been depressed at the rehearsal, but said that
Peter sang the Mozart aria beautifully. He said there was a test of listening in the
storm in the Grimes Interludes: – one instrument was playing a 5th too low, and
he couldn't discover which it was: – it was the first time he'd ever been defeated
by such a thing. When we'd left Erwin and were walking downstairs I asked him
to let me carry his scores to spare his arm, but he'd got them in the left hand and
said it was all right, and that the metal banister was "cool and soothing" to his
right hand: – I said "is it as bad as all that?" and he said "Yes". This was almost
more than could be borne, but he said "it's a <u>holiday</u> tomorrow".

Britten's arrangement with Decca Records, who had agreed to release their
recordings of music from the Festival 'of which the profits would accrue to the
Festival funds,'[180] was now coming to fruition. The company wanted to put
out records from the opening concert, comprising the Mozart Mass, the two
Arne choral works, the Purcell anthem and the *Variations on an Elizabethan
theme.*

<u>Friday July 31st</u>. I got to Chester Gate at 10.45 – pouring rain – Peter was
out shopping. Ben said that on the whole the Serenade had gone well – it had
sounded so beautifully clean. Erwin had not been able to find the corrected score
of Gloriana – had I taken it away by mistake? I told him I'd left it with Erwin in
his office, and I rang up Erwin about it and he'd already found it. Ben said he was
worried about Erwin and he just began having an outpouring about it but at that
moment Peter & Jeremy came in. So we went to Decca's studio in Hampstead and
listened to the Aldeburgh Festival records which sounded <u><u>very</u></u> much better than
I'd dared to hope. The Mozart was <u>most</u> beautiful: – really moving. Ben obviously
enormously impressed – (he said afterwards that he even felt more cheered
about his conducting.) The session lasted a <u>very</u> long time, because of comparing
the records of the performance with the tape recording of the rehearsals. They'd
had to leave the Rolls in a yard at the back of the building and it was agony for
Ben having to turn it and I <u>longed</u> to tell Peter to take the wheel from him but
remembered just in time that that <u>wasn't</u> my job – for the last bit Peter did
help him.

[179] The original vocal score of June 1953 gives these words a different emphasis,
with the first two notes given to 'for' and the last only to 'its'.
[180] Minutes of the Executive Committee, 4 March 1953.

We got back to Chester Gate at a quarter to 2 and had a marvellous meal in the kitchen – bacon & scrambled egg cooked by Peter. While we were waiting for Beth, Ben and Peter went through bits of the St John Passion – Peter tried to make Ben take the $\frac{12}{8}$ bass Aria slower, but Ben said "no, it MUST be that speed; – the Adagio refers to the chorale."

Then we drove to Aldeburgh. 5 of us with a lot of luggage, Ben driving. With Jeremy & Peter both in the car I'd hoped he could have spared his arm. But he let Peter take over halfway. We stopped for tea at Westbury House: – the sun was shining and none of the neighbours had got their radios on and Iso was at the top of her form – they both enjoyed it and it was lovely and peaceful. They dropped me at the end of my lane & picked me up at home later for the ghastly party at Marjorie Spring-Rice's. When I said they deserved haloes for going, Ben said "it's quite a good thing to be let down gently at the beginning of a holiday".

August 1953

Britten's holiday rest began with a pre-arranged meeting of the local gramophone society at Crag House. Pears, who was hosting the evening, began the proceedings mischievously with a recording of Beethoven's rarely heard *Wellington's Victory*, otherwise known as *The Battle of Vittoria*, op. 91.

Sunday August 2nd. There were over 60 people at the gramophone recital at Crag House: – Peter did it beautifully: – they began with a ghastly Beethoven Battle of something or other and everyone looked puzzled and people began muttering "surely Beethoven never wrote that", and Ben's backview looked as innocently wicked as when we were singing "cast a-down the proud" outside Mrs. Close's house last Christmas. They provided drinks for everyone when it was over, and it was awful seeing Ben insisting on carrying trays.

On 4 August IH part-moved temporarily into a studio of her own, but continued to sleep in the houses of local friends. She had now moved next door from Herons to stay in Rhoda Backhouse's house, Gulland. By 12 August she was, according to her appointments diary, 'camping out' at the studio during the week and returning to Gulland only at weekends, whilst working at the planning of the Aldeburgh Music Club's first public outing, a concert in the parish church scheduled for 26 August.

Britten, meanwhile, was using his relaxation time to explore a wide range of musical byways.

Thursday August 6th. I went in to Crag House directly after breakfast to give them the photostat copy of G's "I love my love",[181] which Peter had wanted. They were in the garden, finishing their coffee. The holiday going not altogether well all the time – chiefly because Peter had been having hay fever quite badly. I told Ben about the apocryphal St John's reasons for having a holiday and his eye lit up when it got to the bit about the bow not always being stretched.[182] He talked about the infancy legends and said he must read them again. Peter asked me to go there to dinner that evening.

When I got there at 7.30 Ben was in a silent mood. Peter and I looked through recorder music for the programme on the 26th while Ben read Hungarian scores that he'd been sent to criticise. It seemed an odd way of doing nothing. He said he was suffering from too much family: – even Roguey had begun to pall. "Beth's all right", he said. "But we're all mad." I said what a good thing, and where would we be if they weren't. He said "no: – I like sanity." I said I liked sanity too, but I liked the madness that was the opposite of what families were when they never did anything mad, and he said "no, we're all too tied up into knots and shy.[183] I like people to be easy and open and simple." Then Peter suggested putting on the very beautiful record of the two African goatherds, and Ben said it was heartbreakingly beautiful.[184] They began to listen to one of the Kodaly records that Ben had been sent,[185] but it was impossible to hear it clearly, and Miss Hudson said the food was ready. Peter and I had hot lobster but Ben hates lobster so had sole, and they were both very disappointed because Miss Hudson had given them tinned peas. It certainly did seem a mistake, with the runner beans at the height of their season. We drank very sweet white wine with chunks of ice in it and agreed that it was good not to have the usual snobbish disapproval of the

[181] No. 5 of GH's *Six Choral Folk Songs*, op. 36.

[182] The story tells of how St John, while he was gently stroking a partridge, was approached by a hunter with a bow and arrows, who wanted to know why a man of such reputation was amusing himself with such a trivial pursuit. John asked the hunter why he didn't carry his bow fully stretched all the time, to which the man responded that if he were to do so, the strength and tension of the bow would be lost. John then justified his own relaxation, arguing that he had sometimes to ease and relax his mind, to prevent it growing slack through unbroken rigour, and thus unable to respond to the power of the Holy Spirit. IH's knowledge of the passage may have come from its close proximity in the 'Acts of John' to texts set by GH in *The Hymn of Jesus.*

[183] Originally IH had also written 'and loyal'. This she crossed out.

[184] 'Goatboy calls: Kigezi Uganda', an unpublished 78 rpm recording, coupled with some pygmy harp music.

[185] Probably *Folksongs of Hungary*, vol. 2: *A csitári hegyek alatt régen leesett a hó*, arranged by Zoltán Kodály; performed by Leslie Chabay, tenor and Tibor Kozma, piano (New York: Bartók Records, *c.*1952).

> *English. We talked again about the apocryphal legends when we were finishing
> our wine in the sitting-room. Then Peter began talking about the Rothschild
> book on Bach & Ben said he simply couldn't understand a word. They began
> to discuss the <u>Adagio</u> of the 18th century and Ben said Bach used it when he
> wanted the normal tempo to be different for a while. He began playing Bach on
> the harpsichord: – marvellous mixtures, such as 16 ft for the triplet semiquavers
> in the D minor prelude, which sounded <u>absolutely</u> right. He said it was probably
> like the sound of an 8ft. they had in those days. He was playing all his left hand
> quavers legato and when I said I wanted the descending 7ths, 6ths, etc. semi-
> staccato, (also the ascending minor 3rds at the beginnings of bars) he agreed.
> Then he played Buxtehude organ preludes on the piano and then it was time to go
> home – he insisted on taking me home in the car and defeated all my arguments.*

The next morning IH received a letter from Captain Aubrey C. de Brisay, president of the Aldeburgh Choral Society, who complained that his members 'were
feeling some measure of anxiety for the future' as they felt that the Music Club,
which offered 'a higher level of practice and performance of music than we can'
was inadvertently poaching the Society's best singers.

> *<u>Friday Aug. 7th.</u> Lovely sunny day. Went to Crag House at 11 to rehearse recorder
> trios with Peter & Father Jolly. Ben was lying full length in the garden. in his
> bathing shorts* [words erased]. *He told me he'd had a tiresome letter from
> Decca's about a hum in one of the records which made it impossible to patch.
> He said – "it can't have been as bad as all that or I should have noticed it." I
> showed him the difficult letter about the Music Club, & then I lent him my 1st
> edition Rameau & then Fr Jolly arrived & Peter came down. We practised for
> over an hour; – when Fr Jolly had to go Peter & I played di Lasso duets – then
> Ben came in & lay full-length on the bed and they both talked about the Music
> Club – Choral Society problems & then Ben said "let's have a drink" so we went
> down and the Rameau was open on the harpsichord, looking thoroughly at home,
> and he had been looking at it & was thrilled with it – said the introduction was
> very useful – and he liked the curves of the groups of semiquavers. He'd had two
> schoolboys from the Ipswich Grammar School in to see him – they were writing
> an opera, but the composer hadn't learnt any rudiments. He'd given them advice
> for over an hour, bless him. He saw me out the garden way and told me not to
> worry about the letter because it would come all right.*

Britten had wanted to correct some mistakes in the Aldeburgh concert tapes by
patching in bits from the rehearsals, but Decca found the results unsatisfactory
because of a perceived hum on the performance tape. Responding to Britten's

comments, they observed that 'although you did not perhaps notice the hum ... when they attempted the joining it was made obvious by the contrast'.[186]

Having consulted Britten and Pears about her 'difficult letter', IH replied on 7 August, undertaking to pass the matter to the Aldeburgh Music Club committee, and sympathizing with the Captain's difficulties, observing that 'it is a problem that I have come across so often ... in so many parts of England.'[187]

Britten and Pears spent part of their weekend umpiring a school cricket match in Framlingham, while on the Saturday night IH's *Welcome Joy and Welcome Sorrow* was broadcast in a performance by the BBC Women's Chorus conducted by Leslie Woodgate. Returning to work on Monday, IH reviewed the sleeve notes for Decca's recordings from the Festival. When she took the proofs round to Crag House she found more visitors: James Bernard, a composer whom Britten had known since his schooldays at Wellington College, and his partner Paul Dehn, a writer who was about to collaborate with Lennox Berkeley on the libretto for *A Dinner Engagement*, to be produced by the EOG in 1954. Britten had also been working on his pet project with the strings of the Aldeburgh Music Club, coaxing them into learning Schubert's String Quintet in C.

> <u>Monday Aug. 10th.</u> *The proofs of the Decca write-up had come, so I went in after breakfast with them: Miss Hudson said they'd only just begun breakfast, so I waited about 20 mins & then asked her if I should go through, and she said "Do <u>you</u> go in, do it'll be 10 oclock" just as if it were Thaxted. So I went out into the garden in the brilliant sunshine and Ben & Peter & Jim Barnard and Paul Dehn were sitting drinking coffee, naked to the waist, in shorts, looking as if they were in the South of France. I'd been a bit anxious about Jim because I was afraid he might think I'd done him out of a job in copying out Gloriana, but he was the very last person who'd ever have a grudge; – easy, and good to look at. Ben described the Saturday afternoon cricket match which he & Peter had umpired & scored for the small boys – the winning team never made more than 3 runs, but there were 39 byes. Then he & Peter went through the proofs & made several suggestions and I took them away.*
>
> *At 5.30 I went in to rehearse recorder trios with Peter & Father Jolly: – Peter depressed because he couldn't get his top notes. Went back again at 8.30 & heard Rhoda, Biddy, Ben, Mrs. Vales*[188] *& Dot play the 1st movement of the Schubert 5tet <u>most</u> beautifully – it was like a miracle.*

[186] 10 August 1953; BPL.
[187] 7 August 1953; BPL.
[188] Shirley Bayles.

James Bernard had worked with Britten on preparing the full score of *Billy Budd*, after which Britten had advised him to 'break out on your own', so IH had no need to fear that she was doing him out of a job.[189]

The next morning Pears was travelling to London on his way to giving a concert in France, but was having second thoughts. Millions of French workers had gone on strike to protest against austerity measures, and stories were circulating of thousands of British tourists left stranded by rail stoppages either in Paris or in immobilized carriages in small railway sidings in the country.

IH meanwhile had decided to write a book about Britten, and was also trying to interest him in conducting some of her father's music on record. Britten in turn was trying to cajole IH into taking on another of his protégés, this time James Bernard, to follow in the footsteps of James Butt and Benjamin Zander. He was also using his holiday to embark on the composition of some songs to poems by Thomas Hardy, to add to the setting of 'Wagtail and Baby' he had made in Ireland in the spring, and to give further thought to writing a work based on the Apocryphal Acts. A host of friends continued to pass through Crag House, including Paul Rogerson, Michael Tippett and the family of Otakar Kraus, the baritone, who had sung in the Festival production of *Albert Herring*. And as usual he was taking every opportunity to go swimming. Perhaps most significantly, he was using this rare period of relaxation to begin to develop far-reaching plans for establishing a school of music in Aldeburgh, with IH as its head.

> *Tuesday Aug. 11th. Ben had asked me to go in & finish the metronome marks in Gloriana; – as I was walking in on the main road I met him taking Peter to Saxmundham in the Rolls – they asked me to get in the back & go with them: – they'd got to drive fast or Peter would miss his train. It was absolutely thrilling & felt just like flying: – my skirt filled like a balloon & nearly lifted me out of the back, & the hedges made a marvellous whooshing sound as we rushed past them. When we got to the station the train had just come in. Going back, Ben said that he hoped Peter wouldn't stay too long in France if the strike conditions were still bad.*
>
> *Then he said "I've got a new baby for you", and he began to tell me all about James Bernard and how he'd been talking to him very firmly about the need to get a job and the need to have regular composition lessons with someone who would be ruthless, and he asked me if I'd take him on. One of the reasons for suggesting me had been that "as we work together so closely, we'd be able to look at his*

---

[189] Bridcut, *Britten's Children*, p. 255.

things together." He said very shrewd things about his charm & frivolousness,
and said that he felt there was a need for "weekend composers".

When we got back we went through Act III for metronome marks: – I tried to
persuade him to save his arm and not play too much, but it was hopeless – he
played with a passion that the orchestra has not yet achieved. He wrote in an
extra entry of the tune in canon in the last scene ("in some unhaunted") where
he'd felt it was too naked. When we'd finished we walked along the beach and
talked to Otakar Kraus & his family & Ben told Bill that Paul was coming the
"day after tomorrow, for a long weekend, till Monday or Tuesday". He also told
me that Michael Tippett was coming down on Tuesday for 4 days – that he
hadn't been well – Ben said rather ruefully "I don't much *want to have an invalid*
just now." Stephen Potter & his sons were just going to swim – so they waited
for Ben, & when they were standing at the edge of the water it was impossible
to tell from their backviews which was Ben & which were the two young boys in
their late teens or early 20s. When the Potters had gone, Ben & I had our lunch
in the garden – it was the most wonderful day with a cloudless blue sky and just
enough breeze. Afterwards, while we were finishing our cider, he talked again
of the apocrypha and asked me which five or six incidents I'd have if it were me:
– he said he thought not *the resurrection, as it was to be the human [bits].*[190] *I*
suggested the temptation, and he said "yes – a time of agony" and he went on to
speak of Gethsemane. Then he asked me how I was getting on with my book and
asked if he might read it. I told him I'd learnt so much recently that I was having
to rewrite the beginning, and he said "Oh!" Then I asked him if I might copy out
the Hardy songs so as to get to know them – he was doubtful, as he's still not
sure of several things in them. He asked me to help with the next opera. (!!!) He
then talked about teaching, and how much did I want to do any, & I said I must
have one day a week in London, but didn't want to get too involved and he said
"you mustn't get too many pupils to be able to be Principal of our new school of
music when we get it." Then he said he & Peter had been discussing it with Eric
Harrison,[191] *& had decided that a school must be residential and* needn't *be in*
London – in fact, it would be an advantage for it not *to be. I said that it would*
need a terrible *lot of money, or else being run by the education authorities; & that*
being out of London must *add to the expense of running it. He said "I don't see*
the advantage of sending the students to hear Sir Malcolm conducting."[192]

---

[190] '[bits]' added later.
[191] Possibly the pianist of that name, who was a professor at the Royal College
of Music.
[192] Sir Malcolm Sargent.

*Then I plucked up courage & told him about the Decca Planets & Egdon Heath
and asked him if he'd do them when his arm was better and he said no he couldn't
do the Planets, & said "van Beinam is the man, with that orchestra, and you
could go over there and go through them with him. <u>But don't let him do Egdon
Heath</u>." When I said I wished he'd do both he said "The trouble about the Planets
is that it needs a virtuoso conductor" so I said "nonsense, it isn't such bad music
as all that: – and <u>you</u> think it's better music than I do!" and his eye lit up with
that particular gleam that comes into it every now & then when something one
has said has made a direct appeal to him. He was most touchingly pleased at
being asked, which took me by surprise, although it is so characteristic of him.
Then he went out sketching with Mary Potter.*

Back in 1948, after hearing *The Planets* on the radio in a performance conducted by Sir Adrian Boult, Britten had commented to IH: 'I do see the weaknesses, the problems not really solved, but there is such musicality there &
above all a really wonderful imagination ...'[193] Eduard van Beinum had conducted the first performance of Britten's *Spring Symphony* in 1949, and would
record *The Young Person's Guide to the Orchestra* and the *Four Sea Interludes*
from *Peter Grimes* for Decca in September 1953. Nothing came of Britten's idea
that van Beinum should record GH's music with the Concertgebouw Orchestra, however.[194] IH's book on Britten was not finally completed and published
until 1966.

*<u>Wed Aug 12th</u>. Went in at 11.30 to see Jeremy and check the lists of metronome
marks – feeling like death after an awful night of indigestion, (thought it might
have been yesterday's pork, & afraid Ben might also have suffered.) As I opened
the front door I heard him playing quiet chords: – I crept upstairs but he heard
me – he looked cheerful so he can't have suffered. Jeremy had just gone. Ben
followed me into his room while I did the lists and wanted to know if I thought
Otakar Kraus's 5 yr old boy was too young to start learning the piano. He said
Peter was coming back that evening and possibly not going to France after all
because of the strikes. Then I checked the lists, and as I went out I saw that he
was in the sitting-room so I said give my love to Peter, and he said ought we to
have a Festival meeting, and I said Peter said to wait till Sept., and Ben said "by
then, we <u>must</u> get on", and when I said we'd have the finance meeting by then he*

[193] 27 October 1948; BPL.
[194] Britten's interpretation of *Egdon Heath*, on the other hand, was captured in
a live performance from Orford Church in 1961, and was released in 1999 by
BBC Worldwide in the 'Britten the Performer' series on CD. Not surprisingly
IH considered it the best performance of the work that she had heard.

said "it ought to have been <u>much</u> sooner" and when I said that Peter said it would
always be as late as that he said "it <u>won't</u>". So then I told him that Peter thought
he was going ahead too fast about the theatre, and he said "we'll have the theatre,
& you shall perform to me in it and I'll perform to you." Then I went home, still
feeling v. middle-aged but a <u>bit</u> younger.

Britten's enthusiasm for the new theatre was prompted in part by the financial losses sustained by the 1953 Festival; he told Elizabeth Mayer that despite
'lovely large audiences', the event had 'of course lost money – shall do, in fact,
until we can build a theatre bigger than the Jubilee Hall'.[195] Nevertheless, planning for the 1954 Festival was now underway, and Britten was interested in
a suggestion by Tony Mayer that the renowned Couraud Choir from France
should visit Aldeburgh and take part. But although such impending commitments had begun to cast a shadow over the holiday atmosphere, Britten continued the summer in relaxed mood, playing tennis, swimming and planning
an outing with Richard Kihl, a local schoolboy who often partnered him on the
tennis court. In preparation for this trip, Britten wrote down a list of brasses in
Suffolk churches on the back of a letter from Decca of 7 August, gleaned from
his copy of Arthur Mee's *Suffolk*.[196]

Not all was well, however. Ernst Roth at Boosey & Hawkes had written with
bad news about a projected production of *Gloriana* at La Scala, Milan, under
its music director Victor De Sabata. The previous summer, discussions between
De Sabata and Boosey & Hawkes had concluded that La Scala would have the
first performance of *Gloriana* after London, and in April Roth had returned
from Italy to tell Britten that La Scala would indeed mount the opera 'as the
first novelty of next season, in the first two weeks of January 1954'.[197] By August
all this had changed. Roth reported De Sabata's 'unfavourable impression',[198]
having seen *Gloriana* surreptitiously on 18 June, following which La Scala had
decided finally that they would not mount it.

<u>Friday</u> Aug. 14th. Peter came round to my studio and said would I go out brass
rubbing with them. He told me that Ben had had an awful letter from Roth
saying that Milan was <u>not</u> going to do Gloriana after all, because Sabata didn't
like it. He said Ben was terribly depressed. I went round at 12 & found them
just going to have a bathe – Ben, Peter, Paul, Mary and a v. nice schoolboy called

[195] 30 August 1953; BPL.
[196] Arthur Mee, *Suffolk, our Farthest East*, The King's England (London: Hodder
       & Stoughton, 1941); BPL.
[197] 21 April 1953; BPL.
[198] 10 August 1953; BPL.

> *Richard. Then we packed into the car with lots of food & drink and materials for brass*[199] *rubbing and went to Pettistree – picnicked in a lovely field with a stream and immense trees. The brasses in the church were on the wall which was too difficult to begin on, so we went to Orford*[200] *where there were about 15 beauties on the floor: – it was very exciting trying to do the rubbings. Ben straight away did his very much better than anyone else! He was lovely to everyone and it was a good day.*

The 'awful' tone of Roth's letter resulted from persistent difficulties in his relationship with Britten, which had come to a head in the *Gloriana* negotiations. According to Roth, Britten's friends had told him that Roth was 'not interested in "Gloriana"', and the publisher was keen to defend himself both against the 'persistent vilifications' that he suffered at the hands of Britten's friends and the composer's 'readiness to listen to them'.

Next morning some test pressings of the Aldeburgh Festival records arrived for Britten's inspection.

> *Sat. Aug. 15th. He'd asked me to go in and hear the Aldeburgh record at 10.30. It sounded awful, terribly distorted, and Alfred's voice coarse and harsh.*[201] *Then quite by chance Ben discovered that they'd been using the wrong pick-up! The right one much better: – but Ben furious that they were insisting on having the performance rather than the rehearsal of the Berkeley, because of the missed harmonic. And Peter was depressed that they wouldn't patch the bit in the Purcell where he'd put in an extra beat – they'd said they would in London. Ben then talked about the French singers and players for the Festival – said he'd been thinking about it during his depressing night.*

Britten's depression was the result of his having spent the previous evening in earnest discussions with Paul Rogerson, who was spending his last days on the Suffolk coast, prior to starting his novitiate. IH meanwhile had taken up the suggestion made back in March that she, Pears and Britten should host a visit from some students. To this end, she was arranging to bring her new group of singers to Aldeburgh for four days of rehearsals and a performance of Bach motets, together with music by Monteverdi and Schütz, at the end of August.

Earlier in the year, Britten had been involved in negotiations with Boosey & Hawkes and two record companies regarding the possibility of a recording

[199] 'brass' added later.
[200] Pettistree is to the west of Aldeburgh, near the town of Wickham Market; Orford is to the south, near the mouth of the River Alde.
[201] Alfred Deller, who had sung the countertenor solos in the Coronation Choral Concert.

being made of the first performance of *Gloriana*. For a variety of contractual reasons, and much to Britten's frustration, this never took place, but some private tape recordings of parts of the first broadcasts were circulating, and IH took the opportunity the next day to listen to these.

> *Monday Aug. 16th.*[202] *Went to Crag House after breakfast to give Miss Hudson my rations.*[203] *She told me that Ben had sprained his ankle the evening before, playing tennis. So I went out into the garden & there he was sitting with it bandaged & propped up, while Peter was in his bathing things. Ben said "This is a judgment, isn't it!" He was obviously in pain & feeling wretched: – Paul's last day & he was out in Fr Jolly's boat, and Ben had meant to go with them. He minded not being able to swim in that heavenly sunshine. Peter asked me to go to lunch as there were a good many things to talk about. I told them how thrilled I'd been with the tape-recording of Gloriana in Ipswich the night before: – Ben asked a lot of questions about balance etc.*
>
> *When I went back later at 12.30 Mary Potter was there: – Ben was saying that he could never remember that he was older than some of the very mature young men who seemed so much more assured than he was. When Mary had gone, Ben & Peter drank beer: – Peter was looking through his earliest concert programmes & getting them filed in order, and Ben was teasing him about his highbrow choice of solos in the "miscellaneous" sections. Then we went and ate and Ben asked what Conrad Noel's* Life of Jesus[204] *was like and I said I'd been trying to get a copy for them & Peter said they'd got one somewhere and Ben asked a lot of questions about Conrad and how much still went on, and had he & G been great friends, and so on. Then Ben began to talk about Paul and how he'd asked him about the 15 years the night before. Ben hated the very word "Jesuit", and was appalled to think that Paul mustn't take* any *possessions away to his novitiate. Then we went out into the garden and sat in the sun – it was windy but lovely & bright. Peter began going on sorting out his programmes and Ben was horrified – gave him a disapproving glance as much as to say "not in front of our guest", which was* so *like G, and of course so utterly unnecessary, Peter smiled a very sweet smile at me and said "I shall still be available," and I smiled back and said something about I wouldn't look in the direction of his files because they reminded me of my unanswered letters. But he stopped sorting, and a deep gloom descended on them both and an utter silence. I wasn't going to begin making conversation. After*

---

[202] Actually 17 August.
[203] Sugar and butter were removed from the ration regime a month later, but meat was to remained rationed until July 1954.
[204] Conrad Noel, *The Life of Jesus* (London: Dent, 1937).

a while Ben asked several questions about the music club – and we discussed things quite rationally. Then Ben asked us if we'd drawn up a programme for the students' 4 days in Aldeburgh, and Peter left me to tell Ben what we'd arranged. Then Ben asked Peter if the wind was too much for him and he said no. Then Ben said "what's the matter with you?" and Peter didn't answer and for the very first time I felt really uncomfortable in their presence, apart from the few moments when I've heard Ben swearing at Peter in times of extreme exhaustion. I tried to remember that Ben was in pain & that Peter was quite likely struggling to keep off an attack of hay fever. So then I said I must go home, & when Peter got up to see me out I asked Ben if I might deputise for Jeremy if he'd got any letters to be done.

That evening, at the Music Club rehearsal, I asked Peter what time Paul was leaving – he said 9.

Following Paul Rogerson's impending departure the next day, Britten and Pears were to host a visit from the Bedford family, who had a cottage in Snape. That weekend Michael Tippett was coming to stay, before Aldeburgh Music Club rehearsals began again in preparation for a concert in Aldeburgh Parish Church the following Wednesday – the first time, as the *Leiston Observer* remarked, that the Club would 'face an audience'.[205] With his holiday nearly at an end, Britten's arm remained worryingly troublesome.

Tuesday Aug. 17th.[206] Got to Miss Hudson's door at 9 but Peter leaned through the hatch & said he was catching the 10.30 after all. He asked me in but I said I'd come back at 10 & wave to him. At 10 I waited outside the front door: Paul came out to fetch me in. All three were in tears, Ben being the calmest & most matter-of-fact. He hobbled to the front door to see them off and I waved from the middle of the road till the car had turned the corner. I had to walk off without looking back at Ben which was agony, but there was nothing ... to do for him. I knew the best thing for Peter would be for him to cry for as long as he wanted to. But it was appallingly difficult [words erased] and leave him alone.

In the afternoon I went into the kitchen at Crag House to do my ironing and one of the Bedford boys came in to fetch the tea things – his whole family was there and Ben had suggested tea on the beach – his ankle was so much better that he could manage to get as far as that. I made the tea for them & said I'd take out the kettle when it boiled again. Ben lying on the pebbles looking much

---

[205]   21 August 1953.
[206]   Actually 18 August.

better but with the tight look across his face which he gets when he's tired or worried. Then Peter came in from playing golf and Ben was frightfully pleased that he'd won his game. The Bedfords were talking about organs – "how would you define a baroque organ?" Peter tried to pass it on to me but I wasn't having any, so he began describing it, but Ben said "What you are all forgetting is that the nineteenth century invented the Diapason – it didn't exist on Bach's organ," and went on to explain how it destroyed the clarity of Bach's fugues. Then the Bedford father asked "were the organs equal tempered?" and I said that some were & some weren't and Bach used to go round playing them & was shocked when they weren't equal tempered & would play things in the keys that sounded most out of tune, to the discomfort of the owner of the organ, and he said "That sounds as if Bach must have been rather like Ben – it's just the sort of thing he'd do!" Ben cheered up quite a lot. Then Peter suggested we should practise recorders so we went in.

Friday Aug 21st. Ben peevish & obviously wanting to begin work again. Insisted on playing tennis.

Sunday Aug. 23rd. Rehearsal of the Music Club programme at Crag House in the evening. Ben's ankle completely recovered. He told me he'd been to see me several days ago but I'd just gone out, so "about 18 people" told him. He looked well and cheerful. Michael Tippett was there for the weekend.

Tuesday Aug. 25th. Rehearsed in the church. The things went well on the whole. I longed for them to practise getting into place for each item like we used to at Dartington: – Ben saw the point & suggested to Peter that we should have a "silent rehearsal". When the ordinary rehearsal was over they practised their Bach slow movement from the double concerto – Ben sounded lovely on the viola though quite a lot of it was awkward for him.[207] He asked me rather anxiously if it was all right when he went down after having been up, & I told him yes but that I didn't like the end being loud.

Wed. Aug. 26th. Music Club concert in evening. Great success – church full, about 500 people there. Everything went well. "This have I done" was inspired.[208] Ben & Peter asked me round to a drink when it was over. Several guests there. When they'd gone & only Peter's cousins left, Ben asked me to go with them to Framlingham where the cousins were staying.[209] It was a marvellous moonlight

[207] IH typescript note: 'because of the trouble he'd been having with pain in his arm'.

[208] GH's 'This have I done for my true love', for SATB, op. 34 no. 1.

[209] Probably with Pamela Hope-Johnstone and her children.

night. On the way back, sitting all three in front for warmth, with Peter driving,
Ben talked a lot: – said he'd talked to Fr. Jolly who'd been very reassuring about
Paul. He said Michael was calmer, but madder than usual. They brought me home
to my door – getting on for midnight.

Following this success IH proposed a new challenge for the Music Club to
accept at its next committee meeting – Purcell's *The Fairy Queen*. The meeting
also had to consider the outstanding business of its relationship with the
Aldeburgh Choral Society.

Thursday, Aug 27th I went round to Crag House at breakfast time with the full
score of The Fairy Queen to go through it with Peter. They were having breakfast
in the garden – Billy was there, Ben in white shorts & naked to the waist, looking
well. When Bill had gone they began talking about next year's festival – the
possibilities of appealing for a new theatre, and difficulties in office work. When
Peter was indoors Ben said "What we three have got to remember is that we're
going to have a music school here one day". Then he went to dress, to go out
sailing, & Peter & I went through the Fairy Queen for the next Music Club
meeting.

Following the meeting, the new club secretary Norah Nichols reported to
Captain de Brisay the members' unanimous conclusion that 'time given to the
Music Club and/or the Choral Society is solely the affair of the individuals concerned and not a matter that either your committee or ours can decide.'[210] The
Society struggled on until March 1954, when Captain de Brisay announced that
they would not be giving an Easter concert because of their depleted numbers,
commenting that 'there were other musical activities in which not unnaturally
our members may equally wish to share. We do not exclusively claim loyalties,
neither have we lost any.'[211]

IH's students arrived on Saturday 29 August and were billeted in Crag House,
Gulland and elsewhere, among them Rosamund Strode. She had been busy preparing for their arrival, copying out parts, as she later recalled, 'by hand from
the collected editions; we had no photo-copying machines in those days.'[212]

That evening, with a repertoire including music by Schütz, Monteverdi's
madrigal 'Hor ch'il ciel' and Bach's motet *Jesu meine Freude*, they were to be
pitched straight into an intensive schedule of rehearsals. Pears, whose enthusiasm for teaching had been nurtured by IH, threw himself into the project while

[210] 28 August 1953; BPL.
[211] *Leiston Observer*, 12 March 1954.
[212] IH, 'Not *too* educational'.

Britten, at least to begin with, kept away. The following day they were to have a second rehearsal at 41 Crag Path, the home of Biddy and Dot Row.

Sunday Aug. 30th. The singers & string players[213] *arrived in time for tea at Crag House in the garden – Peter very welcoming, Ben looking as if he wished they weren't there. He disappeared as soon as possible and Peter took the first rehearsal of "Hor ch'il ciel" – After supper we rehearsed the Bach motet: – a good rehearsal.*

Monday Aug 31st. Began rehearsing Bach at 41 Crag Path – then Peter rehearsed the Schütz – it sounded lovely with strings. Evening rehearsals at Crag House – Ben still keeping out of the way.

September 1953

Rehearsals continued into the following week, with a concert scheduled for 2 September in the parish church at Southwold, a resort town to the north of Aldeburgh. Britten was soon drawn into the proceedings, which were, however, briefly overshadowed by concern arising from the late return from Holland of his sister Beth's husband Kit Welford and their son Sebastian. Meanwhile Basil Douglas was coming to stay to discuss plans for *The Turn of the Screw*. IH's own domestic arrangements were finally settling down, as she had now taken a flat on Crag Path, into which she would be able to move at the end of the month.

Tuesday Sept 1. I had a picnic lunch on the beach with Ben & Peter & the singers who were staying with them: – lovely sunny day and everyone feeling happy. Ben was talking about Kit & Sebastian being long overdue on their return journey from Holland. Someone said "if anything had gone wrong we'd have heard about it immediately". Ben agreed. I said "I didn't manage to persuade you about that the day after Peter had missed his night train." Ben said "No, but then you took quite a time making yourself believe it." Which was very revealing, because I had believed it all the time quite firmly, but Ben's own anxiety must have been so much stronger than anything else that I must have apparently caught some of his doubts – it was also revealing to know how easily he sees everything that goes on. Ben had[214] *got a sore throat and was feeling mouldy. Only got a glimpse of him between rehearsals that evening – he said the Schütz sounded lovely. He rehearsed the Mozart G min. 4tet marvellously with the strings.*[215]

213 IH: '(i.e. our 1st students)' added in green pencil in the text.
214 Originally 'He'd'; altered by IH in green pencil.
215 Mozart's Piano Quartet in G minor, K478.

*Wed. Sept 2nd. Pouring wet day. I'd had a 2nd sleepless night, so after the Bach
rehearsal I left Peter doing the Schütz and went and had a bath at Crag House
and lay on Rosamund's bed, where Miss Hudson found me – she was very kind,
bless her heart. Ben was trying fragments over at the piano – perhaps bits of the
Turn of the Screw? (No: Hardy songs).[216] At 12 when I went down he & Peter &
Basil were having drinks & I felt so awful that I accepted one instead of refusing.
Ben v. sympathetic about sleepless nights, & when I said how could one possibly
not get over-excited with Peter rehearsing Schütz & him doing the Mozart, and
he agreed there was nothing to be done about it. Somebody said I ought to take
sleeping-pills, & when I said it would be the end & I'd get more and more like
Harriet Cohen if I began taking drugs Ben said "Oh no, your sight is much too
good!" which was very funny.[217] We drove to Southwold and the rain cleared
up on the way and the sun came out by the time we got there. Beautiful church
– almost as light as Thaxted. Lovely for sound. We had a short rehearsal, but the
audience began turning up very early, so we had to stop. The performance went
well, and the Bach motet was really good: – several mistakes in the basses but the
phrasing was good and the lightness of the runs in "Ihr aber seid nicht fleischlich"
was better than its ever been before. When it was all over Ben put his arm round
me and said "That was certainly a first performance of Jesu meine Freude." He
was truly happy about it which gave me the greatest up since Rejoice in the Lamb.*

*We went and had an excellent tea – Ben thoroughly relaxed. He enjoyed it when I
told him Roguey's remark in church, immediately after the programme was over:
– "Now they're going, can we have a music lesson?" And he loved the Clemens
"Sanctus",[218] and asked me when I was going to bring out the English equivalent
of Der Kanon.[219] Then we went on the pier, and Peter and I had a long talk
about the next time we have students at Aldeburgh. They provided a wonderful
picnic meal at Crag House for everyone: – Miss Hudson had slaved all day. Ben's
throat was so bad that he couldn't eat. In a moment of quietness when we were
in the sitting room with only Peter & one of the students in the room I told them
that I'd taken a flat in Crag Path for a year, and Ben was frightfully pleased and
embraced me to celebrate – Then people began turning up to listen. Monteverdi
went well – Ben playing a thrilling continuo. The Mozart G minor also lovely:
– he was very pleased with the way the strings had done it. And he was thrilled*

[216] '(No: Hardy songs)' added later.
[217] Harriet Cohen underwent two eye operations in the 1950s.
[218] A five-part round by Jacobus Clemens non Papa, which IH later included in
her collection *Singing for Pleasure* (1957).
[219] *Der Kanon: ein Singbuch für alle*, ed. F. Jöde (Wolfenbüttel, 1921). Pears had
recently acquired the two volumes of this historical anthology of vocal music.

with Peter's Honeysucking Bees.[220] *The Buxtehude Easter solo cantata was thrilling. Altogether a good evening. Ben took through the Marsh Flowers and we ended by sight-reading Green Broom. As it was midnight we then went home. I'd felt all the time, in spite of extreme exhaustion, that it was the beginning of our music school, and a good beginning.*

Britten's *Five Flower Songs* had been a favourite of IH's at Dartington, and performing two of them in informal surroundings in Aldeburgh brought her new and old worlds satisfyingly together. The singers departed the next day, and Britten began to emerge from his holiday mood – he confessed to Ronald Duncan that 'a little work has gone on under the desk' – and he had begun to think ahead to the big projects for 1954: the Aldeburgh Festival and *The Turn of the Screw* in Venice. But first he had unfinished business to complete, in the form of his new Hardy songs and an orchestral suite from *Gloriana*, to include the Courtly Dances, promised to Boosey & Hawkes. On 3 September Britten and Pears went to London, where Britten consulted an osteopath – Dr Charles W. Barber of 140 Park Lane – about his arm and also dealt, as he told Duncan, with 'Income Tax, Dentist & happy things like that'.[221]

[Ben & Peter in London Sept 3rd and 4th.]

Sat. Sept 5th. Went in at breakfast time and they said they'd just been talking about me & were coming along to see me. Ben said there was lots of work to do: – orchestral suite of dances in Gloriana, and Hardy songs. Also that we must plan next year's festival. They asked me to go to dinner that evening. When I got there at 7.30 they were still in tennis flannels, Ben having had one visitor after another, and Peter busy wall-papering the top back bedroom. So I practised the harpsichord while they had baths. The food was incredibly good – sherry in soup (after having had a Vermouth), meat done in wine, and Zabaglione with peaches and strawberries! Ben said he was sure his mother's milk had tasted just like Zabaglione. He's got a new doctor for his arm, an osteopath, who thinks he'll be able to cure him. While we were having coffee he talked again of Jesu mein Freude and said what violent music it was. Then we tried to plan the festival, but the meal had been far too good, and they both got sleepier and sleepier – Peter lying full length on the sofa. Ben didn't want to do a Mozart concert, but gave in. I asked him if he'd write something for the Amadeus to play with him, & he said he wouldn't have time this year. We hadn't got very far by 11 pm. Ben insisted

---

[220] 'Sweet honeysucking bees', a madrigal by John Wilbye.
[221] Letter of 25 August 1953; BPL.

on taking me home in the car. He talked about Hardy: – said that Jude wasn't unbearable – that he minded the first bit more than the last.

Sunday Sept 6th. Ben had asked me to go in after breakfast to get on with the Gloriana dances. He played the suite straight through to me: – it sounds good. He's going to let me do it for piano – Hurray! He said "Do work as slowly as you can, my dear, so that you earn a lot of money!" I said that if I was paid by the hour I really should get the sack: – so then I settled down and finished the 32 pages by twenty to two.[222] *(He asked me if he could send my love to Paul, who was going in tomorrow. He'd decided not to go & see him off.)*

Monday Sept 7th. When I went in at breakfast he thanked me for the 3 Hardy songs, said he'd written another the evening before; – couldn't find the right one to begin with – they were all so depressing. He wanted another philosophical one like Before Life & After. Peter had suggested calling them "Winter Words" Which is good. Then a photographer came[223] *& he was angry. When I'd checked the Gloriana pages & mended the splits in the paper I went to the studio to copy out the next 2 Hardy songs. Finished them by 3.30.*

Tuesday Sept 8th. Asked if I could copy the new Hardy "At the Railway Station, Upway," and Ben said "yes." He also said "It's rather good." He asked for the piano part on one stave, as in his sketch, "as it's really violin music". I took it back that afternoon: – meant to leave it for him but he came out of the sitting-room just as I arrived. I asked if he'd got another for me, & he said no, he'd been working all the morning trying to do one less depressing, but it wouldn't work, and they'd just got to be gloomy. I said it would be all right because of the last one, & he agreed.

Easing himself back into work, Britten mixed composition of the Hardy settings with a level of sporting recreation that belied the pain in his arm, and played host to a visit from the Harewoods and their son, his godson, the three-year-old David Lascelles.

Wed. Sept 9th. I didn't go in that morning because I knew he wouldn't have had time to work any more with the Harewoods there. Went to the cricket match in the afternoon. Peter played magnificently. Ben in last man – looking thin and vulnerable. I didn't stay long while the other side were batting, because I couldn't bear knowing that his arm hurt him all the time.

[222] IH typescript note: '(i.e. filling-in and corrections).'
[223] Possibly Roger Wood, who had taken the photographs of the first production of *Gloriana*.

The match – an annual fixture – was played out at Thorpeness between Britten's team and A. S. Ogilvie's XI. Britten described the drawn game, in which Stephen Potter's two sons and George Harewood also played, to Elizabeth Mayer, observing that his team had come 'near to winning. Peter & George excelled themselves – I not so good, but I have an excuse of a bad arm'.[224] Pears scored 32 and Harewood 21 (including a six); Britten was bowled for 2. The next day he travelled to London for a scheduled visit to Dr Barber's clinic. Back in Aldeburgh, the Decca records of the 1953 Festival had arrived, comprising music from the first half of the opening Coronation Choral Concert, with Britten conducting the *Variations on an Elizabethan Theme* and IH conducting the two Arne pieces and the Purcell anthem.

On Friday Britten planned to take his houseguests to Shingle Street, a long beach to the south-east of Woodbridge, at the mouth of the River Alde.

Thursday Sept 10th. Went in at breakfast time – Ben gone to London for the day to have treatment for his arm, thank goodness.

Friday Sept 11th. After breakfast Ben was playing with David; looking cheerful & very gentle & loving. He was annoyed that Decca hadn't removed the two heraldic soldiers from the sleeve of the Aldeburgh record and I realised that I'd never told him of the letter I'd had from Boas[225] about it. Alas.

At 2.30 I went back for a festival discussion with Ben, Peter and Fidelity. We sat in the sun and it was peaceful, though a somewhat depressing meeting. At 3.30 when Fidelity had gone, Peter asked me to go with them to Shingle St for the afternoon. It was lovely. When we started in the car, David was in a questioning mood, asking "Why?" all the time, & Marion and Nannie[226] said "*please* no why this afternoon". But when we were going up the hill he pointed to the church & said "Why is that church standing there?" So I said "It's standing there so that Bim's[227] music can be played in it", and Ben put a hand on mine with a gesture of protest but at the same time seeing the point. Later on Nannie began talking German to David & everyone joined in – Ben's accent much better than Peter's.[228] They were seeing how many birds they knew in German – someone asked what

---

224 30 August 1953; BPL. Britten often wrote long letters over a number of days; this letter, started at the end of August, was still under way ten days later.

225 Robert Boas, who worked in the Publicity Department at Decca. The letter itself is lost.

226 David's nanny Hillo von Stockert, who was Austrian.

227 IH typescript note: 'David Lascelles' name for Ben'.

228 IH typescript note: 'i.e. better than Peter's conversational accent, not his singing accent'.

a Hawk was, & Ben murmured "Beschwippst und Habichte",[229] *which was
really very funny. When we got to Shingle Street Beth & the 3 children were
there: – they bathed and we had a wonderful tea. Peter told me that they'd been
working at the Hardy songs that morning. I asked him if Ben had found the right
poem for the first one yet, & he said no, that he'd been trying to persuade him
to set the one about Proud Songsters, and when he'd told him that Finzi had set
it, "that seemed to spur him on a bit."*[230] *Going home in the car Ben said "The
songs sound all right when Peter sings them". Then he asked if I felt happy about
the afternoon's discussion with Fidelity, & said "I wish I could feel that it was the
right decision." He also said that he'd refused a request from America to bring out
the Carols for mixed voices; it was all very well having separate numbers but they
wouldn't do as a work for anything but equal voices.*

Tony Gishford had made the request for an edition for mixed voices of the
complete *A Ceremony of Carols* on 8 September, on behalf of the New York
office of Boosey & Hawkes. Britten scrawled a decisive 'NO!' across the
suggestion.

*Sat Sept 12th. Peter asked me to go and play recorder duets with him at nine in
the evening. When I got there, he & Ben were both looking weary but cosy, with
a log fire. Ben immediately began talking about the theatre, and thanked me for
the five pages I'd written him that afternoon, & said it was true that we'd got to
begin planning now. They were both depressed at the thought of the amount of
hard work it would mean, & they wished they could think of the right treasurer
with energy & experience. Then Ben said "Why don't you play your duets here?"
So we did, and both got the giggles because every time Peter missed a note Ben
did a mixture of a grunt & a chuckle.*

Two days later the Council of the Aldeburgh Festival met and Britten outlined,
as the Minutes reported, his 'plans for the building of a theatre in Aldeburgh, to
be taken on by a body specially constituted and not by the Festival Committee.
He had the option on a suitable site, not disclosed at this stage'. The meeting
also reviewed the unhappy financial picture following the 1953 Festival, which
had sustained a loss of about £900, partly as a result of the public's 'cutting
down of expenditure, thought to be traceable to the Coronation celebrations'.

The next day IH had a visit from her old friend and colleague from Dartington, Winsome Bartlett.

---

[229] I.e. 'Boozy and Hawks'.
[230] Gerald Finzi's setting had been published in his collection *Earth and Air and
Rain* (1936).

Sept 15th. Copied out The Little Old Table, & took it round. He'd already written another. Proud Songsters; said Peter had probably wanted "Down in a forest something stirred"![231]

Sept 16th. Copied out Proud Songsters, & took it round. They were discussing the order the songs should be in, and said they'd do them in the evening. Went round with Winsome and they sang the whole eight. At first Peter wanted to leave out the Wagtail, but Ben included it in the end. They are magnificent, especially both the railway ones, and the last.

Sept. 17th. Got up very early to see them off; – Ben going to Denmark.

Britten went first to see Dr Barber once more in London. He was on his way to Denmark to record *A Ceremony of Carols* with the Copenhagen Boys' Choir, who had performed the work to great acclaim, and the composer's approval, at the Aldeburgh Festival of 1952, under their own conductor Mogens Wöldike. With Enid Simon playing the harp, the recording took place between 20 and 22 September at the Danish State Radio Studios, Copenhagen. In his absence IH took the first Music Club rehearsal for *The Fairy Queen*, an 'unexpected pleasure!', as Stephen Potter recalled.[232]

It was to be ten days before IH saw Britten again, by which time he had returned to immerse himself in *The Turn of the Screw*, and the beneficial effect of his visit to the osteopath had worn off. IH tried to lighten Britten's mood by presenting him with 'my father's copy of Hardy's novel', *The Return of the Native*, 'from which he had quoted on the title page of Egdon Heath'.[233] Under her father's signature on the flyleaf she inscribed the copy 'To Ben with love; a thank you for having written the Hardy songs. Sept. 53'.

Sept 27th. Went round after breakfast to see if there was any work I could do for him, but he was busy working on the new opera with Myfanwy. His arm bad; – not able to write.

Sept 28th. Ben asked me in to dinner. Peter lost his train, so we were late. Marvellous meal. Ben excited about the new opera, and forgetting the pain in his arm. I made him promise not to write out anything that I could do for him. He was pleased with the present of G's Return of the Native.

In spite of his arm Britten had committed himself to a heavy fortnight of

---

[231] Probably a reference to Landon Ronald's then popular setting of Harold Simpson's words, from his song collection *A Cycle of Life* (1906).

[232] Diary of Stephen Potter, 25 September 1953.

[233] IH typescript note. The copy is preserved at the BPL.

touring with Pears, centred on the Leeds Triennial Festival. Before they went, however, he was keen to sort out some of the planning for his own 1954 Aldeburgh Festival.

> *Sept 29th. From 4 pm onwards we had a meeting discussing Festival plans with Beth, Fidelity and Elizabeth. Ben wanted to cut the Mozart concert. His arm was so bad that I couldn't bear to think of him having to start a concert tour next day. There wasn't a chance to say anything, as the meeting went on till 7, and then the Potters arrived for a drink, so I ran back afterwards with a note, imploring him to get his doctor to summon a conference about him, and telling him he won't just get through on endurance, like G. tried to do. I felt it was an awful risk saying this, as it wasn't my job, but it mattered so much that it was worth getting the sack for if necessary.*

> *Sept 30th. Went round at 10 oclock to see them off on their tour. Ben with his arm in a sling. He thanked me for the note, and I was relieved that he wasn't furious & so worried to see him looking so ill, that I wept. (Miss Hudson very tactful.). Peter appeared with a tightly rolled umbrella so we laughed about the "perfect gentleman" in the Wagtail song, & then I told Ben he must try and think of his arm as if it were Peter's throat, and then it was time for them to go.*

On 30 September, IH finally moved into her new home at 45 Crag Path. She then took the opportunity of Britten's absence to spend a few days in Dartington, from 3 to 5 October.

October 1953

> *(Ben & Peter on tour, in Harewood & Leeds, 1st performance of Hardy Songs Oct. 8th.)*

On 1 October Britten and Pears gave a 'Coronation Concert' of English Song in Nottingham. Two days later they were in Leeds for the Triennial Festival, where Pears sang the tenor solo in Vaughan Williams's *Sancta civitas* on the first night, with Josef Krips conducting Schubert's Symphony no. 9 with the London Symphony Orchestra. The next afternoon Krips directed Pears again in Britten's *Serenade*, and on the 7th in Stravinsky's *Oedipus Rex*. On 8 October Britten and Pears gave the first performance of *Winter Words* (still called 'Hardy Songs') at Harewood House, in a concert shared with the LSO Wind Ensemble. Britten was then scheduled to join Krips in a performance of Schubert's Fantasy in F minor on Saturday, but had to cancel because of the discomfort in his arm.

Better news came, however, with Britten's discovery, whilst in Leeds, of a
new osteopath, Stanley Ratcliffe, of 32 Park Square. Visiting him for the first
time on Friday 2 October, Britten finally received a diagnosis of his condition:
bursitis.

October 11th. Sunday. Went round at breakfast time, left them some butter &
said I'd go back in half an hour. When I got back, they were in their bedroom
with Miss Hudson, having long arguments about laundry, Ben accusing Peter of
borrowing all his white waistcoats. Gradually I gleaned bits of information – Ben
said he'd found a wonderful osteopath in Leeds who had been really helpful. Peter
said that Ben had got to stop all playing for 2 months, after the end of this week's
concerts. Later he told me what his trouble is: – inflammation of the "bursa"
– a pad between the joints of the elbow. Ben said that after the osteopath's
treatment he'd been able to brush his hair without his arm hurting for the first
time since May. Harewood had been grim: – very tense, with lots of unnecessary
fussing, as it had been the first concert they'd ever given there. The new songs
had not gone very well, particularly the last, which Peter had his doubts about.
Afterwards Ben told me that he'd got to learn to write with his left hand, that he
couldn't dictate ("at any rate, not until I'm 70") that if he'd got to give up playing
for some months (the doctor had said "the whole season", but he'd wait & see how
the treatment worked) he'd have to get on with the things he was going to write,
and that the thing to do would be to discover together the easiest way of writing
for him which would save him so that I could copy it out. They asked me to lunch
– Miss Hudson's superb Sunday dinner. Ben teased Peter about how bad his
carving was, and they told priceless stories of the trials of Harewood, including
Princess Mary catching wasps with a pair of painted tongs. Afterwards we went
to Minsmere with Mary Potter – a wonderful day: – Eastbridge looking beautiful.
Peter went to sleep on the beach & Ben & Mary & I walked along the high ridge
and they looked at birds through Stephen's wonderful binoculars. (Ben said
Southwold looked like Tyre & Sidon). The light on the strips of water was lovely
– as beautiful as on that intoxicating day in March in the middle of Gloriana. We
had a picnic tea in the car, & then on the way home looked at Leiston Old Abbey
which is for sale – we only looked from the road, but it looked a good-shaped
house – wonderful grounds, and it was that magical moment in the early evening
when everything looks like heaven, & I could tell that Ben was pining to live out
there or at Eastbridge, instead of in the middle of Aldeburgh.

Monday Oct 12th. Council meeting in the Moot Hall at 6. Not too bad. Peter said
Ben wouldn't be able to do the Ipswich concert because he'd got to stop playing
for 3 months. So now they know. When Mr Cullum said that it would cost money

to provide badges for people to wear when they went into the Festival Club,
Ben muttered (but so that it was audible the whole length of the room) "The
Friends can provide the safety pins." Afterwards, over a drink, he said he'd had a
depressing day with his London doctors who'd made him have another £14 worth
of X-rays.

In addition to badges the Council discussed other ways of raising money for, and during, the Festival. The next day, Pears and Britten were going to Peterborough to give a recital in the Cathedral, in which they performed a wide range of works by Handel, Purcell, Guédron, Rosseter, Dowland and Rameau, in addition to Britten's own Canticle I: 'My beloved is mine' and Fauré's *La bonne chanson.*

Throughout the war years IH had been heavily involved in furthering the cause of refugee musicians, and had served on the Bloomsbury House Refugee Committee, working for some of those displaced from Austria and Germany. She was now championing the case of Norbert Brainin, the leader of the Amadeus Quartet, who had been briefly interned during the war at Prees Hill, Shropshire, and was now seeking support to become a naturalized citizen. IH had first taken the violinist under her wing five years earlier; having heard him play at a masterclass, she had invited him to Dartington for a few days, where she discovered that he was out of work and 'was having difficulty really in finding the next meal'. He had already decided not to return to Vienna because of his belief that 'the centre of music in the future will be in England'.[234] IH encouraged him to start the ensemble that became the Amadeus Quartet, and she remained among his staunchest champions.

Encouraged by the recent experience of his uncle's family into thinking that the process of naturalization would be straightforward, Brainin had first applied in 1946.[235] But he had been in trouble with the Home Office following his release from internment, as he had both played at, and occasionally been paid for, soirées for refugee musicians in London, which took him away from his 'essential' war work as a machine tool fitter. The repercussions of this were now frustrating his attempts to obtain naturalization.

Tuesday Oct 13th. Went in at 11 to wave them off. Pouring wet day, Ben looking
grey and weary. Peter looking worried. When Ben was out of the room he said
that I probably wouldn't approve, but they were thinking of doing some BBC
recordings <u>next</u> Tuesday before Ben begins his treatment. I told Ben I'd been

---

[234] Cox and Dobbs, *Imogen Holst at Dartington*, p. 26.
[235] Letter from Brainin to IH, 22 December 1946; HF.

*practising writing crotchets & quavers with my left hand & it was much easier
than I thought. He began trying it. I asked his help about getting Norbert's
naturalisation through. He said George would certainly do it, and suggested
Kenneth Clark for the Arts Council, but said he didn't think he was any use
himself as he wasn't respectable enough. "Oh yes, you're all right now," said Peter.
Then it was time for them to go.*

Pears's confidence in Britten's 'respectability' was possibly based both on the
royal approval of *Gloriana* and the award of a Companion of Honour to the
composer in the Coronation honours list. But in the post-war climate, conscientious objectors and pacifists were still viewed with suspicion, and Britten
would not have forgotten the recent cancellation of his holiday, resulting from
his support of democracy in Greece. And behind all this must have lurked a
sense of insecurity arising from the open secret – certainly in the artistic world
– of Britten's homosexuality and his relationship with Pears; it was around this
time that Britten was interviewed by the police, who were actively engaged in
'stepping up their activities against the homosexuals'.[236]

Britten, Pears and the Amadeus String Quartet were the Festival Artists
for the Milngavie Festival in Glasgow, along with Dennis Brain and Cecil
Aronowitz. Quartets by Haydn, Britten, Schubert, Mozart and Beethoven
formed the basis of a programme that also included Pears singing Vaughan
Williams's *On Wenlock Edge* with the Amadeus and Britten, and the Schumann
Piano Quintet.

In Britten's absence Drs McCready and Barber examined the composer's most
recent set of X-rays and concluded that the presence of unusually prominent
'cervical ribs' in his neck was contributing to the 'various pressure symptoms in
the shoulder and arm region'. Dr McCready wrote to the composer, suggesting
that he consult a 'good orthopaedic surgeon' and suggesting that while 'in
certain cases the condition can be much helped by improving the muscle tone
and position of the shoulders; in more difficult cases operations have been
performed.'[237]

*Monday Oct 19th. They got back about 2 and I went in at 3 to see them. Ben
looking much better: – Peter said it was such a relief to him to have got through
playing all the week. Ben said the performances had been wild: – they hadn't
rehearsed anything: – in the Schumann they hadn't even arranged about repeats,
and Norbert went back while he & the others went on. But the Scottish festival*

[236] Percy Elland, then editor of the *Evening Standard*, quoted in Carpenter,
Benjamin Britten, p. 335.
[237] 16 October 1953; BPL.

had been worth it. He again said how fond he was of the Amadeus as people. I took the Carey & Daniel Purcell to copy out a vocal line only, for Peter to sing from.

IH had recently realized Daniel Purcell's 'By what I've seen I am undone' and four songs by Henry Carey: 'The Beau's Lament for the Loss of Farinelli', together with three numbers from his *Musical Century* (1737) – 'Polly's Birthday', 'Justification for living', and 'Advice to a friend in love'.[238] Pears made a recording of the songs for the BBC with George Malcolm, which was broadcast on 16 December, the first of four programmes of seventeenth- and eighteenth-century songs, devised by Basil Douglas. Britten, meanwhile, was developing plans for his theatre, and wanted to meet the Arts Council to discuss the possibilities for funding. The next day, Britten and Pears were travelling to Rotterdam.

> *Tuesday Oct 20th. Went in about 11 to say goodbye but they weren't going till a later train. They talked about the Music Club and the difficulties of people not getting on well together. Ben was looking weary again. Every now and then he looks* exactly *like G used to – in gesture & expression & tone of voice. Peter had got on a rainbow coloured tie and Ben was obviously pleased that I admired it so much. We talked a bit about the theatre & Ben asked me if I'd be able to go & see the Arts Council with him. He then talked about the immediate future – Gloriana dances, and the long suite, and he said there'd be lots of work for us to do. He also said he liked my Carey & Daniel Purcell arrangements: – I wish I could hear him play them. Then he asked me to copy out a folk song arrangement he'd just done – The Brisk Young Widow, and then I went.*

'The Brisk Young Widow' was to be first performed by Britten and Pears on 24 January 1954, at the Victoria and Albert Museum, London. Britten sent it to Tony Gishford at the end of March although it was not published until 1961.

Planning for the 1954 Festival was now in full swing, with Britten still optimistic about the possibility of attracting the Couraud Choir to Aldeburgh. IH's plans included conducting Bach's *St John Passion*, with Pears as the Evangelist and Britten playing the harpsichord continuo. Unhappy with the available English translations of the choruses, she found an ally in Pears, who had already made some translations of the Evangelist's part for his own use, and the two undertook to prepare a new English edition for the Festival performance. More immediately, *Peter Grimes* was being revived at Covent Garden in November.

---

[238] IH's realizations of these songs are in the BPL, including a solo line transcription of 'The Beau's Lament', heavily annotated by Pears.

Pears was once again to sing the title role, and, with Britten indisposed, the production would be conducted by Reginald Goodall.

> *Oct 23rd, Fri. In London: – got to Chester Gate at 12.30. Ben looking tired, but* <u>much</u> *more cheerful – his doctor working with another; no operation,* <u>no</u> *work, i.e. playing for 3 months, but he can write with his left hand; treatment in London in the middle of the week. Not to go to Grimes rehearsals because of not being "het up". Then he said "and how are you?" and when I said I felt better after his news, he said "Well, if it wasn't for you I shouldn't be taking it so seriously, but should be struggling on with performances." So it was worth all the panic about writing him that letter.*
>
> *We went to Prunier's*[239] *for the lunch with the Arts Council people – got there before they did – he asked me about Engel Lund (I'd mentioned her) and then we talked frivolously about how ugly the fashionable women's clothes were, and then the others came & we talked about the Festival & the Theatre all through lunch. Afterwards, at Chester Gate, a meeting with Tony Mayer about the French choir & soloists. Ben agreed to play with Fournier if necessary.*

Engel Lund, the Icelandic singer and folksong collector, was known to IH through their shared interest both in folk music and in the well-being of German and Austrian émigré musicians during the war. IH had worked in support of the efforts led by Vaughan Williams and Myra Hess to have these musicians released from internment, among them Norbert Brainin and Peter Schidlof, later of the Amadeus Quartet, and Ferdinand Rauter, Lund's partner and accompanist, who, after internment, went on to establish the Anglo-Austrian Music Society (of which Britten and Pears were founder members). Working through CEMA, IH had arranged for Lund and Rautner to give a series of concerts in Somerset and Cornwall in 1941 and 1942.

The cellist Pierre Fournier was an old friend of Mayer's and had expressed an interest in Britten writing a 'Suite for Orchestra and Cello' for him early in 1952. Mayer was encouraging Fournier to come to Aldeburgh for the 1954 Festival.

> *Sunday Oct 25th. Went to Crag House after breakfast & Ben & Peter asked me to stay to lunch. Worked with Peter at translations of the St. John Passion, – heavenly day, sat in the garden all the time. Ben writing his score with his left hand. He came down to discuss* <u>soloists</u> *for the Bach – he disapproved of my suggestion of Deller. After the meal, which was* <u>excellent</u>*, Peter went to play golf & Ben typed a letter to Morgan. In the evening they took me to dinner at*

---

[239] A fish restaurant on St James's Street.

Glemham²⁴⁰ to discuss Theatre & Festival with Fidelity and her husband. Lovely easy evening – Ben relaxed & enjoying it.

Monday Oct 26th. Music Club rehearsal of The Fairy Queen at Crag House that evening – Ben looking ill – he went to bed half way through it.

Thursday Oct 29th. Peter had said that Ben would be coming home about 4, so I walked round about 5.30 & met him in Crag Path – he'd had a wretched time and was feeling sick, but was very patient about it.

That day Britten wrote disconsolately to Plomer: 'here I am, with everything cancelled, hobbling up to London once a week for treatment, otherwise sitting gloomily here in Aldeburgh trying to learn to write music with my clumsy old left hand! ... Imo can DECIPHER it enough to transcribe it for the world to read. It does at least prevent one becoming absolutely suicidal – having something to do – but the situation, you can imagine, is pretty blackish ...²⁴¹

Friday October 30th. Ran in for 2 minutes at mid-day to see him before my train left – he was a bit better.

November 1953

November began with an Aldeburgh Music Club Night, the members putting on twenty-one numbers from Purcell's *The Fairy Queen*, conducted by IH. The next day Britten and IH began work on final corrections to *Gloriana* in preparation for the publication of the second edition of the vocal score. Also at the start of the month Britten received a letter from his osteopath in Leeds, which left little room for doubt as to the seriousness of his arm condition. In response to Britten's gratitude for his treatment, Stanley Ratcliffe had written: '... no matter what kind of treatment you have, unless you rest it the results will be negligible – because you will be duplicating the conditions under which the whole thing first became manifest if you work it ... God knows, I know little about the piano and nothing about conducting, but I can't see that you are going to get any more out of an orchestra by sending all the shoulder muscles into a spasm and then using brute force to try and make the shoulder move.'²⁴²

Sunday Nov 1st. Music Club performance in the evening – it went much better; – Peter played the harpsichord superbly, & Ben filled in timps with his left hand and some of the most important viola bits, making the old worn-out piano sing

²⁴⁰ Great Glemham House, home of the Earl and Countess of Cranbrook.
²⁴¹ 29 October 1953; BPL.
²⁴² 1 November 1953; BPL.

like a viola. When they'd all gone we went into the dining-room & ate & drank
whatever was still on the table and laughed a lot. It was late, & Peter had to get
up very early, so I came away.

The following week the Soviet composer Aram Khatchaturian, together with
David Oistrakh and a host of other musicians, was in the UK as part of 'the
largest Russian cultural delegation to visit' since the war.[243]

Monday Nov 2nd. A wonderful day with Ben; – I was too het up and weary to
take it in without a sense of strain, but all the same it was good. He'd asked me
to go round & work at Gloriana mistakes in the score: – he began by talking about
general criticisms. Tony Gishford had felt the character of Essex was incomplete
in the libretto – We discussed it, & he said again, what he'd said months ago, that
Joan & Peter's love scenes were all right for a small theatre but wouldn't do in
Covent Garden, and I said they were right because they'd got the right English
restraint which was in keeping with the music & that that's how English opera
ought to be, and when I quoted the hesitating low-level of Aeneas's first entry he
was <u>frightfully</u> pleased.[244] Then a telegram came asking him to meet Katchurian
on Friday and he was frightfully upset at having to refuse it and took ages trying
to find the right words for the reply-paid telegram.

He talked about Purcell, and said he'd wanted to see my realisation of The Fatal
Hour[245] but that Peter had taken it to London. He then said that he thought
my realisations were better than his (!!) because they were a better compromise
between imagination and suitable notes, and that his were too elaborate and
that he wanted to rewrite them all. This was difficult to take calmly, and it was a
comparative relief to get back to Gloriana. He was <u>very</u> patient with the mistakes
I'd made. He talked of altering several details – the bar before "Love's better than
fear" – which always hangs fire. He said was it wrong in the music? It always
sounded wrong at each performance, yet when he played it on the piano it was all
right. He decided to add horns. He also altered the strings' dynamics at Essex's
first entry, from sfp to f $\diagup\!\!\!\diagdown$, and added a perc roll & cresc to take out the
abruptness of the trumpets' quavers. And he marked down the muted trumpets
at the "Jackal" to pp from mf – I was enormously relieved, because it's always
been too loud. At the beginning of the Masque scene he took <u>all</u> the strings dims
out, saying that it had been an error of judgment, as the wind & brass had the

[243] *The Times*, 27 October 1953.
[244] Aeneas's dramatically unassuming first entry in Purcell's *Dido and Aeneas*:
  'When royal fair, shall I be blest, / With cares of love and state distrest?'
[245] 'The Fatal Hour comes on', from Purcell's *Orpheus Britannicus*, vol. 2 (1702).

dims. I saw the point, as the strings represent the quivering vibrations in the air. Then at 1 we broke off and he put on the new Decca record of the Danish boys doing the Ceremony of Carols, which he'd made a few weeks ago. <u>Heavenly</u> singing, perfectly in tune and lovely tone & wonderful rhythm. When I said how lovely the chord on "The Prince himself" was, he said "that's one of the things I learnt from your father, the enharmonic change and the extraordinary effect it has on the note that is changed." This was <u>terribly</u> exciting, and I could hardly eat the meal because it was just what I'd guessed and hoped. During the meal he said he might be going to Germany to stay with the Hesses for a bit in December while Peter was away.

He looked <u>much</u> better, and it was a relief to see him enjoying work on Gloriana. At tea at the Potters, Stephen said something about "backing a horse both ways", & Ben immediately thought of "backing" as trying to get it into reverse! Charles[246] was there, and they were very happy together.

Britten was now being encouraged by his doctors to spend some weeks abroad during his three months' enforced rest from playing, and an opportunity now arose for him to do so. The previous year George Harewood had introduced him to a cousin, Prince Ludwig of Hesse and the Rhine and his wife Margaret, and Britten was invited to spend Christmas with the Hesses at their home at Schloss Wolfsgarten, near Frankfurt.

The next day Britten and IH were planning to work on the suite from *Gloriana*, before fulfilling a promise to go and visit the newly-weds Billy and Barbara Burrell for tea. Married on 10 October, they had moved into a flat on the high street opposite the cinema, above the hairdressing business which the new Mrs Burrell shared with her sister.

Tuesday Nov. 3rd. A <u>wonderful</u> day; – bright blue sky, brilliant sunshine and a calm sea. I got to Crag House at 10; Ben was still in bed so I began work on copying out his left hand score of the Gloriana dances. When he came in we went through the rest of the corrections and alterations in the full score.

At the beginning of Act III Scene I he wanted to add viola at the half bar to help the cellos at the peak of their phrase. I took my courage in my hands and suggested that the trombones shouldn't be f, and he agreed, and altered it in <u>every</u> case! We discussed the f passages in Bach where the long semiquaver runs can't possibly have every note played loudly. He said "the ideal thing would be to have, as in Bach, only a very few general directions about f or p and then leave

it to the conductor". Later on, he marked up the trombone's declaiming passages
from f to ff ("that'll shake 'em!") He found it difficult to concentrate because the
sea was looking so beautiful, and there were boats out, with heaving nets, and
ducks flying. Just before 1 oclock he said "let's go for a walk on the beach, we
mustn't miss all this sun". When we got out there Billy was just going out to take
in the catch from his nets, so Ben asked Miss Hudson to keep back the meal, &
we went with him for half an hour – absolutely beautiful, lovely boat, and Billy
looked very beautiful with the reflected sunlight on his face. When we came
in, Ben talked about his beauty and how unconscious it was. Then we had a
marvellous meal – my first fresh herrings of the season, superbly cooked. Ben
began saying that [name erased] had lost her sparkle, & I said it couldn't be too
easy living with a woman who had money when one hadn't any oneself, & Ben
said "It's never been difficult with any of the men I've lived with: – Lennox had
much more money than I had, but was all right", so then I said yes but that men
were more sensible about money than women, because women have not yet got
used to being independent, and he said "Yes, do you know, my sister Barbara
actually borrows money from the woman she lives with and then pays her back!"
He also talked about scientists and how naive they were about not realising
where their research & discoveries were leading us. Then he was very funny about
how Michael had told him that whenever he saw any English composer, whether
it was Walton or Bliss or Rawsthorne, they'd always draw him aside and say
confidentially, "Of course, the only people who are keeping things going are you
and me and Ben."!

He wanted to go on & finish the full score after lunch. There wasn't much left to
do. In the street scene he marked up the Bass clarinet trills. There were very few
alterations in the last scene. Then he wanted to go for a walk; he didn't look too
well & I said was he sure he felt strong enough but he said yes. When we'd started
he admitted that he felt sick again, & supposed he was bound to feel like that
every now & then. We walked to Slaughden, and the sunlight – bright orange
– on the mud & water, was wonderful. And there were curlews, which cheered him
a lot. He wanted to go into the Martello Tower, but there were huge gaps in the
wooden bridge across to it, and I wouldn't let him do it with one hand; – it looked
terrifyingly ricketty, and I couldn't bear the thought of him doing it while feeling
mouldy, as he might easily have lost his balance. On the way back he told me he'd
had a depressing letter from his Leeds doctor saying that the trouble in his arm
might come back again if he used his arm very violently. This was appalling – I'd
hoped the doctors would have the sense not to mention the future until he'd done
his three months' rest & treatment. He said he'd have to learn to conduct with

*very small movements, and it would be a lesson in control, which was what he felt
he needed more and more. We got in just before 5, & he'd promised Bill that we'd
both go to tea there at 6. When I asked him if he felt equal to it he said yes he'd
be all right. So I went home & changed, and got back at 6 to find Ben drinking
brandy & listening to the Ceremony of Carols to cheer him. He insisted that he
was well enough to go out: I had to nag him to put his coat over his shoulders,
although he'd just had a bath and the night was cold. We had a lovely tea party
at Bill & Barbara's house but the food was the worst possible for Ben – Indian tea
and rather heavy cakes – I hoped he'd refuse things, but he didn't, & he was very
cheerful with them. We didn't get away till after 8 and when he got inside his
front door it was obvious that he was in pain. He went straight to bed.*

*Wed Nov 4th. Ben was leaving for London early that morning – I went round
to wave him off – he was feeling better, but not looking too good. I asked him to
get his doctor to say what he was to do when he felt mouldy – he said "oh, I don't
think there's anything one can do."*

The next evening IH's First String Trio was broadcast on the Third Programme
in a concert sponsored by the Society for the Promotion of New Music. E. M.
Forster was coming once again to Crag House for the weekend, which would
also feature a meeting of the Friends of Aldeburgh Festival, in which tapes of
Gloriana were to be played.

*Sunday Nov 8th. Went into Crag House after breakfast to borrow the score of
Gloriana – EM Forster staying the weekend – looking very well and magnificent
in a check black & white wool shirt which he wore hanging down as if it were a
jacket. Ben came in and asked me to go back to lunch with them. They were both
enjoying their weekend, and obviously all the upheavals on the last occasion had
been washed out. Morgan talked of Cambridge, & the advantages of living in
King's, and Billy. I came away early, as Beth's children were coming over for a
lesson. Ben asked me to look in after the gramophone evening, and was very kind
asking if there was anything he could do to help.*

*The records of Gloriana at the Friends of the Festival meeting went on longer
than I'd expected, and it was nearly half past ten when I got to Crag House, & I
expected he'd have gone to bed. But he & Morgan were sitting talking by the fire,
Ben in his dressing gown, having had his arm done for the night, and looking, as
he always does in pyjamas, very thin and vulnerable, but glowing in the firelight.
I was still intoxicated with hearing Gloriana again, which pleased him, and he
suggested a drink of brandy. Morgan acted host & went to fetch it, even though
it meant going upstairs to Ben's bedroom for it, and while he was out of the room*

Ben embraced me for having enjoyed Gloriana so much. It was a good drink;
– Ben made me have most of his as well as mine, & I went home at 11 quite light-
headed.

Stephen Potter was also present at the gramophone evening and wrote: 'In the
evening a full and friendly Friends' first annual meeting – and it went very well
– I was as cheerful as an old horse nearing home … Then Dr Hayden and Mr
Brown play their tape recording of Gloriana – and I marvel at the della Robbia
positions of ecstatic discipleship of Immo as she listens.'[247]

(In London, Nov 9th to 17th.)

*Thursday Nov 12th. Went to Chester Gate at 6 oclock, to do translations with
Peter. Ben & Myfanwy were working at the Screw – Hayward[248] came in for
a drink. Everyone a bit strained. Then he went, & we worked at our different
jobs till after 8, & had a meal with red wine and a very good round of beef from
Aldeburgh – I felt proud to think that my meat ration had gone into it. Peter
finding it difficult to carve, & Ben being frantic because there was no guard to
prevent the carving knife from slipping. Then Myfanwy had to catch her train
home – Peter and I went on for about ½ an hour, while Ben typed a letter to Paul
who was coming out of his retreat next day, "I'm telling him that we went out
fishing in Bill's boat," he said. I sent my love to him, & then went home, because
Peter had got to go to bed early before his dress rehearsal of Grimes.*

The first performance of the *Peter Grimes* revival was to take place on Saturday
night. IH was intending to go with Peter Cox, but as he was unable to attend,
she was accompanied by Arthur Caton.

*Friday Nov 13th. Waited for Ben at the stage door at Covent Garden, as they
weren't letting anyone in to the dress rehearsal. He said "I hope you don't mind,
you're my secretary." He went down to the stalls, so that he could be near Goodall.
I listened from the stalls circle. A very good rehearsal, overwhelmingly moving to
hear it again after Lucretia and Budd and Gloriana.*

*Sat. Nov 14th. First night went well – I went with A. Peter sang superbly – Ben
got a tremendous ovation at the end.*

[247] Diary of Stephen Potter, 9 November 1953.
[248] G. Heywood Hill, the Mayfair bookseller and brother-in-law of Fidelity, Countess of Cranbrook, whose mother-in-law had a house at Snape Priory, where
Hill and his wife Anne frequently stayed. Hill had recently presented Britten
with a copy of Michael Innes's newly published detective thriller *Christmas at
Candleshoe* (London: Gollancz, 1953), which the composer had taken with him
to read on his trip to Leeds at the beginning of October.

> *Tuesday 17th Nov. Got back to Aldeburgh just after 5 and went to Crag House to*
> *get some work to do. Ben & Myfanwy working. Miss Hudson said he was better*
> *– he'd been "queer" in London & had felt sick all Saturday. But he was worried*
> *about Peter's cold. Ben came out into the hall while I was talking to her, and*
> *asked me to come back next morning & go through the score to mark which pages*
> *he'd need for the Gloriana Suite.*

That night Pears broadcast from the Royal Festival Hall as both singer and
speaker with Arda Mandikian, Joan Cross and the EOG Chorus and Ensemble
conducted by Paul Sacher. The concert featured the first UK performance of
Stravinsky's *Cantata* (1952) and Walton's *Façade*.

Meanwhile IH's continuing work on the evolving *Gloriana* suite once again
raised the question of how, and how much, she should be paid.

> <u>Wed. 18th Nov.</u> *I went at 11, and he was not yet up. Then he came in, and*
> *asked me if I'd go to dinner that night, as Mary Potter was coming. He talked*
> *about the Festival Hall broadcast – was very angry that Peter had had to do*
> *so much experimenting with the amplifying of the Walton, which hadn't come*
> *through well. He was v. worried about his cold – he was cancelling Wednesday's*
> *recording and Thursday's broadcast. He talked about the Stravinski and how*
> *unsatisfactory it was – the tempi all wrong (Stravinsky's tempi, not Sacher's)*
> *and the contrast of Western Wind*[249] *the wrong kind of exciting: – he thought*
> *they'd played it superbly. Said it was cruel writing, especially for oboes.*
>
> *Then we got down to the suite – he talked about wanting the dances to look*
> *continuous, and asked me if I'd copy them so that they just joined up with a thin*
> *double bar – we discussed Bach's manuscripts and how his $\frac{12}{8}$ arias went straight*
> *on from his $\frac{3}{4}$ choruses. I suggested that I should do the dances on the same sized*
> *paper as the full score, so that they could fit into the suite – he was appalled at*
> *the thought of my having to do the March all over again, but I pointed out that*
> *it was <u>very</u> short. Then he said he'd never paid me for copying the Hardy songs,*
> *so I said he couldn't pay me for those as they were part of my education and he*
> *said "my dear you underestimate your I.Q. if you think they are <u>education</u>", and*
> *I said "no, you underestimate your music". Then he said that he must pay me for*
> *them or he wouldn't be able to ask me to do any more, and I said he could pay*
> *me union rates for the Gloriana Suite score, but <u>not</u> the songs, so we left it at*
> *that. Then I made a list of the pages he needed, and then it got to the problem of*
> *how to join the last movement onto the end of the dances, and he wanted me to*

---

[249] Igor Stravinsky had set 'Westron Wynde', an anonymous Middle English lyric,
  in the sixth movement of his *Cantata*.

play bits, but it was the agonisingly difficult scales, so I left those to him and we played the dances as a duet, his left & my right, to arrange the repeats. I wasn't a bit happy at the idea of beginning the 4th movement with Penelope & Q.E. doing their hammer-and-tongs.[250] *He said he wanted those scales, and I said he would probably have to rewrite a bit of it, and he said he wanted the Suite to be good but he didn't want to give* too *much thought & energy to it, and anyhow bits of opera were hopeless, the Grimes Interludes were hopeless except for those who'd never heard the opera. Then we went upstairs to finish numbering the pages, & then it was 1 and he'd invited Pam to lunch, and going downstairs he asked me how Grimes had sounded after all these years, and I said I couldn't go into that if he'd got a guest waiting, and I just had time to say that I could recognise how Peter had grown in those years owing to the things he'd written, which pleased him. He said he was appalled by the way Grimes sounded so* spread, *but I said no, it was economical. He said he couldn't see that it was economical; – but there was a certain naivity about it that suited the subject. Then I went. At dinner that night he was in good form, talking to Mary about painting, and exchanging anecdotes about the Cliveden set.*[251]

In an echo of IH's sentiments Britten wrote to Elizabeth Mayer that Pears had 'grown greatly in stature, and gives a staggering performance'.[252] The next day, instead of going to the BBC, where he had been due to record *Winter Words* for its first broadcast scheduled on 28 November, Britten went out exploring churches with Mary Potter. They visited the village of Thornham Parva, with its famous retable of the Crucifixion, which, four metres long by a metre high, remains the largest surviving altar-piece from the English Middle Ages.[253]

Back in Aldeburgh IH had received a letter from Anthony Gishford, regarding a series of music for recorders that IH and Britten were planning, and which Boosey & Hawkes had agreed to publish. IH, who was to do the lion's share

[250] In Act III Scene 3 of the opera, Lady Penelope Rich pleads for mercy for the Earl of Essex, infuriating the Queen, who is moved thereby to sign the death warrant.

[251] A group of political and literary figures prominent in encouraging a Germanophile foreign policy in Britain before the war, and perceived in some quarters to have urged the appeasement of Hitler. They often gathered at Cliveden, the Buckinghamshire house of the 2nd Viscount Astor and his wife Nancy.

[252] 21 November 1953; BPL.

[253] This tiny church, serving a parish of only fifty, is steeped in Britten resonances; in the graveyard are buried both Frederick Grinke, the violinist who played Britten's *Suite*, op. 6. with the composer in the 1930s, and Basil Spence, the architect of Coventry Cathedral, for which Britten composed his *War Requiem*.

of the editorial work, wanted to include substantial contributions from new young composers, but Gishford, writing on behalf of Ernst Roth, was advising her against this.

> *Thursday Nov 19th. I ran in at 9.pm to ask him about Tony Gishford's letter:*
> *– Miss Hudson had said he was dining alone. But Mary Potter was there – they'd*
> *had a wonderful afternoon exploring Thornton Parva, and he showed me a*
> *photograph of the 14th cent. Retable of the crucifixion – very beautiful. He also*
> *produced the pictures he'd got from the Book of Kells – wonderful endless Knots*
> *like on the celtic crosses. When I showed him Tony's letter he was* very *angry*
> *with Roth for not wanting to risk giving the young composers a chance, and he*
> *gave me permission to fight it tooth & nail. Then I asked him to sign the appeal*
> *for Norbert's naturalisation, and he again said that he wasn't respectable, and*
> *I reminded him that Peter had said he was, but he insisted "no, I'm not" and I*
> *saw a strained look in his eye and it made me wonder whether he was feeling*
> *persecuted – it was one of those agonising moments when one sees more than one*
> *is meant to. He soon cheered up, and produced brandy to drink, and then it struck*
> *10, so I went home as 10 is supposed to be his bedtime.*

Following Britten's advice IH wrote back to Boosey & Hawkes to fight what she perceived as the firm's antipathy towards new music. Gishford countered that 'Roth still feels that you should introduce your young contemporary composers with a good deal of circumspection', as 'both teachers and music dealers are fairly conservative'. He told IH that she could bring young composers on later in the series, and that 'Dr. Roth speaks with great experience and since your objective and ours are identical, I do think this point of view must command respect'.[254]

The following Sunday was Britten's fortieth birthday. In recognition of their joint project, IH presented him with a descant recorder, and the autograph fair copy of GH's 'The Fields of Sorrow', one of the three-part canons that he had so admired when IH had shown them to him in September 1952.

> *Sunday Nov 22nd. I was working in my studio all the morning and then Ben &*
> *Barbara and Basil Douglas walked in and invited me to lunch. As we walked*
> *down Crag Path Ben said he'd had lots of "lovely" presents. (He liked his descant*
> *recorder, & played "Winter Ade"*[255] *on it). Beth & the children had arrived – we*
> *had Schnapps, with beer out of silver mugs, and then with the meal we had*
> *champagne with the most* wonderful *food – chicken & Christmas pudding and*

---

[254] 8 December 1953; BPL.
[255] 'Winter, ade! Scheiden tut weh', a German folksong.

really good brandy butter. I took the children off to give them a lesson and then
went back to tea – Paul's parents had sent Ben a large red wax candle, like
an Austrian one, and we had it alight in the middle of the table. When I went
home about 6 Ben gave me the dance suite score to copy, and thanked me for my
birthday letter and said it meant so much to him to have me helping to keep his
spirits up, and he hoped it wasn't too much of a tie, so I said it was the sort of tie
they had in the Book of Kells that joins up with everything else.

Ben in London all the next week.

Britten spent the week at Chester Gate, going for intensive sessions on his arm
each day with a Miss M. G. Fellows in Devonshire Street. He found time also
to go to *Hamlet* at the Old Vic on 23 November. That weekend, the Harewoods
and William Plomer arrived for a visit.

Sunday Nov 29th. My bus got in at 9 pm and I went round to Crag House to get
George's signature for Norbert's appeal. Marion looking very beautiful. William
in terrific form, <u>pricelessly</u> funny – but his hair looks whiter. Ben looked ill and
worn – he must have had a bad week in London, being anxious about Peter's
throat. We drank brandy & I came home when it had struck 10, hoping they
wouldn't keep him up too late.

December 1953

Tuesday Dec 1. Ben & Peter came round while I was copying out St John Passion
translation and invited me to go to Thornton Parva with them & Mary Potter, to
see the 14th century retable. It was a <u>wonderful</u> day: – brilliant sunshine – we
picknicked in the car – The retable was very beautiful: Ben was happy.

Wed. 2nd. Annual general meeting in the evening in the Moot Hall – Peter did it
beautifully – Ben said "he gives me a feeling of confidence as soon as he gets on
his feet".

On 4 December IH and her choir were at Cecil Sharp House, where she
delivered a lecture and where Vaughan Williams named the group 'The Purcell
Singers'. Nearly five months were to pass before they gave their first concert
under this name, at Aldeburgh on 23 April 1954, conducted by Pears and IH.

Fund-raising for the Festival continued in Aldeburgh on Sunday 6 December,
with an event based on *The Brains Trust*, a BBC Radio discussion programme,
usually of political or philosophical issues, during which listeners submitted
questions that were then discussed by a range of experts. For the Aldeburgh
event, Britten had volunteered to be on the panel.

Sunday Dec 6th. Went round about 10 to find to my dismay that Ben had already gone out to Framlingham to fetch Richard[256] home for the day. So I took the score of the dances, and an orchestral version of a French folk carol he wanted copied,[257] & worked at them all day & took them round at tea time. Erwin & Sophie there. In the evening there was the Friends of the Festival Brains Trust; – Ben did his bit brilliantly, with great ease and humour, answering questions on whether opera should be sung in its own language or not, and whether composers wrote at the piano or not, and so on. Also his comments on the questions about painting were very much to the point. He disagreed violently when Stephen Potter and the actor said that films were an art, but Stephen took advantage of being in the Chair to change the subject. When it was over we had drinks in Crag House with all the speakers, and in the middle of it the telephone rang & Ben came back looking distraught saying that Noel had killed himself. He didn't let everyone know, and carried on being a host.

Noel Mewton-Wood had committed suicide on 4 December. His partner Bill Fedricks had recently died from complications following an operation for a ruptured appendix and Mewton-Wood, already beset with self-doubt, was overcome with grief and guilt. After one failed suicide attempt, it seemed to his friends that he was getting over the loss, and on 3 December he wrote to Britten, thanking him for his letter of condolence over Bill's death, informing him of his imminent tour of Germany and 'expecting to be back round about Christmas'. He hoped to 'pop down & see you some time in January', and expressed his sympathy with Britten's difficulties over his arm.[258] In fact this was one of more than forty informal notes that the pianist wrote before taking a lethal cocktail of gin and cyanide; he was found dead the next morning, next to his Steinway, in his living room in Harley Street.[259]

Monday Dec 7th. Went round after breakfast for the next bit of work on the suite from Gloriana and began by correcting the mistakes in the photographed pages. Then Ben called me into his bedroom. He was looking grey & worried, & talked of the terrifyingly small gap between madness and non-madness, and said why was it that the people one really liked found life so difficult. Peter had rung up,

---

[256] IH typescript note: 'Kihl'.

[257] Probably 'Le Noël passée', the first of the *Folk Song Arrangements*, vol. 2: *France* (1942). Britten had prepared orchestrations of five of these songs in 1945–6, but the date of arrangement of this one has previously been unknown. The ink manuscript at BPL is in IH's hand.

[258] 3 December 1953; BPL.

[259] See Cyrus Meher-Homji, CD booklet to *Noel Mewton-Wood: the Legendary Recordings* (ABC Classics, 2001).

and was "in a state". He also talked of the difficulty of finding anyone else to take his[260] *place. He'd had an awful time being rung up by newspapers. Then he went on to talk about the difficulties of Boosey & Hawkes, and then I began work on the other movements of the Suite. Stayed all day – he cheered up in the afternoon when we played recorder duets & laughed till we cried.*

Friday 11th Dec. In London. Ben asked me to go to Chester Gate that evening. He was feeling terribly depressed. He went through the joins in the last movement of the suite, and then Sue[261] *gave us a meal, and afterwards, sitting by the fire, he talked of Noel's death and of how all his friends had done all they could to help him, & that it was sheer bad luck that he'd had to go back to his music room to practise for his German tour. I went away early, as he was looking so weary.*

Soon after moving into Chester Gate, Pears had taken on his niece, Sue Pears, as a paid housekeeper and cook. She later recalled that Mewton-Wood's friends had agreed that he should never be left on his own, but that he had somehow slipped through the net on this occasion.

Despite the pervading sense of tragedy, routine soon prevailed, as the Music Club convened for a concert of chamber music on 13 December, featuring works by Purcell, Somervell, Corelli and Edward German's Quartet 'on an old French Carol'. In a mixed programme, Britten's 'Old Abram Brown' and 'Green Broom' were also performed along with a Morley madrigal and some recorder ensemble music.

Sunday Dec 13th. Went in after breakfast to work on the last movement. Basil Coleman was there. Ben asked me to stay to lunch, and during the meal they discussed alterations in the production of Gloriana & when it got to the dressing room scene Ben asked me to tell Basil about the entrances & exits being the wrong way round. Basil was lovely about it. I went straight back to work afterwards. In the evening the Music Club did their bits – Ben suffered tortures during the Edward German 4tet, but enjoyed nearly all the rest of it.

Britten's painful arm did not prevent him from enjoying some music-making of his own that evening; Stephen Potter reported that 'Ben and Immo play a duet on the recorders, Ben (right arm in sling) only using left hand. He practises and practises – eg in bed ... and playing he gets such giggles that his eyes swell, his ears grow scarlet and his whole face is suffused with tears.'[262]

---

[260] IH typescript note: 'i.e. Noel's'.
[261] IH typescript note: 'Sue Pears, later Sue Phipps'.
[262] Diary of Stephen Potter, 13 December 1953.

The following night a meeting of the Aldeburgh Festival Council was held to hear plans for the 1954 Festival.

> *Monday Dec 14th. Ben looked really ill when I went round to work, and thinner than ever in his pyjamas. He seemed nervy & upset, but as always was very patient with me when I'd left bits out or had made mistakes. Luckily Peter came down for the 24 hours. By tea time I'd finished the score & looked in on them in the sitting-room, doing their Christmas lists, & ringing up agents about future programmes, & studying the balance sheet before the Council Meeting. The Council Meeting was awful – the Vicar brought out his bit about the Rape & when it wasn't funny there was time to realise how awful it was. But the worst of all was the rudeness of* [name erased]. *Peter was absolutely magnificent: – I was so thankful he was there, as Ben would never have been able to do it without him. When it was over I went straight home, but met Peter who'd run back to Crag House for a letter for Fidelity – he called out "Was I too angry?" so I took his arm & walked back with him & unburdened about how desperate I felt about it all, and then I saw Ben looking ill and grieved and I couldn't bear it any longer and hung onto him and wept on the fur collar of his coat, which was a mistake, as it's the first time I've ever leaned on him since I began working for him. But he was very calming, & just said "It's all right, my dear, they're always like this." So then I felt better, and he called out to me to go round next morning.*

The minutes of the meeting recorded that the vicar, Rupert Godfrey, 'asked the Committee to consider the possibility of having fewer performances of the RAPE OF LUCRETIA and more of LOVE IN A VILLAGE. The artistic directors explained that this would make it difficult for the Opera Group, and the meeting decided that the plans should remain as originally proposed, there being a strong demand for more performances of LUCRETIA after its success here in a former Festival.' IH was later to paraphrase this story, recording how the 'Festival Office received a request for "less Rape and more Love".[263] In the event *The Rape of Lucretia* was performed at the Aldeburgh Festival on 12 and 14 June 1954, conducted by Norman Del Mar. Arthur Oldham's new version of the 1762 Ballad Opera *Love in a Village*, which had featured at the 1952 Festival, was also given two performances in 1954, in a double bill with Berkeley's new opera *A Dinner Engagement*. Pears also announced that the Stravinsky *Cantata* would be too expensive to perform, and that IH would conduct the Purcell Singers and the Festival Choir in Bach's *St John Passion* instead.

[263] Burrows, *The Aldeburgh Story*.

*Tuesday Dec 15th. When I got there Ben was doing Christmas presents with
Jeremy. He asked me to copy out "I wonder as I wander" for Peter; – and he gave
me a <u>really</u> beautiful watercolour by Mary. And he asked me to stay to lunch
with him. He was feeling mouldy – he'd woken up suddenly in the night with
his heart beating very violently, and it had frightened him. At lunch he talked
of G's nocturne²⁶⁴ which I'd given Sue for a birthday present, and then he asked
me if I'd ever tried writing for piano, & I said I wanted to write some studies
some day, and he agreed, and then I told him the story of Burney calling on CPE
Bach, & Bach showed him the manuscript of the 48, describing it as "exercises
which my father wrote for us to practise when we were children", and Ben was
<u>delighted</u>. It's good to see that however low he's feeling he always lights up at
an idea that appeals to him. He was dreading having to pack – he'd reached the
stage of wishing he hadn't got to go to Germany that night. So I offered to fold his
things for him, and of course it was <u>very</u> difficult, because I'd never packed men's
clothes before. He found he hadn't got any manuscript paper left, so I said I'd run
in with some when I went to see him off. The lovely sunny day turned to fog by
the afternoon – I got there at 5.15 & packed the MS paper, & he was just going
to have high-tea so I asked if I might talk to him while he had it, as he looked
pretty low. He said he felt just as bad as during the night, and he hoped he'd get
there. I told him there was no need for him to go if he didn't feel equal to it, but
he said "if I can manage the journey I'll be all right". He talked of G, & said it was
strange that his career was following so much the same pattern as G's, & that
the reception of Grimes was like the reception of the Planets, and that people
were disappointed with what came afterwards. Then he talked about the festival,
and was angry that the Vicar had objected to asking Soper because he was an
"aggressive pacifist"!! He said "They're <u>frightened</u>, that's what's the matter". And
then, looking me suddenly in the eye, he said "we are <u>all</u> of us frightened", and I
said yes, but we're not all frightened all the time at all the same things, and he
was silent for a bit and then said "Dear Imo, you make us very rich."*

*This was quite unbearable, as I was sitting so close to him, and anchored to
the bench so that I couldn't move. There was absolutely nothing I could say so I
kept quiet, and then he said "I don't know what I should have done without you
during these last weeks, let alone during these last years". I was still paralysed
& couldn't say a word, and then he went on to say he hoped it wasn't taking too
much time from my own work & then at last I could protest, and he, with his*

²⁶⁴ Published by Curwen, the work had been written by GH as a twenty-first
birthday present for IH, and first performed by her at the Royal College of
Music in 1930. Sue Pears had celebrated her birthday on 4 December.

unfailing sympathy, talked about The Screw & future plans, and then it was time for him to go.

Despite his show of anger, Britten would have been well aware that Donald Soper, the Methodist minister and prominent socialist and pacifist (like Britten and Pears he was a member of the Peace Pledge Union), would have been as unwelcome in Aldeburgh as IH's earlier suggestion of Bishop George Bell.

A few days later Britten took the boat train from Harwich to Frankfurt and spent the Christmas and New Year period as the guest of the Hesses. IH went first to London, where she spent a week rehearsing for the BBC at All Souls' Langham Place with Mabel Ritchie and Jennifer Vyvyan and conducting a choral concert in London, which the Steins attended; Erwin Stein reported to Britten: 'Imo's little concert in the church went frightfully well. Peter sung lovely & I enjoyed the whole, as did Sophie.'[265] IH then returned to Aldeburgh to lead the carol singing round the town, before going to Great Dunmow to her mother's house for Christmas.

January 1954

(Ben was in Germany for 3 weeks – and then I was in London & Birmingham, so I didn't see him for 5 weeks)

IH wrote to Britten on 5 January to apologize for not being in Aldeburgh on his return 'but I have to be in London for rehearsals'. The Opera School, founded by Joan Cross and Anne Wood five years earlier, was rehearsing in London for performances of GH's *The Wandering Scholar* (in a version that effectively found a balance between GH's own cued-down orchestration and Britten's chamber orchestra version) and *Sāvitri*, to be given at the Birmingham City Art Gallery on Saturday 15 January as a private concert for the CBSO Society Members' Night. IH travelled to Birmingham on 14 January. The *Birmingham Post* admired the performances by the young Opera School singers, and especially the 'vitality and skill' of IH's conducting and her 'absolutely authoritative interpretations of them … no doubt it was her acute awareness of the Wagnerian hangover in *Savitri* that forbade her to attempt any disguising of it'.[266] Anne Wood wrote to thank IH, and also passed on a message from the orchestra who 'said how much they enjoyed playing under her; and that she certainly knew what she was about, and that anyone who came in at the wrong place had only himself to blame, so clear is her beat and intention'.[267]

[265] 21 December 1953; BPL.
[266] *Birmingham Post*, 18 January 1954.
[267] 20 January 1954; HF.

The following Monday she went to Essex to spend some more time with her mother, before going on to Chester Gate on 19 January, returning finally to Aldeburgh the next day. While she was away, Kenneth Clark had, on her behalf, approached the Home Secretary to plead the case for Norbert Brainin's naturalization. Sir David Maxwell-Fyfe held fast, however, and Clark wrote to IH with the bad news that the minister 'cannot change his decision ... He reminds me that the Home Secretary is excused by statute from giving any reason ...'[268]

Part of IH's holiday had been spent in looking through the edition of Purcell's *Dido and Aeneas* that she and Britten had made for the EOG to perform in 1950–51; on 5 January she had told Britten that 'I've begun going through this, but a lot still to do to it.'[269] The EOG were thinking of reviving the work for 1955, although this idea was eventually dropped because of the difficulties recruiting a sufficiently distinguished cast and a perceived lack of enthusiasm in England for the work. The edition was eventually published in 1960.

Britten returned from Germany refreshed and with some improvement to his arm; although he had done no written work he had generated, as he wrote to Myfanwy Piper, 'lots of ideas' about *The Turn of the Screw.*[270] Once settled, he had immediate business in London. The previous November he had been appointed a Composer-Director of the Performing Right Society and attended his first meeting in this capacity on 14 January. Two days later he was with Pears, who was recording *Les Illuminations* for Decca with the strings of the New Symphony Orchestra, conducted by Eugene Goossens, at Kingsway Hall.

Meanwhile *Gloriana* was to be revived for three performances at Covent Garden on 29 January, 2 and 16 February, with Pears again in the role of Essex and Reginald Goodall conducting.

Wed. Jan 20th. As soon as I got back to Aldeburgh I went round to Crag House to see Ben – he'd only got half an hour as he was going out to play left-handed squash. He was looking much *better, arm out of a sling, but he said it still hurt him quite a lot – "more supple but more painful". He said he wasn't going till Friday, so asked me to go in next day to go through Dido etc. He said there was so much to talk about he didn't know where to begin. (He was very kind & sympathetic about Birmingham.) He said Peter was in terrific form and had sung Les Illuminations* superbly *at the recording.*[271] *He also said he was looking*

---

[268] 18 January 1954; HF.

[269] 5 January 1954; BPL.

[270] 3 January 1954; BPL.

[271] Later released by Decca as LXT 2941, coupled with the *Serenade for Tenor, Horn and Strings.*

*forward to Gloriana with Goodall and was going to be in at all of it if possible.
He seemed full of energy once more, in spite of the pain. Priceless story about
his first P.R.S. meeting – crowd of publishers, and the only composers were
Montague Phillips, Haydn Wood & himself. After the meeting Mr. Phillips came
up & said how glad he was to have him on their side. Ben couldn't think what he
meant, & said something about the publishers being very well represented, but it
turned out that Phillips had meant on the side of "really serious music"!!!*

*Ben was <u>very</u> indignant about the Home Secretary turning down Norbert's
appeal for naturalisation. He told me gruesome stories of some of the things that
are happening in Germany to the political prisoners – He began talking about the
theatre – said he'd had a long talk with Fidelity & her husband about the danger
of floods, & Jock doesn't think Aldeburgh will last more than 20 years.²⁷² Ben
suggests a £10,000 shell without a tower, to house 399. He was <u>very</u> practical,
and eager to get down to it with architects right now.*

*Then he said that he couldn't make up his mind whether to revise his early
concerto for the left hand – there'd been a pirated recording in America, &
Booseys wanted to reissue it after the battle had died down. And Ben couldn't
decide whether it was <u>very</u> bad or worth revising. Then it was time to go.*

On 2 November 1953 the Boosey & Hawkes office in New York reported that
Urania Records had brought out a recording of Britten's *Diversions* op. 21 with
the pianist Siegfried Rapp and Arthur Rother conducting the Berlin Radio
Orchestra, only applying for a licence once the record had been released. In
fact the recording had been made without Rapp's knowledge at a concert in
East Germany and sold on by the radio station. Boosey's advised against legal
action as Rapp was playing the piece regularly in Germany to high acclaim, and
Britten acquiesced and authorized the release of the recording, even though it
included one variation (no. 8) which he had subsequently withdrawn. In the
end he did make some revisions to the piece, sending them to Erwin Stein at
the beginning of February, before recording it himself with Julius Katchen as
soloist with the London Symphony Orchestra on 29 and 30 July 1954.²⁷³

On 24 January Britten and IH travelled to London, where they stayed for five
days. Britten was holding auditions for the child roles of Miles and Flora in *The
Turn of the Screw*. On 24 January, with Pears, he gave the first London performance of *Winter Words*, together with Canticle I, some of his own folksong and

---

²⁷² IH typescript note: '(This was before the new sea defences were carried out).'
  Jock was Fidelity Cranbrook's husband, John, the 4th Earl of Cranbrook.
²⁷³ Released by Decca as LXT 2981.

Purcell arrangements, and Pelham Humphrey's 'As freezing fountains' in IH's realization. Among the audience was Maureen Garnham, soon to start work for the EOG, who later recalled:

> Sitting immediately in front of us was what looked from the back view to be a young girl, her fair hair drawn back into a ballerina's bun, who throughout the concert expressed her rapture by clasping her hands ecstatically and rocking her body … At the interval she stood up and half turned round, and we saw that she was not a girl but a middle-aged woman. She proceeded to thread her way among the crowd towards the platform and the artist' room behind it, and my friend murmured, 'Oh dear! I wonder which one of them it is that she's got a crush on!'[274]

As a result of a major oversight at Boosey & Hawkes, IH soon found herself unexpectedly busy correcting orchestral parts for the impending performances of *Gloriana*, with the assistance of a young Australian composer, Malcolm Williamson, who was then working for the publisher.

Jan 24th, Sunday. In London. Went to the V. & A. for Ben and Peter's recital – Sue told me there'd been a crisis about the orchestral parts of Gloriana – none of the corrections[275] had been put in. The concert was superb – they did my Pelham Humphrey which was such a surprise I could hardly listen with excitement: 1st Canticle very beautiful – The Hardy songs went better than ever before. Huge audience, who liked them. I'd thought that I'd be in an agony about Ben's arm as it was the first time he'd played for 3 months, but as soon as he began I forgot all about it. Went round to the artist's room afterwards; Erwin with a very long face about the orchestral parts. I only got a glimpse of Ben – he looked very white & drawn and it was obviously hurting.

Monday Jan 25th. I rang Ben up just after 9 to ask if I could help write in the parts – he asked me to ring Erwin. I went round to Booseys & Erwin asked me to go with Malcolm[276] to Covent Garden. We worked in the library all day – terrific hard work & concentration. Got a glimpse of Ben & Peter at the end of the rehearsal while I was collecting the full score from Goodall (even the score hadn't got the corrections in!) Got back to Chester Gate about 5.30, v. exhausted. Ben was very kind – asked anxiously about it all and said "what should we do if you weren't there?"

[274] Garnham, *As I Saw It*, p. 58.
[275] Originally 'mistakes'.
[276] IH: 'Williamson' added later in green pencil.

*Tuesday Jan 26th. Went back to the library at Covent Garden – Ben in Henley,
working on the Screw. Finished the corrections, by working non-stop. The
greatest effort in concentration since he began orchestrating it a year ago!*

IH was later to recall, in a green pencilled annotation in the diary, that after
the day's work Williamson was 'completely worn out & said "Do you always
work as hard as this?"'. On 27 January Britten combined more rehearsals with
a second hearing of David Hemmings, who was eventually to take the part of
Miles, at Chester Gate (he had been previously auditioned at the Royal Court
Theatre in December).

*Wed. Jan 27th. Orchestral rehearsal at Covent Garden, Acts I & II. V. anxious
about having missed mistakes. Some of the things we'd put in were no better. The
actual rehearsal appalling; everything slow, heavy, and sounding DULL! As well
as inaccurate and anxious. Ben & Peter were so depressed that they hardly spoke
during our meal together at Chester Gate. In the evening, "in order to relax", we
all went to King John at The Old Vic – it was the first time I'd been to a London
theatre for 10 years! They shouted too much, but bits of it were very good, and the
2nd Act terrific. Ben was very moved by it. Got home and had wonderful supper
of bacon and eggs.*

The cast's 'shouting' had not been noticed by the critic of *The Times*, who found
George Devine's production of this Shakespeare rarity 'unexpectedly satisfactory'; it featured Michael Hordern as the King, with Richard Burton bringing
'silent momentousness' to the role of Philip the Bastard and Fay Compton 'all
her nervous strength' to that of Constance.[277]

*Thursday Jan 28th. Ben took a brass rehearsal at 9.30, & things began to improve.
The trombones at the beginning of Act III sc I sounded much better. When
the orchestra arrived at 10 to tune Ben said to me "Did you hear the opening?
It's much better, isn't it?" And when I said yes he said "It's all your doing, for
suggesting that the brass shouldn't be forte, but lighter, like a dance". This was
unbearably exciting, because it was true, and perhaps the proudest moment
of all, knowing that I'd been able to help him to get nearer to what he wanted.
The rehearsal was infinitely better than the day before – all except the Street
scene, which was still deplorable. They were much more cheerful at lunch. Ben
asked me to stay on to talk about the possibility of an Aldeburgh theatre. It was
extraordinary to see how, as usual, he could put the whole of his mind from one
thing to another, like lightening.*

[277] *The Times*, 28 October 1953.

IH went to the eleventh performance of *Gloriana*, on 29 January, and wrote to Britten and Pears from her mother's house to 'Thank you for a WONDERFUL performance … what an immense amount you have both achieved in making the miracle happen in 48 hours'. Britten was also pleased; after attending a post-performance party hosted by Anthony Gishford, he wrote to thank him, adding that the performance had been 'a great improvement' and hoping that 'the reception at the end may prove that the tide is slightly turning'.[278]

February 1954

With the process of rehabilitation of *Gloriana* under way, Britten turned his full attention to the composition, and arrangements for the first performance, of *The Turn of the Screw*. Unusually, he was experiencing writer's block in trying to find the theme on which the whole work would 'turn'.

> *Feb 4th Thursday – Went round to Crag House after breakfast with the Hardy songs – Ben asked me to go back to lunch with Beth & the children. Then he horrified me by walking round to my studio at 12.30 to say that the BBC wanted me on the telephone! Alas, I must somehow get a telephone of my own. He said he was stuck because he couldn't find the right tune for the variations in the new opera. After I'd given the children a lesson I went back to tea & joined the committee meeting about the Snape bazaar in aid of the Festival – Ben being very practical & helpful but obviously longing to escape.*

At 8 o'clock that night the Hull steamship Kentbrook, on its way from Felixstowe to Goole, ran aground to the south of the Martello Tower in Aldeburgh, after developing engine trouble. As the *Leiston Observer* noted the following day, 'people with short wave wireless sets were able throughout the night to follow the attempts to help the Kentbrook', before messages ceased at midnight. Although the crew was rescued, it was not possible to salvage the ship. On the same night – at 10 p.m. – some of IH's songs were broadcast in a mixed piano and song recital by the BBC Midland Service.

The next night the members of the Music Club were meeting for a rehearsal of Bach's Cantata no. 6, *Bleib bei uns* – 'Bide with us'. Stephen Potter wrote to his sister Muriel, IH's old form teacher from Saint Paul's Girls' School, giving a flavour of the evening ahead: 'On Friday we are rehearsing for the Music Club Bach Cantata, and I am singing bass with Martin the chemist, Att [Mary Potter] is singing alto, Ben is playing the viola and Peter is (very badly) playing the piano. The menace is Mrs Y—, who has a nice soprano

[278] 31 January 1954; BPL.

voice which unpredictably goes treble strength, and everybody starts to giggle'.[279]

> *Friday Feb. 5th Ben asked me to go in to supper before the music club rehearsal at Crag House. (The broadcast of my songs was frightful: – he was v. sympathetic!) Wonderful food – He told me how dramatic the short-wave account of the shipwreck had been the night before. He then said that he was worried about* [name erased][280] *& didn't know how to advise her. He said that nearly all of his friends who were married were unhappy and he couldn't help feeling thankful that he wasn't married himself. And what madness it was to involve oneself for life for reasons that were not after all so terribly important. I wanted to argue here that children were important, but the St. Emilion had mounted to my head and when he talks to me confidentially about personal things I still suffer from paralysis even after all these months. He wanted to refill my glass but it was nearly time for the rehearsal and I'd already broken my rule about no drink before conducting, so I said "no" and he said "oh come on" and to my dismay I gave in and then everything was beautifully relaxed and he said it was a good thing to indulge in a little weakness every now and then – such as giving way – and he looked so happy – like he did before he was ill* [line erased] *and then it was time for the rehearsal, which went fairly well – Ben & Stephen Potter were the only basses!*

> *Sat. Feb 6th. Ben came round to my studio in the morning & said would I walk out to the wreck with him & the Potters that afternoon, & would I go to lunch with him so as to ring up the Amadeus, etc. He made me finish off the red wine from the night before. He asked me if I thought the extra bars in the Midnight on the Gt Western were all right.[281] He said he couldn't face having the Hardy songs published because they were so personal and he didn't want everyone doing them badly. I said he was wrong, because people had got to have a chance to learn about music. When I said I thought they were the best thing he'd written[282] he said that several of them were, & that he was pleased to be able to be so relaxed as in the last one: – "I couldn't have written that a year ago".*

> *The walk to the wreck & back was very dramatic – huge blocks of ice floating on*

[279] Jenkins, *Stephen Potter*, p. 181.
[280] Both his sister Beth's and Mary Potter's marriages were in difficulty at this time, and were to break up in the following years.
[281] The manuscript suggests that Britten took some time to finalize the final two bars of the introduction to the song (bars 7–8).
[282] IH subsequently altered this as a pencil annotation in the edited typescript, to 'one of the best things'.

the river, and a low moon. The Potters couldn't stay to tea as they'd got people
coming, so I made tea and then he produced his recorder and began practising
and we did Tower Hill²⁸³ as a duet – he enjoyed having to remember the right
fingering and got terribly angry with himself when he went wrong. He wouldn't
stop, although he was going out that night.

The next day a new member was added to the Crag House family. John Cranko
had bred some dachshund puppies and Pears brought home 'Clytie', 'the first
of many Dachshunds' as IH noted, starting a trend for owning dogs that would
stay with Britten and Pears until the end of their lives. Sue Pears also acquired
a puppy from this litter, which she called 'Billy Budd'. Meanwhile IH had been
advancing the *Music for Recorders* project by writing 'twenty-five practical
lessons for the beginner', devised to be played as duets by teacher and pupil, to
open the series.

    That night the Aldeburgh Music Club met to perform the Bach cantata.

Sunday Feb 7th. Ben had asked me to a meal before the music club meeting. I
found Peter with his Dachshund puppy – they'd both been puppy-worshipping all
the afternoon. We played recorder trios – Peter angry with Ben for giggling. Then
Ben tried some of my exercises for beginners & said he liked them. We'd left it
v. late for eating and the players began arriving half-way through. The Cantata
went well on the whole, the first chorus much *better than Friday, but the solos*
not so good with Peter's continuo as with Ben's. (Alas, even these few bars of
today had made his arm bad.)

Monday Feb 8th. Discussion 4.30 to 7.30 with Elizabeth *about details for the*
festival. As usual Ben quicker & clearer with ideas than anyone else. Argued
again about not conducting the St John if it's to be recorded. Quite a good
meeting, & a lot achieved, at any rate on paper.

Tuesday, Feb 9th. Motored to London with Ben & Peter, Jeremy driving. – Clytie
on Peter's lap. Ben talked about Mozart, Bach & Gluck having given people
more than they bargained for in their oratorios, Passions, operas. When we were
near London he changed places with Peter, as he'd got a head-ache, and talked
of future plans, and his arm. We had an excellent meal at Chester Gate – the 2
puppies taking up most of the time and conversation!

The next day Britten and Pears travelled to Dorset to give a concert for the
Dorset Music Society at the Corn Exchange, Dorchester. In addition to *Winter
Words*, they performed works by Mozart, Purcell and Pelham Humphrey and

---

²⁸³ 'Tower Hill' by Giles Farnaby, from the *Fitzwilliam Virginal Book*.

some of Britten's folksong arrangements. In their absence, IH planned a visit
to Cheltenham, for where she departed on 15 February, returning two days
later.

> *Wed 10th Feb. They left for Dorset just after breakfast: – Ben was pleased to hear
> that I was going to lecture about him at Cheltenham: it was another glimpse of
> his amazing humility because the idea really gave him pleasure.*

> *Thursday Feb 18th. Went to Crag House directly after breakfast: – Ben depressed
> by the Dorchester concert, because they'd laughed at the tragic bits in the Hardy
> songs, and he said he felt more bewildered than ever. Went back at 2.30 for
> meeting about new theatre with Mr Cullum, Elizabeth and County Surveyor
> (who rang up Ipswich & got their approval!!) after 4 hours of discussions we
> drank champagne to it!*

Following this successful meeting Britten and Pears travelled north for more
concerts. On 20 February they were in Glasgow, where Britten conducted his
Spring Symphony with the Scottish National Orchestra. Two days later they
gave a concert for the North Cumberland Recital Club at the Carlisle & County
High School. Canticle I featured again, with sequences of English songs from
the seventeenth and twentieth centuries, and folksong arrangements by Britten himself and Percy Grainger. IH spent the time in London rehearsing the
Purcell Singers, who were to give their first concert under their new name in
April.

Britten and Pears then travelled directly from Carlisle to London to hold
more auditions for *The Turn of the Screw*. Amidst this, and visits by Ronald
Duncan and others, they began with IH to devote serious time to planning the
details of the 1954 Festival. Meanwhile, Britten had heard that he would, as
Stanley Ratcliffe had predicted, need to undergo an operation on his arm.

> *Tuesday Feb 23rd. Got to Chester Gate; – Ben & Peter returned from their
> Carlisle concert just before choir. Lovely supper together, Basil Douglas stayed &
> we drank draught Guinness. Ben v. weary – I got desperate when he would insist
> on stoking the boiler with his arm so bad, but he said it was "good for it".*

> *Wed 24th Feb. Spent all afternoon at Chester Gate going through programmes
> with Ben & Peter for Aldeburgh. They were both weary, & in wording things
> for the leaflet inclined to leave it to me to finish the sentences for them, which I
> always find a terrific strain. It was a hectic time; – telephone calls most of the
> time, Ronnie Duncan coming in, and then more auditions for the Screw children.
> Ben depressed at having to wait at least a fortnight for the operation on his arm.*

*Yet cheerful in spite of everything: – he is <u>quite</u> different now he's working again,
& no longer in despair as he was during the months before Christmas.*

*(Ben and Peter away on tour in the north of England. Crisis about not being able
to raise money for the Couraud[284] choir at the festival.)*

Britten and Pears went back on the road at the end of the month, touring recitals of Mozart, Schubert and English songs (including Canticle I and *Winter Words*). Travelling widely, they performed first at the Sheldonian Theatre, Oxford, on 25 February, before going on to Birmingham where they gave a recital at the City Art Gallery two days later. Still in Birmingham, Pears performed the *Spring Symphony* with the CBSO under David Willcocks, before the couple moved on to Wolverhampton, where on 3 March they gave a concert at the Civic Hall. After a recital at Rossall School on 5 March they returned to London on 7 March to perform Schubert's *Die schöne Müllerin* at the Victoria and Albert Museum.

Their absence left IH to deal with the sudden withdrawal of the Couraud Choir from the Festival for the reason, as Britten later reported to the Aldeburgh Festival Council on 11 March, that 'the necessary funds [had not been] forthcoming'. The choir had asked for £400 to perform two concerts, a request which included a heavy subsidy from the French Foreign Office, and insufficient private contributions had been raised in France to make the tour economically viable. As Tony Mayer commented to Britten, 'the age of the wealthy private backer has passed, and business firms are hardly sensitive to sentimental, artistic or national motivations'.[285] IH wrote hurriedly to Britten and Pears from Liverpool Street Station ('Forgive extreme haste: – train to Ipswich going in 5 mins.') saying 'it is <u>wretched</u>[286] that you should have such a disaster to worry you in the middle of a tour',[287] and outlining a long list of suggested alternatives.

March 1954

Thursday March 11th. Went round to Crag House after breakfast. Miraculous weather: – we sat in the garden in the sunshine all the morning, without coats on, and had the <u>most</u> depressing discussions about the festival, going through the figures over and over again – £400 to find even after calling on this year's guarantors for 100%. Very painful morning. The council meeting in the early

284 IH has written 'foreign' over the word 'Couraud'.
285 15 March 1954; BPL.
286 Underlined six times.
287 Undated; BPL.

evening was worse, and when it was over Ben & Peter were both so desperate
that they didn't want to have the festival at all this year. I was relieved that
things had come to a head at last, but prospects too bleak for rejoicing.

The Council discussed the 'gravity of the financial situation' of the Festival, and
it was agreed that they should apply to the Arts Council for an increased grant,
seek more guarantors, raise ticket prices, and institute a new series of fund-
raising events. In the end the total losses of the Festival added up to £670, which
was covered by an additional Arts Council guarantee of £750, given in response
to a plea from Britten to Kenneth Clark. Clark responded on 18 March saying
'We considered your cri de cœur yesterday and did what we could. We hope it
will be sufficient help'.[288]

Friday March 12th – *Ben* <u>still</u> *doing figures, reducing the overdraft quite*
considerably. They talked about having only a token Festival in '55 & waiting for
the opening of the theatre. While Peter was ringing up, Ben said that he wanted
in future to be able to "think more and more about less and less." Also that he
was slightly alarmed at the slowness with which he was getting down to the new
opera. I said this was because he'd been feeling mouldy, and that the thing to do
was to get better. That evening they asked me to cut my music club rehearsal and
discuss details of St John Passion. Both of them had <u>very</u> *illuminating things*
to say: – Peter's suggestion that the 2nd & 4th bars of the F♯ minor tenor solo
should have a ▱▱▱ *and actually be taken off before the end of the dotted*
minim; Ben's suggestion that the soprano 'Ich folge dir' should be very simple,
like a boy's singing. In the first chorus he wanted ♩♩♩♩ *on every group. Among*
the things I'd already discovered were necessary he wanted <u>long</u> *stacc. quavers*
for strings and a silence before the E♭ entry. Before we'd got to the end of Part
I, Mary & Sue came back from the rehearsal and we played frivolous recorder
quartets.

Sunday March 14th. They gave me a lift to Dunmow on their way to London in
the Rolls, & we went on talking about the St John on the way. Ben now wants the
D major $\frac{12}{8}$ bass aria <u>slow</u>, *"like a lullaby". We had tea at Westbury House which*
was looking warm and welcoming.

Tuesday March 16th. In London, at Chester Gate. Myfanwy was there, working
with Ben on the opera. We had an excellent meal with red wine, after a
depressing Purcell Singers rehearsal.

That day Britten and Pears had also begun recording *Winter Words* at the Decca studios, completing the work the following afternoon. Pears was finalizing his travel arrangements to Germany, where he was due to sing the role of Evangelist in Bach's *St Matthew Passion* under Eugen Jochum at the Bayerischer Rundfunk, Munich, on 25 and 26 March.

The following day brought for IH a welcome resolution of her delicate problem about how, and how much, Britten should pay her for her work, about which she had sought the advice of her Thaxted friend, Arthur Caton.

> <u>Wed March 17th.</u> *Ben rapidly went through the recorder pieces just before I took them to Booseys. Later that morning he rang while I was with Erwin, and said that Peter had got to go to Germany on Sunday night. (That afternoon they had a 4hr recording session on the Hardy songs.)*[289] *Before I left Chester Gate he insisted on paying me for* <u>all</u> *copying, whatever it was. His arguments were so exactly like A's had been on the telephone the day before that I at once gave way.*

'Rapidly' was no exaggeration, as IH was able to leave Britten and get the 10.30 train for London. By Friday, Britten, Pears and IH were back in Aldeburgh, Pears to prepare for his German trip and Britten and IH to get ready for the Aldeburgh Music Club Night on Sunday, a concert that was to include dry runs of the music that the Club were going to perform in the 'Music on the Meare' concert in the Aldeburgh Festival, together with recorder quartet pieces played by Britten, IH and Mary Potter and her son Julian, and Dvořák's *Bagatelles*, op. 47. IH was now working on copying sections of *The Turn of the Screw* as Britten composed them: this work was gradually to take up more and more of her time, her diary becoming one of the chief casualties; on 18 March she wrote in her appointments diary: 'begin regular work for Ben'.

> *Friday March 19th. Went in after breakfast and he gave me the boy's song in the new opera to copy. He came to the music club rehearsal in the evening and he and Julian sang bass superbly. Afterwards we went into Crag House and practised a recorder 4tet I'd arranged for them, for 3 descants & treble. We drank brandy, and Ben gave me such a large glass that all life's problems vanished.*

> <u>Sat March 20th.</u> *I'd arranged to go round at 5.15, but when I got there just after 5 I found them deep in programme building with Elizabeth, so they asked me to join them – To my dismay Peter said that he thought George Malcolm ought to do the continuo in the St John, to save Ben having it as "a millstone round his neck." Devastated by this. At about 6 we went round to the Potters and practised recorders – Stephen back from Spain & two visitors who were very patient in*

---

[289] Released by Decca as LXT 5095, coupled with the *Seven Sonnets of Michelangelo*, recorded in July 1954.

putting up with the frightful sounds we made. Ben still gets the giggles badly, but Mary and Julian were very good, & Peter is getting superb tone on his low notes. Drinks helped.

Sunday March 21st. Music Club in the evening – sad having no Peter. The singing wasn't too bad, but the S.S.A. part song got wildly out of tune. Ben had been feeling sick all day. He played very well in the recorder 4tet, and didn't laugh once. He had to play the piano part in the Dvorak with strings at the end, which was very dreary and went on for ages. He offered me a lift to London next day.

Monday March 22nd. Ben still feeling mouldy. We had a somewhat hectic early lunch with the telephone ringing nearly all the time, & then drove

Having stopped mid-sentence, IH made no further entries in the diary. When she came to edit it, she wrote: 'This was as far as I managed to get in keeping an Aldeburgh diary; in the following weeks and months and years there was too much work to be done.' The end of the diary coincided with, and may indeed have been precipitated by, Britten going into University College Hospital, London, for the operation on his arm. He emerged a few days later in considerable pain, but immediately resumed work on the composition sketch of *The Turn of the Screw*, writing at first with his left hand, and ably supported by what Basil Douglas called 'the great Imogen Holst machine'.[290] IH was later to recall that the work

> was written with very little time to spare. I had to copy out the vocal score straight away in batches of half a dozen pages at a time and then post them to London the same day. It seemed incredible that a composer could be so sure of what he wanted that he would risk parting with the beginning of a scene before he had written the end of it.[291]

In July IH travelled with Britten to Devon for the Taw and Torridge Festival, where she continued to work ceaselessly on the opera. But she retained her quick sense of humour throughout, as Maureen Garnham later recalled:

> She took her work very seriously ... but not herself ... Imo was working almost day and night on a score of Ben's which he had produced very late. Ben and Basil kept up her strength by taking her daily to the dining-room of a hotel in Barnstaple where the food was good but the atmosphere prim, and sitting her down in front of a nourishing steak. On one

[290] Carpenter, *Benjamin Britten*, p. 335.
[291] IH, *Britten*, 3rd edn, p. 55.

such occasion, into a sudden quiet such as can sometimes inexplicably descend on a crowded room came Imo's clear voice: 'Isn't it *lovely* to be kept by two men!'[292]

Such was the tightness of the schedule that Boosey & Hawkes had no time to prepare a conducting score for Britten to use for the first performance. As the pencilled manuscript full score would have been unreadable in the dim light of an orchestra pit, IH took on the further immense task, at the composer's request, of inking in over Britten's writing to make the manuscript score legible. Yet despite this 'battle against time', which found IH still copying out orchestral parts twenty minutes before the first orchestral rehearsal on 2 August, the opera was completed against the odds in time for its successful première at the Fenice Theatre in Venice on 14 September 1954.

The 1954 Aldeburgh Festival also went ahead, with IH's influence now firmly stamped on proceedings. She directed the Purcell Singers in a concert including works by Pérotin, Scheidt, Purcell, Böhm, and Schütz's *St John Passion*, and conducted a Leoš Janáček centenary concert. Her dream of mounting Bach's *St John Passion* at the Festival also came to fruition on the last Saturday afternoon, 19 June, when she conducted an acclaimed performance featuring Pears as the Evangelist and with, to her undoubted delight, the harpsichord continuo played by Britten. Stephen Potter remembered in his diary 'the tremendous effectiveness' of the performance; Britten told him afterwards that 'he thought it was the best St John he'd ever had.'[293]

With IH's position in the Festival set-up now assured it was only a matter of time before Elizabeth Sweeting would have to depart and, with a significant financial squeeze being applied to the 1955 Festival, it was decided that the paid position of Festival manager could no longer be justified. Tommy Cullum resigned from his post as Honorary Treasurer in protest at her removal. To fill the gap, Stephen Reiss, Sweeting's unpaid successor, suggested the setting up of 'a small sub-committee' to carry through the organization and administration of the Festival. Reiss himself took on the role of 'responsible organizer', while IH was made officially 'responsible for programmes, performers and to be a link with Mr. Pears and Mr. Britten', a role she had effectively been performing for the previous two Festivals.[294]

[292] Garnham, *As I Saw It*, p. 61.
[293] Diary of Stephen Potter, 19 June 1954.
[294] Minutes of the Executive Committee meeting, 9 June 1955.

Part IV ~ 1955–84

CHRISTOPHER GROGAN

11 'The thing that one wants to do most in the whole world': 1955–64

For the next decade the pattern of Imogen Holst's life was to revolve around Britten's intensive compositional schedule and the year-round demands of the Aldeburgh Festival. Her dedication to Britten remained obsessive: Eric Crozier recalled her 'on London trains, enthusiastically conducting from a score in total unawareness of her fellow passengers, or dancing down Aldeburgh High street like a six-year-old because Ben had just said "Good morning" to her', while Billy Burrell remarked that 'She kissed the ground that he walked on.'[1] In consequence of this dedication she 'selflessly submerged her own creativity',[2] and for a few years her writing and composing came to a standstill, to be revived only gradually as she became accustomed to the demands of these two dominating priorities. Nevertheless there were some elements of her musicianship that she was able to transfer seamlessly from Dartington to Aldeburgh. Foremost among these was her by now considerable experience as a conductor of choirs and ensembles, both professional and amateur. One of the immediate attractions of her new setting was the opportunity it afforded her to work with musicians of her own calibre. When she first arrived in Aldeburgh her stature in the professional conducting world was not yet recognized, and the BBC in particular had taken exception to her leading performances even of her father's music. But from her first Aldeburgh Festival as a resident of the town, she was given the opportunity to raise her profile as Britten invited her to share the rostrum for the opening Coronation concert in 1953. Her universally acclaimed interpretation of Bach's *St John Passion* the following year not only cemented her in the Festival's affections as a conductor, but also made the wider musical world sit up and listen.

As with all aspects of her musical life, IH's conducting was distinctive, balancing a sound technique with an individual style which owed much to her days as a dancer. In 1957 the author Ronald Blythe compared her with some of her male contemporaries:

[1] Carpenter, *Benjamin Britten*, p. 311.
[2] Michael Graubart in an obituary notice of IH, *Aldeburgh Festival Programme Book*, 1984.

Conductors achieve their results very variously. Sir Thomas Beecham obviously believes in a certain amount of terrorisation! Sir Malcolm Sargent gets his best results through his ruthless urbanity, and Benjamin Britten ... by an equally ruthless kindliness. But Imogen Holst is the only conductor I have seen who appears to be 'audience-free'. She is a suppliant at the rostrum. Do it for *me*, she seems to say – and, of course, they do![3]

After her death Colin Matthews observed: 'Anyone could have told at a glance that she had been a dancer, and still was. Her conducting ... was a joy to watch – the same dance-like movements, and <u>rhythm</u> – rhythm was everything.'[4]

An important focus of IH's conducting for the next fifteen years was her work with the choir she had founded in London in 1952, now officially designated The Purcell Singers. With this group she had begun to explore new repertories and pieces uncovered by her researches in London, Oxford, Venice and further afield. She was later to recall the 'excitement of working with a small choir of young professionals and of being allowed to choose programmes of little-known music, from 1190 onwards'.[5] For IH research and performance went together, and her approach to the editing of early music, of which in the 1950s she was a pioneer, was pragmatic rather than theoretical. For her editions, if not working from her own manuscripts, she usually used one good source, either from a university library if she was able to escape from Aldeburgh, or more often from her own collections of anthologies and complete editions. She would correct by conjecture, and from her familiarity with a composer's style, rather than by extensive research, although she would sometimes send an assistant (very often Rosamund Strode) to London to peruse and copy from manuscript sources. All this music had to be laboriously written out, of course: for example, in preparing Andrea Gabrieli's *Laudate Dominum* for an Aldeburgh concert on 24 June 1955 she copied out eighteen separate single-line parts. This concert featured a strikingly fresh and varied programme: works by the Venetian composers of the late sixteenth century were set off by early English organ music, and followed by twentieth-century British works, including the first performance of an early motet by Britten, 'New Prince, New Pomp', in which Rosamund Strode sang the soprano solo.

Despite her expressed wish in moving to Aldeburgh to 'cut loose' from amateur music-making, IH soon found that her expertise in this field was as

---

[3] Blythe, 'Imogen Holst – perfectionist'.
[4] Colin Matthews, unpublished typescript, 1984.
[5] IH, 'Recollections of times past'.

indispensable in Suffolk as it had been at Dartington. Her decision to spend much of her spare time helping out local groups such as Women's Institute choirs suggests that she found it more difficult to leave this world behind than she might have anticipated, but Britten and Pears were also more than grateful for the expertise she could bring to the management of the amateurs involved in the Aldeburgh Festival itself, especially in training the Aldeburgh Festival Choir. Managing this particular group was a challenge to her egalitarian principles; unwilling to audition and unable to turn anyone away, she concentrated instead on working hard within the limitations of the singers to produce the best results possible. In the winter of 1954 she began rehearsals for Britten's *St Nicolas*, which had to be mastered in time for a planned recording by Decca in Aldeburgh Church the following April. As one member recalled, she 'bullied the choir into learning most of the music by heart, especially in the men's interjections in the storm scene. It was evidently a struggle, and the choir never really got it quite right.' IH acted as sub-conductor to Britten on the day of the recording and afterwards commented that she regarded the sessions as a 'triumph for the "old" choir'; nevertheless the limitations of some of the singers were undoubtedly evident not only to her but also to Britten, who was kept on his toes during the recording itself by some of their idiosyncrasies:

> There was no disguising the fact that some of the men shouted their pieces in the storm scene just when they felt like it and hoped for the best. One bass had brought the wrong spectacles, and unfortunately his was one of the stronger voices. At one point in the storm passage it came to the turn of a page: not trusting to his memory ('wretched man', said Miss Holst) he actually slowed down in order to turn the page. Incredibly Britten … put in a rubato on the spur of the moment to cope with the slowing up of this voice and, what is more, made it sound inevitable.

Following more intensive rehearsals, some of these problems had been ironed out by the time of the Festival performance in June, after which one critic praised the chorus for having 'gained in brilliance and flexibility'.[6]

Another group to gain lasting benefit from IH's talent for encouraging amateur music-making was the Aldeburgh Music Club. The benefit was undoubtedly mutual, for rehearsing and performing on Club Nights had become for IH, as for Britten and Pears, an important source of relaxation and recreation. In addition to the regular informal concerts, IH rehearsed the group for its

---

[6] Wren, *Voices by the Sea*, pp. 38–41.

'Music on the Meare' appearances during the Festival, when, as one member recalled, 'the singers were in one punt, with IH in another moored parallel. Her energetic and inspiring conducting caused some punt-rocking with result-ant challenge to her balance.'[7] For the 1955 event the singers were reinforced by a recorder group who played two new works by Britten, the *Alpine Suite* and *Scherzo*. From 1956 IH shared the conducting responsibilities with Brit-ten's secretary, Jeremy Cullum, but her involvement remained constant, and in spite of her phlebitis she even played the piano occasionally, contributing in this capacity to an evening of chamber music by Telemann in April 1957. In 1959, together with Britten, she became a Vice-President (Pears was President), and only relinquished regular conducting of the Club in the early 1960s, when Rosamund Strode assumed its musical leadership.

Conducting was also a skill that IH could utilize to generate some much-needed extra income, and it was not long before she began to move beyond the confines of Aldeburgh to find other amateur groups to direct. In this capac-ity the autumn of 1955 saw her establish a new relationship with the choir at Imperial College London, return to Dartington to conduct Bach, and direct her concert version for female voices of Handel's *L'Allegro* with the Buckingham-shire Federation of Women's Institutes. Comfortable and confident in these environments, she secured good performances consistently. Much more nerve-wracking was her appearance at the Grosvenor Chapel on South Audley Street, for an event laid on by the EOG to celebrate Britten's birthday on 22 November. Here she had the responsibility of directing the Purcell Singers in Britten's early choral piece *A Boy was Born*, its first outing since the composer had revised it the previous month. In the event the performance went well and was after-wards repeated at Lancing College. The delighted composer, who missed both concerts as he was touring Europe giving recitals *en route* to a holiday in the Far East, wrote to IH from Istanbul: 'So sorry that things were worrying for the 1st Boy was Born, but relieved that you enjoyed Lancing. I'm sure it sounded glorious there. I long to hear it from you – do let's arrange a performance when we get back – somehow.'[8]

While her conducting put her in the public eye, and programming concerts allowed her to explore new and exciting repertories, IH's role at Aldeburgh, especially for the Festival, also involved a great deal of more mundane, but equally necessary, behind-the-scenes activity. She threw herself into this work with characteristic enthusiasm and did so, very largely, without assistance:

---

[7] Barbara Brook, in Wake-Walker, *Time and Concord*, p. 34.
[8] 1 December 1955; BPL.

Among the 'infinity of things great and small' I found the copying out of
orchestral parts took up more time than anything else. (The complete
St John Passion of Bach took four-and-a-half months of spare time in
the evenings.) After years of copying out anything that anyone needed I
was immensely relieved when Rosamund Strode came to Aldeburgh as
Music assistant to the festival. During the 1950s I was the only orchestral
librarian on duty, which was a real test of endurance; I shall never forget
Britten's look of despair as he told me that one of his leading violinists
had lost *all* her orchestral parts just before a Mozart rehearsal.

Another problem, in the days before we had our Festival Club, was
having to feed the artists after they had been performing late at night.
Once, when I got home to my flat after midnight, I found the conductor of the opera sitting at my writing desk and eating a plateful of eggs
and bacon. (I was lucky to have more than one room; during an earlier
festival Jimmy Blades had had to sit on my bed to eat his supper of fish
and chips.) Then there were all the urgent messages that had to be taken
to singers or players at any hour of the day. If the rehearsal schedule
was suddenly altered and there was no telephone at the house where
the performer was staying I used to have to run the length of Lee Road
at top speed to try and find him. What a blessing it was when the Hesse
students came into our lives! Never again will it be possible for the two
conductors of a choral and orchestral concert to be the only people to
arrive at an empty church half an hour before the morning rehearsal,
with music stands to be put up, and chairs to be arranged and the heavy
brass lectern to be moved out of the way. (I can still remember the distress in Britten's voice when he said, 'Isn't *anyone* coming to help us?')[9]

Perhaps her greatest test of endurance, however, was the preparation of the
programme book:

We used to have hour-long arguments in the office about the punctua-
tion of subtitles and the right position of page numbers – fascinating
from a typographical point of view but exasperating when there was so
much music to be written out and rehearsed. And several of our visiting performers – superb musicians and devoted friends – were utterly
incapable of answering letters or pre-paid telegrams. How much easier
it would have been if one could have chosen their programmes for them
and written their programme notes! It always seemed a miracle that the

[9] IH, 'Recollections of times past'.

programme book was on sale at the opening day of each festival, because bits of information used to arrive at the very last moment. I remember one morning when I was being driven up the hill to a rehearsal in the church and I was stopped at the corner next to the Mill Inn and handed several pages of final proofs which had to be corrected then and there. (In those days there were no yellow traffic lines!)

Her task was not always helped by Pears's apparent disregard of the time and forethought needed to make structural alterations, such as a change of type; he would often bring such suggestions to the three-way meetings involving himself, IH and Britten at a late stage when nothing could be done. Then, in the spring of 1956, she was able to call on some extra help for the latter stages of the production of the book from Ronald Blythe, who recalled:

> I used to work … with Imogen in her flat above a photographer's next door to Tuohy's, the house agent's office where I paid my rent. We sat at her big desk and edited the articles, notes and programmes, whilst all around our feet sprawled the orchestrations she was doing for Ben. At about ten she would make us a little meal and about midnight I would walk home with a long list of queries.[10]

IH's utter dedication to Britten and the Festival in the early 1950s totally eclipsed her own work as a composer. Far from resenting this, however, she was content for the moment to let this part of her creative spirit lie dormant in the service of music that she perceived as of far greater achievement and more enduring worth. On the rare occasions when she was able to make an opportunity for herself to write, she started by making arrangements, focusing on music she was intimately involved with, and writing for the ensemble that she knew best. Late in 1953 she scored the March from the 'Courtly Dances' in *Gloriana* for a concert to celebrate the Suffolk Rural Music Schools' Adult Founders' Day concert to be held in Ipswich the following February. She drew on the opera again to produce music for the Purcell Singers, arranging the 'Choral Dances' for them to sing with Peter Pears in a concert on 15 April 1956, at the Victoria and Albert Museum, which she conducted. She also continued to work on the *Music for Recorders* series for Boosey & Hawkes begun in 1953; although Britten was nominally co-editor, it would appear that most of the selection of pieces, and their arrangement, was in fact IH's work. Prompted by her straitened financial circumstances, IH was obliged to keep the wolf from the door and compiled two sets of vocal arrangements of Scottish folksongs,

[10] Wake-Walker, *Time and Concord*, pp. 45–6.

which were accepted by Boosey's for publication in 1955. The only original work that she had time to compose in the first three years of working with Britten was a motet for female voices, *Lavabo inter innocentes*, commissioned for a wedding that never took place.

Unambitious for her own career as a composer, IH remained determined to promote the cause of her father's music, even when other demands on her time, together with her geographical isolation, made active promotion difficult. In the post-war climate public interest in GH's music was already on the rise, largely as a result of IH's pioneering work on his behalf, and late in 1954 she donated her father's piano and two portraits of him to a grateful Cheltenham Art Gallery and Museum. Through the course of 1955 and 1956 she gave a series of talks promoting his legacy to a wide range of audiences, from local music societies to concertgoers such as the Liverpool Philharmonic Club. On 10 December 1955 she was present when Adrian Boult conducted a programme of GH's lesser-known works at the Royal Festival Hall. The wheel of musical fashion, whereby composers pass into neglect following their deaths, only to have their reputations reinstated over time, was now turning in GH's favour. Recordings, especially of *The Planets*, were proliferating, and by 1955 the listening public could also acquire the suite from *The Perfect Fool*, *The Hymn of Jesus* and the *St Paul's Suite*, together with some of the smaller choral arrangements.

At the beginning of 1956 IH was able to further her cause significantly by reinstating the production of *Sāvitri* originally planned for the 1953 Aldeburgh Festival, but then postponed for financial reasons. With Britten and Pears away on their Far East tour, and IH recently elevated to the position of third Artistic Director of the Festival, her influence on programming had become decisive. The financial picture had also been transformed, and this enabled her to inform Britten:

> You will have heard by now that we've decided on Venus and Adonis and Savitri. One of the extravagances about Savitri is that it won't be wanted anywhere else, but I've decided to raise £100 towards it out of mechanical rights on The Planets – my mother's performing fees have been going up quite a bit during the last 18 months and if they stay as high as this I shall ask the trustees to let me spend some of what's to spare on getting some of his music performed the right way – and possibly reprinting Egdon Heath … Meanwhile, an English Opera Group Savitri is an excellent way to start …[11]

[11] 16 January 1956; BPL.

Aldeburgh was in the grip of an exceptionally cold winter, and IH's letter had been prompted by receiving one from Britten that had 'entirely transformed my life!' after she had visited the dentist and experienced 'a cold, grey, wet journey with two teeth out'. And she had more cause for envy than the weather being enjoyed by the couple on their Balinese holiday; Britten was also making musical discoveries that were to inform the development of his musical style for the next two decades. He wrote to her: 'The music is <u>fantastically</u> rich – melodically, rhythmically, texture (such orchestration!!) & above all <u>formally</u>. It is a remarkable culture.'[12] In bleak contrast, Aldeburgh was suffering from burst pipes, and by 14 February IH was complaining to Britten that 'this is my 13th day without any water in my flat (!!) and everything is getting elephant-grey … you can imagine the depth of snow and the fierceness of the N. E. wind.'[13]

She continued to find both warmth and joy in her work for Britten, however, and the next day found her correcting proofs of his Canticle III, 'Still falls the rain', and editing John Blow's *Venus and Adonis* for the Festival, a task which demonstrated her individual, pragmatic and sometimes mischievous approach to the editing of early music, as well as the sense of sheer pleasure that she was deriving from her working life:

> It's such fun being reckless – he's easier to deal with than Purcell, because there's not so much there to begin with. And as we haven't yet got a producer I'm having it all my own way (as the score has got to be finished this month) and am putting in parodies of Thurston Dart at 'Hast thou been reading those lessons in refined arts?' complete with <u>very</u> slow trills. One of the many advantages of working for you two is that all the jobs which would normally be a hell of a sweat are immediately transformed into the thing that one wants to do most in the whole world![14]

In the absence of Britten and Pears (they did not return from their travels in the far East until 17 March) IH's role in the organization and delivery of the 1956 Aldeburgh Festival was central. She stamped her authority on every aspect of the proceedings, from programming to the choice of the preacher for the Festival service, for which she finally managed to engage her friend the 'humanist and humanitarian'[15] George Bell, Bishop of Chichester. She conducted Handel's oratorio *Samson* in the opening choral and orchestral concert

[12] 17 January 1956; BPL.
[13] 14 February 1956; BPL.
[14] 15 February 1956; BPL.
[15] *Aldeburgh Festival Programme Book*, 1956.

and instituted two other major events that were close to her heart. The first was the scheduling of the Purcell Singers in a wide-ranging programme that included the twelfth-century conductus 'Sol oritor', works by Palestrina, Tomkins, Purcell and Bach, but also the recently completed *Requiem* by Priaulx Rainier, commissioned by Pears for the Purcell Singers and premièred by them at the Victoria and Albert Museum in April. Over time this highly imaginative juxtaposition of different periods and repertories was to be developed by IH into a sophisticated device for the wide dissemination of music that she considered unjustly neglected or forgotten by the passing of the years. Also characteristic is the support of contemporary composers in the context of a studied absence of pieces from the nineteenth century; as Colin Matthews was later to observe, 'with new music she was remarkably perceptive; she knew what she didn't like (and this included a great deal of nineteenth-century music) but towards the twentieth century she was open-minded and generous'.[16] IH's general distaste for the Romantic period of music history embodied more than an aversion to the sound itself; she blamed the German-dominated musical language of the nineteenth century for the stultification of English music that she believed her father had fought so hard, and suffered so much, to reinvigorate.

The concert with the Purcell Singers marked the first time that the Festival had used the imposing surroundings of the church at Blythburgh, nearly 20 miles to the north of Aldeburgh. As the Festival and its audiences grew, the local venues were becoming increasingly stretched and the fulfilment of Britten's vision for a new Festival Theatre to be built in Aldeburgh, shared with IH since 1953, was becoming ever more urgent. Plans were drawn up later in 1956, and some land acquired on a plot opposite the Parish Church. The architect H. T. Cadbury-Brown even wrote an article for the 1957 Festival Programme Book outlining the scheme, but it was dropped soon afterwards, and Britten had once more to revert to his ideas for expanding the Jubilee Hall; this was eventually to happen in time for the 1960 Festival.

The second project close to IH's heart marked another new departure for the Aldeburgh Festival, as she brought together 230 children from East Suffolk schools to give a concert of folk music and items by Purcell, Handel, GH and Britten. During the spring, she had herself undertaken the huge task of auditioning the schools. Both this process and the concert itself proved to be a personal triumph, in spite of some opposition from a source that had come to represent, from the perspective of the Festival, a recurrent thorn in her side:

[16] Matthews, unpublished typescript, 1984.

At one school ... the children sang Gustav Holst's 'O England my Country', not one of Miss Holst's favourites but they sang it superbly. When Imogen Holst, in thanking them, told them that it was her father who had written that music, their faces at first showed blank disbelief: then 'because, if I had been a liar I would not have been standing respectably by their headmistress, the blankness faded, and their eyes grew saucer-like and their grins stretched from ear to ear'. At another school she was very touched and moved by the unselfconsciousness of the little girls, who, as soon as they were let out after singing to her, turned cartwheels in the playground.

It was no wonder, with the sense of joy and freedom that those children had shown, that the concert was such a success ... Imogen Holst held the children in the palm of her hand: her wonderful rapport with them produced performances which were examples to their elders ...

Even here, unbelievably, there was controversy: there was actually a complaint about the singing of the old folk-song 'One man shall mow my meadow' in a church. As Miss Holst says, 'These were little children singing this beautiful song ... it's the 1950s, surely we've got beyond that ... nothing about bottles of beer or anything'. She had already come up against the feeling at Aldeburgh that one should not sing motets in Latin about the Virgin Mary in the Parish Church.[17]

That Britten should have allowed IH so much freedom in the planning and execution of the 1956 Festival testifies to the trust and confidence he had in her musicianship and organizing abilities, as well as her gift for bringing new ideas and a fresh look to the event. It also reflects, however, how busy he was in that year, working on a score that was causing him unprecedented difficulties in transferring his thoughts on to paper – the ballet *The Prince of the Pagodas*. Arriving back in England in March, he was faced with a deadline to submit the work by August which soon began to keep him awake at night. Faced herself with the massive task of preparing the full score, IH had brought in Rosamund Strode to help; Britten told her: 'I've never written so many notes in my life – all those bits of thistledown dancing on the stage actually need a tremendous amount of music'.[18] To his immense relief the indisposition of Covent Garden's preferred conductor Ernest Ansermet gave the composer a five-month reprieve, and after the summer he went to Switzerland to work in a

---

[17] Wren, *Voices by the Sea*, p. 44.
[18] Carpenter, *Benjamin Britten*, p. 373.

medieval castle belonging to the Hesses; IH accompanied him for some of the time and immersed herself in copying the full score as Britten orchestrated the ballet.

By the time of the Covent Garden rehearsals Ansermet had backed out altogether, and Britten, despite a recurrence of the bursitis which meant that he 'couldn't carry his own case with the music in it because his arm was so bad', was obliged to take on the conducting. Protective as ever of the composer, IH – who had disagreed with his reluctant decision to conduct – watched with increasing frustration as he was beset on every side by demands from those who, in her view, were far less important to the success of the ballet than Britten himself. More than twenty years later she remained astounded by the treatment he had received:

> Covent Garden persuaded him against his will and said that ... they couldn't do it without him. And I was in the stalls at Covent Garden when Ninette de Valois came and sat down by his side and argued as women do ... and I saw, then and there, Ben being defeated by this woman and having to give way. And it wasn't of course just by the woman, it was that he, I suppose, realised that if the thing had got to be done he'd got to do it himself. It wasn't only that his arm was bad but in those days he'd <u>no</u> experience of conducting a <u>huge</u> orchestra in a <u>very</u> long work in an orchestral pit ... he learnt by trial and error when conducting *Prince of the Pagodas* in Covent Garden, that you do <u>not</u> begin a dance offstage without an upbeat; and I say that's a thing he could have learned at the RCM ... You can't begin cold. And he had to learn all that, you see.
>
> Ninette de Valois was <u>impossible</u> about Beriosova, and wanted Beriosova's <u>most beautiful</u> solo to be altered ... she came up, again, in the stalls, and said 'But you see, Ben, she's a tall girl, she's got a very long back.' My <u>God</u> – that's nothing to do with Ben's <u>music</u> ...[19]

Even harder for her to accept was the seeming indifference of Peter Pears, whom IH felt had no interest in the success of the work because 'it hadn't got singing things in it, and that therefore <u>all</u> that support that he gave Ben in <u>all</u> his compositions with a part for him in, which kept Ben going, was absolutely cut off at the main'. When the situation came to a head, Pears's actions dismayed IH to such an extent that she began to nurture a distrust of him that, for all their enduring friendship over the next thirty years, she was never able entirely to dispel:

[19] Interview with Donald Mitchell, 22 June 1977; BPL. Svetlana Beriosova was dancing the leading role of Belle Rose in the ballet.

The climax of that lack of interest was in this very painful – I think the last full rehearsal before the performance – when Peter, having blown in for a little while, in the coffee break, halfway through, said to Ben 'Well, I'm going now; I'm going to have a haircut.' And walked out of the theatre, leaving Ben bewildered and in pain and trying to fix up [a] doctor; no one to get him a taxi, no one but me to carry the bag or anything; and it wasn't my job to encourage Ben, because I didn't do that side. I did it through the music, but nothing else ... I thought if there was ever a moment in a composer's life when he needed his very, <u>very</u> nearest beloved just by his side ...

Following the divorce of Stephen and Mary Potter, Britten was able in 1957 to fulfil his dream of moving to a more isolated house 'not in the middle of Aldeburgh', for which IH had observed him 'pining' in October 1953. That The Red House – which they exchanged with Mary Potter for Crag House – should have been already so familiar to Britten and Pears undoubtedly increased its attraction, and they were to stay there until the end of their lives.

Later that year IH was given the first real opportunity to expand the scope of her creative endeavours beyond Aldeburgh, when the National Federation of Women's Institutes asked her to edit a song book for women's voices. Despite her extremely busy schedule, this was an invitation that struck close to her heart, and she accepted enthusiastically. Still haunted by the 'disappointed faces' of those isolated rural folk who had requested copies of the songs she had taught them as a Music Traveller but had been unable to provide, she set to work and produced a wide-ranging collection of eighty-one pieces from the thirteenth to the twentieth centuries; folk and unison songs, rounds and two-, three- and four-part settings, with and without simple piano accompaniments. Creative considerations aside, the project also offered a significant financial incentive, although she came to regret her business naïveté when the collection became a huge success: 'The publisher purchased the copyright for £150. I ought not to have agreed to this, but I was hard up. It has sold very well indeed, and I shall never again make this mistake!'[20] But she enjoyed every aspect of preparing the volume, from the selection to the proofreading, made easy for her because 'the tunes are so excellent that they are always welcome, and can never lose their freshness'. Of the selection process she wrote:

No song book has ever been large enough to contain everyone's favourites. During the Committee meetings which were held to discuss the

[20] Unpublished list of works, 1968; HF.

plans for this book, several distinguished members of the N.F.W.I. kept on saying, 'Oh, can't we have that one?' and the publisher, Mr. Alan Frank, kept on having to remind them of the rising costs of production.

In whittling down the number of pages we have given preference to those songs which are most needed and which are least accessible in other collections. The accumulative folk songs and the short, easy rounds are included and, for experienced choirs, there are duets by Bach and Handel which can be practised week after week. For *Singing for Pleasure* is essentially a book that can be shared by all, including the newest W.I. member who has so far opened her lips only to sing Jerusalem, as well as the conductors of those choirs which took part in the first performance of Vaughan Williams' *Folk Songs of the Four Seasons* in the Albert Hall.[21]

Singing for Pleasure was published early in 1957, the year in which IH celebrated her fiftieth birthday. Ronald Blythe offered an assessment of her to the readers of *The Lady*, which illustrates how busy, and yet settled and content, she appeared at this time:

> At fifty, there are scarcely enough hours in her day. She works in a tall, narrow-roomed flat perched up high amongst the roofs of Aldeburgh. Drawings by Theodore von Holst and Kokoschka[22] hang on the walls. It is a feminine, but not a fussy room, and reverting once more to that fancied likeness of her creative integrity to Virginia Woolf's, most decidedly a 'room of one's own'. It is to this demure eyrie that she has brought her collection of rare scores and texts, her wit and charm, and her unique gifts.
>
> Watching her as she works steadily on the latest pages sent over from Britten's study across the street, one feels certain that here, at least, is an artist where she was intended to be.[23]

To mark the anniversary Britten sent her the manuscript of *The Prince of the Pagodas*, which he had dedicated jointly to her and Ninette de Valois. His accompanying letter demonstrates how, after five years of working closely with her on a sequence of major compositions, the composer's appreciation and affection for his amanuensis had not dwindled:

[21] IH, 'Singing for pleasure'.
[22] Oskar Kokoschka's 'King David', a chalk portrait inscribed 'For Imogen / she hears – from OK'.
[23] Blythe, 'Imogen Holst – perfectionist'.

A rather tactless present – is there anything you would rather <u>less</u> have than this beastly Ballet which has confused, obscured, & nearly wrecked two years of your life?? But, dear Imo, there may be (here & there) the odd semiquaver which is worth just a little & if it is any comfort to you, that has been made possible by your selfless encouragement, devotion & tireless work. I can't begin to say thank-you, only just ... thank God it is over & done with (all except those .... metronome marks).

With love, thanks, & many happy returns of the first half-century: may we be together on your 100th birthday (but I promise you NO BALLET for that).[24]

IH herself chose to mark her fiftieth year by expanding her dedication to the revival of early music through the Aldeburgh Festival and the Purcell Singers. The solution, radical for its time, was to institute a series of late-night concerts to be held in Aldeburgh Parish Church at 10.45 p.m. For this first experiment in the format she decided not to expose the Purcell Singers, but instead persuaded Charles Mackerras to lead singers from the English Opera Group and the Aldeburgh Festival Orchestra in a series of five concerts featuring Buxtehude's *The Last Judgment*, a cycle of cantatas with related texts. With no guarantee that the concerts would draw large audiences, she had to justify to her fellow directors the expense of the new venture: this she did by approaching the BBC and persuading them to support the late-night concerts through their Transcription Service. The arrangement came into place the next year, and the relationship was to flourish until 1971, doing much to encourage the revival of early music in its Aldeburgh manifestation, by providing a vehicle for the performance of unfamiliar music by emerging instrumental and vocal groups that would never have been possible within the constraints of the Festival's own budget. The model of late-night concerts was itself to prove immensely popular, extending to festivals all over the country, including eventually the Proms.

Writing in 1984, John Thomson noted the breadth of IH's contribution to the early music revival at a time when a new understanding of repertories and performance practice was just beginning to emerge:

Any scholarly assessment of her role in the early music revival would have to need to draw together her manifold activities, the various editions and concert versions of works she prepared for the Aldeburgh festival, her illuminating programme notes and articles, and the paths she chose both for her late night concerts and for the Purcell Singers ...

[24] 13 April 1957; BPL.

She always seemed a pivotal figure in the early music world. She had contributed significantly to that splendid revival of Purcell's music [while] her involvement in ethnic music ... prepared her admirably to respond to and anticipate the patterns of the early music revival and the important cross-fertilization between European and other cultures.[25]

Central to these activities was the other new idea that she brought to the 1957 Festival, the development of 'themed' programmes of early music devised to draw attention to particular repertories or important anniversaries. That year there was a single concert, designed to celebrate the Thomas Morley quatercentenary, but the idea expanded over the years to comprise as many as seven concerts in a late-night series. Her direction of the Purcell Singers in the Morley concert, given at Great Glemham House, drew critical acclaim: 'it was described as a *tour de force*, her expressive hands and fingers attending to the behaviour of every voice'.[26] She must have been equally pleased with the public response to her conducting of Bach's *St John Passion* the following week, in a performance that was generally acknowledged to be equal to her groundbreaking interpretation of the work three years earlier. It was also the source of an anecdote which says much about her single-minded dedication to making music, and her ability to forget herself in the process:

She came onto the rostrum, bowed to the audience and turned to face the choir and orchestra. So unconscious was she of anything but the task in hand, that she picked up the hem of her long black dress, took off her glasses, polished them with the dress, dropped the hem again, and began the performance. Such simple touches endeared her to all who ever played or sang under her direction.[27]

Equally endearing to those who knew IH at this time was her generous encouragement of the young composers who came within the orbit of the Festival. Malcolm Williamson recalled that when he asked for her advice the 'benefit of her clear and profound mind was incalculable': he was also able to benefit from a generosity of spirit that belied her continuing paucity of means:

Once in the late 1950s I was staying in Southwold. Imo invited me to lunch. It was a generous spread, and we sat on the beach at Aldeburgh enjoying it as she spoke with encyclopaedic knowledge of choral music from Stanford onwards. I found out later by chance that Imo had given

[25] Thomson, 'Imogen Holst', pp. 583–4.
[26] Wren, *Voices by the Sea*, p. 46.
[27] Wren, *Voices by the Sea*, p. 45.

extra music lessons that morning to earn the money for the lunch. That was characteristic.[28]

Amidst the ever-increasing administrative and organizational burden of the expanding Festival, IH was at least able to let go of one of her most time-consuming duties when in 1957, through a chance encounter, she succeeded in delegating much of her work on the programme book to Mary Harrison, a local resident who was keen to get more involved:

> One day, as Arthur and I were walking along Crag Path, we met a very worried looking Imo … 'Oh dear!' she said, 'I have a very interesting article for the Programme Book on "The Flora of Suffolk" … by Lord Cranbrook, and I don't know where to turn to check all these botanical names. Do you know anything about botany?'
>
> I confessed I knew a little and I had quite a number of botanical books. The paper was immediately thrust into my hands and Imo continued on her way, perhaps a little relieved. I took the article home … I took the article back to Imo, duly corrected, the next morning and that started my thirteen years as so-called editor.[29]

Respected and admired for her successes both as organizer and participant at the Festival, IH remained unassuming and modest about her achievements. For her, Britten's music remained at the heart of proceedings and the 'greatest excitement of all was helping in the early stages of each new Britten work'. The composer continued to involve her closely in the formation of his ideas, and thus it was that late in 1957 she was with him when, 'on a long wet walk over the marshes with the rain streaming down our necks'[30] he shared with her his plans for *Noye's Fludde*. But as the year drew to a close, two difficult situations arose that were to pull IH into more uncomfortable territory, with her loyalties to Britten and the Festival forced into conflict both with her principles and with other important friendships.

IH had by this time been coaching the Aldeburgh Festival Choir for six years. Adhering to principles learnt from her father, that in amateur music-making dedication and commitment were more important than a high standard of musicianship, she had never reauditioned the singers. But as the Festival expanded, with a greater range of internationally renowned performers and with increasingly knowledgeable audiences becoming accustomed to higher

[28] Williamson, 'Remembering Imo'.
[29] Wake-Walker, *Time and Concord*, p. 51. 'Arthur' was Muffet's husband.
[30] IH, 'Recollections of times past'.

standards, it was perceived that the Festival Choir was lagging behind, and was even in decline. Pears decided to tackle the issue head on, but IH, who regarded all the members as her friends, felt unable to take the lead. Nevertheless she acquiesced to his suggestion that they bring in a new choir trainer, Charles Cleall, to work with her to reaudition the choir for 1958. Inevitably a large number of long-serving singers were dismissed. Several went to IH in distress, but she was unable to offer them any consolation; for herself the experience was wounding, and brought, perhaps for the first time, an element of harsh reality into the otherwise generally idyllic world of her musical life at Aldeburgh.

Another unwelcome intrusion involved Britten's decision at this time to dispense with the services of Basil Douglas, the General Manager of the EOG, with whom IH had developed a strong friendship through their work together over the previous six years. As a close confidante of Britten, IH knew what was in the wind, but was unaware that Britten, who disliked confrontation, had not yet informed Douglas of the decision. As a result, when IH went into the EOG offices and declared: 'Basil, I want you to know that, whatever happens, I'll always love you', this was the first that Douglas had heard of his impending dismissal. Such was the strength of their friendship that she remained in close touch with him as he left Aldeburgh and set up his own business as an agent; moreover, as Maureen Garnham, Douglas's business partner in the new venture, recalled, she demonstrated her support by giving his agency 'the representation of the Purcell Singers, by that time burgeoning into a first class professional choir with some important engagements in the offing. This she did without fuss and as though it were the most natural thing in the world, despite the fact that we were "out" with Ben. Imo had a very strong mind of her own.'[31]

IH's relationship with Britten was, in the event, unaffected by this difficult course of events. During the early months of 1958 he continued to work on *Noye's Fludde*, a project especially close to her heart as it enshrined her desire to increase the participation of schoolchildren in the music of the Festival. In fact children became involved in the work at an earlier stage than even she had envisaged. While orchestrating, Britten had a conversation with some members of the Aldeburgh Youth Club, who were rehearsing handbells for a concert. He invited them to play for him and

> was so enchanted by the sounds they made that he gave them a part to
> play at the supreme moment of the drama in *Noye's Fludde*, when the

---

[31] Garnham, *As I Saw It*, p. 60.

rainbow appears in the sky and the Voice of God promises that all wrath and vengeance shall cease in the newly-washed world.

No other sound could have suited that moment so well; which helps to prove that composers need amateurs just as much as amateurs need composers.[32]

To see one of the maxims of her own musical philosophy borne out in this way would have pleased IH immensely. Equally rewarding was her own significant contribution to the orchestration of *Noye's Fludde*, for which she was able to draw on her own experience as a Music Traveller of improvisation with amateurs. Britten asked her advice on how to replicate the sound of raindrops, and she remembered that

> by great good fortune I had once to teach Women's Institute percussion groups during a wartime 'social half hour', so I was able to take him into my kitchen and show him how a row of china mugs hanging on a length of string could be hit with a large wooden spoon.[33]

IH took her advisory role one step further by accompanying Britten to Mrs Beech's shop on the High Street, where together they 'purchased lots of mugs with 'A Present from Aldeburgh' written on them'.

The past was to catch up with her again when on 20 May 1958 she took part, with the Purcell Singers, in the Diamond Jubilee Concert of the Folk Song Society at Cecil Sharp House. To a great extent, and possibly as a tactic for survival in her busy life, IH had learnt to maintain distinct boundaries between the different strands of her musical world since taking up residence in Aldeburgh. Colin Matthews, who knew her much later in life, observed her 'tendency to put the people she worked with into separate compartments when she might have gained more by bringing them together', although he also recognized the benefits of a strategy that 'enabled her to concentrate on individuals and to get the best out of everyone.'[34] Britten was out of sympathy with the Cecil Sharp–Vaughan Williams axis of the folksong revival, and IH did not try and interest him in her continued forays into this area of interest, where she moved among a circle of colleagues and friends for whom he would have had little time. For the Society's celebrations she had been hard at work preparing another set of songs for publication. The selection for *A Jubilee Book of English Folk Songs* had already been made by Kenneth Loveless, a member of the editorial board

---

[32] IH, *Britten*, 3rd edn, p. 62.
[33] IH, 'Working for Benjamin Britten', p. 202.
[34] Matthews, unpublished typescript, 1984.

of the EFDSS Journal; IH was then invited to arrange them for unison voices and piano. The resulting volume was designed, as the editors noted, to 'reflect the ever-growing popularity of the folksongs since the first steps were taken to preserve them sixty years ago.'

Back in Aldeburgh IH had made the discovery since the winter that her release from training the Festival Choir allowed her more time for research. She used this freedom to devise a new series of late-night concerts for the Purcell Singers, comprising a selection of early settings of the Magnificat by such composers as Dunstable, Obrecht, Josquin, Monteverdi, Victoria, Schütz and Buxtehude. She was by now able to use her reputation within the early music field to draw in both established and promising younger exponents, and for this Festival Raymond Leppard was invited to conduct his new realization of Monteverdi's *Il ballo delle ingrate* under the auspices of the EOG, a work for which Pears had translated the libretto with his friend Iris Holland Rogers. IH shared with Britten the conducting of the first choral and orchestral concert in a programme dedicated to Bach, and also persuaded the composer to direct a concert of mostly Baroque music from the harpsichord. She satisfied another of her particular musical appetites by inviting the Asian Music Circle to present a concert of Indian music and dance, the first ethnic music event to be heard at the Festival and a precursor to her meeting with Ravi Shankar at the Leeds Festival that October. With all this new activity something of her previous Festival routine had to give way, and she was glad to be able to pass on the conducting of the Aldeburgh Music Club's 'Music on the Meare' to Jeremy Cullum.

Since the early 1950s Britten and IH had worked on a number of projects for which she had readily put in most of the work with Britten coming in towards the end, providing corrections, suggestions and, most importantly, lending his name. In 1958 they applied this arrangement for the first time to a book, *The Story of Music*, nominally by Britten and IH, but in fact written almost totally by the latter, who submitted her drafts in batches to the composer for his approval. Her last major job for the composer that year was to prepare the vocal score of his *Nocturne* for tenor, seven *obbligato* instruments and string orchestra.

This period of relative calm allowed her to address herself to one of her key priorities for 1959, the celebration of the tercentenary of Henry Purcell. Her research over the years, and in particular her work on *Dido and Aeneas*, had led her to the identification of numerous 'practical problems of editing Purcell's works for performance', and she decided to address these in print by bringing together a collection of essays by several performers and musicologists in the field. In her preface she addressed the central problems directly:

Even those of us who have been brought up on his music are still woefully ignorant when it comes to such questions as whether a note should be doubly-dotted or whether it should be a flat or a natural. One longs to know what balance of singers and players Purcell had at his first performances and whether certain parts were sung by a counter-tenor or an ordinary tenor with light, easy, top notes.

For her contributors she ranged widely, calling on Britten to write about continuo realization, and Robert Donington, a Froebel contemporary as a child, to bring his unique knowledge of the performance of early music to bear on modern Purcell interpretation. For elucidation on the problem of sources, she enlisted the help of the young American scholar Franklin B. Zimmerman, outlining in her preface the particular difficulties she had encountered: 'Perhaps our greatest need, when puzzled by the conflicting guesses of different editors of his music is to know where to find the manuscripts, and, having found them, to know how to recognize if they are autographs or not.'[35]

Many of the issues discussed in the book were especially pertinent to IH at this time, as she and Britten were contemplating a revised version of their edition of *Dido and Aeneas*. But they had a wider application also, for she would encounter many of them again when she came to catalogue her father's manuscripts. She knew, however, that that was an undertaking which would have to wait. A more pressing task in the promotion of her father's legacy was the completion of an edition of the letters between GH and Ralph Vaughan Williams, jointly edited with the latter's widow Ursula, and entitled *Heirs and Rebels*; this too was to be published in 1959.

The Aldeburgh Festival that year reflected recent changes, with IH taking no part in the first choral concert, deferring to Charles Cleall and Bryan Balkwill. Her influence on programming, however, remained as strong as ever, and she ensured that the two anniversaries closest to her heart – the Purcell tercentenary and the centenary of the birth of Cecil Sharp – were both celebrated appropriately. For Sharp she organized a programme of folk dancing by children from Bungay, including some who had been in the première of *Noye's Fludde* the previous year. For Purcell she devised a series of late-night concerts on the theme of 'Purcell and his Predecessors', inviting a variety of groups to perform the programmes she had put together. These included the Deller Consort and the Cambridge University Musical Society, in addition to the Purcell Singers; there was also a programme for voices and viols performed by The Elizabethan Players.

35 IH, *Henry Purcell*, Preface.

Towards the end of the year IH attained a further publishing success by her contribution to another, less trumpeted, tercentenary. Her arrangements for SSA of ten songs from John Wilson's *Cheerfull Ayres and Ballads* were performed by the Purcell Singers on 1 October, in a concert to mark the centenary of music at Oxford University Press. In printing the arrangements, the publisher noted that it was

> three hundred years since 'Cheerful Ayres or Ballads' was published, 'this being the first essay ... of printing music that ever was in Oxford', as the Preface correctly remarks. Thus, to put it another way, 1959 is the tercentenary year of music publishing at Oxford, and the occasion has been marked by the present publication of this selection of ten songs.

For all her successes in 1959, some of which demonstrated a distinct move away from the almost entirely Britten-centred outlook that had preoccupied her for seven years, not everything in her life was free from tension. Perhaps partly in reaction to the first spreading of her wings, for the first time small cracks began to appear in her relationship with Britten, who was at times finding her difficult to work with. His patience with what Rosamund Strode has called her 'disciple-at-his-feet' attitude had begun to wear thin, exemplified in her tendency to carry dutifulness to extremes; Rosamund Strode also recalled his irritation when hearing that IH would wait at home, telling people 'I can't come out in case Ben rings up.' On 17 February 1959 he had written to Pears following a session of work: 'Imo good, but pretty wild – I'm doing my best to keep my temper!'; five days later he wrote again, describing "Imo's panics" as "*ff* staccato".[36]

These problems became exacerbated towards the end of the year as Britten embarked in October on a new opera, *A Midsummer Night's Dream*, which was to have its first performance in the newly extended Jubilee Hall the following June. By the end of November he had finished the sketch of Act I, and IH was at work on the vocal score; three months later he had completed the orchestral score of Act II but not yet sketched much of Act III. Disaster then struck as IH was taken to hospital with suspected appendicitis. Once the emergency was over, and the diagnosis less life-threatening, she wrote Britten a letter from hospital in which her disregard for her own health is contrasted sharply with her overriding concern for Britten's opera:

---

[36] Carpenter, *Benjamin Britten*, p. 391.

I AM sorry to be such a bore. I didn't have the emergency operation they'd prepared for me last night, because the surgeon was not sure that it really was appendicitis ... I'm having ex-rays this afternoon and probably an 'exploratory abdominal' operation on Saturday ...

I HATE to think of leaving the next batch of master sheets unchecked, and Dido vocal score with no double bars worked out, and the unwanted slurs in those two pages not crossed out – the only thing I've looked at is your HA! HA![37]

If you want Rosamund to do checking of master sheets, the office will have her address and telephone number ...[38]

On 26 February she wrote again to update the composer on her likely date of return, and to offer some suggestions:

I'm to have an operation at 2 oclock this afternoon. As it's possible that they may have to take out the womb, this will I'm afraid take a bit longer than I'd hoped. They tell me I'll have to stay here for a fortnight at least, and they can't say how long it will be after that before I begin work again. Could you find someone else to do Act III? Jim Bernard perhaps? Rosamund would be able to prepare the full score ...

I wondered if you'd be very kind and write a note to my mother when I'm safely through with the operation – would you? I don't want her to know its happening until it's over ...

Britten dutifully wrote to Isobel Holst, and received a reply implicitly criticizing the workload he had imposed on her daughter:

I have been worried for a long time about her health because I do think she is doing too much – too many jobs, & too much uncomfortable travelling – working against time, which is so wearing especially for a woman. However it is her choice and she loves her work, so what can one do?[39]

The operation – to remove an ovarian cyst – took place as planned, and IH was instructed not to return to work for six weeks. She travelled to Dartington to recuperate, still feeling guilty about not being able to finish the vocal score of Act III, a task undertaken in her stead by Martin Penny. After visiting her mother, she returned to Aldeburgh on 11 April, when she wrote to Britten:

[37] A reference to the witches' chorus in Act II of Purcell's *Dido and Aeneas*.
[38] Undated, February 1960; BPL.
[39] 1 March 1960; BPL.

'I can now walk Andante un poco Allegretto and it no longer hurts to laugh, so things are looking up.'⁴⁰ But the episode, and her extended absence from Aldeburgh, had undoubtedly altered Britten's perception of her, and his continued admiration and affection were now sometimes tinged with a sense of exasperation, expressed in occasional gentle mockery. Myfanwy Piper, while recognizing IH's 'spark of genius [and] real quality', considered her a 'joke' and Rosamund Strode noted that 'Britten was dismayed by her frequent, studiedly casual references to [the] gynaecological operation she had recently undergone' which became 'a slightly naughty Red House joke. She had no idea how it curled Ben up.'⁴¹

Britten successfully completed *A Midsummer Night's Dream* in time for it to feature as the opening work of the 1960 Aldeburgh Festival, although the delays resulting from IH's indisposition meant that George Malcolm, who was training the boy fairies, did not receive the vocal score for Act III until two weeks before the performance. IH was on hand during the rehearsals, and was called upon, with Rosamund Strode, to assist in reshaping the two harp parts for a single instrument three days before the first night, when one of the harpists abruptly dropped out. Another direct result of her illness was that IH's participation as a performer in the Festival was somewhat reduced. Nevertheless, she devised a series of 'Medieval Sacred Music' programmes for the late-night concerts and recruited the specialists Francis Baines and John Becket to perform on a wide range of early instruments, including hurdy-gurdy, pipes, tabors, crumhorns, rebecs, bagpipes and viols. Charles Cleall took charge of the main choral concert, which included two of GH's *Hymns from the Rig Veda*, although in a further twist to the saga of IH's strained relations with Aldeburgh Parish Church she had to alter some of the words.

Throughout this time, and in spite of ever-increasing returns from performances and recordings of GH's music, IH continued to live in Spartan conditions, and remained, as Rosamund Strode noted, 'entirely without money – she had made over her share of Gustav's estate to her mother'.⁴² Since her early days of working with Britten, however, she had at least learnt to be more assertive in claiming what was hers. The occasional tensions in her working relationship with the composer may have also made her more forthright than usual, for on 6 August she wrote a strong letter to his secretary Jeremy Cullum:

⁴⁰ 11 April 1960; BPL.
⁴¹ Carpenter, *Benjamin Britten*, p. 429.
⁴² Carpenter, *Benjamin Britten*, p. 391.

Might I remind you that I haven't had a retaining fee cheque since Dec 59? … I enclose details of telephone calls I've made from my flat which were entirely on Ben's behalf. He also owes me for the duplication of Purcell songs & Folk Songs last October …

On 5 September IH was described by Dilys Rowe in *The Guardian* as a 'business-like visionary', a description that accurately summed up her approach to organizing the Aldeburgh Festival, but which could not yet be as aptly applied to her personal situation. Nevertheless she continued to eke out money by making arrangements and writing texts aimed at the educational and general interest markets.

In 1958 Geoffrey Faber had commissioned her to write a book with the suggested title *Tune*; she worked on this through the summer and autumn of 1960, when, for a space, she had little to do for Britten, who essayed no major compositions for six months after the completion of *A Midsummer Night's Dream*. She completed the book in April 1961, very soon after Faber's death. *Tune* is a landmark in her career as an author. Written in her own time and at her own pace, it exudes a refreshing tone and light humour that captivate the reader and reflect no doubt a gathering self-confidence in the strength of her own ideas and her ability to articulate them. Its content was aimed at the non-specialist and includes a wealth of down-to-earth observations, of which this is a typical example: 'It is just as difficult to separate the rhythm from the intervals in a well-constructed tune as it is to separate the butter from the eggs in a well-made omelette.'[43] But the deliberately light tone of the writing is underpinned by rigorous scholarship. Quoting from sources as disparate as Roger North and Stravinsky, and drawing for its musical references upon a wealth of traditional and contemporary music, as well as the early Renaissance and Baroque, the book also demonstrates – in, for example its discussion of Deryck Cooke's then recently published *The Language of Music* – the extent to which IH, despite all the pressures on her time, had been able to keep pace with the music scholarship of the day.

Tune encapsulates a theory of the development of music – especially in England – that had been forming in IH's mind and writings ever since her European travels at the end of her studies at the Royal College of Music. Taking a broadly chronological view of the evolution of tunes, she singles out Purcell, particularly the recitatives in *Dido and Aeneas*, as the perfect exemplar of how to set English words idiomatically. Following his death, English music

[43] IH, *Tune*, p. 15.

was slowly engulfed by Germanic influences, reaching a nadir at the end of the nineteenth century:

> Elgar's 'Land of Hope and Glory' was fated to sound as it does, with the stressed and unstressed syllables of 'glory' evenly ironed out, and with the rising phrase giving the word 'and' an unwanted prominence which is further emphasized by the falling fourth that follows it. Heard side by side with 'Fairest Isle', the tune is a convincing proof of the need for expressing the energy of English words.[44]

In IH's view it had been left to her father to recover the memory of Purcell's genius and to Britten to complete the restoration of idiomatic English text-setting; in his music, 'the gesture and energy have been learnt from Purcell, but the language is Britten's own, and it takes what it needs from all that has happened in music since 1695 ...'[45] Contemporary tunes needed to be recognizable and singable, by amateurs and children as well as professional musicians. Against these criteria, the composers of serial music had, in IH's estimation, put themselves at a significant disadvantage:

> Another reason that twelve-note melodies are difficult to learn is their refusal to go back on a note. There is no twelve-note equivalent of 'Sally go round the moon' for twentieth-century five-year-olds to begin on.[46]

The publication of *Tune* marked a further step in IH's recognition as a major musical force in her own right. On 5 December 1960 she was invited by the Arts Council of Great Britain to become a member of its Music Panel, an appointment which she took up the following March. On 13 December she led the Purcell Singers in a concert of Christmas music at Cecil Sharp House, given for the Vaughan Williams Memorial. The programme included two arrangements she had recently made of folksongs noted by Vaughan Williams, published in the collection *A Yacre of Land*. Moving into Britten's world had not dampened her affection and admiration for Vaughan Williams as composer, teacher and her father's most valued friend, and she had been greatly saddened by his death in 1958.

Britten's new music remained, nonetheless, one of her chief joys and she continued to be trusted and sought out by him for her opinion. In December he began a cello sonata for Mstislav Rostropovich, reporting to Pears on 17 January 1961 that he had 'played it to Imo who was quite impressed', certainly

[44] IH, *Tune*, p. 156.
[45] IH, *Tune*, p. 160.
[46] IH, *Tune*, p. 167.

an understatement of her response to hearing a work by Britten for the first time. By now she had once more plunged herself into the organization of the Aldeburgh Festival, devising a series of late-night concerts entitled 'Music in Venice 1500–1750.' She also conducted Schütz's *St John Passion* with Pears as the Evangelist and achieved a long-held ambition by persuading Britten to conduct *Egdon Heath*, the work of her father's that she most admired and in which she had first tried to interest Britten back in 1948.

Once the Festival was over, she became immediately immersed in another major project for Britten. In October 1958 the composer had accepted an invitation to write a choral work for a festival being planned to mark the consecration of the new cathedral in Coventry. By November 1960 the details of the commission were finalized, and Britten began composing in April 1961. Work on the vocal and full scores of *War Requiem* was to occupy IH for the rest of the year, although she did also find time to achieve a milestone with the Aldeburgh Music Club when she conducted them on 30 September in Purcell's *Dioclesian*, the masterpiece that her father had resurrected for its first modern performance half a century before. And in the same month a new extension of the Aldeburgh Festival was launched with the institution of Bach weekends in the village of Long Melford; at the inaugural event IH conducted the Suffolk Singers, an offshoot of the Aldeburgh Festival Choir, in a selection of cantatas.

The first months of 1962 found IH completing the copying of the full score of *War Requiem*, which Britten had finished on holiday in Greece in January. In April she found some light relief in rehearsing the London Boy Singers for a performance of Britten's 1959 *Missa Brevis*. She wrote to the composer on 16 April that she was 'completely thrilled with working at the Missa Brevis: – it's lovely to come to it after the Requiem'. But her joy was overshadowed by the recurrence of a theme in her domestic life that was to become ever more dominant during the next few years – the declining health of Isobel Holst: 'For the last 2 days I've been with my mother: – she's getting a bit shaky and has been alone for 2 ½ months, but the Lord has provided a new companion who is coming just before Easter, so it will be wonderful to start a new life without those particular ostinato crises!' Britten's *War Requiem* was first performed in Coventry on 30 May 1962 to almost universal acclaim. IH attended and amidst the clamour of praise that followed wrote to the composer afterwards with her own simple and touching words of gratitude: 'Thank you for the Requiem: it has been more wonderful than anything else in life to have listened to a conviction equal to Bach's'.[47]

47 3 June 1962; BPL.

IH's dedication to the restoration of her father's reputation reaped further rewards at the Festival that year, when David Willcocks chose to conduct GH's *Ode to Death* in the opening concert shared with Britten and attended by the Duke of Edinburgh. IH's own series of late-night concerts of Flemish music reflected her new interest in this repertory, but its achievement was eclipsed by an event that marked her return to an old, and much-loved, stamping ground of research and performance. This was the production by the EOG of a new version, edited by IH and Britten, of *Dido and Aeneas*. For their 1951 edition the collaborators had used as their primary source the earliest surviving manuscript, at Tenbury. In the years that followed, however, IH heard of another source, and she painstakingly tracked this down to Japan, obtaining a microfilm that arrived in Aldeburgh in June 1959, during the Festival's Purcell celebrations. In the Festival programme book IH described the process of the manuscript's rediscovery and the editing that followed – a characteristic blend of pragmatism and scholarship to create a viable 'performing' version:

> Various legends have sprung up concerning this Tokyo copy. At one time it was considered as 'lost'. Later on, there was a rumour – fortunately unfounded – that it had been sold to an American collector in Baltimore, who had locked it up in a cellar, refusing to let anyone have a look at it. After many searches had been made, the manuscript was traced by the Tokyo representatives of the British Council, and the present owner, Mr. Kyuhei Oki, generously allowed a photographed copy to be used in preparing the edition ...
>
> It was an exciting moment when the microfilm from Tokyo reached Aldeburgh. Our first glance was for the end of Act II, in the feverish hopes of finding the missing music to the last six lines of the libretto. Alas, it was not there. But throughout the photographed pages of this 1800 manuscript there were fascinating details where the music differed from the more familiar version.
>
> The new edition ... is based on a collation of the two manuscripts, in which we have aimed at getting as near as possible to the composer's intentions, reaching each decision partly as the result of contemporary evidence but mostly as the result of a working familiarity with other music by Purcell.

Purcell apart, one of IH's favourite avenues of exploration continued to be the music of India. In September 1962 this passion, probably shared by very few in Aldeburgh, became a point of discussion for the town's councillors, as the *Leiston Observer* reported in a paragraph entitled 'Stuffy':

Members of the Aldeburgh Public Health and Planning Committee were faced with an unusual problem at a recent meeting, where they were asked to waive a by-law calling for every room of a dwelling-house to have at least one window which will open.

The applicant was said to be fond of listening to Indian music for many hours at a time, and in order not to disturb neighbours had had a room made soundproof – an essential part of which was a double-glazed, fixed window.

The committee felt that suffocation might well be an occupational hazard for this devotee of the weird and wonderful melodies of the Orient, and much as they appreciated the desire to spare neighbours who might not have similar musical tastes, they felt that some other means of ventilation would have to be introduced to the room … As one councillor said: 'Even Indian music must be preferable to dead bodies.'

IH's concern not to upset her neighbours came about as a result of her moving, that month, to Church Walk, where a bungalow had been designed and built for her on the edge of the site of the proposed Festival Theatre by the architect H. T. Cadbury-Brown, who, once that scheme had been abandoned, had purchased half of the plot from the Aldeburgh Festival primarily to erect a house for himself and his wife. IH was to remain there for the rest of her life.

If 1962 had proved particularly significant for IH's achievement in the cause of two major composers she particularly admired – Britten and Purcell – it was also the year in which she began to regain confidence in her own abilities in this field. Fired by the success not only of her work for others but also of her own books and vocal arrangements, her creative imagination now impelled her to return, after a decade of dormancy, to original composition. She signalled her intent by taking up a commission for the Rural Music Schools' Association from which Malcolm Arnold had withdrawn. The *Variations on 'Loth to Depart'* for string quartet and two string orchestras was first performed on 3 November 1962, in the Royal College of Music Concert Hall, by the RMSA players conducted by Sir Adrian Boult. The concert was given in honour of IH's friend Mary Ibberson, who had founded the first Rural Music School in Hertfordshire in 1929 and had gone on to direct an association of ten similar schools across the southern half of England by the time of her retirement in 1962. IH had got to know her well in her days working for CEMA and Dartington and was delighted to share in this tribute. The critical reception of the work was exceptionally favourable, with one commentator noting:

No other work in the world could have been more fitting, for it wittingly and cunningly enshrines some of the characteristics of all the individual R.S.M.s and of the R.M.S.A. itself, and it was most excitingly and sincerely performed. But it is much more than a piece for an occasion: it is a work of real beauty which will enchant listeners ...[48]

Soon afterwards she received another commission, this time from another Dartington friend, Pamela Hind O'Malley, for a cello piece to be performed at a Wigmore Hall concert the following February. *The Fall of the Leaf* for solo cello was composed in November 1962 and followed almost immediately by an original work for SSA, *The Twelve Kindly Months*. This was written for Valda Plucknett, for several years a répétiteur with the English Opera Group. The singing of her Ipswich Girls' Choir at the Aldeburgh Festival had impressed Britten and Pears, and also IH, who was moved to write this unaccompanied part-song for them, to a text by the sixteenth-century Suffolk agriculturalist poet Thomas Tusser. It was first performed by its dedicatees on 8 February 1963 in a pre-recorded broadcast for the BBC Midland Home Service.

After this burst of creative energy, there followed a pause at the end of 1962, as IH redirected her attention to a major new score being composed by Britten. He was engaged in writing a Symphony for Cello and Orchestra for Rostropovich, setting thereby a new challenge for IH who took on for the first time the task of preparing a piano reduction for a non-vocal composition. With the first performance scheduled for the Aldeburgh Festival in June, she worked quickly, and submitted the first two movements to Boosey & Hawkes on 3 January 1963. In the event, however, Rostropovich was unable to attend the Festival, and the première had to wait until March 1964, when Britten and Rostropovich performed the work in the Great Hall of Moscow Conservatory.

The rehabilitation of Gustav Holst as a major figure in twentieth-century British music was symbolically achieved on Thursday 25 April 1963, when IH attended the unveiling of a plaque at no. 10 The Terrace, Barnes, a monument which she, with the enthusiastic collaboration of the Sponsors of the Holst Plaque Commemoration Fund, had done much to secure. At the unveiling Herbert Howells marked the significance of the occasion thus: 'We would wish this plaque to be a constant reminder that here, in our midst, this illustrious composer and most rare man once lived and worked to the certain enrichment of our musical lives and to the greater glory of our national heritage.' Britten had been one of the subscribers to the fund, which had raised £157, of which £50 was given to GH's daughter 'to further performance of her father's works'. For

---

[48] *Making Music*, no. 51 (Spring 1963).

IH, the work on behalf of her father had only just begun, and she was already starting to conceive new and long-term plans for the securing of his reputation and musical legacy. As the year progressed, these began to dominate her thoughts to the partial exclusion of other priorities, including the music of Britten.

At the 1963 Festival IH enjoyed the satisfaction of hearing her first Aldeburgh première since *Welcome Joy and Welcome Sorrow* in 1951. Her String Trio no. 2 was performed by the Oromonte Trio, who had commissioned it for this concert; they repeated the work at the Wigmore Hall the following week. 1963 also marked the quatercentenary of the birth of John Dowland, and for the late-night Festival concerts she had devised her most extended series of programmes to date, seven concerts comprising the music of Dowland and his contemporaries. The BBC Transcription concerts, which since 1959 had become her special responsibility, had by now expanded from their original late-night scheduling; one was given at 5.30 p.m. on 27 June in the Country Club, Thorpeness, and another, including Tallis's forty-part motet, *Spem in alium*, 'in the round' in Orford Church at 5 p.m. five days later. This was performed by the Purcell Singers, now an established and highly professional ensemble, frequently used by the BBC for broadcasts and including amongst its members singers who were to make their names internationally as soloists and conductors in the coming years. Later in life IH recalled auditioning 'John Shirley-Quirk, who was then earning his living as a schoolmaster ... he said he could join the first basses in the Purcell Singers at the Aldeburgh Festival if he might bring his exam papers to correct between rehearsals.'[49] Other male voices in the ensemble had included Ian Partridge, Robert Tear and Roger Norrington; they were joined in 1963 by the young Philip Langridge, who retained vivid memories of his first Festival appearance:

> I was, of course, rather young and over-awed to be singing in Aldeburgh with such an elite group of singers. Imogen was always very precise with her dynamics, so when she put her finger to her mouth for 'sshh' just before we began the first unaccompanied piece, we knew that we should begin *ppp*. Unfortunately, with the first beat no one was able to sing at all, we were all so terrified. When we did finally make a sound, it was unfortunately not the soft, beautiful tone that Imo was after.
>
> The other memorable moment was also in the Purcell Singers, this time forty of us, again under Imogen Holst, in Orford Church. We sang the Tallis forty-part motet *Spem in alium*. To be singing in a choir, but

[49] IH, 'Recollections of times past'.

at the same time as soloist, in such a great work will remain with me forever. God bless Imo (and God bless Thomas Tallis!)[50]

Towards the end of the year IH became involved, through Britten and Pears, in a major regional educational initiative, the founding of a music department at the new University of East Anglia. The first Vice-Chancellor, Frank Thistlethwaite, felt inspired to 'bridge the gulf peculiar to this country, between universities and music academies whereby a bright and musically gifted eighteen year old has to choose between a performing career and sacrificing the university experience or vice versa.'[51] He approached Britten for advice. The composer's interest was stirred, and in March he and Pears met the Vice-Chancellor for an exploratory meeting. Britten remained encouraging, but, with time pressing for other matters, passed the detailed negotiations over to IH.

In a long memorandum she set out her vision for the new department, drawing extensively on her own educational philosophies and her experience of working at Dartington. Characteristically she conceived the department as attracting a wide range of participants, not just typical music students but also performers, teachers and those with a more recreational interest. She envisaged a very practical course with orchestras, choirs, composition, sight-reading and, very much in the model of Dartington, instrument maintenance. Thistlethwaite was appreciative but at first inclined to consider her ideas more appropriate to a training college than a university, for which he felt they lacked sufficient academic rigour. He told Britten that 'as an academic discipline, on all fours with the other humanities, the emphasis will inevitably be on music history and criticism.' But he undertook nevertheless to combine this with the practical work for teachers that IH had envisaged. Ever mistrustful of universities, Britten remained uneasy about 'the return to a more academic view of the position' and reasserted his own view that the School should seek to combine practical composition and performance with academic studies. At the Vice-Chancellor's request, he also suggested some possible names for the first Director of Music. The following year Philip Ledger, a close friend of both IH and Britten, having performed at Aldeburgh for three years, was appointed to the post. IH kept in close contact with Thistlethwaite, and the University and went on to deliver the first of the Arthur Batchelor lectures endowed by his daughter Diana in January 1966, on the subject of 'Some East Anglian Composers.'[52]

[50] Wake-Walker, *Time and Concord*, p. 190.
[51] Sanderson, *The History of the University of East Anglia*, p. 94.
[52] Arthur Batchelor was an artist who lived in Norwich from 1912. His daughter Diana played in amateur orchestras run by IH and drew a memorable cartoon of her for an EFDSS competition in the late 1930s; see plate 13.

Britten's initial meeting with Frank Thistlethwaite had been delayed by his absence from Aldeburgh through the beginning of 1964. By the end of 1963 it had become impossible for him to maintain his work routine at The Red House and he had decided to work abroad on his new composition, the church parable *Curlew River*. He settled in Venice, where he was joined by Colin Graham, who was to produce the drama for the Festival that year, and IH, who worked on the vocal score while Britten composed. Rosamund Strode in Aldeburgh was by now heavily involved as IH's assistant; on 9 February 1964, with Britten and IH still in Venice, the composer warned her:

> Imo & I are going to have a long session on the parts (vocal & instrumental) & score problems, before she leaves, & she can tell you the work, rather than me have to write it! But I think it'll be panic stations from about March 10th onwards!'[53]

Four days later IH had returned and Rosamund reported to Britten, who was suffering in the 'arctic' climate of Venice, that 'Imo is in fine form, I'm <u>so</u> glad things went well both with her book & yr own work. Aldeburgh seems tropical (as she infers) after the Venetian climate.'[54] IH was using any spare time to compile *An ABC of Music*, a step-by-step introduction to the language of music intended for school and amateur use; in writing it she held in her mind the example of her friend Winsome Bartlett, who enshrined for her the type of 'unschooled' amateur musician whom she felt might benefit.

By 2 April 1964 Britten was able to report to William Plomer, the librettist, that the writing of *Curlew River* was 'all finished, & the machinery is grinding away at producing parts for everyone to learn.' That machinery had recently gained a new 'cog' in the person of Rosamund Strode. In the very near future, however, it was to lose a yet more integral part of its mechanism, as once she had completed her work on the new church parable, IH decided finally to retire from her post as Britten's music assistant.

[53] BPL.
[54] 13 February 1964; BPL.

12 'The immense joy of learning about Holst via Britten': 1964–76

Imogen Holst's decision to step back from her role as Britten's amanuensis was undoubtedly the most difficult of her professional life, but had become inevitable in the face of the mounting pressures on her time from other sources, her wish to look after and develop her father's musical estate and his legacy, and the increased opportunities being offered to her as a respected and sought after composer, writer and speaker in her own right. Although she had intended to carry on in the role until she was sixty, three years hence, the pattern of her life had demonstrated a keen instinctive awareness on her part of when the time was right to move on, even when, as at Dartington, she had been sorely tempted to settle down for life. Now, while working on *Curlew River*, she realized that this time had come again. There was one important difference, nevertheless. Her departures from Eothen, CEMA and Dartington had all been followed by a period of rest and travel while she worked out the direction which she wished her life to pursue. On ceasing to work for Britten, she took no holiday: instead she embarked on a further journey the paths and major milestones of which she had already to a great extent marked out.

Foremost among these milestones was the centenary of GH's birth in 1974. Although this was as yet a full decade in the future, IH had already begun to conceive a major project to locate, identify and catalogue his music manuscripts. She also wanted to encourage further performances and recordings to bring her father's music to an ever-wider public, and to set up the affairs of his estate on a sound footing. In May 1964 the World Record Club released her recording of GH's *Choral Fantasia* and *Psalm 86*, an event that she later told Ursula Vaughan Williams was pivotal in attracting a wider audience. She was also quick to see the potential for the promotion of GH's music offered by the establishment, by Donald Mitchell, of Faber Music. Initially set up to meet Britten's need for a sympathetic, responsive and innovative publisher, the new company would soon be looking for other composers to represent and high-profile projects to secure its reputation. At the same time IH's own music was also beginning to re-establish a following; the String Trio no. 2 she had written for Aldeburgh, for example, had recently gained a second London performance on 15 July 1964 at Leighton House.

It seems likely also that IH may have seen the writing on the wall in respect of her working relationship with Britten. Throughout the years she had known him, Britten had gained the reputation of discarding friends and working associates who had, in his view, either let him down or served their purpose. IH herself had been witness to the dramatic cooling of relations with Eric Crozier, had been complicit in the departure of Elizabeth Sweeting and personally upset by the sacking of her friend Basil Douglas. But she knew and respected Britten's high standards, however challenging these were for those around him; she later recalled: 'What Ben expected from professionals working for him, they couldn't live up to it. I mean one nearly died at the strain of trying to keep up to what he wanted.'[1] For herself, she felt that she had let Britten down badly during the composition of *A Midsummer Night's Dream* and although this situation had been recovered, Britten's dependence on her utter reliability must have become increasingly difficult to satisfy as a myriad other demands impinged upon her time. Unprepared to compromise on her standards or to cut down the time she dedicated to Britten's scores, she realized that the only solution was a clean break. From a personal point of view, she would have found the wrench enormous, but she was sufficiently self-aware to recognize that her complete and uncritical devotion was by now having a claustrophobic effect on the composer. Ultimately therefore, as Fidelity Cranbrook observed, she 'had the wisdom to leave of her own accord'[2] and do so at the right time, after seeing *Curlew River* through the press. With hindsight she would have judged her timing as perfect, for paradoxically, by choosing to place herself at a greater distance from Britten, she was able to retain his affection and regard; as a result the two remained intimate friends for the rest of the composer's life.

While her devotion to Britten remained constant, the personal and domestic politics surrounding his music had certainly begun to depress her. For IH Britten's music was everything; she was unable to understand, and had little time for, those whom she saw as putting themselves between the composer and his creative process. Soon after taking the decision to leave, she was party to an episode that would only have helped confirm the hard choice she had made:

> When Ben was writing *Curlew River* I was working <u>desperately</u> hard on the score, because already by then I was about to have to give up working for Ben … And Stephen [Reiss] came in uninvited one Sunday morning

---

[1] Interview with Donald Mitchell, 22 June 1977.
[2] Carpenter, *Benjamin Britten*, p. 429.

when I was working hard there, and went on arguing for over an hour, saying that we must stop Ben writing this because of what people would think about Peter singing a woman's part. And I said 'But you <u>can't</u> think of that kind of thing when it's <u>Ben's music</u>. It just doesn't come into it at all' and of course I couldn't convert him. So he went on and on, and I suppose to lots of other people too. All that was a <u>frightful</u> strain.[3]

Having set out on her new course, IH set to work and for the first time took on a part-time secretary, Helen Lilley. She now felt ready to begin the huge undertaking of identifying and cataloguing her father's manuscripts. In February 1966 she described the beginnings of this process and her progress thus far in a presentation to a UK branch meeting of the International Association of Music Libraries. The talk, published in their journal *Brio* the following year, demonstrates the seriousness of purpose and commitment with which IH approached this new challenge, for which she was supremely equipped through working both for Britten and on the rediscovery of early music:

When I was asked last year if I would write a short article for BRIO, I was in the middle of cataloguing my father's manuscripts, and I hoped that by the spring of 1967 the search would have gone far enough for me to offer a detailed list for publication. But the search is still going on, and all that I have to offer is a glimpse of some of the problems that I am trying to solve.

Fortunately there are very few problems connected with his unpublished works. Nearly all the manuscripts mentioned in his own dated list of unpublished compositions have been in the British Museum for the last fifteen years (details in the handlist in the Manuscripts Students' Room, Add. MSS 47804–38). One or two early songs and a 1903 wind quintet are missing, but all the longer works are there, beginning with 'Opus 1, *The Revoke*; an opera in one act, 1895', and ending with fragments of an unfinished symphony he was writing just before he died in 1934.

A large number of manuscripts of the eighteen-nineties were not included in his list of compositions. He kept them, however, and tied them up in brown paper parcels which he labelled 'Early Horrors'. These are still on my own shelves. I go through them from time to time, and a few weeks ago I decided that several of them are worth hearing. There is a poignant setting of 'On the green banks of Shannon', for solo voice and

[3] Interview with Donald Mitchell, 22 June 1977.

piano, written in 1891 when he was at the Cheltenham Grammar School, and an expressive S.A.T.B. part-song, 'The Autumn is old', written in 1895 when he was a student at the Royal College of Music in London: both of these will be sung later this year by the Purcell Consort of Voices. But what am I to do with all the other 'Early Horrors'? They should certainly be preserved, but would it be right to ask the British Museum to house them?

The British Museum is surely the right future home for all the available autograph manuscripts of my father's published works, and I am grateful to the Keeper, Mr T. C. Skeat, for welcoming this suggestion. I am asking the various publishers if they would be willing to release the manuscripts in their possession, and their response has been most generous. It is fascinating going through each work in detail, and one can learn so much that is helpful. For instance, in *The Evening-Watch*, which has been out of print for twenty-five years, there is a descending scale for tenors and basses which has always been difficult to sing in tune. The manuscript shows my father's suggestion in the margin for an alternative enharmonic notation in flats instead of sharps. This is much easier to sing, and I have been able to include it in the new edition which Faber Music has recently published.

The new collection of Holst manuscripts for the British Museum will not be complete. To begin with, there will be gaps where works have already been given to other libraries; to the Bodleian, the Fitzwilliam, the Royal College of Music, the Library of Congress in Washington and the University of Michigan. Then there are manuscripts that have been lost. I shall go on hoping that these may eventually be discovered. (After I had been searching for nearly thirty years for the original manuscript of one of his best works, the publisher concerned, who shall be nameless, came across it while looking for something else on the top shelf of a cupboard in a store-room!)

It will not be easy to trace the missing autographs of some of the scores published by J. Curwen and Sons. When I wrote to ask about them several years ago, Maurice Jacobson replied: 'Many works taken over by us from Goodwin and Tabb were engraved in Germany, and probably the manuscripts were never given back'.

Then there are the manuscripts which my father gave to his friends. These include the first sketches of some of his greatest music. Fortunately one of the most interesting of these sketches is already in the British Museum. It is the complete original draft of the *First Choral*

Symphony, which differs considerably from the printed score. This was the only work he ever had the chance of writing during a long period of leisure. Normally he had to compose in the intervals between teaching schoolchildren and conducting amateur choirs and orchestras, but at the time when he was writing the symphony he had been ordered a year's rest. He sent this first sketch of the work to his friend Jane Joseph with a letter saying:

> I want you to keep it as a memento of all that you have done in the last fifteen months to make the symphony possible ... Later on, when it is published, you can compare your sketch with the finished article and learn either one or the other of the following lessons in composition:
> (a) The virtue and advantage of careful and prolonged study and rewriting.
> (b) The vice and futility of careful and prolonged study and rewriting.
> I wonder which it will be!

The late Jane Joseph was one of the three friends who helped him more than anyone else in music-copying and proof-correcting. The other two friends are Miss Nora Day and Miss Vally Lasker. A few years ago Miss Day gave the British Museum the autograph sketch of his *Choral Fantasia* (Add. MS 48369). And a few months ago Miss Lasker sent me three of his manuscript note-books, dated 1923–6, 1926 and 1932. These will join the three note-books already in the British Museum dated 1928, 1929 and 1933–4.

It is a pity that some of the pages of these very interesting note-books are difficult to read. This is not only because my father occasionally wrote his tunes while walking in the country or while travelling to work on a London bus: it is also because he liked to use a very soft pencil. The writing is badly smudged in places, and is too far gone for fixing.

The autograph full scores, which are all in ink, are in fairly good condition, though I am still struggling to rub out other conductors' indelible blue pencil marks and trying to avoid making holes in the paper. (There are at least half a dozen original scores which have obviously been sent out on hire for forty or fifty years.)

My next problem is how to indicate what is in my father's writing in the 'partly autograph' scores. Like many composers, he was too busy to prepare the layout of his orchestral scores himself, or to write out the voice parts in the vocal scores. And he needed more help than most other composers, owing to the neuritis in his right arm which he suffered from during his whole life. In the eighteen-nineties the pain was so bad that he was often unable to hold a pen and had to try and write with a nib tied to his middle finger. This is the reason for the straggling appearance of many of his early manuscripts. His neuritis was never again as bad as this, but he was seldom free from the worry of having to 'save' his hand for conducting, and I can remember, in the nineteen-twenties, hearing him say that his arm felt 'like a jelly charged with electricity'. It is remarkable that he managed to write so clearly, and that quite a number of his manuscripts are completely autograph.

Some of the 'partly autograph' scores are easy to describe in a catalogue. One can say of the *Ode to Death* that it is 'entirely autograph except for the duplication of words on pages 2–5'. But what can one do about *The Planets*, (Bodleian, MS. Mus. b. 18/1–7) where nearly every page is in a mixture of two or three different hands?

It is surely important from a practical point of view to be able to recognise what the composer has written himself. During a rehearsal for a recent recording of my father's *Seven Part-Songs* with words by Robert Bridges I had doubts about several metronome-marks in the printed copy. When I looked at the autograph manuscript I found that none of the metronome-marks were in his own writing, which made me feel less guilty about disregarding some of them.

There is also, I think, a certain historic importance in knowing what is autograph and what is not. (Having worked as Britten's amanuensis from 1952 to 1964 I am very much aware of this: it was acutely embarrassing to find a glossy magazine triumphantly reproducing a bit of the first page of the manuscript full score of the War Requiem in which practically everything was in my writing instead of the composer's.)

When I look at my father's 'partly autograph' scores I feel burdened by the expert knowledge that will die with me. It would be easy to sit by the side of a musicologist in the Bodleian and skim swiftly through the seven movements of *The Planets*, pointing to each bar and whispering 'autograph' or 'not autograph'. But how can I indicate all these details in writing for the students of the twenty-first century? I have been wondering whether it would be possible to have a facsimile with the autograph bits outlined in red and the rest of it shaded in some other colour ...

It was inevitable that this article, which was meant to impart information, should turn into an appeal for help. After all, music librarians are,
without any doubt, the most helpful people on earth.

Although she was no longer Britten's amanuensis, IH's connections with the
Aldeburgh Festival as Artistic Director and performer remained as strong as
ever, and in 1964 she shared with Pears the task of once more reauditioning the
Festival Choir. Her late-night concerts that year were built around the theme of
'Bach's Predecessors', to elucidate which she wrote an extended article for the
programme book entitled 'The Music that Bach was brought up on':

> At this year's Festival the late half-hours of music in the Parish Church
> have been planned to include cantatas, motets, preludes, fugues and
> suites that Bach either sung or played or listened to or copied out during
> the years 1693 to 1703. In nearly every work one can hear hints, if not
> actual 'quotations' that suggest the music he himself was to write many
> years later.

Allowing herself to bask in the reflected glory of Britten's enormous success
with *Curlew River*, she would have been equally delighted by the inclusion of
concert of modern music 'for children and amateurs' devised by Eric Roseberry
and Donald Mitchell, and performed by schoolchildren from Huntingdonshire
with Malcolm Williamson playing the piano.

Behind the scenes, she continued to organize events with tireless efficiency,
although she had by now learned to delegate many of the chores that she had
once taken on single-handed. In particular she could now call on the Hesse
students, who were given bursaries to come and experience the Festival in
exchange for helping out in many practical ways. Rosamund Strode recalled
that the majority of them were employed in 'endless chair-moving', although
'Imo used to nab the most musical ones for turning over and other sorts of
musical stooging'. The following year, one of the Hesse students kept a diary
which paints a delightful picture of IH's style of delegation:

> By great good fortune, four of us were chosen by Imogen Holst to help
> her with some scores. We spent the morning in her delightful bungalow
> up near the Parish Church, earnestly rubbing out all the pencil marks in
> various scores. Imogen kept us supplied with biscuits and orange juice,
> and chatted away to all of us like our dearest friend! – she is such a lovely
> character. And we all got one of her music books for children, signed
> with a 'thank you'.[4]

4 Hazel Fehr, in Wake-Walker, *Time and Concord*, p. 80.

Once emancipated from her duties for Britten, IH's life began to take flight across a wide territory of musical activity. Late in 1964 she addressed herself to serious composition for the first time since leaving Britten's employment. Grayston Burgess, one of the countertenors of the Purcell Singers, had decided to form an offshoot of the ensemble for six solo voices. The Purcell Consort of Voices had come into being in 1963, and IH had encouraged them from the start; she wrote *As Laurel Leaves that Cease not to be Green* for a concert they were to give on 30 March 1965 at the Wigmore Hall. A month before that performance she delivered a talk reminiscing on her father and her childhood for the BBC's *Woman's Hour*, while in March her music was included in a programme of compositions by women composers at the Commonwealth Institute. May saw the publication of her study of *Bach* for the Faber 'Great Composers' series.

In the same month Britten asked her, together with Stephen Reiss, to be a trustee of his Benjamin Britten Aspen Fund, established to encourage young composers: Nicholas Maw was the first beneficiary. IH's encouragement of young English composers had taken root at Aldeburgh, and her particular view of English musical history had achieved the status of received wisdom for a whole generation of scholars. These two strands were brought together in an essay written by Donald Mitchell for the 1965 Programme Book. Entitled 'A second Renaissance for English music?', it highlighted the achievements of Maw, Williamson and Richard Rodney Bennett, and harked back to a view of the 'first' Renaissance seen very much through IH's eyes. In this interpretation folksong had contributed much to the establishment of 'an identity-card' for English music, although, echoing GH, 'at one time it did seem as if English music were in danger of rhapsodising itself to death'. GH and Bridge, Britten's teacher and one of his main influences, were admired as 'exceptions in remaining open to influence by the new European music of their day'. IH's own dedication to the promotion of contemporary music was manifested in the new direction she took for her series of late-night concerts, juxtaposing English church music of the fifteenth century with its modern equivalents, and including along the way works by Birtwistle, Mathias, Gordon Crosse and Jonathan Harvey.

By 1965 the pressure on the Festival to find a new concert venue had become intense. With Britten's plans for a Festival theatre in Aldeburgh abandoned, and IH now living on a corner of the site where it would have stood, Britten was casting his eye around more widely. Others were yet to grasp the full extent of his ambitions, however, and IH was perhaps typical in her view at this time that expansion of the Festival would not only always be limited by the size of Aldeburgh itself but was, in any event, not very desirable. In an interview published on 10 June 1965 she told the *Radio Times*:

> People sometimes ask: 'What about the future? Will it grow bigger?' It can't. Aldeburgh itself is kept within bounds by the sea and the river and the marshes. The Jubilee Hall still holds just over three hundred people, though it has been enlarged since the days when there was no room in the orchestra pit for the harp or the percussion and they had to be played in the auditorium behind barriers of brightly coloured eiderdowns.
>
> First-night audiences, during the intervals of an opera, can still step out on to the pebbly beach where the fishermen's nets are spread to dry, and can stand in the shelter of the life-boat while they breathe huge lungfuls of our strong north-east wind. Unexpected things may happen to the Festival in the future, but it is safe to say that as long as it lasts it will remain 'modest' and its concerts will always be given by friends.

The 'unexpected' was about to happen more quickly than IH had anticipated, however, and on a scale that she could not have foreseen. That autumn, Stephen Reiss discovered that the disused Maltings at Snape, five miles inland from Aldeburgh, was available to lease. Britten, who had lived in a house with a view of the site when writing *Peter Grimes*, was immediately inspired. Ove Arup, who had worked on the Sydney Opera House, was called in to advise, and eventually Derek Sugden of Arup Associates was appointed to oversee a project to convert the Maltings into a concert hall. Less than a year after IH's interview with the *Radio Times*, building work had begun.

Meanwhile IH was expanding her own horizons by accepting two commissions for major works from the type of amateur group to whom she felt her own brand of 'useful' music was best suited. *The Sun's Journey*, a twenty-five minute cantata for female voices and small orchestra, was written at the request of Helen Anderson, then Music Adviser to the National Union of Townswomen's Guilds; she had known IH since 1941, when they both worked for CEMA. The NUTG wanted a work for a National Music Festival with a strongly competitive element, so IH provided for this when composing a work that also succeeds as a musically satisfying whole. The 1967 NUTG annual report commented that her 'skilful writing of two-part and three-part pieces of comparable difficulty ... enabled choirs of different sizes to compete on equal terms'. Nine winning regional choirs (from an initial entry of 511) took part in the final in London before joining together in the first performance of the cantata on 24 May 1967 at the Kingsway Hall, London. IH herself conducted the soloists Noelle Barker and Pauline Stevens, with the massed choirs of the NUTG and the Jacques

Orchestra. The other major commission that she undertook in 1965 had a more local interest. She was asked to provide an orchestral piece for the enterprising Trianon Music Group for young players and singers, based in Ipswich. IH had heard of the group during her stay in hospital in the spring of 1960, when one of her nurses had been the mother of the Group's director Christopher Green. She composed the *Trianon Suite* in April and May 1965, and heard the Trianon Youth Orchestra give the first performance in Ipswich School Great Hall on 18 September.

The beginning of 1966 represented an exceptionally busy period for IH, which took her frequently away from Aldeburgh and her research. She began the year by delivering a series of talks on East Anglian composers at the University of East Anglia. While still working on *The Sun's Journey* she travelled to Dartington to attend the opening of the new Music School on 7 February, before going to London to present a television programme on GH for the BBC *Sunday Night* series on 13 February. The following week found her directing the English Chamber Orchestra and the Purcell Singers in a concert of Bach cantatas, also for the BBC, and on 25 February she conducted a recording of GH's band works, *Hammersmith* and *A Moorside Suite*. During a brief respite in Aldeburgh, she was visited by Ursula Vaughan Williams, who was writing a piece for the journal of the Performing Right Society. When it was published in May the article presented a vivid portrait of IH enjoying her independence and the hectic lifestyle that came with it:

> Imogen Holst is a slight, fair-haired figure, usually armed with masses of work to do in trains or other unlikely places, finding time to seem to be in at least three places at once and to write at least three books at a time. She loves walking and rejoices in the cold winds of her beloved East Anglia. She likes food and wine, and her friends know what excellent company she is. She describes her own compositions as 'utilitarian, for learners or when asked', but everything she does has a quality all her own, where perception and imagination grace knowledge and mastery of her subject. The Purcell Singers are one of her contributions to the art of living, and there must be many people all over England who have been her students or have joined in amateur groups she has touched, saying 'let there be music', who owe to her a new dimension in their lives.
>
> Professionals and amateurs, East and West, past and present, have all a part in her being and, perhaps because this is so, she has the power of making each of them appreciate the place and value of the other.[5]

5 Vaughan Williams, 'PRS profile 3'.

In the spring of 1966 Britten's legal and financial advisers, Isador Caplan and Leslie Periton, became involved in IH's affairs, helping her to establish the new company of G. & I. Holst Ltd., superseding the more casual arrangements dating back to 1934 by which IH had been managing her father's estate. Nevertheless, she continued to live frugally, diverting most of the money that she received from the huge increases in income from GH's estate to the care of her mother and the promulgation of GH's music. But she did allow herself one luxury, as Maureen Garnham, then managing the Purcell Singers, recalled:

> I remember ... sitting down with her in a restaurant shortly after a sudden influx of royalties from her father's estate had transformed her life from one of some degree of financial hardship to relative affluence. She slipped off her coat and let it fall lining outwards over the back of her chair, exclaiming without regard to who might be overhearing her, 'It's so *nice* to be able to do that without being ashamed of the state of the lining'.[6]

Despite this flourishing independence, Britten continued to be a major force in IH's life and to preoccupy much of her time and thought. For the past year she had been writing the book on him that she had first conceived in 1953, and as she did so found herself once again drawing parallels between her subject's life and that of her father. Almost since her first acquaintance with Britten's music, she had seen him as the composer who had solved the compositional problems that had beset her father's music in trying to develop an idiomatic language. In IH's view, where her father had stumbled into dryness of expression and austerity of style, Britten, born two generations later, had attained fluency and lyricism. It was not surprising therefore that as she edited GH's scores for publication she should keep her unique knowledge of Britten's creative processes in mind. In March 1966 she wrote to him in a spontaneous outpouring of gratitude:

> I wanted to tell you how thrilled I've been while working at my father's Lyric Movement for viola and small orchestra to find, over and over again, how his mind and your mind so often work in the same way ... The Lyric Movement is full of difficulties: – there are so many problems about phrasing & dynamics, because he wrote so few directions and he died before he could revise it for publication. I've been getting panic-stricken about having to record it, because there are rhythmical

---

[6] Garnham, *As I Saw It*, p. 59.

problems I haven't yet solved. But whenever I work at it really hard I find
that the problems solve themselves if I just think of <u>your</u> music and learn
from it as I go on. So this is a thankyou, and to tell you that if <u>anything</u>
could make up for my desolation at not helping with <u>The Fiery Furnace</u>
it would be the immense joy of learning about Holst via Britten.[7]

The Burning Fiery Furnace was the first major work the Britten had produced
since IH had ceased to act as his amanuensis; however much she was now
enjoying her new freedoms, it was clear that her decision to walk away from
that role had retained some painful resonances for her.

In the same month Faber published IH's study of Britten. Written with the
memory of working for him still fresh in her mind, the book sparkles with
anecdotes and insights that only she could have supplied, dressed in prose that
is at once affectionate yet suitably detached. Her continuing intimacy with the
composer had also led her into a serious miscalculation, however, as she chose
to omit from her survey the contributions to Britten's achievement made by
creative associates with whom he had since broken contact. These included
Montagu Slater, Ronald Duncan and, most starkly, Eric Crozier, the librettist
of works from *St Nicolas* to *Billy Budd* and a co-founder of the English Opera
Group and the Aldeburgh Festival. Crozier was outraged, and suspected that
she had 'suppressed all mention of my name in order to please Britten, even
without such a wish having been consciously expressed by him'.[8] IH was forced
on to the defensive and in subsequent editions of the book went some way at
least to acknowledging the importance of Crozier's contribution.

Among her research interests, IH had recently developed a passion for
the neglected music of East Anglian church composers from the fifteenth to
seventeenth centuries. These composers had formed the basis of her talks at
the University of East Anglia at the start of the year, and for the 1966 Aldeburgh Festival she devised a fascinating series of late-night concerts built on
their work. She also delivered a lecture, illustrated by the Purcell Singers, on
the much larger theme of 'What <u>is</u> Musical History?' As she explained in the
programme book, she had been stung into addressing this subject by 'coming
across an astonishing sentence in Grove's Dictionary (1954) stating that "Lully's
harmony is not always correct". The misplaced confidence of this casual remark
led to a search for similar utterances.'[9] In the audience was a regular visitor to
the Festival, Joyce Grenfell, who wrote to a friend afterwards:

[7] 2 March 1966; BPL.
[8] Carpenter, *Benjamin Britten*, p. 19.
[9] *Aldeburgh Festival Programme Book*, 1966.

It was utterly fascinating and absolutely first class. She came on trippingly, head down. Not a trace of powder or lipstick on that fifteenth-century head painted on wood. A pale beige dress blending in with face and hair. Almost invisible really. And then she began. It was a miracle of erudition, simplicity, interest, passion and *wit*. Haven't enjoyed anything more during the whole festival, and it's been a very good festival.[10]

In July IH was called away to Thaxted after her mother suffered a fall. For the next few weeks she found it was 'impossible to make plans',[11] and stayed in Isobel's house, travelling each day to visit her in a nursing home in Cambridge. While in Thaxted she received on 22 July the welcome news that she had been made a Fellow of the Royal College of Music. Once her mother had returned home and IH had installed a new companion to take care of her, she returned to her hectic schedule, recording a variety of her father's works with the English Chamber Orchestra and the Purcell Singers for the Argo Record Company, and seeing through the press Faber's new editions of his *Six Choruses* and *Seven Part-Songs*. In a determined effort to catch up with her work following the frustrations of the summer, she fell ill herself, causing further delays to her work and, most distressingly, preventing her from attending the Covent Garden revival of the Britten opera that continued to mean to her perhaps most of all. Rosamund Strode wrote to Britten on 3 November that

> Imo is still not really well, but improving all the time ... She has heard from several people what a long time this particular thing takes to right itself, & this (luckily) makes her feel better about it & not depressed by a comparatively slow rate of progress. She will not, alas, be able to come to Gloriana on Saturday, which of course is a great blow to her.

By Christmas she was much improved and wrote a letter to Britten and Pears in effusive thanks for their respective Christmas presents:

> BLESS YOU for the WONDERFUL presents. Peter – that will be my best hat throughout 1967! Ben – the ecstasy of the M. S. is such that I can't come down to earth at all, but float in a perpetual state of elevation ...[12]

For everyone associated with Aldeburgh and its Festival, 1967 would be dominated by the opening of the new concert hall at Snape Maltings, for Britten the

[10] Wake-Walker, *Time and Concord*, p. 84.
[11] Letter to Britten, 6 July 1966; BPL.
[12] 30 December 1966; BPL.

realization of a dream that he had cherished from 1952. The conversion of the buildings had been in progress since May of the previous year, and IH had been consulted on numerous matters, taking a particular interest in the acoustics and the seating: she memorably told Derek Sugden that the chairs 'mustn't be too comfortable! ... They should make people sit properly. And when there's something special in the music, they should be able to *sit up straight!*'[13] The Queen and the Duke of Edinburgh had consented to open the new concert hall on 2 June on the first day of the Festival and to attend the opening concert. As in the Coronation tribute in 1953, IH shared the rostrum with Britten. The evening was for her a personal triumph. A member of the Aldeburgh Festival Singers recalled that 'the whole choir had tears in their eyes at the marvellous performance of *St Paul's Suite* conducted by Imogen Holst. Several of us said we would be happy to die there and then!'[14] One critic was prompted to declare: 'It was as if the composer's spirit descended upon her. She lived the music so vividly that it would have been no surprise if she had suddenly risen in a state of levitation.'[15] Although it had been decided that there would be no curtain-calls, Britten had to go backstage to lead IH out to acknowledge the applause.

Now sixty, IH had decided to retire from conducting the Purcell Singers; to Maureen Garnham she 'declared that she had ten years' worth of editing and writing to do, and was therefore giving up conducting in order to complete this work by the time she was seventy.'[16] She had devised for the Festival a series of four programmes of William Byrd's church music, but she handed over the concerts themselves to the care of Grayston Burgess and the Purcell Consort of Voices. Other events at the Festival of 1967 – the twentieth – also seemed to symbolize a gradual passing of the torch from the first generation of performers to the next, especially in the field of early music. Another of the Purcell Singers, Roger Norrington, had recently founded the Heinrich Schütz Choir, and he presented a concert dedicated to Schütz's music, thereby assuming responsibility for a composer whom IH had championed since the 1940s. Two of the Bedford children, David and Steuart, who had visited Britten during the early 1950s while holidaying in Snape, had now grown up and featured as composer and performer in a concert celebrating the achievements of 'Two Musical Families'.

While welcoming this new generation of artists and composers, IH herself

---

[13] Carpenter, *Benjamin Britten*, p. 469.
[14] Rowena Westbury, quoted in Wake-Walker, *Time and Concord*, p. 90.
[15] Wren, *Voices by the Sea*, p. 82.
[16] Garnham, *As I Saw It*, p. 61.

remained a central figure in the proceedings, which featured the first performance of her version for concert performance of Purcell's *The Fairy Queen*, co-
edited with Britten. Her programmes of English Church music of the seventeenth and twentieth centuries for the late-night concerts formed a roll-call
of her favourite composers, and touchingly also included a short piece – 'A
Hymn for Whitsuntide' – by Jane Joseph. Finally she had one of her own works
performed: the *Leiston Suite* had been written for and dedicated to the band at
Leiston Modern School; they gave the first performance on 24 June 1967 under
their director Hugh Connell.

Now no longer cloistered together for long periods, IH and Britten had rekin-
dled the relationship of mutual respect and real affection that they had enjoyed
through the early 1950s. Their renewed friendship was touchingly exemplified
in an exchange of letters during March 1968. While working on his church
parable *The Prodigal Son* Britten was taken ill with sub-acute bacterial endo-
carditis, an infection of the heart that put him in hospital for four weeks. IH
wrote regularly and received a warm reply once the composer was well enough
to write from his hospital bed:

> Your notes & cards have been so very comforting & welcome – thank
> you so much for thinking of me, & helping! It is going to be a long busi-
> ness, but everything is going to be all right …

On 28 March she replied:

> Thank you for your LOVELY letter, which I treasure more than any
> words can ever say. It was so sweet of you to have written, when you
> should have been spending every ounce of your energy on just getting
> better …

A month later, on 24 April, she stood in for Britten at a ceremony to open the
new Aldeburgh public library.

The Prodigal Son was one of the major new works (together with Birtwistle's
Punch and Judy) featured at the Festival that June. Philip Ledger had joined the
existing triumvirate of artistic directors, and, with the success of the Maltings
project securely under their belts, they planned together a Festival programme
extending over twenty-three days. IH's gradual retreat from her conducting
duties continued, and she restricted herself to directing the Ambrosian Singers in one late-night concert and sharing the conducting of the imaginatively
entitled programme 'Up She Goes: Five Centuries of Folk Music'. Her own
place in the Festival's affections was celebrated in a 'Musical Families' concert
dedicated to the Holsts. Both Britten and Pears contributed to a programme in

which forgotten compositions by eighteenth- and nineteenth-century 'von Hol-sts' were mixed in with songs by GH and IH's own Duo for Viola and Piano, which she had written for the occasion; this was played by Cecil Aronowitz and Nicola Grunberg, who remembered 'rehearsing with Imogen who, although sweetness itself, was very particular.'[17]

In July IH accepted an honorary degree from Essex University; and in September she continued her connection with the county of her childhood when she conducted the Essex Youth Orchestra at the Maltings in a programme that included the *St Paul's Suite*. IH's success in promoting her father's music had been such that her schedule of performances and recordings was more or less continuous. During the autumn she made momentous recordings of the *Lyric Movement* and the *Brook Green Suite* for the British music specialists Lyrita. Her own familiarity with, and affection for, these works had increased substantially through her editing and performing of them, and she now decided that she wanted to set down in print her considered reassessment of GH's work by preparing a new edition of *The Music of Gustav Holst*. In it she acknowledged that her former sometimes harsh criticisms had been perhaps too influenced by the surrounding musical landscape of 1951, although she doubted, in her new preface, if a simple revision of these earlier thoughts was sufficient recompense for a composer whose achievement she believed deserved a more comprehensive reassessment:

> During the last few years it has been encouraging to hear young musicians disagree with many of the things I have written in this book ... They have been able to listen to the music without being harassed by any problems of style, because the phrases that stood out as old-fashioned in 1948 have been swallowed up and digested in the process that we call history. Is it therefore a mistake to allow the opinions of twenty years ago to be brought back into print? It would be much more satisfying to start all over again.

GH was not the only composer to benefit from IH's mellowing of attitudes. Writing a programme note for Colin Davis's performance of Elgar's 'Enigma' Variations at the 1968 Festival she observed how, in the 1940s, 'the new generation of young composers had their doubts about it: some of them found the *nobilmente* mood of the music embarrassing ... Today, those unwanted false associations are completely forgotten, and listeners of any age can hear the music, unencumbered, as a masterpiece.'

[17] Correspondence with Christopher Grogan, 24 October 2006.

The early months of 1969 saw IH return to her schedule of recordings and lectures. Then on 16 April all these activities came to an abrupt halt with the death of her mother at the age of ninety-two. In her last days, Isobel had been found a place at Stow Lodge, near Stowmarket, through the good offices of one of the Aldeburgh Festival Choir members, Dr John Agate. The move from Thaxted, where IH's lifelong friend Arthur Caton had faithfully kept a close eye on Isobel, had eased IH's concerns and also allowed her to visit her mother more frequently towards the end. The funeral took place five days later at Ipswich Crematorium. Rosamund Strode drove IH to the funeral, and when she got home wrote an extended description of the day to Britten:

> Well, the Ipswich appointment with Imo this afternoon went all right, entirely simple & uncomplicated & no fuss. Five in the congregation (Imo, her mother's daily help, the woman who 'came in to sleep in the house' & their Thaxted taxi driver, & me) & the old parson who is laid on when there isn't anybody special to officiate: the retired Vicar/Rector of St. Peter's Ipswich (Wolsey's Church, as he told us) who lives conveniently on the other side of the Bypass. He was all right, with a good bass reading voice only slightly tinged by ecclesiastic elocution. The congregation, by special command, wearing its 'everyday clothes' (no hats, no black etc.); & a charming undertaker from Stowmarket called Mr Greengrass (which pleases Imo no end!) & his 4 minions in inky black: top hat & all, looking almost Venetian in the totality of his blackness (though a motor isn't so good as a funeral gondola, is it.) So I think all that bit was really done properly & nicely.
>
> Coming home I failed to turn down the vital lane towards Bealings from Tuddenham so we went past, then into, Culpho church – a funny little small place that looks like part of something bigger, but maybe it wasn't, really ... Then I thought a rural ride home seemed a good idea, so we trundled round a bit before emerging above Ufford: through Ufford itself & to look at its church which (shame!!) neither of us had seen, & Imo hadn't even heard of its C15th font cover, wh. I had at least – (which makes not going there even worse). So that was a huge success (C15th is her century, after all!) & we got back in good style at about 3.30.[18]

A week later she reported that IH was 'back into her 4–years-behind-schedule normal working scheme'.[19]

[18] 21 April 1969; BPL.
[19] 28 April 1969; BPL.

A new and pleasing development occurred later in the year when Michael Short, an ex-student of Morley College, arrived in Aldeburgh intending to write an extended study of GH's life and music. Having carried the torch for her father single-handedly for so long, IH could have been forgiven for being cautious about this intrusion. Instead she welcomed the visitor with open arms, as heralding the onset of a new generation of scholars dedicated to GH's music and legacy. Short later recalled his first visits to Aldeburgh, where he found his hostess consistently 'kind, thoughtful and attentive':

> From the start of our association she offered full exchange of information about her father's life and music … Her capacity for work was insatiable; her diminutive and apparently frail physique concealing an iron-willed determination to attain her objectives. Late in the evening of our first day's work, I enquired what time I should return the following morning. 'Any time you like, Dear', was the reply. 'Would nine o'clock be alright?' – 'yes, of course, but I shall have done three hours' work by then!'
>
> By way of respite from our labours, she would occasionally don raincoat and sou'wester to stride out into the bitterly cold wind along the Aldeburgh sea-front, coming back glowing with health and energy …[20]

Following the triumphs of the first two Festivals held at the Maltings, expectations were high for the success of the 1969 event. These were dashed, however, on the opening night, when the Maltings was gutted by fire soon after the end of the evening concert. IH was immediately involved in helping Britten and Pears reschedule programmes and arrange alternative venues, and Blythburgh Church was made available to host what was to prove a landmark performance of Mozart's *Idomeneo*, conducted by Britten. At short notice IH took up her baton on 15 June to conduct GH's *A Fugal Concerto* in the same venue, replacing a planned performance of Elgar's 'For the Fallen' – designed for a much larger orchestra than Blythburgh could accommodate – that Britten was to have conducted in the Maltings; the rest of the programme was unaffected. IH also contributed a talk in memory of Dorothy Elmhirst in the Jubilee Hall, at which her own setting of *In heaven it is always Autumn* was performed, and she took the opportunity to speak movingly of the 'unforgettable' experience of working with the Elmhirsts at Dartington.

Following the end of the Festival on 3 July IH was awarded another honorary degree, this time a doctorate from the University of Exeter. In September she witnessed the dedication of a Gustav Holst Memorial Window at James Allen's

---

[20] Short, *Gustav Holst*, p. v.

Girls' School, and on 6 October went to the 'Women of the Year' luncheon in London. These marks of celebrity extended to encompass a wide range of civic occasions. On 15 October, for example, she opened the new buildings at Saffron Walden College, while in December acquiesced to planting a copper beech tree in her role as President of the Woodbridge Orchestral Society. This last occasion was a labour of love; she had been president of the Society since 1960, and had respect and affection for its conductor, Bernard Barrell. Before Christmas she completed work on the *Woodbridge Suite*, the first of three pieces she was to write for the Society, which duly gave the first performance on 4 May 1970. The first movement became a 'signature-tune' for the orchestra and was used on many subsequent occasions to open its concerts.

In the years immediately following her father's death IH had bewailed the absence of performers and students willing to champion the composer's cause. Thirty-five years on, this situation was transformed when she came into contact, initially through his work for Britten, with the young composer and scholar Colin Matthews. On 14 May 1970 she wrote to thank him for doing some work for her:

> Thank you VERY much for the most beautiful copying! I am indeed grateful. I enclose a cheque for the Astorga,[21] and I have sent a bill for the other things to the Festival Office.

Matthews's involvement with IH's work (they had not yet met) had become necessary as a result of her failing health during the spring, when she had developed bronchitis and had to be taken into hospital. On 4 March Rosamund Strode told Britten there was 'no fresh news on the Imo front, though Helen Lilley says she sounds in good form on her daily telephonings, but she admits to being very thin'. The following week she was 'back at home, looking terribly thin and rather tired but glad to be there. She still has a strict régime to follow & has sent round a résumé of what this means: a penicillin injection daily; 31 pills daily (!! Horrors ...); no engagements, meetings or travelling for 3 weeks; & so on. I think she really is better basically however, it's the usual story of a spell in hospital leaving one less strong than before although they seem well on the way to vanquishing the virus which is the main thing. She is planning to go away for a week in April (has been invited to Dartington by both Leonard & Winsome, I know, so it's probably there that she's going) which one HOPES will

---

[21] The Sonata no. 2 in G major by Juan Oliver y Astorga (1733/4–1830), which was programmed for one of the late-night concerts of eighteenth-century chamber music to be given at the Festival. The work had not been reprinted for 200 years, hence the need for it to be recopied.

really set her up.'[22] By 24 April she was 'perking up nicely & planning a Lake District holiday', which she took in May.

For *The Observer* of 7 June 1970 John Lucas wrote a piece on the Aldeburgh Festival entitled 'At the court of Benjamin Britten', in which he mischievously made fun of the founders of the event and their entourage in the context of the Festival hosting another royal visit by the Queen to open the rebuilt concert hall. 'Their court has a princess, Imogen Holst, and two princes, Ledger and Graham. There is a Lord Chamberlain, the very efficient Stephen Reiss ... and there are numerous courtiers.'[23] Underlying this gentle mockery was undoubtedly a feeling that the older generation at the Festival had formed a clique that was difficult for new artists to break into. In fact, IH was now limiting her active role in the Festival considerably. She conducted pieces by Henry VIII and Byrd during the opening 'Music for a Royal Occasion' and contributed to a rumbustious concert of folk music arrangements 'Up She Goes Again' to celebrate the reopening, in which was included her new and stylistically adventurous setting of 'Gipsy Davy'. Although she devised programmes of Spanish music for the late-night concerts, however, she now let others direct them. Gratifyingly for her, the Festival at last featured the Aldeburgh première of *The Planets*, with Charles Groves conducting the Royal Liverpool Philharmonic Orchestra. In her programme note she was happy to acknowledge the suite as another work which through its use as 'snippets for background music' had developed a 'clutter of unwanted associations' but which had 'survived as a masterpiece, owing to the strength of Holst's astonishing invention'.

Another graduation ceremony beckoned in July, and she went to the Royal Academy of Music to receive an honorary degree. In the same month Lyrita Records, strong supporters of IH's drive to set down as much of her father's music as she believed to be of appropriate quality, released her recording of the Double Concerto with the English Chamber Orchestra. For IH, who had been the rehearsal pianist for the first performance of the work more than forty years earlier, this recording event had a special significance. Another occasion symbolic of the passing of the years occurred that October, when she conducted the Aldeburgh Music Club for the last time, in GH's arrangement for chorus, strings and wind of 'All people that on earth do dwell'.

Throughout these contradictory times, when her life seemed to veer between valediction to much that was familiar and the continued exploration of new vistas, it was Britten's music that provided both a fixed point of reference and a

[22] 11 March 1970; BPL.
[23] Headington, *Peter Pears*, p. 233.

source of continual refreshment. During the autumn of 1970 he was at work on a new opera, and on 22 November IH, who had seen some of the music, wrote to him:

> THANK YOU for <u>Owen Wingrave</u>. I can think of nothing else, all the time. It is the miracle of miracles that your music can go on getting better & better every time, when its previous best is already so staggering …

She remained equally inspired by his conducting, which she had come to regard as a model for others to follow. On 13 January 1971 she wrote:

> This is a FAN MAIL, and you won't have time to read it, but I've just been listening to the broadcast of your King's Lynn concert, and the Mozart symphony made me realize all over again why there is all the difference in the world between your conducting & other people's conducting … With you the rhythm really <u>is</u> 'flow', so that, from the first note to the last, every tiny detail is the shape of the music itself, instead of one thing after another …

In a letter dated 27 March she returned to another favourite theme, her gratitude to Britten for the clarity he had contributed to her reassessment of her father's music:

> THANK YOU for the <u>Hammersmith</u> rehearsal. There are no words to tell you what it means to me to have you working at his best music and solving its problems and bringing it to life in the way that he wanted it to sound …

Britten himself was no longer a well man, however, and IH was one of many who noticed with distress 'how white and drawn he looked' after conducting an extraordinarily intense performance of Mozart's *Requiem* at the Festival on 20 June that year. But while her concerns for Britten's health cast a shadow over proceedings, IH nevertheless enjoyed some lighter moments at the Festival, one of which was later recalled by Mary Clarkson, a soprano and pupil of Peter Pears. IH had planned a series of late-night concerts of English church music to take place in Aldeburgh Parish Church. Prior to these performances the concerts were to be recorded for the BBC earlier in the day in the church at Framlingham, where

> At one recording session a bird had got into the church and decided to sing with the performers … Imo told us all to leave the church; she would ask the bird to leave and explain that we loved the birdsong but

that time was important and this was a recording. The door remained open and soon Imo came out triumphant. The bird had left.[24]

By the beginning of 1972 IH was finally in a position to deliver to her publishers the fruits of her previous decade's work on GH's music. Rosamund Strode wrote to Britten on 26 January to tell him that it was 'Imo's Great Thematic Delivery Day today, I believe. I'm sure she's probably desperate'. Britten, who had received a stream of 'fan mails' from IH over the past few months, was now able to turn the tables and sent her a letter of congratulations; on receiving his message IH replied on 31 January:

> Thank you for your lovely letter … It's cheered me up enormously, because I'd been fairly depressed at having to part with a typescript that was so full of queries and gaps. (I've got to find the answers before the proofs stage – also to get two more books to Faber's before May 1st, so life is still interestingly full!)

June saw the publication by Faber Music of her new study score of *The Wandering Scholar*, followed in quick succession by her latest contribution to Faber's 'Great Composers' series. This study of William Byrd placed her thinking firmly in line with an older generation of scholars for whom Byrd and Tallis represented the first full flowering of an idiomatically English music. But her views caused 'some consternation in early music circles as … she aroused the ire of some of the younger scholars, who felt she regarded English music too exclusively as starting with the Elizabethans'. It was perhaps too easily forgotten that through her late-night programmes at Aldeburgh she had been instrumental in bringing to wide attention the music of earlier English composers, and that 'her performances had shown her love [not only] for the Tudor tradition [but also] what lay behind it'.[25]

IH had by now effectively retired from conducting, although she was persuaded to lead one item – GH's *This I have done* – in a mixed concert for 'Voices and Percussion' at the Aldeburgh Festival on 17 June, at Blythburgh. Research and editing were now her main focus, but she did not completely neglect her skills as a composer and in the summer she provided the orchestra of the Incorporated Association of Preparatory Schools with the *Iken Fanfare* for school wind band. This was performed for the first and only time by the IAPS Orchestra on 22 July 1972, in the Maltings. After the concert had finished, somebody remarked that an important tune in the work closely resembled the

[24] Wake-Walker, *Time and Concord*, p. 191.
[25] Thomson, 'Imogen Holst'.

title theme of a weekly regional television series then running. Disturbed at the implication of plagiarism, IH (who, as the orchestra's administrator Robin Wilson pointed out, 'lived too far outside the current world to possess a television set' and never watched one) withdrew the work. More successful was her setting of *Hallo My Fancy, Whither Wilt Thou Go?*, composed that autumn for the Purcell Consort of Voices, who gave the first performance at the Wigmore Hall on 21 May 1973. In a note for a later performance IH stated: 'I wrote this partsong in the autumn of 1972, as a tenth birthday present for the members of the Purcell Consort, in gratitude for the many performances we worked at together when they were in the Purcell Singers.' IH's achievements were further publicly recognized at the end of October, when she accepted an invitation to be the castaway on the BBC's *Desert Island Discs*. October also saw a visit from the photographer Edward Morgan, who was working on a project entitled 'Artists in East Anglia'. He initially found his subject somewhat cold and detached, but once the subject of their conversation had turned to dance – a field in which Morgan had done extensive photographic work – IH opened up completely and he was able to capture her in a memorable series of images.[26]

Developments at Snape Maltings, meanwhile, were beginning once more to gather pace. Back in the summer of 1953 Britten had mooted the idea of establishing a school of music in Aldeburgh, and had told IH that she should be its first Principal. Apart from the visit that year of a small group of students, who rehearsed choral music and a Mozart piano quartet with Britten, Pears and IH, however, this idea had lain dormant in Britten's mind until the conversion of the Maltings in 1967. That done, Britten started to lay further plans for the expansion of artistic activities on the site, including the fulfilment of his vision for a school. The idea was fully supported by Pears, who, unlike Britten, was himself a keen teacher, and by IH, for whom teaching and performing had always represented two sides of the same coin. In September 1972 the initiative got under way with a weekend of classes for young professional singers led by Pears and Lucie Manén and preceded by a recital by Britten and Pears that included *Winter Words*. Over the next few years the project was to develop into the Britten–Pears School for Advanced Musical Studies, with courses designed to bridge the gap between conservatory training and the realities of the performing world, and with its own Snape Maltings Training Orchestra. The plan for the school also included the provision of a library, prompting IH to consider donating her own collection of books and music in memory of her father.

---

[26] Conversation with Christopher Grogan, November 2006. Three of these images are reproduced as plates 37–9.

It was IH who had, through her example at Dartington, first convinced Pears of the power of effective teaching, and now, much later in their lives, it was through her also that he now developed an interest in research. In May 1973 he asked her to sponsor his application for a British Museum reader's card, and she responded with enthusiasm: 'I'm enormously honoured to be able to help you enter my 'home-from-home' at the B.M.'

In June the Aldeburgh Festival featured another new Britten opera, *Death in Venice*, but the composer was too ill to attend. IH wrote to him on the morning after the performance: 'Last night was more wonderful than can ever be told, and it was as if you were with us all, the whole time.' The sadness that she felt at Britten's absence from the Festival was intensified at the end of the month when Winsome Bartlett died on 29 June in Dartington. Although some areas of her past seemed to be inexorably fading from view, she nevertheless continued to look forward and to plan new initiatives, particularly for the celebration of the GH centenary which was now only a year away. Donald Mitchell at Faber Music had recently raised the possibility of producing a complete scholarly edition of the composer's work, an idea which filled IH with enthusiasm:

> I couldn't believe it – it sounded too good to be true. Well, about the first thing that happened was, we found that it couldn't be done, in publication: they couldn't reprint things as the costs would have been enormous, even if the other publishers had been willing. So I suggested that it should be facsimile of the manuscripts. To begin with, I find manuscripts fascinating to look at, and also it would give a chance of seeing my father's unorthodox way of writing things down.[27]

Colin Matthews had joined her on the project, with publication of the first volumes planned for the centenary together with the already completed Thematic Catalogue. Earlier in the year Matthews had been heavily involved with preparing the score of *Death in Venice*, but he was now able to find more time for IH's work; a letter of 1 August shows the tireless commitment and sense of urgency that she, after so many years, could still apply to the promotion of her father's music:

> Thank you for your letter. I'm sending you by separate recorded delivery the photostats of the aut[ograph] M.S. of the Lyric Movement and my own corrected printed score. As you see, I've done most of the work needed for Facsimile Vol II on this particular score, but I'd be glad of your

[27] Interview with Christopher Headington, 1979.

eagle eye! It was published posthumously – I've made some corrections for a 2nd impression, at the same time as I prepared the pft reduction.

Have you been able to list the collation of the Double Concerto? And what about the Fugal Concerto? We ought to get Facs. Vol II ready as soon as possible because things take so long. We can discuss both St. Pauls Suite & the Brook Green Suite when you are here Aug. 13–17. Would you very kindly ask Rod [Biss], as from me, what the position is about Facs. Vol I (Savitri & Wandering Scholar) which is due out on sale before the end of this year? I've not seen any suggestions for binding etc. And I've not heard whether Halstan's have finished their job on the Wandering Scholar.

I've found several mistakes in the music examples for the Thematic Catalogue but they can all be corrected when we go thro' the new proofs of the music examples together to see if they've put the words in properly.

Thank you for your help. (You needn't feel 'guilty'! Just wait to see what I get you to do for me during the next few months!!)

After IH's death Matthews wrote of these days: 'Editing music with her was exhilarating and exhausting … she knew exactly what she wanted, but she could, with difficulty, be persuaded to another opinion – when she would not only be magnanimous, but positively delighted to be able to change her mind.'[28] Despite her own sense of urgency, however, IH willingly released Matthews for more important work at the end of September, when she wrote to him:

> Faber's will have told you that we've had to cancel your visit to Oxford next week to look at the manuscript of the Planets in the Bodleian owing to the urgency of getting Ben's alterations to D in V ready for Covent Garden. I'm so sorry about this: we'll find a later date for you to go without me. I shall go myself, & concentrate on amanuenses' handwriting, not on corrections.[29]

The year 1974 saw the culmination of the work begun by IH a decade earlier after she had made the life-changing decision to stop working as Britten's music assistant and direct her energies to preparing for her father's centenary. Now that the celebratory year had arrived, she plunged herself into a whirlpool of activity, attending concerts and events, many of which she had organized

---

[28] Matthews, unpublished typescript, 1984.
[29] 27 September 1973.

and encouraged into being, lecturing and continuing work on the Collected Facsimile Edition. The previous year she had negotiated with Keith Grant at Covent Garden for two performances of *Sāvitri* and *The Wandering Scholar* to be given at Sadler's Wells; these new productions, by David Pountney, were first seen at the festivals in Aldeburgh in June and Cheltenham in July, conducted by Steuart Bedford, before travelling to London in September. A party was held at Aldeburgh on 3 June at the start of a Festival that included not only performances but also an exhibition of GH's life and music; a second exhibition was held at the Royal Festival Hall. Britten was unable to attend the party but sent a telegram, prompting IH to reply the next day, thanking him for the 'lovely surprise, [which] started the party, by making all the organizers feel happy!' IH must also have been especially gratified by the host of performances undertaken by amateur groups across the country. At St Paul's Girls' School a number of events were organized, including the recording for the first time of the music for *The Vision of Dame Christian*. The year also saw the publication by Faber of *A Thematic Catalogue of Gustav Holst's Music* and the announcement of the forthcoming Collected Facsimile Edition, uniformly designed to an exceptional standard in olive-green covers, calculated to underline the quality and distinction not only of the music itself, but also of the project that IH had brought to fruition. Plans were also finalized to commemorate GH's life and work by opening to the public the house in Cheltenham in which he was born. This was put into effect by the local Borough Council, with the aid of a public appeal launched by Arthur Bliss, Master of the Queen's Musick; the opening ceremony was carried out by the Duke of Beaufort on 25 October the following year.

IH now had the satisfaction of knowing that her father's achievements and legacy had become established unassailably as an integral part of English twentieth-century culture. The growth of mass-media had ensured that his music was now recognized at every level of public consciousness, while her editorial and recording labours over the past decade had awakened musicians to the unique quality and variety of his output. In recognition of her work she was awarded a CBE in the New Year's Honours List of 1975.

Unsurprisingly, the hectic schedule of touring, lecturing, broadcasting and myriad public appearances, coupled with her continuing publishing endeavours, took their toll on IH, aged sixty-seven in the year of her father's centenary. Towards the end of 1974 she was taken ill. At first it was generally believed that she was suffering from simple exhaustion; Rosamund Strode wrote to Britten from Aldeburgh on 10 October:

> Imo was back here briefly yesterday (G & I. Holst meeting in London
> today) & we had a good natter in the evening. Her travels & Centenary
> do's seem to have gone off pretty well, though she had torrential rain in
> Dartington (!not unusual) & in Cheltenham, which was obviously trying.
> She looked tired & not too well (though all right "in herself", very much
> so) & goes into Burton Ward for 3 days' investigations on Monday.

Once in hospital it became apparent that the problem was more serious, and
IH wrote to Britten herself on 28 October with the news that 'I've recently had
a few days in hospital, and I've got to go back in January to have my right kidney
removed: I'm not to be allowed to begin normal work again until June.'

Now semi-invalided himself by the major heart operation that he had had
to undergo after the completion of *Death in Venice*, Britten had been using his
convalescence to write a suite on English folk tunes, a project that was particularly close to IH's heart. Britten wanted the first performance to take place
at the 1975 Aldeburgh Festival, and on hearing that IH would be meeting the
Queen Mother at a Holst concert at the beginning of December, he asked her
to find out if the Festival's royal patron would be happy to consider it for her
'Patron's Choice' concert. IH delivered the message and wrote to Britten the
next day:[30]

> The Queen Mother was thrilled at the news of the Suite, and would be
> <u>delighted</u> to have it in Patron's Choice. I gave her your greeting while
> I was sitting next to her in the box, & I told her exactly what you said
> about how you wished you could have a slip of the tongue and call it
> 'love'. She <u>glowed</u> with pleasure; – at that moment the next item on the
> programme began and she couldn't go on talking. But at the end when
> we'd all said goodbye she called out to me over the heads of all the grand
> people who were bowing between the guard of honour: – 'Thank him
> for his lapsus linguae!'[31]

For a number of reasons the bond between Britten and IH had recently developed a new strength. Both haunted by ill health, they found comfort and reas-
surance in discussing the achievements and experiences of their shared past.
Britten's illness had, as Humphrey Carpenter has noted, 'radically altered' his
relationship with Pears, who was now away from Aldeburgh for long stretches:
his performing career in the USA had found a new lease of life after his critically

---

[30] 3 December 1974; BPL.
[31] The concert took place on 13 June 1975. Britten and Pears entertained the
      Queen Mother to lunch at The Red House beforehand.

acclaimed interpretation of the role of Aschenbach in *Death in Venice* in New York. When Pears was in Aldeburgh early in 1975 friends noticed a new emotional distance between the two, emphasized by the presence of younger men whom Pears had invited to stay at The Red House. These developments must have troubled IH, whose affection for Pears had always depended heavily on her recognition of his place as Britten's chief comfort and inspiration. Recognizing the composer's increasing isolation from his muse, IH did her best – on the musical level to which she had long since resigned herself – to provide encouragement. At the start of the year she wrote him another of her 'fan mails', in response to his invitation to her to attend a rehearsal of his new Canticle V, 'The Death of Narcissus', which Pears and the harpist Osian Ellis were preparing for its first performance in Germany a fortnight hence:

> This is to thank you for letting me have the wonderful experience of listening to Peter & Osian rehearsing your new Canticle. I've been haunted by it ever since. It's supremely great music.[32]

In his response Britten paid brief but significant tribute to the contribution that she had made to his own life over the past thirty years:[33]

> Thank you so much for your 'fan' letter – that is something to treasure. But you must remember how much I have learned from you – so it's really 'all-square'!

Four months later Britten was able to express his gratitude to her for a significant achievement of her own, the publication by Faber of the first volume of the Gustav Holst Collected Facsimile Edition, comprising *Sāvitri* and *The Wandering Scholar*. IH sent a copy to Britten and Pears, which the composer acknowledged on 23 May:

> I am so delighted to have Vol I of the Complete Facsimile Edition. I was just about to order it from Fabers ... but how much lovelier for Peter & me to have it from you. I think it is a publishing and editorial triumph & I congratulate you (& Colin) on it. I have just read it through from cover to cover ...

Two days later IH shared her satisfaction with Colin Matthews: 'Vol. I of the Facsimile edition is MAGNIFICENT. Very many thanks for everything. I gave a copy to Ben, & he's delighted with it, & congratulates you most warmly.'

---

[32] 2 January 1975; BPL.
[33] 24 January 1975; BPL.

It was now several years since IH had played an active role as a performer at the Aldeburgh Festival. In 1975, however, she was tempted out of retirement by the opportunity to conduct some of her father's music in very special circumstances, at an open air concert at Framlingham Castle. The background to the event was later recalled by Trevor Sharpe, director of music at the Royal School of Military Music, Kneller Hall:

> Gustav Holst wrote a number of works for wind band that have become established classics ... IH had similar interests and on one occasion visited the Royal Military School of Music, Kneller Hall, to proof various publications of her father's scores. She also conducted the celebrated Kneller Hall Band in its summer-season concerts.
>
> These activities all led to the RMSM being invited to give a Festival concert at Framlingham in 1975. I was Director of Music at the time and we agreed that IH should be Guest Conductor of one of her father's pieces for this occasion.
>
> The Holst Suite in E flat was not going all that well so IH stopped and in her charming but precise manner said 'No, that is not quite right ... I think my father would have liked it like *this*.' Thereupon she proceeded to explain quite clinically to a more than attentive Kneller Hall Band what 'Father' would have wanted. The result produced sounds and shapes that previously we had never realized. A music lesson I, for one, wished had come much earlier in my career.[34]

Among the audience was Hester Agate, who recalled:

> In spite of the wonderful spectacle the evening was a little lacklustre (mainly due to a persistent drizzle) until a diminutive figure in a special scarlet dress – 'to match the stripes down the soldiers' trousers' – took the conductor's baton. The band was transformed and played Holst's Suite as it can never have played it before – for Imo.[35]

The beginning of 1976 found IH returning to composition to provide a new piece for her favoured amateur group, the Woodbridge Orchestral Society. *Joyce's Divertimento*, for viola and orchestra, was written, according to Bernard Barrell, for his wife Joyce 'for her being willing to attend to Imo's washing during a stay in Ipswich Hospital when she had a major operation there'. The conductor remembered that, as Joyce Barrell's mother was also ill and the soloist

---

34 Wake-Walker, *Time and Concord*, p. 193.
35 Wake-Walker, *Time and Concord*, p. 193.

would therefore have little time to practise, 'with typical understanding, Imo produced a most interesting work that both tested the orchestra suitably, yet gave pleasure in rehearsing'.[36] The work was first performed on 17 May 1976 in Woodbridge, Suffolk, by its dedicatees.

Despite his grave illness, Britten was also continuing both to compose and to arrange some of his earlier music for performance. Through late 1975 he set out to revise *Paul Bunyan*, his ballad opera from 1940, and the first performance for more than thirty years was given on BBC Radio 3 on 1 February, conducted by Steuart Bedford. The work was generally well received, and IH wrote her own note of congratulations and gratitude on 9 February: 'I've been living on (and in) Paul Bunyan ever since that wonderful first performance … as always with your music, it is just right for NOW!'

Following her operation in January IH's own health was now much improved, and she was able to attend two important conferences during the year. Between 22 and 29 April she was at the European String Teachers' Association Conference in Elmau, Austria, where she delivered a paper recounting her first discovery of early music while at the Royal College of Music half a century earlier. She then went to the Durham Oriental Music Festival, an event that 'filled her mind with so many speculations that she felt compelled to communicate them', and on her return to Aldeburgh she wrote an article entitled 'A Learner's Questions' for the journal *Early Music*. She knew the editor, John Mansfield Thomson, and had provided encouragement and support to him when the new journal was getting under way. Now a subscriber, she remained absorbed in the questions posed by early music and the study of performance practice; as Thomson was to recall 'whenever we met (often at the railway platform at Ipswich) she would throw herself into animated discussion on a topic in the latest issue'.[37]

IH had another opportunity to hear *Paul Bunyan* at the Aldeburgh Festival that year, and on 12 June she went to the garden party at The Red House held to celebrate the award to Britten of a life peerage. But she knew, as did all the composer's friends, that his time was now fast running out. On 23 October she was present beside him in the box at the Jubilee Hall for a concert entitled 'Cabaret', at which Pears sang 'Tell me the truth about love', one of the composer's *Cabaret Songs*. Ostensibly organized to celebrate the thirtieth anniversary of the Festival, the event actually took place eight months in advance of this in unspoken acknowledgement that Britten would be unlikely to live long enough to share that landmark. As Rosamund Strode noted in her copy of the

---

[36] Undated letter from Bernard Barrell to Christopher Tinker.
[37] Thomson, 'Imogen Holst'.

programme, the concert was indeed to be Britten's 'last public appearance'. IH wrote to Pears on 17 November: 'I'm thinking of you all the time, now and for ever. All my love to you both'. Five days later she went to a birthday party for Britten at The Red House at which the composer, in bed upstairs, asked for his closest friends, IH included, to go individually and say goodbye to him. He died on 4 December, and was buried in the churchyard in Aldeburgh three days later. To the surprise of some of his friends, Pears then immediately set out to complete some concert commitments, travelling to Cardiff, Birmingham and Winchester before returning to Aldeburgh on 19 December, in time for the first performance of Britten's Third String Quartet given by the Amadeus Quartet at the Maltings. He found a letter awaiting him from IH:

> It's good to know that you've got such LOVELY people looking after you ... I hope they'll take away all the pain before it begins. And I hope that you'll sleep and SLEEP and SLEEP.[38]

---

[38] 16 December 1976; BPL.

13 'Old age – Protest against disintegration – Gradual calming down – Acceptance': 1977–84

The comforting and affectionate tone of Imogen Holst's letter to Pears just before Christmas 1976 concealed its writer's more troubled and ambivalent feelings towards Britten's life partner and muse. With the composer now dead, these feelings came quite suddenly into stark focus. In 1952 IH had quickly come to realize, once she moved to Aldeburgh, the crucial effect that Britten's personal and musical relationship with Pears had on his creativity. It was this knowledge, combined with her own feelings of protectiveness, which had caused her to be so dismayed by the tenor's behaviour during the rehearsals for *The Prince of the Pagodas* twenty years earlier. IH was never drawn personally to Pears as she had been to Britten, and she had, moreover, developed over the years a degree of mistrust in his musicianship. This had come to the fore in the early 1960s during a Bach performance at Long Melford when Britten had been obliged to intervene in a dispute between Pears and IH about the correct tempo for an aria in one of the cantatas which he was singing under her baton. William Servaes, who worked with her on Festival matters in the 1970s, recalled that she was 'hooked on the memory of her father, and on Ben – not on Peter.' Colin Matthews recalled that 'she didn't trust Peter on a musical level. She once said to me, "Peter is a philistine".'[1]

Pears's behaviour in the days surrounding Britten's final illness and death reinforced many of IH's negative feelings towards him. She was not alone in being dismayed when he chose to disappear on tour to the USA and Canada in November, leaving Britten isolated and alone, and she must have been surprised at the haste with which he returned to touring immediately after the composer's funeral. More troubling, however, was his behaviour on the day of the funeral itself, when the funeral party returned to The Red House:

> When the guests had gone ... there were a few of us left. There was Peter and Peg,[2] and Rosamund and me ... in the Library and Peter suddenly à

[1] Carpenter, *Benjamin Britten*, p. 310.
[2] Peg Hesse.

propos of nothing said, 'Slava[3] says I must conduct.' ... Just like that. On the day of the funeral. And then I said, 'You can't – you've got to have a technique. Remember that it took Ben twenty years to learn, and that in the beginning he didn't even know ... how to raise his arm for an upbeat; and we've seen him year after year get better and better, and it's taken him twenty years.' So Peter said, 'Oh well, I haven't got twenty years. Where do I begin? On the Snape Maltings Training Orchestra?' And then I went on about it, and I said 'You must realise that conducting, like singing or playing the violin, has a technique.' I said, 'You wouldn't ask me to sing.' And – he couldn't take it.[4]

Clearly IH was as upset by what she perceived as Pears's suggestion that he could become a conductor overnight as she was by the timing of his announcement.

Tensions continued to mount as IH and Pears ran a two-week Bach course at the Maltings in the spring of 1977. IH soon became exasperated by what she perceived as Pears's lack of organizing ability, his wrong-headed scholarship (he interpreted a misprint in the *Bach Gesellschaft* as an example of Bach beginning a piece on a 'howling discord') and his amateurish conducting. By the end of a 'painful' fortnight she felt 'defeated ... physically and almost spiritually', and decided then and there that if she and Pears were to maintain a personal friendship, she would have to stop working with him. Nearing her seventieth year she was also becoming exhausted by endless committee meetings, as she had done during the CEMA days, while as Managing Director of G. & I. Holst Ltd., her business life was far from slack. Consequently she decided, following the end of the 1977 Festival, to step down as an Artistic Director and also announced, significantly, that she would 'not be doing any more work for the educational courses at Snape Maltings'.[5] Professional frustrations thus set aside, she was able to sustain a mutually warm relationship with Pears until her death. She also accepted the post of Artistic Director Emeritus of the Festival while Pears in turn became a director of G. & I. Holst Ltd.

One final task that IH was happy to undertake for the Festival was to rehearse the Snape Maltings Training Orchestra, together with Cecil Aronowitz, for a concert to be conducted by André Previn. At the last moment, however, Previn became indisposed, and IH and Aronowitz stepped into the breach and shared the rostrum. She also delivered the interval talk, the text of which reveals the

3 Mstislav Rostropovich.
4 Interview with Donald Mitchell, 22 June 1977; BPL.
5 Typed memorandum, June 1977.

extent to which, soon after Britten's death, she was already exploring ways of perpetuating his legacy:

> This concert that you are listening to was the first that the Snape Maltings Training Orchestra has given during an Aldeburgh Festival. Two years before this, Cecil Aronowitz had begun coaching a group of young string players, aged 16 and upwards, at a weekend of rehearsals in the Maltings. On the Sunday afternoon they gave a performance to a very small audience; people hadn't turned up because they didn't know if the experiment was going to work. Those who did come were astonished at the exciting sound. It was the real thing, and the listeners wondered how the players had managed it in such a short time. Well, it certainly helped that many of them already knew each other, and that a fair number of them were Cecil Aronowitz's own pupils. But there was more to it than that. For these young players weren't just good soloists in their own right; they were all chamber-music players, and they listened to each other.
>
> When that first experimental performance was over I went behind the stage to thank Cecil and told him what a joy it was to hear Mozart phrased like that. He said: 'It's only what I've been learning all these years from Ben.' And that's what the Snape Maltings Training Orchestra is about.
>
> Since that first weekend the players have gone on from strength to strength, with large audiences and London concerts. Several critics have objected to the name that we've given to them. But it is a 'training' orchestra; that's the whole point.
>
> As long ago as 1953, when I'd just begun working in Aldeburgh for Benjamin Britten, he said to me: 'What you and Peter and I have got to remember is that we're going to have a music school here one day.' That was long before the Maltings had been thought of. But Britten had meant what he said, and only a few months later he invited several students to his house on the sea-front and rehearsed the Mozart G minor piano quartet with them.
>
> Britten was not a teacher; he said so himself. But throughout his working life, at every rehearsal he took, his players and singers learnt from him. The music school that he'd hoped for came to birth at the Maltings in 1973[6] with a weekend for singers directed by Peter Pears. Britten was by then an invalid, but during the next three years he was

---

[6] Actually 1972.

able to help us with his criticism and encouragement. Since his death, the Britten–Pears School of Advanced Musical Studies has become his memorial. We are building practice rooms in an unused wing of the Maltings, for until now the students have had to practise wherever they could fit themselves into an odd corner of the Concert Hall; under the stairs, in the wardrobe-room, or in the passage where the scenery is brought in. Members of the training orchestra have put up with this discomfort because of the luxury of the superb acoustic in our hall. If you are going to listen to the second half of this concert after the interval you will hear in my father's *Brook Green Suite* a very quiet pizzicato passage; while we were rehearsing it I thought: 'Can we possibly risk playing as quietly as that? Will the people at the back of the hall be able to hear?' They did hear every note, for there is magic in the way the walls and the roof respond to the music that is offered to them.

The Snape Maltings Training Orchestra is one of many things that are happening in the Britten–Pears School; there are string quartets, and madrigal groups, and rehearsals of Bach obligato arias where the singers and players can learn from listening to each other. And I'm hoping that one day students will be taught conducting at the School, so that they can discover the need for a technique. And when they've got a technique, they may perhaps be able to convey what they have learnt about rhythm from listening to Britten's recordings, where the music never sounds like one thing after another, but the rhythm and the form are always inseparable. This sense of 'wholeness' in the music is something that can't be expressed in words; it is what the players in our Training Orchestra are aiming at, and they get nearer to it in each performance.

The beginning of 1978 brought IH a welcome surprise in the discovery that she was a beneficiary of Britten's will. Long since settled into a frugality of lifestyle that eminently suited her temperament, she did not keep the cheque to herself but decided rather, as she told Pears on 7 February to 'spend it on several intelligent children, aged 10 to 13, whom I think Ben would have approved of.' Five days later she and Pears attended a memorial concert for Britten at Dartington, before she returned to Aldeburgh to dedicate her time to GH's music. Primarily this involved working with Colin Matthews on the Collected Facsimile Edition. At this stage it was hoped that this would eventually comprise a complete edition, of the major scores at least. Work was progressing well on Volume IV, for which Matthews was organizing the photography of manuscripts of the shorter orchestral works, and Volume III – containing

The Planets – of which IH was now editing proofs. Volume V was to include IH's favourite *Egdon Heath* and some other orchestral works, and Volume VI the works for band.

Meanwhile she continued to host research visits from Michael Short and others, and to oversee recording projects. Lyrita remained committed to recording her father's lesser-known works, and on 24 May she asked Matthews to tell the company that 'I DON'T think Carnival from Suite de Ballet is worth doing'; clearly her extended re-evaluation of the quality of GH's output had not compromised her critical faculties. To coincide with the production of the facsimile edition of *The Planets*, the two collaborators were also planning a new edition of the printed score: a phone call from Adrian Boult at the end of May reminded them how pertinent this task remained:

> Adrian Boult rang me at 7.30 last evening (he'd been conducting Mars & Saturn during the day for a new EMI recording!! – Jupiter & Mercury already done) in distress because the LPO full score being used had got strings *fff* at IV – (parts were all right.) I assured him the correction had been made but promised to mention it to you!

In preparing the new score she bore in mind the same principles that she had applied for many years to her editions of early music. Speaking of the proliferation of errors in the available editions, she told Christopher Headington: 'Those mistakes we've been trying our utmost to put right. The new Faber Music score [is] timed to be published simultaneously with the facsimile edition. We're just hoping that it's nearer to the real thing. Well it *is* nearer – we're hoping that it's accurate.'[7] The facsimile edition of *The Planets* was eventually issued by Faber in April 1979, with Curwen publishing IH's and Matthews's revised edition of the score soon afterwards. Adrian Boult wrote on 3 April to report that 'a wonderful parcel has come from Fabers with the lovely facsimile in it, & a long introduction which we shall read with very great interest'.

For the first time since 1949 IH attended the Aldeburgh Festival of 1978 solely as a member of the listening public. In an essay written for the programme book she expressed her relief that 'now I am no longer an Artistic Director and my Aldeburgh responsibilities have come to an end, I am looking forward to the luxury of having time to listen to the 1978 concerts.'[8] Her cutting loose from the Festival was underlined by a rebuke suffered by a new assistant, Jarrah Wickham, who recalled:

[7] Interview with Christopher Headington, 1979.
[8] IH, 'Recollections of times past'.

I had left her waiting for me to drive her home after a concert while I was busy putting up the seats, as an usher does after a performance at the Maltings. Apologizing as I did of course for keeping her waiting, she said sternly, 'Dear, when you work for me, you work for no-one else as well!'[9]

IH's gradual unburdening of her administrative responsibilities was to continue into 1979, as her colleagues at G. & I. Holst tried to persuade her to concentrate on the 'really important' tasks of writing and editing, and to leave them to handle on her behalf the 'endless requests from record companies and tortuous arguments about copyright'.[10] To some extent she was by now a victim of her own success, in that GH's music had become so ingrained in the public's consciousness that it was being used for a huge range of often unauthorized purposes. Most notorious was an electronic version of *The Planets* by Tomita, which IH had to work hard to prevent being distributed in the UK. At Colin Matthews's suggestion she now agreed to become President of the Company, with Matthews himself stepping into the role of Managing Director, allowing IH to 'concentrate exclusively' on her more important work.

On 28 April 1979 the Queen Mother visited Snape to open the new buildings of the Britten–Pears School. IH was able to show the royal guest round the new library, now stocked with the rich collection of books and music that she had donated. The previous December she had prepared a press release for John Trew of the Aldeburgh Festival office in which she set out her vision of the Library:

The Gustav Holst Library will be a working library for the use of the students. It is being called after him in gratitude for his music and for his teaching. Some of the volumes of music in it will be those that he used with his own pupils.

The establishment of the Holst Library was for IH a further important stage in a process of letting go. Never particularly enamoured of worldly possessions, she had now discovered a joyous freedom in giving them up. She set out her philosophy of ageing in an essay entitled 'Advantages of Being Seventy' for the Aldeburgh Festival programme book of 1980:

'It is best as one grows older to strip oneself of possessions' says Lolly Willowes in Sylvia Townsend Warner's novel. I always used to think this

---

[9] Wake-Walker, *Time and Concord*, p. 192.
[10] Letter from Colin Matthews to IH, February 1979.

was a sign of Lolly's generosity, but now I know by experience that it was a proof of her practical self-interest. During the last two years I have discovered the advantage of giving away most of my books and music to the Maltings library, for it has put an end to my anxieties about dust or condensation or the occasional unexplained disappearance of a volume now that the things are being catalogued and repaired under the expert guidance of Martin Thacker.

Shedding responsibilities is not nearly as difficult as it is made out to be. Even having to give up conducting has its advantages, for it means that there is time to listen to some of the other conductors. And giving up organising is undoubtedly a blessing. Among other benefits it cures the occupational fallacy of believing that if one doesn't do the job one-self it probably won't be right. For many years I have insisted on mak-ing my own decisions about my father's unpublished manuscripts and have edited them myself for future performance. But now that Colin Matthews is Managing Director of G. & I. Holst Ltd I have learnt the advantage of leaving a good deal of the hard work to him. And when we do happen to disagree about a technical detail, our arguments are enjoy-able as well as useful.

One of the unexpected benefits of being over seventy is the delight-ful freedom from having a guilty conscience. No effort is needed to get rid of it; it just goes away of its own accord. Other benefits include the joy of never again having to travel on the London Underground during the rush hour and the relief of not having to write out orchestral parts until three in the morning so as to finish them for a 10 am rehearsal. In fact, there is no more need to be in a perpetual hurry in order to get through the day. This is such an immense advantage that even after several years' experience of being in the seventies I'm still finding it a miracle. It makes up for no longer being able to run or skip or leap. And if one lives in Aldeburgh there are advantages in walking at an *Andante piacevole* speed, for it leaves time to look at the changing colours of a sunset or at the pattern of bare branches of a tree or the contrapuntal circling of the gulls as they fly above Crag Path.

Not being in a hurry means that there is time to listen to one's favour-ite composers and performers on Radio 3. Until fairly recently I had to limit my listening to whatever music happened to be connected with my work, but now I enjoy the luxury of sitting at the breakfast table and hearing a Haydn quartet or a Shostakovich symphony. (It is true, alas, that the *very* lowest level of a pianissimo passage for pizzicato double basses has a distressing way of becoming inaudible, but even this is not an irreparable loss, for it is possible to follow the score while listening and to imagine the sound of the few missing notes.)

Another advantage is being able to make time for non-professional occupations such as learning elementary arithmetic or memorising Shakespeare sonnets or beginning Russian grammar. The list of possible benefits could stretch beyond the number of words allowed me by the editor of the programme book. I must, however, make room to include the blessing of not having to go on buying new clothes when the old ones are not only tougher but are also much more beautiful. (For special occasions in the Directors' box at the Maltings I'm still wearing the wool-embroidered evening jacket I bought for £5 in South Kensington in 1928 on my way to a lesson at the Royal College of Music.)

And the greatest blessing of all is *still* having too much to do.

Her closest working colleague at this time, Colin Matthews, later set down his memories of IH in this autumnal phase of her life:

How can one begin to describe Imogen Holst to anyone who never met her or heard her voice? The voice first, perhaps, measured, modulated and careful, beautifully enunciated, a surprisingly deep laugh for such a bird-like figure contrasting with a short, sharp and quintessential 'ha!' of amusement … Her appearance: bird-like in a way, but extraordinarily graceful, no sharp movements … Colours: soft yellow ochres, browns and olive greens predominated in her clothing and her surroundings – she did not like bright colours, and had a loathing of a particular shade of purple which publishers inevitably seemed to choose for covers of books and scores (a score of *The Planets* in that uniform was kept permanently wrapped in brown paper). And as with colours, so, of course, with noise: the roar of a London street could cause her physical pain.

Listening to music with her was a lesson in concentration – intensity radiated from her, and her displeasure at poor musicianship could be alarming to see … She combined great patience with an uncompromising attitude to work. She could not tolerate incompetence (she would quote her father: 'there is no room in music for the second-rate'), and could be very hard on those who did not measure up to her standards. But she could also be far too unassuming in fields where she felt (often wrongly) that others knew better than her. She was essentially one who inspired, who by her beliefs and actions set a standard for others to follow.[11]

IH's total concentration when listening to music, so often throughout her life viewed as eccentric or comical by casual observers, put her in touch with an interior life of which she seldom spoke or wrote; expressive also of her independent spirit, it could be traced back to her years as a child at the Froebel Institute, when she would spend her free time 'usually play[ing] some quiet game alone'.

For the 1980 festival IH once more brought herself out of retirement, to help devise a gala concert to celebrate the seventieth birthday of Peter Pears. For this she assembled, from the music of Tchaikovsky, Rubinstein, Bach, Britten and Purcell, the aptly titled *A Greeting*, which was performed on 20 June 1980 by the singers Marie McLaughlin, Heather Harper and Sarah Walker, with Murray Perahia at the piano. The process of assembling this score seems to have jolted her creative mind, and she experienced over the next four years a late flowering as a composer. This began with occasional pieces for friends. *About Ship*, a piano-duet arrangement of a traditional English dance, was written at Christmas 1981 for the retirement of William Servaes, General Manager of the Aldeburgh Festival; IH was aware as always of the limitations of her intended performers, and the technically challenged dedicatee only had to play a single repeated note. *Song for a Well-Loved Librarian* was composed the following August for another retirement, that of the first Librarian of the Britten–Pears Library, Fred Ferry. More significantly she reapplied herself for the first time in many years to the rigours of chamber music, and in the first half of 1982 wrote a String Quintet, in response to a request from the cellist Steven Isserlis for a work for the Cricklade Festival. His choice of IH reflected his fondness for her earlier work for solo cello *The Fall of the Leaf*, which he had learnt at Aldeburgh in 1977 and continued to perform regularly ever since. The Quintet was first performed on 2 October 1982 at St Sampson's Church, Cricklade, by the Endellion String Quartet, with Isserlis playing the second cello. In her note on the piece IH recalled that 'in their invitation they mentioned that they wanted a piece to mirror some of the characteristics of the River Thames. I was glad to agree to this request because the music festivals I have worked for have always had local roots'.

To IH's great delight, the String Quintet was accepted for publication by Faber Music in recognition of her seventy-fifth birthday, and Colin Matthews

---

[11] Matthews, unpublished typescript, 1984.

and Howard Skempton offered to help see the work through the press. On 24 July 1983 she wrote to Matthews:

> I got back to Aldeburgh feeling a lot better after my holiday, but when I'd read your approval of my 5tet I felt <u>still</u> better!! Bless you. And thank you and Howard for checking the parts; will you please both make out an enormous bill at Union rates for this, & send it to me so that Helen can write Company cheques for you both (because the Company get PRS fees etc for it.)

On seeing the proofs of the printed score she is reported to have commented to friends 'I feel like a *real* composer!'

Despite this flurry of compositional activity, GH's music was not forgotten, and IH, with Colin Matthews, was now preparing an edition of *The Mystic Trumpeter*, a 'scena' for soprano and orchestra which her father had composed in 1904. He had thought well enough of the piece to revise it in 1912, but it had never been published. IH herself had many misgivings about its quality, but had allowed the piece to be recorded by Lyrita. The recording was broadcast by the BBC on 9 September 1983 in their 'Music for Pleasure' programme on Radio 3. The next day IH wrote to Matthews:

> I thought the Mystic Tpt. sounded all right, but alas the homing USA planes chewed the VHF into small bits on several occasions. I'm still unable to listen to the work impartially, but this is MY FAULT and no-one else's. I thought Sheila A [Armstrong] was absolutely MAGNIFICENT.
>
> Tony F-G [Friese-Greene] rang me yesterday morning to ask about details of its 1st performance, so I dictated (slowly!) to him out of the Thematic Catalogue. I mentioned that you had been worried (on behalf of G & I Holst) that the 1st broadcast was not on 'Stereo Release' or 'New Records' and he said that 'another producer' (he didn't say who) was interested in putting out one of the other works on this record & I said I'd pass this 'information' on to you. He also said that the numbers of listeners to Mainly for Pleasure was now very large, and I rudely said that I'd learnt ½ a century ago not to be influenced by numbers, because most of the so-called listeners were attending to something else at the time, & that the thing that mattered to me (& to G & I Holst) was the quality of the concentrated listening. He then said that [Richard] Itter was delighted that the recording was going on the air so soon, and I was silent because there was no appropriate comment to make!

> I'll be thinking of you this evening at David [Atherton]'s concert. (I'm
> still up-and-down in my recovery, and am leaving decisions about work
> to my doctor when I see him next Thursday.)

Despite the undoubted benefits it had afforded her lifetime campaign to promote her father's works, IH remained ambivalent about the mass-media dissemination of music: to her, casual listening was as hard to tolerate as a per-
functory performance or lazy scholarship.

For the past few years IH had suffered from angina, and towards the end of
1983 was increasingly concerned about her health. Nevertheless she continued to plan ahead, and on 28 November she accepted an invitation from Ian
Chance of Wingfield College to be Guest of Honour at a concert the following
June which was to feature her new String Quintet and *The Fall of the Leaf*. But
at the same time, in a further gesture of letting go, she decided to donate her
Holst manuscripts to the Holst Foundation, and to pass all her Britten materials to the Britten–Pears Library.

Following the success of the Quintet she was back in demand as a composer.
She began 1984 with no fewer than four commissions to fulfil. The previous
autumn she had begun work on *Homage to William Morris*, commissioned
by the William Morris Society to commemorate the 150th anniversary of the
designer's birth. IH was invited to compose this work partly because it was
known that her father had held William Morris in high regard. Her own interest stemmed from childhood when GH, during their walks along the Thames
towpath, would point out Morris's home, Kelmscott House. Throughout her
life she had remained sympathetic to his egalitarian principles, which had
informed her own view of music education and had also been central to the
Elmhirsts' philosophy at Dartington. Choosing texts from Morris's lectures,
she completed the work – for the distinctive combination of bass voice and
string bass – speedily, and it was first performed on 24 March 1984, soon after
her death, by Peter Rose and Mary Scully at the Institute of Contemporary
Arts, London. In the programme note, the Society paid fulsome tribute to the
composer: 'The willingness with which she responded to [our] invitation to
compose a new work ... the advice and encouragement she gave us in our first
venture in promoting new music, her help with practical arrangements for the
concert; and her generosity in presenting [the manuscript] to the society; these
are all characteristic of her, and they place us deeply in her debt'.

Having handed over one commission IH embarked immediately on the next,
a Sextet for recorders requested by Evelyn Nallen, vice-president of the Guildford branch of the Society of Recorder Players. IH wrote a programme note

for the first performance (which was to take place on 12 May), from which it is clear that she intended the work to represent an affectionate, and no doubt valedictory, musical reminiscence of her involvement with the recorder over the entire course of her long professional life:

> The last [movement], Salutation, is a brief gesture of gratitude to some of the recorder players who have been my friends, beginning with Miles Tomalin, whose playing first converted me to the recorder as a 'real' instrument; he is represented by a Purcell hornpipe. The second tune, Nonsuch, is a Thankyou to the recorder players in my amateur orchestra at Cecil Sharp House half a century ago; they taught me to try and make the sound of music convey the feel of the dance. The third tune is a jig from Britten's *Gloriana* which he allowed me to transcribe for the series of recorder pieces we were editing together. He used to enjoy playing recorder trios during his free evenings at Aldeburgh, and he was president of the Society of Recorder Players from 1959 until his death in 1976.

The recorder also featured in the next commission that IH undertook, a Recorder Concerto intended for the 1984 Cricklade Festival. At the same time she began work on a Duo for Violin and Cello, requested by her champion Steven Isserlis for the Deal Festival. For the last movement of this piece she sketched out a programme; the work was to end with a portrayal of old age, passing from a 'Protest against disintegration' through a 'Gradual calming down' to end in 'Acceptance'.

On 3 February IH gave an unscripted interview to Stephen Wilkinson of BBC Manchester. A week later she wrote Colin Matthews a characteristic letter displaying her continued interest in the minutiae of the Aldeburgh Festival and her generosity towards other musicians:

> I'm sending you a strictly confidential copy of the Aldeburgh Festival proof for their brochure. Please see my enclosed letter to Ken Baird, and IF any detail of the 'in association' etc is wrong, please let him know.
>
> I'd like to contribute personally (anonymously) to the fees of my two performers for the William Morris programme on June 19 afternoon. BUT what about Late Night II? (Ought this to be Holst Foundation??)

The late-night concert was to feature IH's String Quintet and her father's early String Trio in G minor. Through the rest of the month she worked on another treasured project, a new revision of *The Music of Gustav Holst*, requested by Oxford University Press. Unlike the second edition of 1968, for which IH had been unable to make the changes that she felt were necessary, she had been allowed this time to contribute an entirely new set of chapters under the heading 'Holst's Music Reconsidered'. Dedicating these to Colin Matthews, she used essays on 'The need for thinking again' and more practical topics (covering problems of editing, notation and performance) to explore the general critical re-evaluation of GH that her own work had prompted, exemplified in John Warrack's contention that 'Holst seems to go on getting more and more modern'. She still regarded her life's work on GH's music as unfinished, and ended her comments with the acknowledgement that 'the reconsidering is still going on all the time'.[12]

Work on the Collected Facsimile Edition, in contrast, had ceased. The project had proved to be very expensive, and sales had failed to recuperate the costs of production, so that after Volume IV, IH, with typical realism, drew a line under this particular ambition. She was continuing to work on a study of Henry Purcell for the Faber Great Composers Series, but probably feared that she would never complete it, as she discussed with Matthews the possibility of handing it over to someone else.

By now, it was clear to her friends that her health was deteriorating rapidly. She tired more quickly than before, and it took longer each morning for her to be ready for the day ahead. Helen Lilley recalled that on the morning of Friday 9 March:

> she telephoned to ask if I could go round earlier than we had arranged, which I did. Arrving at about 9.30, I found her still in bed, propped up with pillows, and she told me that she had already telephoned the surgery. Dr Ian Tait arrived almost at once, and after being with her for a short time, told me that it would be better for IH to be in the local hospital, and he went straight off to arrange this.
>
> She said that she was thirsty so I fetched some water and stayed by the bed to help her with the cup. She smiled and thanked me in the usual Imo way. Everything was still. Her head drooped gently sideways and I felt she had slipped away, absolutely peacefully, and without fuss. I was so glad that she had not been alone.[13]

IH had died of a heart attack. Rosamund Strode was in Norwich when she heard the news and rushed back to help Helen Lilley with arrangements. The funeral was organized for 14 March. IH was buried in Aldeburgh churchyard,

---

[12] IH, *The Music of Gustav Holst*, 3rd edn, p. 158.
[13] Helen Lilley, unpublished typescript, 2006.

in a plot adjacent to Benjamin Britten's. Peter Pears, who had been in the USA on the day she died, read a passage from GH's translation of *The Hymn of Jesus*, and the final chorale from Bach's *St John Passion* was played as the church slowly emptied. After most of the mourners had retired, the handful left behind, reluctant to move, sang a spontaneous valediction: the five-part *Sanctus* by Clemens non Papa, a canon that IH had taught to many gatherings. She had introduced it to Britten in 1953 and later included it in *Singing for Pleasure*. The round was one of IH's many 'useful' pieces, designed to be able to be sung in any circumstances by rote and by singers with no access to the printed music; its performance at her graveside provided a final, moving exposition of the principles of music-making that she had championed throughout her life.

Following IH's death the Aldeburgh Festival programme book included a two-page selection of the many reminiscences and tributes that Rosamund Strode and her colleagues had received. It was left to John Thomson in his obituary in the journal *Early Music*, however, to sum up the unique presence that IH had brought to Aldeburgh, and to define the empty, and unfillable, space that she had left:

> Her presence will always be felt in Aldeburgh Parish Church, especially at night, when with the usually forlorn North Sea in a groundbass in the background, the lights in the church throwing shadows against the white walls, the dark woodwork and the stained glass, IH would appear, stride to the rostrum purposefully, quickly acknowledge applause, and turn to the matter in hand, to bring iridescently to life facets of that tradition to which her own life had been dedicated and which she presented as a continuing source of strength and wonder.[14]

14 Thomson, 'Imogen Holst'.

29   *top* With the Purcell Singers at Blythburgh Church, 19 June 1956.
Pears and Britten stand to the left; Rosamund Strode is on the far right, in the front row.

30   *bottom left* At a performance of *Noye's Fludde*, late 1950s.

31   *bottom right* Talking to a policeman at Blythburgh, Aldeburgh Festival, 1962

32 Manuscript of the vocal score of the semi-chorus 'Farewell to Spring,'
no. 6 from *The Sun's Journey* (1965)

33 *top* With Arthur Caton, Thaxted, 1966

34 *bottom left* Rehearsing for the inaugural concert of the Aldeburgh Festival,
June 1967, to celebrate the opening of the Snape Maltings Concert Hall

35 *bottom right* With the percussionist James Blades at the Aldeburgh Festival, 1968,
at the first performance of Britten's *The Prodigal Son* on 10 June

36 *top left* Outside Blythburgh Church at a concert of 'Voices and Percussion' June 1972.

37–9 *top right, bottom left, bottom right* At 9 Church Walk, 17 October 1972

40 *top* At the 'Notes & Embellishments' Exhibition, Snape Maltings, June 1975

41 *bottom* With Robert Tear and Philip Ledger on Aldeburgh beach, June 1975

42 *left* IH's house at 9 Church Walk, Aldeburgh

43 *below* Conducting the Band and Trumpeters of the Royal Military School of Music (Kneller Hall) in an open-air 'Concert with Fireworks' at Framlingham Castle, 22 June 1975

44 *left* With Steven Isserlis and the score of *The Fall of the Leaf*. Isserlis played the piece on 17 June 1977 in an 'anniversary' concert to celebrate IH's 70th birthday

45 *below* With Janet Baker, Snape, 1977. Baker had returned to repeat her acclaimed interpretation of Britten's *Phaedra* in the first festival since the composer's death

46 In discussion with Cecil Aronowitz, Snape, 15 June 1977. The two shared the conducting of an orchestral concert that night after André Previn became indisposed

47 *top left* In Aldeburgh Church, listening to a quartet led by Malcolm Layfield
rehearsing for a performance of Haydn's Quartet op. 76 no. 1, 14 June 1978

48 *top right* At Church Walk, 9 November 1978

49 *bottom* With Peter Pears and HRH Queen Elizabeth the Queen Mother
at the opening of the Britten-Pears School building, 28 April 1979

Preparing 'A Greeting' for the concert in honour of Peter Pears's 70th birthday, Snape Maltings, 22 June 1980

50 *left* With the producer Colin Graham, who was to introduce the concert

51 *below* With the performers Sarah Walker, Marie McLaughlin, Heather Harper and Murray Perahia

52 *top* With Colin Matthews, Aldeburgh Festival, 1981

53 *bottom* Mourners at IH's funeral, Aldeburgh Parish Church, 14 March 1984

Part V ~
The Music of Imogen Holst

CHRISTOPHER TINKER

14 'A *real* composer': an introduction to Imogen Holst's musical style

A first glance at the size of the catalogue that follows reveals the perhaps surprising amount of music that IH composed, edited and arranged through her career. Altogether this comprises a notable achievement to add to the enormous contribution she made to British musical life in so many other spheres.

IH's career as a composer began auspiciously. She entered the RCM in 1926, and won an open scholarship for composition in 1927, followed by the Cobbett Prize in 1928 and an Octavia travelling scholarship in 1929. For the next few years she was viewed as one of a number of rising women composers in England, and had works performed and broadcast alongside those of Elisabeth Lutyens and Elizabeth Maconchy, among others. But once she had joined the staff of the EFDSS and begun work as a school music teacher, her creative activity moved into the sphere of arrangements, principally of folk dance and song, either for educational purposes or for the EFDSS. Although her list of compositions began to grow again in the following decade (during which she founded and directed the music department at Dartington), the quantity and quality of her work remained little recognized. When she began work for Britten in 1952 her own compositional activity ceased, and it was not until 1962 that a remarkable burst of creative energy signalled a return to composition that was to result in a late flowering of nearly thirty works before her death in 1984.

Many of IH's unpublished compositions and arrangements have lain dormant since their early performances, but study of them reveals a unique and personal style that merits further investigation by scholars and performers alike. Her style was influenced by a number of factors, including her natural and inescapable relationship with the English musical establishment, the strong shadow cast by her father's music during her formative years as a composer, the affinity she felt towards folksong, and the correlation between her compositions and other musical activities. As a result of these varied influences, her development followed a very different path from that of contemporaries such as Maconchy and Lutyens. Whereas Maconchy's technical processes might be matched with those of Bartók, and Lutyens's to her own brand of serialism,

IH's music represents much more a twentieth-century recasting of older traditions, not as a neo-classicist but through an historic awareness which had been
initiated by her father. Early on, the style of many of her student works was
touched with a soft Romanticism, though later, during the 1940s, she adopted
a starker approach. European advances did not infiltrate this decidedly English mind to any substantial degree, her preoccupation with English music of
the sixteenth and seventeenth centuries and with folksong resulting in a linear
style and a modal outlook. Similarly, her later advances towards dissonance
arose not from any great familiarity with Continental models, but simply from
her own peculiarly independent approach to melodic and harmonic intervals.

Educational music and music for amateurs

To modern audiences IH is undoubtedly best remembered for her folksong
arrangements. She wrote and arranged for a wide range of ensembles, including bamboo pipes, piano, string classes and of course voices – 'useful music', as
she would have put it. The demand for music for pipes led her to make arrangements of repertoire ranging from country dance tunes from Playford's *Dancing
Master*, to the music of Morley, Purcell, Lawes, Weelkes and Gustav Holst, all
of which was designed to extend the musical experience of novices as well as
being suitable for its primary function. Similarly, in the piano pieces, which
resulted from her teaching during the 1930s, she approached matters of fingering and independence of hands in two lovely volumes of simple compositions,
along with some arrangements. Ex. 1 is taken from 'On the Lake', the first of *Six
Pictures from Finland* (1934).

IH also arranged for larger ensembles, by all accounts undertaking a great
deal of such work, though little survives. She arranged not only traditional
country dance tunes for brass and military bands, but also pieces for a variety

Ex. 1

of ensembles designed to lead country dancing by members of the EFDSS. Indeed, some public recognition for her endeavours in this field resulted from the occasional BBC broadcast of concerts and festivals promoted by the EFDSS, and also from the 78s of her arrangements made for the Gramophone Company in 1934.

The small amount of material for string classes was composed during IH's years at Dartington when she had Sybil Eaton on her staff. Characteristic in their style and intent are the *Six Canons for Violin Classes* which appeared in 1946, and for which a note in the front of the published score states that 'the least experienced players will be able to take an easy part in contrapuntal music that is not confined to the familiar tonic and dominant seventh ...' Suitable for violinists of varying abilities, even the simplest line has something of interest (ex. 2).

The corpus of IH's own educational music from her Dartington years is supplemented by books of compositions written by students of her composition classes, which survive in the library there. They include music for recorder, cello classes, three-part SSA choir and canons.

Following her visit to India in 1951, when she explored in depth its indigenous folk music, a variety of arrangements based on Indian tunes might have been expected to follow; in fact she produced just one such collection, the *Ten Indian Folk Tunes* for recorder in 1953. This instrument was to feature heavily within her activities as an arranger over the next decade, primarily through her work on the series 'Music for Recorders', a collaboration with Benjamin Britten, published by Boosey & Hawkes. Although this was a new venture for the publishers, the combination of Britten, an enthusiastic player, and IH, with her extensive teaching experience, resulted in a highly successful venture. Boosey's also published IH's *Dolmetsch Descant Recorder Book* in 1957, of which Carl Dolmetsch recalled: 'Her book was written at the instigation of Boosey & Hawkes, who were marketing Dolmetsch plastic recorders at that time. They wanted to tie in Imogen's book with our recorders as a selling factor for both.'

The last twenty years of IH's compositional career were characterized by her readiness to accept commissions and requests from amateur groups, often for suites of dance movements and sometimes for the large forces of an orchestral society or brass band. She always worked happily with, and wrote sympathetically for, such amateur groups, but perhaps not surprisingly did not often rise to the heights of her creative abilities in these comparatively unsophisticated works. In the final analysis, her abilities in this field should not be judged upon the music itself, but upon the suitability of the music for the occasion, by which criterion she always succeeded admirably. Nevertheless, perhaps IH's greatest

Ex. 2

achievement in her non-vocal 'useful music' was her ability, on occasion, to transform everyday materials into something of substance. Certain pieces stand out: from her educational music, the *Four Easy Pieces for Viola* (1935) with the beautiful piano accompaniment (reminiscent of her father) to the viola's open strings; and from the music for amateur orchestra, the *Variations on 'Loth to Depart'* (1963). This is a set of variations for string quartet and two string orchestras which caters for a professional string quartet and two amateur orchestras, where the second orchestra is intended for less experienced players.

Inspired by the success of her recently published instrumental arrangements in the early 1930s, IH turned next to choral arrangement, and particularly to the combination of SSA. Judging by the amount of time she spent on such arrangements over the next twenty-five years, either her appetite for choral arrangements was insatiable or the offers from publishers too generous to refuse; certainly many of these arrangements, largely of popular folksongs, appeared in print. Stylistically, her approach is simple, never self-indulgent, resulting in a plain and natural treatment of the original modal material (Dorian being the most common in arrangements, and Phrygian in compositions). The arrangements retain the strophic or strophic variation forms of their originals, and thus provide a contrast with her own vocal and choral compositions which avoid strophic form and are usually through-composed, following the texts which were of such importance to her. Many of the compositions and arrangements, though currently out of fashion, remain excellent material for choirs, in particular those for female voices for whom she wrote with a rare originality. Ex. 3, from *The Virgin Unspotted* (1935), is typical.

Ex. 3

Further stylistic hallmarks include oblique motion away from and back to the unison, the tonal centre E, the interval of the second, and some notable rhythmic invention. Taken together, these features lead to an unmistakeable individuality. The rhythmic delay in ex. 4, from 'There was an old woman lived in Athlone', one of the *Twenty Traditional British Folksongs* (1967) is more a trait of composition than arrangement, here leading to a natural *ritardando* in the closing bars of a lively song – there is some humour here too.

Ex. 4

IH's style here is markedly more linear in approach than much of the heavy, chordal work prevailing in England at the time. Yet more adventurous is *Gypsy Davy* (1970), written for Russell Burgess's Wandsworth School Choir, which features changes of time signature, difficult intervals, arresting harmonies and unpredictable dynamic contrasts coming together to sustain fever pitch. This free arrangement has a more potent compositional element than is customary within the arrangements. IH allows herself imaginative scope in the chorus 'Rattle-Tum a Gypsen Davy', developing the original material (as set out in ex. 5a) with great resourcefulness (ex. 5b).

Ex.5a

Choral works

A full measure of IH's worth as a musician can only be understood through a study of the music she wrote for professional choirs and ensembles, a corpus of work that embodies the core of her musical personality. Within this category there are only about thirty titles, choral and instrumental, but these scores are far removed from the folksong arrangements and suites for amateur ensembles; within them can be found the best qualities of her work as an original composer. Through her student works she developed a warm and melodious style, which can still be discerned as late as 1940 in her setting of John Donne's 'In what torn ship so ever I embarke' (ex. 6).

Through the 1940s IH's musical style becomes increasingly stark, however, a trend that is perceptible in an expanded musical vocabulary, notable for its harmonic economy, the preference for quartal as opposed to triadic chording, and the pursuit of semitonal dissonance which can be associated with the initial semitone of the Phrygian mode. The texts she chose to set, always high in literary quality, seem to have encouraged this developing musical style. The settings from the 1940s are rarely tuneful, perhaps in reaction to the simple tunefulness of the folksong arrangements with which she worked so frequently. Melody tends to be fragmented, although imitative passages successfully build the texture. Rhythm, used discreetly, plays a significant role, and changes of time signature often throw the beat to follow the text. The *Three Psalms* (1943) for mixed chorus and string orchestra make use of a variety of *ostinati*, secundal and quartal dissonance, and much conjunct movement, especially when approaching dissonance which might otherwise be difficult for singers to pitch. In the setting of Psalm 56 the deployment of a seven-beat *ostinato* within a

Ex.5b

3/4 time signature is particularly effective. The string harmonization above the bass is limited to four two-part chords which are used freely to create maximum harmonic tension; ex. 7 is from the introduction.

Ex. 6

Ex. 7

Although this work is important within the framework of IH's musical growth, its overall shape is damaged by insufficient contrast of pace. In comparison, the *Four Songs from Tottel's Miscellany* (1944) for soprano and piano sparkle throughout both vocally and pianistically. The piano was IH's own instrument, and it is good to see her exploring its potential in a more demanding context than was possible in the educational music of the previous decade and a half. The work remains unpublished, but a few published titles for female voices followed, including the extended cantata *The Sun's Journey* (1965) for female

Ex. 8

voices and orchestra. This displays a curious mixture of style: more demanding music for soloists and semi-chorus set against a number of rounds and canons for chorus, devices she had always used as a choir trainer. But it is not until 1972 that we arrive at perhaps the most testing of all her choral works, *Hallo my Fancy*, a setting of poetry by William Cleland, written for the Purcell Consort of Voices. IH uses her own personal scales in this score, one for each verse, and harmonies develop naturally from a directional pull (contrary motion) into added-note chords built on fourths. Clusters which result from this linear style retain tension until a final resolution, usually to the unison (a common trait). Ex. 8 is taken from verse 1; note the countertenor melody based on a locrian F♯ scale and the harmonies which surround it.

The last of IH's vocal compositions to be published was the *Homage to William Morris*, written for the curious combination of bass voice and string bass. In ex. 9 an appogiaturic use of the minor second is often employed, the resulting dissonance used to add strength to the musical articulation of the text.

Ex. 9

Chamber works

Chamber music represents a small but significant element in the portfolio of IH's compositions. Her works in this idiom encompass both familiar ensembles such as string trio and quartet, and some less usual combinations, such as flute, viola and bassoon. The viola has a strong representation, with a solo suite and a duo with piano, and the recorder also features prominently, with two trios in 1943. Most of these works are quite short, a factor which might stand in the way of more frequent performance; indeed, one critic described the String Trio no. 2 after its first performance as 'tantalizingly short' and 'not really substantial enough to hold its own in a programme of normally proportioned works' (*The Times*, 25 June 1963).

The fingerprints of IH's style, already noted in her choral works, became clearer and more personal during the 1940s, and can all be found in her mature chamber music. There are three principal elements, all of them closely linked: the use of modes and other scales, often juxtaposed in conflict; the significance of the interval of a second; and the establishment of tonal centre (very often E) rather than key. Experiments with scale patterns may be discerned in her first (student) period, the whole-tone scale appearing, for example, in the

Suite for solo viola (1930), and mode-based movements occurring elsewhere. But if some of the earlier works share that Aeolian pastoralism so personal to Vaughan Williams and others, IH soon began to experiment with formulating scales of her own. She confined herself firstly to six notes of a mode, omitting either the sixth or seventh of the original seven-note version. The modal colouring of such patterns soon decreased, with intervals of the second and fourth effecting a growing dissonance. Eight-note scales which included both the major and minor third became the source of a number of passages, the scale in ex. 10 providing the basis for the *Theme and Variations* for solo violin (1943).

Ex. 10

In ex. 11, taken from the String Trio of 1944, two scales form the basis of the passage, E major in the cello and a Lydian C in the viola.

Ex. 11

A similar juxtaposition is found in the String Quartet no. 1 (1946), and this conflict extends to polymodality, the earliest example being from the *Serenade* (1943). Later on the *Duo* for viola and piano (1968) provides a good example of a more exploratory use of scales. The eight-note synthetic scale in ex. 12 provides the basis, with transpositions and inversions, for the entire first movement.

Ex. 12

The second movement makes use of a six-note scale throughout, both instruments strictly adhering to it without transpositions. The last movement adopts a twelve-note technique which is used in free style. Towards the end, a descending scale reminiscent of music from both the previous movements is heard once more, this time in an eleven-note form, the twelfth note (E) added by the piano just before the conclusion of the work (ex. 13).

Ex. 13

Along with her original use of these scales, IH tended, as in her choral out-put, towards a linear rather than chordal style. In ex. 14, taken from the first movement of the String Quartet no. 1, the contrapuntal approach largely over-rides harmonic considerations. The interval of the minor second at the head of this imitative passage becomes increasingly important, as does the tritone

Ex. 14

encompassing the second to fifth notes of the scale (F to B). Combined with a further semitone (a C after the B), there emerges a harmonic structure which IH used both throughout this quartet and elsewhere in her string music (ex.15); it occurs powerfully at the very beginning of the work (ex. 16).

Ex. 15

Ex. 16

The prominent use of fourths in ex. 15 is another distinguishing fingerprint; the *Theme and Variations* for solo violin (1943) provides another instance, with the falling fourths of the theme forming an *ostinato* that underpins the first variation (ex. 17):

Ex. 17

In the music for strings the two most commonly found tonal centres are E for the rollicking *scherzi* reminiscent of GH (indeed, the Phrygian chill in this context is one influence of her father that never left her), and a deep and resounding C which is favoured in the broader movements, exploiting of course the lowest open strings of the cello and viola. It is this rich resonance that characterizes the opening of the String Quintet (1982) (ex. 18).

This final published chamber work stands as the culmination of a compositional achievement which undoubtedly merits more attention that it has so far received; most of the works discussed here deserve to be heard and played, but at present many have only received a single performance. Composition was the area in which IH excelled as a student, and though her life was to take on many tasks essential to the vitality of the English musical scene in the mid-twentieth century, her talent for composition never left her, and indeed reached its fruition in the works of her last years. She spoke little of it, but was heard to remark on the publication of her String Quintet: 'Ah! I feel like a *real* composer!'

Ex. 18

Catalogue of Imogen Holst's works

CHRISTOPHER TINKER & ROSAMUND STRODE
revised and updated by CHRISTOPHER GROGAN

Introduction

This catalogue sets out to list chronologically IH's musical output in all its forms. So much of her creative activity involved an element of original work – whether through arrangement, realization or editing – that it has seemed appropriate to deal with all her works together; where desired, the index of works can be used to isolate IH's entirely 'original' compositions from her arrangements and editions. The exceptions to the single chronological sequence relate to the editorial and arranging work that she performed for the two composers to whom she dedicated most of her creative energies – Benjamin Britten and Gustav Holst. The piano and vocal scores that she prepared for Britten's works from 1953 through to 1964 are listed separately as are her editions and arrangements of her father's compositions.

It should be said at the outset that because of the nature of IH's music-making, and in particular her attitude to music as something to be 'useful', this catalogue can have no pretensions to be complete. IH habitually made editions and arrangements of music to suit the frequently amateur and *ad hoc* performing forces assembled for a single event, not to mention the transcriptions she made of medieval and Renaissance music for the Purcell Singers. As she was in no sense a hoarder, much of this work will have been dispersed or even destroyed, perhaps irretrievably, although it is hoped that the publication of this catalogue may in itself help to bring lost items to light. The editors will certainly be very pleased to hear from any readers with additions and emendations.

The catalogue is divided into three main sections:

A Compositions, arrangements and editions
B Editions of music by Gustav Holst
C Vocal and piano scores of music by Benjamin Britten

followed by two indexes:

D Index of first lines and titles
E Index of names

The order of the catalogue is as chronological as has proved possible, given the level of uncertainty surrounding the composition of much of IH's work. She abandoned the use of opus numbers while still a teenager, after her 'op. 4', and the dating of many works has had to be based on stylistic and contextual evidence. In addition, many of her works and collections were assembled over a number of years. For each year, therefore, the following order has been adopted, following the principle of moving from the general to the specific:

1 Works begun in a known year spanning a number of years
2 Works conjecturally assigned to the year (dates in square brackets, with a circa designation), ordered alphabetically
3 Works known to have been written in that year, ordered alphabetically
4 Works known to have been completed on a certain date within the year, ordered by date.

This order has been overridden, however, both at the beginning and the end of the sequence. At the beginning IH's use of opus numbers gives a clear reading of the chronology; at the end the final two entries comprise works that she left incomplete. In the sections relating to her work on the music of Gustav Holst and Benjamin Britten, the chronological arrangement is by date of publication (or first performance for unpublished works).

Details of **manuscript holdings** are given where known. They are, as might be expected, usually in IH's hand, but copyists are identified wherever possible. Lost manuscripts, of which there are many, are listed as 'Whereabouts unknown', in the hope they may yet reappear. **First performance** details are given when they have been traceable; press reports are mostly confined to those in the national press and readily available music periodicals. **Durations** are inevitably approximate, given the paucity of performances of IH's works, and have only been recorded in the case of works that last for 5 or more minutes to assist performers in their choice of repertoire. Other commentary has been added where it adds to our understanding of a work and its composition and performance history.

A Compositions, arrangements and editions

August 1918
Sonata in D minor, op. 1
for violin, viola, cello and piano
   One movement only
Manuscript non-autograph; two fair
   copies, both in the hand of Mabel
   Rodwell Jones: (a) 4pp, (b) 6pp; HF
Notes Composed at Thaxted. Mabel
   Rodwell Jones was an ex-pupil of GH,
   and was on the staff of James Allen's
   Girls' School, Dulwich, one of the
   schools where he taught.

1918
Four English Christmas Carols, op. 2
   1. A Christmas Lullaby: Sleep, baby,
      sleep, the mother sings (J. A.
      Symonds)
   2. Out of the Orient
   3. Now thrice welcome Christmas
   4. Gabriel that Angel bright
Words Nos. 1–3 from *Ancient English
   Christmas Carols, 1400–1700*, ed. Edith
   Rickert (London: Chatto & Windus,
   1914)
Manuscript 2pp, incomplete, separate
   words; HF
Notes The music consists of
   unaccompanied tunes only; the
   fourth carol is unfinished. IH's copy
   of Rickert's collection is inscribed 'To
   Imogen to help her do her Opus II
   and in honour of Opus I from Father,
   Thaxted, August 1918'. IH continued
   to use the book as a source for texts
   through her career, calling on it for the
   last time in December 1968 for *Out of
   your sleep*. The first carol is listed in
   the programme for the distribution of
   Prizes and Certificates at James Allen's
   Girls' School on 19 December 1918.

1918
Duet for Viola and Piano, op. 3
Manuscript non-autograph, 2pp; HF. IH's
   annotation, 'handwriting unknown',
   was added at a much later date.

1920
The Masque of the Tempest, op. 4
   1. Nymphs' Dance, for fl, cl, tri, strings
   2. Shepherd's Dance, for strings
Manuscripts 1. 3pp non autograph; 2.
   4pp. Sets of parts for both movements
   also exist; hands include those of Jane
   Joseph (a former pupil of GH at St
   Paul's Girls' School and on the music
   staff at Eothen School) and a little by
   GH; HF
Dedication 'To R.M.'
Notes Eothen school magazine for 1920
   lists, in the School Calendar of Events,
   the following entry for 9 July: 'Dance
   of Nymphs and Shepherds, composed
   and arranged by I. Holst'. At this
   time IH hoped to be a dancer, so her
   talents were combined in this school
   performance; as well as arranging
   the dancing, she took the part of first
   nymph. GH heard the performance
   and commented: 'I wish I could have
   written anything as good at that
   age'. The style of the 'Nymphs' Dance'
   reveals the helping hand of a teacher,
   the 'Shepherd's Dance' being more
   obviously unassisted work.

1921
Resonet in Laudibus
Carol arranged for unison voices and
small orchestra
1.1.1.0–1.0.0.0–tri–strings
Words From *Piae cantiones*
Manuscript 8pp, incomplete; HF

Notes Probably written in the autumn 1921 during IH's first term at SPGS, the carol was orchestrated by Nora Day, one of the music teachers at the school.

Spring–Summer 1925
An Essex Rhapsody
for orchestra and treble choir
2.2.2.1–2hn–timp–strings; voices in
   unison
Duration 5'
Manuscript 22pp, some pencil
   annotations by GH; HF
First performance 28 July 1925, at St
   Paul's Girls' School Speech Day
Notes The folk song 'As I walked out' on
   which this work is based was noted in
   1904 by Vaughan Williams. IH wrote
   this single-movement Rhapsody in
   her last term at SPGS, when she was a
   composition pupil of Herbert Howells.
   After the work's first outing she was
   promised a performance in the USA
   by an unnamed American, but nothing
   appears to have come of this.

August 1925
Three Songs
for treble voice, two violins and cello
   1. The Willow: Leans now the fair
      willow, dreaming
   2. The Fool's Song: Never, no never,
      listen too long
   3. Exile: Had the gods loved me
Words Walter de la Mare
Manuscript 14pp in all; HF

February 1926
Two Four-part Rounds
for equal voices
   1. Come sit aneath this pine tree (from
      The Greek Anthology)
   2. I wander north, I wander south
      (translated from the Chinese)
Manuscript 2pp; HF

May 1926
Weathers
   This is the weather the cuckoo likes
A Song for Voice and Piano
Words Thomas Hardy
Manuscript 4pp; HF

October–December 1926
Theme and Variations
for piano solo
Duration 13'
Manuscript 20pp; HF
First performance 5 July 1927, at an RCM
   Informal Concert, played by IH
Notes The Holsts had given up their
   London house as soon as IH left school
   in 1925, so as a student, she lodged for
   some time at Bute House, the boarding
   house for SPGS, where this work,
   comprising eleven variations on an
   original theme, was written.

January–March 1927
Mass in A minor
for SSATB
   Kyrie
   Gloria
   Credo
   Sanctus – Osanna – Benedictus
      – Osanna
   Agnus Dei
Duration 18'
Manuscript 54pp; HF

April 1927
Suite in F for Strings
   Allegro assai
Manuscript 21pp; HF
Notes This suite movement, together
   with the one that follows and the
   preceding Mass, would have been
   written at Bute House as part of IH's
   work with George Dyson, then her
   composition professor at the RCM.
   The two manuscripts are similarly
   presented; the first is named 'Suite in

F for strings – First movement' and the second, using augmented forces, 'Suite for small orchestra – Slow movement'. If there ever were any other movements, they do not seem to have survived.

April–May 1927
Suite for Small Orchestra
2.2.2.1–2hn–timp–strings
  Moderato
Manuscript 17pp; HF

1928
Quintet
for oboe and strings
  1. Moderato
  2. Allegro assai
  3. Lento
  4. Allegro
Manuscript whereabouts unknown
Dedication 'To Sylvia Spencer'
First performance 3 December 1931, Ballet Club Theatre, Ladbroke Road, by Sylvia Spencer and the Macnaghten String Quartet
Notes The first performance took place as part of the first year of the Macnaghten concerts, which were to provide a platform for new chamber works by (especially) women composers. IH's *Suite for Viola* (1930) was also performed in the 1931 series of concerts. The Oboe Quintet was reviewed in *The Times* on 5 December 1931.

1928
Sonata in G
for violin and piano
Manuscript whereabouts unknown
First performance 29 May 1928, at an RCM Informal Concert, by Victoria Reid and IH
Notes The violinist (later Mrs Ingrams – a lifelong friend of IH's since their SPGS

days) believed that the manuscript was lost or destroyed. Details of the movements are not recorded.

July 1928
Phantasy
for string quartet
Duration 9'
Manuscript 2 scores, both of 23pp; HF
First performance 27 February 1929, RCM, by Reginald Morley, Barbara Pulvermacher, Mary Gladden and Olive Richards
Notes Written as an entry for the 1928 Cobbett Prize, which it won, with Grace Williams placed second. The work was reviewed in the *Monthly Musical Record* of February 1929 and April 1929; two subsequent performances and a BBC broadcast in 1930 were reviewed in the *Daily Telegraph* (14 July 1930), *Daily Mail* (29 October 1930) *The Times* (14 October 1930) and the *Liverpool Post and Mercury* (22 October 1930). Among those who congratulated IH on this achievement was the poet John Masefield, who sent her a book of tales on hearing of her success.

Autumn 1928
Suite
for flute, oboe, clarinet and bassoon
  1. Prelude
  2. Contredanse
  3. Minuet and Trio
  4. Gigue
Duration 6'
Manuscript set of parts only, 23pp in all (not all autograph); HF
First performance probably 3 December 1928, the County Secondary School, Clapham, by Lilian Cook, Sylvia Spencer, Inez Sworn and Miriam Brightman

1929
Overture 'Persephone'
for orchestra
3(3 = picc).2.corA.2.2.dbsn–4.3.3.1–timp–
    perc–cel–hp–strings
Duration 12′
Manuscript 68pp; HF
Dedication 'To E.B.' [E. B. Worthington]
First performance 5 July 1929, RCM, at a
    Patron's Fund 'Rehearsal', by the New
    Symphony Orchestra, conducted by
    Malcolm Sargent
Notes Reviewed in the *Daily Mail*, the
    Daily Telegraph and *Manchester
    Guardian* of 6 July 1929, and *The
    Musical Times*, August 1929.

1929
Suite 'The Unfortunate Traveller'
(a) for brass band
(b) arranged by IH for strings (1930)
    1. Introduction
    2. Scherzo
    3. Interlude
    4. March
Manuscripts (a) 53pp; HF. (b) 32pp,
    incomplete; lacking the end of the
    Interlude and the March; HF
Dedication 'To St. Stephen's Band,
    Carlisle'
First performance (a) 12 February 1933,
    Her Majesty's Theatre, Carlisle, by St
    Stephen's Band, Carlisle, conducted by
    IH; (b) 15 July 1930, RCM, by the Strings
    of RCM Third Orchestra, conducted by
    W. H. Reed
Notes In the summer of 1930 IH, by
    then a composition student of Gordon
    Jacob, submitted a brass band score to
    the examining professors for her last
    grading examination at the RCM. *The
    Unfortunate Traveller* was suggested by
    Thomas Nashe's picaresque romance
    of the same title, published in 1594,
    of which a modern edition had been

brought out in 1920. Several Morris
dance tunes are introduced during the
course of the music, including 'Bonnie
Green Garters', 'Shepherd's Hey', 'The
Rose' and 'The Wind Blaws Cauld'. The
first known performance of the Suite
was given in its string version so that
the work could be played at the RCM
just before IH left in July 1930.

The original brass band version was
included in a concert of Holst works
given in Carlisle on 12 February 1933 to
honour the memory of GH's maternal
uncle, Dr Henry Ambrose Lediard, a
local physician; proceeds from the
concert went towards the Mayor's
Fund for Unemployment. GH himself
conducted St Stephen's Band in a
performance of his *A Moorside Suite*
and, while working out the programme
beforehand with his pianist cousin,
Mary Lediard (who was organizing the
event) he had suggested that IH's Suite
for brass band might also be included.
In an interview at the time with a *Daily
Mail* correspondent IH said, '... it is
the first time, so far as I know, that a
woman has conducted a brass band at
a public concert ... it has been a delight
to rehearse the St Stephen's Band. It
was their performance at the Crystal
Palace festival that inspired me to write
this Suite, which I have dedicated to
them.'

The first performance of the brass
band version was widely reviewed in
the press, including the *Daily Mail* (13
February 1933) and a range of regional
newspapers.

[*circa* 1930]
What Man is He?
for SATB chorus and orchestra
2.2.2.2–2.2.1.0–timp–organ *ad lib*–strings
Duration 6′

Words From Book of Wisdom IX:13–17

Manuscript 19pp; HF

Notes The date of this composition is not known for certain, but the musical style suggests 1930; a later setting of the same text dates from Spring 1944.

1930

Ballet: 'Meddling in Magic'

for orchestra

1(= picc).1.2.1–2.2.1.0–timp–perc–strings

Duration 35–40'

Manuscript 161pp; HF

Notes The Camargo Society was formed early in 1930 (after the death of Diaghilev) by Lydia Lopokova, Constant Lambert and others, in order to put on ballet in London; it was to lead to the development of the Vic-Wells Ballet Company. *Meddling in Magic*, based on the story of the Sorcerer's Apprentice, and with choreography by Dorothy Osborne, was seriously considered by the Society in 1930 and 1931, and was even announced in the *Daily Mail* in September and October 1930; however, it was never staged.

Summer 1930

Suite

for unaccompanied viola

1. Prelude
2. Cinquepace
3. Saraband
4. Gigue

Duration 9'30"

Manuscripts (a) Sent by IH to Bernard Shore in 1934, now at the RCM. (b) Fair copy, given as a wedding present in June 1932 to Leila Andrews, a friend and contemporary of IH at SPGS.

Published Roberton, 1991

Dedication 'For Leila, with love from Imo, June 1932'

First performance 14 December 1931,

Ballet Club Theatre, Ladbroke Road, by Violet Brough

Notes The concert including the first performance, which also featured works by Elisabeth Lutyens, Patrick Hadley and Elizabeth Maconchy, was reviewed in the *Morning Post* and the *Daily Telegraph* on 15 December 1931.

October–November 1930

Sonata

for violin and cello

1. Allegro ritmico
2. Adagio
3. Presto, molto leggiero

Duration 17'

Manuscript 31pp; HF

Notes Written while the composer was visiting Vienna on the travelling scholarship gained at the RCM. There is no record of any performance of this work.

1932

A Book of Tunes for the Pipes

collected and arranged by IH

PART 1: Country Dance Tunes (taken from Playford's *The English Dancing Master*)

1. If all the world were paper (2 players)
2. All in a garden green (3)
3. My Lord Byron's maggot (2)
4. Jamaica (3)
5. Never love thee more (3)
6. Argeers (3)
7. The Dargason (3)

PART 2: Madrigals and Part Songs

8. Robin-A-Thrush (3) Folk song
9. My bonnie, bonnie Boy (4) Folk song
10. My Johnny was a shoemaker (3) Folk song
11. Now is the month of maying (5) Thomas Morley
12. Come again, sweet love (4) John Dowland

13. A measure to pleasure your leisure(5)
   G. B. Martini, arr. GH
14. Pastoral (3) GH
Manuscript whereabouts unknown
Published Cramer, 1932, under the
   auspices of the Pipers' Guild. In later
   reprints the title became *First Book
   of Tunes* and the original no. 10 ('My
   Johnny was a shoemaker') was moved
   to the end of the book, giving a more
   practical page layout to the last five
   pieces.
Notes The Pipers' Guild was founded
   in 1932, thanks to the activity of
   Margaret James, a Gloucestershire
   schoolteacher who had for some time
   been teaching children and amateur
   musicians how to make their own
   pipes (fipple flutes) out of bamboo,
   and then to play them in consort. Her
   classes and demonstrations attracted
   many EFDSS musicians, and IH
   recognized the value that these home-
   made instruments could have in the
   enjoyment and teaching of music. (All
   this was, of course, several years before
   mass-produced, inexpensive recorders
   became freely available for beginners.)
   Playford's *The English Dancing
   Master* was a favourite source book for
   IH, who returned to it many times.

November 1932
Morris Suite
arranged for small orchestra
1.1.2.1–timp–perc–strings
Manuscript 37pp; HF
First performance 6 December 1932,
   Cecil Sharp House, London, by the
   BBC Theatre Orchestra, conducted by
   Stanford Robinson
Notes IH's lifelong enthusiasm for folk
   music began even before she became
   a member of the EFDS in 1923, when
   she reached the qualifying age of

sixteen. By 1932 she was working as
an occasional member of staff for the
EFDSS, and this Suite formed part of
the broadcast programme celebrating
the coming of age of the Society. It
consists of a continuous arrangement
of four Oxfordshire morris dance tunes
collected by Cecil Sharp – 'Bonny
green garters', 'I'll go and enlist',
'Shepherd's Hey'and 'The rose'. The
Suite was often performed on later
EFDSS occasions, and was broadcast
twice in the spring of 1934.

1933
Eighteenth Century Dances
selected and arranged for piano, with
directions for performance
   1. The Penelope
   2. Whitehall Minuet
   3. I often for my Jenny Strove
   4. Manage the Miser
   5. The Tub
   6. Joy after Sorrow
   7. The Cuckoo
Manuscript whereabouts unknown
Published OUP, 1933
First performance probably 19 April 1933,
   in a BBC Scottish Regional broadcast;
   four titles only, played by IH
Notes IH performed four of these at the
   Summer Festival of the English Folk
   Dance Society at Reading, 1933, playing
   them on the virginals. (Another title
   on this programme was 'The Duchess',
   which was not to be published until
   1937.) The tunes are taken from the
   seventeenth edition of Playford's *The
   Dancing Master* and arranged for
   junior grade pianists. New, easy dances
   'invented in the style of the older forms
   of country dance' are substituted for
   the original ones, which IH felt lacked
   interest for young people.

1933
A Second Book of Tunes for the Pipes

collected and arranged by IH

PART 1: Country Dance Tunes (taken from Playford's *The Dancing Master*)
  1. Milk Maid's Bobb (2)
  2. Pretty Peggy's minuet (3)
  3. Maiden Lane (3)
  4. Have at thy coat, old woman (2)
  5. Ginnie Pug or Strawberries and cream (3)
  6. Black and gray (3)
  7. Pity, or I die (3)
  8. The fit's come on me now (4)

PART 2: Songs
  9. Wilton Fair (3) Hampshire Folksong
  10. On Monday morning (2) Hampshire Folksong
  11. Thou Shepherd, Whose intentive eye (3) Henry Lawes
  12. A Christmas lullaby (3) IH
  13. Trip it, trip it in a ring (3) Henry Purcell
  14. Late in my rash accounting (3) Thomas Weelkes

Manuscript whereabouts unknown
Published Cramer, 1933, under the auspices of the Pipers' Guild
First performance The first known performance was on 5 June 1934 in the Aeolian Hall, by the Pipers' Guild Quartet at a concert given by the Oriana Madrigal Society.
Notes No. 12 appears to be an arrangement of an original part song by IH, but no other version has been found.

1933
Two Scottish Airs

arranged for cello and piano
  1. My only Joe and dearie
  2. Come under my plaidie

Manuscript whereabouts unknown

Published Novello, 1935
First performance probably 19 April 1933, in a BBC Scottish Regional Broadcast, by Peggie Thomson and IH
Notes The work attracted favourable reviews in the *Monthly Musical Record* (May 1935) and *The Musical Times* (March 1936); it was the first of IH's arrangements to be published by Novello.

1934
Five Short Airs on a Ground

for pipes
  1. Quick and light (5 players)
  2. Fairly slow (3)
  3. Very quick (3)
  4. Slow and sustained (3)
  5. As fast as possible (5)

Manuscript whereabouts unknown
Published Cramer, 1934, under the auspices of the Pipers' Guild
Notes These original airs are prefaced by a note: 'In each of these pieces the 'ground' is meant to be played by beginners, and can, if necessary, be played on unfinished pipes with only two holes. The grounds themselves, different for each Air, are for treble pipe in D.'

1934
Five Short Pieces

for piano solo
  1. Prelude
  2. March
  3. Canon
  4. Toccata
  5. Nocturne

Manuscript whereabouts unknown
Published OUP, 1935 (Oxford Piano Series; no. 212. Grade B). A shortened version of no. 4 is included as no. 21 of *Piano Time Pieces*, ed. Pauline Hall (OUP 1989).

1934
Four Oxfordshire Folk Songs
arranged for two sopranos with piano accompaniment
1. Pretty Caroline
2. Now the winter is gone
3. The seeds of love
4. A bunch of green holly and ivy
Manuscript whereabouts unknown
Published Novello, 1936 (separately, in the series 'Novellos's Schools Songs')
First performance 'Pretty Caroline' and 'Now the winter is gone', probably on 3 March 1934, at the Assembly Rooms, Oxford, the first as a solo song by Doris Aldridge of Burford
Notes Three of the tunes were originally noted by Cecil Sharp; no. 4 was noted by the Revd C. F. Cholmondley and Miss Janet Blunt. The concert on 3 March 1934 was the last that GH ever attended.

1934
Four Somerset Folk Songs
arranged for SSA
1. Hares on the mountains: If all those young men
2. It's a rosebud in June
3. Sweet Kitty: As he was a-riding
4. The crabfish: There was a little man
Manuscript whereabouts unknown
Published Novello, 1934 (separate leaflets)
Dedication 'To the singers at Eothen' (no. 4)
First performance Folk Music Festival, 1936, organized and adjudicated by IH. The first two songs appear on the programme.
Notes The four songs on which these arrangements are based had been noted by Cecil Sharp when, staying with friends in Somerset, he first

became aware of the living English folksong tradition, 1903–4.

1934
Love in a Mist or The Blue Haired Stranger
arranged for orchestra from music by Scarlatti
Manuscript whereabouts unknown
First performance 19 January 1935, in the Rudolf Steiner Hall, London, orchestra conducted by IH.
Notes One of three folk dance ballets choreographed on the occasion of a fund-raising event for the International Folk Music Festival of 1935, by Amy Stoddart, a gifted part-time staff member of the EFDSS who taught geography at SPGS. No details of the Scarlatti pieces used by IH, or of their orchestration, have come to light. The ballets, which included one to GH's *St Paul's Suite*, were performed again on 29 February 1936 at Morley College under Arnold Foster, in aid of their Gustav Holst Memorial Fund.
   The first performance was reviewed in the national press, by *The Observer* (20 January 1935), *The Times* and the *London Evening News* (21 January 1935).

1934
Nowell and Nowell
Folk song. Collected by Cecil J. Sharp and arranged for mixed voices [SSATBB]
Manuscript whereabouts unknown
Published Novello, 1934 (in *Musical Times*, no. 1102, December 1934)
Dedication 'To the Westhall Hill Singers'
First performance December 1934, Westhall Hill, Burford.
Notes Westhall Hill, Burford, Oxfordshire, was the home of Captain and Mrs W. R. W. Kettlewell, influential members of the EFDS since its beginnings and themselves

enthusiastic musicians and dancers. Their house became the focus for much musical activity; IH stayed there often, to conduct and train a small group of local singers and to direct the music at occasional weekend gatherings.

This arrangement of a Cornish version of the familiar 'First Nowell' carol was written with its Burford dedicatees much in mind – for instance the bass pedal notes were for the fine bass voice of Eric Reavley, pharmacist. In addition to its Burford première in December 1934, the carol was also sung that Christmas season in a carol service at Chichester Cathedral, where the ashes of Gustav Holst had been interred the previous June.

1934

Six Pictures from Finland

for piano solo
1. On the lake
2. The dancer in the red skirt
3. The old woodcutter
4. The spinner's song
5. A shower among the birch trees
6. Night piece

Manuscript whereabouts unknown
Published OUP, 1935 (Oxford Piano
  Series; no. 211. Grade A)
Notes These easy piano pieces were
  written while IH was teaching at
  Eothen and Roedean Schools. She had
  visited Finland in September 1933 as
  a member of a team from the EFDSS,
  which had taken part in a British–
  Finnish Trade Week.

1934

Six Scottish Folk Songs

arranged for voice and pipes with piano
accompaniment
1. Cauld blaws the wind
2. I'm owre young to marry yet
3. Ca' the yowes

4. Go to Berwick Johnnie
5. The auld man
6. Baloo, loo, lammy
Manuscript whereabouts unknown
Published Lyrebird Press, 1934

1934

Traditional Country Dances

arranged variously for the Cecil Sharp
House Orchestra and EFDSS
1. Heartsease
2. Morpeth rant (Northumberland)
3. My dear mother (Hungary)
4. The Dargason
5. Catching of quails
6. Adson's sarabande
7. Queen's jig
8. The round
9. Juice of barley
10. The slip

Manuscript whereabouts unknown
First performances no. 1: 20 May
  1934, in a Concert of Folk Music at
  the Shakespeare Memorial Theatre,
  Stratford on Avon; nos. 2 and 3: 29
  November 1934, by the Cecil Sharp
  Orchestra, conducted by IH.
Notes IH made three 10-inch records
  of folk-dance music in March 1934 for
  the Gramophone Company, including
  the last seven titles in the above list.
  The demand for such arrangements
  was considerable: on 23 August 1933
  Douglas Kennedy had written to
  her: 'Can you write me two foxtrots
  and a waltz based on "Picking up
  sticks", "Morpeth rant" and "A virgin
  unspotted"? A blues based on "Death
  and the Lady" and a rumba written
  around and behind "A Gypsum Laddie".
  Put your fertile and subtle brain to
  the possibilities and tell me what you
  think ...'

1934
A Wedding Hymn: 'Father in Thine Almighty Hand'
for SATB
Words Eleanor Spensley
Manuscript whereabouts unknown
Published privately printed by J. Calvert Spensley
First performance 17 March 1934, St Mary's Church, Stoke D'Abernon, Surrey
Notes Composed for the marriage of Jane Schofield (a schoolfriend of IH) to Henry Fosbrooke. The author of the words was the bride's godmother.

July–August 1934
The Song of Solomon
Incidental music for a Hollywood pageant
for full orchestra
Words Libretto by Vadim Uraneff
   1. Bacchanal
   2. Panic Music
Manuscript whereabouts unknown
Notes At the time of his death on 25 May 1934 GH left unfinished some incidental music for this projected pageant. He had written some small vocal settings, and somewhat reluctantly agreed to the librettist's request that extracts from *The Planets* should also be used, but two sections remained unwritten. To fulfil her father's obligation, IH herself composed the music for the missing numbers, an Egyptian Bacchanal – a ballet to last about 5 minutes – and a short linking passage for a 'moment of panic in the palace', both at the end of Act I of Vadim Uraneff's play. On 30 August 1934 Uraneff enthusiastically acknowledged the receipt of her manuscript score, set for full orchestra, but nothing further was ever heard of either the music or the Pageant, a grandiose affair in which it was hoped that John Barrymore and Katherine Hepburn would appear, with Eugene Goossens conducting.

[*circa* 1935]
Four Easy Pieces
for viola with piano accompaniment
   1. Timothy's trot
   2. A farewell
   3. Mill-Field
   4. Jenny is dancing
Manuscript whereabouts unknown
Published Augener, 1935
Dedication 'For A.F.C.' [Arthur Caton]

[*circa* 1935]
On Westhall Hill
for small orchestra
1.1.1.1 (*ad lib*)–timp–perc–strings
Duration 5'15"
Manuscript 22pp; HF
Notes A single movement based on two folk tunes, not identified. 'Westhall Hill' was the house in Burford where Captain and Mrs W. R. W. Kettlewell lived. The date of the work is not known, but IH moved to the address given on the title-page (54 Ormonde Terrace, NW8) in October 1935, and in later life she herself assigned it to the 'mid 1930s'. Evidently a tribute to the Kettlewells, the piece was very likely written for one of the many special events for which IH directed the EFDSS orchestra at this time.

1935
Concerto for Violin
and string orchestra
founded on traditional Irish tunes taken from the Petrie Collection
   1. Allegro
   2. Andante molto moderato
   3. Vivace
Duration 13'30"

Manuscript 43pp; HF

First performance 15 November 1935, at an RCM Patron's Fund 'Rehearsal', by Elsie Avril, with the London Symphony Orchestra, conducted by IH.

Notes Elsie Avril was for many years principal violinist to the EFDSS. The performance was reviewed in *The Times*, 16 November 1935.

1935
Four Folk Tunes from Hampshire
for violins [unison] and piano

1. Allegretto grazioso
2. Moderato
3. Andante cantabile
4. Vivace

Manuscript whereabouts unknown

Published Novello, 1935 (Novello's 'Elementary and School Orchestra Series', no. 9)

Notes Novello's 'Elementary and School Orchestra Series', published from 1933 to 1939, under the general editorship of W. H. Reed, was primarily concerned with violinists. There were four grades of difficulty, with additional parts for string orchestra available in Grades 3 and 4. IH's *Four Folk Tunes from Hampshire* fall into Grade 2 ('can be played in first position') and are in two sets of two tunes each, forming no. 5 (tunes 1 and 2 above) and no. 6 (tunes 3 and 4) of this grade. The titles and provenance of the folk tunes themselves have not been identified. In 1959 *Four Folk Tunes* were reissued, with additional parts by Denis Wright for extended school orchestra; these two sets were then renumbered as no. IX (tunes 1 and 2) and no. X (tunes 3 and 4). IH's original versions for violins and piano are retained intact in the full scores.

1935
Intermezzo from First Suite in E flat
Gustav Holst, arranged for orchestra by IH

Manuscript whereabouts unknown

First performance 24 March 1935, Cecil Sharp House, London, conducted by IH.

Notes The arrangement was made for a Gustav Holst Memorial concert given by the EFDSS. IH does not mention it in her own *A Thematic Catalogue of Gustav Holst's Music*.

1935
My Bairn, Sleep Softly Now
I saw a sweet and simple sight

Carol for unaccompanied female voices (SSSAA) or for soprano voice and pipes

Words Anon, taken from *Ancient English Christmas Carols*, ed. Rickert

Manuscript whereabouts unknown

Published Cramer, 1935, under the auspices of the Pipers' Guild

First performance The first known performance was on 15 July 1936, by the Carlyle Singers under Iris Lemare. This occasion was the 25th anniversary of the foundation of the Society of Women Musicians.

1935
The Virgin Unspotted
Folk song arranged for SSA

Manuscript whereabouts unknown

Published Novello, 1935

Notes A tune from Shropshire, originally noted by Cecil Sharp in December 1911.

1936
Canons for Treble Pipes
Manuscript whereabouts unknown

Published Cramer, 1936, under the auspices of the Pipers' Guild

Dedication 'For the Pipers at Eothen'

Notes Twelve canons, progressing from two to ten parts, dedicated to IH's pupils at Eothen School, Caterham. IH had boarded there as a child and taught at the school from March 1933 to Easter 1939.

1936

Fly Away Over the Sea

Two-part song [for two sopranos and piano]

Words Christina Rossetti

Manuscript whereabouts unknown

Published Cramer, 1936 (Cramer's Library of Unison and Part Songs, no. 130)

1936

Great Art Thou, O Lord

Canon for five equal voices

Words Biblical

Manuscript 2pp; HF

Notes Although this canon is included on the same publisher's contract as the three surrounding songs (all Cramer, 1936), in fact it never appeared in print.

1936

Lady Daffadowndilly

Growing in the vale by the uplands hilly

Two-part song for treble voices and piano

Words Christina Rossetti

Manuscript whereabouts unknown

Published Cramer, 1936 (Cramer's Library of Unison and Part Songs, no. 123)

1936

Now Will I Weave White Violets

Part-song for SSA

Words Meleager 'Romance'; translated from the Greek by William M. Harding

Manuscript whereabouts unknown

Published Cramer, 1936 (Cramer's Library of Unison and Part Songs, no. 122)

Dedication 'For Becky and Kay'

First performance 15 July 1936, by the Carlyle Singers under Iris Lemare, on the occasion of the 25th anniversary of the foundation of the Society of Women Musicians

Notes The dedicatees, Becky Ridley and Kay Freeston, were good friends of IH at this time.

1936

Twelve Old English Dance Airs

arranged for pipes ... from Playford's *English Dancing Master*

1. Paul's steeple (3 players)
2. Rose is white and rose is red (3)
3. Kettle drum (3)
4. Millisons jegge (4)
5. Glory of the west (3)
6. Petticoat wag (3)
7. Prince Rupert's march (4)
8. Skellemesago (3)
9. New new nothing (3)
10. Crosbey Square (3)
11. Chirping of the nightingale (2)
12. Staines morris (4)

Manuscript whereabouts unknown

Published Cramer, 1936, under the auspices of the Pipers' Guild

Notes All the tunes save one are taken from Playford's *English Dancing Master* of 1651. The exception (no. 10) comes from the eleventh edition of 1701.

1936

Wassail Song

The wassail, the wassail throughout all the town

Folk song arranged for chorus of men's voices (unaccompanied), from the original setting for mixed voices by Gustav Holst

Manuscript whereabouts unknown

Published Curwen, 1936 (The Apollo Club, no. 725)

Notes GH's setting (H182) was written between 1928 and 1931, and is dedicated 'To the Huddersfield Glee and Choral Society', who gave the first performance.

1937

The Cobbler

I am a cobbler bold

Folk song from Hampshire. Collected by G. B. Gardiner. Arranged for SATB unaccompanied

Manuscript whereabouts unknown

Published Novello, 1937 (Novello's Part-Song Book, no. 1496)

1937

A Cornish Wassail Song

The mistress and master our wassail begin

Collected by Cecil J. Sharp. Arranged for SATB unaccompanied

Manuscript whereabouts unknown

Published Novello, 1937 (Novello's Part-Song Book, no. 1498)

1937

Coronation Country Dances

A selection arranged for band by IH and Gordon Jacob

1. Norfolk long dance (IH)
2. Speed the plough (IH)
3. Galopede (GJ)
4. Circassian circle (GJ)
5. Morpeth rant (GJ)
6. Long eight (IH)
7. Yorkshire square eight (IH)

Manuscript whereabouts unknown

Notes To celebrate the Coronation of King George VI on 12 May 1937, the record company Columbia issued an album of 'Coronation Country Dances' selected by the EFDSS. The dances, played by the Morris Motors Band under the direction of Mr S. Wood, are preceded on the recording (DB1671–4) by an 'Opening Flourish' by Vaughan Williams, and the National Anthem.

A companion volume, *A Coronation Country Dance Book*, was published at the same time by the EFDSS; it contains instructions for the seven easy dances, set to piano arrangements by Arnold Foster, Cecil Sharp and Vaughan Williams.

1937

Nicodemus

A Mystery by Andrew Young with incidental music by IH for chorus (SATB) and orchestra

1.1.1.1–1.1.1.0–(*ad lib* organ when no woodwind or brass)–timp–perc–strings

1. Introduction to Scene 1
2. Behold how good a thing it is (Hymn)
5. The Lord's my Shepherd (Hymn)
8. Thou crownest the year
10. He will not suffer thy foot to be moved
11. I bless the Lord
16. Ye gates, lift up your heads
17. Amen

There are 17 short sections in all, the others (instrumental only) are without titles.

Manuscript National Library of Scotland (Andrew Young Collection)

Published Jonathan Cape, 1937; a short score of the music is included after the text of the play

First performance 21 March (Palm Sunday) 1937, St Andrew's Presbyterian Church, Cheam, where the Revd Andrew Young was the minister. The first broadcast performance was given on 23 January 1944 by a chorus (not identified) and the BBC Northern Orchestra and BBC Choir, conducted by Julius Harrison.

1937

Six Old English Dances

The melodies from Playford's *The Dancing Master*. Arranged for pianoforte

1. The Duchess
2. Hang sorrow
3. Beautiful Clarinda
4. Good advice
5. Dearest and fairest
6. Bullock's hornpipe

Manuscript whereabouts unknown
Published Lyrebird Press, 1937
Notes Although published by the Lyrebird Press, this is described in a review as being 'sponsored by the OUP', the publishers of IH's 1933 collection.

1937

A Sweet Country Life

Folk song from Gloucestershire. Collected by Cecil J. Sharp. Arranged for SATB unaccompanied
Manuscript whereabouts unknown
Published Novello, 1937 (Novello's Part-Song Book, no. 1497)

1937

Twelve Songs for Children

from the Appalachian Mountains. Collected by Cecil Sharp. Piano accompaniments by IH

BOOK 1

1. Bye, bye, baby
2. Swing a lady
3. Sourwood mountain
4. The frog in the well
5. Putman's hill
6. Sing, said the mother

BOOK 2

7. Snake baked a hoe-cake
8. The Bridle and saddle
9. Sally Anne
10. I wish I was a child again
11. The mocking bird
12. The farmyard

Manuscript whereabouts unknown
Published OUP, 1937 (in two books)
Notes All the songs are taken from volume two of *English Folk Songs from the Southern Appalachian Mountains*, ed. Maud Karpeles (OUP, 1932), with the exception of no. 6, which IH describes in a footnote as 'not a traditional folk-song'.

5 June 1937

Little Thinkest Thou, Poore Flower

for voice and piano
Words John Donne
Manuscript 3pp; HF

1938

The Rival Sisters

Suite for small orchestra by Henry Purcell Arranged, from figured bass, for strings and ad lib woodwind [1.1.1.1.] and percussion [timp–perc]
Duration 6'
Manuscript whereabouts unknown
Published Novello, 1938
Notes This suite of Purcell's original music for a play by Robert Gould is in seven short movements, scored for not very advanced string players.

1938

Ten Appalachian Folk Songs

arranged for voice and piano

1. The Lady and the dragoon
2. The brown girl, or Fair Sally
3. I must and I will get married
4. When Adam was created
5. The brisk young lover
6. Married and single life
7. My dearest dear
8. The Irish girl
9. The chickens they are crowing
10. The Twelve Apostles, or The Ten Commandments

Manuscripts separate songs, each of 2–4 pp; HF

Notes In the spring of 1938 Maud
Karpeles (former colleague and
executrix of Cecil Sharp) approached
the OUP with a plan to publish a
volume of arrangements for voice and
piano of thirty-five of the *English Folk
Songs from the Southern Appalachians*
which Sharp had collected in 1916–18.
Apart from four songs arranged (or
partly arranged) by Cecil Sharp himself,
the composers involved were Arnold
Foster, IH, Michael Mullinar, Ralph
Vaughan Williams and Arnold Walter.
However, for some reason the scheme
failed, so the ten settings by IH were
not published.

No. 10 is an accumulative question-
and-answer song for more than one
voice. In 1962 IH suggested this song
to Benjamin Britten, who arranged
a version of it for tenor, boys' chorus
and piano for an Aldeburgh Festival
concert.

1938
Three Songs
Pelham Humphrey. Edited and arranged
for voice and piano
  1. As Freezing Fountains
  2. In Vain does Nature's Bounteous
     Hand Supply
  3. A Lover I'm Born
Manuscript whereabouts unknown
Published Lyrebird Press, 1938
First performance Probably 20 March,
1938, when IH presented a concert of
music by Pelham Humphrey in Cecil
Sharp House. Of the performances,
The Musical Times wrote: 'by this
time it was apparent that Miss Holst's
enthusiasm for this hitherto neglected
composer had become infectious and
there followed a really exquisite song'.

1939
Prelude and Dance
for piano solo
Manuscript 5pp; HF

October 1939
Eothen Suite
for small orchestra
1.1.1.0–strings
  1. March
  2. Slow Air
  3. Jig
  4. Air on a Ground
Duration 7'
Manuscript 18pp; HF
Notes Written for the orchestra of
Eothen School, although IH had ceased
to teach there at Easter 1939.

circa 1940–6
Six Traditional Carols [First Set]
arranged for SSA
  1. The holly and the ivy
  2. Joys seven
  3. A Virgin most pure
  4. I saw three ships
  5. Bedfordshire May Day Carol
  6. Matthew, Mark, and Luke and John
Manuscript whereabouts unknown
Published OUP, 1947
Notes The first of four similar sets of six
carols arranged for unaccompanied
female voices. They are prefaced
by the following note: 'These short
simple settings of traditional carols
are intended for village choirs and
Women's Institutes where some of the
singers may still be in the early stages
of trying to read their notes. Each part
is easy enough to be learnt by rote if
necessary. Every verse is sung to the
same setting so that choirs can learn
the carols by heart for singing out of
doors in the dark.'

It is not possible to date each of these arrangements precisely, though no. 4 certainly existed in 1940.

circa 1940
The Cherry Tree Carol
for SATB unaccompanied
Manuscript copy only; HF
Notes A single-verse carol probably written as an exercise for the benefit of IH's students.

circa 1940
Nymphs and Shepherds
A pastoral scene arranged for SSA, strings and optional recorders
The original by Henry Purcell
Duration 8′
Manuscript string parts in the hand of a copyist; HF

circa 1940
Six Shakespeare Songs
The original Elizabethan melodies arranged for recorder trio
  1. Mistress mine (*Twelfth Night*)
  2. Jog on, jog on (*A Winter's Tale*)
  3. How should I your true love know? (*Hamlet*)
  4. Tomorrow is St. Valentine's Day (*Hamlet*)
  5. It was a lover and his lass (*As you Like it*)
  6. When that I was and a little tiny boy (*Twelfth Night*)
Manuscript whereabouts unknown
Published Schott, 1941
Notes The words of each song are printed with the Recorder 1 part in the score. The Publisher's Note includes the hope 'that these settings of Shakespeare Songs may prove useful to producers of the plays'.

1940
Come All You Worthy People
Dorset folk carol arranged for SSA
Manuscript 6pp; HF
Notes Mentioned in a letter to IH in October 1940 from Sir Walford Davies, then based in Bristol with the BBC, in connection with a proposed broadcast programme in the 'Music Makers' Half Hour' series.

1940
Five Airs
by Pelham Humphrey arranged for Recorder Trio
  1. Charm me asleep
  2. The shady grove
  3. The birthday
  4. Hey down a down
  5. Fare thee well
Manuscript whereabouts unknown
Published Schott, 1941
Notes The published score includes the following details: 'The first two Airs are from songs published with unfigured bass in the late 17th century. The other three are from an unpublished Birthday Ode: Nos. 3 and 4 have figured basses, and No. 5 has an unfigured bass'.

April 1940
A Hymne to Christ
In what torne ship soever I embarke
for SATB chorus
Words John Donne, 'A Hymne to Christ', verses 1−2
Manuscript 5pp; HF
Published B&H, 1998
First performance The first known performance was on 25 October 1987, in Lincoln Cathedral, by Sedbergh School Choir, directed by Christopher Tinker.

[*circa* 1941]
Offley Suite
for recorder trio
  1. Lament
  2. Dance in Canon
  3. Interlude
  4. Rondo
Duration 6' 30"
Manuscripts (a) 9pp; HF. (b) Schott
Notes Offley Place near Hitchin was
  used for thirty-five years for weekend
  courses and summer schools put on
  by the Hertfordshire Rural Music
  School and the RMSA. During World
  War II the CEMA Music Travellers
  held conferences there; IH certainly
  attended in the early 1940s, and may
  have written the Suite for one of these
  meetings.
    Although IH noted in 1968 that
  this work had been published by
  Schott in 1942, it never appeared in
  print. On 1 October 1946 she wrote
  to the publisher: 'I had very nearly
  forgotten the existence of my "Offley
  Suite" for recorders. I am wondering
  now whether it is worth publishing.
  My second suite for recorders, called
  the "Deddington Suite" is, I think,
  much better. I cannot remember now
  whether you have seen it or not. I am
  enclosing a copy … Perhaps you will
  let me know what you think about the
  second Trio and which of the two you
  prefer to publish.' In the event, Schott
  published the Deddington Suite in 1947.
    The work is quite different from IH's
  later piece of the same name, written
  for elementary string class.

1941
Nature's Homily
Song by Pelham Humphrey, arranged for
baritone and pianoforte
Manuscript HF

[*circa* 1942]
Deddington Suite
for recorder trio
descant (or treble), treble (or descant),
  tenor (or treble)
  1. Fairly slow
  2. Quick and light
  3. Slow
  4. Quick
Duration 6'
Manuscript 9pp; HF (on loan from
  Schott)
Published Schott, 1947
Notes Written for Marjorie Wise,
  headmistress of a large school in
  Dagenham evacuated to Deddington
  in north Oxfordshire during the war.
  In London she had studied with IH
  at Cecil Sharp House. A friend of the
  Elmhirsts of Dartington Hall, it was she
  who had introduced IH to Dartington
  in 1938.

1942
As When the Dove
George Frideric Handel, continuo
realized by IH
Manuscript HF

1942
A Bach Book for the Treble Recorder
Twenty passages from the flute parts in
the church cantatas
Selected and edited by IH
Manuscript copy only; British Library
Published Cramer, 1942
Notes The preface describes the selection
  as 'intended as a practice book for
  solitary recorder players. Nearly all
  the tunes are taken from the opening
  bars of a flute *obbligato* in an *aria*
  for solo voice … the original key has
  been altered where it does not suit the
  compass of the recorder.'

1942
Three Carols from Other Lands
1. Noel nouvelet (French)
2. Fonteine, moeder (Flemish)
3. Es ist ein Ros' entsprungen (German: Michael Praetorius)

Manuscript whereabouts unknown
First performance probably 20 December 1942, by the Dartington Hall Music Group (three solo singers, string quartet and keyboard) for whom the carols had been arranged, to perform on their Christmas seasonal tour that year

August–September 1942
Serenade
for flute, viola and bassoon
1. Salutation for a birthday
2. Dance in Exile
3. Lament
4. Exorcist
5. Nocturne

Duration 12′30″
Manuscript 14pp; HF
First performance 4 June 1943, Wigmore Hall, London, by Eve Kisch, Jean Stewart and Anne Joseph
Notes Led by Marjorie Wise, some of the many friends IH had made in the field of amateur music wrote to her in July 1942 to say: 'We all feel that it is high time that you had a LONDON CONCERT, both as a COMPOSER and as a CONDUCTOR, but it must be professional not amateur. We are prepared to do the work of getting the necessary funds and audience.' More than 300 people subscribed, and the concert given at the Wigmore Hall exclusively of music by IH included first performances of three substantial works, the *Serenade*, *Suite for String Orchestra* and *Three Psalms*. The event was reviewed in *The Times* (7 June

1943), *Daily Telegraph, Daily Mail, Gloucestershire Echo, Liverpool Daily Post* (all 5 June 1943) and in the *RCM Magazine* vol. 39 no. 3.

circa 1943–50
[Counterpoint Exercises]
in two parts
Manuscript 5pp; HF
Notes Written at Dartington, the manuscript was annotated thus in the 1970s by IH: 'These I think I wrote for counterpoint exercises for people to get used to different intervals.' There are eleven short, simple tunes over held bass pedal notes, demonstrating intervals within the octave.

circa 1943–8
Of a Rosemary Branch Sent
Such green to me as you have sent
arranged for SATB with strings
Manuscript set of parts; HF
Notes Probably intended for a combined music day; the parts (stamped 'Arts Department') indicate that it may date from *c.* 1943–8.

1943
All Under the Leaves or The Seven Virgins
Shropshire folk-carol collected by Cecil Sharp. Arranged for SSA
Manuscript whereabouts unknown
Published OUP, 1943 (Oxford Choral Songs, no. 570)
First performance probably 4 June 1943, Wigmore Hall, London, by the BBC Singers, conducted by IH. See note to the *Serenade* above.

1943
Cherry, Holly and Ivy
Cornish folk-carol. Collected by
T. Miners and J. Thomas. Arranged for
SATB
Manuscript Dartington Hall Archives
(copy given by IH to Dorothy Elmhirst)
Published OUP, 1943 (Oxford Choral
Songs, no. 850)
First performance probably 4 June 1943,
Wigmore Hall, London, by the BBC
Singers, conducted by the composer.
See note to the *Serenade* above.

1943
Suite
for string orchestra
1. Prelude
2. Fugue
3. Intermezzo
4. Jig
Duration 11′30″
Manuscript 34pp; HF
First performance 4 June 1943, Wigmore
Hall, London, by the Jacques String
Orchestra, conducted by IH. See note
to the *Serenade* above.

March 1943
Three Psalms
for chorus (SSAATB) and string
orchestra
[minimum no. of players 2.2.2.2.1]
1. Psalm 80: Give ear, O shepherd of
Israel
2. Psalm 56: Be merciful unto me, O
God
3. Psalm 91: He that dwelleth in the
secret place of the most high
Words From the Authorized Version of
the Bible (1611)
Duration 14′30″
Manuscript 33pp; HF
First performance 4 June 1943, Wigmore
Hall, London, by the BBC Singers and
Jacques String Orchestra, conducted by
IH. See note to the *Serenade* above.

September–November 1943
Theme and Variations
for solo violin
Duration 16′30″
Manuscripts (a) and (b) both of 11pp;
HF. (c) Private possession
Dedication 'For Joyce'
Notes Written at Dartington for Joyce de
Groote. The original theme is followed
by fourteen variations. In 1946 IH gave
a copy to Edward Bor, a departing
student, telling him she had 'written it
as an exercise'.

1944
Concerto for Oboe
and orchestra
1. Prelude
2. Nocturne
3. Scherzo
Manuscript whereabouts unknown
First performance 11 February 1945,
Wembley Town Hall, by David Tucker
and the Pinner Orchestra, conducted
by Kenneth Tucker.
Notes Written for and dedicated to David
Tucker (a former pupil at Dartington
Hall School) in his first year as a
student at the RCM. The music is lost.

1944
First String Trio
for violin, viola and cello
1. Andante
2. Presto
3. Un poco lento
4. Andante
Duration 14′
Manuscript 21pp; HF
Dedication 'For the Dartington Hall
String Trio'
First performance 28 May 1944,
Dartington Hall, by Robert Masters,
Nannie Jamieson and Muriel Taylor
Notes These three players, the core of
the former Dartington Hall Music
Group, continued to work as a trio

during the war while the pianist Ronald Kinloch Anderson was serving in the RAF. The London première of IH's First String Trio took place on 17 July 1944 at a National Gallery concert given by the dedicatees, who were to play it on many subsequent occasions. The work received its first broadcast on the BBC Third Programme on 28 September 1951.

February–March 1944

Five Songs

for SSSAA

1. Evening Prayer: Upon my right side I me lay (Anon. 15th century)
2. Hail be thou, maid, mother of Christ (Anon. 15th century)
3. O years and age, farewell (Robert Herrick)
4. What man is he that can know the counsel of God? (Wisdom IX, 13–17)
5. In Heaven it is always Autumn (John Donne)

Manuscript HF (no. 5 only); cyclostyled copies of all five songs in IH's hand, inscribed 'For Dorothy with love from Imogen March 1944', are in the Dartington Hall Archives. HF has another similar set.

Published No. 5 only: OUP, 1947 (Oxford Choral Songs, no. 576). Republished with 'The twelve kindly months' as *Two seasonal part songs for upper voices* (Thames, 1998).

Dedication 'For Dorothy Elmhirst' (no. 5)

Notes Nos. 3 and 5 were performed at Dartington on 4 February 1945 at a concert given in memory of Joan Lennard, a promising singer, who had died in February 1944.

May 1944

Four Songs

for soprano and piano

1. Brittle beauty
2. Why fearest thou thy outward foe?
3. Shall I thus ever long?
4. As lawrell leaves

Words From *Tottel's Miscellany* (1557)

Manuscripts 13pp: 1. and 2. HF. 3. Dartington Hall Archives. 4. in private possession

Notes Written for Mary Williams, one of IH's first Dartington students, who sang the songs there on 12 July 1945. Richard Tottel was a London printer who published the earliest anthology of English poems.

circa 1945

Cantata no. 79 'God the Lord is Son and Shield'

J. S. Bach, edited for SSA

Manuscript full score, edited in IH's hand; incomplete; HF

circa 1945

Hierusalem

for eight-part female voice chorus

Words 'F.B.P.', from *Tottel's Miscellany* (1557)

Manuscripts (a) 16pp; (b) 12pp. Both HF

circa 1945

Offley Suite

for elementary string class

violins 1, 2, 3 and 4 (open strings), viola (*ad lib*), cello, double bass (*ad lib*)

1. Prelude
2. Toccata
3. Nocturne

Manuscript 10pp; HF

Notes An entirely different work from the 1942 *Offley Suite* for recorders.

circa 1945
The Tempest
Henry Purcell. An arrangement for piano, flute, descant recorder, oboe, clarinet, strings
Manuscript piano score and parts of 24 bars; Dartington Hall Archives

circa 1945
Three Somerset Folk Songs
arranged for small orchestra; the songs collected by Cecil Sharp and published by Novello
    1. The crystal spring
    2. A-roving
    3. The sailor from the sea
Manuscript Autograph parts (except two in another hand); Dartington Hall Archives. No score was prepared; the conductor was to use the Novello piano edition.

November–December 1945
Young Beichan
A Puppet Opera in seven scenes for soloists, chorus and orchestra [1.1.1.1–string quartet–dbass]
Words Libretto by Beryl de Zoete (founded on the traditional ballad of Lord Bateman)
Duration 65'
Manuscript 99 pp (piano score); Dartington Hall Archives
Dedication 'For Dorothy with love from Imogen, Dartington, January 1946'
Notes An 'open rehearsal' of the music took place at Dartington on 3 June 1946, without puppets, and with piano accompaniment, the singers sight-reading their parts. The principal singers were April Cantelo, Patrick Harvey and Richard Wood. There are no indications that the work was ever performed again, and no orchestral score or parts have emerged. A carbon copy of the libretto is with the

manuscript. 'Young Beichan' contains five versions of the traditional Lord Bateman tune (from Britain and Kentucky) and four other folk songs are also used.

circa 1946
Duet for 2 Treble Recorders
Manuscript 5pp; HF (on loan from Schott)
Notes On 1 October 1946 IH wrote to Schott, enclosing a copy of the *Deddington* Suite and also 'a copy of a more recent recorder piece, a short Duo for treble recorders'. Schott chose to publish the suite, but not the duet.

1946
Six Canons for Violin Classes
    1. Pastoral
    2. Jig
    3. Lament
    4. Dance
    5. Slow Air
    6. Nocturne
Manuscript HF
Published OUP, 1948
Dedication 'For Sybil Eaton'
Notes A prefatory note explains that 'these canons in eight parts are intended for graded violin classes where the least experienced players will be able to take an easy part in contrapuntal music that is not confined to the familiar tonic and dominant seventh, while the most experienced players will find several technically difficult passages that need practising.'

    Detailed performance instructions follow. The dedicatee, the violinist Sybil Eaton, was very interested in the RMSA and its work with amateur string players. She had been the prime instigator of the CEMA Music Travellers scheme, and for three years was herself the senior Traveller. She had a serious illness in 1945 and spent a year recuperating at Dartington; she said of IH 'She taught me how to phrase.'

August 1946

Festival Anthem: 'How Manifold are Thy Works'

A setting of the 104th Psalm
for choir [SSATB] and organ [or piano]
Duration 14′30″
Manuscripts Both of 32pp: (a) Dartington Hall Archives; (b) HF
Dedication 'For Dorothy with love and gratitude September 21st 1946'
Notes The Elmhirsts had a chalet on the cliffs at Portwrinkle, just over the Tamar into Cornwall, and lent it to IH for a quiet holiday, which she used to write this anthem together with the String Quartet no. 1 and the *Four Canons for Winsome*.

August 1946

Four Canons for Winsome

for female voices
  1. Give not over thy mind to heaviness (3 voices) (Ecclesiasticus)
  2. Let the words of my mouth (4) (Psalm 19)
  3. I sent you out with mourning (4) (Baruch)
  4. Set me as a seal upon thine heart (5) (Song of Solomon)
Manuscript 10pp; HF
Notes Written at Portwrinkle. Winsome Bartlett taught craft skills and folk dancing to the music students at Dartington.

August 1946

String Quartet no. 1

  1. Lento
  2. Presto
Duration 15′
Manuscripts each of 35pp: (a) Dartington Hall Archives; (b) and (c) HF

Dedication 'For Dorothy with love from Imogen, January 1947'
First performance possibly 24 April 1990, the Baptist Chapel, Aldeburgh, by The Brindisi Quartet (Jacqueline Shave, Patrick Kiernan, Katie Wilkinson, Jonathan Tunnell)
Notes Although it may have been played through soon after its composition there is no record of any performance during IH's lifetime. The work has since been recorded by the Brindisi Quartet (Conifer CDCF196).

1947

Folk Songs of the British Isles

selected and set for piano
  Oh, Yarmouth is a pretty town
  Chevy Chase
  Lord Willoughby
  Greensleeves
  The Coventry carol
  A brisk young lad he courted me
  Bedfordshire Mayday carol
  The valiant lady
  Agincourt song
  The gallant poachers
  Portsmouth
  I must live all alone
  Robin's last will
  Robin Adair
  Loch Lomond
  Ye banks and braes
  Annie Laurie
  Come o'er the stream, Charlie
  Milking croon
  O saw ye my wee thing?
  Ca' the ewes
  The Laird o' Cockpen
  When the kye come hame
  The cockle gatherer
  The bells of Aberdovey
  The blackbird
  The stratagem
  The gallows tree
  Londonderry Air

When Johnny comes marching home
Arran boat song
Manuscript HF
Published B&H, 1947
Notes Comprising thirty-one song tunes
in simple arrangements, each one
headed by a few lines from the song
itself. French and Spanish translations
are provided, by M. du Chastain and C.
Alonso respectively.

24 August 1947
A Birthday Canon for Winsome
 Open me the gates of righteousness
for four voices, SATB
Manuscript 2pp; HF
Note Winsome Bartlett's birthday fell on
1 September.

30 August 1947
A Birthday Part-Song for Winsome
 The loppèd tree in time may grow again
for SSSAA
Words Robert Southwell
Manuscript 6pp; HF
Notes The title page claims that this
is 'with/ NO time signature/ NO
bar-lines/ NO key-signature/ NO
sharps/ NO flats/ NO naturals'. As
an adult beginner, Winsome Bartlett
found difficulty in grappling with the
rudiments of music; in 1963 IH's book
An ABC of Music was to be written
with her in mind.

circa 1948
I stand as still as any stone
Round for four voices
Manuscript HF; comprising two small
manuscript copies in the hand of
Winsome Bartlett, annotated by IH (at
some point after WB's death in 1973)
as 'a round that I wrote for her 25 years
ago'

1948
Six Traditional Carols [Second set]
arranged for SSA
 1. O little town of Bethlehem
 2. In dulci jubilo
 3. God rest you merry, gentlemen
 4. This endris night
 5. Lord Jesus hath a garden
 6. Joseph dearest
Manuscript whereabouts unknown
Published OUP, 1948

1949
Lullay my Liking
Gustav Holst. Arranged for female voices
(for SSA with solo soprano)
Manuscript whereabouts unknown
Published Curwen, 1950 (Choruses for
equal voices, no. 2213)

1949
Six Christmas Carols [Third set]
arranged for SSA and SSAA
 1. Wassail song
 2. Coventry carol
 3. Rejoice and be merry
 4. Es ist ein Ros' entsprungen (from the
setting by Michael Praetorius)
 5. Little one (from the setting by J. S.
Bach)
 6. In the bleak midwinter (from the
hymn by Gustav Holst)
Manuscript whereabouts unknown
Published OUP, 1949
Notes The slight change of title for this
collection reflects the inclusion of
carols by three named composers.
The Praetorius carol had been set
previously by IH for a concert at
Dartington on 20 December 1942.

1949
String Quartet no. 2
 Largamente, ma appassionato
Manuscript parts only, each of 2 or 3pp
(11pp in all); HF

Notes This unfinished piece, of which only the first movement survives, was heard at Dartington on 24 July 1949, but the players' names were not recorded. IH apparently abandoned the work.

1950–1; rev. 1958–9
Dido and Aeneas
Henry Purcell, realized and edited by IH and Benjamin Britten
Manuscript (a) 'Ah! Belinda', pencil composition sketch (Britten); (b) 'Witches' Dance', ink copyist's score (c) Full score, pencil and ink (IH and Britten); BPL
Published B&H, 1960 (vocal score); 1961 (full score and miniature score). Orchestral parts available for hire.
First performance 1 May 1951, the Lyric Theatre, Hammersmith, by Nancy Evans (Dido), Bruce Boyce (Aeneas), the English Opera Group Chorus and Orchestra, conducted by Benjamin Britten. The first staged performance of the revised version was on 16 May 1962, at Drottningholm, Sweden, with Janet Baker (Dido), John Lawrenson (Aeneas), the Purcell Singers and the EOG Orchestra, conducted by Benjamin Britten.

circa 1950
Four Songs for Recorder Ensemble
arranged for recorder ensemble from the originals of Purcell
 1. Silvia, now your scorn give over
 2. Hail to the myrtle shade
 3. Celia, that I once was blest
 4. I'll mount to you blue Coelum
Manuscript HF

circa 1950
Greensleeves
 Alas, my love, you do me wrong
arranged for SSA
Manuscript whereabouts unknown

Published OUP, 1950 (Oxford Choral Songs, no. 584)

circa 1950
Seventeen Songs of Purcell
Arranged for piano and two violins and cello *ad lib*
 1. I resolve against cringing
 2. When first Amintas sued for a kiss
 3. There's nothing so fatal as woman
 4. Rashly I swore
 5. Sweet tyraness, I now resign
 6. More love or more disdain I crave
 7. She who my poor heart possesses
 8. Cease, O my sad soul, cease to mourn
 9. Let formal lovers still pursue
 10. Tell me no more
 11. Oh! How you protest
 12. No watch, dear Celia
 13. Though you make no return
 14. Take not a woman's anger (*The Rival Sisters*)
 15. Love's power in my heart
 16. Ask me to love no more
 17. Now the fight's done (*Theodosius*)
Manuscript HF

1950
I Must Live All Alone
A folk song arranged for SSA
Manuscript whereabouts unknown
Published OUP, 1950 (Oxford Choral Songs, no. 585)
Notes IH's source for this song was Lucy Broadwood's *English Traditional Songs and Carols* (1908).

July–August 1950
Prometheus
Incidental music for voices (soprano, mezzo-soprano and baritone solos, chorus) and viola
Words From the *Prometheus* of Aeschylus in a translation by Edith Hamilton

Manuscripts (a) solo part (baritone) 6pp + 3pp; HF. (b) solo part (soprano); in private possession

Notes Prometheus formed the First Image of 'The Family of Man', a composite dramatic presentation in four 'images' given at Dartington on 25 and 26 August 1950 as the culmination of the American University Theatre Summer School, which had taken place there over the previous four weeks. IH was a member of the international staff for the Summer School. Her unaccompanied music for *Prometheus* is in thirteen numbered sections. Three additional short movements with manuscript (a) probably also relate to 'The Family of Man'.

October 1950

Welcome Joy and Welcome Sorrow

Six part-songs for female voices (SSA) and harp (or piano)

1. Welcome joy and welcome sorrow
2. Teignmouth
3. Over the hill and over the dale
4. O sorrow
5. Lullaby
6. Shed no tear

Words John Keats

Duration 12′

Manuscript 34pp; in private possession. HF has a photocopy.

Published OUP, 1951

Dedication 'For the Aldeburgh Festival'

First performance 9 June 1951, the Jubilee Hall, Aldeburgh, by the Northgatean Singers and Enid Simon (harp), conducted by IH

Notes Written at Dartington, this work marked IH's first direct involvement with the Aldeburgh Festival, and was written (at Benjamin Britten's request) for a Serenade concert given at the fourth Festival.

1951

Ten Indian Folk Tunes from the Hill Villages of the Punjab

transcribed for solo descant recorder by Prabhakar Chinchore and IH

Manuscript 6pp; HF (on loan from Schott)

Published Schott, 1953

Notes These untitled Punjabi folk songs were collected by Prabhakar Chinchore, who used them to introduce IH to the intricacies of the classical music of India when she visited Santiniketan, the Tagore University of Western Bengal, in December 1950 and January 1951.

Spring–Summer 1951

Benedick and Beatrice

A one-act opera in twelve scenes, the libretto adapted from Shakespeare's *Much Ado About Nothing*, for mixed voices (soloists and chorus) and speaking parts; violin, viola, cello, piano, f1, 3 treble recs (1 doubling descant), 2 obs, bsn, hn, tpt, pipe and tabor, bells, gong; 3 on-stage violins

Duration 75′

Manuscripts (a) Sketches (marked 'incomplete' by IH) 112pp; HF. (b) Incomplete performing material (three single-line solo voice parts and cello only); HF. (c) Piano part; HF

First performance 21 July 1951, The Barn Theatre, Dartington Hall, by the staff and students of the Arts Department, with the assistance of Cecil Cope (Don Pedro) and Walter Todds (Benedick) and members of the Playgoers' Society. Spoken scenes produced by Miriam Adams. The opera produced and conducted by IH.

Notes The single performance of this opera, given as the second part of a double bill, took place before an invited audience on IH's last weekend as Director of Music at Dartington. It involved all her staff and students – the singers included Noelle Barker (Beatrice), Kathleen Kelly (Hero) and Roger Newsom (Claudio) – and, in three spoken scenes, members of the amateur drama group as Dogberry, Verges, Watchmen etc. IH was adamant that it should not be performed again.

1952
L'Allegro, il Penseroso ed il Moderato

George Frideric Handel. A shortened version arranged for equal voices and orchestra (and *ad lib* soprano and alto soli)

Duration 60'

Manuscript vocal score, HF

Published Curwen, 1953. The songs 'Come with native Lustre shine' and 'These delights if thou canst give', and the choruses 'Populous cities please us then' and 'Thy Pleasures, moderation give' were also published separately.

29 April 1952
Rejoice in the Lamb

Benjamin Britten. Festival Cantata, op. 30, for soloists, chorus and orchestra, orchestrated IH

1.1.1.1–1.0.0.0–timp–perc–hp–organ (*ad lib*)–strings

Duration 16'

Manuscript whereabouts unknown

Published B&H (score and parts on hire)

First performance IH's orchestration was first performed on 21 June 1952, in the Parish Church, Aldeburgh, by the Aldeburgh Festival Chorus and Orchestra, conducted by Benjamin Britten.

Notes The orchestration was made at Britten's invitation; its success contributed directly to his asking IH, later in the year, to come to Aldeburgh and work as his assistant on *Gloriana*.

October–November 1952
Sellenger's Round

transcribed from Byrd's setting for the Virginals

for string orchestra

Manuscript whereabouts unknown; dyeline copies of IH's fair copy of the complete *Variations on an Elizabethan Theme* are at the BPL

First performance 16 June 1953, in a broadcast by the BBC Third Programme from London, conducted by Benjamin Britten

Notes IH made this transcription to provide the theme for the *Variations on an Elizabethan Theme* commissioned from six composers for the coronation celebrations during the Aldeburgh Festival 1953, where the work received two performances.

circa 1953
The Fatal Hour Comes On

Henry Purcell, realized by IH

Manuscript whereabouts unknown

Notes The song occurs in vol. 2 of *Orpheus Britannicus* (London, 1702). IH's arrangement prompted a conversation between her and Britten, recorded in her Aldeburgh diary, on 2 November 1953, in which Britten said that said that 'he thought my realisations were better than his (!!) because they were a better compromise between imagination and suitable notes'.

1953
By What I've Seen I Am Undone
Daniel Purcell, edited and realized by IH
Manuscript whereabouts unknown
Notes The realization was broadcast in
a recital by Peter Pears and George
Malcolm on 10 December 1953.

1953
[Four songs]
Henry Carey, edited and realized for
voice and piano by IH
1. The beau's lament for the loss of
Farinelli
2. Polly's birthday
3. Justification for living
4. Advice to a friend in love
Manuscripts 1. 3pp + 2pp, including a
solo vocal line heavily annotated by
Peter Pears; 2. 2pp; 3. 3pp; 4. 4pp
+ 1p, including additions by George
Malcolm. All BPL
Notes Nos. 2–4 are all taken from Carey's
Musical Century (1737), and featured in
a BBC broadcast by Pears and George
Malcolm on 10 December 1953.

1953
O Lord, Grant the Queen a Long Life
Henry Purcell, edited and realized by IH
Manuscript HF
First performance 20 June 1953, at the
Aldeburgh Festival, by the Aldeburgh
Festival Choir and Orchestra,
conducted by IH
Notes IH prepared the work for
its performance at the opening
Coronation Choral Concert of the 1953
Aldeburgh Festival. Decca recorded the
concert and released it later in the year
on LP as LXT 2798.

1954
March from the Courtly Dances
from Benjamin Britten's *Gloriana*
arranged for orchestra
Manuscript whereabouts unknown
First performance 24 February 1954,
Ipswich
Notes IH 'scored the March for the
Suffolk Rural Music School's Adult
Founders' Day concert … it may have
been completed some time before the
performance, to allow for adequate
rehearsal time' (Banks and Strode,
'*Gloriana*: A List of Sources', p. 134).

1954–9
Music for Recorders
A series published by B&H between 1954
and 1959 under the general editorship of
Benjamin Britten and IH for which, apart
from the specially written contemporary
pieces and those otherwise noted, all the
detailed editorial work was undertaken
by IH.

The series was a direct outcome
of amateur music-making with the
Aldeburgh Music Club at which Britten,
taught by IH, would play the descant
recorder. He had been a founder-member
of the Club in 1952.

Duets for Descant Recorders
Twenty-five Practical Lessons for the
Beginner
Manuscript whereabouts unknown
Published B&H, 1955 (Music for
Recorders, no. 1)
Notes A publishers' note about this tutor
reads 'These little duets are so devised
that the less easy part is of interest
to the teacher, while the pupil has a
simple line involving at first only one
note, progressing to the full range of
two octaves.'

Folk Songs for Three Descant Recorders

Thirty-three short arrangements of folk songs from different countries in six sets, each set printed on its own playing-score leaflet and available separately, or all six complete in a folder. Published with the reference number 'FSR', as below.

FSR1 Four Scottish Folk Songs
1. Robin's last will
2. The cockle gatherer
3. The blithesome bridal
4. Ca' the ewes

FSR2 Seven French Folk Songs
1. Fais dodo
2. Le rosier
3. Entrez la belle en vigne
4. On dit que l'amour
5. Le nez de Martin
6. Le chat à Jeanette
7. Mon père avait cinq cents moutons

FSR3 Five Norwegian Folk Songs
1. The suitor
2. Norwegian dance
3. Will you help me to sing?
4. Herdsman's song
5. The bailiff's fine mare

FSR4 Six Irish Folk Songs
1. The little red lark
2. The breeches on
3. I lost my love
4. If all the young maidens were blackbirds and thrushes
5. Nursery song
6. Plough whistle

FSR5 Seven Flemish Folk Songs
1. The good man
2. Van Hanselijn
3. Rosalie, will you dance with me?
4. Wake up
5. Under the trees so green
6. The message
7. New Year's song

FSR6 Four Welsh Folk Tunes
1. Y Gwcw fach (The cuckoo)
2. Clycha Aberdyfi (The Bells of Aberdovey)
3. Bugail yr Hafod (When I was a shepherd)
4. Ap Shenkin

Manuscript whereabouts unknown
Published B&H, 1955 (Music for Recorders, no. 3)

Recorder Pieces from the 12th to the 20th Century

Eighteen numbers in three groups of six, each number printed on its own playing-score leaflet and available separately, or each group complete in a folder. Published with the reference number prefix RP, as below.

Nos. 1–6
Published B&H, 1955 (Music for Recorders, no. 2)

RP1 **Scherzo** (1955) by Benjamin Britten for d, tr, ten, b (or ten 2)
Dedication 'To the Aldeburgh Music Club'
First performance 26 June 1955 by the dedicatees at an Aldeburgh Festival concert conducted by IH; the performers were in moored punts on Thorpeness Meare.
Notes The first performance of Britten's *Alpine Suite* for two descants and one treble recorder (published separately in the *Music for Recorders* series) was given in the same Festival programme as *Scherzo*. It was composed on a Swiss skiing holiday in February 1955 when the dedicatee, the artist Mary Potter, had injured her leg and needed distraction.

RP2 **Two Motets**
Pérotin, transcribed and edited by Arnold
Dolmetsch
　1. Vir perfecte for 2 tr
　2. Haec dies for 2 tr, ten

RP3 **Air from 'Persée'**
Jean Baptiste Lully
for 2d, tr, ten, b (or ten 2)

RP4 **Five Pieces from 'Mikrokosmos'**
Béla Bartók
for d, tr
　1. Dor hangsor / In Dorian mode
　2. Napkeleten / In Oriental style
　3. Délszlávos / In Yugoslav mode
　4. Sípszó / Duet for pipes
　5. Népdalféle / In the style of a folksong

RP5 **Canzonet**
　Desus, nostre treille de may
Adrian Willaert
for d, tr, ten

RP6 **Canon**
　On the death of a nightingale, K229
W. A. Mozart
for 3 tr

Nos. 7–12
Published B&H, 1955 (Music for
　Recorders, no. 2)

RP7 **Allegro**
Lennox Berkeley
for 2 tr

RP8 **Six Rounds**
Henry Purcell
for 3 tr
　1. Once in our lives
　2. True Englishmen
　3. Since time so kind to us does prove
　4. Young Colin
　5. Of all the instruments
　6. To all lovers of music

RP9 **Gavotte**
Gustav Holst
for d, tr, ten, b
Notes IH's note on this score reads 'From
　an unpublished movement for string
　orchestra'. This was the original second
　movement of *Brook Green Suite* which
　Holst decided to cut (leaving the other
　three movements) after hearing an
　informal performance in March 1934.

RP10 **Two Motets**
Gregor Aichinger
for 2 d, tr, ten
　1. Jesu, Rex admirabilis
　2. Jesum omnes cognoscite

RP11 **Traditional Irish Tunes**
from the Petrie Collection
for descant solo
　1. A Clare Jig
　2. The gooseberry blossom
　3. Jig
　4. Take her out and air her
　5. Jig from Cork
　6. John Dwyre of the Glyn
　7. Jig

RP12 **Two Chorales**
Johann Walther
for d, tr, ten, b
　1. Aus tiefer Not
　2. Christ lag in Todesbanden

Nos. 13–18
Published B&H, 1957 (Music for
　Recorders, no. 2)

RP13 **Four Chorales**
J. S. Bach
for d, tr, ten, b
　1. Christ is risen (Erstanden ist der
　　heil'ge Christ)
　2. I will not leave Thee, Lord (Von Gott
　　will ich nicht lassen)
　3. Ah God, what sighs (Ach Gott, wie
　　manches Herzeleid)

4. Lord, now lettest Thou Thy servant (Herr, nun lass in Friede)

RP14 Morris Dance from *Gloriana*
Benjamin Britten
for 2 d

RP15 Five Rounds
John Blow, from *The Pleasant Musical Companion*
for 3 tr
Notes The original titles of these rounds are not given.

RP16 Two Madrigals
Ludwig Senfl
for 2 tr, ten, b
1. The fair maid fetching a bucket of water (Es woll't ein Maidlein Wasser hol'n)
2. I mourn the day (Ich klag den Tag)

RP17 Dance
James Butt
for 2 tr, ten

RP18 Four Pieces
P. I. Tschaikowsky
for d, 2 tr
1. Folk Song
2. Old French Song
3. Russian Song
4. March of the Tin Soldiers

One Hundred Traditional Irish Tunes from the Petrie Collection
for descant solo
Published B&H, 1955 (Music for Recorders, no. 4)
Notes The antiquary and artist George Petrie (1789–1866) was an important early collector of Irish folk music, though his volume *The Ancient Music of Ireland* (1853–5) contained only a handful of the 2,148 tunes he had noted. Two of the airs among the hundred selected by IH for this tune book appear elsewhere in the recorder series, as FSR4/5 and RP11; see above.

The Book of the Dolmetsch Descant Recorder
with a note on breathing by Peter Pears
Published B&H, 1959 (Music for Recorders, no. 6)
Notes The publishers' note reads: 'A fully illustrated tutor for home and school, this book is designed for beginners, and includes the most elementary rudiments of music (which may be omitted by the more experienced pupil), half-tone photographs, diagrams, and many carefully selected and graded music examples.' The examples include the 'March' from Britten's *Gloriana*, arranged for descant recorder.

1954
The Second Lute Song of the Earl of Essex
from Benjamin Britten's *Gloriana*
arranged for voice and piano
Manuscript whereabouts unknown
Published B&H, 1954
Dedication 'For Peter Pears'
Notes 'The arrangement derives directly from the vocal score except for the introduction and piano coda which embody some slight recomposition of the corresponding music in the opera.' (Banks and Strode, '*Gloriana*: A List of Sources', p. 124)

1955–6
Choral Dances
from Benjamin Britten's *Gloriana*
arranged for tenor solo and SATB
1. Introduction
2. Time (SATB)
3. Concord (SATB)
4. Time and Concord (SATB)
5. Country girls (SA)
6. Rustics and fishermen (TTBB)
7. Final dance of homage (SATB)
Duration 9'

Manuscripts (a) MS copy (introduction only), (b) MS solo part, (c) interim copies and dyelines; BPL

First performance 15 April 1956, the Victoria and Albert Museum, London, by Peter Pears and the Purcell Singers, conducted by IH.

Notes 'Prepared by IH for Peter Pears for concerts of unaccompanied music which he gave with the Purcell Singers in the later 1950s … most of the solo tenor line derives from the role of Spirit of the Masque, whose solos connect the dances in the opera, and accompanies the chorus in the final dance.' (Banks and Strode, '*Gloriana*: A List of Sources', p. 136)

circa 1955
A Christmas Canon
arranged for recorder quartet from an original by J. S. Bach
Manuscript HF
Notes Probably written for the Aldeburgh Music Club.

1955
For Ever Blessed Be Thy Holy Name
George Frideric Handel, realized for voice and piano
Manuscript 2pp; BPL

1955
O Can Ye Sew Cushions?
Benjamin Britten. From *Folk Song Arrangements*, vol. 1
arranged for SSA and piano
Manuscript whereabouts unknown
Published B&H, 1955
Notes Britten's arrangement of this Scottish song (for solo voice and piano) was first published in 1943 by Boosey & Hawkes as no. 4 in his *Folk Song Arrangements*, vol. I. IH retains his piano accompaniment unaltered.

1955
Six Scottish Songs
arranged for SSA unaccompanied
1. My heart is sair for somebody (Robert Burns)
2. A Highland lad my love was born (Robert Burns)
3. Afton Water (Robert Burns)
4. The piper o' Dundee (Anon.)
5. My boy Tammie (Hector MacNeil)
6. Bonnie Lesley (Robert Burns)
Manuscript whereabouts unknown
Published B&H, 1955

1955
Traditional Songs of Scotland
arranged for SSA unaccompanied
1. Ca' the ewes to the knowes (Robert Burns)
2. Come o'er the stream, Charlie (James Hogg)
3. I'm owre young to marry yet (Anon.)
4. O, saw ye my wee thing (Hector MacNeil)
5. The winter it is past (Anon.)
6. The birks of Aberfeldy (Robert Burns)
Manuscript whereabouts unknown
Published B&H, 1955
First performance no. 6 only: a BBC broadcast on 30 December 1955, by the Purcell Singers, directed by IH

1955
Under the Greenwood Tree
Thomas Arne, realized for voice and piano
Manuscript 5pp; BPL

May 1955
Lavabo inter innocentes
Motet for SSSAA
Words From Psalm 25:6–12
Manuscript HF
Dedication 'For S. and M. with love from Imogen'

Notes Intended as a wedding anthem, but the marriage for which it was written did not take place.

1956
Sally Brown
arranged for voices and recorders
Manuscript whereabouts unknown
First performance 24 June 1956, by the Aldeburgh Music Club singing and playing in punts on Thorpeness Meare at an Aldeburgh Festival concert conducted by IH.
Notes A setting of a sea shanty collected by Cecil Sharp.

1956
Venus and Adonis
realized from the original by John Blow
Manuscript HF
First performance 15 June 1956, at the Aldeburgh Festival, by the English Opera Group, with Heather Harper (Venus), Thomas Hemsley (Adonis), conducted by Charles Mackerras, in a double-bill that also featured GH's *Sāvitri*.
Notes For this edition IH used a British Library manuscript of 1682, and a later manuscript in the Bodleian Library, Oxford. She also used Anthony Lewis's 1949 edition (L'Oiseau Lyre) as a working copy.

1957
Singing for Pleasure
A collection of songs edited for female voices
 The National Anthem (piano only)

FOLK SONGS
1. Jack Jintle (Manchester)
2. Twenty, eighteen (Essex)
3. Donnybrook Fair (Essex)
4. I will give you a paper of pins (Appalachian)
5. Claudy Banks (Hampshire)
6. My boy Billy (Appalachian)
7. It rains and it hails (Appalachian)
8. Hob y deri dando (I'm a shepherd born to sorrow) (Welsh)
9. Maa bonny lad (Northumbrian)
10. Migildi, magildi (Welsh)
11. Plannu coed (Planting trees) (Welsh)
12. Hinkin, winkin, *or* The straw cradle (Manx)
13. The twelve Apostles (Appalachian)

UNISON SONGS
14. Greensleeves (Anon.)
15. Never weather-beaten sail (Thomas Campion)
16. It was a maid of my country (Anon.)
17. The songsters *or* Love in their little veins (Henry Purcell)
18. Water parted from the sea (Thomas Arne)
19. Love will find out the way, *or* Over the mountains (Anon.)
20. How happy could I be with either (Anon.)
21. Under the greenwood tree (Thomas Arne)
22. Hey, dorolot (André-Ernest Grétry)
23. In gentle murmurs (G. F. Handel)
24. The self banished (John Blow)
25. As far as east lies from the west (J. S. Bach)
26. In dulci jubilo (*harm.* J. S. Bach)
27. Cradle song (Franz Schubert)
28. Hen wlad fy nhadau (Land of our fathers) (John James)
29. I vow to thee, my country (Gustav Holst)
30. Let us now praise famous men (Ralph Vaughan Williams)

ROUNDS
31. Hark! the bells (4-pt) (Hauptmann)
32. Where is John? (3-pt) (Anon.)
33. Humming round (4-pt) (E. O'Hanrahan)
34. Hey ho, nobody at home! (5-pt) (Anon.)

35 Oh, blow the wind southerly (4-pt)
(IH)

36. Hot cross buns (5-pt) (Samuel
Webbe)

37. Derry ding ding dason (3-pt) (Anon.)

38. For us a child (5-pt) (Anon.)

39. Lady, come down and see (4-pt)
(Anon.)

40. As I me walked (4-pt) (Anon.)

41. Joy in the gates of Jerusalem (6-pt)
(Anon.)

42. Praise God from whom all blessings
flow (8-pt) (Thomas Tallis)

43. Happy is he (3-pt) (William Byrd)

44. Sanctus (5-pt) (Clemens non Papa)

45. Praise ye the Lord (3-pt) (Palestrina)

46. Jerusalem, O that thou had'st known
(3-pt) (Anon.)

47. Laudate Deum (3-pt) (Henry Purcell)

48. Alleluia (3-pt) (William Boyce)

49. Death and sleep (4-pt) (Joseph
Haydn)

50. Fa la la (4-pt) (W. A. Mozart)

51. Laugh and be glad (2-pt) (Ludwig van
Beethoven)

52. Oh, welcome, welcome smiling May
(3-pt) (Franz Schubert)

53. Pretty bird, sitting in yonder tree
(4-pt) (Johannes Brahms)

54. Welcome, sweet pleasure (3-pt) (G. B.
Martini)

55. One, two, three (3-pt) (Henry
Purcell)

56. Prithee, why so sad? (3-pt) (Henry
Purcell)

57. My dame has in her hut (3-pt) (Henry
Purcell)

58. O ever against eating cares (3-pt)
(Hayes)

59. Adieu, sweet Amaryllis (3-pt) (Anon.)

60. He that will an alehouse keep (3-pt)
(Anon.)

61. Oaken leaves in the merry wood
(3-pt) (Anon.)

62. Sumer is icumen in (Anon., 13th
century)

TWO-PART UNACCOMPANIED

63. Make we merry (Anon.)

64. Here is joy for every age (*Piae
cantiones*, alto by G. Holst)

65. Up in the morning early (Traditional
Scottish)

66. To drive the cold winter away (Anon.,
17th century)

67. Sigh no more, ladies (Richard
Stevens)

TWO-PART ACCOMPANIED

68. Now O now I needs must part (John
Dowland)

69. It was a lover and his lass (Thomas
Morley)

70. Happy, happy we (G. F. Handel, *Acis
and Galatea*)

71. Bring the laurels, bring the bays (G. F.
Handel, *Samson*)

72. How blest are thy children (J. S. Bach,
Cantata 184)

73. Sing, sing, ye Muses (Henry Purcell,
Bonduca)

THREE-PART ACCOMPANIED

74. Welcome home! (Henry Purcell)

75. The Linnet (C. W. Gluck, *Alceste*)

76. The cock's in the yard (J. B. Lully)

THREE-PART UNACCOMPANIED

77. Y Gwcw fach (The cuckoo) (Welsh
folk song)

78. Though Philomena lost her love
(Thomas Morley)

79. Tune thy music to thy heart (Thomas
Campion)

80. Alle, psallite (Anon., 13th century)

FOUR-PART UNACCOMPANIED

81. While I live will I sing praises (J. S.
Bach)

Manuscript whereabouts unknown

Published OUP, 1957, in collaboration
with the National Federation of
Women's Institutes

Notes A wide-ranging collection of
eighty-one pieces from the thirteenth
to the twentieth centuries; folk and

unison songs, rounds, and two-, three- and four-part settings, with and without simple piano accompaniments. In her foreword IH makes several helpful suggestions to both the less and the more experienced conductors, singers, and pianists.

In her own list of published works (1968) IH wrote: 'The publisher purchased the copyright for £150. I ought not to have agreed to this, but I was hard up. It has sold very well indeed, and I shall never again make this mistake!'

1958
A Jubilee Book of English Folk Songs
selected by Kenneth Loveless
Arranged for unison voices and piano

SEA SONGS
The Watchet sailor
Johnny Todd
Admiral Benbow
The coast of the High Barbaree

SONGS OF COUNTRY LIFE
Roving in the dew
The green grass

CAROLS
On Christmas night
Wassail song

LOVE SONGS
Blow, ye winds, in the morning
She's like the swallow
Green bushes

BALLADS
High Germany
The Barkshire tragedy
The three ravens

CHEERFUL SONGS
Stow Fair
The farmer's curst wife
The beggar
My boy Willie

Carrion crow
The Derby ram
Manuscript whereabouts unknown
Published OUP, 1958
Notes A note on the title page reads: 'The Diamond Jubilee of the Folk Song Society, 1898–1958. The songs in this book reflect the ever-growing popularity of the folk songs since the first steps were taken to preserve them sixty years ago. It is to the pioneers of these early days that this book is dedicated.'

The Folk Song Society celebrated here merged at the end of 1931 with the English Folk Dance Society (founded in 1911) to form the English Folk Dance and Song Society. A true collaboration, this *Jubilee Book* has a preface by Douglas Kennedy (Director of the EFDSS from its formation until 1961), while the Revd Kenneth Loveless, who made the selection, was a member of the Editorial Board of the EFDSS Journal. The Librarian of Cecil Sharp House, Sara Jackson, provided fully informative notes on each song, several of which had migrated with settlers to North America. There is a publisher's note on the simple alternative guitar accompaniments by Patrick Shuldam-Shaw, which are printed only in the small-sized Melody Edition, with a caution that they 'are independent of the piano accompaniment and use different harmonies'.

In the Full Edition IH encourages the pianist in her note: 'As in some of Cecil Sharp's country-dance accompaniments (where the same eight bars may have to be repeated a dozen times), the printed version can be taken as a starting-point for the player's own variations. There are almost endless possibilities for changing the texture of the accompaniment while keeping to its main harmonic structure. All that is needed is courage and an unshakable familiarity with the words of the song.'

1958

Six Traditional Carols [Fourth set]
arranged for SSA and SSSA
unaccompanied
1. Nowell sing we, both all and some
2. The moon shines bright
3. The Salutation Carol
4. Quem pastores
5. Unto us is born a Son (SSSA)
6. A Boy was born in Bethlehem (SSSA)
Manuscript whereabouts unknown
Published OUP, 1958
Notes In her preface to this fourth and final set IH has added 'schools' to the suggested list of performers.

1959

Ten Songs
from John Wilson's *Cheerfull Ayres and Ballads* (1659).
arranged for SSA voices
1. From the fair Lavinian shore
2. Fly hence, shadows
3. Full fathom five
4. For ever let thy heavenly tapers
5. Now the lusty Spring is seen
6. So have I seen a silver swan
7. Come, silent night
8. Where the bee sucks
9. Do not fear
10. Lawn as white as the driven snow
Manuscript whereabouts unknown
First performance 1 October 1959, by the Purcell Singers, in a concert for the OUP centenary in London
Published OUP, 1959
Notes The publisher's note reads: 'It is three hundred years since 'Cheerful Ayres or Ballads' was published, "this being the first essay ... of printing music that ever was in Oxford", as the

Preface correctly remarks. Thus, to put it another way, 1959 is the tercentenary year of music publishing at Oxford, and the occasion has been marked by the present publication of this selection of ten songs ... arranged by Imogen Holst for SSA voices.'
The first performance was reviewed in the *Yorkshire Post* (3 October 1959) and *Music and Musicians* (December 1959).

circa 1960

Fifty Tunes for Recorder
Arranged from originals by J. S. Bach
Manuscript Dartington Hall Archives
Notes Compiled for Leonard Elmhirst.
Under IH's tutelage Leonard Elmhirst had become a keen recorder enthusiast. On 6 October 1959 IH wrote to him from Aldeburgh: 'Your lovely letter about your recorder progress was a real joy to read. BLESS YOU: – I shall never forget hearing you practising at dead of night after all those concerts!'

circa 1960

[Forty Rounds]
Thomas Ravenscroft, prepared for publication by IH
Manuscript HF

circa 1960

Ten Bach Tunes
arranged from originals by J. S. Bach
Manuscript Dartington Hall Archives
Notes Compiled for Leonard Elmhirst

1960

A Yacre of Land
Sixteen folk-songs from the manuscript collection of Ralph Vaughan Williams edited by Imogen Holst and Ursula Vaughan Williams. Arranged for unison voices and piano or for unaccompanied part-singing by IH

1. A yacre of land (SAB)
2. John Reilly (SAB)
3. The week before Easter (SAB)
4. Willie Foster (SAB)
5. The jolly harin' (SAB or TBB)
6. Nine joys of Mary (SAB)
7. Joseph and his wedded wife (SATB)
8. The Lord of life (SSA or SSAB)
9. Over the hills and the mountains (SSA)
10. The foxhunt (SSA)
11. Come all you young ploughboys (SSA)
12. A bold young sailor (SA or SAT)
13. The pretty ploughboy (SA)
14. Seventeen come Sunday (SA)
15. It was one morning (SA)
16. My coffin shall be black (SA)

Manuscript whereabouts unknown

Published OUP, 1961

First performance nos. 6 and 7 only: 13 December 1960, Cecil Sharp House, London, by the Purcell Singers conducted by IH, at a concert of Christmas music given for the Vaughan Williams Memorial

Notes An informative introductory note to this selection by its two editors outlines some of the difficulties encountered by folk song collectors and editors: 'From the large body of collected songs, he [RVW] chose for publication the ones he considered best; others were printed in the Journal of the Folk Song Society. A great number remained unpublished and it is from them that we have chosen these sixteen.' Ursula Vaughan Williams has since acknowledged that, apart from a little translation, IH did all editorial work for the collection.

1961

Nineteen Songs

from *Folk Songs of Europe*, edited by Maud Karpeles

for the International Folk Music Council

arranged, with piano accompaniment

1. The red rosebud (Denmark)
2. Flowers red and blue (Sweden)
3. Hark to the cuckoo (Finland)
4. Down by the tanyard side (Ireland)
5. The snow-white bird (Netherlands)
6. All on the grass (Belgium)
7. O I did climb a tree-top (Germany)
8. Spin, spin (Germany)
9. Waltz song (Austria)
10. The white chestnut tree (Portugal)
11. Little partridge (Greece)
12. Cretan dance song (Greece)
13. Military song (Roumania)
14. The cricket takes a wife (Hungary)
15. The wedding garland (Czechoslovakia)
16. The warrior princess (Poland)
17. River Wisla (Poland)
18. Girl's dance song (USSR)
19. When I was a child (Estonia)

Manuscript whereabouts unknown

Published Novello, 1961 (School Song Book, no. 383)

Notes The publisher's note identifies the source from which IH worked: '*Folk Songs of Europe* (Novello, 1956) is an anthology of 183 songs from thirty European countries in which the original texts are given as well as metrical English translations for all songs in foreign languages. The melodies are given without accompaniment.' The accompaniments of the nineteen songs in this collection can be used with the original words as well as with the English translations. Only the English texts are printed for these songs and a publisher's acknowledgement indicates their authors.

August 1961
Tunes from Kentucky
Appalachian Folk Songs
arranged for equal voices with junior
orchestra
Manuscript HF
Notes An incomplete project intended
to be 'a first step in an anti-Orff
campaign in experimental school
classes'. (IH evidently disapproved of
the approach taken by Carl Orff's work
in this field.) From several titles she
had selected, only one specimen was
prepared in full; the instrumentation
includes '*ad lib* percussion, home-
made harps, xylophones etc. with *ad
lib* recorders (descant), bamboo pipes
and elementary violins' with detailed
instructions on how to rehearse.

1962
The Fall of the Leaf
Three short studies for solo cello on a
sixteenth-century tune
   Theme: Andante meno mosso
   1. Vivace
   2. Poco adagio
   3. Presto
   Theme (da capo): Andante molto
      moderato
Duration 9′
Manuscript in private possession
Published OUP, 1963
Dedication 'For Pamela Hind O'Malley'
First Performance 4 February 1963, the
   Wigmore Hall, by the dedicatee
Notes The tune, by Martin Peerson, is
   taken from the *Fitzwilliam Virginal
   Book*. The work was written at the
   request of Pamela Hind O'Malley for
   a piece to include in a Wigmore Hall
   recital. A pupil at SPGS from GH's last
   year, she was later to learn much from
   IH while herself teaching on the music
   staff at Dartington. The piece was later

taken up by Steven Isserlis, who learnt
it at IH's request for an Aldeburgh
Festival concert in 1977.

1962
**The Passion According to Saint
John**
Heinrich Schütz; edited, with English
translation, by Peter Pears and Imogen
Holst
for soloists and chorus (unaccompanied)
Manuscript HF
Published OUP, 1963
Notes This edition arose out of earlier
   performances for which IH had
   prepared her own manuscript parts
   based on the Eulenberg miniature
   score. Her work on it had begun at
   least as early as 1953, as the Passion was
   performed under her direction at the
   1954 Aldeburgh Festival by the Purcell
   Singers, with Peter Pears singing the
   role of Evangelist.

1962
The Twelve Kindly Months
   A kindly good January freezeth pot by
   the fire
for SSA
Words Thomas Tusser (*c.* 1520–1580)
Manuscript whereabouts unknown
Published OUP, 1963. Republished with
   'In Heaven it is always Autumn' as *Two
   seasonal part songs for upper voices*
   (Thames, 1998).
Dedication 'For Valda Plucknett and the
   Ipswich Co-operative Girls' Choir'
First performance 8 February 1963 in a
   pre-recorded broadcast on the BBC
   Midland Home Service by the Ipswich
   Co-operative Girls' Choir, conducted
   by Valda Plucknett
Notes Valda Plucknett was for several
   years a repetiteur for the English Opera
   Group, especially at the Aldeburgh
   Festival. The singing of her Ipswich

Girls' choir at the 1962 Festival impressed Britten and Pears, and they were invited back to perform at Aldeburgh in a programme of music by Tippett and Schumann. This concert in turn moved IH to write this unaccompanied part-song for them, to a text by Thomas Tusser, the sixteenth-century Suffolk agriculturalist poet.

1962
Variations on 'Loth to Depart'
for string quartet and two string orchestras
    Theme: Slow and expressive
    Var. 1. Cinquepace ('Sinkapace')
    – Lively and energetic
    Var. 2. Lament – Fairly slow
    Var. 3. Pastorale – Flowing. Tranquil and unhurried
    Var. 4. Moto Perpetuo – Quick and light
    Var. 5. Chaconne – Fairly slow
Duration 12' 30"
Manuscript RMSA, Little Benslow Hills
Published OUP, 1965
Dedication 'For Mary Ibberson'
First Performance 3 November 1962, RCM Concert Hall, by the RMSA players, conducted by Sir Adrian Boult, in a concert in honour of Mary Ibberson.
Notes IH was not the original choice of composer for the occasion, but offered to write this piece after Malcolm Arnold had pulled out. The sixteenth-century theme, harmonized by Giles Farnaby, is taken from the *Fitzwilliam Virginal Book*. Variation 2 is built on the notes A–D–E (German for 'Farewell'), and Variation 3 uses a different version of the theme, published by Thomas Ravenscroft in *Deuteromelia*, 1609, as a canon. The last movement depicts the activities

of the Association and its Schools and culminates in a final 'farewell' statement of the theme.

By the time she retired in 1962 Mary Ibberson, who had founded the first Rural Music School in Hertfordshire in 1929, was Director of an Association of ten similar schools scattered across the southern half of England. She recognized the needs of would-be musicians in (mainly) country areas long before peripatetic teachers were funded by education authorities, and the value of her work was from the start appreciated and supported by many professional musicians. From 1940 to 1943 the CEMA Music Travellers had been looked after and helped by the RMS Council and from 1943 the RMSA naturally maintained a close connection with IH's training scheme at Dartington Hall, which was to provide several outstanding teachers for the expanding RMSA after the war.

The *Variations on 'Loth to depart'* was completed in a relatively short space of time during a year in which IH renewed interest in her own composition following a decade devoted almost entirely to working for Britten. The first performance was widely noticed, with reviews in the *Sunday Telegraph* (4 November 1962) *The Times* (5 November 1962) and the *Times Educational Supplement* (9 November 1962).

December 1962
String Trio no. 2
for violin, viola and cello
    1. Andante
    2. Allegro
    3. Adagio
    4. Poco lento
    5. Presto

Manuscript violin and cello parts only; in private possession

Dedication 'For the Oromonte Trio'

First Performance 24 June 1963, the Jubilee Hall, Aldeburgh, at the Aldeburgh Festival, by the Oromonte Trio (Perry Hart, Margaret Major, Bruno Schrecker)

Notes The second String Trio was written for an Aldeburgh Festival concert 'Music in England 1963', one of a series of programmes which also included the years 1763 and 1863. The first performance was reviewed in the *Daily Telegraph* (26 June 1963), and *The Times* (25 June 1963).

1964

As Laurel Leaves that Cease Not to Be Green

for SSA [C-T]

Words From *Tottel's Miscellany* (1557)

Manuscript 4pp; HF

Dedication 'For the Purcell Consort of Voices'

First performance 30 March 1965, the Wigmore Hall, London, by the Purcell Consort of Voices

Notes In IH's copy of *Tottel's Miscellany* (Edward Arber's edition, London, 1897) this poem by an unknown author is headed 'The promise of a Constant Lover'.

The founder members of the six-voice Purcell Consort (two sopranos, counter-tenor, tenor, baritone, bass), all of whom had sung with IH in the Purcell Singers, formed themselves into a solo group in 1963 under the direction of the counter-tenor Grayston Burgess. From the start they received IH's encouragement and support, and she was very happy that they too should take on Purcell's name, which her chamber choir had borne for ten years. The Purcell Singers was to

cease to exist as a group after IH gave up conducting it in 1967.

1964

That Lord that Lay in Asse Stall

for SATB

Words Fifteenth century, from a manuscript in the Bodleian Library, taken from *Religious Lyrics of the XVth Century*, ed. Carleton Brown (Oxford: OUP, 1938)

Manuscript whereabouts unknown

Published Cambridge University Press, 1967 (no. 169 of *The Cambridge Hymnal*, ed. David Holbrook and Elizabeth Poston)

Notes One of the many new settings specially commissioned from twenty or so contemporary composers for *The Cambridge Hymnal*.

1964

A Wee Bird Cam' to Our Ha'Door

Scottish traditional song arranged SSATB

Manuscript HF

Dedication 'For Basil Douglas'

Notes Written for the Purcell Singers to celebrate the fiftieth birthday of Basil Douglas (4 March 1964) at an informal gathering in his house. He was a keen amateur tenor, and a founder-member of the Singers.

1965

Make Ye Merry for Him that is to Come

Salvator mundi, Domine

for SSATB

Words Fifteenth century

Manuscript whereabouts unknown

Published OUP, 1965 (no. 14 in *Carols of Today*)

Notes The collection of carols by contemporary composers in which this appears is subtitled 'Seventeen original settings for mixed voices', although not all were in fact new compositions.

1965
Not Unto Us, O Lord
for two choirs of trebles and altos, organ
and optional tubular bells
Words Psalm 115
Manuscript 11p; HF
Dedication 'Written for the dedication of
the chapel at Felixstowe College'
First performance 3 June 1965, Felixstowe
College, by the school choir with organ,
conducted by Daphne Cornford
Notes It was intended that tubular bells
should be used at the performance,
but when they arrived they were a
semitone out, and had to be abandoned.
(The *ad lib* bells part is anyway cued in
for organ.)

1965
The Passion According to Saint Luke
for unaccompanied voices
edited for performance from anonymous
manuscripts, *c.* 1440
Manuscript HF
First performance 21 June 1965, in
Aldeburgh Parish Church, at the
Aldeburgh Festival, by Ian Partridge
(Evangelist), Christopher Keyte
(Christus), the Purcell Consort
of Voices and the Purcell Singers,
conducted by IH
Notes According to the programme
note, the work was originally written
probably for St George's Chapel
Windsor; IH's source was the British
Library manuscript Egerton 3307. Of
the edition, she wrote: 'Any twentieth-
century performance must be guess-
work: no two editors are likely to agree
about which written B natural should
be sung B flat.'

1965
The Passion According to Saint Matthew
Heinrich Schütz; edited, with English
translation, by Peter Pears and IH
for soloists and chorus (unaccompanied)
Manuscript HF
Published OUP, 1965
Notes This edition arose out of an
earlier performance for which IH had
prepared her own manuscript parts.
Pears's involvement in the work had
begun before its performance at the
Aldeburgh Festival on 18 June 1952,
where he had sung the Evangelist in
a performance by The Renaissance
Singers directed by Michael Howard.

1965
The Sun's Journey
A cantata for sopranos and altos and
small orchestra (or piano)
2 flutes, strings, piano, percussion (1
player)
Words John Ford and Thomas Dekker,
adapted from *The Sun's Darling* (1623)
1. Recit.: Phoebus, make holiday! (solo
mezzo-soprano or unison semi-
chorus. This applies to all recitatives)
2. Chorus: *Fancies are but streams
(SSA)
3. Recit. and Chorus: Hark the fair
hour/ Glorious and bright (canon for
4 equal voices)
4. Chorus: *Spring song (SSA)
5. Recit. and Chorus: Music, take Echo's
voice/*Echo's song (canon for 2 equal
voices)
6. Semi-chorus: *Farewell to Spring
(unison sopranos)
7. Recit.: I'll bring you to the court of
the Sun's Queen
8. Pastorale: [instrumental, on a 12th-
century theme]

9. Chorus: *Song of summer (SA) and
   *Folly's song (unison)
10. Recit. and Semi-Chorus: A health
    to Autumn's self!/ *Autumn's song
    (SSAA)
11. Chorus: *Revellers' song (unison)
12. Semi-Chorus: *Winter's song (SA)
13. Recit. and Chorus: See, what strange
    light appears!/ *The Sun is up!
    (unaccompanied round)
14. Recit. and Chorus: Thy sands are
    number'd/ Here in this mirror (SSA)

   * These songs may be sung as separate
     numbers

Duration 25′
Manuscript 42pp; HF
Published OUP, 1965
Dedication 'For the National Union of
Townswomen's Guilds'
First performance 24 May 1967, the
Kingsway Hall, London, by Noelle
Barker (soprano), Pauline Stevens
(mezzo-soprano), massed choirs of
the National Union of Townswomen's
Guilds and the Jacques Orchestra,
conducted by Imogen Holst
Notes *The Sun's Journey* was written at
the request of Helen Anderson, then
National Music Adviser to the NUTG,
who had known IH since 1941, when
they both worked for CEMA. The
NUTG wanted a work for a National
Music Festival with a strongly
competitive element, so IH provided
for that when composing a musically
satisfying whole. The 1967 NUTG
annual report comments 'Miss Holst's
skilful writing of two-part and three-
part pieces of comparable difficulty
… enabled choirs of different sizes to
compete on equal terms'. Nine winning
regional choirs (from an initial entry
of 511) took part in the final in London
before joining together in the first
performance of the cantata.

The minimum instrumentation,
with a string quartet at least, calls
for experienced players, but for most
tutti numbers there are parts for a
larger body of strings 'less experienced
players') and *ad lib* parts for wind
(recorders, oboe, 2 clarinets, bassoon)
and extra percussion. If no orchestra is
available, piano accompaniment alone
may be used, played from the vocal
score. The twelfth-century theme on
which no. 8 is based comes from an
'Alleluia' by Leonin.

April–May 1965
Trianon Suite
for orchestra
2.2.2.2–2.2.2.1–percussion–piano–strings
 1. Fanfare
 2. Dialogue
 3. Toccata
 4. Intermezzo
 5. Nocturne
 6. Ostinato
Duration 8′ 30″
Manuscripts (a) 16pp; HF. (b) in private
possession
First performance 18 September 1965,
Ipswich School Great Hall, by the
Trianon Youth Orchestra, conducted
by Christopher Green
Notes The enterprising Trianon Music
Group for young players and singers
(aged thirteen to twenty-five) was
based in Ipswich. IH heard of the
group during a stay in hospital, where
one of her nurses was the mother of
the Group's director, Christopher
Green, and she became its President in
1961. The Suite takes all sections of the
orchestra into account, and the third
movement has an important part for
piano solo.

1966
I Will Lift Up Mine Eyes
Thomas Tudway, realized for soprano and
continuo by IH
Manuscript HF
First performance 10 June 1966,
   Aldeburgh Church, at the Aldeburgh
   Festival, by the Purcell Singers, directed
   by IH, in a concert of 'East Anglian
   Church Music 1013–1931', one of a
   series of five concerts devised by IH

1966
O Jesu, Look
George Kirbye, edited for SSATB
Manuscript HF
First performance 9 June 1966,
   Framlingham Church, at the Aldeburgh
   Festival, by the Purcell Singers, directed
   by IH, in a concert of 'East Anglian
   Church Music 1013–1931', one of a
   series of five concerts devised by IH

1966
Two Fanfares
   1. For the Grenadier Guards, for three
      trumpets, horn, two trombones
   2. For Thaxted, for two trumpets, flute,
      bells
Manuscript HF
First performance no. 1: 13 December
   1966 in a BBC broadcast
Notes A review of the first broadcast
   performance appeared in *Musical
   Opinion* in February 1967.

1967
The Fairy Queen
Henry Purcell; shortened version for
concert performance devised by Peter
Pears; edited and realized by Benjamin
Britten and IH
Harpsichord part realized by Philip
Ledger
Duration 96'
Manuscript whereabouts unknown
Published FM, 1970

First performance 25 June 1967, the
   Maltings Concert Hall, Snape, as part
   of the Aldeburgh Festival, by soloists
   including Jennifer Vyvyan, Alfreda
   Hodgson, James Bowman, Peter Pears,
   Owen Brannigan; the Ambrosian
   Opera Chorus and the English
   Chamber Orchestra, conducted by
   Benjamin Britten.

1967
Leiston Suite
for brass quartet
   1. Entry Music
   2. Jig
   3. Interlude
   4. Slow March
   5. March to the tune of a kettledrum
Duration 5' 45"
Manuscript HF
First Performance 24 June 1967, at the
   Aldeburgh Festival, directed by Hugh
   Connell
Notes The first performance was
   dedicated 'To the players' (from
   Leiston Modern School) as noted on
   the programme, which also included
   arrangements by IH of a 'Prelude' by
   Pezelius and a 'Canzona' by Gabrieli of
   which nothing now survives.
      Leiston Modern School had strong
   connections with Aldeburgh. Because
   it could boast a handbell team and
   a recorder group, it was invited to
   take part in the first performance of
   Britten's *Noye's Fludde*, and also made
   recordings and broadcasts.

1967
**The Passion According to Saint
John, BWV245**
J. S. Bach, edited by Benjamin Britten
and IH; English translation by Peter Pears
and IH
Duration 120'
Manuscript HF
Published FM, 1967 (hire only)

First performance 26 July 1967, Royal
   Albert Hall, London, by Peter Pears
   (Evangelist), Thomas Hemsley (Jesus),
   Ambrosian Singers, The English
   Chamber Orchestra, conducted by
   Benjamin Britten
Notes Although not published until 1967,
   IH's work on the edition extended back
   to her performance at Dartington on
   20 March 1948. IH's Aldeburgh diary
   records considerable input into the
   translation and edition by Peter Pears
   and Benjamin Britten, prior to its
   performance on 19 June at the 1954
   Aldeburgh Festival, with Pears as the
   Evangelist, and the Aldeburgh Festival
   Choir and Orchestra, conducted by IH.

1967
Suite from Persée
edited by IH and Emanuel Hurwitz from
the original by Lully
Manuscript score and parts; HF
First performance Aldeburgh Festival, 21
   June 1969, by the Youth Music Centre,
   director Kay Hurwitz
Notes IH wrote in the programme book
   that 'this short suite has been adapted
   from the 1682 score and specially
   arranged for large string orchestra
   without harpsichord'.

1967
Three Carol Arrangements
for three equal voices unaccompanied
   1. As I sat under a holly tree
   2. We have been a-rambling
   3. There was a pig
Manuscript whereabouts unknown
Published FM, 1967
Notes Planned for inclusion in the
   Twenty Traditional British Folk Songs
   (see below), these three carols were
   published separately in time for
   Christmas 1967.

1967
Twenty Traditional British Folk Songs
arranged for unaccompanied equal voices,
in two, three and four parts
   1. I've been to France (2 voices)
   2. There sits the hand (2)
   3. We will all so merry, merry be (2)
   4. Oh shepherd, oh shepherd will you
      come home? (3)
   5. Of all the horses in the merry green
      wood (3)
   6. There was an old woman liv'd in
      Athlone (3)
   7. Shule, shule, shule amogalay (2)
   8. My father gave me an acre of land (3)
   9. Come to the woods (3)
   10. There was a wee cooper who liv'd in
      Fife (2)
   11. Fine new pickled salmon! (2)
   12. Hi! Shoo all 'er birrds! (2)
   13. Will you buy my sweet lavender? (3)
   14. All kinds of fancy chairs (2)
   15. Harf-stones! (3)
   16. Fine and young green watercress! (4)
   17. We have been a-rambling (3)
   18. As I sat under a holly tree (3)
   19. May Day Carol (3)
   20. There was a pig went out to dig (3)
Manuscript whereabouts unknown
Published FM, 1967 and 1968. The
   three carols (nos. 17, 18 and 20) were
   published separately in autumn 1967
   in time for Christmas, before the
   complete volume appeared in 1968.
Notes The tunes and words of these
   songs were 'taken from various late
   19th and early 20th century collections
   in the Journals of the Folk Song
   Society and the English Folk Dance
   and Song Society'. Full details about
   the singer and source of each tune in
   this collection are given in IH's notes
   printed at the end.

1968
How Blest Are They
Henry Purcell; wedding anthem for
mixed voices and soprano and bass soli
with organ.
Realized and translated by Philip Ledger
and Imogen Holst
Manuscript HF
Published OUP, 1968

March 1968
Duo for Viola and Piano
in three movements
1. Allegro molto
2. Poco lento
3. Vivace
Duration 9'
Manuscript 25pp; HF
Dedication 'For Cecil Aronowitz and
   Nicola Grunberg'
First Performance 26 June 1968, the
   Jubilee Hall, Aldeburgh, by the
   dedicatees
Notes This stylistically important work
   was written for Cecil Aronowitz and
   his wife for a 'Musical Families' concert
   at the Aldeburgh Festival, at which
   compositions by five generations
   of Holsts were performed. Cecil
   Aronowitz, principal viola of the
   English Chamber Orchestra, was
   associated with the Aldeburgh Festival
   from 1949 until his sudden death in
   1978. He was the first Director of String
   Studies at the Britten–Pears School for
   Advanced Musical Studies.

December 1968
Out of Your Sleep Arise and Wake
for unaccompanied mixed chorus
(SSATTB)
Text Anon., *c.* 1450, from *Ancient English
   Christmas Carols*, ed. Rickert
Manuscript HF
Published FM, 1970

Dedication 'For John Agate'
Notes The tune is founded on the
   plainsong hymn 'Nunc Sancte nobis
   Spiritus' for the first Sunday in Advent.
   The dedicatee, Dr John Agate (a keen
   amateur singer), was at this time the
   geriatric consultant in East Suffolk, and
   had become a friend of IH's through
   his care for her aged mother, Isobel, in
   her last months.

1969
Badingham Chime
for handbells
Manuscript HF
First performance 24 June 1969, by
   Leiston Modern School, directed by
   Hugh Connell, in Badingham Church,
   Suffolk during a 'church crawl' which
   took place as part of the Aldeburgh
   Festival. The music is marked 'slow, but
   flowing'.

1969
The Glory of the West
Theme and seven variations for brass
band
Manuscript 39pp, Redbridge Music
   School
Dedication 'For the Redbridge Youth
   Brass Band'
First Performance 23 March 1970, the
   Fairfield Halls, Croydon
Notes The theme is taken from Playford's
   English Dancing Master.

1969
Remember Not, O Lord
arranged for male voices from the
original by Henry Purcell
Manuscript HF
First performance 27 October 1969, St
   Sepulchre's Church, Holborn, by the
   Baccholian Singers, on the occasion of
   the Memorial Service for Isobel Holst

November–December 1969
Woodbridge Suite
for orchestra
2.2.2.2–1.2.1.0–timp–perc–strings
  1. Preamble
  2. Musette
  3. Jig
  4. Nocturne
  5. Homage to Leonin
  6. Woodbridge greeting on a ground
Duration 7′
Manuscript 30pp; HF
Dedication 'For the Woodbridge
  Orchestral Society'
First performance 4 May 1970,
  Woodbridge, Suffolk, by the
  Woodbridge Orchestral Society,
  conducted by Bernard Barrell
Notes The first of three works written by
  IH for this amateur orchestra (founded
  in 1907), of which she was President
  from 1960 until her death. The first
  movement became a 'signature-tune'
  for the orchestra and was used on
  occasions to open its concerts. An
  arrangement for military band of the
  suite was made by Major (Ret'd) Brian
  Keeling MBE and first performed on 10
  October 1992 in the Maltings Concert
  Hall, Snape, by the Band of the 1st
  Battalion, The Royal Anglian Regiment,
  conducted by W/O Tim Parkinson.

1970
Browning
William Byrd, edited for violin, 2 violas
and 2 cellos
Manuscript HF
First performance 28 June, 1970, the
  Maltings Concert Hall, Snape, as part
  of the Aldeburgh Festival.
Notes The concert, based on folk music
  settings was entitled 'Up she goes
  again', an oblique reference both to
  a similar programme given at the

end of the 1968 Festival and to the
concert hall itself, rebuilt just in time
for the 1970 Aldeburgh Festival after
a disastrous fire the previous summer.
The programme for this final concert
of the 1970 Festival also featured IH's
arrangement of *Gipsy Davy*.

1970
Fantasia on Hampshire Folk Tunes
for string orchestra
  1. Eggs in her basket
  2. The female farmer
  3. The outlandish knight
  4. Claudy banks
Duration 6′
Manuscript HF
First performance 26 June 1983, in a BBC
  broadcast
Notes Four tunes from an unpublished
  string quartet by Gustav Holst (1916,
  H135) revised and arranged by IH at
  the time she was preparing *A Thematic
  Catalogue of Gustav Holst's Music*
  for publication in 1974. She prepared
  a note on the piece, detailing how
  the original, for all its 'unhelpful
  repetition' and 'padding', contained
  many enjoyable passages, and how
  she decided in the 1960s to 'revise
  it ruthlessly' and recast it for string
  orchestra, enlivening the texture of the
  original by introducing contrapuntal
  entries, and inventing new variants for
  several phrases.

1970
Gipsy Davy
  It was late in the night when the squire
  came home
English folk-song from the Southern
Appalachian Mountains arranged as a
ballad for unaccompanied chorus
Manuscript 10pp, HF
Dedication 'For the Wandsworth School
  Choir and Russell Burgess'

First performance 28 June 1970, the
Maltings Concert Hall, Snape, by the
Wandsworth School Choir, conducted
by Imogen Holst
Notes The first performance of this
arrangement of a tune originally
collected by Cecil Sharp in 1916 took
place during the final concert of the
23rd Aldeburgh Festival; see note to
Browning above.

1972
Iken Fanfare
for school wind band
Manuscript whereabouts unknown; copy
HF
Dedication 'For Arthur Harrison and the
IAPS'
First performance 22 July, 1972, the
Maltings Concert Hall, Snape, by the
IAPS Orchestra
Notes Arthur Harrison, retired
headmaster of a boys' preparatory
school and then living in Snape,
was secretary of the Incorporated
Association of Preparatory Schools. He
had enlisted the support of Britten and
IH in forming the new IAPS orchestra.
The parish of Iken is on the river Alde,
almost opposite Snape.

  After the first performance
somebody remarked that an important
tune in the Fanfare was very similar to
the programme theme from a weekly
regional television series then running.
Disturbed at the implication of
plagiarism, IH (who, as the orchestra's
administrator Robin Wilson pointed
out, 'lived too far outside the current
world to possess a television set' and
never watched one) withdrew the work.

September–November 1972
**Hallo My Fancy, Whither Wilt
Thou Go?**
for SS C-T TBB
Words William Cleland
Duration 7′
Manuscripts (a) 11pp; HF. (b) in private
possession
Dedication 'For the Purcell Consort of
Voices'
First performance 21 May 1973, the
Wigmore Hall, London, by the Purcell
Consort of Voices
Notes In her programme note for a later
performance of this (given at Snape
in August 1973) IH remembered: 'I
wrote this part-song in the autumn of
1972, as a tenth birthday present for
the members of the Purcell Consort, in
gratitude for the many performances
we worked at together when they were
in the Purcell Singers.'

1974
Farewell to Rod
for solo voice and continuo
Words IH
Manuscript HF
First performance 28 June 1974
Notes This short 'farewell' was written
for Roderick Biss (music editor and a
director of Faber Music) as he and his
wife Dorothy were returning to their
native New Zealand after many years
in England. IH was unable to attend
their leaving party, but sent along this
recitative and aria in her place. By way
of mock tragedy and sentimentality,
and with something of Purcell about it,
the piece offers a rare glimpse of IH's
humour in musical terms.

January 1976
Joyce's Divertimento
for viola and orchestra
2.2.2.2–1.2.1.0–timp/perc–strings
    1. Entry music
    2. Tide mill
    3. New Year's welcome
Duration 6′30″
Manuscript in private possession
Dedication 'For Joyce and Bernard
    Barrell and the Woodbridge Orchestra'
First performance 17 May 1976,
    Woodbridge, Suffolk, by Joyce Barrell
    and the Woodbridge Orchestral Society,
    conducted by Bernard Barrell
Notes According to Bernard Barrell, the
    work was written for his wife 'for her
    being willing to attend to Imo's washing
    during a stay in Ipswich Hospital when
    she had a major operation there'. The
    conductor remembered that, as Joyce
    Barrell's mother was also ill and the
    soloist would therefore have little time
    to practice, 'with typical understanding,
    Imo produced a most interesting work
    that both tested the orchestra suitably,
    yet gave pleasure in rehearsing'.
       Woodbridge, on the River Deben, has
    a famous ancient tide mill, the subject
    of the second movement. The third is
    'founded on a traditional dance tune'.

November–December 1977
Deben Calendar
for orchestra
1.1.2.1–2.2(2 *ad lib*).2.0–timp–perc–
    strings
    1. January resolutions
    2. February frost
    3. March gales
    4. April rain
    5. May morning
    6. June haysel
    7. July ebbtide

    8. August holiday
    9. September mist
  10. October vintage
  11. November strikes
  12. December feasts
Duration 10′
Manuscript 40pp; in private possession
Dedication 'For the Woodbridge
    Orchestral Society'
First performance 15 May 1978,
    Woodbridge, Suffolk, by the
    Woodbridge Orchestral Society
    conducted by Bernard Barrell
Notes The last work written by IH for
    this amateur orchestra. Some of the
    movements depict the river Deben and
    its countryside, and 'November strikes'
    may perhaps refer to the widespread
    industrial unrest (and consequent
    frustrations) of November 1977.

1978
A Dialogue Between Two Penitents
Pelham Humphrey and John Blow,
realized for two tenors and continuo
Manuscript HF
First performance 14 June 1978, the
    Maltings Concert Hall, Snape, as part
    of the Aldeburgh Festival, by Peter
    Pears and Ian Partridge (tenors) and
    Steuart Bedford (continuo)
Notes The dialogue is taken from the 1714
    edition of the first book of *Harmonia
    Sacra or Divine Hymns and Dialogues*.

1980
February Welcome
for handbells
Manuscript HF
Dedication 'To Barbara Brook and her
    handbell ringers'
First performance Easter 1980,
    Aldeburgh Parish Church

Notes Barbara Brook, a former
   headmistress of Aldeburgh Primary
   School, retired to live in the town
   after a distinguished career as an
   educationalist. *February Welcome* was
   written at her request for her group
   of junior ringers to play. (A few weeks
   later, on 8 June, they were to join in the
   opening Festival service in the same
   church at which John Piper's memorial
   window to Britten was dedicated. The
   service ended with the final hymn
   from *Noye's Fludde*, complete with
   handbells.)

February 1980
A Greeting
for two sopranos, mezzo-soprano and
piano
Manuscript 4pp; copy at BPL
First Performance 20 June 1980, the
   Maltings Concert Hall, Snape, by Marie
   McLaughlin, Heather Harper, Sarah
   Walker and Murray Perahia
Notes Devised 'with the help of several
   composers' works in the Britten–Pears
   and Maltings libraries', *A Greeting* was
   written as a surprise item for the gala
   concert given at the 1980 Aldeburgh
   Festival in celebration of Peter Pears's
   seventieth birthday. The sources, as
   written out by IH herself, are:

'Accompaniment based on the Welcome
   Scene Act II of *Gloriana*
Tchaikovsky's part-song in honour of Anton
   Rubinstein
The Turn of the Screw
Bach's Dramma per Musica 'Zerresisset,
   zersprenget'
The birthday chorus in Purcell's *The Fairy
   Queen*'

The inclusion of a Russian text was
founded on the expectation that
Mstislav Rostropovich and Galina
Vishnevskaya would be taking part, but
in the event they were unable to attend.

1981
About Ship
Traditional seventeenth-century English
dance; arranged for piano duet
Manuscript HF
First performance Christmas 1981
Notes William Servaes, General Manager
   of the Aldeburgh Festival, retired in
   1981. His wife was a good pianist, but
   Bill was distinctly limited in his skill,
   hence the simple part for the second
   player.

1982
Song for a Well-Loved Librarian
for soprano, mezzo-soprano, tenor and
baritone
Words Richard de Bury (1281–1345),
   translated by E. C. Thomas
Manuscript BPL
Dedication 'For Fred'
First performance 30 August 1982, the
   Britten–Pears Library, Aldeburgh, by
   the library staff
Notes Written for the retirement party
   for Fred Ferry, the founding Librarian
   of the Britten–Pears Library.

1982
String Quintet
for two violins, viola and two cellos
Duration 12' 45"
Manuscript in private possession; copy
   HF
Published FM, 1984 (score and parts)
Dedication 'For the Cricklade Festival'
First performance 2 October 1982, St
   Sampson's Church, Cricklade, by the
   Endellion String Quartet and Steven
   Isserlis, cello
Notes The cellist Steven Isserlis
   suggested that IH might write a quintet
   for the 1982 Cricklade Music Festival, a
   choice reflecting his fondness for her
   earlier work for solo cello, *The Fall of
   the Leaf* (1963). IH's note on the piece

recalled that 'in their invitation they mentioned that they wanted a piece to mirror some of the characteristics of the River Thames. I was glad to agree to this request because the music festivals I have worked for have always had local roots.'

The performance was recorded by BBC Bristol and broadcast on 20 March 1983; it received a report in *The Listener* on 17 March 1983.

1983
Seven Tunes
Gustav Holst; arranged for easy piano
  1. Jupiter's theme (*The Planets*)
  2. Slow dance (*St Paul's Suite*)
  3. Carol: A dream of Christmas
  4. Song (*The Coming of Christ*)
  5. Entry tune (*The Wandering Scholar*)
  6. Mr Shilkret's march (*Capriccio*)
  7. Air (*Brook Green Suite*)
Manuscript whereabouts unknown
Published FM, 1983

1984
Homage to William Morris
for bass voice and string bass
Words From lectures and *News from Nowhere* by William Morris
Duration 7'
Manuscripts (a) The William Morris Society (b) copy, pencil score and sketches; HF
Published The William Morris Society, 1985
First performance 24 March 1984, Institute of Contemporary Arts, London, by Peter Rose and Mary Scully, for the 150th anniversary of the birth of William Morris
Notes IH was invited to compose this work partly because it was known that her father had held William Morris in high regard. Her own interest in Morris stemmed from childhood,

when GH, during their walks along the Thames towpath, would point out to her Morris's home, Kelmscott House. The musical tribute to mark the 150th anniversary of Morris's birth was a new departure for the Society, and IH's death only two weeks before the first performance greatly saddened the concert organizers, who wrote in the concert programme: 'Without her inspiration and help, today's events could not have taken place. The willingness with which she responded to [our] invitation to compose a new work ... the advice and encouragement she gave us in our first venture in promoting new music' her help with practical arrangements for the concert; and her generosity in presenting [the manuscript] to the society; these are all characteristic of her, and they place us deeply in her debt.'

IH originally conceived the work to be for tenor and viola as she had mistakenly believed Peter Rose to be a tenor. The choice of string bass came about at Peter Rose's suggestion.

February 1984
Sextet for Recorders
An Anniversary Serenade
for sopranino, 2 descants, 2 trebles and tenor recorders
  1. Entry Music
  2. Night Piece
  3. Dance
  4. Song without words
  5. Salutation (with tunes from Playford, Purcell and Britten)
Duration 8' 30"
Manuscript HF
Dedication 'For the Society of Recorder Players'
First performance 12 May 1984, at the Guildford Recorder Festival

Notes The Sextet was commissioned by Evelyn Nallen, vice-president of the Guildford branch of the Society of Recorder Players, in 1983. It was recorded for BBC Radio 3 in September 1984. In a programme note IH wrote: 'The last [movement], Salutation, is a brief gesture of gratitude to some of the recorder players who have been my friends, beginning with Miles Tomalin, whose playing first converted me to the recorder as a 'real' instrument; he is represented by a Purcell hornpipe. The second tune, Nonsuch, is a Thankyou to the recorder players in my amateur orchestra at Cecil Sharp House half a century ago; they taught me to try and make the sound on music convey the feel of the dance. The third tune is a jig from Britten's *Gloriana* which he allowed me to transcribe for the series of recorder pieces we were editing together. He used to enjoy playing recorder trios during his free evenings at Aldeburgh, and he was president of the Society of Recorder Players from 1959 until his death in 1976.'

1984
Concerto
for recorder and string orchestra
Lament
Manuscript HF (sketches only)
First performance 5 October 1984, at the Cricklade Music Festival, the solo recorder played by Evelyn Nallen
Notes The single-movement 'Lament' forms the central movement of an unfinished Recorder Concerto intended for the 1984 Cricklade Music Festival. Colin Matthews, who edited it for performance, wrote in

the programme note: 'When I first looked at the sketches for the concerto it seemed that it might be possible to reconstruct the whole work. But while the first movement, a brief pastoral introduction, and the second movement, entitled "Lament", were nearly complete in the sketch, it soon became clear that the finale, a buoyant Allegro, was too fragmentary to put into shape without a great deal of composing being necessary. The first movement does not really make sense without the finale to balance it, so I have completed and scored the "Lament" as a separate movement.'

1984
Duo for Violin and Cello
Manuscript sketches only; HF
Notes Steven Isserlis has revealed that this duo was intended for the Deal Festival (1984) for the violinist Roger Raphael and himself. The final word should come from IH herself, in the form of a quotation from the sketches for the second (final) movement of this last work; the programme for these sketches is revealing, and makes a fitting conclusion to this catalogue:

Air *wind in leaves, reeds, trees*
Water *stormy sea, rippling stream, fountain trickling in sunshine*
Colour-and-sound *rainbow, sunlight on dew, sunlight on frost*
Fire deep under earth *creation-warmth bringing growth*
Living things *fishes, insects, birds*
Humans *children skipping, athletes running, ballet dancers*
Old age *OAPs hobbling ('col legno')*
Protest against disintegration *climax*
Gradual calming down
Acceptance

B Editions of music by Gustav Holst

Throughout her composing career IH had occasionally made arrangements of her father's music, both vocal and instrumental; these are listed in the main catalogue above. Then in 1964, she embarked on the preparation of new and revised editions of his music, for performance and publication, in tandem with her work on *A Thematic Catalogue of Gustav Holst's Music* (London: Faber Music, 1974), and including a notable series of facsimile editions, which appeared between 1974 and 1983.

Two Pieces
for piano
Edited by IH
  1. Nocturne
  2. Jig
Published FM, 1965

The Harper (1891)
for voice and piano
[Edited by IH for its first performance in 1967]
Unpublished

The Autumn is Old (1895)
for SATB
[Edited by IH for its first performance in 1967]
Unpublished

The Planets, op. 32
Suite for large orchestra
Full orchestral score
Revised by IH
Published Curwen, 1969

Lyric Movement
for viola and small orchestra
Reduction for viola and piano by IH
Published OUP, 1971

The Wandering Scholar, op. 50
a chamber opera in one act
Vocal score, Study score
Edited by Benjamin Britten and IH
Published FM, in association with G. & I. Holst, 1968 (vocal score); 1971 (study score)

Capriccio
for orchestra
Study score
Edited by IH
Published FM, in association with G. & I. Holst, 1972

Sāvitri, op. 25
an episode from the Mahabharata
Revised edition by IH
Published Curwen: FM, 1973; Eulenburg (with foreword by Imogen Holst), 1976

Chamber Operas
  1. Sāvitri, op. 25
  2. The Wandering Scholar, op. 50
Edited by IH
Published FM, in association with G. & I. Holst, 1974 [Collected facsimile edition of autograph manuscripts of the published works; vol. 1]

First Choral Symphony, op. 41
Vocal score, Full score, Study score
Revised 1973 by IH
Published Novello, 1974

Seven Part-Songs, op. 44
for female voices and strings
Vocal score, Full score
Revised 1973 by IH
Published Novello, 1974

Works for Small Orchestra

1. St Paul's Suite, op. 29 no. 2
2. A Fugal Concerto, op. 40 no. 2
3. Double Concerto, op. 49
4. Brook Green Suite
5. Lyric Movement

Edited by IH; assistant editor Colin Matthews
Published FM, in association with G. & I. Holst, 1977 [Collected facsimile edition of autograph manuscripts of the published works; vol. 2]

Terzetto (1925)

for flute, oboe and viola (or clarinet)
[Revised by] IH; clarinet adapted from the viola part by R. James Whipple
Published Chester Music, 1978 (The Chester Woodwind Series)

Nunc Dimittis

for SSAATTBB unaccompanied
[Revised by] IH; keyboard reduction added by Desmond Ratcliffe
Published Novello, 1979

The Planets, op. 32

Suite for large orchestra
New edition, prepared by IH and Colin Matthews
Published Curwen, 1979; B&H, 1983 (Hawkes Pocket Scores; 22); Ernst Eulenburg, 1985

The Planets, op. 32

Suite for large orchestra
Edited by IH and Colin Matthews

Published FM, in association with G. & I. Holst, 1979 [Collected facsimile edition of autograph manuscripts of the published works; vol. 3]

First Choral Symphony, op. 41

Edited by IH and Colin Matthews
Published FM, in association with G. & I. Holst, 1983 [Collected facsimile edition of autograph manuscripts of the published works; vol. 4]

Wind Quintet in A flat, op. 14/H67

Study score
Edited by IH and Colin Matthews
Published FM, 1983

The Lure (1921), H149

Ballet music for orchestra
Score
Introduction by IH and Colin Matthews
Published FM, 1984

Four Part-Songs

for unaccompanied chorus
Edited by IH
Published Novello, 1988

The Mystic Trumpeter, op. 18/H71

scena for soprano and orchestra
Study score
Edited by Colin Matthews and IH
Published Novello, 1989

Five Part-Songs, op. 12

'Her eyes the glow-worm lend thee' completed by IH
Published FM, 1992 (Choral programme series)

C *Vocal and piano scores of music by Benjamin Britten*

IH prepared the vocal and piano scores for most of Britten's major compositions from her arrival in Aldeburgh in September 1952 until 1964, when she ceased working for him in order to be able to dedicate her time to editing and cataloguing her father's music. For the sake of completeness, the list that follows also includes her text adaptation of Psalm 127 for the overture that Britten wrote for the opening of the Maltings Concert Hall, Snape, in 1967, and her much later introductory note to the published full score of *Curlew River*. IH's arrangements and orchestrations of Britten's music are, however, included in the main catalogue above.

Gloriana, op. 53
an opera in three acts
[Original version, 1st edition]
Vocal score by Imogen Holst
Published B&H, 1953

Gloriana, op. 53
an opera in three acts
[Original version, 2nd edition]
Vocal score by Imogen Holst
Published B&H, 1954

The Turn of the Screw, op. 54
an opera in a prologue and two acts
Vocal score by Imogen Holst
Published B&H, 1955

The Prince of the Pagodas, op. 57
a ballet in three acts
[Piano reduction by Imogen Holst and
    Erwin Stein]
Published B&H, 1957 (hire only)

Noye's Fludde, op. 59
the Chester miracle play ...
Vocal score by Imogen Holst
Published B&H, 1958

**Cantata Academica, Carmen
Basiliense, op. 62**
Vocal score by Imogen Holst
Published B&H, 1959

Nocturne, op. 60
for tenor solo, seven obligato instruments
    and string orchestra
Vocal score by Imogen Holst
Published B&H, 1960

**A Midsummer Night's Dream,
op. 64**
opera in three acts
[1st and 2nd editions]
Vocal score by Imogen Holst and Martin
    Penny
Published B&H, 1960

Billy Budd, op. 50
an opera in two acts
Revised version, 1961
[Vocal score alterations by IH]
Published B&H, 1961

War Requiem, op. 66
Vocal score by Imogen Holst
Published B&H, 1962

Cantata Misericordium, op. 69
Vocal score by Imogen Holst
Published B&H, 1964

Symphony, op. 68
for cello and orchestra
Reduction for violoncello and piano by
    Imogen Holst; cello [part] edited by
    Mstislav Rostropovitch
Published B&H, 1965

Curlew River, op. 71
a parable for church performance
Rehearsal score by Imogen Holst
Published FM, 1965

The Building of the House, op. 79
overture with or without chorus
Words Psalm 127, adapted by IH from
  The Whole Book of Psalms
Published FM, 1968

Gloriana, op. 53
an opera in three acts
Revised edition 1968
Vocal score by Imogen Holst
Published B&H, 1968

Curlew River, op. 71
a parable for church performance
Full score
Introduction by Imogen Holst
Published FM, 1983

D Index of first lines and titles

References to IH's works in the main text will be found in the General Index.

References in bold type refer to main entries in the catalogue
Names of composers whose music IH has edited, arranged, realized or transcribed appear in italics.
The form of the edition, transcription or arrangement appears in parentheses.

Key to collection references

E Catalogue of IH's works: index of names

This index comprises references in the Catalogue of Works to the named authors and composers used as sources by IH in her own compositions and arrangements.

Bibliography

Full references are supplied here for sources quoted in the text. Of Imogen Holst's own writings the selection given here aims to give a broad overview of the range of interests and enthusiasms that encouraged her into print. From the mid-1930s and thence throughout her life she contributed short articles on folk music and much else to a wide range of magazines and journals, as well as programme notes for concerts, festivals and record sleeves. In addition she delivered many other unpublished broadcast talks and public lectures, drafts of many of which are preserved at the Holst Foundation in Aldeburgh.

Banks, Paul, ed. *Britten's Gloriana: Essays and Sources*. Woodbridge: Boydell Press, 1993.

Banks, Paul and Rosamund Strode. '*Gloriana*: a list of sources'. In Banks, *Britten's Gloriana*, pp. 95–170.

Blythe, Ronald. 'Imogen Holst – perfectionist'. *The Lady*, 20 June 1957.

Bridcut, John. *Britten's Children*. London: Faber, 2006.

Burrows, Jill, ed. *The Aldeburgh Story*. Aldeburgh: Aldeburgh Foundation, 1987.

Carpenter, Humphrey. *Benjamin Britten: a Biography*. London: Faber, 1992.

Cohen, Harriet. *A Bundle of Time: the Memoirs of Harriet Cohen*. London: Faber, 1969.

Cox, Peter, and Jack Dobbs, eds. *Imogen Holst at Dartington*. Dartington: Dartington Press, 1988.

Cox, Peter. *The Arts at Dartington, 1940–1983*. Dartington: Dartington Hall Trust, 2005.

Garnham, Maureen. *As I Saw It: Basil Douglas, Benjamin Britten and the English Opera Group, 1955–1957*. London: St George's Publications, 1998.

Harewood, Lord. *The Tongs and the Bones: the Memoirs of Lord Harewood*. London: Weidenfeld & Nicholson, 1981.

Headington, Christopher. *Peter Pears: a Biography*. London: Faber, 1992.

Holst, Imogen. 'New ways of making music'. *Home and Country*, July 1935.

—— *Gustav Holst: a biography*. London: Oxford University Press, 1938; 2nd edition 1969.

—— 'Rural music'. *The RCM Magazine*, vol. 36 no. 3 (Summer 1940).

—— 'Amateur music'. *The Year's Work in Music*, 1949–50, pp. 19–28.

—— 'The Suffolk Rural Music School'. *Aldeburgh Festival Programme Book*, 1950, p.10.

—— 'Britten's *Let's Make an Opera*'. *Tempo* no. 18 (1950–1), pp. 12–16.

—— 'Equal temperament: some problems of intonation'. *The Chesterian*, vol. 26, no. 167 (1951), pp. 130–2.

—— 'Elizabethan music'. *Aldeburgh Festival Programme Book*, 1951, p.10.

—— *The music of Gustav Holst*. London: Oxford University Press, 1951; 2nd edition, 1968; 3rd rev. edition (with *Holst's Music Reconsidered* as a supplement), 1985.

—— 'Britten and the young'. In Mitchell and Keller, *Benjamin Britten*, pp. 276–86.

—— 'The influence of folk song on twentieth-century music'. *The Chesterian*, vol. 30, no. 183 (1955), pp. 6–9.

—— *The Book of the Dolmetsch Descant Recorder*. London: Boosey & Hawkes, 1957.

—— 'Singing for pleasure'. *Home and Country*, May 1957.

—— and Benjamin Britten. *The Story of Music*. London: Rathbone, 1958.

—— 'Cecil Sharp and the music and music-making of the twentieth century'. *Journal of the EFDSS*, vol. 8 no. 4 (1959), pp. 189–90.

—— 'Folk songs'. *Aldeburgh Festival Programme Book*, 1959, p.16.

—— and Ursula Vaughan Williams, eds. *Heirs and Rebels: Letters Written to Each Other and Occasional Writings on Music, by Ralph Vaughan Williams and Gustav Holst*. London: Oxford University Press, 1959.

——, ed. *Henry Purcell, 1659–1695: Essays on his Music*. London: Oxford University Press, 1959.

—— 'Music in Venice'. *Aldeburgh Festival Programme Book*, 1961, p.12.

—— *Henry Purcell: the Story of his Life and Work*. London: Boosey & Hawkes, 1961.

—— *Tune*. London: Faber, 1962.

—— *An ABC of Music: a Short Practical Guide to the Basic Essentials of Rudiments, Harmony, and Form*. Oxford: Oxford University Press, 1963.

—— 'Indian music'. In *Tribute to Benjamin Britten on his Fiftieth Birthday*, ed. Anthony Gishford. London: Faber, 1963, pp. 104–10.

—— 'The music that Bach was brought up on'. *Aldeburgh Festival Programme Book*, 1964, p.49.

—— *Your Book of Music*. London: Faber, 1964.

—— *Bach*. London: Faber, 1965

—— *Britten*. London: Faber, 1966; 2nd edition, 1970; 3rd edition, 1980.

—— 'Gustav Holst's manuscripts'. *Brio*, vol. 4 no. 2 (1967), pp. 2–4.

—— 'Audiences'. *Aldeburgh Festival Programme Book*, 1970, p. 11.

—— *Byrd*. London: Faber, 1972.

—— *Holst*. London: Novello, 1972.

—— 'Holst's debt of gratitude to Vaughan Williams'. *Folk Music Journal*, vol. 2 no. 2 (1972), pp. 171–2.

—— *Conducting a Choir: a Guide for Amateurs*. London: Oxford University Press, 1973.

—— 'Holst's music: some questions of style and performance at the centenary of his birth'. *Proceedings of the Royal Musical Association*, vol. 100 (1973), pp. 201–7.

—— 'Wind bands'. *Aldeburgh Festival Programme Book*, 1973, p. 7.

——, comp. *Gustav Holst: a Guide to his Centenary*. Cambridge: Cambridge Music Shop in association with G. & I. Holst Ltd, 1974.

—— 'Gustav Holst and Thaxted'. *Thaxted Bulletin*, 1974.

—— 'Gustav Holst's Debt to Cecil Sharp'. *Folk Music Journal*, vol. 2 no. 5 (1974), pp. 400–3.

—— 'Not *too* educational'. *Aldeburgh Festival Programme Book*, 1976, p. 7.

—— 'A learner's questions on Eastern influences'. *Early Music*, vol. 5 no. 3 (1977), pp. 364–8.

—— 'On Grace Williams'. *Welsh Music*, vol. 5 (1977), pp. 19–21.

—— 'Working for Benjamin Britten'. *Musical Times*, vol. 118, no. 1609 (March 1977), pp. 202–3.

—— 'Recollections of times past'. *Aldeburgh Festival Programme Book*, 1978, p. 8.

—— *Holst*. London: Faber, 1974; 2nd edition 1981.

—— *A Thematic Catalogue of Gustav Holst's Music*. London: Faber Music, in association with G. & I. Holst, 1974.

—— *A Scrapbook for the Holst Birthplace Museum*. East Bergholt: Holst Birthplace Museum Trust in Association with G & I Holst, 1978.

—— 'Advantages of being seventy'. *Aldeburgh Festival Programme Book*, 1980, p. 10.

—— 'Holst's *At the Boar's Head*'. *Musical Times*, vol. 123, no. 1671 (May 1982), pp. 321–2.

—— 'Holst in the 1980s'. *Musical Times*, vol. 125, no. 1695 (May 1984), pp. 266–7.

Howard, Patricia, ed. *Benjamin Britten: The Turn of the Screw.* Cambridge: Cambridge University Press, 1985.

Jenkins, Alan. *Stephen Potter: Inventor of Gamesmanship.* London: Weidenfeld & Nicholson, 1980.

Malloy, Antonia. 'Britten's major set-back? Aspects of the first response to *Gloriana*.' In Banks, *Britten's Gloriana*, pp. 52–3.

Marshall, Arthur. *Life's Rich Pageant.* London: Hamish Hamilton, 1984.

Mitchell, Donald, and Hans Keller, eds. *Benjamin Britten: a Commentary on his Works from a Group of Specialists.* London: Rockliff, 1952.

Reed, Philip. 'The creative evolution of *Gloriana*.' In Banks, *Britten's Gloriana*, pp. 17–47.

Sanderson, Michael. *The History of the University of East Anglia, Norwich.* London: Hambledon & London, 2002.

Short, Michael. *Gustav Holst: the Man and his Music.* Oxford: Oxford University Press, 1990.

Sinclair, Andrew. *Arts and Cultures: the History of the 50 Years of the Arts Council of Great Britain.* London: Sinclair-Stevenson, 1995.

Strode, Rosamund. 'Working for Britten (II)'. In *The Britten Companion*, ed. Christopher Palmer. London: Faber, 1984.

Summers, Dorothy. *The East Coast Floods.* Newton Abbot: David & Charles, 1978.

Thomson, J. M. 'Imogen Holst'. *Early Music*, vol. 12 no. 4 (November 1984), pp. 583–4.

Tinker, Christopher. 'Imogen Holst's music, 1962–84'. *Tempo*, no. 166 (1988), pp. 22–7.

—— 'The Musical Output of Imogen Holst'. Ph.D. diss., University of Lancaster, 1990.

Vaughan Williams, Ursula. 'PRS profile 3 – Imogen Holst'. *Performing Right*, April 1966.

Wake-Walker, Jenni, comp. *Time and Concord: Aldeburgh Festival Recollections.* Saxmundham: Autograph Books, 1997.

Walker, Patrick, and Valerie Potter, with Rosamund Strode. *Aldeburgh Music Club: 1952–2002.* Aldeburgh: Aldeburgh Music Club, 2001.

Williamson, Malcolm, *et al.* 'Remembering Imo'. *Aldeburgh Festival Programme Book*, 1984.

Wren, Wilfred J. *Voices by the Sea: the Story of the Aldeburgh Festival Choir.* Lavenham: Terence Dalton, 1981.

General Index

This index continues the practice of using the abbreviations 'IH' and 'GH' to refer to Imogen and Gustav Holst; in addition, it uses 'BB' and 'PP' to refer to Benjamin Britten and Peter Pears. References in **bold** type are to the plates.

Karpeles, Maud Pauline 81, 404
Katchen, Julius 280
Keeling, Major Brian 434
Keller, Hans 176–7
Kelly, Kathleen 126, 415
Kelmscott House, Hammersmith 367
Kennedy, Douglas 47, 74, 81, 83, 398, 423
Kennedy, Mrs Douglas 36
Kensington Musical Competition Festival
    (1928) 44
Kentbrook (steamship) 283, 284
Kettlewell, Captain and Mrs W. R. W.
    84, 397, 399
Keys, Julia 195
Keyte, Christopher 429
Khatchaturian, Aram 265
Kihl, Richard 245, 246, 274
King's College, Cambridge 268
King's Lynn Festival 234–5
King's Theatre, Stockholm 58
Kingsway Hall, London 279, 334, 430
Kipling, Rudyard: *Puck of Pook's Hill* 8
Kisch, Eve 92, 407
Kjöhler, Maja 3, 58, 63
Kleiber, Erich 67, 192
Klemperer, Otto 66
Knappertsbusch, Hans 60
Knight, Esmond 193
Kodály, Zoltán 53, 63, 239 n. 185
Kraus, Otakar 195, 242, 243, 244
Krauss, Clemens 61, 63
Křenek, Ernst: *Reisebuch* 52
Krips, Josef 213, 258
Kutcher String Quartet 53, 63

Laban, Rudolf von 104
Lambert, Constant 50, 66, 68, 394
Lancaster, Osbert 172
Lancing College, Sussex 216, 217, 297
Landowska, Wanda 51
Langridge, Philip 323–4
Lanigan, John 192
Lascelles, David 254, 255
Lasker, Vally 10, 17, 20, 330
Lasso, Orlando di 44, 57, 107, 240
Lawes, Henry 80, 373
Lawrenson, John 413
Le Fleming, Christopher 114
League for Democracy in Greece 207–8
Ledger, Philip 324, 340, 345, **41**
Lediard, Dr Henry Ambrose 393

Lediard, Mary 75, 393
Leeds Triennial Festival 258, 312
Leighton House, London 327
Leiston Abbey 185
Leiston Modern School 340, 431, 433
Leiston Observer 163, 185, 231, 248, 250, 283,
    320–1
Leith Hill Music Festival (1936) 86
Lemare, Iris 36, 42, 45, 54 n. 9, 86, 400
Lennard, Joan 409
Leppard, Raymond 312
Letchworth Morris Team 33
Lewis, Ronald 195
Library of Congress, Washington 329
Lilley, Helen xvii, 328, 344, 369
Lincoln Cathedral 405
Liszt, Franz 70, 161
Livery Hall, Worshipful Company of
    Goldsmiths 221
London Boy Singers 319
London Contemporary Music Centre 53
London Philharmonic Club 300
London Philharmonic Orchestra 199 n. 117,
    361
London Symphony Orchestra 19, 35, 86,
    258, 280, 400
London Symphony Orchestra Wind
    Ensemble 258
Long, Kathleen 52, 60, 83
    teaches IH piano 33, 35, 40, 43–4, 46, 55
Lopokova, Lydia 394
Loveless, Rev. Kenneth 311–12
Lovett, Martin 110
Lowestoft Festival (planned) 163
Lund, Engel 263
Lutyens, Elisabeth 54 n. 9, 372
Lyrebird Press 42 n. 4, 89
Lyric Theatre, Hammersmith 413
Lyrita Records 341, 345, 361, 366

Mackerras, Charles 307, 421
Macmillan, Hugh Pattison, Baron 92
Macnaghten-Lemare Concerts 54, 392
Maconchy, Elizabeth 54, 372
Mahler, Gustav 61, 67
Major, Margaret 428
Making Music (journal) 93–7
Malcolm, George 144, 176, 199, 212, 262,
    289, 316, 416
    BB on 174, 177
Mandikian, Arda 270